A Cruising Guide
The Southern Bahamas

From Cat Island South to the Turks and Caicos

and the Dominican Republic

by
Stephen J. Pavlidis

Seaworthy Publications, Inc.
Cocoa Beach, Florida

A Cruising Guide to the Southern Bahamas

Stephen J. Pavlidis
Copyright © 2017 Stephen J. Pavlidis
ISBN 978-1-892399-29-8
7.0

Published in the USA by:
Seaworthy Publications, Inc.
2021 N. Atlantic Ave., Unit #226
Cocoa Beach, Florida 32931
Phone 321-610-3634
email orders@seaworthy.com
www.seaworthy.com - Your Bahamas and Caribbean Cruising Advisory

CAUTION: Sketch charts are not to scale and are not to be used for navigational purposes. They are intended as supplements for NOAA, DMA, or British Admiralty charts and no warranties are either expressed or implied as to the usability or the information contained herein. The Author and Publisher take no responsibility for their misuse.

A publication like this is actually the result of a blending of many people's knowledge and experiences. I would like to take this opportunity to thank the following for their help in this effort: Simon Anderson of *South Side Marina* on Provo, Turks and Caicos; Andy and Star on the S/V Moria, for their help with the dive sites; Capt. Lee Bakewell on the S/V *Escape Cay* for his help with programming; Gene Ballou on the S/V *Harrison*; Dean Bernal; Alicia Bonnet; A1 Broadshad of Spanish Wells; Mike and Lee Brown of the S/V *Wings*; BASRA Nassau, Chris Lloyd, Ken Waton, and Courtney Curtis; Caicos Marina and Shipyard; Judd Clarence; Steven Clareridge; Mike and Suzi Cope of the S/V *Awakening*; Craig and Paige on the S/V *Caribbean Soul*; Roger and Beth Day on the S/V *42*; Titus H. DeBoer of the *Bamboo Gallery*; Doug and LouAnn on the Schooner *Whisper*; Dan Doyle, skipper of the R/V *Sea Dragon* for once again making his vast knowledge of these waters available to all; Anne and Norm DuPont of M/V *Carpe Diem*; the folks at the Forfar Field Station; Captain Bob Gascoine of the M/V *Aquanaut*, whose years of experience in these waters made my job that much easier; Tom Gill on the S/V *Windrider* for his help with the hardware; Rev. David Goodrum on the S/V *Ephesians*; Jane and Gordon Groves of the S/V *Goombay*; Herman on the S/V *Trident*; Ralph Higgs of the Turks and Caicos Tourist Board; Captain Willis Jennings of South Caicos; Chuck and Alexis Kehn of S/V *Caicos Sol* and *Tropic Sol*; Manny and Ora Mae Lacour at Hawks Nest Resort And Marina; Andy Lowe and Star Droshine of the S/V *Moria*, for their help with the diving sections and areas around Provo; Professor Josiah Marvel, Turks and Caicos historian and proponent of the *Grand Turk Landfall Theory*; Captain David Matthews of the S/V *Tao*; the late John McKie; Beryl Nelson; Nicolas Popov of Island Expeditions; *Leeward Marina* and Dockmaster Dwayne Pratt; Bob Rader (NU4P) and Anita Martinec (WZ4U) for enriching this publication by sharing the wisdom of their years of experience and experiences in the Bahamas; Scooter Bob's; Pierre Seymour, Deputy Chief Conservation Officer of the DECR on Providenciales, Turks and Caicos; Captain Tom Shepherd, Treasure Island, Florida; Surfer 1%er Chicago Outlaw, retired National President of the *Outlaws M.C*; David Taylor; Jack and Pat Tyler of the S/V *Whoosh*; Bruce and Rosa Van Sant; Craig and Jan Scott, S/V *Seabbatical*; Carolyn Wardle; Lenny Williams of *Lenny's Photo*; Yon on the S/V *Asapwal*; and last but not least Gene Zace of the S/V *Joshua*. If there is anybody that I have neglected to mention here, rest assured that it is an oversight and I sincerely apologize. A very special thanks goes out to Captain Paul Harding of *Safari Seaplanes* for his aerial photographs.

Cover Design by Ken Quant, *Broad Reach Marketing*, Milwaukee, WI.

Library of Congress Cataloging-in-Publication Data
Pavlidis, Stephen J.
  The southern Bahamas guide : from Cat Island south to the Turks &
Caicos--Dominican Republic north coast / by Stephen J. Pavlidis.
     p. cm.
  Rev. ed. of: On and off the beaten path. c2002.
  Includes bibliographical references and index.
  ISBN-13: 978-1-892399-29-8 (pbk. : alk. paper)
  ISBN-10: 1-892399-29-6 (pbk. : alk. paper) 1. Boats and boating--
Bahamas--Cat Island--Guidebooks. 2. Boats and boating--Turks and
Caicos Islands--Guidebooks. 3. Boats and boating--Dominican Republic--
Guidebooks. 4. Pilots guides--Bahamas--Cat Island. 5. Pilots guides--
Turks and Caicos Islands. 6. Pilots guides--Dominican Republic. 7.
Nautical charts--Bahamas. 8. Nautical charts--Turks and Caicos
Islands. 9. Nautical charts--Dominican Republic. I. Pavlidis, Stephen J.
On and off the beaten path. II. Title.
  GV776.24.A2P38 2009
  797.109729'6--dc22
                    2008050783

Introduction

Only the hardiest of cruisers head south of George Town, Exuma, for the islands of the Southern Bahamas, Turks and Caicos, and the entire Caribbean. This guide is designed to take you from George Town, through the Southern Bahamas and Turks and Caicos, and deposit you on the northern coast of the Dominican Republic where Puerto Rico will likely be your next stop.

Many of these islands lie well off the beaten path and are rarely visited by yachts. Those that do stop in are usually in transit southward from The Bahamas to the Caribbean or northward from the Caribbean to the U.S. Some of these areas are extremely isolated and if you get weathered in you may find yourself the only boat in the anchorage for days, and sometimes, weeks at a time. The cruiser in these waters definitely needs to be as self-sufficient as possible. Extra jerry cans of fuel are a good idea, a necessity if you have a small fuel tank and motor a lot. In places like the Jumentos, the residents get their fuel in 55-gallon drums from Nassau and there may be little if any to spare for visiting yachtsmen as most of it must go to fuel their fishing boats. Adequate medical supplies and the knowledge to use them properly are a necessity.

A well-stocked pantry is a prime consideration. When leaving George Town or Long Island make sure that you provision well, some of the stores in the outer islands, although they might carry a few staples, often lack a lot of the luxuries that you may be used to such as cigarettes, fresh milk, eggs, veggies, meat, and even alcoholic beverages, which are not sold at Landrail Point on Crooked Island. You may become like the islanders themselves, waiting on a mailboat that is late or that may not even arrive at all for weeks. However, if you can fish, you can eat, so sharpen your hooks and spears, and grab a line to string up some conch and have at it! The fishing is superb. If you are used to conch such as are found in the Exumas, you will find that the conch in the outer islands are plentiful and much larger. Of course, once you arrive in Providenciales, you will find shopping the equal to what you'll experience in Nassau. In the DR, provisioning is wide open and inexpensive.

Here in these outer islands, with their many open lee-side anchorages, you will learn a new dance, "The "Out-Island Roll," and no matter how hard you try, you will not escape performing it somewhere down the line. Usually a bridle arrangement, or a stern anchor, setting your bow into the swell is your only salvation, and that may not be enough if the wind picks up. I have rolled for days at a time at *Abraham's Bay*, Mayaguana with 25-knot easterly winds and southeasterly swells working their way around Guano Point and over the reef. If I adjusted my bridle to meet the swells, I rolled with the wind waves, if I adjusted my bridle to ride the wind waves; I rolled from the swells coming in over the reef. It was not a dangerous situation by any means, but highly uncomfortable and it makes for poor sleeping.

But all these things are minor. The provisioning and medical supply situations can, and should, be thought out well ahead of time. The roll, well, you'll get used to it, and when you find a peaceful harbor such as Attwood or French Wells you will be all the more grateful for it. As for fuel, usually someone will come to your assistance and let you have a few gallons, enough to get you to someplace where you can purchase fuel. With a little preparation, determination, and a definite desire to have fun, you will succeed in doing just that. These outer islands are not to be missed. The people are the some of the friendliest in The Bahamas and you may even learn some new tricks from them. For instance, people on Crooked Island are very aware of the moon's influence on our lives. They tell the tide not by the height of the water, but rather by the position of the moon. Some can even predict the kind of a day they are going to have by whether or not the moon is "on the right or on the left." Enjoy. Open your mind and your heart and you'll have an unforgettable time as you voyage from the Exumas southward to the inviting Caribbean.

Stephen J. Pavlidis

Table of Contents

The Basics

Anchoring

Just as important as getting your vessel moving and keeping her heading along your chosen courseline quickly and efficiently is the fine art of keeping your vessel from moving. Many of the anchorages in this book are swept by swift tidal currents, sometimes up to 3 knots, and to avoid bumping into your neighbor in the middle of the night or putting your vessel on the rocks or beach, two anchors, such as in a Bahamian Moor, are required.

Anchor choice is basically a personal preference. Some skippers prefer *CQRs*, while others swear by a *Bruce, a Rocna,* or a *Danforth*. Of the lot, you will find that a *Danforth* holds as well or better than a *CQR* or *Bruce* in sandy bottoms while the *CQR* or *Bruce* is preferred when anchoring in rocky bottoms. Whatever your choice of anchor, you must deploy your anchor correctly and with sufficient scope to hold you when the tide changes, if a front approaches, or if a squall should blow through at 2:00 a.m. (which seems to be the time they choose to blow through). Your anchor should have a length of chain (at least 15') shackled to your anchor to keep your rode from chafing against coral or rocks and to create a catenary curve that helps absorb shock loads while lowering the angle of pull on your anchor. Too high an angle may cause your anchor to pull up and out of the bottom. Some cruisers prefer all chain rodes with a nylon snubber to absorb the shock loads. This is an excellent arrangement but a windlass may be needed unless you prefer the workout involved with hauling in the chain and anchor every time you move.

In many of the leeward anchorages in The Bahamas you will find that you can lie quite comfortably to only one anchor. When setting your anchor do not just drop it and let your rode run out, piling itself on top of your anchor. Lower your anchor to the bottom and deploy the rode as you fall back with the current or wind until you have at least a 5:1 scope out, 7:1 is preferable but not always possible. When calculating the amount of scope required, be sure to allow for high tide as well as the height of your anchor roller or fairlead above the water. Without being precise, you can figure on a 2½'-3' tidal rise in The Bahamas although occasionally you may find a 4½' rise, and in general a little more rise during a full moon and a little less with no moon (remember that the soundings in this guide are at *MLW, Mean Low Water*, this means

that it is possible to have a lower tide with less depth that what is shown). When you have secured your rode, back down with the engine at about ½ throttle to set the anchor. If you have not succeeded in securing your anchor, try again. To check the set it is best to dive on your anchors or at the very least, look at their set through a glass bottom bucket from your dinghy. You may find that you will have to set them by hand, especially in rocky areas.

If there are other boats in the anchorage when you arrive and they are riding to two anchors, or if you are in an area beset by tidal currents, it is best to set two anchors in a Bahamian Moor. Although one anchor may be fine if you have the swinging room, when the tide changes it may pull out and fail to reset. These anchorages are often very crowded and while you may swing wide on your one anchor and not find yourself endangered by the rocks or beach, you and your neighbor may go bump in the night because his two anchors have kept him in one spot. If unsure the best thing to do is follow the lead of those boats that are there before you. Conversely, if you arrive at an anchorage and everyone is on one anchor and you choose to set two, do so outside the swing radius of the other boats. If you are riding on one anchor and find that you are lying to the wind but that the swell is rolling you, position another anchor at an angle off the stern so as to align your bow into the swell making for a more comfortable night. Another option is to rig a bridle which allows your vessel to lie to the swells and not the wind.

To set a *Bahamian Moor,* you must first decide where you wish for your vessel to settle. You will lay out two anchors, one up-current and one down-current of that spot which will keep you swinging in a small circle. Head into the current to where you will drop your first anchor and set it properly. Let out as much scope as you can, setting your anchor on the way by snubbing it, until you are at the spot where you are to drop your down-current anchor. If the wind has pushed you to one side or the other of the tidal stream, you will have to power up to the position where you will set your second anchor. Lower your second anchor and pull your vessel back up current on your first rode, paying out the rode for the second anchor and snubbing it as you maneuver back up current to your chosen spot. You may want to dive on your anchors to check their set. Keeping your rodes tight will keep you swinging in a tighter circle. Check your anchor rodes daily as they will twist together and make it extremely difficult to undo them in an emergency.

In some tight anchorages you will be unable to set your anchors 180° apart. An alternative is to set them 90° apart in a "Y" configuration perpendicular to the wind. A skipper with a large swing radius in very tight quarters is apt to find out what his neighbors think of his anchoring technique as soon as the wind shifts. Responsible anchoring cannot be over-stressed.

Always set an anchor light. Some cruisers feel this is unimportant in some of the more isolated anchorages. What they probably do not understand is that many locals run these islands at all hours of the night, even on moonless nights, and an anchor light protects your vessel as well as theirs. There are no "designated anchorages" in The Bahamas.

It is important to note that the lee-side anchorages, especially those in the outer islands (Inagua, Plana, etc.), can get rolly at times (yes, you will learn a new dance, "The Out Island Roll"). The Atlantic Ocean surge seeks out any way it can to round the tips of these islands to cause you seemingly no end of discomfort and there is not much you can do about it except possibly use a second anchor or bridle arrangement to keep your bow or stern into the swell. If using a bridle, set up your line on the opposite side that you wish to turn your vessel. For instance, if you need to turn your bow to port to face the incoming swells and make for a calmer ride, run your bridle line from a winch to a block on your starboard quarter and then forward outside your shrouds to your anchor line. Either tie it to your rode or, if you use all chain, attach it to the shackle where your nylon snubber (be sure to use a long one, at least 10'-20' if you are setting up for a bridle arrangement) hooks to your chain. After your anchor is set, simply crank in your bridle line bringing your bow to port and off the wind.

Anchorages on the eastern shores of the Bahamian out-islands are all daytime anchorages only due to the prevailing winds and should be used only in settled or westerly weather.

Never anchor in coral, even with your dinghy anchor. An anchor can do a great deal of damage to a very fragile ecosystem that will take years to recover if it is to recover at all. Besides, sand holds so much better anyway.

In the summer months and on into the early fall, or when there is no wind, you may wish to anchor a good distance from shore to keep away from the relentless biting insects. Cays with a lot of vegetation or mangroves will have a higher concentration of biting insects.

Proper anchoring etiquette should by practiced at all times. For instance, if the anchorage is wide and roomy and only one boat is at anchor, do not anchor right on top of them, give your neighbor a little breathing room and some solitude. You would probably appreciate the same consideration should the situation be reversed. Cruisers often exhibit a herding instinct where they seek the comfort of other nearby cruisers, anchoring much too close at times. Many boaters, after a long, hard day in rough seas or bad weather, anxiously await the peace and tranquility of a calm anchorage. The last thing they want is noise and wake.

If you have a dog aboard that loves to bark, be considerate of your neighbors who do not wish to hear him. They do have that right. Jet skis can be a lot of fun, but only when you are astride one. Many cruisers have little tolerance for the incessant buzzing back and forth of high speed jet skis. It is a good show of manners to slowly leave the anchorage where you can have your high speed fun and games and not disturb anyone. The same can be said of water skiing which is prohibited within 200' of the shoreline in The Bahamas unless the skier is approaching or leaving the shore at a speed of 3 knots or less. If at all possible, try not to run your generators at sunset or after dark. At sunset, many cruisers are sitting in their cockpits enjoying cocktails and watching the sun go down and do not want a generator disturbing their soft conversations. Courtesy shown is usually courtesy returned.

Charts

The best charts that you can buy for the Turks and Caicos Islands, besides the ones in this publication, are TC-001, TC-002, and TC-003 by Captain Bob Gascoine, (*Wavey Line Publishing*, Bob, the dean of Turks Islands divers, has done a remarkable job and created some truly accurate and reliable charts that also show all the major dive sites along the shores of the Turks and Caicos Islands. His charts go into a bit more detail in the area of the *Caicos Bank* where he shows the *Damn Fool Channel* route, a small boat or shallow draft route through an incredibly beautiful area that I do not cover for the simple reason that the vast majority of cruising boats are restricted from entry by their draft. Captain Gascoine also has a new chart out for Hispaniola and several for The Bahamas.

Clothing

If you are heading to the Bahamas or the Turks and Caicos Islands you will enter a tropical climate where the theme for clothing is light. You will likely live in shorts and T-shirts (if that much). Long pants and sturdy, comfortable shoes are preferred when hiking for protection from the bush and the rugged terrain. Long sleeved shirts (or old cotton pajamas) and wide brimmed hats are important in keeping the sun off you. Polarized sunglasses (helpful for piloting) and suntan lotion (suntan oil tends to leave a long lasting greasy smear all over everything) should be included in your gear. In winter months it is advisable to bring something warm to wear, especially in the evenings. Long pants and sweaters are usually adequate and a light jacket would be a good idea as some frontal passages will occasionally drop the temperature to 60° F.

It is important that men and women dress appropriately when entering settlements. Skimpy bathing suits for men as well as women are excellent for the beach or boat but in town they are not apropos. Men should wear shirts in town as some local inhabitants are quick to remind you to cover up. Remember, you are a visitor here and that entails a certain responsibility.

Currency

The Bahamas

The legally acceptable currency of The Bahamas is the Bahamian dollar whose value is on par with the American dollar. American money is readily acceptable throughout the islands at all stores, marinas, and hotels. Bahamian coins come in 1¢, 5¢, 10¢, and 25¢ denomination while Bahamian paper money comes in $.50, $1, $3, (yes, a three dollar bill), $5, $10, $20, $50, and $100 denominations.

The Turks and Caicos Islands

The legally acceptable currency of the Turks and Caicos is the American dollar. The treasury also issues a Turks and Caicos crown and quarter. If you are arriving in the Turks and Caicos from the Bahamas you will want to cash in your Bahamian money in the Bahamas prior to your arrival at Provo. The banks in the Turks and Caicos will not accept Bahamian money and you'll be stuck with it unless you find a cruiser heading north. Traveler's checks are accepted almost everywhere and many places,

including some grocery stores, take major credit cards. If you are coming from someplace without a sales tax such as the Bahamas, restaurant and grocery bills will take some getting used to as the Turks and Caicos charges a 10% sales tax on food items. There are no company or personal income taxes in the Turks and Caicos Islands. The government's budget is derived from the 10%-30% customs duty on incoming goods. There is a $35 departure tax when flying out of the Turks and Caicos Islands.

The Dominican Republic

In the Dominican Republic the currency in usage is the Peso (RD$) and you may change your dollars into pesos at *Claró* in Luperón (you may also withdraw pesos on your credit or debit card here). At the time of this writing in 2014 the exchange rate was RD$43.49=US$1. Some other locations will give you a slightly higher rate.

Please note that the rate mentioned will certainly have changed by the time this guide is published. It is the nature of this work that business listings change and rates fluctuate, I can only give you a guideline here.

Foreign currency can also be changed into Dominican pesos at *Banco de Reservas* booths at the airports, major hotels, or at commercial banks. Banking hours are 0830 to 1500, M-F. Airport booths remain open to service all incoming flights, up to 24-hours if necessary.

Traveler's checks and major credit cards are widely accepted. Cash advances are available at some commercial banks. When tipping, a 10% gratuity (as well as an 8% sales tax) is often included in the bill. Please note that the practice of tipping taxi drivers is not the custom in the DR but it is widely practiced.

Don't change very much more money than you plan to spend, only 30% of Dominican currency exchanged by visitors can be changed back into dollars upon departure (a tip - save your currency exchange receipts). Although it's extremely tempting, one should avoid changing money on the black market. Absolutely no more than US$5,000 may be taken out of the country when you leave. Arrests have been made for even small currency-law violations.

Customs and Immigration

The Bahamas
Ports of Entry

ABACO: Grand Cay, Green Turtle Cay, Marsh Harbour, Spanish Cay, Treasure Cay, Walker's Cay

ANDROS: Congo Town, Fresh Creek, Mangrove Cay, Morgan's Bluff

BERRY ISLANDS: Chub Cay, Great Harbour Cay

CAT CAY: *Cat Cay Marina*

CAT ISLAND: Bennet's Harbour, Arthur's Town, New Bight, Airport

ELEUTHERA: Governor's Harbour, Harbour Island, Rock Sound, Spanish Wells, Cape Eleuthera

EXUMA: *Emerald Bay Marina*, George Town

GRAND BAHAMA: Freeport Harbour, Port Lucaya (*Port Lucaya Marina, Lucayan Marina Village, Sunrise Marina*, West End (marina)

INAGUA: Matthew Town

LONG ISLAND: Stella Maris, *Flying Fish Marina*

MAYAGUANA: Abraham's Bay

NEW PROVIDENCE: Nassau (any marina), *Lyford Cay Marina*

NORTH BIMINI: Alice Town (any marina)

RAGGED ISLAND: Duncan Town

SAN SALVADOR: Cockburn Town

SOUTH BIMINI: *Bimini Sands Marina*

All vessels entering Bahamian waters must clear in with *Customs* and *Immigration* officials at the nearest Port of Entry shown above. Failure to report within 24 hours may subject you to a penalty and make you liable for confiscation and forfeiture of your vessel. When approaching your selected port of entry be sure to fly your yellow "Q" flag. Tie up to a dock or marina and await the officials if directed. In places like Bimini (where the dockmasters will usually have the necessary forms for you) or Green Turtle Cay, only the captain of the vessel may go ashore to arrange clearance and no other shore contact is permitted until pratique is granted. I

In some places, such as Nassau, *Customs* will actually come aboard your vessel. Some of the marinas that you use may levy a charge for using their dock, Cat Cay and Chub Cay in particular. If any marina does not charge you, good manners suggest that you at least make a fuel purchase.

Most southbound vessels usually clear in long before reaching the outer islands while those northbound skippers have a choice of ports of entry.

The *Customs* and *Immigration* fee structure has changed considerably over the last decade and it has caused a tremendous amount of contention in various segments of the cruising community. Regardless, cruisers still come to The Bahamas. The cruising permit fee is $150 for vessels to 30' in length, and $300 for vessels over 30', and is valid for one year (tenders over 18' are charged an additional $150). This fee allows the owner to keep the vessel in Bahamian waters for up to one year without paying duty, and also covers the cost of Immigration charges for up to 4 people. Also included are all transportation and overtime charges as well as a one-year fishing permit for up to six reels. This fee allows you to also leave The Bahamas within 90 days of your first clearance and return without having to pay the duty a second time (this may change by the time this edition has been published). It is sometimes possible to get an extension for this permit for $500, but it is at the option of the *Customs* officer on duty. If you wish to leave your boat permanently in The Bahamas you will have to pay a 27% duty on vessels under 30' and 6% on vessels from 30-100'. A $15 departure tax is included for those of your crew who choose to fly home but they'll need a copy of your cruising permit when flying out so they won't have to pay the $15 departure tax a second time.

U.S. citizens need a passport, but visas are not required for visitors from the U.S., Canada, and persons from any British Commonwealth country. If you are flying in and returning by way of a boat in transit you need some proof that you are able to leave the country. It is suggested that you purchase a round trip ticket and leave the return reservation open. When you return aboard your boat you may then cash in your unused ticket or use it for a future flight. Check with the airline when buying your ticket as to their policy in this matter.

If yours is a pleasure vessel with no dutiable cargo, the captain will fill out a Maritime Declaration of Health, Inwards Report for pleasure vessels, and a crew list. Do not mistakenly call your crew "passengers" or it may be interpreted that you are running a charter. An International Marine Declaration of Health in duplicate will be accepted in lieu of a Bill of Health from vessels arriving in The Bahamas. Smallpox vaccination certificates and cholera inoculation certificates are required only if the vessel is arriving directly from an infected area.

Each crew member will fill out and sign an *Immigration* form. You will be asked to answer several tourism related questions. You can ask for and receive a stay of up to eight months however some Immigration Officials will only give three or four months for reasons that are clear only to them. This is an inconsistency that one sees every now and then as you talk to different cruisers and find out about their clearing-in adventure. An Immigration official in Nassau explained that it is up to the individual officer to determine how long a stay to permit. If you have guests flying in they also must have a return trip ticket and proof of citizenship.

The captain will be issued a Cruising Permit (Transire) for the vessel that is valid for up to 12 months. This permit must be presented to any *Customs* official or other proper officer (if requested) while in The Bahamas. If you wish to keep your vessel in Bahamian waters for longer than one year without paying import duties, special arrangements must be made with Customs (see above). Spare parts for installation aboard your vessel are duty free. If the parts are imported as cargo they are subject to a 6% duty. Bicycles and motorcycles (including scooters), are required to be licensed at the yacht's port of entry. If they are to be brought ashore they may be subject to a *Customs* duty or a bond in the form of a cash deposit.

If you have pets on board they must have an import permit. An application for the permit may be requested by writing to the Director of the Department of Agriculture, P.O. Box N-3704, Nassau, Bahamas (242-325-7502, fax # 242-325-3960). Return the completed application with a $10.75 fee in the form of a Postal Money Order or International Money Order payable to the Public Treasury. This will hasten the process of obtaining your permit although you should allow three to four weeks processing time. Rabies certificates are required of all animals over three months old and must be more than 10 days but less than 9 months old and should be presented when you clear Customs and Immigration. If you wish your permit to be faxed to you, include a fax number and an extra $5 in the money order.

Non-residents of The Bahamas entering aboard a foreign vessel are not required to obtain permits nor pay duties on firearms during their visit to the islands. This exemption is for three months following the arrival of the vessel at a designated port of entry. After three months a certificate must be obtained from the Commissioner of Police. All firearms must be kept safe from theft under lock and key and be declared on your cruising permit with an accurate count of all ammunition. Firearms may not be used in Bahamian waters nor taken ashore. Hunters should contact the Department of Agriculture and Fisheries in Nassau for information on hunting in The Bahamas. Completely forbidden are tear gas pens, military arms such as artillery, flame-throwers, machine guns, and automatic weapons. Exempt are toy guns, dummy firearms, flare guns, and spear guns designed for underwater use.

In the summer of 2009, the Government of The Bahamas passed an amendment to the Tariff Act reinstating the Duty Free exemption for printed matter and original artwork. The amendment also reinstates the original exemption for printed matter and original artwork. All Bahamian *Customs* Officers have been informed of this change, but if you should happen to come across an official who insists on charging duty on these items, you can call Bahamas Entry Checking in Nassau, 242-302-3509, for assistance.

The U.S. department of Customs and Border Protection (CBP) has implemented the Local Boater Option (LBO) program. This option is available to frequent small boat users in the Tampa, Miami, Puerto Rico and U.S. Virgin Islands areas. The LBO will allow CBP to expedite the arrival reporting process to low risk boaters.

Enrollment in the LBO Program is voluntary, free of charge and will facilitate your clearance procedures. All U.S. citizens are eligible to join. In order to participate in the LBO you must contact CBP at the nearest registration location designated by the port of entry. The registrant will be provided an appointment to present all required documentation to CBP officials.

American flag vessels are not required to obtain clearance when departing U.S. ports. If clearing back into the United States you must, upon entry, call the U.S. Customs Service to clear in. You are required to go to a nearby telephone immediately upon arrival and dock nearby. You can dial 1-800-432-1216, 1-800-458-4239, or 1-800-451-0393 to get a Customs officer on the line to arrange clearance.

Each resident of the United States, including minors, may take home duty-free purchases up to

$800 U.S. if they have been outside the U.S. for more than 48 hours and have not taken this exemption in 30 days. This includes up to 2 liters of liquor per person over 21 provided that one liter is manufactured in The Bahamas or a member of the Caribbean Basin Initiative (CBI). A family may pool their exemptions. Articles of up to $1000 in excess of the duty-free $800 allowance are assessed at a flat rate of 10%. For example, a family of four may bring back up to $3200 worth of duty-free goods. If they were to bring back $7200 worth of goods, they would have to pay a duty of $400 on the $4000 above the duty-free allowance. This flat rate may only be used once every 30 days. If the returning U.S. resident is not entitled to the duty-free allowance because of the 30 day or 48 hour restrictions, they may still bring back $25 worth of personal or household items. This exemption may not be pooled.

Antiques are admitted to the U.S. duty-free if they are over 100 years old. The Bahamian store selling the antique should provide you with a form indicating the value and certifying the age of the object. Importation of fruits, plants, meats, poultry, and dairy products is generally prohibited. More than $10,000 in U.S. or foreign coin, currency, traveler's checks, money orders, and negotiable instruments or investment securities in bearer form must be reported to *Customs*. Importation of Bahamian tortoise or turtle shell goods is prohibited. Many medicines purchased over the counter in The Bahamas such as 222, a codeine-aspirin-caffeine compound, are not allowed entry. Although you can buy Cuban cigars in Nassau, enjoy them on your cruise and do not attempt to bring them back into the U.S. The *U.S. Customs Service* frowns on Americans spending money on Cuban products. Hopefully that will change in time.

The Turks and Caicos Islands
Ports of Entry
PROVIDENCIALES: *South Dock, Turtle Cove Marina, Caicos Marina and Shipyard*
SOUTH CAICOS: Cockburn Town
NORTH CAICOS: airstrip (not for boaters)
GRAND TURK: *South Base*

All vessels entering the waters of the Turks and Caicos must clear in with *Customs* and *Immigration* officials at the nearest port of entry listed above. Failure to report within 24 hours may subject you to a penalty and make you liable for confiscation and forfeiture of your vessel. When approaching your selected port of entry be sure to fly your yellow "Q" flag. Only the captain of the vessel may go ashore

to arrange clearance and no other shore contact is permitted until pratique is granted. During normal working hours, 0800 to 1630, Monday through Friday, the only fee charged is a mandatory $50.00 boarding fee (clearing in or out), whether the officer actually boards your boat or not. At South Dock (*Sapodilla Bay*), you'll clear ashore and no officer boards your boat, but if you're in a marina the Customs officer will come to you. If arriving outside normal hours or on holidays you may expect to pay overtime charges, usually a $6.00 overtime fee Monday through Friday, and an $8.00 fee overtime if you clear in on Sundays and holidays.

As of 2012, vessels staying in the islands for 7 days or less pay a fee of $100, even if the stop is to purchase fuel. If you intend to stay more than seven days you must get a cruising permit from Customs at a charge of $300 for 90 days. But first you must report to Immigration to secure a Visa. Visas are granted for periods not to exceed 30 days and can be renewed twice, each renewal costs $50 per passport. If your cruising permit expires you can renew it for another 90 days. If you wish to stay in the Turks and Caicos for longer than 180 days must pay an Import Duty that is currently 11% of local valuation or leave the country and not return until the following calendar year

North Americans need proof of citizenship. If you are flying in and returning by way of a boat in transit you need some proof that you are able to leave the country. It is suggested that you purchase a round trip ticket and leave the return reservation open. When you return aboard your boat you may then cash in your unused ticket or use it for a future flight. Check with the airline when buying your ticket as to their policy in this matter. As soon as the captain has cleared Customs, you must take down your yellow "Q" flag and replace it with the British courtesy flag. Canadian citizens need a valid passport or some proof of identity such as a birth certificate along with a photo ID and a return ticket if arriving by air and a visa is not required. Australian, New Zealand, EU, and Japanese citizens need a valid passport and a return ticket, but no visa is required. Citizens of countries not listed above should check with the embassy or consulate in their home country for details on entry requirements.

Vessels leaving the Turks and Caicos are now required to clear out 24-hours in advance of their scheduled departure time. If you're in a marina, have the dockmaster notify Customs for you and an officer will soon arrive to clear you out of the country. If you're in *Sapodilla Bay* you can go to South Dock for your outward clearance. If you clear out and must wait on weather in some place like Great Sand Cay (if you're bound for the DR) it is fine to await weather at the cay, however you cannot clear out and then anchor at an inhabited cay. If you are in *Turtle Cove Marina* or Leeward Going Through and wish to stopover at *Sapodilla Bay* before heading to Luperón, do not call Customs to come to you for an outward clearance, instead, when you arrive at *Sapodilla Bay*, go to South Dock to clear.

Most vessels heading across the banks and venturing south to the DR or Puerto Rico leave Provo and head to Ambergris Cay and then Sand Cay. As long you do not stop at any other inhabited islands in the Turks and Caicos Islands, you may proceed straight across the banks and stage your trip from Sand Cay. When clearing out of Sapodilla Bay, you can clear out in the afternoon and not actually leave until the next morning, as long as you are gone before Customs opens. This enables you to have an early morning start to get to Ambergris before dark. There are no fees to clear out unless you choose to do so outside of normal working hours. The same rates for overtime are charged as for clearing in. If you or your guests are flying out, be advised that the airport departure tax is US$15 for visitors over the age of 12.

Firearms, including those charged with compressed air, must be declared and brought in to Customs with you when you clear. Unless you have prior approval in writing from the Commissioner of Police, Customs will impound them and store them for you at the police station until your departure. Spear guns are also illegal and must be brought in to Customs when you clear. There is no quarantine period on pets, all pets must be declared and have a recent bill of health (dated within one month of the date of your departure) from a certified veterinarian. Pets must also have a recent rabies shot. The importation of controlled drugs and pornography is illegal in the Turks and Caicos Islands.

Anyone over the age of 17 may bring certain items duty free including personal effects such as wearing apparel and ship's stores. If you are staying seven days or less each crew member is permitted 50 cigarettes, 25 cigarillos, or 60 grams of smoking tobacco, plus one liter of wine (less than 25% alcohol by volume), or .5 liters of potable spirits. If you are

staying in the country for less than 24 hours you are permitted 25 cigarettes, 12 cigarillos, 6 cigars, or 30 grams of smoking tobacco. Crew who are staying in the Turks and Caicos Islands for more than 7 days receive the full statutory allowance of tobacco and spirits: 1 liter of alcohol or 2 liters of wine, 200 cigarettes, 100 cigarillos, 50 cigars or 125 grams of pipe tobacco. Fifty grams of perfume or .25 liters of toilet water are also permitted. Dutiable goods, up to a value of $200.00 and purchased outside the Turks and Caicos, may be brought in by visitors as gifts and must be declared when clearing in. Persons arriving in the islands with the intention of working are allowed to bring in personal effects duty free, providing they intend to remain in the islands not less than 12 months. Duties on imported goods run in the neighborhood of 10%-33% depending on the particular item. In the spring of 1998, the government of the Turks and Caicos dropped all duties on computer products so you might not have to pay duty for parts shipped into the country. For more information you may telephone the Collector of Customs on Grand Turk at 649-946-4241, 649-424-4776, 649-424-4450.

Dominican Republic
Ports of Entry
Barahona, Manzanillo, Luperón, Cofresi (*Ocean World Marina*), Puerto Plata, Samaná, *Puerto Bahia Marina*, Salinas, Santo Domingo, Boca Chica, Casa de Campo

Firearms must be declared upon arrival and the *Commandante* will keep them for you until you are ready to depart DR waters. Pets must have a valid rabies inoculation and a health certificate.

In 2009, the Dominican Republic passed a new law that pertains to cruisers arriving and clearing in at marinas only. The law states that only two officials may board your vessel and they are not permitted to ask for compensation of any sort. After the officials leave you must go to the *Immigration* office to have your passports stamped. For a typical 90-day stay some new fees have been set up. The vessel must pay 5% of the dockage fee as a tax and 2% of any fuel bill as a tax.

In most places the officials involved with clearance will come aboard your vessel (and no, they will not remove their shoes in most instances) to grant clearance and inspect your vessel. Generally, but not always, you will be visited by *Immigration*, *Customs*, *Agriculture*, *Drug Enforcement* (you are permitted to accompany this official as they inspect your vessel),

Defence Force vessel

the Dominican *Coast Guard (Marina de Guerra)*, and occasionally *M-2*, the *Dominican Intelligence Agency*.

If you opt to clear at a government dock you will also deal with someone representing *Portuario* (*Ports*). I have experienced *Ports* trying to hit me up for a fee when I cleared at Luperón, you must be careful and not be afraid to say "No." You may even be asked for a tip for the *Commandante* or for a T-shirt.

If you clear at a marina you will pay more for their services since they are taking care of everything for you. You will still be boarded by a gang of officials.

Pets are permitted in the DR though you will be asked for a health certificate in some places.

The Dominican Republic requires that vessels transiting her waters obtain a *despacho* for moving from one harbor to the next (obtained from the *Marina de Guerra*). If you ask for a *despacho* with *puntos intermedios* you will not get one. That means if you go from Samaná to Cap Cana you cannot stop anywhere in between unless it is a "rest stop," a provisioning stop, bad weather, or the stop is required for "repairs." A *despacho* will not be issued for harbors that are NOT a port of entry.

You must also obtain a *despacho* when you clear out.

The Defence Force

The *Royal Bahamas Defence Force* officially came into existence on March 31, 1980. Their duties include defending The Bahamas, stopping drug smuggling, illegal immigration, poaching, and to provide assistance to mariners whenever and wherever they can. They have a fleet of 26 coastal and inshore patrol craft along with 2 aircraft.

I have been associated with a number of *Defence Force* personnel through my efforts at Exuma Park and I have developed a healthy respect for these men and women. Every officer and seaman that I have met has been highly intelligent, articulate, dedicated, and very professional in regards to their duties. These are not the thugs and hoodlums that so many cruisers have come to fear over the last few years. As late as 1991, horror stories were coming out of Nassau concerning improprieties during routine boardings. The *Defence Force* has taken corrective steps and reports of trouble caused by boarding parties are almost non-existent now. What complaints I have heard I have found to have two sides, and quite often cruisers take the boaters side instinctively while giving no thought to the other side of the coin. There is no reason to dread the gray boats as they approach. The *Defence Force* has a very difficult job to do and it often becomes necessary for them to board private pleasure vessels in routine searches. The boarding party will do everything they can to be polite and professional, however, due to the violent nature of the criminals they seek, standard procedure is to be armed. Unfortunately, in the process of protecting themselves, they inadvertently intimidate cruisers. Please do not be alarmed if a crewman bearing an automatic weapon stays in your cockpit while the officer conducts a search below decks in your presence.

If you are boarded you will be asked to sign a statement saying that the search was carried out politely and in the presence of the owner or skipper. I have been boarded and found the boarding officer and crew to courteous and professional. It is not unusual for the *Defence Force* to enter an anchorage and board all the vessels anchored there. Normally they will not board a vessel that is unoccupied, preferring to keep an eye out for your return.

Cruisers often ask why single me out, why search my boat? What are they looking for? Besides the obvious problem with drugs, The Bahamas has problems with people smuggling illegal weapons and ammunition into the country. With bullets selling for $5 and more a piece on the street in Nassau a boater could fatten his or her cruising kitty very easily. You must keep accurate records on all your weapons and ammunition and make sure you record them on your cruising permit when you check in.

The *Defence Force* also must defend the richness of the marine fisheries in The Bahamas. It is not unknown for a boat to cross over from the states without a permit and fill up its freezers with Bahamian caught fish, conch, and lobster. In 1997, a boat from south Florida was boarded upon its return to Florida and the owners and crew arrested and charged under the *Lacy Act*. The *Defence Force*, if they board your vessel, will probably want to see your fishing permit and ask you whether you have any fish aboard. For most cruisers this does not pose a problem. If, however, you have 100 dolphin aboard, you will find yourself in a world of well-deserved trouble. You might have a better understanding of what the *Defence Force* goes through if you learn about the four *Defence Force Marines* who died a decade ago when Cuban MIGs sank their boat after the rest of the

crew boarded Cuban fishing boats illegally operating in Bahamian waters along the southern edge of the *Great Bahama Bank*. Theirs is a serious business.

Dinghy Safety

Most cruisers spend a considerable amount of time in their dinghies exploring the waters and islands in the vicinity of their anchorage. It is not unknown for a dinghy engine to fail or a skipper to run out of gas miles away from the mother vessel. For this reason I urge boaters to carry some simple survival gear in their dinghies. First, I would recommend a handheld VHF radio for obvious reasons. If there are any other boats around this may be your best chance for getting some assistance. A good anchor and plenty of line are also high on the list. I do not mean one of those small three pound anchors with thirty feet of line that is only used on the beach to keep your dinghy from drifting to Cuba. It may pay to sacrifice the onboard room and use a substantial anchor with a couple of feet of chain and at least 100' of line. Just as you would go oversize on your mother vessel do the same with your dinghy. If you are being blown away from land a good anchor and plenty of line gives you a good chance of staying put where someone may find you.

Next, a dinghy should have a supply of flares. Local boaters often carry a large coffee can with a rag soaked in oil lying in the bottom. If they get in trouble lighting the rag will produce an abundant amount of smoke that can be seen from a quite a distance. A dinghy should be equipped with survival water, a bottle or some small packages manufactured by a company called *DATREX*. It would be a good idea to throw in a few *MRE*'s. These are the modern, tastier version of *K-Rations* that our armed forces survived on for years. Each *MRE* also contains vital survival components such as matches and toilet paper. Another handy item that does not take up much room is a foil survival blanket. They really work and take up as much space as a couple of packs of cigarettes.

Please don't laugh at these suggestions. I have seen people forced to spend a night or two in a dinghy and these few items would have made their experience much more pleasant if not entirely unnecessary. I have run out of gas and used flares to attract some local attention even though one of my boat mates was ready to dive in and swim for the nearest island to fetch some help. Now, I never leave in my dinghy without my little survival bag stashed away in the dink. It doesn't take much effort to prepare a small bag for your dinghy and it will be worth its weight in gold should you need it.

One final word, if you find the need to skirt a large sandbank lying to leeward of a cay remember that even though the sandbanks stretch out quite a way to the west, there is usually a channel of slightly deeper water nearer the shoreline of the cays.

Diving

From shallow water reef dives to deep water wall drop-offs, the diving in the Bahamas and the Turks and Caicos Islands is as good as it gets anywhere and much better than most places. You don't need scuba equipment to enjoy the undersea delights that are available; many reefs lie in less than 30' and are easily accessible to those with snorkels, dinghies, and curiosity.

Providenciales is a hotbed of diving activity with more than a half-dozen different diving shops offering dive trips, charters, and complete instructions. In the waters between *Grace Bay* and Pine Cay you'll find wonderful spur & groove coral reefs, which consist of central reefs with arm-like lateral extensions and grooves. The spur and groove coral generally runs perpendicular to the wall, which runs parallel to the shoreline. West Caicos is known for its many great dives just off its dramatic limestone cliffs.

Grand Turk represents a wealth of tremendous experiences for the diver. Less than a quarter of a mile off shore and starting in just 25'-45' of water, a coral wall runs the full length of the island, with profiles ranging from steeply sloping terrain to interesting coral undercuts and perfectly vertical drop-offs.

The sponge growth and fish populations are spectacular and distinctively different from the other Turks and Caicos sites. You can expect manta rays in the summer, turtles year-round and humpback whales in the winter, this is a primary corridor for migrating humpback whales from December through April.

Some of the world's best wall diving can be found within 300 yards of the western shore of Grand Turk. Here coral cliffs drop from 30' below the surface to over 7,000' deep. Mooring buoys protect the delicate coral structure and there are several dive operations working these waters.

Although the waters in The Turks and Caicos are crystal clear and the obstructions plainly visible in the ambient light, divers must take proper precautions when diving in areas of current. Experienced divers are well aware of this, but it must be stated for novices and snorkelers. Tidal fluctuations can produce strong currents that must be taken into account when diving. Waves breaking over and around inshore reefs can create strong surges that can push or pull you into some very sharp coral. Only experienced divers should penetrate wrecks and caves.

Most of the dive sites in the Turks and Caicos have moorings installed by the *National Parks Committee* and maintained by the many dive boats that use them. Please do your part to protect these fragile coral eco-systems and don't anchor on the reefs; anchor nearby in sand, it holds better anyway.

While summer waters run about 82°F-84°F at the surface, it is certainly warm enough for swimsuits though most divers welcome protection in the form of a light cover-up. In the winter, water temperatures of 74°F-78°F would suggest the use of a wetsuit. Dive computers are an advantage owing to the multi-level nature of the diving in the Turks and Caicos.

Fishing

Fishing in the Bahamas is hard to beat. Trolling in the *Gulf Stream*, the *Atlantic Ocean*, *Exuma Sound*, or *Crooked Island Passage* you are likely to hook a dolphin, wahoo, or tuna, all excellent eating. Trolling on the banks you will usually catch a barracuda although it is possible to bring up a snapper, jack, or grouper. Bonefish can be found in the tidal flats scattered throughout the islands. Chris Lloyd of *BASRA* in Nassau offers this little ditty to those who are unsure what color lure to use for trolling offshore. Chris says:

Red and black-Wahoo attack.
Yellow and green-Dolphin fishing machine.

Chris works Monday through Friday at *BASRA* HQ in Nassau (http://www.basra.org/) and is quite an authority on fishing Bahamian waters. If you have any questions stop in and ask Chris. He loves visitors and is a wealth of fishing and diving information. Chris reminds us that the cooler months are ripe for wahoo while dolphin are more abundant from March through May.

The back of your fishing permit will have a brief but incomplete description of the fishing regulations in the Bahamas. Only six lines are permitted in the water at one time unless you have paid for a commercial permit (very expensive). SCUBA is illegal for the taking of marine life and an air compressor such as a *Third Lung* or similar type of apparatus, must have a permit issued by the *Minister of Agriculture*. Spear guns are illegal for fishing in the Bahamas. You may only use a Hawaiian sling or pole spear for spearfishing. It is illegal to use bleach, firearms, or explosives for fishing. Spearfishing is illegal within one mile of New Providence and within 200 yards of any family island (defined as any cay with a residence). The capture of bonefish by net is illegal as is their purchase or sale.

Possession of a hawksbill turtle is prohibited. The minimum size for a green turtle is 24" and for a loggerhead, 30". The bag limit for kingfish, dolphin, and wahoo is a maximum combination of 6 fish per person aboard.

Crawfish, the spiny lobster that is such a treat as well as being a large part of the economy for local fishermen, has a closed season from April 1-August 1. The minimum limits are a carapace length of 3 3/8" and a 6" tail length. It is illegal to possess a berried (egg laying) female or to remove the eggs from a female. As of 2004, the Government of the Bahamas has declared that the month of January is a closed season for Nassau Grouper. This has a serious effect on the economy of the local fisherman who remain very vocal in protest. The future of this ban is uncertain, it may be lifted or it may be expanded. Ask when you clear. Also, you may not take any live corals while in the Bahamas.

In the out-islands there are far fewer jobs than there are people looking for jobs. The people here must eke out a living the best way they can. Remember that when you are fishing. Please catch just enough to eat and maybe put some away for tomorrow. So often cruisers come through this area with huge freezers just waiting to be filled to the brim to help their owners offset vacation costs. If you over-fish an area you may be taking food out of the mouths of children. To help protect the livelihood of the people of the Bahamas, some of richer fishing spots will not be mentioned in this guide.

Although you can no longer take conch, FYI, conch can usually be found on the bottom in beds of sea grass or soft corals where they prefer to feed.

They are usually in areas with a swift current such as in the cuts between cays. The conch that you don't plan to eat right away can be left in a dive bag hanging in the water or may be put on a stringer. Punch or drill a small hole in the lip of the conch shell and string four or five together and set them on the bottom, they won't go far. After you clean the conch, save the tough orange colored skin and put it in your freezer for later, it is an excellent fish bait and a small piece of it should be placed on all lures to give them an attractive aroma to fish.

The reefs in the Bahamas can provide you with a plentiful supply of fish such as grouper, snapper, hogfish, turbots (trigger fish), and grunts. How many you can get is dependent on your skill with the spear. Groupers are especially wary and prefer holes in which to hide.

When near cays, the drop-offs are excellent for game and food fish. You may find yourself hooking a dolphin, wahoo, shark, kingfish, or tuna.

Crawfish is the principal delicacy that most cruisers search so hard for and which are getting increasingly difficult to find. They prefer to hide during the day under ledges, and rocks, and in holes where the only visible sign of them will be a pair of antennae resembling some sort of sea fan jutting out from their hiding spot. If you are fortunate enough to spear a few, and they are large enough, do not overlook the succulent meat in the base of the antennae and in the legs. So many cruisers ignore these pieces and just take the tail. Watch a Bahamian as they prepare a lobster, very little goes to waste.

The drop-offs around the Turks and Caicos Islands offer fishing that is as good as it gets anywhere. The annual *Provo International Billfish Tournament*, usually held in mid-summer, results in a great number of billfish including blue marlin and swordfish being weighed-in. In 1996 for example, a 599 lb. blue marlin was hauled in, the largest ever caught in the Turks and Caicos Islands. Of course you can also find dolphin, wahoo, kings, yellowfin, and bonita in large numbers when trolling offshore. The Caicos Banks are ideal bonefishing grounds and there are several guides around the Provo area to choose from.

There are several different categories of fishing permits. Most visiting skippers only need a regular sportfishing license. Tournaments and charter sportfishing boats have separate categories. If you intend to fish on the *Mouchoir Banks* you will need a special permit for that privilege. A regular sportfishing permit cost $15 for thirty days and is renewable. They can be purchased at the *DECR, the Department of the Environment and Coastal Resources* (sometimes just referred to as *Fisheries*), upstairs from the *Public Treasury* in Provo or at their office on Grand Turk. Licenses can also be picked up at *Turtle Cove Marina* ($16 as of this writing) at Sellar's Pond on Provo, and at *J & B Tours* at *Leeward Marina,* also on Provo. Remember that you are not allowed to fish within the boundaries of any national park in the Turks and Caicos Islands, and especially at the drop-off along the reefs bordering Provo.

Fishing permits are only valid for hook and line fishing, the use of spear guns, pole spears, and Hawaiian slings are not permitted in the Turks and Caicos Islands. Every July the *Minister* must go before the *Executive Council* to lift the ban on the use of hooks to catch lobsters for the local licensed commercial fishermen. This allows the commercial fellows to use a hook on the end of a pole to snag the lobster and also to have a Hawaiian sling in the water with them for protection (visiting skippers may also have a Hawaiian sling with them in the water for protection but if caught the burden is on you to prove its necessity; fines for violations of Turks and Caicos fishing regulations can go as high as $50,000 and/or 12 months in jail and yes, *Fisheries* does patrol their waters!).

Lobster and conch may not be taken from the waters of the Turks and Caicos by visitors to these islands. The use of SCUBA and hookah rigs for fishing are also not permitted in the Turks and Caicos Islands. Even with a fishing permit, you are only allowed 10 pounds of fish per day for consumption. In other words, you are not allowed to fill your freezer. Skippers holding a valid license may remove one fish from the Turks and Caicos for trophy mounting purposes.

Garbage

When I first began cruising I had this naive idea that all cruisers lived in a certain symbiosis with nature. My bubble finally burst with the bitter realization that many cruisers were infinitely worse than common litterbugs. So often they have the attitude of "out of sight, out of mind." I sometimes wonder if they believe in supernatural beings, hoping that if they dump their trash somewhere imaginary

garbage fairies will come along and take care of the disposal problems for them.

One cruiser leaves a few bags of garbage in some secluded (or not so secluded) spot and the next cruiser says "My, what a good spot for a garbage dump. Ethel, bring the garbage, I've found the dump!" This is why you often go ashore on otherwise deserted islands and find bags and piles of bags of garbage. Nothing is worse than entering paradise only to discover some lazy, ignorant, slob of a cruiser (no, I have not been too harsh on this type of person, I can still think of plenty of other adjectives without having to consult a thesaurus) has dumped his bags of garbage in the bushes. Please do not add to this problem. Remember, your garbage attracts all kinds of foul creatures such as rats (and other careless cruisers).

Nobody likes storing bags of smelly garbage aboard but if you cannot find a settlement nearby to take your garbage for free, you will have to make an allowance in your budget to pay for the local garbage disposal service. If you are nowhere near a garbage facility you should stow your trash aboard separated into three groups for easier disposal. First cans and bottles (wash them first to remove any smells), then into another container stow the organic stuff such as food scraps, rinds, and eggshells, and finally paper and plastic trash. Your food scraps, stored in a large coffee can with a lid, can be thrown overboard on an outgoing tide. Paper and plastic should be burned completely and the ashes buried deep and not on the beach. Cans and bottles should be punctured or broken and dumped overboard in very deep water at least a few miles offshore. Cut off both ends of the cans and break the bottles overboard as you sink them. If you cannot implement a garbage disposal policy aboard your vessel, stay home, don't come to these beautiful islands. Do not abuse what we use

Ham Radio

Amateur radio operators will need a Bahamian reciprocal license, C6A, to operate in the waters of the Bahamas. To obtain one you must write at least two months before you will leave for the islands and actually need your license. Send a copy of your valid General class or better license along with a copy of the photo page of your passport and a US Postal Money Order (no personal checks) for $10.00 to: Utilities Regulation and Competition Authority(URCA), Utilities Regulation and Competition Authority, Frederick

House, Frederick Street, P.O. Box N 4860, Nassau, Bahamas. URCA's phone number is 242 396-5200, fax number is 242 393-0153, and their email is info@urcabahamas.bs.

The following is a listing of ham nets you may wish to participate in during your cruise through the waters of The Bahamas and the Turks and Caicos Islands.

Net Name	Time ET	Freq. KHz
Bah. Am. Radio Society	0830 Sundays	3,696
Bah. Wx Net	0720	3,696 or 7,096
Caribbean Net	1100-1200 UTC	7,420*
Computer Net	0900 Fridays	7,268
CW Net - slow	0630 M,W,F	7,128
CW Net - fast	0630 T, T, S, S	7,128
Hurricane Net	As needed	14,325; 14,275; 14175
Intercontinental	1100 UTC	14,300, 14216*
Maritime Mobile	After Intercon.	14,300, 14216*
TACARS	0800 Sundays	3,780
Waterway Net	0745	7,268

*This frequency changes often

All visitors to the Turks & Caicos Islands on production of a valid Amateur Radio License from their own country, with the necessary application form and fee, will receive a VP5/Home-call License. Maritime Mobile visitors within 12 nautical miles of the Turks & Caicos Islands must apply for and have a Visitors License before operating

The Wireless Telegraphy (Amateur Radio Operator Licensing) Regulations 2004 designates the Turks and Caicos Amateur Radio Society, ("TACARS") as the certifying organization of qualified persons to operate amateur radio in the Turks & Caicos Islands. Qualified persons are those that hold a valid un-expired amateur license from another country and have complied with the necessary application processes. Additionally, residents who have passed a properly administered test of TACARS and have complied with the necessary application processes may also be qualified to operate amateur radio in the Turks and Caicos Islands. Every license issued is valid for the calendar year in which it is granted and

expires on 31 December in that year (except special event licenses, see below).

To get a visitor's license, you will need to submit a completed application form (you can download one at http://www.tacars.org/license.pdf), a copy of your current home amateur radio license, and a check payable to T.A.C.A.R.S. for $35.00 in U.S. currency (if a Special Event license is requested include an additional $35.00). Send all of this via *FedEx* to Jody Millspaugh (the *FedEx* recipient phone number is 649-946-4436), *Cherokee Road,* Providenciales, Turks and Caicos Islands, B.W.I.

If you wish to check on the status of your application via the Internet, Jody's email address is jody@carbisurf.com. Reciprocal licenses may be collected by the operator upon arrival in Providenciales or Jody will send you a copy prior to your departure, your regular license will still need to be picked up in person after your arrival in Provo. You can phone Jody Millspaugh, VP5JM, at 649-946-4436 to arrange for pickup. If you arrive in the Provo without a reciprocal, you can call Jody at the above mentioned number and she will arrange to meet you so you may apply for your license. Jody will give you a receipt that will allow you to transmit until your regular license arrives.

The Turks and Caicos do not have a third-party agreement with the United States; this means that you cannot make a phone patch from the Turks and Caicos Islands to the U.S. If you head offshore at least twelve nautical miles you will be in international waters and can make a phone patch from there without using your VP5.

Holidays

The Bahamas

New Year's Day - January 1
Good Friday
Easter Sunday
Easter Monday
Whit Monday - six weeks after Easter
Labour Day - first Friday in June
Independence Day - July 10
Emancipation Day - first Monday in August
Discovery Day - October 12
Christmas Day - December 25
Boxing Day - December 26

Holidays that fall on Sunday are always observed on Monday. Holidays that fall on Saturday are also usually observed on Monday. Bahamians are very religious people so expect stores and services to be closed on Sundays as well as on Holidays. Some businesses may be open all day on Saturday but may close for a half day on Wednesdays. A must see is the *Junkanoo* parade that begins about 0400 on *Boxing Day* and *New Year's Day* in Nassau and Freeport.

The following public holidays are observed in

The Turks and Caicos

New Year's Day - January 1
Commonwealth Day (March; date varies)
Good Friday
Easter Sunday
Easter Monday
National Hero's Day (May; date varies)
Her Majesty The Queen's Official Birthday (usually the second Sunday)
Emancipation Day - August 1
National Youth Day (September; date varies)
Columbus Day
International Human Rights Day - October 24
Christmas Day
Boxing Day - December 26

Holidays that fall on Sunday are always observed on Monday. Holidays that fall on Saturday are also usually observed on Monday.

The following public holidays are observed in

The Dominican Republic

New Year's Day - January 1
Epiphany - January 6 (usually celebrated on the closest Friday or Monday)
Our Lady of Altagracia Day - January 21
Juan Pablo Duarte's Birthday - January 26 (usually celebrated on the closest Friday or Monday)
Independence Day - February 27
Good Friday
Easter Sunday
Easter Monday
Labor Day - May 1
Ascension Day - varies
Feast of Corpus Christi - varies in May and June
Restoration of the Republic Day - August16
Our Lady of Mercedes Day - September 24
Columbus Day
Christmas Day

Dominicans love festivals and the calendar year has several for you to enjoy. Carnival in Santo Domingo

takes place along the Santo Domingo Malecón the week of February 27 during the *Independence Day* celebrations. The famous *Merengue Festival* is a lively celebration of the country's national music, with *Merengue* bands performing at most major hotels and along the Santo Domingo Malecón. This huge party takes place from the last week in July through the first week of August.

The term *Merengue* refers both to the music and the dance, which evolved in the Dominican countryside among the happy people of a divided island. The history of the *Merengue* is woven into the fabric of Dominican history itself. This Afro-Caribbean dance became part of country life and is still danced today around the squares of small villages, next to bonfires on secluded beaches, in ballrooms, and in nightclubs throughout the world. In the traditional countryside settings, the music is provided by a *Perico Ripiao*, a small band made up of an accordion, a drum, a guiro and a box bass. Puerto Plata's *Merengue Festival* is held during the second week of October. Christmas celebrations begin in early December and end on *Epiphany Day* on January 6.

One of the biggest celebrations in Luperón is the huge *St. Patrick's Day* party, a great mix of locals and cruisers which has started drawing crowds of 1,000. There's music and a pig roast on the beach and each boat contributes a few pesos to cover the cost of the food they eat.

Hurricane Holes

THERE IS NO SUCH THING AS A HURRICANE HOLE!

There is no anchorage so secure that it cannot be decimated by a strong hurricane and a high storm surge. There are no guarantees; there is no Fort Knox to hide in when a named windstorm threatens. Now, with that out of the way we can discuss how to protect yourself in those special places that offer the best hurricane protection. Let's begin our discussion with what constitutes protection and pass along a few hints as to how to secure yourself as well as get along with your neighbors.

First, make sure your fuel is topped off and you have enough food and water for an extended period. Also, make sure you have enough cash to see you through as phone lines may be down for a while which would prohibit credit card usage. Once your tanks, lockers, and wallet are topped off, you can head for protection. Some skippers prefer to head to sea when a hurricane threatens. Some will take off at a ninety-degree angle from the hurricane's forecast path, usually heading south to Venezuela. I cannot advise you as to what course to take, but I for one, unless absolutely necessary, will not gamble with racing a storm that is unpredictable no matter what the forecasters claim.

For protection, most of us would prefer a narrow creek that winds deep into the mangroves where we will be as snug as the proverbial bug-in-a-rug. These creeks are rare, and to be assured of space you must get there early. When a storm threatens, you can bet that everybody will soon be aware of it and the early birds will settle in the best places. Sure, those early birds might have to spend a night or two in the hot, buggy mangroves, but isn't that better than coming in too late and finding the best spots taken and your choices for protection down to anchoring in the middle of a pond with a bit of fetch and no mangroves to offer protection? Hint number one..get to safety early and secure your vessel.

So how do you secure your vessel? Easy! First, find a likely looking spot where you'll be safest from the oncoming winds. Try to figure out by the forecast path of the storm where the wind will be coming from as the storm passes and plan accordingly (remember that the winds blow counterclockwise around the center in the northern hemisphere). If your chosen spot is in a creek that is fine. Set out bow and stern anchors and tie off your vessel to the mangroves on each side with as many lines as you can, including lines off the bow and stern to assist the anchors.

Use plenty of chafe gear (I like old fire-hose, leather, and towels) as the lines lead off your boat and rig your lines so that they don't work back and forth on the mangroves as well. If chain can be used to surround the mangroves that will help. If other boats wish to proceed further up the creek past your position, remove your lines from one side of your boat to allow them to pass. Courtesy amongst endangered vessels will add to the safety factor of all involved, especially if somebody needs to come to somebody else's aid later on.

If your only choice is to head into the mangroves bow or stern first, always go in bow first; it stands to reason that if you place your stern into the mangroves serious rudder damage could result. I prefer to go

bow-in as far as I can, until my boat settles her keel in the mud (trying to keep the bow just out of contact with the mangroves), tie off well, and set out at least two stern anchors. If other boats will be tying off into the mangroves in the same manner on each side of you, courtesy dictates each skipper assist the other in the setting of anchors (so that they don't snag on each other) and the securing of lines in the mangroves (and don't forget to put out fenders).

If you must anchor in the open, away from the mangroves, place your anchors to give you 360° protection. The greatest danger to your vessel will likely be the other boats around you, and in the Caribbean there's going to be a better than average chance that you'll be sharing your hole with several unattended boats, often times charter boats that are not secured in the best of manners. A good lookout is necessary for these added dangers.

Once secure, your next step is to strip everything off your boat and stow it below. Sails, bimini top, dodger, awnings, rail-mounted grill, wind-generators, solar panels, jerry cans, and anything small and loose that can become a dangerous object should it fly away at a hundred plus miles an hour. And, don't forget to secure your dinghy as well! Keep a mask and snorkel handy in the cockpit, you might need it to stand watch. Also, keep a sharp knife close at hand; you never know when you might need it. Pack all your important papers in a handy waterproof container, and in the most severe of circumstances, use duct tape to secure your passport, wallet, and/or purse to your body. Plan ahead as you secure your vessel so that you will not have to go on deck if you don't absolutely have to, it is most difficult to move about in 100-knot winds.

If you are going to be cruising in The Bahamas from June through November, hurricane season, you should always keep a lookout for a safe hurricane hole. In the northern and central Bahamas you're never too far away from some sort of refuge, some holes are better than others but like the old adage advises: Any port in a storm. With that in mind let me offer a few of the places I consider hurricane holes. Bear in mind that if you ask ten different skippers what they look for in a hurricane hole you're likely to get ten different answers. Some of these holes may not meet your requirements. I offer them only for your consideration when seeking safety for your vessel. The final decision is yours and yours alone. For the best information concerning hurricane holes always check with the locals. They'll know the best spots.

The Bahamas

Abaco

The best protection in the Abacos lies in places like *Treasure Cay Marina* where you can also anchor in the narrow creeks surrounding the marina complex. There is a man-made canal complex called Leisure Lee lying just south of Treasure Cay on Great Abaco. Here you will find excellent protection from seas in 8' but you will have to tie off to the trees along the shore as the entire complex is dredged and the holding is not good. Green Turtle Cay offers *White Sound* and *Black Sound*. I much prefer *White Sound* though there is a bit more fetch for seas to build up. *Black Sound,* though smaller, has a grassy bottom and a few concrete mooring blocks scattered about. At Man Of War Cay you can choose either anchorage. Just to the south on Elbow Cay, Hope Town Harbour boasts very good protection. If you arrive early enough and your draft is shallow enough you may be able to work your way up the creek for better protection. There is an old hurricane chain stretched across the harbour to which you may be able to secure your vessel. Ask any local where to find the chain. Just a few miles away lies *Marsh Harbour* with that wonderful sand/mud bottom that anchors so love (but the harbour is open to the west for a fetch of over a mile).

For small shallow draft (3') monohull vessels there is a small creek on the eastern side of the harbour just to the east of the *Conch Inn Marina*. Get there early. Farther south you might consider Little Harbour though it is open to the north with a 3' bar across the mouth. Between Marsh Harbour and Little Harbour lies Snake Cay which has excellent protection in its mangrove lined creeks. To the north, you can try Hurricane Hole on the SE end of Allan's Pensacola Cay. Excellent protection can be found in 6'-8' of water but the bar at the entrance will only allow about 4'-6' at high water, depending on the tidal height that particular day. Small shallow draft vessels can work their way well up into the creeks at Double Breasted Cay if unable to get to better protection to the south.

Andros

An excellent spot for vessels drawing less than 4' is in the small pocket at *Stafford Creek* that lies north of the bridge. Enter only at high tide. If you draw over 6' and are in Andros when a hurricane threatens

you would be better off to get to New Providence or someplace in the Exumas, although I know several boaters that weathered *Hurricane Michelle* at the dock in *Fresh Creek* (the eye of the hurricane passed over *Fresh Creek* with winds in excess of 100 mph).

The Berry Islands

There are only three places to consider in the Berry Islands and two of them were hit hard by powerful *Hurricane Andrew*. *Chub Cay Marina* is a possibility if you didn't mind a slip or perhaps tying off between pilings. The marina was devastated by Andrew and quite a few boats destroyed. Something to remember when it's decision making time. Another possibility would be to work your way into Little Harbour. There is a winding channel into the inner anchorage where you can tuck into a narrow channel just north of the Darville's dock in 7'-11' of water with mangroves to the east and a shallow bar and a small cay to the west. Little Harbour is open to the north but there is a large shallow bank with 1'-3' over it just north of the mangroves. By far the best place to be in a hurricane is in Bullock's Harbour at *Great Harbour Cay Marina*.

Bimini

The best protection in the Biminis is up the creeks of South Bimini by way of *Nixon's Harbour*. Seven feet can get in over the bar at high tide where you'll find plenty of secure water inside. On the west side of South Bimini lies the entrance to the Port Royal canals. Five feet can make it over the bar with spots of 7'-10' inside. Be sure to tie up in vacant areas between houses.

On the north side of South Bimini is another entrance to some small canals with a 4' bar at the entrance from the harbour at North Bimini. Take into consideration that these canals have plenty of wrecks lining the shores along with old rotten pilings jutting up here and there. The surrounding land is very low and the canals may become untenable in a high storm surge.

Cat Island

Unless you have a small, shallow draft vessel and can get up *Orange Creek* or *Bennett's Creek* along the western shore of Cat Island, your only choice may be *Hawks Nest Creek* on the southwestern tip of Cat Island. Six feet can enter here at MLW and work its way up the creek. *Bennett's Harbour* offers good protection but it is small and open to the north.

Crooked/Acklins

The only protection here will be found in the maze of creeks between French Wells and Turtle Sound for boats with drafts of 3' or less, or by going through The Going Through towards the *Bight of Acklins*. Here you will find a maze of shallow creeks leading to numerous small mangrove lined holes, perfect little hidey-holes for the shallow draft cruiser (up to 4' or less draft) seeking shelter.

Eleuthera

There are a few holes in Eleuthera but they all suffered considerable damage from *Hurricane Andrew*. Royal Island offers excellent protection and good holding, but during *Hurricane Andrew* the fleet washed up on one shore only to be washed up on the other shore after the eye passed. *Hatchet Bay* is often considered a prime hurricane hole but it too has a history of damage as the hulls along the shore will testify. At Spanish Wells you will find *Muddy Hole* lying off the creek between Russell Island and St. George's Cay. *Muddy Hole* is the local hurricane hole and 4' can enter here at MLW if you get there early. Every boat (and there are a lot of them) at Spanish Wells will be heading there also. Some skippers like *Cape Eleuthera Marina* at Powell Point but I wouldn't use it as shelter unless I had no other choice.

The dogleg marina channel is open to the west and large seas easily work their way into the basin rocking and rolling everybody. The huge concrete breakwater at the bend in the dogleg has suffered considerable damage and offers testimony to the power of the seas that enter the marina. Just south of Powell Point lies No Name Harbour, Un-Named Harbour on some charts. Seven feet can enter here at MLW and 6' can work farther up the small coves that branch off and offer fair protection. You might consider tying your lines to the trees and setting your anchors ashore here, the holding is not that great being as this is a dredged harbour.

The Exumas

The Exumas Cays are home to some of the best hurricane holes in The Bahamas. From the north you should consider the inner pond at Norman's Cay. The pond offers excellent protection and good holding although there is a mile long north-south fetch that could make things rough at best. Shroud Cay has some excellent creeks with a reputation as good hurricane holes. Dr. Evans Cottman rode out a fierce

hurricane here as documented in his book *Out Island Doctor*.

Compass Cay has a snug little cove for protection with moorings, a marina, and creeks for shallow draft vessels. Farther south at Sampson Cay you may be able to tie up in the marina on the eastern side of the complex in the shallow and well-protected basin. I have known people to anchor between the Majors just north of Staniel Cay for hurricane shelter though I personally would try to find someplace a little more protected. At the north end of Great Guana Cay lies a small, shallow creek that gives fair to good protection for one or two small vessels drawing less than 5'.

Cave Cay is an excellent hurricane hole with room for four boats in 6' at MLW. Many experienced captains like the pond at Rudder Cut Cay as a refuge but I see the eastern shore as being very low. I believe a strong hurricane with a large storm surge and high tide might make this anchorage a death trap. The George Town area is home to what may be the finest holes in The Bahamas. Holes #0, #2, and #3 at Stocking Island are excellent hurricane holes in every sense offering protection from wind and wave. The only problem here is that these holes will be crowded and Hole #3 is usually full of stored boats with absentee owners. The inner cove at Red Shanks offers good protection if you can get in close to the mangroves. Another possibility is inside the western arm of Crab Cay.

Grand Bahama

If you're in the area of Grand Bahama Island you might consider tying up at *Old Bahama Bay Marina* at West End. Although the marina offers excellent protection a direct hit by a major hurricane would likely do considerable damage to this complex. From the north of Grand Bahama you can consider entering *Hawksbill Creek* though it only has 2' over the bar at its entrance with 5'-6' inside at MLW. The *Grand Lucayan Waterway* offers very good protection. You can tie up anywhere deep within its concrete lined canals but you cannot pass under the *Casuarina Bridge* unless your height is less than 27' at high water. The canal has a fairly uniform depth of 5' throughout although the northern entrance has shoaled to around 3'-4½' at MLW. Another option would be to tie up at *Lucayan Marina* or in the small coves surrounding the complex that offer some very good protection.

New Providence

Here, in the capitol of The Bahamas, Nassau Harbour has fair to good holding along with a long east-west fetch. There are two hurricane chains crossing the harbour whose approximate locations are shown on the chart for Nassau. If you're fortunate enough to know someone in *Coral Harbour* you may be able to use their dock to escape the seas. On the southwestern shore of Rose Island is the entrance to a very good hurricane hole shown as Salt Pond on charts. It is a circular harbour with a small island in the center. The channel is easily 50'-60' wide and 7'-9' deep. Anchor and tie off between the shore and the island. Get there early as everyone in Nassau and the northern Exumas will have the same idea.

Long Island

If I had to find a place to hide from a hurricane while visiting Long Island my first choice would be in the canals that wind behind the marina at Stella Maris. Some skippers have suggested Joe's Sound but I find the land to the west too low and a tidal surge like the one in *Hurricane Lili* (9'-14') would make this anchorage untenable. Another consideration is in the mangrove tidal creeks in the Dollar Harbour area but the best protection is hard to get into unless you have a draft of less than 4'.

The Jumentos and Ragged Island

There are only two possibilities here and both are in the vicinity of Ragged Island. A boat with a draft of less than 5' can work its way up the mangrove lined channel to anchor in the harbor at Duncan Town. Here you will find 4'-6' at high water with mangroves and cliffs surrounding you. This would be a fantastic hurricane hole if it were just a couple of feet deeper. The people of Duncan Town are in the process of having their channel re-dredged, perhaps they will do something with the harbour area also. Just south of Ragged Island is a small hole called Boat Harbour that some Ragged Islanders use as a hurricane hole. There is 9' inside but there is a winding channel with a 3' bar at the entrance. Ask any Ragged Islander for directions, they'll be happy to help.

The Southern Bahamas

If you are cruising the southern Bahamas from Crooked-Acklins to Mayaguana or Inagua you will not find a truly safe hole. Although I have heard about a large sailboat riding out *Hurricane Klaus* lying between Samana and Propeller Cay I would not attempt to test my luck. I would either head north to better protection at George Town or continue on to The Turks and Caicos for protection at Sellar's Pond or up the canals at *Discovery Bay* lying northeast of Five Cays, at Leeward Going Through, or up *North Creek* at Grand Turk. If I had enough time I would try to make Luperón in the Dominican Republic, which is as good a hole as any in the Caribbean.

The Turks and Caicos Islands

In the Caicos Islands, Providenciales offers several dredged canals that offer an opportunity to get well inland, hopefully away from any damaging seas though you may still be affected by a storm surge. On the south side of Providenciales, the canals at *Cooper Jack Bight* are a favorite place for local boaters and are well protected. A 6½' draft can enter here at high water. Bear in mind that when anchoring in any of the dredged canals around Provo, that the bottom will likely be poor holding; you'll have to set some of your anchors on shore here.

A small, narrow, shallow canal, leads northward from *Caicos Marina and Shipyard* to some private residences in the *Long Bay Hills* section of Provo and offers excellent protection but draft is limited to 3'-4' at low water; the canal entrance, through a small bascule bridge, prohibits wide multihull vessels.

In Leeward Going Through there is a small canal leading into the Leeward community. The bar at the entrance restricts entry to vessels with drafts of less than 5' at high tide. Leeward Going Through has often been used as a hurricane hole by some skippers and should also be considered as well as the cuts between Pine Cay and Fort George Cay, Ft. George Cay and Dellis Cay, and between Dellis Cay and Parrot Cay. A word of warning about the tides here during hurricanes. When a storm surge approaches from the south across the banks, the water rushes in the southern sides of these cuts at a good clip. One past hurricane raised the water level in Leeward Going Through by over 6'. You can probably imagine the current involved with the movement of that much water, so use extreme care when securing your vessel. On the northern shore, folks were walking around in knee-deep water in the central portion of *Turtle Cove Marina* during *Hurricane Frances* in 2004, that's an approximate surge of six to eight feet.

On the northern shore of Providenciales, skippers should consider Sellar's Pond and *Turtle Cove Marina*, a very well protected spot. But check with the marina first for space availability; they might not want to take on any other boats. Just west of Sellar's Pond is small Thompson's Cove, a private dredged community with a sign warning that all unauthorized boats will be removed. Drafts of less than 5' can work their way in here on a high tide. There are several undeveloped lots and if one did not have permission to tie up inside, one would have to hope that the land owners would understand that a life threatening storm chased you inside and you would not leave until the danger passed. As well protected as Thompson Cove is, I would probably make it my last choice.

Shallow draft boats, those with drafts of less than 3', could work their way into some of the creeks between North Caicos, Middle Caicos, and East Caicos if needed. South Caicos' Cockburn Harbour is excellent in most conditions but it is unsuitable to me as a hurricane shelter.

In the Turks Islands, the only choice for shelter is to round the northern tip of Grand Turk and seek shelter inside North Creek if conditions allow entry (see text in *Part II, The Turks Islands, Grand Turk, The North Creek Anchorage*). The entrance channel is limited to about 6½' on a normal high tide but once inside the water deepens to over 12' in places. There is quite a bit of north/south fetch to take into consideration.

The Dominican Republic

Along the northern shore of the Dominican Republic the best hurricane hole is in the harbor at Luperón, which is probably one of the best hurricane holes in the entire Caribbean. And although the rivers on the southern shore of the Dominican Republic look inviting and offer good protection, caution must be exercised as torrential rains will cause flooding and very strong currents, not to mention all manner of flotsam and jetsam floating down on you.

JoJo the Dolphin

JoJo is a very, very unique Atlantic bottlenose dolphin. Since 1980 JoJo has been plying the waters of the Turks and Caicos Islands centering on the Provo area. This friendly dolphin has become a powerful symbol for nature conservation in the Turks and Caicos Islands.

JoJo is one of the few dolphins around the world who have chosen to voluntarily interact with human beings in his own natural habitat. Much loved by the islanders, the government has proclaimed JoJo a National Treasure and in 1987 appointed a special Warden, Dean Bernal, to protect him. Dean first met JoJo in 1985 when JoJo began following Dean on his long swims out to the reefs off Providenciales. At that time JoJo was already a popular figure along the beachfront but he was known to bite people and he had a dangerous reputation. What most people did not know is that JoJo only bit those who tried to touch him as he cavorted in the shallows. It seems that for some wild dolphins, a human's attempt to touch the mammal is considered a threat and JoJo was simply defending himself.

At the time, Dean was employed as a Dive Instructor on Providenciales and each day after Dean's dive instructions, usually about 5:00 P.M., JoJo and Dean would begin their reef swim. They would swim out to the reef where Dean would meet a dive boat to conduct a night dive, and then Dean and JoJo would swim back to shore in the dark. Their nightly dives became a regular part of Dean's daily regimen and the relationship between Dean and JoJo grew stronger steadily. If JoJo showed up before the SCUBA lessons ended, he would playfully pull on Dean's regulator hose trying to drag him away from his students. Sometimes he would swim in high-speed circles around the group, effectively reducing the visibility to zero and canceling the instruction. Occasionally he would patiently wait, hovering just over Dean's shoulder, for the lessons to end. One time JoJo herded an 8' shark into the middle of the group to break up the day's class. Knowing that Dean will stay in the water with him for hours when they are with other marine life, JoJo has brought Dean fish, lobsters, turtles, manta rays, whale sharks, an occasional bull and nurse shark, and he has even herded in a baby humpback whale along with its mother. JoJo's playful antics are often aimed at others. Quite often water skiers in the waters off Provo would suddenly find themselves paddling water. JoJo likes to come up underneath the ski and butt it skyward throwing the skier. JoJo once took a diver's $3,000 camera and hid it in the reef but playfully returned it 15 minutes later.

Through patient observation since 1987, Dean has compiled an impressive collection of data providing a rare and complete look into a wild dolphin's life in the open ocean. Diaries, data sheets, video and film materials now form a library and a wealth of information on the behavior of dolphins in their natural habitat. Dean has been fortunate to witness and document

JoJo's behavior and interaction with whales, sharks, manta rays, other dolphins, numerous other forms of marine life, submarines, people and even terrestrial animals. Over the years, Dean has documented JoJo's growth through puberty, his competing for his position in a pod, his sickness and his well-being. Because of the Dean's ongoing *Dolphin Project*, the development of trust in his and JoJo's relationship, and Dean's position as a Warden, JoJo's life has been saved on numerous occasions. Dean has been able to treat JoJo's wounds caused by such incidents as entanglement in turtle nets, infections from stingray barbs, confrontations with sharks, and impacts from water ski boats. Dean has contacted *Club Med* about putting guards on their ski boats at a cost of about $200. *Club Med* refused and hired a lawyer for $400 to fight the case. Doesn't make sense, does it? It shows where *Club Med's* priorities lie. JoJo's first and worst injury came from a jet ski and Dean is fighting the new PWC rental business that just opened in Leeward Going Through.

As JoJo grows older, Dean's research is becoming far more complex. Since JoJo has expanded his 26-square mile home range around Provo to 260 miles (in 1997 JoJo was seen off Grand Turk, thirty miles across the deep Columbus Passage), it makes the research much more challenging, not to mention interesting and rewarding. JoJo is now mating and travelling with other dolphins intermittently, finding new feeding grounds, utilizing new habitats and migratory routes, and continuing to expand his experiences of what a young free-roaming, wild dolphin should be living and experiencing.

JoJo and Dean

Thanks to the JoJo Dolphin Project (http://www. marinewildlife.org/jojoProject.php), the importance of this information from a conservation and animal welfare perspective has given Dean the opportunity to develop his work into a full-time research project. Never before has the chance to learn about the behavior, interaction, health, habitat and needs of a single wild dolphin been so clearly available for study. The information is vital to the conservation of all dolphins because it provides a rare, intimate and relatively complete look at the dolphin's life in the wild.

JoJo is easily recognized. JoJo prefers the waters between Grace Bay and Pine Cay on the northern shore of Providenciales, but may be seen just about anywhere. If a dolphin approaches your vessel, sticking his head out of the water to look at you, or perhaps circling your boat at anchor, the chances are that this is JoJo. If you're diving and a large dolphin approaches you it will likely be JoJo. JoJo has numerous prop marks and scars on his body and fins and this makes him almost unmistakable.

JoJo has been known to approach divers very closely, getting as close as a foot or two away to satisfy his curiosity. If you are in the water and JoJo appears, there are several things you need to remember for your protection and his. First, understand that although JoJo is a wild creature, he is capable of expressing his feelings and his personality as well as aggression and anger. Never reach out to touch him, especially around the blowhole at the top of his head; this is his nose and he breathes through it. Do not approach JoJo, remain passive and let him come to you. Don't swim after him, he might perceive it as a threat and act defensively. If provoked he may bite or use his tail to slap you. If JoJo shows any behavior that you are uncomfortable with, do not panic; exit slowly from the water. Dean reminds us not to lie on our backs in the water as JoJo gets unpredictable at this. Actually he gets very amorous (if you follow my drift). He once tried to mate with the SCUBA tank of a female dive instructor I know in Provo.

JoJo is now a commercial entity as well. You can choose from the *JoJo Collection* of jewelry at the *Royal Jewels Duty Free* shop in Provo.

Junkanoo

The culture of The Bahamas, its heart and soul, the eyes through which it sees and is seen, is Junkanoo, with its spirit, music, dancing, singing, costumes and color. Standing along *Bay Street* in Nassau in the

early hours of *Boxing Day or New Year's Day*, one cannot help getting caught up in the frenzy that is Junkanoo. Junkanoo must be experienced on the street, where the clamor of the bells, whistles, and goombay drums approaching in the distance creates an electric feeling in the crowd who sway and jostle with the building excitement. The source of all this energy is the participants, organized groups and "scrap gangs," throbbing forward to the rhythm of the music. Groups vie in a heated competition for awards for best music, costumes, and dance.

Junkanoo was introduced to the American colonies by slaves from Africa's western coast. From there it quickly spread to Jamaica and The Bahamas. Its exact origins are unknown and the numerous derivations of the name *John Canoe* further complicate the matter. The West African name *Jananin Canno* was derived from a combination of the Quojas tribe's *Canno*, a supreme being, and *Janani*, who were the dead who became spirits and were seen as patrons or defenders of the tribe. The Jamaican John Canoe, a slave who insisted on his people having the right to their celebration, was known in eastern North Carolina as *John Kuner, John Kooner, John Canoe, Who-Who's*, and *Joncooner*. A West African trait often attributed to the origin of Junkanoo was an Ashanti figure known as *Jankomo*. *Jankomo* was famed for his dance in which he took two steps forward and one step back, a form of Junkanoo dancing prevalent in today's festival. Some researchers theorized that the name is a corruption of the French *gens innconnus* which, roughly translated, means unknown people or masked people.

Junkanoo developed as a celebration during the pre-emancipation days when slaves were allowed a special Christmas holiday. Not wanting to waste any of their holiday, they took to beginning their celebration well before dawn. It is said that the wild costumes, masks, and makeup were used by the slaves as a way to disguise themselves while exacting revenge upon their masters and settling grudges with fellow slaves. During the late 1800s, Junkanoo began taking on added dimensions and significance for Bahamian people. It became a vehicle for political expression and a catalyst for social change. The *Street Nuisance Act* of 1899 was aimed directly at Junkanoo attempting to reduce the amount of noise and length of celebration of the event in the hopes that Junkanoo would extinguish itself. Junkanoo continued, albeit a little quieter. During the economic depression of the early 1900s, Junkanoo

Junkanoo Reveler   Photo Courtesy of Alicia Bonnet

thrived on various parts of New Providence however and was back on *Bay Street* by 1947.

Junkanoo today is basically the same with some minor changes. It is no longer considered a social taboo to participate in Junkanoo and more and more women are parading in this once male dominated event. Junkanoo is a national event on the edge of becoming an international festival.

The heart of Junkanoo is the music which has changed little over the last 50 years. A typical Junkanoo band consists of lead drums, second or bass drums (goombay), cowbells, clappers, bugles, trumpets, horns, conch shells, and whistles. A few obscure instruments, such as the fife, are no longer used.

The drum is the core of the music. Drums are made every year from goat or sheep skin and represent a sacrifice, the spilling of blood to make a drum. Drummers often place a flame inside the drum or heat it up over a fire, this is called "bringing it up" and helps produce various drum tones. The combined effect of the music, the bells and drums and horns, all fueled by the emotion of the participants, is overwhelming

The costumes create a tremendous visual effect and are painstakingly manufactured by hand. The costumes are brightly colored and usually represent some theme. There are no weight restrictions on costumes and one single piece may weigh over 200 pounds. Competition among the various groups is fierce and members are very secretive about their upcoming productions.

was characterized by rival masked and costumed gangs from the various districts of New Providence. Money was scarce and the costumes changed from cloth to papier-mâché and became more frightening and grotesque.

World War I saw the suspension of Junkanoo when the white inhabitants of Nassau felt the celebrations were unsuitable considering the wartime conditions and Junkanoo was banned from Bay Street until well after the war. It moved to the "over the hill" section of Nassau where it grew and prospered. The prosperous bootlegging period of the 1920s in The Bahamas was reflected in more flamboyant costumes and headdresses. Junkanoo moved back to *Bay Street* in 1923 when its potential for increasing tourism revenue became apparent. It was at this time that Junkanoo became a competition with prizes being awarded.

Junkanoo was again banned from *Bay Street* in 1942 when riots broke out due to labor unrest and all public gatherings were banned. Junkanoo still

Mailboats

You do not have to own a yacht to see The Bahamas by sea. You will find you can go almost anywhere within the island chain by mailboat. One need only approach the dockmaster on Potter's Cay for schedules and costs. Shipping times are announced three times daily on ZNS radio in Nassau. The mailboats are subsidized by the Bahamian government for carrying the mail, but they also take on freight and passengers. It is an inexpensive and rewarding way to see the out-islands. If you book passage you will gain a different view of the Bahamian people as travel by mailboat is a cultural experience as well as being a mode of transportation.

People on the outer islands would find life hard indeed if not for the mailboats, they are the lifeline of the Bahamian out-islands and the arrival of the mailboat is somewhat of a celebration. Costs range from $30.00 for a trip to Little Farmer's Cay to slightly higher for George Town or Inagua. Some mailboats include food in the fare. For more information on schedules and fares, visit the office on Potter's Cay.

And while we're on the subject of mailboats, let me clarify something. I've heard people say that if you can't find the way you wish to go, follow a Mailboat. This is fine for deepwater passages, but you must remember that Mailboat captains know these waters and they accept the fact that they must frequently pay the price for error, which does happen no matter how well somebody knows the waters. To be more succinct, the mailboats carry spare props, do you?

Medical Emergencies

The Bahamas

There are two hospitals in Nassau, *Princess Margaret Hospital* (http://www.pmh.phabahamas.org/) on *Shirley Street,* and *Doctor's Hospital* (http://www.doctorshosp.com/) on the corner of *Shirley Street* and Collins Ave. On Lyford Cay, also on the island of New Providence, is the *Lyford Cay Hospital and Bahamas Heart Centre* (http://www.cmp-bahamas.com/Heart/index.php).

If more medical assistance is needed the patient will be flown into Nassau, usually to *Princess Margaret Hospital*. *National Air Ambulance* out of Ft. Lauderdale, Florida (305-359-9900 or 800-327-3710), can transport patients from the Bahamas to the United States. If you join *DAN*, the *Divers Alert Network (http://www.diversalertnetwork.org/)*, for a small yearly fee, you are covered under their *Assist America Plan*. This program offers emergency evacuation for any accident or injury, diving related or not, to the nearest facility that can provide you with adequate care. After you have been stabilized to the satisfaction of the attending physician and the *Assist America* doctor, *Assist America* will arrange your transportation back to the United States, under medical supervision if necessary. Bear in mind that this is a reimbursement policy, make sure you are clear on this matter before joining.

The *Bahamas Air-Sea Rescue Association, BASRA (http://www.basra.org/),* has stations in Nassau, Black Point, and George Town in the

Exumas, Salt Pond in Long Island, and at Landrail Point on Crooked Island. All *BASRA* stations monitor VHF ch.16, while *BASRA* Nassau monitors 2182 KHz and 4125 KHz on marine single sideband from 0900-1700, Monday through Saturday. *BASRA*, Nassau, can be reached by phone at 242-322-3877. Bear in mind that the *BASRA* stations in the out-islands are staffed strictly by volunteers and they may not monitor the VHF 24-hours a day.

The Turks and Caicos

Provo has a few medical centers to fill most any need. On Leeward Highway is *the Menzies Medical Practice and Interisland Medical Services* (946-4242/4321, and 941-5252; menzies@tciway.tc). Here are three full-time physicians, a dentist, an optometrist, a chiropractor, a psychologist, and a pharmacy. Services include an emergency room and ambulance, general family practice, and trauma care. Divers will be happy to know that *Menzies* has a hyperbaric chamber on site staffed by trained personnel. *Menzies* offers a Florida lab linkup and obstetric ultrasound. *The Myrtle Rigby Health Clinic* (941-3000) is a government run facility with a full time Physician and nursing staff that is also located on *Leeward Highway*. *Rigby's* offers family practice, X-ray, obstetrics and ultra-sound, lab services, casualty reception, and a maternity unit.

The *New Era Medical Centre* (941-5455/3233) is located in Blue Hills and is staffed by one doctor offering family practice, a pharmacy, lab, emergency defibrillation and *EKG* units, delivery and post-natal care. *New Era* is open 24 hours and monitors VHF ch. 82. Other medical services include Dr. Steve Bourne (231-0000; bourne@tciway.tc), Dr. Dawn O'Sullivan (231-1350, dawnos@tciway.tc); the *Associated Medical Practices* on Leeward Highway in Provo (946-4942); *Dental Services Ltd.* (946-4321), an optometrist (941-5842), and a chiropractor, Dr. Kathleen Sims (941-3393). If you need a veterinarian call *Whichdoctor* on VHF ch. 16, or call 946-4353.

On North Caicos there are three government clinics at Bottle Creek, Kew, and Sandy Point. There are two resident nurses, three nurse's aides, and a government doctor visits weekly. Two environmental health officers work weekdays from 0800 to 1630. In case of emergency call 941-3000 or 946-5422. There is a clinic on South Caicos (946-3216) with a visiting doctor and two full time nurses.

On Middle Caicos there is a government clinic at Conch Bar (946-6985) with a trained nurse. At Lorimars and Bambarra there are community health aids. A doctor visits every two weeks.

On Grand Turk you will find the *Grand Turk Hospital* (946-2040/2110) north of the *Front Street Anchorage*. The hospital is staffed by four physicians and can handle emergency cases, general medicine, surgery, geriatric care, obstetrics, and pediatrics. Also on Grand Turk is the government-run *Downtown Clinic* (946-2328) open from 0800 to 1230 and from 1400 to 1630.

You will find that all government offices, from post offices to these government clinics are all closed for lunch from 1230 to 1400. Just south of Grand Turk at Salt Cay you will find a government clinic (946-6985) with a full-time nurse and a doctor that visits every two weeks.

National Air Ambulance out of Ft. Lauderdale, Florida (305-359-9900 or 800-327-3710), can transport patients from the Turks and Caicos to the United States. You might also try *AAA Air Ambulance*; call collect to 612-479-8000. If you join *DAN*, the *Divers Alert Network* (http://www.diversalertnetwork.org/), for a small yearly fee you are covered under their *Assist America Plan*. This program offers emergency evacuation for any accident or injury, diving related or not, to the nearest facility that can provide you with adequate care. After you have been stabilized to the satisfaction of the attending physician and the *Assist America* doctor, *Assist America* will arrange your transportation back to the United States, under medical supervision if necessary.

The Dominican Republic

In the DR, the phone number for a medical emergency is 911, but don't count on it working all the time. Most medical centers are bi-lingual, many accept international insurance, and the costs can be 1/3 of the prices in the U.S. All the clinics are free to residents of the Dominican Republic and cruisers, but the more serious medical problems, such as those that require a visit or a stay at one of the hospitals in Puerto Plata or Santiago can cost quite a bit. Most medical insurance is accepted throughout the DR and drugs that can only be acquired by prescription in the U.S., are available without a prescription in the DR, and most are very inexpensive. It helps to know the Spanish translation of the drug when you head for the *pharmacia*.

There is a medical clinic in Luperón where two of the three doctors in residence speak passable English. The clinic is located at the end of *Calle Luperón*, two blocks south of *Verizon* and then three blocks southwest. While the clinic can deal with most basic health problems, for testing you will be referred to the *Laboratory Luperón*, just across from the *guagua park*. If you have your samples in before 1200 you can usually get the results by 1700. If you need a dentist try the *Medicon Dental Implant Center, Independencia No. 9*, (phone 829-947-5977 ext: 24368C).

If you need medical attention in Puerto Plata visit *Centro Médico Bournigal* (809-586-2342, Fax: 809-586-6104 or email them at info@bournigal-hospital.com).

In Santiago you can find medical attention at *HOMS*, the *Hospital Metropolitano de Santiago, Duarte Highway* Km 2.8 (829-947-2222 Ext. 5000, Fax: 829-947-2223, or you can reach them by email at info@homshospital.com

In Sosúa or Cabarete you can visit the *Medical Center Carretera Sosúa-Cabarete* Km 1, Sosúa, 809-571-4696, or you can reach them by email at cmc.sosua@gmail.com. In Cabarete visit *Servi-Med* Dr. Gidion or Dr. Naurio Carretera, *Cabarete 25* (809-571-2903). If you need a vet in Sosúa or Cabarete, visit *Dr. Bob's*, on the main road from Sosúa to Cabarete. (24-hour phone number 809-430-5503). After *El Choco Road* you will come to a *Coastal* gas station, just past the station is the *Dr. Bob's* sign.

In Samaná, Dominican Republic, quality medical care can be found at the *Medical Center* (with ambulance service), located at No.6 *Coronel Andrés Diaz Street*, phone: 809-538-3999, 809-538-3888, or fax them at 809 538-2424. The *International Medical Clinic* is located in the *Plaza Pueblo Principe*, Local 4, in the heart of downtown Samaná and is open 24/7 (809-538-2426 Fax: 809-538 2675). If you need a dentist in Samaná, visit Dr. Elizabeth Frias de Martinez, her clinic is located at *Calle Peter Vander Horst No.2* (809-538-3180, Cell: 809-988-1705).

In Santo Domingo, *Clinica Abreu*, at *Av. Independencia y Beller,* has 24-hour emergency service and free treatment for foreigners. the *Padre Billini Hospital* is located on *Calle Padre Billini y Santomé, Zona Colonial*, and offers free consultations. If you need an ambulance call *Movi-Med Ambulance Evacuation Service* at 809-532-0000.

National Parks-Turks and Caicos

One of the largest misrepresentations that visiting cruisers have of the Turks and Caicos concerns its national parks system. I consistently hear misinformed cruisers moaning and groaning to themselves, and others, that they cannot anchor or fish in the Turks and Caicos Islands because of the many national parks. The worst part is that they often impart their lack of knowledge to other cruisers, who may be considering a Turks and Caicos cruise, often ruining their cruise before it even begins.

In 1992, the Government of the Turks and Caicos Islands created a national park system and set aside 33 specific protected areas to protect their scenic environments and habitats, both to preserve and conserve them for future generations as well as make them available for public recreation. The listing includes 11 national parks, 11 nature reserves, 4 sanctuaries and 7 historical sites totaling more than 325 square miles. Two hundred and ten square miles of this total amount are sensitive and ecologically essential wetlands ratified under the Switzerland based *International Ramsar Bureau*. Some of these protected areas include marine replenishment areas as well as breeding grounds for turtles, seabirds and other creatures. All the national parks are under the supervision of the *DECR*.

The Turks and Caicos have five different classifications for their protected areas. At the top of the list is the *UNESCO (United Nation Educational, Scientific, and Cultural Organization) Heritage Site*. Next is the *National Park* allowing access, recreation, and some development. A *Nature Reserve* allows limited use, recreation, and development. A *Sanctuary* does not allow development and only allows limited access with a permit issued by the *DECR*. A *Historical Site* allows access and limited development.

Vessels under 60' in length may anchor in any national park on any clear sand bottom. Damaging any corals by misuse of your anchoring privileges may result in a fine. Vessels over 60 in length may not anchor or take a mooring. Moorings must be vacated at the request of a dive boat. If bad weather is threatening or repairs must be made, vessels over 60' may anchor anywhere except in coral. Water skiing and jet skis are not permitted in any protected area in the Turks and Caicos Islands.

Provisioning

The Bahamas

If you are on a tight budget, it would be best for you to stock up on provisions in the United States prior to your Bahamas cruise. Take enough for the length of your cruise and then some. The cheapest place after the U.S. for provisioning is Puerto Plata (or Santiago, both are easily reached by car or bus from Luperon) in the Dominican Republic. With few exceptions, prices in the Bahamas are considerably higher than American prices. Beer and cigarette prices will seem outrageous with cigarette prices some 2-3 times higher than in the States.

The local Bahamian beer, *Kalik* (named after the sound that cow bells make when clanged together), is very good and more reasonably priced than foreign beers. Try the *Kalik Gold Label*, it is more full-bodied and a little stronger. Rum, as one would think, can be very inexpensive while American whiskies and certain Scotches are very high. Staples such as rice, beans, flour, and sugar are just slightly higher than U.S. prices. Vegetables can be quite reasonable in season. The vegetable market on Potter's Cay in Nassau is a good spot to pick up a large box of mixed vegetables for around $15.00 in season. Meats, soft drinks, and milk all are considerably higher than in America.

As you shop the various markets throughout the Bahamas you will find some delightful items that are not sold in the U.S., foreign butter and meats for example. The shopping experience will give you the opportunity to purchase and enjoy some new treats. Of course, the prices on fresh fish, conch, and lobster are all open to bargaining with the local fishermen.

Good drinking water is available throughout the islands from some of the cisterns and wells on various cays. Well water will have a higher salt content than cistern water, which is rainwater. Always check with the owners before you remove any water. Most stores sell bottled water and you can buy reverse osmosis water in quite a few places.

I have found prices on Long Island, particularly at Salt Pond and southward to Mangrove Bush, to be equivalent to and sometimes better than prices in George Town, Exuma. Prices in Provo, Turks and Caicos, are equivalent to Nassau prices and sometimes better with some prices near stateside levels.

If you plan to dine out while in the islands, you will find the prices to be higher than stateside prices. It is common for dining establishments in the Bahamas to include a 15% gratuity in the check.

If you want quality foodstuffs delivered to you anywhere in The Bahamas, visit *Food Store 2Go* at www.FoodStore2Go.com.

The Turks and Caicos

If you are on a tight budget, it might be best for you to stock up on provisions in the United States or at Puerto Plata or Santiago in the Dominican Republic prior to your Turks and Caicos cruise. Take enough for the length of your cruise and then some. Although the prices in the Dominican Republic are increasing, there are still plenty of deals to be had, especially on locally made products.

With few exceptions, prices in The Turks and Caicos are a little higher than American prices but generally lower than Bahamian prices on most goods. Food items are taxed in the Turks and Caicos. Beer and cigarette prices will seem outrageous with cigarette prices some 2-3 times higher than in the States.

Rum, as one would think, can be very inexpensive while American whiskies and certain scotches are very high. Staples such as rice, beans, flour, and sugar are just slightly higher than U.S. prices. Vegetables can be quite reasonable in season. Meats, soft drinks, and milk all are considerably higher than in America. As you shop the various markets throughout the Turks and Caicos you will find some delightful items that are not sold in the U.S. - foreign butter and meats, for example. The shopping experience will give you the opportunity to purchase and enjoy some new treats. Of course, the prices on fresh fish, conch, and lobster are all open to bargaining with the local fishermen, with the South Caicos fishermen giving you the best deal.

If you plan to dine out while in the islands, you will find the prices to be comparable to or higher than at home. I have found that it is difficult for two people to have a decent lunch in Provo with a couple of sodas or beers for under $20.00. It is common for dining establishments in the Turks and Caicos to include a 10%-15% gratuity on the check on top of the 10% government tax.

Tides and Currents

The Bahamas

The islands of the Bahamas are affected by the west setting *North Equatorial Current* on both their eastern and western extremities. After entering the Caribbean the *North Equatorial Current* splits into two branches, the northern branch flowing northeast of the Bahamas off Abaco, Eleuthera, Cat Island, and Long Island as the Antilles Current with an average velocity of approximately ½ knot. To a lesser extent the *Antilles Current* also flows through the *Old Bahama Channel* along the northern coast of Cuba and through the islands of the Bahamas themselves. The more southern branch of the *North Equatorial Current* makes its way around the Caribbean and the Gulf of Mexico and enters the *Straits of Florida* as the *Gulf Stream* with an average velocity of approximately 2.5 knots in a northward direction (for more information see the chapter *Crossing the Gulf Stream*).

Once north of The Bahamas the stronger *Gulf Stream* merges with the weaker *Antilles Current* and bears off north and northeastward across the North Atlantic. The *Sailing Directions for the Caribbean Sea* (*DMA#* SDPUB147) advises that the eastern entrance to the *Northwest Providence Channel* has a northwest setting current of approximately 2-3 knots which may reverse to a southeast set after strong northwest to north winds. Within the *Northeast* and *Northwest Providence Channels* themselves the current is nominal although after strong northerly winds the set may be easterly with a velocity of approximately 1 knot.

Where the shallow banks drop off to deeper ocean waters in such areas as the Abacos, the Berry Islands, the Biminis, the Exumas, and the Jumentos, tidal currents flow in and out the passes and cuts sometimes reaching 2-4 knots in strength and even more in a few of the more narrow passes. Some cuts may be impassable in adverse wind conditions or in heavy swells that may exist with or without any wind. Even in moderate conditions, onshore winds against an outgoing tide can create very rough conditions.

As a rule of thumb you can estimate the tidal rise and fall to be about 2½ '-3' at most times. Where the banks drop off to the deeper waters of the Atlantic Ocean, the *Straits of Florida*, the *Tongue of the Ocean*, or Exuma Sound for instance, the tides ebb and flow in and out the passes and cuts with ferocity in places, sometimes reaching 2-4 knots in strength and even more in a few of the more narrow passes. All tides in the Bahamas are based on the tides in Nassau, which have a mean rise of 2.6'. Tides immediately after the first and last quarter of the moon, rise approximately ½' less, while tides after new and full moons rise approximately ½' more.

During Spring tides, when the moon is nearest the Earth, the range is increased by another ½'. Cruising through the Bahamas during Spring full moon tides will give you some of the lowest lows and highest highs. It is quite easy to run aground at this time on some of the banks routes. Boats with drafts of 5' have reportedly run aground in what is normally a 6' depth at low water during this time. To receive tidal information while in the Bahamas see the section entitled *Weather* later in this chapter.

When attempting to predict the state of tide at any time other than at slack tide, you can use the *Rule of Twelfths* for a generally reliable accuracy. To do this take the amount of tidal fluctuation and divide it into twelfths. For example, if high tide in Nassau is expected to be 3.0' and the low water datum is 0.0', the tidal fluctuation is 3', and each twelfth is 0.25' or 3". To predict the state of tide at different times you can use the *Rule of Twelfths* in the following table. The table is merely to demonstrate a point and uses an imaginary charted high tide of 3'. Always consult your chart tables or listen for tidal information broadcasts and calculate accordingly.

Time of Low Water	Tide Datum - 0 Feet
1 hr after low, add 1/12	¼' above datum-3"
2 hr after low, add 3/12	¾' above datum-9"
3 hr after low, add 6/12	1½' above datum-18"
4 hr after low, add 9/12	2¼' above datum-27"
5 hr after low, add 11/12	2¾' above datum-33"
6 hr after low, add 12/12	High Water-3'*

*Caution: assumes a 3' tidal fluctuation.

Chart tables give the times and heights of high and low water but not the time of the turning of the tide or slack water. Usually there is little difference between the times of high and low water and the beginning of ebb or flood currents, but in narrow channels, landlocked harbors, or on tidal creeks and rivers, the time of slack water may vary by several hours. In some places you will find that it is not unusual for the currents to continue their direction of flow long after charted predictions say they should change. Strong winds can play havoc on the navigator attempting to predict slack water. The current may often appear in places as a swift flowing river and care must be taken whenever crossing a stretch of strong current to avoid being swept out to sea or onto a bank or rocks.

Some of the currents may flow from 2.5 to over 4 knots in places and in anchorages with tidal flow two anchors are a must. Some cuts may be impassable in adverse wind conditions or in heavy swells that may exist with or without any wind. Even in moderate conditions, onshore winds against an outgoing tide can create very rough conditions.

The Turks and Caicos

The islands of the Turks and Caicos are affected by the west setting *North Equatorial Current* on both their northern and southern extremities.

As a rule of thumb, you can estimate the tidal rise and fall in the Turks and Caicos to be about 2'-4' at most times with a mean rise of 2.6'. Neap tides, those after the first and last quarter of the moon, rise approximately ½' less, while tides after new and full moons rise approximately ½' more. During spring tides, when the moon is nearest the Earth, the range is increased by another ½'. Cruising through the Turks and Caicos during spring full moon tides will give you some of the lowest lows and highest highs. It is quite easy to run aground at this time on some of the Banks routes. Boats with drafts of 5' have reportedly run aground in what is normally a 6' depth at low water during this time. To receive tidal information while in the Turks and Caicos see the section *Weather*.

Tides in the Turks and Caicos use *Hawk's Nest Anchorage* at Grand Turk as their datum location. Low tides at this location are usually 14 minutes before Nassau tides and high tides at Grand Turk are 19 minutes before Nassau tides. Both high and low tides run generally .5' less than Nassau tides. Tides at Provo and Leeward Going Through are approximately one hour later than tides at Grand Turk. Tides on the *Caicos Banks* are generally northwest on the flood and southwest on the ebb with an average strength of approximately 1 knot.

Printed tide tables can be purchased for $5 in Providenciales at the *DECR*, just above the *Public Treasury*, across from *Island Pride Supermarket*.

Tides are sometimes unpredictable around Providenciales. Strong northeast winds will sometimes keep the tides on the southern side of Provo low for days at a time while strong southern winds will give the southern shore higher tides than normal. The tides at Leeward Going Through are erratic at best. While the tides in Provo are generally thought to be about ½ hour after Nassau, this is not the case in Leeward. I have seen tides there occur three hours after Nassau tides and the floods generally tend to flow for a shorter period than the ebbs. I have seen the flood tide only last three hours during strong southeast winds.

The Dominican Republic

In the passage between Great Sand Cay and Luperón in the Dominican Republic, you can expect to find a west/northwest setting current of about ½ - ¾ knots, and sometimes a bit stronger in periods of easterly winds.

VHF

The Bahamas

The regulations pertaining to the proper use of VHF in the Bahamas are basically identical to those in the United States. The *Public Utilities Commission* now handles all licensing for VHF, SSB, and amateur radios. In the Bahamas, channel 16 is the designated channel for hailing and distress. Please shift all traffic to a working channel when you have made contact with your party.

The *Public Utilities Commission* requests that all vessels in Bahamian waters use ch. 68 as a hailing frequency and then switch to a working channel after contact is made. This works fine in most places, except in Nassau where so many fishermen use ch. 68 that people often revert back to ch. 16 because they don't care to listen to the fishermen all day.

People throughout the Bahamas use the VHF as a telephone. You will often hear businesses announcing their latest deals, or the local restaurant describing the delights of their upcoming seafood night and inviting you for a meal in exchange for a small amount of cash. Technically this is illegal and improper by American as well as Bahamian laws.

Bear in mind that this is a way of life in the Bahamian Out Islands and that you are a visitor here and only temporary. There are a few cruisers who bring with them into this paradise the very things that many of us are here to escape. Some of these people insist on playing radio vigilante, sitting by the VHF anxiously awaiting an opportunity to spring into action and place the restrictions of the dreaded "proper radio etiquette" that have been placed on them, upon someone else. If you are one of the Radio Police, please relax. You are doing nothing but making an unpleasant situation intolerable and increasing your blood pressure in the process. This is just the way it is on ch.16 and 68 in the Bahamas and you had best learn to live with it. There is absolutely nothing that you, the Bahamian government, or the *Public Utilities Commission* can do to change things. Besides, you will find few other cruisers that will agree with you. If you don't wish to hear the ads or traffic, simply turn your radio off.

When you are using your VHF assume that at least a half-dozen of your neighbors will follow your conversation to another channel. Even if you have a "secret" channel it will not take too long to find you. It is a fact of life that everybody listens in to everybody else.

The Turks and Caicos

In the Turks and Caicos, Channel 16 is the designated channel for hailing and distress. Please shift all traffic to a working channel when you have made contact with your party. Most of the local marine interests usually monitor VHF ch. 68, so if you can't find somebody on 16, then try 68 and move off to another channel after making contact.

The Dominican Republic

In Luperón, the primary hailing channel is 68. There is a boater's net every Sunday and Wednesday on VHF ch. 72 at 0800. Here you can hear the latest goings on in Luperón such as who has what deal on this or that, who has a dinner special, and what time the nautical flea market begins at *Puerto Blanco Marina* on Sunday. An announcement will be made on ch. 68 prior to the net.

Weather

The weather throughout the Bahamas is sub-tropical with a rainy season from June through October, coinciding with hurricane season. In the winter, temperatures in the Out Islands rarely fall below 60°F and generally are above 75°F in the daytime. During the summer months the lows are around 75°-78°F while the highs seldom rise above 90°F. Seawater temperatures normally vary between 74°F in February and 84°F in August.

Humidity is fairly high all year long, especially during the summer months, but there is usually a breeze to lessen the effect. In the summer, winds tend to be light, 10 knots or less from the southeast with more calms, especially at night. In the winter, the prevailing winds tend to be more easterly or north of east and stronger. It is not unusual to get a week of strong winds, 20 knots or better, during the winter months as fronts move through.

These fronts tend to move through with regularity during the winter months and become more infrequent as spring approaches. The wind will usually be in the southeast or south before a front and will often be very light to calm. As the front approaches with its telltale bank of dark clouds on the western and northwestern horizon (sometimes there may not be an associated bank of clouds), the winds will steadily pick up and move into the southwest, west, and northwest as the front approaches. Strongest winds are usually from the west and northwest and this is the direction from which the squalls usually arrive.

After the front passes the winds will move into the north and northeast for a day or two before finally settling back into an east/southeast pattern until the next front. Winds just after a front tend to be strong and the temperature a little cooler.

Depending on its speed and strength, a front passing off the southeast Florida coast will usually be in Nassau in about 12-24 hours; from there it may arrive in the Exumas within 12-36 hours, and the Turks and Caicos about 12-36 hours later.

In the summer the weather pattern is typically scattered showers with the occasional line squall. Although the main concern during June through November is hurricanes, The Bahamas are more often visited by a tropical wave with its strong winds and drenching rains. Tropical waves, sometimes called easterly waves, are low-pressure systems that can strengthen and turn into a tropical depression or hurricane. Cruisers visiting The Bahamas during hurricane season are advised to monitor weather broadcasts closely and take timely, appropriate action (also see previous section on *Hurricane Holes*).

The Turks & Caicos and the Dominican Republic are cooled by the trade winds, the steady current of air that originates off West Africa and that pushed Columbus' ships to the New World. The consistent breezes of the trade winds protect the islands from excessive heat, contributing to an ideal average temperature of 83°F. Climatic extremes are unheard of here, and about 20"-40" of rainfall leave the skies clear for much of the year.

As a general rule of thumb, the Turks and Caicos Islands are warm and dry. They lie along the path of the northeast trade wind belt which brings somewhat of a cooling effect to the cays. Temperatures usually stay in the neighborhood of 70ºF to 85ºF. Winter temperatures in the Turks and Caicos rarely fall below 60°F and generally are above 75°F in the daytime. The average year-round temperature in the Turks and Caicos is 83º F.

During the summer months the lows are around 75°-78°F while the highs seldom rise above 90°F except in the hottest months of September and October when highs can soar to 95ºF. Seawater temperatures normally vary between 74°F in February and 84°F in August. The trade winds also bring rain to these islands, not very much by some standards, but enough it seems. Grand Turk averages 20" per year while the Caicos group averages around 40" per year. These islands are dry with a lot of cactus; they can almost be described as desert-like. The rainiest month is May; the summer months may see a lot of rain depending on the actions of tropical waves and hurricanes. In the winter, rainfall is dependent upon frontal passages.

Staying in touch with weather broadcasts presents little problem in the Bahamas and southward, even if you don't have SSB or ham radio capabilities. From Nassau you can receive the local Bahamian radio station *ZNS I* at 1540 KHz which also broadcasts simultaneously on FM at 107.1 MHz. *ZNS II* on 1240 KHz and *ZNS III* at 810 KHz can usually be picked up in the northern Exumas. *WGBS* also from Miami at 710 KHz has weather four times an hour 24 hours a day. In the New Providence area you will be able to pick up *BASRA* Coral Harbour giving the weather and tides at 0715 every morning. *BASRA* will place a call on VHF ch.16 and then move to ch. 72 for weather information. Skippers can contact the *Nassau Marine Operator* on VHF ch. 27 and ask for the latest weather report from the Nassau Meteorological Office.

On Grand Turk, *Flagstaff* comes on VHF ch. 16 at 8:00 a.m. local time and informs those who want to hear the latest southwest North Atlantic weather forecast to shift to VHF ch. 13. You can frequently pick up *Flagstaff's* weather transmissions as far away as South Caicos. When *Flagstaff* is off the island Brian Riggs (of the *National Museum*), handles the weather broadcasts using the call *Bluewater*.

If you have ham radio capabilities you can pick up the *Bahamas Weather Net* every morning at 0720 on 3.696 MHz, lower sideband. The net begins with the local weather forecast and tides from the *Nassau Met. Office*. Next, hams from all over the Bahamas check in with their local conditions which are later forwarded to the *Nassau Met. Office* to assist in their forecasting. If you are interested in the approach of a front you can listen in and learn what conditions hams in the path of the front have experienced. The local conditions in the weather reports follow a specific order so listen in and give your conditions in the order indicated.

At 0745 on 7.268 MHz you can pick up the *Waterway Net*. Organized and maintained by the *Waterway Radio and Cruising Club*, this dedicated band of amateur radio operators begin the net with a synopsis of the weather for South Florida and then proceed to weather for the Bahamas (with tides), the southwest north Atlantic, the Caribbean Sea, and the Gulf of Mexico.

The *United States Coast Guard* in Portsmouth, Virginia weather broadcasts can be received on your SSB on 4428.7 KHz (ch. 409), 6506.4 KHz (ch. 601), 8765.4 (ch. 816), 13113.2 KHz (ch. 1205), and 17307.3 (ch. 1625) at 0600, 0800, 1400, and 2200.

All cruisers suffered a loss when David Jones passed away in November of 2003. But the *Caribbean Weather Center* continues to provide all the same services that David provided with Chris Parker at the microphone from his sailboat *Bel Ami*. Chris' weather nets are conducted 6 days a week, Monday through Saturday, but also Sundays when Tropical or other severe weather threatens. Chris' summer schedule, April to October, begins on 4.045 MHz at 0630 AST/EDT; then Chris moves to 8.137 MHz at 0700 AST/EDT; Chris is back on 4.045 MHz at 0800 AST/EDT; then Chris moves to 8.104 MHz at 0830 AST/EDT; Chris moves up to 12.350 MHz at 0915 AST/EDT; and finishes up at 6.221 MHz at 0930 AST/EDT. When severe weather or tropical weather systems threaten

Chris will also transmit in the evenings, usually on 8.104 MHz at 2000 AST/EDT and Chris will usually announce this on the morning net.

Chris' winter schedule, November to March, begins at 0700 AST/0600 EST on 8.137 MHz; Chris then moves to 4.045 MHz at 0730 AST/0630 EST; Chris can then be found on 8.104 MHz at 0830 AST/0730 EST; Chris them moves up to 12.350 MHz at 0930 AST/0830 EST; Chris then finishes on 6.221 MHz at 1000 AST/0900 EST. Quite often during the winter months Chris may be late in getting to the 12 meg frequency. When severe weather or tropical weather systems threaten Chris will also transmit in the evenings, usually on 8.104 MHz at 1900 AST/1800 EST and Chris will usually announce this on the morning net. Chris begins the net with a 24-48 hour wind and sea summary followed by a synoptic analysis and tropical conditions during hurricane season. After this, Chris repeats the weather for those needing fills and finally he takes check-ins reporting local conditions from sponsoring vessels (vessels who have paid an annual fee for this service). Those who seek more information about weather, weather patterns, and the forecasting of weather, should pick up a copy of Chris Parker's excellent publication: *Coastal and Offshore Weather, The Essential Handbook*. You can pick up a copy of Chris Parker's book at his web site: http://www.mwxc.com.

Another well-respected forecaster is a ham operator named George Cline, KP2G. George can be found on the *Caribbean Maritime Mobile Net* (http://users.isp.com/kv4jc/) located at 7.241 MHz, lower sideband at 0715 AST, 15 minutes into the net. George gives an overview of the current Caribbean weather from the Turks and Caicos to Trinidad as well as the western Caribbean basin. At 0730 AST, George moves to 7.086, lower sideband for further Caribbean weather information and questions and answers. The same weather information is then transmitted in a weatherfax format. George returns to the airwaves at 1630 AST, on the afternoon cocktail net at 7.086 lower sideband.

Using the Charts

For the soundings on the charts I use my dinghy with a computer-based hydrographic system consisting of an off-the-shelf GPS and sonar combination that gives a GPS waypoint and depth every two seconds including the time of each observation. The software used records and stores this information in an onboard computer.

My first objective is to chart the inshore reefs after which I plot all other visible hazards to navigation. These positions are recorded by hand on my field notes as well as being recorded electronically. I rely primarily on my on-site notes for the actual construction of the charts. The soundings taken by the system are later entered by hand but it is the field notes that help me create the basis for the chart graphics. Next I will run the one-fathom line as well as the ten-fathom line and chart these. Finally, I will crisscross the entire area in a grid pattern and hopefully catch hazards that are at first glance unseen. It is not unusual to spend days sounding an area of only a couple of square miles.

Due to the speed of my dinghy, each identical lat/long may have as many as ten or twenty separate soundings. Then, with the help of *NOAA* tide tables, the computer gives me accurate depths to one decimal place for each separate lat/long pair acquired on the data run. A macro purges all but the lowest depths for each lat/long position (to two decimal places). At this point the actual plotting is begun including one fathom and ten fathom lines. The charts themselves are still constructed from outline tracings of topographic maps and the lat/long lines are placed in accordance with these maps. The soundings taken are shown in feet at MLW, *Mean Low Water*, the average low tide. Since MLW is an average, cruisers must be aware that there are times that there will be less water than shown, particularly on Spring low tides, during the full moon and new moon.

These charts are as accurate as I can make them and I believe them to be superior to any others. However, it is not possible to plot every individual rock or coral head so piloting by eye is still essential. On many of the routes in my guides you must be able to pick out the blue, deeper water as it snakes between sandbanks, rocky bars, and coral heads. Learn to trust your eyes. Remember that on the banks, sandbars and channels can shift over time so that what was once a channel may now be a sandbar. Never approach a cut or sandbar with the sun in your eyes, it should be above and behind you. Sunglasses with polarized lenses can be a big help in combating the glare of the sun on the water. With good visibility the sandbars and heads stand out and are clearly defined. As you gain experience you may even learn to read the subtle differences in the water surface as it flows over underwater obstructions. The only true way to gain the ability to read the water is to get out there and do it. Explore. Keep one eye on your depth sounder and one on the water around you. Soon you'll be an expert.

All courses shown are magnetic. All waypoints for entrances to cuts and for detouring around shoal areas are only to be used in a general sense. They are meant to get you into the general area, you must pilot your way through the cut or around the shoal yourself. You will have to keep a good lookout; GPS will not do that for you. <u>The best aids to navigation when near these shoals and cuts are sharp eyesight and good light</u>. The charts will show both deep draft vessel routes as well as some shallow draft vessel routes. Deep draft vessel routes will accommodate a draft of 6' minimum and often more with the assistance of the tide. Shallow draft vessel routes are for dinghies and small outboard powered boats with drafts of less than 3'. Shallow draft monohulls and multihulls very often use these same routes.

Not being a perfect world, I expect errors to occur. I would deeply appreciate any input and corrections that you may notice as you travel these waters. Please send your suggestions to Stephen J. Pavlidis, C/O Seaworthy Publications, 2023 N. Atlantic Ave., Unit 226, Cocoa Beach, Florida, 32931, or email me at stevepavlidis@hotmail.com.

Legend

☐	water depth less than 1 fathom	☐	water depth over 10 fathoms
☐	water depth between 1 fathom and 10 fathoms		
- - -	large vessel route-6' draft	↓	light
- · -	shallow vessel route	⚓	anchorage
+	rock or coral head	⊕	GPS waypoint
++++	reef	●	tower
══	road	⚓	wreck–above hw
m	mooring	⊕	wreck-submerged
dm	dinghy mooring	☐	building

List of Charts

**The prudent navigator will not rely solely on any
single aid to navigation, particularly on floating aids.**

CAUTION:
The Approach and Index charts are designed strictly for orientation, they are <u>not</u> to be used for <u>navigational purposes</u>. <u>All</u> charts are to be used in conjunction <u>with</u> the text. <u>All</u> soundings are in feet at <u>Mean Low Water</u>. <u>All</u> courses are <u>magnetic</u>. Projection is transverse Mercator. Datum used is WGS84.

Differences in latitude and longitude may exist between these charts and other charts of the area; therefore the transfer of positions from one chart to another should be done by bearings and distances from common features.

The author and publisher take no responsibility for errors, omissions, or the misuse of these charts. No warranties are either expressed or implied as to the usability of the information contained herein.
Note: Some *NOAA* and *DMA* charts do not show some of the reefs and heads charted in this guide. Always keep a good lookout when piloting in these waters.

Chart #	Chart Description	Page #
Cat Island		
CT-1A	Springfield Bay	51
CT-1B	Flamingo Hills Marina	52
CT-1	Hawk's Nest Creek	53
CT-2	Hawks Nest Creek to Whale Creek	54
CT-3	Whale Creek to Fernandez Bay	56
CT-4	Fernandez Bay, Smith's Bay	58
CT-5	Smith's Bay to Gaitors	60
CT-6	Bennett's Harbour	60
CT-6A	Bennett's Harbour	62
CT-7	Arthur's Town, Orange Creek	63
CT-8	Half Moon Cay	66
Conception Island		
CO-1	West Bay	69
CO-2	East Bay	71
Rum Cay		
RC-1	Flamiongo Bay	73
RC-2	Port Nelson	75
San Salvador		
SS-1	Cockburn Town	79

Chart #	Chart Description	Page #
SS-2	Graham's Harbour	82
SS-3	French Bay	83
Long Island		
LI-1	Cape Santa Maria to Hog Cay, Calabash Bay	96
LI-2	Hog Cay to Millerton, Stella Maris	99
LI-3	Simms	102
LI-4	Salt Pond	104
LI-5A	Deadman's cay	107
LI-5	Dollar Harbour	110
LI-6	Clarence Town	112
LI-7	Little Harbour to Burrow's Harbour	114
LI-8	South End, Gordon's Anchorage	115
The Jumentos		
JU-1	Nuevitas Rocks to No Bush Cay	119
JU-2	Pear Cay to Stony Cay	121
JU-3	No Name Cays	121
JU-4	Water Cay to Lanzadera Cay	122
JU-5	Torzon Cay to Flamingo Cay	123
JU-6	Flamingo Cay to Man of War Cay	126
JU-7	Man of War Channel, Jamaica Cay	127
JU-7A	Jamaica Cay Anchorage	127
JU-8	Seal Cay to North Channel Cay	129
JU-9	Nurse Channel	129
JU-10	Frog Cay to Buena Vista Cay	130
JU-11	Raccoon Cay, Northern Tip	130
JU-12	Raccoon Cut	132
JU-13	Margaret Shoal	132
JU-14	Ragged Island Harbour, Duncan Town	136
JU-15	Duncan Town to Little Ragged Island	138
JU-16	Little Ragged Island to Hobson Breaker	138
Crooked/Acklins District		
CA-1	Bird Rock to Landrail Point	141
CA-2	French Wells	143
CA-3	Long Cay to North Cay	147
CA-4	The Fish Cays	148
CA-5	Snug Corner to Camel Point	150
CA-6	Camel Point to Jamaica Cay	151
CA-7	Jamaica Cay to Binnacle Hill	152
CA-8	Cotton Bay Cay to Rokers Cay	153
CA-9	Salina Point to Jamaica Bay	153

Chart #	Chart Description	Page #
CA-10	Castle Island	154
CA-11	Mira Por Vos	155
CA-12	Major's Cays Harbour	156
CA-13	Lovely Bay	157
CA-14	Attwood Harbour	159
CA-15	Propeller Cay	162
CA-16	The Plana Cays	163
Mayaguana		
MG-1	Pirate's Well to Betsy Bay	166
MG-2	Start Bay	167
MG-3	Abraham's Bay	169
MG-4	Southeast Point	171
Hogsty Reef		
HR-1	Hogsty Reef	172
Inagua		
IN-1	Northwest Point, Alfred Road	176
IN-2	Matthew Town	177
IN-3	Southwest Point	179
IN-4	Little Inagua	180
The Caicos islands		
TCI-C1	The Caicos Islands	191
TCI-C2	Providenciales	192
TCI-C3	North West Point, Malcolm Roadstead	195
TCI-C4	West Harbour to Wiley Point	195
TCI-C5	Sandbore Channel, Western Entrance	197
TCI-C6	Sandbore Channel, Sapodilla Bay	197
TCI-C7	Five Cays to Long Bay	204
TCI-C8	Cooper Jack Bight, Discovery Bay	206
TCI-C9	Juba Point Creek, Caicos Marina & Shipyard	206
TCI-C10	Sellar's Cut, Turtle Cove Marina	208
TCI-C11	Stubbs Cut to Pine Cay	211
TCI-C12	Leeward Going Through	212
TCI-C13	The Caicos Cays, Pine Cay to Parrot Cay, Ft. George Cut	216
TCI-C14	West Caicos	219
TCI-C14A	West Caicos Marina	219
TCI-C15	French Cay	221
TCI-C16	North Caicos	223
TCI-C17	Middle Caicos	225
TCI-C18	East Caicos, South Caicos	226

Index of Charts

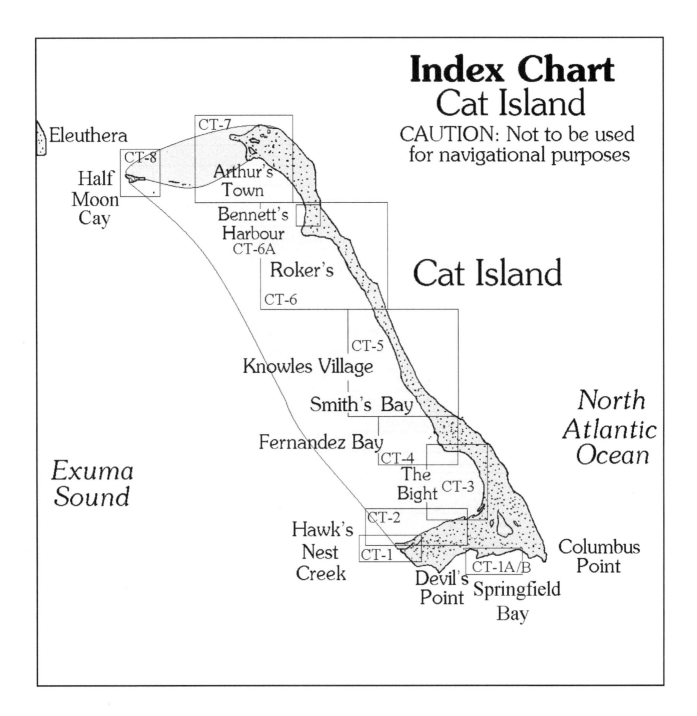

Index Chart
Cat Island
CAUTION: Not to be used
for navigational purposes

Cat Island

North
Atlantic
Ocean

Eleuthera

CT-7

CT-8

Half
Moon
Cay

Arthur's
Town

Bennett's
Harbour
CT-6A

Roker's

CT-6

CT-5

Knowles Village

Smith's Bay

Fernandez Bay

CT-4

The
Bight CT-3

Exuma
Sound

CT-2

Hawk's
Nest
Creek

CT-1

CT-1A/B

Devil's
Point Springfield
Bay

Columbus
Point

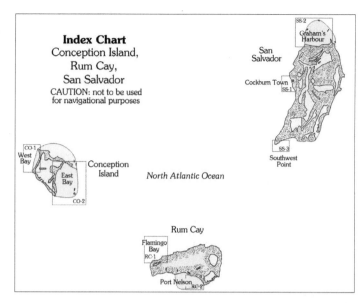

Index Chart
Conception Island,
Rum Cay,
San Salvador
CAUTION: not to be used
for navigational purposes

San Salvador

Graham's Harbour
SS-2

Cockburn Town
SS-1

SS-3
Southwest Point

North Atlantic Ocean

CO-1
West Bay

East Bay

Conception Island

CO-2

Rum Cay

Flamingo Bay
RC-1

Port Nelson
RC-2

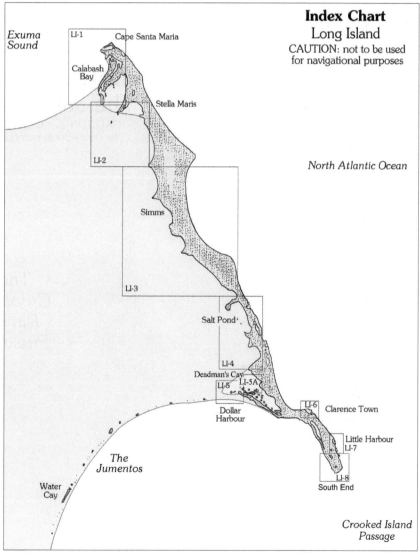

Index Chart
Long Island
CAUTION: not to be used
for navigational purposes

Exuma Sound

LI-1
Cape Santa Maria

Calabash Bay

Stella Maris

LI-2

Simms

North Atlantic Ocean

LI-3

Salt Pond

LI-4

Deadman's Cay
LI-5A
LI-5

Dollar Harbour

LI-6
Clarence Town

Little Harbour
LI-7

The Jumentos

Water Cay

LI-8
South End

Crooked Island Passage

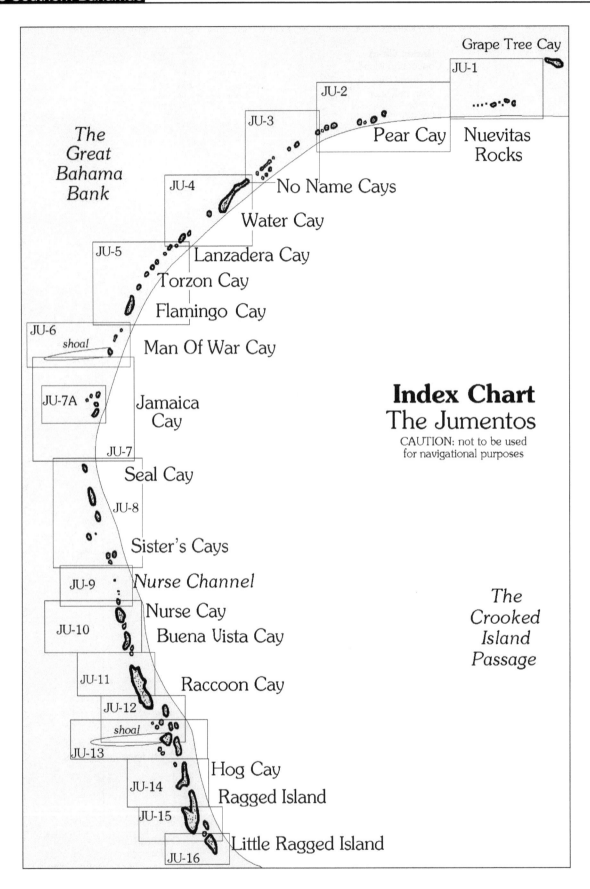

Grape Tree Cay

JU-1

JU-2

JU-3

*The
Great
Bahama
Bank*

Pear Cay   Nuevitas
Rocks

JU-4

No Name Cays

Water Cay

JU-5   Lanzadera Cay

Torzon Cay

Flamingo Cay

JU-6
shoal   Man Of War Cay

JU-7A   Jamaica
Cay

Index Chart
The Jumentos
CAUTION: not to be used
for navigational purposes

JU-7

Seal Cay

JU-8

Sister's Cays

JU-9   *Nurse Channel*

Nurse Cay
JU-10   Buena Vista Cay

*The
Crooked
Island
Passage*

JU-11

Raccoon Cay

JU-12

shoal

JU-13

Hog Cay

JU-14   Ragged Island

JU-15

Little Ragged Island

JU-16

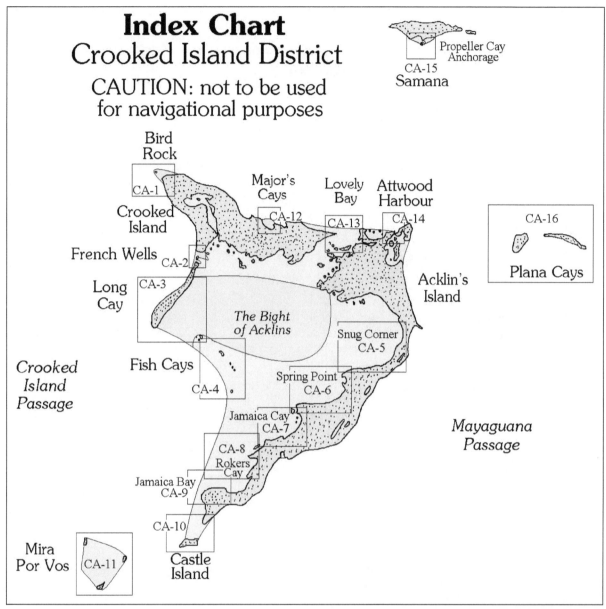

Index Chart
Crooked Island District
CAUTION: not to be used
for navigational purposes

Propeller Cay Anchorage
CA-15
Samana

Bird
Rock
CA-1

Major's
Cays
CA-12

Lovely
Bay
CA-13

Attwood
Harbour
CA-14

CA-16
Plana Cays

Crooked
Island

French Wells
CA-2

Long
Cay
CA-3

Acklin's
Island

*The Bight
of Acklins*

Snug Corner
CA-5

Fish Cays

Spring Point
CA-6

CA-4

*Crooked
Island
Passage*

Jamaica Cay
CA-7

*Mayaguana
Passage*

CA-8
Rokers
Cay

Jamaica Bay
CA-9

CA-10

Mira
Por Vos
CA-11

Castle
Island

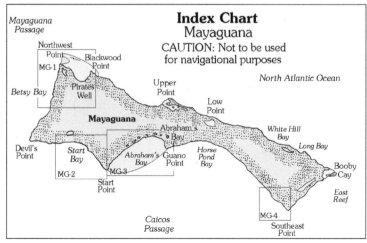

Index Chart
Mayaguana
CAUTION: Not to be used
for navigational purposes

Mayaguana Passage
Northwest Point
Blackwood Point
MG-1
Betsy Bay
Pirates Well
Mayaguana
Upper Point
Low Point
North Atlantic Ocean
White Hill Bay
Long Bay
Abraham's Bay
Devil's Point
Start Bay
Abraham's Bay
Guano Point
Horse Pond Bay
MG-2
MG-3
Start Point
Booby Cay
East Reef
MG-4
Southeast Point
Caicos Passage

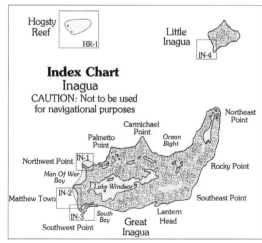

Hogsty Reef
HR-1
Little Inagua
IN-4

Index Chart
Inagua
CAUTION: Not to be used
for navigational purposes

Northwest Point
IN-1
Palmetto Point
Carmichael Point
Ocean Bight
Northeast Point
Rocky Point
Man Of War Bay
Matthew Town
IN-2
Lake Windsor
Southeast Point
IN-3
South Bay
Lantern Head
Southwest Point
Great Inagua

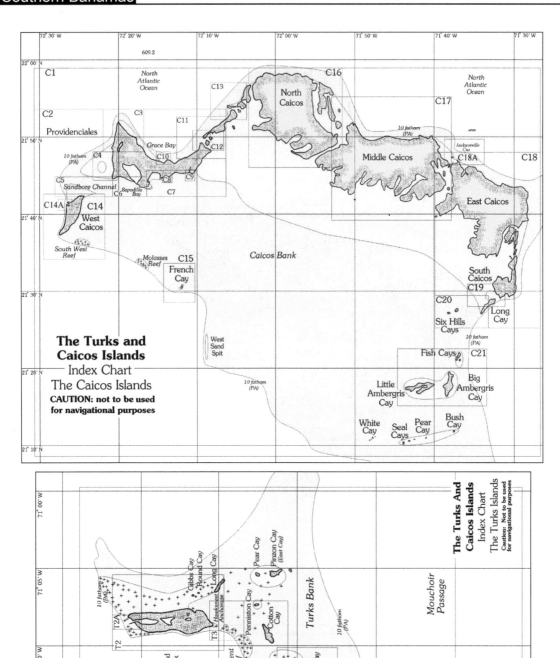

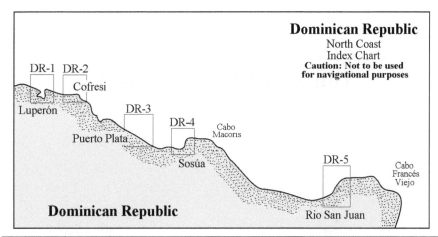

Dominican Republic
North Coast
Index Chart
**Caution: Not to be used
for navigational purposes**

DR-1 DR-2
Cofresi
Luperón
DR-3
Puerto Plata
DR-4
Cabo
Macoris
Sosúa
Cabo
Francés
Viejo
DR-5
Rio San Juan

Dominican Republic

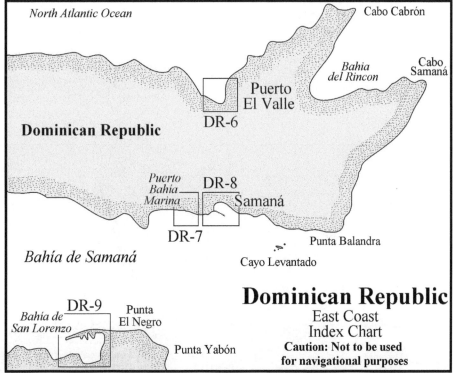

North Atlantic Ocean
Cabo Cabrón
Bahia
del Rincon
Cabo
Samaná
Puerto
El Valle
DR-6

Dominican Republic

Puerto
Bahía
Marina
DR-8
Samaná
DR-7
Punta Balandra
Cayo Levantado

Bahía de Samaná

Dominican Republic
East Coast
Index Chart
**Caution: Not to be used
for navigational purposes**

DR-9
Punta
El Negro
*Bahía de
San Lorenzo*
Punta Yabón

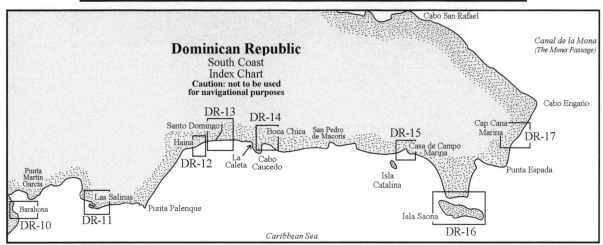

Cabo San Rafael

Dominican Republic
South Coast
Index Chart
**Caution: not to be used
for navigational purposes**

*Canal de la Mona
(The Mona Passage)*

Cabo Engaño

DR-13 DR-14
Santo Domingo
Boca Chica
San Pedro
de Macoris
Haina
DR-12
La
Caleta
Cabo
Caucedo
DR-15
Cap Cana
Marina
DR-17
Casa de Campo
Marina
Punta
Martín
García
Isla
Catalina
Punta Espada
Barahona
DR-10
Las Salinas
DR-11
Punta Palenque
Isla Saona
DR-16
Caribbean Sea

The Southern Bahamas

Cat Island to the Turks and Caicos

MARKET BOAT GEORGETOWN   DON REYNOLDS © 1996

Cat Island

Ports of Entry:
Smith's Bay, New Bight, Airport, Bennett's Harbour
Fuel: *Hawk's Nest Resort and Marina*
Haul-Out: None
Diesel Repairs: Ask at *Hawk's Nest Resort*
Outboard Repairs: Arthur's Town
Propane: Arranged by Mailboat from Nassau
Provisions: Arthur's Town, New Bight, Old Bight, Orange Creek
Important Lights:
Bennett's Harbour: Fl W ev 4 sec
Smith's Bay: Fl W ev 4 sec
Devil Point: Fl W ev 5 sec

The original Lucayan name for Cat Island was *Guanima,* but after the time of the Spanish explorers the island was called *San Salvador.* Some of the older families still retain land titles referring to the island by that name. Some of these same older residents insist that Columbus' first landfall was at Cat Island instead of the more widely accepted San Salvador. Cat Island acquired its current name in the 18th century, some say the island was named after William Catt, a little known pirate or British sea captain, depending on whose side you take. Another opinion is that the island was named after the hordes of feral cats that the English discovered on the island in the 1600s, descendants of tame cats orphaned by the Spanish in their quest for gold. In the 1700 and 1800s the island was home to many fairly successful Loyalist cotton plantations.

Cat Island, one of the finest agricultural producers in The Bahamas, is approximately 45 miles long, from Orange Creek in the north to Port Howe in the south, and the island averages about 4 miles in width. Cat Island is akin to Eleuthera in that it is bordered by the North Atlantic Ocean along its windward eastern shore, while the leeward western shore sits on a large shallow bank with many possibilities for lee anchorages.

The culture of Cat Island is very traditional, some residents still cook in outside ovens. Cat Islanders are warm, friendly, and very proud of their island. Tradition dictates that when the last of a generation dies his house is left for the spirit to reside in and the remaining family members gather stones from the site to construct a new dwelling. Elsewhere, particularly in the northern end of the island, homeowners place spindles atop their houses to keep harm from befalling anyone who resides there, a lightning rod for evil spirits of sorts. Many believe that the spirits of the dead still walk Cat Island. Obeah, a form of magic, is still practiced on Cat Island though most residents won't talk about it except in covert whispers and only if they know you. Many Cat Islanders are hesitant to enter the inland blue holes, possibly due to the stories of monsters lurking within or perhaps because things floating in the hole one week are found in the Atlantic the next week. Bush medicine is widely practiced and the people of Cat Island are known for their longevity, less so today than two centuries ago when a certain Daddy Sundown died in 1810 at the young age of 120.

One of the traditional types of music of Cat Island (as well as most of the islands of The Bahamas) that you will likely hear on Cat Island is the well-known *Rake n' Scrape.* The instruments may consist of, but are not limited to, a bass, similar to an American washtub bass and made of a length of wood, an old tin tub, and a piece of fishing line, a rhythm section containing a conch shell horn, a harmonica which is just a paper covered comb, a concertina, and a carpenter's saw scraped with a piece of metal. Setting the beat is the smoking drum made out of goatskin with a flame inside to heat it up.

Although far from remote, Cat Island is seldom visited mainly due to its lack of all-weather harbors and protection from fierce northers. The only true protection being at *Bennett's Harbour*, *Smith's Bay*, and in *Hawk's Nest Creek* although smaller, shoal draft vessels may find shelter in some of the extensive creek systems along Cat Island's western shore. In prevailing winds, cruising Cat Island's western shore is truly pleasurable. Even if the wind is blowing 20 knots or more, you can sail right in the lee of the land ½ mile or less offshore in most places and sometimes within 50 yards of the shoreline in 9' of water. There are only three large sandbars to avoid, one at Hawk's Nest Point, another at Bonefish Point, and the largest at Alligator Point.

There are no propane filling facilities on Cat Island, all tanks must be shipped to Nassau by mailboat for filling.

Approaches

From *Calabash Bay,* Long Island, Hawk's Nest Point bears 007° at a distance of 31.1 nautical miles. From *Conch Cay Cut* at George Town, Exuma, Hawk's Nest Point bears 34° at a distance of 38.8 miles. If approaching Hawk's Nest Point from Conception

Island, beware of the reefs off the southern shore of Cat Island that lie some two miles off the land.

Vessels heading north along the western shore of Cat Island should be aware that the drop off to the deeper water of *Exuma Sound* lies just off Hawk's Nest Point in the south and follows the contour of Cat Island northward staying between 8 and 9 miles to the west of Cat Island. This area is unsurveyed and although deep reefs exist all along the drop off, there may be some shallow heads or reefs also. Likewise, there may be any number of shallow heads or reefs inshore of the drop off between the 10-fathom line and Cat Island's western shoreline. Caution is advised when traversing this area.

The vast majority of cruisers visiting Cat Island do so from south to north as Spring approaches and the chance of a frontal passage is lessened. We too shall visit Cat Island in that direction.

The Southern Coast

The southern tip of the "foot" of Cat Island was a lair for pirates and wreckers. Stretching from Columbus Point at the "heel" to *Devil's Reef* at the "toe," the southern coast was treacherous to shipping. Between Columbus Point and Devil's Point is the deceptively named Port Howe. Port Howe really is not a port, rather it is a place where wreckers once lit fires to lure passing shipping into contributing to the local economy. It is said that the buccaneer Arthur Catt used these same wreckers for his piratical schemes.

Navigational Information

Residents on the south end of Cat Island are encouraging boaters to try the anchorage at Port Howe. Also known as *Reef Harbour*, this anchorage is entered by a gap in the reef located approximately at 24° 08.77' N, 75* 21.35' W. Good visibility is required for safe entry. Be forewarned that this area has not been charted for this guide yet.

Once inside the reef, you can turn right and go as far as your depth allows. The spacious anchorage is well protected by land to the north and by the wide shallow reef to the south. Very little swell makes it over the reef. This anchoring spot provides an alternative to Old Bight with good protection from clocking winds when winter fronts pass through (a good spot to rid out a norther). A few ex-cruisers live here who have installed permanent moorings. If you wish to rent a car, contact Donny Newbold at 242 342-5041.

Port Howe was named after Admiral James Howe, the first English Commander during the Revolutionary War. Today Port Howe has an airstrip and it is more noted for its coconut palms and lush pineapple fields. An interesting stop is the ruins of the *Andrew Deveaux Plantation*. Col. Andrew Deveaux earned fame for driving the Spanish from Nassau in 1783, and for this feat was rewarded with 1,000 acres on the southern end of Cat Island. Still intact is the mansion with its hand-pegged kitchen.

One mile to the east of Port Howe is a lovely day anchorage at *Winding Bay* with good holding and an easy entrance although less protected.

What You Will Find Ashore

Columbus Point is believed to be where Columbus landed on Cat Island. At the roundabout, a landmark on the road that stretches the width of the foot of Cat Island, is a conch shell monument utilizing some 570 conch shells that has been erected here to commemorate that event. West of the roundabout lie McQueens, *Hawk's Nest Creek*, and Devil's Point. East of the roundabout lies Port Howe and Bain's Town, home of Cat Island's *Masonic Lodge* and *The Galleon Bar*. The reef offshore along the 12 mile front is very popular with SCUBA divers. Wall diving begins at 50' and drops to the bottom between 2,000 and 6,000' with a myriad of coral canyons, caves, and tunnels. Nearby *Cutlass Bay* is an adult's only resort with a nude beach.

In Greenwood, nine miles north of Port Howe, the *Greenwood Beach Resort* sits a hundred feet above the *Atlantic Ocean* and boasts an 8-mile long stretch of pink beach and their restaurant offers fine dining. *The Cat Island Dive Center* is also on premises and offers a full service dive shop facility for those wishing to explore the reefs of Cat Island. They conduct shore dives, night dives, and also provide boats for wall diving off the eastern shore and Port Howe. They accommodate all divers and certification is available with dive gear and accessories for rent.

North of the roundabout is *Armbrister Creek* where at one time a small railroad came from the other side of Cat Island bringing sisal to be shipped to Nassau. Little remains of it today, almost all the rail was sent to England during World War II for armament manufacture although a few lengths can be found supporting cauldrons in backyard kitchens. The nearby *Pilot Harbour Restaurant* offers Cat Island seafood and boasts a beautiful sunset view from its waterfront location. Dean's Wood, just east of the road, contains what is left of a government forestation project from the 1930s. Madeira (mahogany) trees were planted to make furniture and some still remain in the wild.

Standing upon a crest above the *Atlantic Ocean* near the roundabout, about 500' off the road, are the remains of an octagonal fortress divided by a double-faced chimney. This was used as a lookout to signal islanders when pirates were approaching so they could run to nearby caves and hide. It is also said that it was used by pirates scanning the waters for passing prey. There are tales of pirate gold buried here.

South of Cat Island in the mouth of *Exuma Sound* lies the *Tartar Bank*. The *Tartar Bank* is a huge underwater mountain, which rises to within 7 fathoms of the surface from the surrounding depths. The top of the bank is only a few hundred yards in diameter and the walls slope away from it like a cone. This creates some excellent diving opportunities for the SCUBA enthusiast, but you must be wary of the currents. The tidal action in the mouth of *Exuma Sound* creates strong currents that swirl around and over the bank and even the most experienced divers should exercise the utmost caution when diving in this area.

Skippers too should be alert as to dangerous sea conditions on the bank when wind and tide oppose. Needless to say the fishing in this area is superb.

Springfield Bay

Springfield Bay - 1.5 nm S of Dolphin Head
24° 07.00' N, 75° 24.50' W

The one place on the southern coast of Cat Island that offers amenities to the cruising boater is at the *Flamingo Hills Resort and Marina* at the eastern end of *Springfield Bay* (see Chart CT-1A).

The full-service marina (see Chart CT-1B), which is still in the early stages of construction as of this writing, boasts a 12' dredged entrance channel leading to a protected basin with 102 slips that can accommodate vessels up to 180' LOA with drafts to 12', even at the marina's fuel dock. The resort is planning the sale of 39 home sites, each with a slip in the marina. Owners not wishing to use their slip can put it into the pool for rent to visiting boaters.

I shall chart and detail the entrance channel as soon as it has been dredged and the marina open for business.

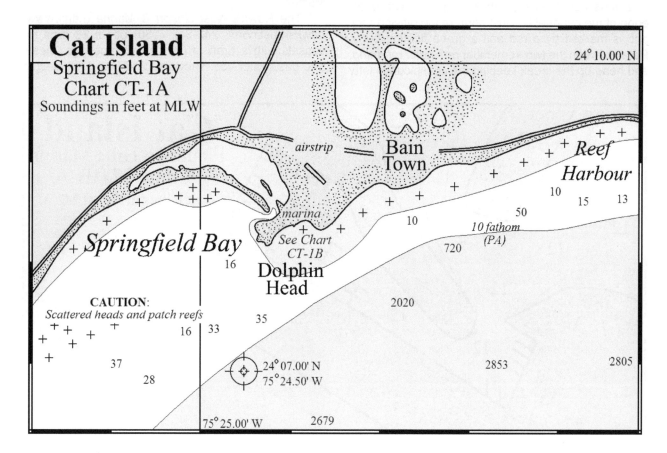

Hawk's Nest Creek

Hawks Nest Point-1 nm W of point:
24° 08.55' N, 75° 32.45' W

Navigational Information

At the very toe of the "foot" of Cat Island, is Hawk's Nest Point and *Hawk's Nest Creek*. The creek will take 6' over the bar at low water, but it shallows quickly once past the marina. As you approach McQueen's the water even gets too shallow for most dinghies. Hawk's Nest is one of the oldest British settlements on Cat Island, being originally settled in the 1600s but later destroyed by Pirates in 1717.

Hawk's Nest Creek may well be an important stop on your Cat Island cruise. The creek and marina offer excellent protection from frontal passages and almost anything short of a hurricane, but the holding in the creek is questionable. If really strong winds threaten, I would rather get a slip in the marina than try to anchor in the creek.

A waypoint at 24° 08.55' N, 75° 32.45' W, will place you approximately ¾ mile west of the entrance to *Hawk's Nest Creek* as shown on Chart CT-1. Contact the marina on VHF ch. 16 if you have any questions about entering their channel. The outer edge of the channel lies just north of the offlying rock and is marked by a red and a green floating buoy. Pass between the two, remember *red, right, returning*, and head up the creek keeping the conspicuous jetty

to port. There is a shallow spot at the mouth of the entrance channel with 6' at low water and another spot about 150 yards further in with the same depth. Once past the end of the jetty the marina's fuel dock will be immediately to port. Just past this dock the marina basin opens up to port with 28 slips accommodating drafts up to 7'.

If you wish to anchor in the creek, head up stream past the marina and anchor wherever your draft will allow. A 5' draft can work up stream a good way and shallow draft vessels even further. I must caution you about anchoring in *Hawk's Nest Creek*. The bottom is very, very rocky, and it's hard to get an anchor to set in the thin sand. As if that was not enough, the strong current threatens to drag you along with it; there are countless stories of skippers who have dragged their anchors in this creek. The further up stream you go, the better the holding, but not much better. Make sure your anchor is well set, dive on it if you can before you turn in for the night. And don't forget the bug juice, this anchorage is notorious for those vile, biting insects we all love so much.

What You Will Find Ashore

Marina

The *Hawk's Nest Resort & Marina* (http://www.hawks-nest.com/; 242-342-7050) offers 28 slips for vessels with a draft of up to 7', 3 moorings, diesel and gas, water, ice, showers, *Wi-Fi,* and full electric

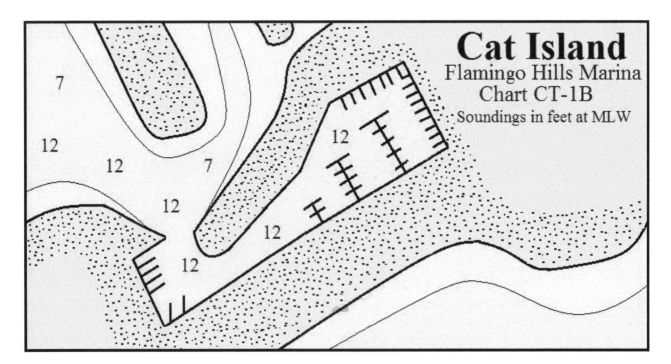

Cat Island
Flamingo Hills Marina
Chart CT-1B
Soundings in feet at MLW

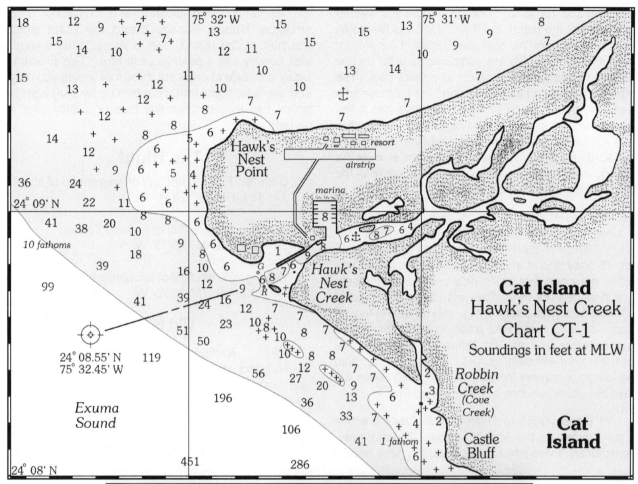

18 12 9 + 7 + + 75° 32' W 15 15 13 75° 31' W 8
15 14 10 + 7 + 13 12 11 15 10 9 9 7
15 13 + 12 11 10 13 14 7
+ 12 12 10 8 7 7
14 + 8 8 6 + 7 7
12 + 9 6 + 5 + Hawk's resort airstrip
36 24 + 5 4 + Nest marina
24° 09' N 22 11 6 6 + Point

41 38 20 8 10 fathoms 18 9 6 8 1 8 6 8 7 6 4
39 16 6 10 9 6 ☩
99 41 39 24 16 12 G 7 6 Hawk's
51 23 9 R 6 8 Nest
50 10 8 + 7 Creek
56 10 8 8
196 27 12 +++ 7 7
106 20 13 9
451 286 33 7 6

24° 08.55' N
75° 32.45' W 119

Exuma
Sound

24° 08' N

Cat Island
Hawk's Nest Creek
Chart CT-1
Soundings in feet at MLW

*Robbin
Creek
(Cove
Creek)*

2
3
2
4
41 1 fathom 6 Castle
Bluff

**Cat
Island**

Entrance to *Hawk's Nest Creek* and marina   Photo Courtesy of Paul Harding

(50 amp and 100 amp) hookups. There is a washer and dryer at the resort, but if you don't feel like doing your own laundry the staff can handle it for you for a small fee. Bicycles are complimentary for marina or resort guests and the resort also rents cars. The office at the resort has a phone and fax for those who need to keep in touch. The marina store has a few basic marine supplies. The dining room at the resort has a beautiful waterfront view and serves up some extraordinary cuisine. Folks come from all over the island, even from the other resorts to sample the dining at the *Hawk's Nest Resort.*

The resort has 10 rooms and two 3-bedroom houses for rent (the *Blue Marlin* and the *Sailfish*; 242-342-7050). For more information call them on VHF ch. 16 or by phone at 242-357-7257. The resort has a fully equipped dive facility on site with a compressor and dive gear for rent. They also have a 44' center console boat (with captain) available for dive or fishing charters. If you would like a fishing guide contact the marina office and ask for Nathaniel Gilbert or one of their other excellent guides. The resort can also handle your request for bait fish. Bonefishermen will love the upper reaches of *Hawk's Nest Creek.*

At the entrance to *Hawk's Nest Creek* are two small houses on the northern shore. The old, gray, ramshackle, three story house is said to have hosted the ex-Panamanian dictator and convicted drug smuggler Manuel Noriega during the years when this part of Cat Island, due to its secluded airstrip, was heavily into a positive cash flow. The structure today is unsafe to enter but if you look inside you may see the false floors that were torn up by drug agents when they closed down this hive of activity over a decade ago.

The Bight

Bonefish Point-¾ nm SW of western tip of shoal:
24° 16.50' N, 75° 28.90' W

New Bight-¾ nm SW of Batelco Tower:
24° 16.75' N, 75° 25.75' W

Old Bight-¾ nm NW of anchorage:
24° 13.40' N, 75° 25.20' W

Old Bight

Navigational Information
Heading north and east from *Hawk's Nest Creek*, you must clear the small sand bar off the northwestern tip of Hawk's Nest Point (Chart CT-1 and Chart CT-2) to continue east. Once past the bar you can head directly for New Bight, *Fernandez Bay,* on continue along the coast to Old Bight staying ¼ mile offshore.

About 5 miles northeast of Hawk's Nest Point, situated on a hillside overlooking the long beach at the southern end of The Bight, is McQueen's as shown on Chart CT-2. The homes are very traditional, stone and thatched roofs, and the inhabitants are primarily Rolles from Exuma. Pre-Columbian Lucayan cooking areas were found in the vicinity of McQueen's. You can tuck in close to anchor off the beach at McQueen's, but watch out for the small patch reefs and shallow heads just offshore (they're easily seen and avoided). Never try to come in close to this shore at night.

At the south end of The Bight, in the crook of the "foot" of Cat Island, is the community of Old Bight. As shown on Chart CT-3, a waypoint at 24° 13.40' N, 75° 25.20' W, will place you approximately ¾ mile northwest of the anchorage area off Old Bight as shown on Chart CT-3. Head in to the beach in prevailing winds as far as you can and drop the hook in excellent holding sand. Many cruisers heading northbound from George Town make this their first stop. Never anchor here in strong winds from southwest to northeast.

What You Will Find Ashore
Old Bight is home to the old *St. Francis of Assisi Catholic Church*, which was also built by Father Jerome who also built *The Hermitage* at New Bight (read a little further in this section for more information on Father Jerome). The church's Gothic facade, frescoes, and detailed interior sculptures are quite impressive.

The largest goat farm in The Bahamas, the *Mango Hill Ranch*, is located here in Old Bight. One mile south of the road to Greenwood, look up the *Straw Lady of Cat Island* for excellent straw work.

Dinghy Dock
Access to Old Bight is via *Old Bight Landing*.

Dining
For dining out try the *Peter Hill Restaurant, Pilot's Harbour, Beaches Delight*, the *Pass Me Not Restaurant and Pool Parlour*, and *C.A. Rolle's Bar*.

Provisioning
For groceries you can pay a visit to *Southern Food Fair* and *Dawkin's Food Store*.

Medical Assistance
There is a government clinic located in town, the *Old Bight Community Clinic* (242-342-3121), and it is open from 0900 to 1700 M-F except holidays. Old Bight is also home to *The Corner Drugstore*.

New Bight
New Bight is the capitol of Cat Island and sits at the northern end of The Bight. Most cruisers stay north of the town at *Fernandez Bay*, but some anchor off the town, where you'll find a good lee anchorage in winds from northeast to southeast as shown on Chart CT-3.

Navigational Information
Vessels heading northward from Hawk's Nest Point can head straight to New Bight once they clear the sandbar lying northwest of Hawk's Nest Point. Another alternative is to cruise the western coastline of Cat Island staying about ¼ mile offshore. A waypoint at 24° 16.75' N, 75° 25.75' W will place you in The Bight approximately ¾ mile west/southwest of the *Batelco* tower. Anchor wherever you choose off the town. There is no longer an active navigational light at The Bight, the *Batelco* tower more than makes up for its loss though, it is a great landmark, day or night.

What You Will Find Ashore
At the head of the dock, under the *Batelco* tower, is the *Government Administration Building* and the *Batelco* office. Across the street are the ruins of the old *Armbrister Plantation*, easily seen from the waterfront. These are the ruins of the great house of Henry Hawkins Armbrister, which was burned by slaves during a revolt during those heady days prior to emancipation. The house was actually pre-Loyalist period, it was built in the 1760s.

The local hotel, *The Bridge Inn* (242 225-1357), offers 12 regular guest rooms and 6 two-bedroom condominium units close to the beach at reasonable rates and has a restaurant on premises. You can access town by using the town dock located by the *Batelco* tower. In town you will find the *Commissioner's Office* and *Police Station* in the *Government Building*.

Dinghy Dock
You can land your dinghy at the government jetty or on the long white beach off town.

Dining
Just south of the dock is the *Bluebird Restaurant and Bar*. In Doud's you can dine at the *Two Corners Inn*.

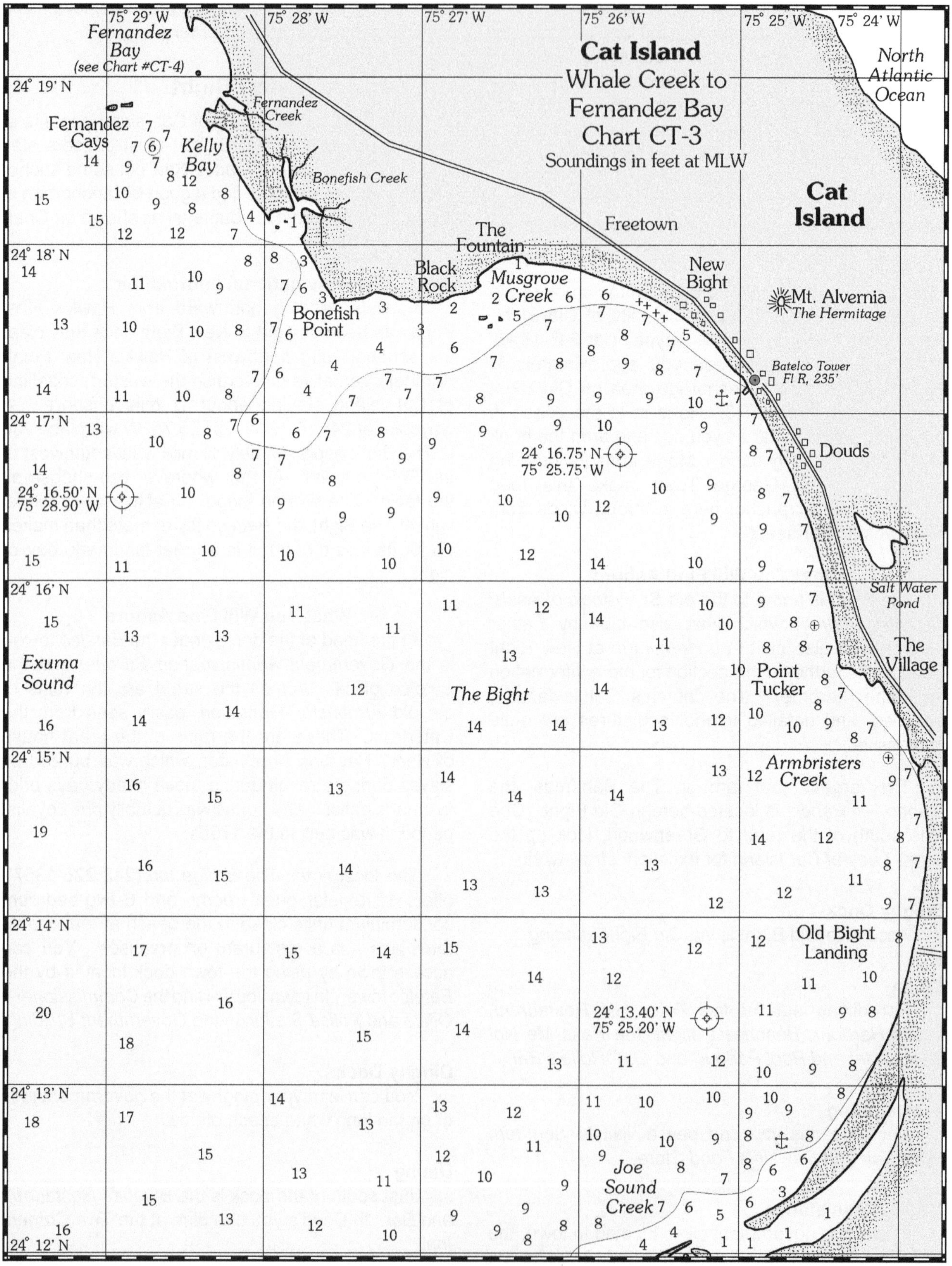

75° 29' W   75° 28' W   75° 27' W   75° 26' W   75° 25' W   75° 24' W

Fernandez Bay
(see Chart #CT-4)

Cat Island
Whale Creek to
Fernandez Bay
Chart CT-3
Soundings in feet at MLW

North Atlantic Ocean

24° 19' N

Fernandez Creek

Fernandez Cays

Kelly Bay

Cat Island

Bonefish Creek

24° 18' N

The Fountain

Freetown

Black Rock

Musgrove Creek

New Bight

Mt. Alvernia
The Hermitage

Bonefish Point

Batelco Tower
Fl R, 235'

24° 17' N

Douds

24° 16.75' N
75° 25.75' W

24° 16.50' N
75° 28.90' W

24° 16' N

Salt Water Pond

Exuma Sound

The Bight

Point Tucker

The Village

24° 15' N

Armbristers Creek

24° 14' N

Old Bight Landing

24° 13.40' N
75° 25.20' W

24° 13' N

Joe Sound Creek

24° 12' N

Fuel

In town there is a *Shell* gas station, the *New Bight Service Station*; you will have to jerry jug your fuel.

Mechanical Assistance

If you need a mechanic hail *New Bight Service* on VHF ch. 16, they are the *Shell* station in town.

Provisioning

In town you can find plenty of places to spend your money on groceries such as the *New Bight Food Store* (the best grocery on the southern side of Cat Island), the *Honourable Harry Bethel's Wholesale Bar*, *Idelle Dorsete's Convenience Store* (fresh bread here), *Virie McKinney's Convenience Store*, the *Sweet Things Confectionery*, and *Romer's Mini Mart*. Most of these places are on the main road north of the *Batelco* tower.

The Hermitage

One of the most interesting places in The Bahamas, *The Hermitage*, is probably the most noted tourist attraction on Cat Island. *The Hermitage* is situated just outside of New Bight atop 206' high *Mt. Alverna* (sometimes called *Mt. Comer*) the highest point of land in The Bahamas. *The Hermitage* is a monument to the faith of one man, John Hawes, known as Father Jerome. Father Jerome, born in 1876, spent five years studying at the *Royal Institute of British Architecture* before entering *Lincoln Theological College* to become an Anglican Minister. In 1911, Father Jerome went to Rome to study three years for the Catholic Priesthood. He built both St. Paul's and St. Peter's Churches in Clarence Town, Long Island (see the chapter *Long Island, Clarence Town*). He later went to Australia to pursue the callings of his faith as a bush priest, but when it came time to retire he chose Cat Island. Father Jerome received permission from the Catholic Bishop in Nassau to retire on Cat Island as a hermit and in 1939 he arrived and surveyed *Mt. Alverna*. In 1940, he began construction of *The Hermitage*, a miniature replica of a European Franciscan Monastery. Father Jerome built the entire structure by himself out of native rock including the *Stations of the Cross*. He chose a place where he could look to the east and see the cobalt blue of the Atlantic Ocean and to the west where he could gaze upon the emerald and turquoise waters of the banks. Father Jerome lived here until his death at age 80. He is buried beneath *The Hermitage* that he so lovingly built with his own hands.

The Hermitage is only a 20 minute-walk from town; after you pass the portal inscribed "*Mount Alverna*" take the path that bears off to the right and winds straight up the hill past the *Stations of the Cross*. You must signal your approach by striking a stone on a piece of scrap metal left hanging there for that purpose at the turnoff.

Navigational Information

Vessels headed north must detour around Bonefish Point and its shallow bar that stretches about a mile southwest of the point. This bar actually starts well to the east at the north end of The Bight as shown on Chart CT-3. A waypoint at 24° 16.50' N, 75° 28.90' W, will place you approximately ¾ mile southwest of the southwestern tip of the bar. From here you can head straight to *Fernandez Bay*, *Smith's Bay*, or points north as you wish.

Fernandez Bay

Fernandez Bay-¾ nm W of:
24° 19.10' N, 75° 29.55' W

Fernandez Bay is home to the *Fernandez Bay Village Resort* (http://www.fernandezbayvillage.com/) and has one of the most beautiful beaches on Cat Island. *Fernandez Bay* has been in the Armbrister family, one of the oldest families on Cat Island, since the 1780s, although the resort has only been open a little over 40 years. Jacqueline Onassis once stayed aboard her yacht just offshore here. The resort is a well-laid out series of villas, each with a kitchen and maid service, and guests can take their choice of activities such as snorkeling, windsurfing, skiing, or sailing. A divemaster on premises leads SCUBA divers and snorkelers to deep-water reefs some 7 miles west of *Fernandez Bay*. Among the features are coral heads 100' in diameter and wall diving in water from 70'-100' deep. Certifications and dive gear rentals are also available for guests of the resort. The restaurant offers fine dining serving breakfast, lunch, and dinner (with reservations by noon), an open-air beach tiki-bar is simple to use, it works on the honor system, make your drink, sign your name, and pay later. The resort also has a book-swap that you are welcome to use.

Navigational Information

The anchorage off the horseshoe shaped beach at the *Fernandez Bay Village* resort is easy to enter and offers good holding in 8' over a sandy bottom. As shown on Chart CT-4, a waypoint at 24° 19.10' N, 75° 29.55' W, will place you approximately ¾ mile west of the entrance to *Fernandez Bay*. Steer eastward between the northern tip of the bay and the small, unnamed rock in the middle of the entrance, slightly favoring the north side of the channel. The best holding is in the northern end of the bay and if you head too far to the east the bottom gets rocky and the holding is poor. If your draft is not too deep, less than 6', you can tuck in close to the northern shore if west and northwest winds threaten. Although you can anchor in the southern part of *Fernandez Bay* to escape southerly winds, the bay is not a pleasant place to be in the prelude to a frontal passage.

If the wind is forecast to be strong out of the south to west, a better place to be would be north about a mile at *Smith's Bay* (see the next section: *Smith's Bay*). If you have a draft of less than 3', and bad weather threatens, you might be able to work your way in over the bar at high tide into *Armbrister Creek*

where some local fishing boats are moored. There are a couple of spots inside the creek where the depths are 3' at low water but the entrance is about 1' at low water. Sound the entrance carefully before attempting to enter.

There is an excellent lee anchorage just south of *Fernandez Bay* called *Kelly Bay*. Here you'll have good protection from winds from the north/northeast to the east/southeast. The sandy bottom is excellent holding and the pretty beach is deserted, no one from the resort comes here. The Fernandez Cays are home to a colony of white-crowned pigeons, please don't disturb their fragile nesting sites.

What You Will Find Ashore
Fernandez Bay Village Resort is a small, family-run operation. "A little manners goes a long way!" as the staff says. Their honor bar is a wonderful thing. The resort has a common area under the casuarinas

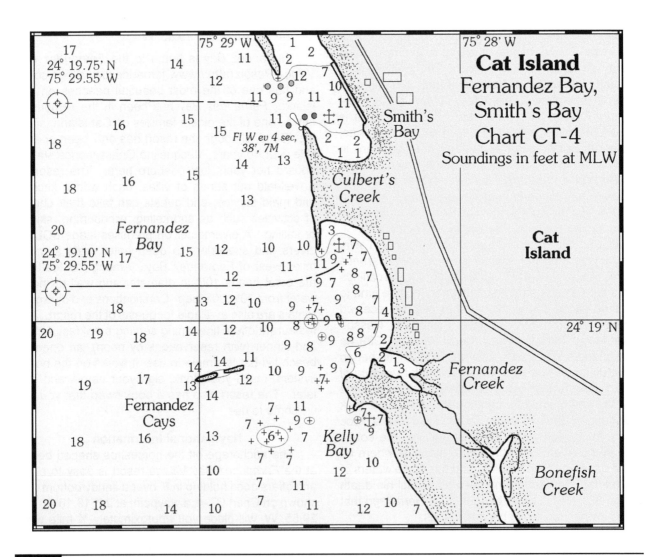

where all the deck chairs are and boaters are welcome to use this area and relax. The hammocks are to be saved for guests and the guest areas off to either side of the common area are for guests only. For a good meal visit the *Blue Bird Cafe*.

Smith's Bay

Smith's Bay--¾ nm W of:
24° 19.75' N, 75° 29.55' W

This area of Cat Island is heavily agricultural and *Smith's Bay* is most noted for its government packing house. Prior to its construction in 1971, growers had to ship their produce to Nassau, a headache for all involved necessitating a middleman or family member in Nassau. Now growers receive a check from the packing house, which handles everything involved with its shipment and sale.

Smith's Bay residents make their living farming and fishing as do most of the people you will meet along this shoreline. *Smith's Bay* was once a much larger settlement, which will be obvious when you notice the layout of the buildings. In town there is a tree called the *Passion Tree* because it is said to bleed a red liquid at Easter.

Navigational Information
A waypoint at 24° 19.75' N, 75° 29.55' W, will place you approximately ¾ mile west of the entrance to the harbour at *Smith's Bay* in *Culbert's Creek* as shown on Chart CT-4. Head generally eastward to pass between the opening between Cat Island and the small, unnamed cay to the north. There is a lighted range (Fl R) to lead you in. The front range is a white pole topped with an orange daymark and a red light; the rear range is an inverted triangle as a daymark. You'll have 9' at the entrance and it deepens inside to 11' just off the long concrete dock. If approaching from *Fernandez Bay* you can stay ¼ mile offshore and you'll be there before you have hardly a chance to warm up the engine or trim the sails.

The only place deep enough to anchor in *Smith's Bay* is between the dock and the entrance. *Smith's Bay* offers good protection in a frontal passage but a good size sea can work its way in with westerly winds. If you intend to anchor here to get out of bad weather don't block access to the dock as the mailboat calls in here on a weekly basis, usually on Wednesdays, and other freight boats are in and out at other times. If you need fuel you can make arrangements with the station in New Bight to deliver to the dock in *Smith's Bay*.

What You Will Find Ashore
Four miles to the east along the path is a surfer's beach on the Atlantic shoreline. North of *Smith's Bay* lies friendly *Tea Bay* and Knowles Village, with its colorful primary school sitting just a few paces from the water's edge (see Chart CT-5). *Tea Bay* got its name from the plantation owners who would meet here daily in the shade of a large tree for tea.

A little further north, The Cove sits approximately midway down the western shore of Cat Island, the halfway point. The town was originally called Jesse Cove and was first inhabited by a Loyalist. Off *The Cove* on the Atlantic shore are the wrecks of the *Whisky* dating back to the last century and the *S.S. Modegard*, which sank on the reef in 1910. On the western shore, partially hidden by the casuarinas, are some fuel tanks that feed the large power station just inland, a small antenna tower marks the power station.

Further north are the settlements of Stephenson, Industrious Hill, Cairey's, and Gaitor's. Stephenson has an area known as Poitier Village where the few residents claim kinship to their native son, the famous actor, Sydney Poitier. Inland of Stephenson two caves that are home to a healthy population of bats. There is a small cave at the point just above Stephenson on the western shoreline. I have not investigated this cave so I can tell you nothing about it. Perhaps you might check it out and tell me. Any takers?

Nearby, Industrious Hill is not so industrious, it is more agricultural than anything and it's the home of the multi-chambered *Bat Cave*, another dark hole in the ground spelunkers will want to climb into and explore. Cairey's was founded by Eleuthera pineapple farmers in the late 1800s when Cat Island and Eleuthera were the major pineapple growers in The Bahamas.

North of Gaitor's at Ben's Bluff, Chart CT-6, is a small cave mouth on the western shore of Cat Island just above the water's edge. The cave consists of a main tunnel with a large chamber off to the left and an even larger one at the rear of the cave. The entire cave is only 50'-60' long, the largest chamber is about 20' x 40' x 15' high and is home to a large number of bats. You must check this one out, even if you're not a spelunker.

Customs and Immigration
Smith's Bay is a *Port of Entry* and there is a *Customs* and *Immigration* office here.

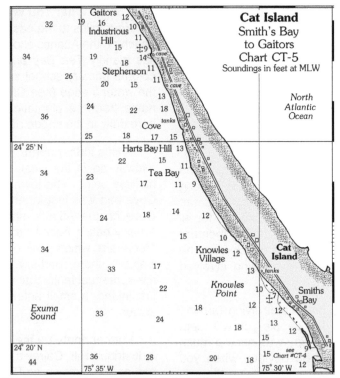

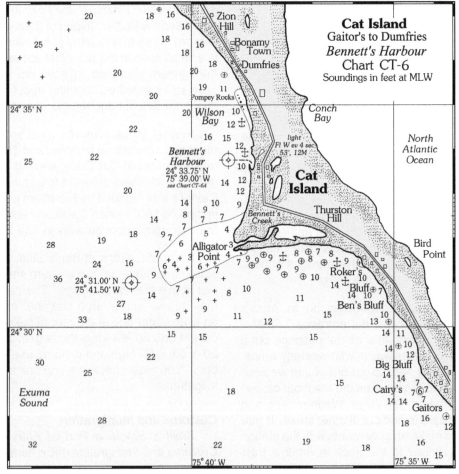

Provisioning

Shoppers can visit *The Heritage Convenience Store* for groceries. In T*ea Bay* you can get groceries at *Linnette's Convenience Store*, spirits at *The Liquor Store*, and other goodies at the *Snack Counter and Vegetable Stand*. In Knowles Village you will find groceries at *Moncur and Sons Grocery* and *Issie's*. In The Bluff you will find a well-stocked grocery store, the *Island General Shopping Center*.

Dining

The *Haulover Restaurant and Bar* is just across from the dock and nearby is the *Wayside Restaurant*. If you would like a cold drink visit *Hazel's Hideaway Bar*, sometimes called the *Sea Side Bar,* and other times simply called *Hazel Brown's Bar,* with its distinctive bright green exterior. Owner Hazel Brown offers cold drinks, the coldest beer in The Bahamas she claims, and pleasant company. In Knowles Village you can enjoy the Bahamian fare served at the *Bachelor's Restaurant and Bar*.

Medical Assistance

If you have a medical emergency you can contact the *Smith's Bay Community Clinic* at 242-342-2160 (resident doctor and nurse). The clinic is open from 0900-1700, Monday-Friday, except holidays.

Navigational Information

Vessels heading north from *Smith's Bay* have no dangers if they stay at least ¼ mile offshore. This part of the coast is basically one long lee anchorage. Just tuck in close to shore in prevailing winds and drop the hook wherever you like. A small string of rocks lies about 200 yards offshore just north of *Smith's Bay*. They all sit on the edge of the one fathom line with the exception of a small break north of *Smith's Bay*. Here cruisers can head in towards the southern end of the first beach lying about ½ mile north of the entrance to *Smith's Bay*. Pass south of the large rock lying off the beach, you must eyeball your way into the bay. The area between the rocks has 7' at low water and there is up to 9' inside.

Just to the east of Alligator Point, around Roker's, is an excellent anchorage in winds from the north to northeast as shown on Chart CT-6. Here a long white beach stretches east from Alligator Point to Roker's where it follows the curve of Cat Island as it turns southeastward. In northerly winds anchor just south of the long beach, but watch out for the shallow stray heads and small patch reefs that this area is strewn with.

Never attempt this at night. In easterly winds you can anchor in the lee of Roker's.

Bennett's Harbour

Alligator Point-½ nm SW of southwestern tip: 24° 31.00' N, 75° 41.50' W

Bennett's Harbour-½ nm W of entrance: 24° 33.75' N, 75° 39.00' W

Bennett's Harbour, Chart CT-6 and in greater detail on Chart CT-6A, was originally settled by freed slaves and this community of some 400 is spread around a small harbour that is alleged to have hidden pirates in days of old.

Navigational Information

Vessels heading north for *Bennett's Harbour* must first round Alligator Point with its long, shallow, rocky bar. A waypoint at 24° 31.00' N, 75° 41.50' W, will place you approximately ½ mile southwest of the shoal's southwest tip. From here you can head generally northeast towards *Bennett's Harbour.* At Alligator Point, *Bennett's Creek* (also shown as *Pigeon Creek*) is alive with sea life (good bonefishing) and worth the time to explore by dinghy. The mouth of the creek is blocked by a bar with less than 2' at low water. Shallow draft vessels can find a good anchorage inside the creek in 5' of water a bit over ¼ mile from the mouth of the creek at the spot that *Bennett's Creek* winds northward and *Pigeon Creek* continues eastward.

A waypoint at 24° 33.75' N, 75° 39.00' W, will place you approximately ½ mile west of the entrance to *Bennett's Harbour.* From this position steer generally east and round the spit of land and its offlying shoal and turn to starboard to anchor in the small harbour as shown on Chart CT-6A. This is a small anchorage and there is no such thing as swinging room if there is more than one boat present. Don't block the dock as the mailboat and other freight boats call here regularly. This is a good spot to ride out a front although it gets a little choppy inside when strong winds from the northwest to north push in the seas. There's also a lot of current here, two anchors are a must. *Bennett's Harbour* has room for two to three vessels of moderate draft, no more than 6' or so. If the weather is settled or out of the NE-SE, you'll find a fine anchorage at the northern end of the little cove north of the dock at *Bennett's Harbour,* south of Pompey Rocks.

Bennett's Harbour   Photo Courtesy of Paul Harding

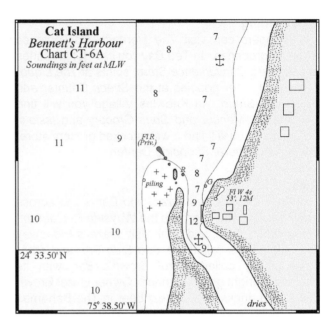

Cat Island
Bennett's Harbour
Chart CT-6A
Soundings in feet at MLW

24° 33.50' N

75° 38.50' W   *dries*

What You Will Find Ashore

North of *Bennett's Harbour* is Dumfries. Originally settled by Loyalists and once named Ways Green, Dumfries is home to the dramatic *Great Crown Cave*, said to stretch for over three miles and which should only be visited with the help of an experienced guide from Dumfries or Arthur's Town, ask for Mr. Gaitor in Dumfries. This vast labyrinth and its chambers is a spelunkers delight and you can ask for directions at *C&S Farm Supply* (they also carry hardware, plumbing supplies, and occasionally fresh produce). The path north of the *Gossip Bar* leads to this cave passing through a huge stretch of 40' tall mangrove.

Dining

After your visit to the earth's innards, you might enjoy stopping at *The Turning Point Club* which features the occasional *Rake and Scrape* band. The restaurant's mutton souse is excellent. For another dining option you can visit *Ducky's Restaurant.*

Provisioning

For groceries try *Tito's* or *Better Value.* Fresh produce, when in season, can be found at the produce exchange after the mailboat calls. You can also find some provisions at the *Wayside Convenience Store.*

Arthur's Town

Arthur's Town-½ nm SW of:
24° 36.80' N, 75° 41.20' W

North of *Bennett's Harbour* is Arthur's Town, the commercial center of Cat Island with an 8,000' long airstrip. Arthur's Town was raided by the Spanish inthe 1700s and later in that century was settled by Loyalists from America. It is said that Sydney Poitier lived here for a time as a child.

The first weekend in May finds Arthur's Town hosting the *Annual Heritage Festival,* an exhibit of historical artifacts while the first weekend in August you'll find the annual *Cat Island Regatta* in full swing.

Navigational Information

Boats heading to Arthur's Town from Alligator Point or *Bennett's Harbour* have deep water all the way with few obstructions save a few shallow heads very close inshore. The 200' *Batelco* tower makes an excellent landmark day or night. A waypoint at 24° 36.80' N, 75° 41.20' W, will place you approximately ½ mile southwest of Arthur's Town. Vessels can anchor anywhere, north or south of Arthur's Town as shown on Chart CT-7, the water is deep and the holding good. This is a lee anchorage, prevailing winds only.

What You Will Find Ashore

Dinghy Dock

You can land your dinghy in the small basin near the large coconut grove by the *Batelco* tower, or you can tie to the town dock as long as it's not being used. At the head of the town dock is the *Commissioner's Office* and the *Police Station.* These buildings sit right on the large grassy town square called *Christie Park.*

Mechanical Assistance

If you need a mechanic or if you just need something welded or fabricated, visit *Captain Black's Welding.*

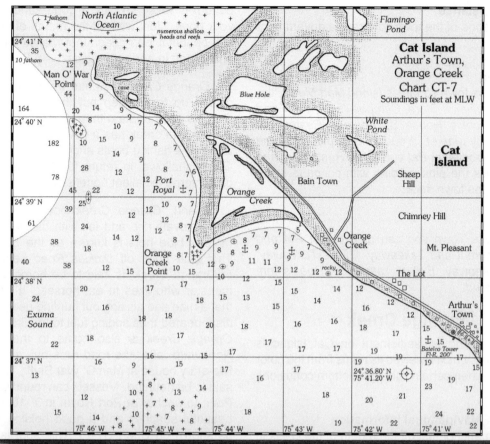

Arthur's Town

Photo Courtesy of Paul Harding

Medical Assistance

ON the edge of the town square is a government clinic.

Provisioning

Nearby the town square is *Island Mart Meats,* the *Jabon Convenience Store, Campbell's Big Bull Food Store,* the *Cookie House Bakery and Restaurant,* and the *Family Market,* You can also pick up some nice baked goodies at *Pat and Dell's Restaurant and Takeaway,* it's the pink building with concrete steps just north of the town dock.

Dining

In Arthur's Town you can dine out at *Pat and Dell's Restaurant and Takeaway, Gina's Takeaway, Nancy's Takeaway, E & K Takeaway, Dean's Inn,* and *In The Mud.*

Orange Creek

The northernmost settlement on Cat Island is *Orange Creek,* which received its name from the color of the creek when certain light and bottom conditions exist.

Navigational Information

You can anchor just off the mouth of the creek in 8"-14' of water as shown on Chart CT-7. Some of this bottom is rocky so pick a good sandy spot to drop your hook. Just west of the mouth of Orange Creek is a beautiful long beach that makes for an excellent anchorage in northerly winds.

Orange Creek itself has waters that are in some places up to 7' deep but the bar at the entrance restricts entry boats with drafts of less than 3' at high water. The creek has a few scattered wrecks along with some fishing boats anchored inside. As *Orange Creek* shallows, in return for the loss of depth one gains some excellent bonefishing grounds.

Inland, *Orange Creek* boasts two blue holes whose levels rise and fall with the tide. Their most famous blue hole is known as the *Bad Blue Hole.* This blue hole, off *Dickies Road* behind the town of Orange Creek, is said to be home to a ferocious monster who likes to eat horses. It has been said that a man and his dog out hunting near this blue hole disappeared thus adding fuel to the fire of the legend. *Orange Creek* is also home to the *Griffin Cave.* Northward, after the road runs out, sits a lonesome two-story house at Man O' War Bluff. The structure is said to be haunted. Vessels can round Orange Creek Point to anchor at Port Royal in 7'-10' of water with beautiful beaches and a good holding sand bottom as shown on Chart CT-7. This spot is excellent in northeast to east winds. At Man O" War Point is a

Orange Creek

Photo Courtesy of Paul Harding

large cave right at sea level, definitely worth a dinghy ride. North of Man O' War Point is one the island's most beautiful beaches, inaccessible by road but not by dinghy. About a mile from Man O" War Point you will see a coconut palm grove where you will find the *Drip Cave*, said to be a Lucayan cave.

What You Will Find Ashore

Mechanical Assistance
If you need a mechanic, check at the gas station in town.

Medical Assistance
The Orange Creek Community Clinic (242-354-4050) located in town and is open from 0900 to 1700 M-F except holidays.

Provisioning
It is possible to pick up some groceries (and ice) at the *Sea Spray Inn*, *Orange Creek Inn* (http://www.orangecreekinn.com/), the *Orange Creek Food Store*, and *Seymore's Bayside Grocery*.

Dining
You can dine out while in Orange Creek at *Magnolia's Bar* or *CJ's Eatery*.

Laundry
You can do your laundry at the *Orange Creek Food Store* (they also have a fax service).

Half Moon Cay

(Little San Salvador)
Fuel: None
Haul-Out: None
Diesel Repairs: None
Outboard Repairs: None
Propane: None
Provisions: None
Important Lights:
South shore: Fl W ev 2½ sec

West Bay-1 nm W of anchorage:
24° 34.48' N, 75° 58.60' W

Little San Salvador-1 nm S of light:
24° 32.70' N, 75° 56.30' W

Half Moon Cay, lying between Eleuthera and Cat Island, is an excellent stopover in anything but strong westerly weather. If you wonder why the cay would once be called "Little" San Salvador, being as it is so far from the island of San Salvador, you must remember that Cat Island was known as San Salvador for a long period of time.

In early 1997, the island was purchased by the *Holland America Cruise Line* and developed Little San Salvador into what is now known as Half Moon Cay, an out island paradise strictly for guests of their cruise ships. The lovely anchorage at West Bay is no longer a cruiser's haven, in fact the powers-that-be on the island request that if you must anchor here, do so at the northwestern end of the harbour so as not to interfere with their guest's water sports activities. There are still rumors going around that managers of the operation plan to install moorings on the northwestern side of the harbour for visiting cruisers, but as of this writing none are in place.

While you are permitted by Bahamian law to walk any beach on any Bahamian Island up to the high water line, the caretakers of Half Moon Cay frown on such activity while cruise ships are in the harbour. When the cruise ships are not present (they're usually in port 2-3 days a week) you can hail *Half Moon Cay* on VHF ch. 16 to request permission to come ashore.

Approaches

From anywhere in the Exumas it is a straight shot across *Exuma Sound* to Half Moon Cay. From *Conch Cut* in Exuma Park, a bearing of 68° for 34.6 miles will bring you to the waypoint that lies approximately 1 mile west of the *West Bay* anchorage at 24° 34.48' N, 75° 58.60' W, as shown on Chart CT-8. A vessel leaving the north anchorage at Warderick Wells should steer 82° for 37.7 miles while those departing Staniel Cay at *Big Rock Cut* will run 34.3 miles at a heading of 55°. From *Joe Cay Cut* in Pipe Creek, *West Bay* lies 35.0 miles distant on a course of 62°.

From *Bennett's Harbour*, Cat Island, a course of 93° for 15.6 miles will place you at a waypoint at 24° 32.70' N, 75° 56.30' W, which lies approximately 1 mile south of the light as shown on Chart CT-8. Vessels heading to Half Moon Cay from Arthur's Town or Orange Creek should head to the area of *Bennett's Harbour* to take up the course for the waypoint south of Half Moon Cay. I have traveled west/southwest from Orange Creek and there are a lot of shallow patch reefs lying west of the Long Rocks, especially in the area of 24° 36.00' N, 75° 44.60' W. These reefs are easily seen and avoided

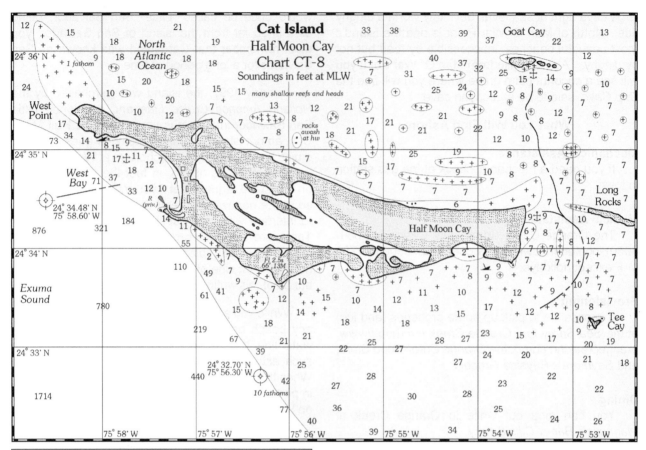

Cat Island
Half Moon Cay
Chart CT-8
Soundings in feet at MLW
many shallow reefs and heads

Half Moon Cay: West Bay to
Tee Cay and Long Rocks

Photo Courtesy of Paul Harding

in good light. All vessels heading to Half Moon Cay from *Bennett's Harbour* or points north must keep well south of the Long Rocks and Tee Cay.

Between Tee Cay and the Long Rocks to its north and east are numerous shallow patch reefs and there are places where there are few if any passages

between them. It's best to avoid this area unless you intend to dive on the reefs. Vessels for their offspring's recreation. Passengers wishing to spend money will find what is described as a shopping center with an art gallery and "native" crafts. There are upwards of 15 full-time employees from Cat Island and at least one management couple living on Half Moon Cay on a day-to-day basis. One bright spot is that the cruise ships will only stay overnight when they do stop.

There is good fishing on the reefs off the rock at the southeastern tip of *West Bay*. At the northwestern tip of the bay, just west of the conspicuous rocks, is the wreck of an old barge in shallow water and there's usually a lot of fish around this site. The northern shore of Half Moon Cay is a fisherman and diver's delight. There are many, many large and small reefs lying along the shoreline stretching eastward past Goat Cay and Long Rocks. There is a huge, shallow reef system that stretches northward for over a mile from West Point at the northwestern tip of Half Moon Cay and I have seen some very large lobsters come off these reefs. The long beach on the northern shore of Half Moon Cay is excellent for beachcombing, especially after a northerly blow.

Along the southern shore of Half Moon Cay are quite a few shallow reefs. The main draw on the southern shore is the shallow entrance to the extensive creek system in the interior. Unfortunately, the owners of Half Moon Cay have placed the lagoon off limits to visitors in their dinghies. East of the creek is a small bay that looks inviting but really isn't, it is very shallow, 1'-2' at low water, and very rocky. Just a little southeast of this beach is the wreck of a large vessel. Part of the bow of this upside down wreck juts above the surface at low tide as shown on Chart CT-8. Heading to Half Moon Cay from *Fernandez Bay* should steer 306° for 27 miles to reach the waypoint south of the light. From the waypoint south of Half Moon Cay, boats can head generally northwest, parallel to the shoreline but not too close in to avoid the shallow patch reefs, and then make the turn into *West Bay*. For those heading to Half Moon Cay from Eleuthera, simply parallel the southwest shoreline of Eleuthera from Cape Eleuthera southward and once clear of East End Point take up a course of 105° for 9.8 miles to the anchorage at *West Bay*.

West Bay

Navigational Information
A waypoint at 24° 34.48' N, 75° 58.60' W, will place you approximately 1 mile west of the anchorage area at *West Bay* as shown on Chart CT-8. From this waypoint simply head straight in and anchor wherever you choose in the northwestern part of *West Bay*, the holding is great throughout the entire anchorage area. *West Bay* is an excellent anchorage in even the strongest north to southeast winds but it is not the place to be in anything westerly.

What You Will Find Ashore
There are several groups of buildings scattered about the beach area. Ashore the cruise ship passengers find all sorts of toys like paddle boats and jet skis to play with as well as a children's play area

Eastern Shore, Goat Cay

If caught at Half Moon Cay with westerly weather threatening, skippers have the option of heading to *Bennett's Harbour* at Cat Island or moving to the eastern shore of Half Moon Cay (one could also head to Eleuthera, but that is quite a bit further and the first leg is to windward if westerly winds are blowing).

From *West Bay*, head southward along the southern shore of Half Moon Cay staying at least ½ mile off to avoid the shallow reefs as shown on Chart CT-8. Work your way towards Tee Cay and then steer north of Tee Cay towards the western end of Long Rocks. Keep an eye out for the shallow reefs and bars that you will want to leave to port. You'll have no less than 7' of water on this route if you're careful. Never, I repeat, NEVER attempt this route at night, even with waypoints it would be too dangerous, a small error could be disastrous (if you must leave at night head downwind to *Bennett's Harbour* staying well south of Tee Cay and the rocks that lie to its east and northeast). Once clear of the reefs you can work your way in to the eastern shore of Half Moon Cay where you can tuck in between the reefs and the shore in 6'-9' of water.

From this area one can head over to Goat Cay which lies a little over a mile north of the eastern tip of Half Moon Cay. I think visiting Goat Cay by dinghy is the best idea, but you can take the big boat over and anchor off the cay in settled weather if you so desire. The anchorage is open to the prevailing east and southeast winds though, only giving a little lee in northerly winds. To head to Goat Cay, follow the directions to arrive along the eastern shore of Half Moon Cay. Passing between the reefs off the northeastern tip of Half Moon Cay and the western tip of the Long Rocks you will have 7' along this route at mean low water. Once between the reefs steer towards Goat Cay, the larger and westernmost of the cays to your north. The water will get progressively deeper as you approach Goat Cay and you will have to zigzag your way through a few shallow reefs that are easily seen and avoided in good visibility. Again, never attempt this at night. Goat Cay is encircled by shallow reefs and the best place to anchor is south of its western end. Dinghy in to the small beach and you can snorkel the reefs right off the beach.

Conception Island

Fuel: None
Haul-Out: None
Diesel Repairs: None
Outboard Repairs: None
Propane: None
Provisions: None
Important Lights:
Southwest Point: Fl W ev 2 sec

N of reef off NW tip of Conception Island:
23° 55.18' N, 75° 05.40' W

West Bay - ¾ nm W of anchorage:
23° 51.00' N, 75° 08.00' W

Southeast point - clears reef SE of Conception:
23° 47.25' N, 75° 04.66' W

Conception Island is the smallest of the three islands that lie just off the mouth of Exuma Sound where it meets the *Atlantic Ocean*. Rum Cay lies to the southeast of Conception with larger San Salvador lying to the northeast. This trio of islands are a popular stop for cruisers heading to or from the Caribbean, but are most often visited by those skippers who are just spending a short time in George Town, Exuma and seek a little break from the hustle and bustle of *Elizabeth Harbour* (hustle and bustle you ask?).

Conception Island is a National Park and is under the protection of *The Bahamas National Trust*. Contrary to popular belief, Conception Island is not a land and sea park, only its land area is protected. This means that nothing on the island may be disturbed, removed, or damaged. You cannot take shells, you cannot have a fire, and most of all, you cannot leave any garbage. This also means that cruisers can fish on the rich surrounding reefs. Good news for cruisers indeed.

Approaches

The high wooded mass of Booby Cay will probably be the first thing you can make out when headed for Conception Island. The land mass of Conception Island is hilly and scrub covered and steep-to along the western shore. From the waypoint to clear *Cape Santa Maria Reef* at the northern end of Long Island it is approximately 15.4 miles on a course of 62° to the waypoint, 23° 51.00' N, 75° 08.00' W, ½ mile west of the anchorage at *West Bay* as shown on Chart CO-1.

Navigational Information

If approaching Conception from Rum Cay, from the waypoint north of the wreck north of Flamingo Bay, a course of 311° for 8.6 nm will bring you to a waypoint at 23° 47.25' N, 75° 04.66' W, which will allow you to clear the reefs that lie southeast of Conception Island as shown on Chart CO-2. From this point keep the reefs well to starboard and round the southern point of Conception Island, Wedge Point, and parallel the shore about ¼ offshore until you arrive at the *West Bay* anchorage. Watch out for the reefs close in along the shore.

Conception Island from the Southeast   Photo Courtesy of Paul Harding

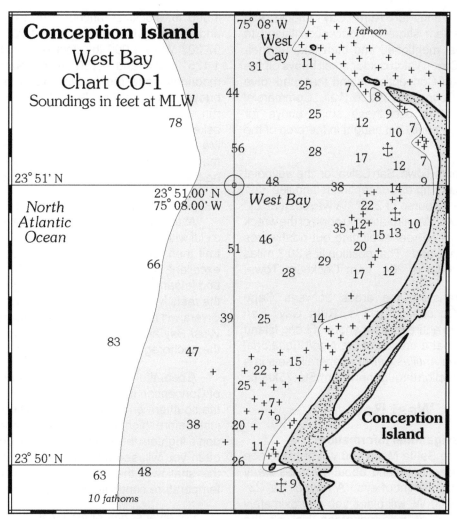

Conception Island

West Bay
Chart CO-1
Soundings in feet at MLW

75° 08' W
West Cay
1 fathom

23° 51' N

23° 51.00' N
75° 08.00' W

West Bay

North
Atlantic
Ocean

Conception
Island

23° 50' N

10 fathoms

East Bay as seen from the North

Wedge Point

East Bay

Conception
Island

Photo Courtesy of Paul Harding

Vessels heading for Rum Cay should sail around the southern shore of Conception Island to the waypoint just mentioned and then take up their course to Rum Cay. Watch out for small buoys off the southern shore of Conception Island that mark dive sites along the *Conception Island Wall*. Commercial dive boat operators use these small buoys for moorings that can easily get caught in the prop of the unwary skipper.

From Cockburn Town, San Salvador, the waypoint at the southeastern tip of Conception Island lies 33.1 miles distant on a course of 250°. A waypoint at 23° 55.18' N, 75° 05.40' W, will place you north of the wreck that lies off the large reef stretching out northwards from Conception Island. That position lies 30.8 miles distant on a course of 264° from Cockburn Town.

Skippers transiting the areas between Cape Santa Maria, Conception Island, Rum Cay, San Salvador, and the entire eastern shore of Long Island must be aware that a branch of the *North Equatorial Current* called the *Antilles Current* generally sets in a northwesterly direction through here from .5 to .75 knots.

West Bay

Navigational Information

Leaving Cape Santa Maria you will begin to see the hills of Conception Island about 10 miles away depending on your height of eye. A waypoint at 23° 51.00' N, 75° 08.00 W, will place you approximately ¾ mile southwest of the anchorage just off the beautiful long white beach as shown on Chart CO-1. Boats can anchor just off the beach in 6'-25' over a beautiful, excellent holding, sandy bottom. This anchorage is good in winds from northeast to almost south but is not place to be in the westerly prelude to a frontal passage. If a front threatens, round the south tip of Conception Island and Wedge Point (see next section: *East Bay*) and anchor in the lee of Conception Island or north near Booby Cay. Along the southern shore of Conception Island is a snug little anchorage in northerly winds as long as there is no surge. The anchorage is just off the small beach that lies west of the entrance to the creeks.

There are three big boat moorings (for vessels up to 150' LOA) located in *West Bay* and installed by the *Bahamas National Trust*. The anchors have GPS positions at 23° 51.091 N, 75° 07.644 W (a 3,000 pound Danforth with 90' of 1.125" chain with a 2" nylon pennant); 23° 51.109 N, 75° 07.382 W (a

1,000 lb. stockless anchor with 90' of 1.125" chain and 1.250" nylon pennant); and 23° 51.099 N, 75° 07.307 W (a 1,000 lb. stockless anchor with 90' of 1.125" chain and 1.250" nylon pennant). All the moorings have red buoys and smaller red pickup buoys with large thimbles in their pennants. Please run your own line through the pennant. You are asked to leave the larger mooring if the MV *Chantal Ma Vie* arrives (these are the folks who donated the moorings and their installation). At this time there are no fees associated with these moorings.

What You Will Find Ashore

At the north end of the beach is a trail leading over a cliff with a rope attached to assist climbers. Another trail then leads to the northern beach, which offers excellent beachcombing through its piles of flotsam and jetsam as well as some exciting camera shots of the reefs lying off Conception Island's northern shore. Divers will love the reefs to the north and south of the *West Bay* anchorage. You don't even have to leave the anchorage for some truly marvelous snorkeling.

A beautiful sight to see are the turtles in the creeks of Conception Island at high tide. Enter the creeks at the southern end of the island, west of Wedge Point, just before high tide and kill your engine, so you don't frighten the turtles with your outboard. Quite often you will see dozens of sea turtles cavorting in the shallows, the warm water making a delightful temperature controlled climate for them.

For diver's, one of the most beautiful reefs in the Bahamas is the *Conception Island Wall* lying just 300' off the beach. Here gigantic coral heads climb from 90' depths to 50' and less. The wall drops in ladder-like steps and is covered with hard and soft corals and sponges. Some of the best spots are south of the island where you will find some dive buoys placed there by dive boat operators. Stretching northward from West Rock some four miles is *Southampton Reef*. At the northern end of *Southampton Reef* you can dive on the remains of a wrecked freighter which sank over 90 years ago. The 300' long hull lies amid Elkhorn and Staghorn corals in 25' of water with its very prominent engines, boilers, anchors, and props.

East Bay

Navigational Information

Vessels caught at Conception Island when a frontal passage threatens have the option of heading around to the eastern side of the island to gain a lee from southwest winds through west and northwest all the way through north to almost northeast. To gain access to the anchorages along the eastern shore of Conception Island pass south of the island, giving the southeast tip (as shown on Chart CO-1) a wide berth to avoid the shallows along that shoreline. Head eastward along the southern shore of Conception Island at least 200 yards offshore taking Wedge Point, the conspicuous pointed bluff, to port as shown on Chart CO-2. Watch out for the reef stretching east from Wedge Point, pass between this reef and Wedge Point. From here, head northward along the eastern shore of Conception Island and anchor wherever your draft allows and where you feel safe from the southwest to north winds. The best spots are north of the unnamed point north of Wedge Point where you can get close in to the beach, and at the northeastern tip of Conception Island, just southeast of Booby Cay,

between the reef and the shoreline. The anchorages on the eastern shore of Conception Island are only good in winds from south/southwest to north/ northeast. When the wind moves into the north on its way eastward, it is time for you to move back around to the shelter of *West Bay*. One can also anchor just south of Booby Rock but there are a lot of shallow patch reefs around that you must steer around. The beaches on the eastern and northern shores of Conception are excellent for beachcombing. Booby Cay, the conspicuous high island at the northern end of *East Bay*, is a protected bird sanctuary.

There is a light on the southern shore of Conception Island that is supposed to flash white every two seconds. It stands 84' above the water, and is visible for 6 nautical miles. Don't expect this light to be working, it has been out of operation for years and when it will be repaired is anybody's guess.

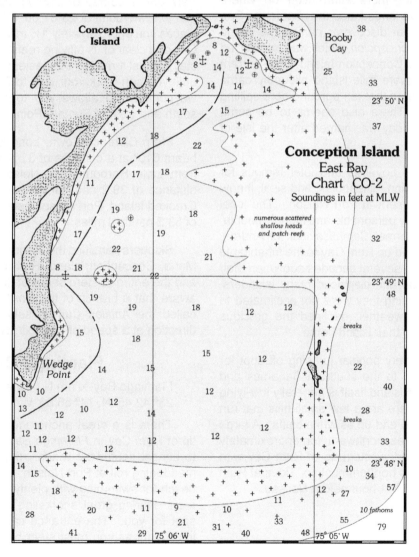

Rum Cay

Ports of Entry: None
Fuel: None
Haul-Out: None
Diesel Repairs: None
Outboard Repairs: None
Propane: Port Nelson
Provisions: Port Nelson
Important Lights
Cottonfield Point: Fl WYR ev 8 sec
Port Nelson Dock: Fxd G

About twenty-five miles southwest of San Salvador and nearly the same distance southeast of Conception Island lies Rum Cay. Lucayan Indians named the cay *Mamana* and it is said to be the second island that Columbus visited on October 15, 1492, of course that's only if you subscribe to the *San Salvador Landfall Theory* (for more information on where Columbus may have landed, see the chapter on San Salvador). The great discoverer named the island *Santa Maria de la Concepcion*, which was transferred over time to nearby Conception Island. The current name of this 30-square mile island allegedly came from an *East Indiaman* that ran aground here spilling its cargo of rum. There also seems to be some speculation that the cay was named after the Isle of Rum in Scotland.

Once settled by Loyalists and later famous for its salt pond production, pineapples, and sisal, it now has only one settlement at Port Nelson. The local inhabitants are a very personable and friendly people. One gentleman, a former *Commissioner* for Andros, even offered free land on Rum Cay to the inhabitants of Tristan De Cunha several decades ago when their volcano blew its top and displaced many islanders. The Tristanians, saying they were not acclimated to the colder English weather, declined the gracious offer and returned to their island home.

Rum Cay is a very popular jumping off spot for vessels southbound to the southern Bahamas and the Caribbean. The island itself is generally low-lying and flat although there are a few small hills that run down to the shore to end up as white bluffs. A large reef system stretches northward for approximately two miles off the northwestern tip of Rum Cay with a visible wreck on its northernmost tip. Tides at Rum Cay run approximately 1 hour before Nassau.

Approaches

From the waypoint that clears the reefs lying southeast of Conception Island a course of 131° for 8.6 nautical miles will bring you to a waypoint just north of the wrecked freighter lying north of Flamingo Bay. Rum Cay will be spotted very shortly after leaving Conception Island, and a waypoint at 23° 38.50' N, 74° 57.30' W, will place you approximately ½ mile off Sandy Point in very deep water. From this position skippers wishing to gain access to Port Nelson may take up an eastbound course staying at least ½ mile south of the shoreline of Rum Cay to avoid the shallow rocks and shoals close in.

From Cockburn Town, San Salvador, a course of 235° for 29.9 miles brings you to a point north of the wrecked freighter lying off the northwest tip of Rum Cay at Flamingo Cay. From Sandy Point at San Salvador, a course of 218° for 22.1 miles will bring you to a waypoint at 23°37.00' N, 74° 47.0' W, which places you approximately 1½ miles southeast of Rum Cay and clear of its offlying reefs. From this waypoint stay at least 1 mile off the eastern and southern shore until you can work your way to Port Nelson and the waypoint which allows you to clear the reef lying south and west of Sumner Point.

From Clarence Town, Long Island, Port Nelson bears 019° at a distance of 31.1 nautical miles while from Little Harbour, Port Nelson bears 006° at a distance of 39.2 nautical miles. From Bird Rock at Crooked Island, Port Nelson bears 338° at a distance of 53.2 nautical miles.

Skippers transiting the areas between Cape Santa Maria, Conception Island, Rum Cay, San Salvador, and the entire eastern shore of Long Island, must be aware that a branch of the *North Equatorial Current* called the *Antilles Current* sets in a northwesterly direction at a speed of approximately ½-¾ knots.

Flamingo Bay

Flamingo Bay-¼ nm N of wreck at entrance:
23° 42.45' N, 74° 56.80' W

There is a great anchorage at the northwestern tip of Rum Cay in *Flamingo Bay* that is good in east to almost southwest winds. If you are tired of the maddening roll at Port Nelson, and you want a great beach for swimming with plenty of shallow and deep reefs offering great snorkeling or diving, this is the spot for you. The entrance can only be navigated in daylight as you must steer between a lot of small

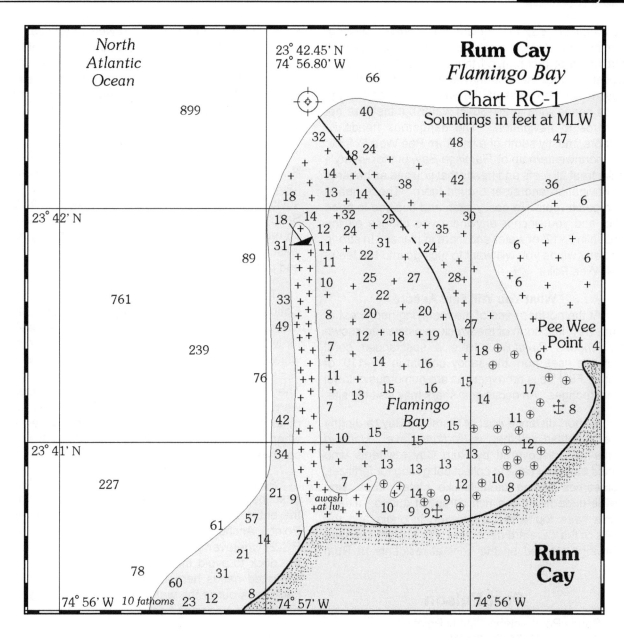

North
Atlantic
Ocean

Rum Cay
Flamingo Bay
Chart RC-1
Soundings in feet at MLW

23° 42.45' N
74° 56.80' W

Flamingo
Bay

Pee Wee
Point

**Rum
Cay**

patch reefs that are easily seen and avoided; but don't fret, there's plenty of room around and between them.

Before entering this anchorage make sure your weather forecast does not call for any westerly to northerly winds overnight because you'll never safely find your way back out in the dark. Over the next few years, perhaps even by the time this edition is published, work will have begun in earnest on a new marina at *Flamingo Bay*. Keep your eyes out for it. The entrance will probably utilize the narrow passage through the southern end of the reef just off the point at the southwestern end of *Flamingo Bay*.

Navigational Information

The entrance, as shown on Chart RC-1, is gained by rounding the northern tip of the reef well north of the remains of an old Haitian freighter. A waypoint at 23° 42.45' N, 74° 56.80' W, will place you approximately ¼ mile north of the wreck at the northern end of the reef. Do not attempt to bring your big boat close to the freighter, use your dinghy for exploring as the shallows extend north of the freighter about 50-100 yards.

From the waypoint steer well east of the wreck giving it a wide berth as you head in for the beach at *Flamingo Bay*. There are two narrow, twisting, turning, entrances through the reef south of the wreck but I cannot recommend them as viable passages. Better to enter the standard way north of the wreck. Just north and east of the wreck are some huge coral heads lying in 20'-30' of water but they are not hazards to navigation. The dangerous heads lie inshore, mostly south of a line from Pee Wee Point to the northwestern tip of *Flamingo Bay*, but for safety's sake treat all reefs and heads that you see as hazards to navigation and steer around them. These heads and patch reefs are easily seen and avoided in good light and you anchor anywhere you choose off the beach in 7'-12' of water and more in places. In strong easterly winds you will want to tuck up into the lee of Pee Wee Point.

What You Will Find Ashore

At the northern end of the reef lying northwest of Rum Cay, just north of the wreck, is a dive site known as *Pinder's Pinnacle*. Here a spectacular coral pinnacle rises from the sandy bottom in 75'-110' of water. Fish life is prominent as are numerous colorful tube sponges. An occasional shark may visit the site.

A short distance east of Flamingo Bay, a dinghy ride in settled weather, is *Hartford Cave*. *Hartford Cave* was discovered by Rum Cay residents who would enter the cave to collect bat guano for fertilizer, sometimes finding utensils like plates, cups, and bowls underneath the rich carpet of guano. These items were found to be Lucayan in origin and the walls of the cave are decorated with ancient Lucayan drawings created by the original residents of Rum Cay.

Port Nelson

Sandy Point - clears Sandy Point:
23° 38.50' N, 74° 57.30' W

Port Nelson - ¼ nm SW of W end of reef:
23° 37.75' N, 74° 51.20' W

Rum Cay - 1½ nm SE of SE tip clear of reef:
23° 37.00' N, 74° 47.00' W

Port Nelson, originally called *Wellington Bay*, is the only settlement on Rum Cay at the present time. In the past there were other communities all over the island with names like Port Boyd, Carmichael, Black Rock, Times Cove, The Village, and Gin Hill. The buildings that remain in these areas are now overgrown with vegetation. After you round Sandy

Point on your approach to Port Nelson you can see the ruins of Black Rock on the southern shore of Rum Cay on a ridge approximately ½ mile east of Sandy Point. There are the remains of numerous slave-constructed stone walls called "margins" all over the island.

Navigational Information

As mentioned earlier, a waypoint at 23° 38.50' N, 74° 57.30' W, will place you approximately ½ nautical mile off Sandy Point in very deep water. Be advised that there is a westerly setting current around Sandy Point. Once you round Sandy Point take up an eastbound course towards Port Nelson staying at least ½ mile south of the southern shore of Rum Cay and passing south of Cottonfield Point.

There is a privately maintained light atop Cottonfield Point (*Fl WYR, 10s, 23m, 10M*) sitting approximately 70' above the water. The light flashes for two seconds every 10 seconds providing two safe white sectors bearing 018° and 087° magnetic to assist vessels wishing to gain access to Port Nelson. The area between 018° and 087° shows amber to warn of some scattered heads. Red shows in all other sectors. The light is obscured by higher land when approaching from the northwest through almost southeast.

Approach Port Nelson and *St. George's Bay* as described and you will be in 20'-30' of water almost the entire way until you come abeam of Cottonfield Point. Anchor just south of the town dock (Chart RC-2) wherever your draft will allow staying well off the dock to avoid the shallows close in. Watch for scattered heads hereabouts. Some of the Elkhorn coral rises out of the water at low tide as if reaching out to snag a passing boat or dinghy.

Heading to Port Nelson from the south, the conspicuous white cliffs just east of Sumner Point make an excellent landmark. Vessels approaching Port Nelson from the south can head to a waypoint at 23° 37.75' N, 74° 51.20' W, which will place you safely south and west of the western tip of *Sumner Point Reef*. From this waypoint head north until well inside the reef and turn to starboard to anchor. Be careful, there are a lot of shallow, dry at low water, patch reefs in this area, especially along the northern edge of *Sumner Point Reef*. In good visibility, that means in daylight with the sun not in your eyes, they are easily seen and avoided.

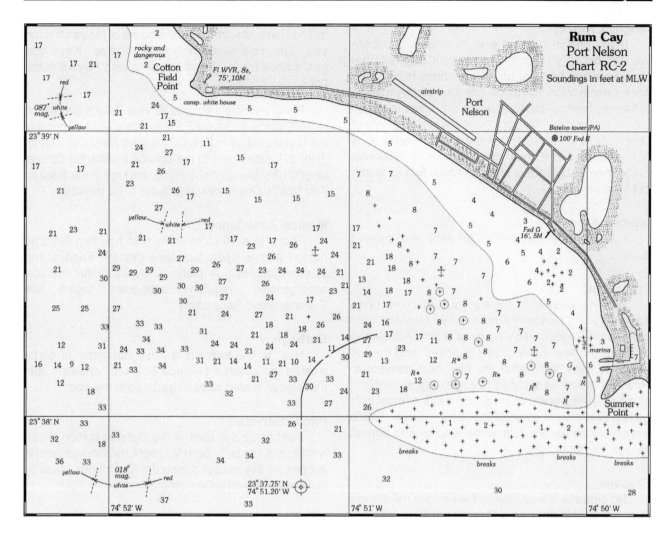

Vessels wishing to gain access at night (not advised), should line up the white light on Cottonfield Point on a heading of 018° to bring their boats into the harbour. The waypoint I have given lies well east of the white sector of the light and is not advised for use at night. Skippers not comfortable with the waypoint given are advised to head in on the light on Cottonfield Point, day or night, on a heading of 018° as this route has been safely used for years. The waypoint given, although clear of all dangers, may place some skippers too close to the reef for their comfort. If this is the case, head in on Cottonfield Point and then head to the anchorage off the dock. There are some deeper pockets surrounding the docks and there's usually a catamaran or two occupying them. Be advised that Rum Cay, although touted as the best spot to wait for weather for southbound cruisers, has a reputation for being a rolly anchorage; a well-deserved reputation.

What You Will Find Ashore

Port Nelson is situated in a beautiful setting of casuarinas and palm trees. Over the last few years a developer began the *Cottonfield Point Project* on the western side of Rum Cay. The builders dug out an area for a new marina, damaging a lot of wildlife habitat, and never connected the area to the sea. Currently abandoned, the future of this project is uncertain.

Marinas

At the southeastern end of *St. George's Bay* lies the entrance channel to the *Sumner Point Marina*. As mentioned earlier, the entrance channel is usually buoyed from the end of *Sumner Point Reef* into the marina. As of the summer of 2015, the marina has closed. An ownership issue has resulted in the marina buildings being bulldozed and the channel dredged to only 4'.

Dinghy Landing

If you anchor out and wish to dinghy in to town you can beach your dinghy or tie your dinghy to the town dock and clamber up. If you chose to tie to the dock, bear in mind that at low tide your dinghy may be extremely hard to reach. There is a 2' lower ledge on the western side of the dock but there is a huge pile of conch shells in the water that are well above the level of low tide and that could possibly hole an inflatable. Fishermen also use this ledge to clean fish so watch out for a mess.

Internet Access

Last Chance has DVD's for rent and internet access.

Provisions

Walking west from Kaye's you will come upon Kaye's *Last Chance Yacht Supply, Grocery, and Ice Cream Parlour.* This name is a little misleading as there are few if any "yacht supplies" and the ice cream is gone soon after the mail boat delivers it. However groceries and fresh veggies are no problem along with gifts, some clothes, and a video rental with quite a selection of some of the latest movies. *Bain's Variety Store* usually has some staples and almost always has fresh eggs.

Propane

No propane is available on the cay, but the marina is happy to help arrange a fill for you.

Dining

George Gaitor is proprietor of the *Two Sisters Take Away* and will deliver to the dock.

Just past the dumpster, look to your right across the road and you will see a purple building. This is *Kaye's Restaurant and Bar* and is a must stop for anybody visiting Port Nelson. Although, as in most places in the out islands, a little notice for a meal is necessary, *Kaye's* has proved quite the exception. I was there one day when 10 yachties showed up spontaneously and wanted lunch. Well, Kaye and her mother, Doris Wilson, cooked a fantastic meal of salad, stewed cabbage, potatoes au gratin, johnny cake, fried conch, and baked grouper and the lunch bill for two people with two *Kaliks* and two sodas was only $22.00. Kaye and Doris created this remarkable feast on a one burner stove and oven. Absolutely the best deal, and the best food, that I have found in these islands, and I have eaten a lot of native cuisine in The Bahamas, strictly in the name of research mind you. The meal was simply unforgettable. Kaye also has a book trade. Don't forget to sign Kaye's guest book.

Party animals will want to visit *Toby's Bar* which is THE place to be on Friday nights (and especially the last weekend in February during *Rum Cay Days*). *Toby's*, located next to the school, boasts the coldest beer on the island. It should be..it's kept in the freezer. Ted Bain's *Oceanview Bar* is not to be missed!

Medical Assistance

There is a clinic in town that has two full-time nurses and is open Mondays through Fridays and in emergencies. A plane is available for medical emergencies (regularly scheduled flights are Tuesdays and Saturdays).

Garbage

Next to the tower is a trash dumpster of sorts, a large tan colored plywood box with wheels. Just place your sealed bags of garbage in the box.

Phone Service

Further up the road is the *Batelco* station if you wish to place a call. Sam Maycock runs the office and is open all day except during the lunch hour. Nearby is Terry Strachan's *One Stop Shop*.

Diving

Snorkelers and *SCUBA* divers alike will be thrilled at what awaits them at Rum Cay. South of Cottonfield Point lies *Cottonfields*. This is an excellent snorkel in calm weather in depths of 5'-18'. The reef is alive with fish and also makes for a unique night dive when the basket stars and red coral shrimp are on display.

The best diving at Rum Cay, and some say the entire Bahamas, lies along the reefs south and east of Sumner Point. The entire reef can be snorkeled and the fishing is outstanding in its waters.

Just south of Sandy Point lies a dive site known as *Snowfields* in 20'-40' of water. Here the currents feed countless small fish, invertebrates, and sponge encrusted corals.

At the western end of the Sumner Point reef lies a site called *The Chimney* in 75'-110' of water. *The Chimney* is a series of large tunnels, one ascending through the reef from about 100' to 75'. It is a narrow vertical tunnel but wide enough for a diver with camera gear.

Directly south of Sumner Point and in 20'-50' of water lies the *Grand Canyon*, with its deep coral canyons and a few tunnels. The fish are very tame here as divers from the old *Rum Cay Club* fed them on a regular basis. The divemasters even named a few such as *Radar*, a Nassau Grouper with a damaged dorsal fin, *Klinger*, a Queen Trigger who thinks she is a grouper, and *Lady Di*, who nibbles food from the divemaster's hands.

All along the reef east and west of Sumner Point are many dive sites with names like *Dynamite Wall*, *The Cathedral*, *Martini's Reef*, and *Jewfish Wall*. You can buy maps in town, actually placemats from the old *Rum Cay Club* that will assist you in finding these sites.

About ½ mile off the centermost of the three prominent sandy bluffs east of Summer Point, and about 200 yards south of the reef, lying almost southeast of Signal Point, is the wreck of the H.M.S. *Conqueror* which sank here in 1861. This wreck, the first propeller driven British warship, lies amid a forest of coral in a gully almost 30' deep. The wreckage that remains today is scattered over the bottom but plainly visible are the main shaft, crankshaft, and the anchor chain. Quite often divers find small trinkets, cannon balls, and bullets at the site hiding in holes and under ledges. Divers are reminded not to take anything from the site and not to disturb it. The site is the property of the government of The Bahamas and is a *National Historic Site*.

San Salvador

Ports of Entry

Cockburn Town
Fuel: Cockburn Town
Haul-Out: None
Diesel Repairs: Cockburn Town
Outboard Repairs: Cockburn Town
Propane: Cockburn Town
Provisions: Cockburn Town
Important Lights:
Dixon Hill Lighthouse:
Gp. Fl (2) W ev 10 sec

By some people's consensus, Columbus' first landfall in the New World on Oct. 12, 1492, was made on San Salvador and no less than four monuments will remind you of that although other islands have at one time claimed the honor. Ask different Bahamians and you will find claims that Columbus first landed on Samana, or Cat Island, it almost depends on who you ask. If you subscribe to the popular theory that Columbus first set foot in the New World on San Salvador, then you will know that the island was originally called *Guanahani* by the Lucayans who lived here at that time. San Salvador was known as Watling's Island until 1925-1926 and was named after the pirate George Watling who was noted for his strict observance of the Sabbath Day. He severely punished his crew if they so much as threw dice on a Sunday. On some old charts the island is spelled *Watland*. The ruins of what is known as Watling's "Castle" (although some say the ruins date to a time later than the pirate's career) still stand some 85' above sea level at Sandy Point awaiting your exploration.

San Salvador is approximately 12 miles long and from 5-7 miles wide. It is surrounded by dangerous reefs and has no all-weather anchorage. There is a beautiful lake in the interior that may be the one Columbus referred to saying that it would hold "...all the ships in Christendom." If that is true he neglected to mention that a canal would have to be dredged through the cay to the sea to accomplish this.

San Salvador was once noted for its breed of horses and other livestock, consignments of which were sent to Jamaica on a regular basis. The island once provided hardwoods such as *lignumvitae* in abundance. The *U.S. Navy* had a submarine tracking station on San Salvador for many years. Some local inhabitants feel that the base, as well as the *U.S. Pan-American Base* also on San Salvador, were bad for the economy in general. True, they brought a boom to the economy when they were here, but they also caused a severe slump when they departed. For over twenty years the young sons and daughters of San Salvador forgot the ways of fishing and farming to earn their money in the employ of the military presence. When they left, the young San Salvadorans faced a decision, return to the ways of their ancestors, or move to Nassau or some other place where they could make better money perhaps and live a lifestyle that they had become accustomed to. Many left, only a few stayed. Now however, San Salvador has come into its own as a tourist destination and hopefully the sons and daughters will not have to leave the island in search of the almighty dollar.

On a side note, the *Bahamas National Trust* is considering opening give new national parks on San Salvador. Keep an eye open for them if you are in the area. The five areas which are proposed national parks are *Southern Great Lake*, *Pigeon Creek* and *Snow Bay*, *Grahams Harbour*, *Green's Bay*, and the dive sites along the western shore of San Salvador..

Approaches

Skippers transiting the areas between Cape Santa Maria, Conception Island, Rum Cay, San Salvador, and the entire eastern shore of Long Island must be aware that a branch of the *North Equatorial Current* called the *Antilles Current* generally sets in a northwesterly direction through here from .5 to .75 knots. Not only must you concern yourself with the current in the area of San Salvador, you must also be on the lookout for large ship traffic. San Salvador marks the northern end of the shipping lane that passes through the *Crooked Island Passage* and the area is heavily traveled, so keep a good lookout and pay attention when sailing these waters, especially at night.

From the waypoint off the reefs that lie southeast of Conception Island, Cockburn Town bears 70° at a distance of 33.1 miles. From the waypoint north of the reef lying north of Conception Island, Cockburn Town bears 84° at a distance of 30.8 nautical miles.

From the waypoint southeast of Rum Cay, Sandy Point bears 38° at a distance of 22.1 nautical miles. From the waypoint north of the reef lying north of Flamingo Bay, Cockburn Town bears 55° at a distance of 29.9 nautical miles.

Sandy Point, San Salvador bears 358° at a distance of 65.1 nautical miles from Bird Rock at

Crooked Island. Sandy Point also bears 41° at 52.9 nautical miles from Clarence Town, Long Island, and 59.0 miles on a course of 22° from Little Harbour, Long Island.

Cockburn Town

Cockburn Town - 1 nm W of anchorage:
24° 02.75' N, 74° 32.75' W

Most cruisers approaching San Salvador will head north along its western shore in the vicinity of Fernandez Bay. Beginning two miles south of Fernandez Bay (sometimes shown on charts as Long Bay) there are a series of reefs close inshore that almost dry at low water. These reefs generally do not break and give little warning of their presence. In Fernandez Bay, about two miles south of Cockburn Town, you will find the *White Cross Monument*, which was erected in 1956 to commemorate Columbus' first setting foot in the New World here. Of course, others say he stepped ashore on the eastern shore first (one cannot imagine why a seasoned seaman like old Chris would attempt to land on a windward shore, the leeward shore at Fernandez Bay makes much more sense). Nearby is the *Olympic Monument*, which was erected to commemorate the transfer of the Olympic flame from Greece to the New World for the *1968 Olympic Games* in Mexico City.

At the northern end of *Fernandez Bay* is the principal settlement of Cockburn Town, pronounced Co'burn Town, and which was once called Riding Rock. Cockburn Town is a pretty, clean, friendly, and extremely busy (by out-island standards) community. Cars are constantly buzzing down the roads, there seem to be a lot of cars here for such a small island. The economy here is in great shape primarily due to *Club Med*. There is almost 100% employment on San Salvador. Anybody who wants to work can find a job, some folks even manage to hold down two jobs.

Navigational Information

The entrance to the anchorage in the bay at Cockburn Town is only to be approached from the west. Give the western shore of San Salvador a berth of at least a mile to avoid the many shallow reefs that abound in this area. Never attempt to parallel the shore close in from Sandy Point or southward from Green Cay. There are numerous shallow reefs inshore, particularly south of Cockburn Town. As

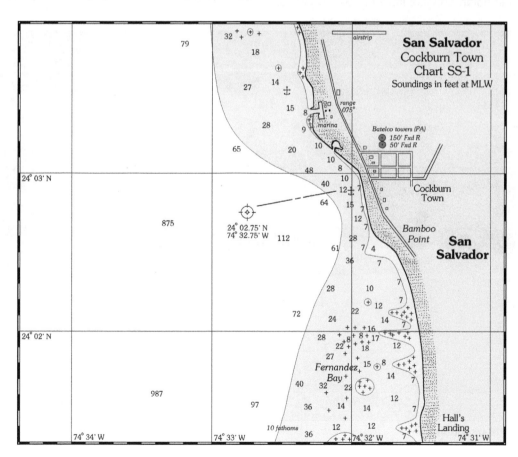

shown on Chart SS-1, a waypoint at 24° 02.75' N, 74° 32.75' W, places you approximately 1 mile west of the anchorage of Cockburn Town. Head straight in on the *Batelco* tower and drop your hook off the town anywhere you like. You can also head south to anchor off the beach but if you head too far south you must dodge a few shallow reefs. Skippers can also anchor north of town near the *Riding Rock Inn*, the long motel-looking building just south of the sprawling, pastel colored, *Club Med* complex.

Approximately ½ mile south of the entrance to the *Riding Rock Marina* (see chart) is the entrance to a small basin where the town dock is located (private, for use by mailboats and other commercial vessels).

What You Will Find Ashore

The town dock is pretty much falling apart these days but you can dinghy up to the beach south of the dock to land your dinghy. Just off the end of the town dock is the *Batelco* office and the *Government Building*, which houses the *Commissioners Office*. The two story salmon colored building right on the waterfront is the *San Salvador Museum*. Here, history buffs will find Lucayan, pre-Columbian, Colombian, and post-Colombian artifacts from the San Salvador

region. The upstairs of the building itself was the seat of government for San Salvador while the downstairs was the jail. If the museum is not open check at the *Batelco* office at the foot of the huge tower and dish that sit just a couple of hundred yards away.

Customs and *Immigration*

Cockburn Town is a *Port of Entry* for The Bahamas and skippers wishing to clear in must tie up at the marina where the dockmaster will give you the forms you need and contact *Customs* for you.

Marina

The *Riding Rock Inn Resort and Marina* is the center of attention for cruisers. Once you locate the jetty (at approximately latitude 24° 03.40' N) at the entrance you can come in on a heading of 75°. There is a range with green lights but the daymarks have been destroyed during the last hurricane. Stay in the center of the channel as the sides are rocky. If you need assistance upon entry call the marina on VHF ch. 06, they don't monitor ch. 16, the marina can also be reached at (242-331-2631, or reservations@ ridingrock.com in fact most of the island monitors VHF ch. 06.

Columbus Monument

Photo by Author

If you need anything such as bread, simply place a call on ch. 06, ch.16 is unusually quiet at San Salvador. *Riding Rock Marina* wants me to advise skippers that the marina is a good spot to ride out a front. Although the marina staff has doubled the length of the jetty, surge still makes it in during strong southwest to northwest winds. If you use plenty of fenders and tie off properly you shouldn't have a problem. The marina can handle 26 boats with drafts to 8' and offers 110v and 220v, 30-amp and 50-amp electric service. The marina also has diesel, gasoline, good well water, *Wi-Fi*, and ice. The marina charges a fee for trash disposal unless you are a guest. The marina is open from 8 a.m. to 5 p.m., Sunday through Friday and is closed on Saturdays.

Marine Repairs

Skippers in need of a mechanic can contact the marina to inquire about a diesel or outboard mechanic. If the job is not too serious the marina will be able to find someone to handle the repairs. Major repairs may require a mechanic flying into San Salvador. Steve, a local mechanic, has a small shop across from the marina behind the *National Insurance Board* office.

Dining

In and around Cockburn Town you will find three fine restaurants, the *Three Ships*, *Club Med*, and *The Driftwood Bar* at the *Riding Rock Inn*. For a night out in town try *Harlem Square,* across the street from the *Three Ships*, or the *Ocean View*, both serve food and drinks and *Ocean View* even has ice cream while *Harlem Square* boasts a pool table and fantastic Friday night buffets. *Carter's Snack Bar* is across the street from the marina and serves up great Bahamian fare!

At the *Riding Rock Inn*, *The Driftwood Bar* is an excellent place to stop and have a cold one and stare at the ceiling of driftwood where visitors have carved their names. *The Driftwood* also serves breakfast, lunch, and dinner. The resort has 42 rooms for those skippers whose crews are tired of bouncing around all the time and need a night ashore. If you wish to rent a car or scooter, the *Riding Rock Inn* can handle the arrangements for you; it's a lot easier to let them do the legwork for you. The *Inn* can also arrange a bus tour of the island if you are interested.

Just north of the *Riding Rock Inn* is the *Club Med* resort with its 300 rooms with all the bells and whistles a full service resort has to offer. This all-inclusive resort offers the best in diving, fishing, sailing, snorkeling, swimming, or just plain relaxing on the beach. If you wish to dine here you'll need a reservation for dinner and the show.

Provisioning

If you're looking for groceries try *Island Distributors*, *Jake Jones Grocery Store*, *Laramore's Snack's*, and *Dorette's Groceries* (who also carries some hardware items).

Medical Assistance

There is a clinic about a mile north of town with a resident doctor and nurse. If you need medicine there is a pharmacy in town, *J's Pharmacy*.

Propane

If you need propane, the *Shell* station in town is the only place to fill your tank.

Laundry

The marina has a washing machine and dryer that takes tokens that you can purchase at the marina office. In town is the *Dutch Laundromat*.

Diving

There is a quality dive center at the marina and *SCUBA* enthusiasts may want to sample some of the magnificent wall diving just off the resort. The marina also has a photo lab on premises that attracts underwater photographers who frequent the nearby dive sites. The photo shop can develop slide film only; in at 1:30 p.m. and you'll have it back before 5 p.m. The wall dives along San Salvador are a diver's paradise, some areas are virtually unexplored and run for 12 miles along the leeward side of the island. Who knows, maybe if you take the time to explore you might get a reef named after you. There is also excellent wreck and reef diving at High Cay, Low Cay, and Middle Cay on the eastern shore of San Salvador. The dive shop at the *Riding Rock Marina* requests that visitors refrain from fishing on the reefs along the western shore of San Salvador. There are a lot of tame grouper on these reefs that the local SCUBA divers feed and do not wish to lose to your frying pan. Remember that Bahamian law prohibits spearfishing within 200 yards of any family island, and most of the reefs along the western shore of San Salvador are within that limit.

Graham's Harbour

Graham's Harbour-1 nm W of entrance:
24° 08.15' N, 74° 31.60' W

At the north end of the island is a nice little anchorage that gives good protection from east through southwest (almost to west) winds. The reefs on the northern side of San Salvador extend for over two miles forming a northward pointing triangle from Cut Cay in the east and Northwest Point in the west. Along the edge of the reefs lie White Cay (wait till you see it-this cay is WHITE!) and Green Cay which have been designated a *National Park* primarily due to their huge bird populations. White Cay, as one might guess from its name, has distinctive white cliffs which are often covered with brown boobies and red-footed boobies.

Navigational Information

There is only one way in and one way out of this peaceful anchorage. Never attempt this route at night or with the sun in your eyes. As shown on Chart SS-2, a waypoint at 24° 08.15' N, 74° 31.60' W, will place you approximately 1 mile west of the entrance channel that lies just south of Green Cay. When heading for this waypoint head for it from the west. Never, I repeat, NEVER try to head to this waypoint from any point along the shore of San Salvador, in other words, do not head north for the waypoint, you must go around the huge reef system off Baker's Point as shown on the chart. Give the western shore of San Salvador a berth of at least a mile due to the numerous shallow reefs that abound in this area.

From the waypoint you can head east staying about 100 yards south of Green Cay as you make your way for a point south of Goulding Cay. There is one small patch reef on this route that has less than 6' of water over it but it is easily seen and avoided. When you are abeam of Goulding Cay you will be in 15' of water or more and can then take up your course for the conspicuous dock at Graham's Harbour. There is one dark patch of water between Goulding Cay and the dock but it is grass. Don't try to head for the dock until you are abeam of Goulding Cay as there are some very shallow reefs that lie northwest of the dock as shown on the chart. Don't try to head to the rust and white checkerboard tower as the reefs are directly on that route, approach the tower from the dock. You can anchor off the dock in 7'-9' of water.

What You Will Find Ashore

Cut Cay is a small cay just separated from the mainland of San Salvador. It is believed that a fort was once situated on the cay as evidenced by a cannon and cannon balls that were found nearby. This also implies that Cut Cay was once part of the mainland of San Salvador within the last 500 years and has only recently been a separate island.

Located in Graham's Harbour is the *Bahamian Field Station* of the *College Of The Finger Lakes* in upstate New York. Here researchers study the island's biological and geological features. Part of the station was once the site of an old *U.S. Navy* base from the 1950s.

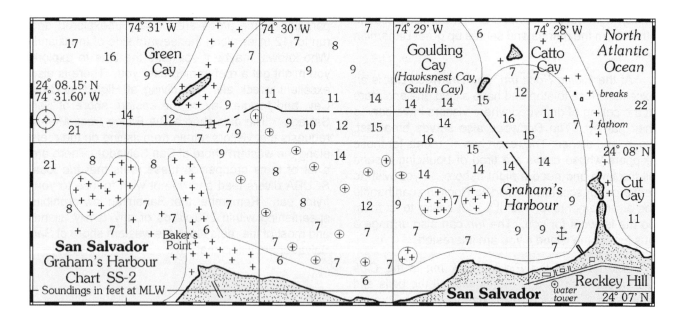

For those venturing inland, a road leads south from the dock and locals will usually give you a ride if you stick out your trusty thumb. A little ways south is Reckley Hill, a small but friendly community where you can find cold thirst quenchers *at Ed's First and Last Bar*. Further south is United Estates, or UE as it is often called, the second largest settlement on San Salvador. If you plan a short stop here, by all means stop by the *Short Stop Club*.

Dixon Hill is easy to find, just look for the lighthouse. *Dixon Hill Lighthouse* was built in 1887 by the *Imperial Lighthouse Service* and you can take a guided tour of the lighthouse and climb 72' above ground level and 163' above sea level to get a beautiful view that is said to stretch 21 miles. *Dixon Hill Lighthouse* is one of the few remaining manually operated lighthouses in the world. For another good lookout try *Mt. Kerr*, just east of the airport. At 140'

Mt. Kerr gives you an excellent view of San Salvador and her creeks. Just south of Dixon Hill is Polly Hill where the Storr family dominate. If you need a few supplies try *Bernie's Grocery Storr*, (no pun intended folks, that's the name).

Along the eastern shore of San Salvador, about ½ mile southeast of Cut Cay, lies Manhead Cay. Here a small colony of iguanas rules over what was once an archeological dig signifying a Lucayan presence. Further south along the mainland shore is another monument to the discovery of the New World, erected in 1892 by the *Chicago Herald* and known as the *Chicago Herald Monument*. You may wish to explore the *Pigeon Creek* area by dinghy (3' controlling depth). Here are a series of excavations offering evidence of Lucayan villages called the *Pigeon Creek Sites*. You can travel up the creek and visit places like *South Victoria Hill* with its small

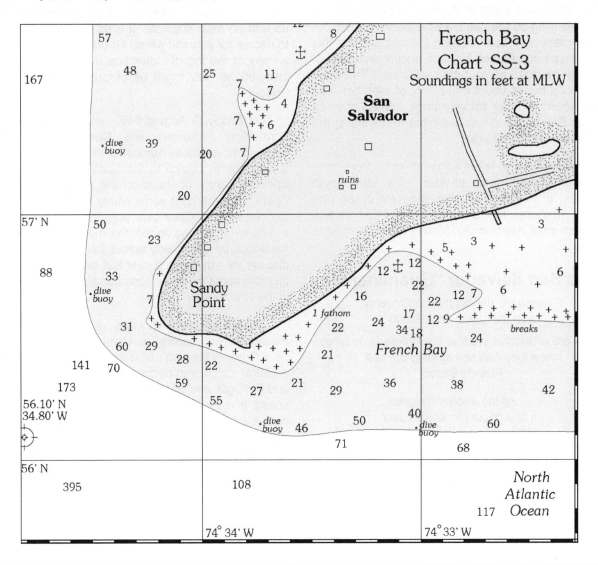

French Bay
Chart SS-3
Soundings in feet at MLW

cement dock and the nearby and almost totally abandoned villages of Farquharson, Old Place, Trial Farm, Montreal, and Allen. Until recently these places were all visited by small boats on a regular basis. The ruins of the *Farquharson Plantation* are known locally as *Blackbeard's Castle* for it is said that he once visited here. The remains include the great house, a kitchen, and a prison.

French Bay

French Bay - ¾ nm SW of Sandy Point:
23° 56.10' N, 74° 34.80' W

Navigational Information

If you need a shelter from northwest to almost northeast winds you might try anchoring in *French Bay* at the southern end of San Salvador. A waypoint at 23° 56.10' N, 74° 34.80' W, will place you approximately ¾ mile southwest of Sandy Point as shown on Chart SS-3. Pass well south of Sandy Point giving it, and the reefs lying off the point, a wide berth. Watch out for the many dive boat mooring buoys located in this area. Head into *French Bay* and anchor well west of the dock as close as your draft will allow. There are a few coral heads about with plenty of sand between them where you can set your hook. When entering *French Bay* be careful to avoid the reef lying to the south and east of the dock.

This anchorage is not good for winds from east/ northeast through south to west. The reefs south and east of *French Bay* offer excellent diving and fishing. In places, tremendous stands of Elkhorn and Staghorn coral rise from 30'-50' foot depths almost to the surface.

Was San Salvador "Guanahani?"

Guanahani, the landfall controversy,
and the *Diario de a Bordo*

*They are ill discoverers that think there is no land,
when they can see nothing but sea.*
Francis Bacon

*All the ancient histories,
as one of our clever wits said,
are not but accepted fables.*
Voltaire
Jeannot et Colin

If you have visited San Salvador you have probably seen the monuments to Christopher Columbus on the island's shores. Most people take

it for granted that San Salvador was Columbus' *Guanahani*, the Lucayan name of the island where Columbus first set foot in the New World. But is San Salvador truly *Guanahani*? It has never been proven beyond a shadow of a doubt either way. Did you ever wonder why, or why not? If you don't care to know the story behind the story, then skip this chapter and go on to the next. However, if you care to learn about the landfall controversy, and especially about Columbus' log, the *Diario*, which is what all the "experts" base their "assumptions" on, then allow me a few minutes to explain. But I must warn you, if you're confused now, you might be even more confused by the time you finish this piece, for the question of "Where?" may well be argued about forever. In this piece I will not attempt to advance a new theory, nor will I attempt to embrace or bash one of the existing theories and in so doing coerce you to follow that lead, but what I will attempt to do is explain how the one document all of this controversy is based upon may be flawed leaving us with no clear solution. It is up to you dear reader to decide for yourself where *Guanahani* lies. Acquire a copy of the log of Columbus and make your own calculations, you might be surprised with what you discover.

On Friday, 3 August 1492, under royal mandate from King Ferdinand and Queen Isabella, the Spanish sovereigns, Admiral Christopher Columbus, a Genoese in service to the Spanish Crown, set sail from the harbor of Palos on the southwest coast of Spain. Commanding some ninety men aboard a fleet of three vessels, Columbus' objective was to reach the coasts of China and Japan, the most eastern parts of the Indies, by sailing west across the ocean. Before we discuss the voyage and eventual landfall, let's learn a bit more about the ships, their handling, and navigation in the 15th century.

Columbus' flagship, the *Santa María*, with Peralonso Niño serving as Columbus' pilot and Juan de la Cosa as the ship's Master and owner, was a *nao*, a beamy cargo ship built to sail the coastline of Spain and Portugal, she was designed for cargo hauling, not speed, and was frequently outsailed by the two swifter *caravels* in Columbus' fleet, the *Niña*, commanded by Vicente Yáñez Pinzón with Sancho Ruiz de Gama as the pilot, and the Pinta, commanded by Vicente's older brother Martín Alonso Pinzón, with Christobal Garcia Sarmiento serving as the pilot. The *caravel* was a more maneuverable Portuguese design developed for long distance exploration by Prince Henry the Navigator. These vessels were usually lateen rigged, but for the downwind Atlantic crossing they were rigged with square sails on their mainmasts. The speeds attained by Columbus' fleet were quite modest by today's standards. Six knots was common while eight knots was fast, but not unusual. The *Niña* boasted a sustained speed of 9.4 knots on Feb. 6, 1493, on her return from the New World. Owing to the construction of his vessels and their sails, Columbus' ships could not sail closer than 70° to the apparent wind, a fact that is important when plotting Columbus' courses after his initial landfall.

The *Santa María* had the deepest draft of the fleet, somewhere in the neighborhood of 7-7½ feet. When anchoring the fleet the captains would seek a lee anchorage giving shelter from the wind and swell. The anchors were secured by ropes in those days, not by chains as they are today, and the skippers wanted nothing more than to be blown away from land if the rode parted, hence the desire for an open roadstead anchorage. Rope rodes also meant that a sandy bottom was preferred, not rock or coral.

We have touched upon his fleet, but what about the man, Christopher Columbus? We use the name Christopher Columbus to describe the discoverer of the New World, but it is really the Anglicized version of his real name Cristóbal Colón. Here too there's a bit of controversy over who Columbus truly was. Was he Cristóbal Colón or Cristoforo Colombo? Was he from Genoa as he claimed, or was he actually from the Greek island of *Chios*, sometimes shown as *Xios*, (which is mentioned several times in his log and where it is known he at one time voyaged for commerce), and was ruled by Genoa? But all of this is another story for another time, for now let's just call him Christopher Columbus. And so to keep it brief, all scholars agree that Columbus was a master seaman with almost two-and-a-half decades of ocean sailing to his credit, a professional who was very skilled at his trade.

And what about navigation on this fabled voyage? How did the *Admiral of All Oceans* navigate his fleet? In his log Columbus daily recorded his course, speed, and the results of his ded (short for deduced) reckoning, a method of navigation that was common practice as the primary means of navigation five centuries ago but today is rarely used since the advent of GPS. In ded reckoning the navigator takes into account the compass course, the vessel's speed through the water, the direction and strength of the wind, the set and drift of the current, and leeway,

the presumed movement of his vessel caused by the wind's force on the ship's rigging and hull. It has been estimated that Columbus' ships made 1.5° of leeway in the northeast trades (with the wind over the helmsman's right shoulder as Columbus described) until about 40° west longitude when the wind came more from astern and leeway was no longer considered a factor. The conclusion is the ship's estimated position and the entire process is, at best, an approximation, but owing to Columbus's skill as a navigator, it was a very good approximation.

Columbus did not use celestial navigation as a primary means of navigation, and only relied on it on a few occasions to fix his latitude by *Polaris*; in fact, he thought his astrolabe was in error so he kept it in its box. The primary navigational instrument in the 15th century, and especially on Columbus' voyage, was the compass. The compass consisted of a magnetized iron needle pivoted on a brass spike mounted to the bottom of a cylindrical wooden case. To the top of the needle a circular paper *wind rose* divided into 32 equally spaced points was attached. North was signified by a *fleur de lys*, which was mounted directly above the north-seeking point of the magnetized needle. When the fleur de lys pointed to the lubber line marked on the inside of the cylindrical case (marking the long axis of the ship), you were heading north. Directions were given in terms of the 4 principal winds (North, South, East and West), the 4 minor winds (Northeast, Southeast, Southwest and Northwest), the 8 half-winds (North/northeast, etc.) and "points," which could also designate one of the 16 quarter-winds. Thus, North-by-northeast could also be expressed as a point (or quarter) northeast of north. A point consisted of 11¼°. The compass rose was derived from the *wind rose* and appears for the first time on medieval *Portolano* charts of the Mediterranean. In these early charts only four or eight directions were drawn based on the winds in the Med which blew from the eight principal and minor directions (and while we're on the subject of charts, I just want to mention that it has been said that Columbus owned a chart of the region long before he embarked on his first voyage to the New World. There is some evidence that as early as 1424, Portuguese explorers had already begun mapping the western North Atlantic Ocean including an island they named *Antilia* along with other mythical islands).

But as exacting a navigator as Columbus was, let's see what happened the day after his landfall, October 13, 1492. On that day Columbus noted in his log that *Guanahani*, the Lucayan name for the island of his landfall, was on the same parallel as the island of Ferro.

By the end of the 15th century, Ferro was drawn on charts at latitude 27° 30' N. Far north of where it is estimated that Columbus made landfall. Columbus also remarked in what is known as his 1493, *Letter to Santángel* (the official announcement of his discovery, the Letter to Santángel, *La Carta de Colón*, dated 15, February, 1493), which consists of Columbus' official report to King Ferdinand and Queen Isabella, the Duke of Medinaceli, Gabriel Sánches, and the city council of Cordoba; the letter is addressed, in accordance with the etiquette of the day, to a court official, Luis de Santángel, the Secretary and Treasurer to the Spanish Sovereigns; the letter was composed on board *La Niña* off the Azores and posted to the court at Barcelona from Lisbon in early March; today a copy resides in the *New York Public Library*), that Hispaniola was "twenty and six degrees from the equinoctial line." While these latitudes are incorrect as we now know, the difference in the two allows one to compute the distance between Hispaniola and *Guanahani,* and the distance between the two, which is subject to the same error and is likely a reliable figure, is about 90 miles. This adds some credence to the *Grand Turk Landfall Theory* as Samana and San Salvador are farther north. However, to add more confusion to an already confused subject, Columbus revised this figure in 1496, judging his original estimate too high.

And what of *Magnetic Variation* you may ask? Ded reckoning navigation which has not compensated for magnetic variation will almost always result in an incorrect position for the terminus of any trans-oceanic voyage. As early as 1450, observations of magnetic variation were made in Germany, and Columbus himself made his own observations of magnetic variation during his 1492 voyage as well as during the return from his second voyage, and once off Isla Margarita on his third voyage to the New World. Sixteenth-century Portuguese and Spanish texts give evidence that in Columbus' time, on the Atlantic side of the Iberian Peninsula, it was customary to use a compass calibrated for local magnetic variation at its place of manufacture, in the case of Seville, five and five-eighths degrees east. The effect of such a calibration, of westerly magnetic variation in the western Atlantic or of both would cause a vessel sailing west across the ocean by ded reckoning to veer imperceptibly to the south. Either condition, or both, would also cause a navigator to perceive lands on the western side of the ocean to lie on a higher latitude than in actuality. In the late 1800s, attempts were made to reconstruct the field of magnetic variation in the North Atlantic Ocean at the end of the 15th century. In 1899, Dutch geophysicist Willem Van

Bemmelen, using the previous work of Eugen Gelcich and American geophysicist Charles Schott (whose study on magnetic variation in the Bahamas at the time of the discovery was commissioned as an appendix to Captain Gustavus Vasa Fox's *Samana Cay Landfall Hypothesis),* concluded that there was no significant magnetic variation in the Bahamas in 1492. This conclusion went unchallenged until 1921, when Antonio Blázquez published the *Livro de las Longitudines* of Alonso de Santa Cruz. This work, written about 1556, contains a report of an observation of westerly magnetic variation of 22° made at Santo Domingo prior to 1536. Santa Cruz also recorded a westerly variation of 28° at Havana for the same period. In January of 1595, Robert Dudley noted a 3° westerly variation off Cabo Rojo, Puerto Rico.

In an interesting tidbit on magnetic variation and Columbus' *Voyage of Discovery*, an incident occurred on Sunday, September 30, 1492. In the course of verifying the compass of the *Santa María*, the pilot, Peralonso Niño, noted the compass needle varying a full point west of north. The crew gave voice to their concern but Columbus quelled their fears for a while asking them to wait until the needle was checked at dawn. At dawn the needle pointed to *Polaris*, the *Pole Star.* Columbus, endeavoring to allay his crew's fears, explained that it was *Polaris* that moved, not the compass. His men, and his pilots, believed his logical argument and for a while they succumbed to the experience, wisdom, and the solid faith of the Admiral.

Less than two weeks after this incident, some nine weeks after sailing from Palos, Juan Rodríguez Bermejo de Triana, the lookout aboard the *Pinta*, sailing in the waters east of the Bahamas saw something that would change the world forever. At 0200 on the morning of October 12, 1492, Triana shouted out as he sighted the moon's reflection on land. Triana spied *las Islas Blancas*, the *White Islands*, 33 days from the Canary Islands. With this, Christopher Columbus changed history as very few men have been able. His arrival on *Guanahani* opened the doors for the propagation of the European civilization while sounding the death knell for the Lucayan civilization that was prevalent throughout the Bahamas at that time and that would be gone forever within one generation, those not taken into slavery died from European introduced diseases such as smallpox and measles.

Several islands in the Bahamas and the Turks and Caicos lay claim to being *Guanahani* and the debates for and against each one are often quite heated. Although many islands, including Grand Turk and Samana Cay, are often suggested as being Columbus' first landfall, as for physical proof there is next to nothing. Early cartographers show several different locations of *Guanahani* thus adding further to the confusion. The number of landfall theories have cited Cat Island, Mayaguana, Conception Island, Rum Cay, Samana Cay, San Salvador, the Plana Cays, East Caicos and Grand Turk in the Turks and Caicos Islands, and even Royal Island and Egg Island off the northern shore of Eleuthera as being *Guanahani.*

Washington Irving gave strong support to the Cat Island landfall theory in his *History of the Life and Voyages of Christopher Columbus.* For many years, residents, noblemen, scholars, even merchant and Navy mariners advocated Cat Island as *Guanahani.* The principal argument seemed to be that Cat Island was once called San Salvador, which is what Columbus named his *Guanahani.* In 1882, a U.S. Naval officer, Gustavus Vasa Fox, advanced the *Samana Cay Landfall Theory* that all but blew the *Cat Island Landfall Theory* right out of the water so to speak, and as a landfall theory, it is still the most serious candidate today. Fox, an experienced seaman and the *Assistant Secretary of the Navy* under Abraham Lincoln, returned to the Bahamas in 1879-1880 after the completion of an illustrious naval career to make his landmark study of Columbus' route for the *U.S. Coast & Geodetic Survey.* A dozen years later, a cartographer named Jacques W. Redway, backed up Fox's theory in an article in *Geographic* in 1894.

In November of 1986, the venerable *National Geographic Society* jumped on the bandwagon by endorsing the *Samana Cay Landfall Theory* in a well thought-out and researched article by then Senior Associate Editor John Judge that deduced by scientific means that Samana Cay was indeed *Guanahani* (of course this scientific deduction was immediately contested by oceanographers from the *Wood's Hole Oceanographic Institute*). Bolstered by a trans-Atlantic track adjusted for current and leeway by Luis and Ethel Marden in 1985 (a similar track created by then Lt. John W. McElroy, USNR, in 1941, was not adjusted for current and leeway and made Columbus' landfall at San Salvador, a full degree of latitude north of Samana Cay), the trans-oceanic track to Samana Cay was also deduced by a computer program called the *Columbus Research Tool*, or *CRT*, a multifaceted interactive computer system developed by the *Control Data Corporation* in conjunction with

National Geographic Magazine. As state-of-the-art as the *CRT* was, it was never employed to analyze all of the landfall possibilities, nor was it programmed to plot Columbus' track based upon different translations of Columbus' log, the *Diario* (which you shall soon learn can be quite varied). Although Samana Cay differs a bit in description from the accepted location of San Salvador (Admiral Samuel E. Morison, one of the world's most respected Columbus' experts, strongly advocated the *San Salvador Landfall Theory* in 1942), both fit the *Guanahani* described in Columbus' log, it's a matter of translation at times. Every expert in the field, every historian, every archaeologist, amateur and professional, is likely to offer a slightly different interpretation of the *Diario.* And for every expert who advocates a certain theory there are several of his colleagues who are all too eager to point out the various holes in his assumption. For now though, let us examine just the physical evidence before we turn to the document in question, the *Diario*, the log of Christopher Columbus.

San Salvador, called Watling's Island until the early 1900s, lies east/southeast of Cat Island and northeast of Long Island, Rum Cay, and Conception Island, well out into the open Atlantic, and has no less than four monuments to Columbus on its shores. In 1793, Juan Bautista Muñoz, who was commissioned by King Carlos III of Spain to write a history of the New World, first introduced San Salvador, then called Watling's Island, as Columbus' landfall. In his *Historia del Nuevo Mundo*, Munoz identifies Watling's Island as Columbus' *Guanahani*, which took the limelight off Cat Island although Cat Island was first shown as *Guanahani* on a map in 1625. As for physical proof, archaeologists have unearthed evidence of a Lucayan civilization on San Salvador that dates to the late 15th century. Also unearthed were seven small, wire-wound glass beads that are similar to those used for trading by the Spanish. Whichever translation of the *Diario* is used, in several instances Columbus mentions giving to the Lucayans "...red caps, and to others glass beads..." and later records trading "... little glass beads and hawk's bells." A coin was also found on San Salvador, a billion *blanca* of Henry IV that was minted between 1471-1474; the term *billion* is used to describe the composition of the coin, in this case it is a copper-based alloy with an 3.97% silver content. In the *Diario* Columbus states that his men gave the Lucayans *ceitis*, but there is no mention of a *blanca.* Also found mixed in with Lucayan artifacts were a small metal buckle (which might have been a shoe buckle), a "D" ring, several small shards of

Spanish pottery, three planking nails, one copper grommet, one metal hook, and some fragments of metal that researchers believe may have once been part of a knife or sword. All of the items found have been shown to be of the late 15th to early 16th centuries in origin.

Although the physical evidence found on San Salvador is circumstantial, it provides the most compelling argument for the island being *Guanahani* regardless of ANY interpretation of the *Diario*. It puts the Lucayans and the Spaniards on San Salvador, together, in the same time period, the end of the 15th century. No other alleged landfall can boast such impressive proof, not Cat Island, not Grand Turk, not even Samana Cay (where Lucayan palmetto ware, shell beads, buttons, and a figure of a Lucayan deity, a *zemi*, have all been found; but to date, no Spanish artifacts have been found on Samana Cay, although a small piece of Spanish pottery dating to the late 15th or early 16th century was found nearby, but researchers cannot prove the origin of the shard or when it arrived in the New World). Some researchers point out that although the items were found on San Salvador, they might not have been left by Columbus. The items found there might have been brought from other islands, including the true *Guanahani*, by other Lucayans. Columbus mentions in his log that three days after landing on *Guanahani*, he came across a Lucayan in a canoe at sea. In the canoe the man had several beads that the Admiral had earlier traded on *Guanahani*.

The *Grand Turk Landfall Theory* was first put forward by the nineteenth century Spanish historian Don Martín Fernández de Navarrete (remember this name, you will see it again). This theory is supported by the work of Robert Power in 1982 and noted Turks and Caicos historian Josiah Marvel of Salt Cay, an associate of Power, and the late Herbert E. "Bertie" Sadler of Grand Turk. The *Grand Turk Landfall Theory* has gained much in the way of acceptance in the last two decades but, as with all theories concerning Columbus' *Guanahani*, its basis is Columbus' log. The descriptions of *Guanahani* in the *Diario* can be interpreted to give a strong argument to a *Grand Turk Landfall Theory*, but there is absolutely no physical evidence whatsoever pointing to Grand Turk as a possible *Guanahani*. The Lucayan sites that have been found on Grand Turk predate Columbus by 500 years (researchers believe that Grand Turk was settled by the Lucayans around 750 AD) though many valuable sites, including the one that may

have proven the theory, could have unknowingly been destroyed by Bermudian Salt Rakers when constructing Cockburn Town in the 17th and 18th centuries. The descriptions in Columbus' log are simply not enough to classify any one particular place as the true *Guanahani* as they can be interpreted to fit several locations (you will learn more about this in a moment). And as I mentioned, Columbus' log itself may have been corrupted several times over the centuries, which leads one to doubt some of the validity of the account in the first place.

Now that we know a bit more about the navigational methods of Columbus and the various landfall theories, let's discuss the log itself, the *Diario*, the daily record of Columbus' voyage from August 3, 1492-March 15, 1493, which became the single document that bridged the gap from the middle ages to the modern age. The *Diario* contains the key to the landfall location in the description of *Guanahani* itself, and more important, in the reporting of the routes taken from *Guanahani* to Cuba and Hispaniola which, when looking at a nautical chart of the area, leaves one with a better sense of Columbus' first landfall, especially if you know these waters and can visualize his passages.

Columbus actually kept two records of his progress across the Atlantic. His primary log, the *Diario de a Bordo, The Onboard Log*, was the distance that he thought his ships had actually traveled which he kept secret from his crew. This log was intended solely for King Ferdinand and Queen Isabella and the distances were measured in common *Mediterranean Leagues*. The second record, the *Cuaderno de a Bordo* (which was more of a personal notebook or journal) was a shorter estimate of Columbus' mileage based on the longer *Iberian Maritime Leagues* which were in use only west of the Iberian peninsula. Columbus allowed his crew to view this log to quiet their fears and hopefully quell any thoughts of mutiny as the lesser number of miles recorded inspired a sense of being closer to home.

In 1983, James E. Kelly Jr., a computer consultant and cartography student, analyzed the double set of figures given for the distance sailed on Columbus' first voyage to the New World. Kelly's analysis showed a linear relationship between the two sets of numbers with a ratio of five to six. Columbus's *Letter to Santángel* supports this conclusion with specific references to *leguas grandes,* or "great leagues," implying that these were different from "short leagues."

Las Casas uses the term *largas leguas* in describing the length of Puerto Rico. Experts in such matters have suggested that Columbus' "false log," the *Cuaderno*, may have been closer to his actual mileage than his secret hidden log, the *Diario*.

The *Diario de a Bordo* was turned over to Queen Isabella shortly after Columbus' return and Isabella immediately commissioned two trusted scribes to prepare an exact copy for Columbus in strictest secrecy (this action is verified by a letter from Barcelona that is dated June 1, 1493). Records testify that Isabella presented Columbus with a copy of his *Diario* on September 5, 1493 (Columbus' copy of this letter was marked received on September 18, 1493) and this copy is known today as the *Barcelona Copy*. Isabella hid the original *Diario* to keep it from falling into the hands of the Portuguese and any others who could profit from the information that it contained. It seems that there was a great amount of interest in the gold that was found in Hispaniola and very little in regards to fixing the position of where Columbus first set foot ashore in the New World. It can be argued that the first corruption of the original *Diario* occurred when Isabella's scribes copied the original, however most experts downplay that theory claiming that the royal scribes were professionals engaged by the King and Queen and for that reason they were not likely to change a word, still others argue that the possibility for corruption still exists at this time. However, Castilian Spanish was not Columbus' native tongue, and it has been suggested that the scribes may have taken it upon themselves to correct the Admiral's grammar and spelling which may have altered vital points of navigational data. Translation errors will be discussed in greater detail in a moment, in the meantime allow me to finish the tale of the loss of the *Diario* before we discuss its reappearance and translation.

The original *Diario de a Bordo* was lost to the world forever when Isabella died in 1504. Conjecture abounds as to where Isabella hid the *Diario*; some say in a monastery, some a library, and other experts claim it was unknowingly destroyed by Napoleon's armies. In the late 1800s, a piece of the original *Cuaderno de a Bordo* turned up. The piece, four pages of folio sheet folded in the center where it had been bound into a book, had been offered for sale to the Duchess of Berwick and Alba by the widow of a librarian who had stolen it from the library of the Duke of Osuna. The Duchess purchased the folio sheet and published it in 1902 in a work entitled *Nuevos*

autógrafos de Cristóbal Colón y relaciones de ultramar. The sheets contain a sketch of the northern coast of Hispaniola and six lines written in Columbus's own hand between the time of his first landfall and his arrival in Hispaniola. The lines read: "*He has pleased thus to give me the reward of these anxieties and dangers. Truly having been voluminous with this great victory, please God may there be reduced the defamers of my honor, who with so much dishonesty and malice have made a mockery of me and my enterprize without comprehension of my opinion and of the service and aggrandizement of their Highnesses.*" Most believe Columbus' remarks refer to Martin Alonzo Pinzón, the pilot of the *Pinta*, whose insubordination in leaving the fleet on his own to seek gold in Hispaniola infuriated Columbus on his first voyage.

The sketch of Hispaniola is remarkably accurate and covers the northern shore from its western cape to a point west of what is now called Cabo Samana. In the sea north of Monte Cristi, on the verso page of the first leaf near the crease where it was bound, is a cross surmounted by two dots. This mark appears where there is neither reef nor land. In 1985, Robert Power first proposed that this cross was a symbol indicating the position, relative to the northern coast of Hispaniola, of *Guanahani*, the island Columbus named *San Salvador*, *Holy Savior* (of course Power favored the *Grand Turk Landfall Theory* which is supported by this marking). Columbus habitually placed his devotional marks in the center of the page on all other documents, and it has been suggested that the cross records Columbus' ded reckoning perception of the longitude of Columbus' *San Salvador* with respect to Hispaniola. This is the only cartographic evidence from the Admiral's own hand that survives today. The map is preserved in the *Archivo de la Casa de Alba*, at the *Palacio de Liria*, in Madrid. Unfortunately, this map of Hispaniola has also been claimed to be a forgery by such experts as Robert H. Fuson who brings up several points. First, Hispaniola is labeled on the map as *La Española*, a term that never appeared in the *Diario* (although Columbus actually did use the term *La Isla Española* in the *Diario*), and second, the settlement that Columbus founded, *La Navidad*, is shown as *Nativida*, a term also not utilized in the *Diario*.

It has been hypothesized that the *Barcelona Copy* survived for a while, at least until 1554. When Columbus passed away in 1506, all of his charts and personal papers, including the *Barcelona Copy*, passed to Don Diego, Columbus' eldest son, probably through the hands of Don Fernando, Columbus' second son. When Diego died in 1526, this inheritance passed on to his son Luis, Columbus' grandson. At this time Luis was a minor under the guardianship of Doña María Álvares de Toledo (Don Diego's widow, Luis' mother, niece of the Duke of Alba, and a cousin of King Ferdinand) and Christopher Columbus' personal papers were not to be entrusted to him for another 23 years. It is suggested that María did not possess the *Barcelona Copy* until after the death of Don Fernando (Ferdinand) Colón, Columbus' illegitimate son and Don Diego's half-brother, in 1539. Fernando was the Columbus family archivist and the only true scholar in the family. Fernando, who accompanied his father on his fourth voyage to the New World in 1502 at the age of fourteen, wrote a biography of his father somewhere around the time of the elder Columbus' death in 1506. Fernando, later the geographic adviser to the Spanish crown, had a grand home on the banks of the *Guadalquivir River* and there he assembled one of the finest private libraries in all of Europe estimated to contain over 15,000 items.

When Fernando passed away in 1539, his library was sealed for five years due to legal complications. In 1544, María removed everything from Fernando's home and placed the bulk of it in the Dominican monastery of San Pablo in Sevilla (where it stayed until 1552 when the Cathedral of Sevilla acquired the collection from the San Pablo monastery). María is thought to have had the *Barcelona Copy* in her possession for approximately five years until her death in 1549 when the copy, and Fernando's personal collection of papers, passed on to María's son, Luis. This was a tragedy. Luis has been described as being "devoid of morality," a man who put women and money first, and not necessarily in that order. Luis was imprisoned for having three wives at one time, and later acquired a fourth in prison by bribing the guards. Luis' only interest in the papers of his grandfather was for their financial worth so he rummaged through Fernando's collection seeking something of value to sell. It is known that Luis actually possessed the *Barcelona Copy* in 1554 when he was granted permission to publish it by the Crown. Luis never published the work and although it is possible that he may have actually lost the *Barcelona Copy*, most experts presume that Luis sold the copy to the highest bidder and that it may (hopefully) be hidden away in a private library somewhere. It is a known fact that Luis sold Don Fernando's biography

of Columbus to a Genoese physician who took it to Venice for publication in 1571.

It has also been suggested that the *Barcelona Copy* was carried to Algeria in the possession of Luis, when he was exiled to Oran in 1565. There is one faint ray of hope that it may one day be found in a chest of papers that was left to Luis' majordomo after his death in 1572, but the search for this chest has so far proved fruitless. Most of the remainder of Don Fernando's collection ended up in the Cathedral of Sevilla, which acquired the collection from the San Pablo Monastery in 1552, but it is doubtful that the *Barcelona Copy* was in the collection at that time for it never surfaced. Today, after centuries of neglect, only about 2,000 volumes of Don Fernando's collection remain in what is known as the *Biblioteca Capitular y Colombina*, and sometimes shown as the *Biblioteca Colombina*, in Seville; some of the volumes contain margin notes in Columbus' hand.

So now we know that we have probably lost, for all time, the original *Diario* as well as the *Barcelona Copy*. So where did we get the *Diario* that all these landfall arguments are based upon, the log that everybody quotes with such authority? *The Diario of Christopher Columbus' First Voyage to the America, 1492-1493,* was actually written by a Dominican friar and close friend of the Columbus family, Fray Bartolomé de Las Casas.

Las Casas was a young Spanish lawyer when his father, who accompanied Columbus on his second voyage to the New World, sent him to Hispaniola to manage his estate in 1502. Las Casas began missionary work on the island and was ordained a priest in 1512, possibly the first ordained priest in the New World. Las Casas later took up the plight of the Taino Indians whom the Spanish had enslaved, and in doing so he mistakenly advocated the use of black slaves from Africa instead. In fact, in 1517, Charles V of Spain authorized Las Casas to enter into a trade that would transport more than five million men, women, and children from the western coast of Africa to the Caribbean, a slave trade that endured for over three centuries. Las Casas decision to import slaves was one he later regretted. His *Historia de las Indias* was a monumental work that he began in 1527 and which he continued to rewrite, edit, and polish for 36 years until 1563, three years before his death at the age of 92.

For the most part, it is believed that Las Casas penned his work based on the *Barcelona Copy* or a copy of it that was made for or by Don Fernando Colón. This copy was purported to have been kept in Fernando's huge private library (this is also the copy that is alleged to have been handed down to his nephew Luis and possibly taken to Algeria). Las Casas never revealed how he came across the copy, but most scholars believe he discovered it in Don Fernando's library between 1544-1552, while Las Casas was residing in the San Pablo Monastery, which at the time housed Don Fernando's entire collection. If this is true, he must have seen the copy before Luis removed it from the collection prior to 1552. Other experts say this period is much too late as Las Casas quotes the *Diario* in his *Historia de las Indias* in a section that was written in Hispaniola between 1527 and 1539. It has also been suggested that Don Fernando may have sent a copy of the log to his brother Don Diego who was residing in Santo Domingo at the time (it is known that Don Diego gave certain materials to Las Casas who also resided in Santo Domingo). Still other experts suggest that Las Casas received the copy from Don Fernando himself during several trips to Spain in 1515 and 1517 or that a copy of the *Barcelona Copy* was made specifically for Las Casas. However he came by his copy, it is fortunate for posterity that Las Casas managed to gain access to it.

From the *Barcelona Copy*, Las Casas created his own handwritten abstract, *El Libro de la primera navegación, The Book of the First Navigation*, the *Diario de Colón*, known today simply as the *Diario*, which is believed to have been written between 1544 and 1552. It has been suggested that Las Casas never intended for his abstract to be used for any other purpose than as a reference for the history he was writing, and some have suggested that Las Casas just borrowed the *Barcelona Copy* long enough to take as much from it as he could before having to return it.

For the most part, the experts agree that Las Casas' version of the *Diario* is no more than three times removed from the original (an opportunity for a corruption argument here as you can see), but let's face it, it is all we have (some scholars have brought to light the fact that Las Casas' *Historia de las Indias* could be viewed as a second source of landfall information as there are details in his history that are not found in the *Diario*, certain sections of which, it is claimed, should be treated as part of Columbus' log itself, but unlike the *Diario*, Las Casas' *Historia de las Iindias* has never been translated into English).

Las Casas version of Columbus' log is composed of 76 folios and, except for the last, each folio, front and back, contains about forty-five lines in Spanish with many abbreviations, cancelled words and phrases, and both marginal and interlinear notes. The work is condensed and also biased with the author's personal views concerning Indian rights in the New World. It has been argued that Las Casas used certain parts of the *Diario* and omitted others for his own interests (although it is claimed that none of the omitted parts concerned navigation). Las Casas says that he transcribed Columbus' *palabras formales*, his actual words, and in instances where he discusses Columbus's landfall and similar descriptions he uses phrases like "In the Admiral's own words..." To most this denotes a direct quote from either the original *Diario* or the *Barcelona Copy*, but to a few scholars that belief is, at best, speculation. In regards to Columbus' *palabras formales*, John Judge, then *National Geographic Magazine's* Senior Associate Editor, wrote in his November, 1986 article, *Where Columbus Found the New World*, that "It is assumed that Las Casas copied this part word for word..." At other times Las Casas states "The Admiral went ashore..." and some scholars consider these references unsubstantiated even though Columbus' son, Don Fernando, made several references to the same effect in his *Life of His Father* (more on that in a moment). In five instances Las Casas makes reference to Columbus' poor Castilian Spanish (as I said previously, it was not his native language), and complains of the scribe's handwriting. There are several mistakes in the manuscript which may have originated with Las Casas, the scribes, or even Columbus himself. There are also some abbreviations, some words that are unreadable, and a few blanks.

A man who is believed to have seen the original *Diario*, or at least the *Barcelona Copy*, was a Catalan monk named Ramón Pané who wrote of his voyage with Columbus. Pané accompanied Columbus on his second voyage and the Admiral charged him with collecting "the ceremonies and antiquities" of the Indians that they were to encounter in the New World. The body of Pané's work, 26 chapters in Castilian, was written between 1494 and 1501. No copy of the original text has survived the centuries but the entire work is incorporated in Don Fernando Colón's biography of his father, *Life of His Father*.

Pané's text bears the simple title *The Treatise of Friar Ramón on the antiquities of the Indians which he as one who knows their language diligently collected by command of the Admiral.* Although Don Fernando's work contains landfall text that is similar to Las Casas', it is suggested that his writings are a reflection of the official geographic perceptions of the 1530s rather than a true recording of his father's own recollections. Don Fernando also had access to the *Barcelona Copy* when writing his biography of his father, usually called the *Historie.* The Spanish original of this work has been lost and all we have to go by is a poor 1571 Italian translation of the original Spanish. There are several tomes by other writers of that era who borrow heavily on Las Casas and Don Fernando, and although Las Casas is indebted to Don Fernando in his own right, most of these other works fall short of the Las Casas *Diario.*

After the death of Las Casas, his *Diario* was lost for nearly two centuries and was not discovered until 1790, when Don Martín Fernández de Navarrete, a young naval officer, and Don Juan Bautista Muñoz, found it in the archives of the Duke del Infantado, nearly three hundred years after the discovery of the New World. The duo had been commissioned by the King to write a history of the New World and Muñoz was granted a royal *cédula* granting him access to all historical repositories in Spain. Navarrete and Muñoz later found another copy of 140 folios in the same archive that was written in a different hand. Navarrete, who originated the *Turks Island* Landfall Theory (see, I told you that you'd hear this name again; as an interesting side note, Navarete's partner, Muñoz, advocated the Watlings Island/San Salvador theory), translated and finally published a collation of these two copies of Las Casas' *Diario* in 1825, over 34 years after he found it and eventually published five volumes between 1825 and 1837. Not only is the modern day *Diario* a copy of a copy of a copy, we now have Navarete possibly corrupting the copies with another work written by an unknown author.

Over the years since, several experts have made their own translations of the *Diario*, each a bit different than the one before and generally leaning toward the author's own suspected landfall location. What has been described as a "reliable" printing of the *Diario* was the 14 volumes of the *Raccolta* published in Rome in 1892, which also included most of the other documents pertaining to Columbus' first voyage. The *Diario* has been translated in whole or in part into almost every language on Earth, and into English several times. Most claim that the first good English translation was by Lionel Cecil Jane in 1930, which was later revised by L. A. Vigneras in 1960. In 1962, Carlos Sanz presented a very well done line by line transcription and in 1976, Manuel Alvar published two volumes of his own translation, the *Diario del Descubrimiento*, what has been described as the first definitive transcription. There have been numerous other translations including those by such esteemed names as Sir Clements R. Markham, Michael Mathis, Samuel E. Morison, and Dr. Eugene Lyon who worked from a photocopy of the original Las Casas manuscript. In advancing his *Samana Cay Landfall Theory*, Vasa Fox used an English translation of Navarete's 1825 edition by the official translator of the *U.S. State Department.* In 1987, Oliver C. Dunn and James E. Kelly, Jr., published the latest definitive transcription (using computer technology to build upon the foundation laid by Manuel Alvar), the only direct English translation of the entire Spanish manuscript, until this edition all previous transcriptions were based upon an intermediary Spanish transcription done by someone else, and no translation is any better than the transcription used.

So how do all these translations differ? One translation moves a period by two words, which relocates a point of land some 45 nautical miles. One translation changes a sunrise to a sunset while another translation has Columbus anchoring in one location and then raising anchor in another harbor several miles away. In some translations you'll find the misuse of the word *isleta, little island.* If the translator thought that Columbus was at a larger island, it is possible that the English word *island* was used rather than *islet.* Some translations have directions changed, distances altered, and weather conditions invented, all to make things "fit."

So what about the physical description of *Guanahani*? San Salvador, Samana Cay, and Grand Turk all fit the bill when it comes to satisfying the log entries that claim *Guanahani.*

A) ...is low and surrounded by a reef,

B) ...had several small ponds in the center, (Columbus claimed *Guanahani* had *muchas aguas, many waters*, which can be either small lakes or rain catchment ponds, after all, Columbus arrived during the rainy season),

C) ...had a rock formation that resembled a quarry (exposed limestone is common in the Bahamas and in some areas the weathered blocks appear almost man-made),

D) ...there is a peninsula attached to the island that can be cut through in two days of digging (using 15th century tools),

E) ...there is a reef-protected harbor that can hold "...*all the ships in Christendom,*" a favorite saying of the Admiral's, and one he also used to describe Little Harbour on Long Island, and finally,

F) ...Columbus' use of the word *laguna*.

Laguna. This particular key word is probably the most argued about, and with each translation the landfall can be made to fit San Salvador, Samana Cay, or Grand Turk. In his log, Columbus makes the statement that *Guanahani* had a large *laguna*, or *lagoon*, in the middle of the island. If *laguna* was made as a reference to an oceanic feature, it could mean a reef-protected body of water, perhaps bordered on one or more sides by land, such as the anchorage on the southern side of Samana Cay. If the Admiral used *laguna* in reference to a terrestrial feature, such as a lake, it would fit better with the topography of San Salvador and Grand Turk. Columbus does use the term in both an oceanic and terrestrial manner in his log and it is up to us to decipher how he meant it to be read.

It is not just the words chosen by the translators that causes confusion and argument, some experts argue about the length of the miles and leagues that Columbus used in his log since at that time there was no true standard. Las Casas claimed four miles to the league, but it is unclear as to how Las Casas viewed a mile. In John Judge's landfall article in the November, 1986, issue of *National Geographic Magazine*, the author suggests that Las Casas may have confused miles and leagues (this occurs several times in the *Diario* and has been reported by other researchers as well). *The National Geographic Society* accepts 4,284' for the Columbus mile or 17,134' to the league (2.82 nautical miles, based on an excerpt from a 1574 book, *A Regiment for the Sea* by William Bourne and backed up by a 1594 book by Thomas Blundeville wherein he states that a Spanish league is 2857 fathoms, one fathom being 6'; many other scholars have accepted 3.18 nautical miles as the length of one *Spanish League*-see the following on Morison). James E. Kelly Jr., a proponent of the *San Salvador Landfall Theory* uses 4,060' per mile and 16,240' per league (2.67 nautical miles). Admiral

Samuel Eliot Morison, also a proponent of the *San Salvador Landfall Theory*, in his translation uses both 4,842' and 4,855' for his miles, but uses a figure of 3.18 nautical miles per league. As you can see, this opens up several different landfall possibilities (not to mention playing havoc with the courses and distances sailed between *Guanahani* and Cuba).

One must also wonder if Columbus followed the sun westward, if he did his landfall would be somewhere between the Caicos Islands and Samana Cay. However you figure it, with either distance employed, and whether or not he followed the sun, Columbus' entire recorded voyage is within 100 nautical miles of the actual 3,100-mile route! Whichever length is used by researchers in determining distance sailed, Columbus was generally within about 9%-10.5% of the true distance from island to island after his initial landfall.

So, just where did Columbus land? I'll leave that up to you to decide and by now you're probably more confused than ever about Columbus' landfall. Don't fret. All the physical evidence points to San Salvador and certain aspects of the description of *Guanahani* in Las Casas' version of the *Diario* can be made to fit San Salvador. But, as anyone who is not an expert in the field can see, there are bound to be holes in any theory based strictly upon the *Diario* with its possibly corrupted text. Still, scholars deny that there is little, if any, corruption of the *Diario*. Nobody wants to admit that the log of Columbus, which is the only way to decipher the puzzle of his landfall, is off the mark in any manner and how dare one even suggest the possibility. These same scholars would rather interpret the log their own way in order to back up their own theories. But until somebody digs up an artifact saying "Columbus arrived here on October 12, 1492" or something to that effect, all these theories will remain exactly that, just theories. But for now I favor the *Samana Cay Landfall Theory*, not because of Luis Marden's 1985 trans-Atlantic track, but because the descriptions of Columbus' voyages from *Guanahani* to Cuba fit so well if begun from Samana Cay. Then again there may be some validity to a Grand Turk landfall, but if some new theory comes along I will gladly consider it after all the experts have cut, shot, and punched holes through it.

As Professor Josiah Marvel of Salt Cay, Turks and Caicos, once wrote: *I believe it is only the controversy that is tedious - not the inquiry.*

Long Island

Ports of Entry

Stella Maris
Fuel: Clarence Town, Stella Maris, Thomson Bay
Haul-Out: Stella Maris
Diesel Repairs: Clarence Town, Stella Maris
Outboard Repairs: Clarence Town, Hamiltons, Mangrove Bush, Salt Pond, Stella Maris
Propane: Clarence Town, Stella Maris
Provisions: Clarence Town, Salt Pond, Stella Maris
Important Lights:
Cape Santa Maria: Fl W ev 3.3 sec
Clarence Town, Booby Rock: Fl W ev 2 sec
South End: Fl W ev 2½ sec

"Long" is quite likely the best description of this island. Long Island is 76 miles in length by 4 miles in width at its greatest breadth and stretches from the southern Exumas and Exuma Sound to the deep Crooked Island Passage. Long Island is similar to Eleuthera and Cat Island in that along its eastern shore (its northern shore according to Long Islanders) lies the *Atlantic Ocean* while to the west (the southern shore according to Long Islanders) lies the shallow waters of an arm of the *Great Bahama Bank*. Long Island has many natural caves with some having guided tours for visitors. A skeleton believed to be the remains of a Lucayan Indian was found in one of Long Island's caves.

In pre-Columbian times the island was known as *Yuma*, *Yumetta*, or *Yametta*, but the great discoverer, who landed there on October 16, 1492, renamed the island *Fernandina* after his King. Long Island was the third stop for Columbus in the New World after San Salvador and Rum Cay. In fact, Columbus's flagship, the *Santa Maria*, went aground on a reef off the northern tip of the island earning the area the name Cape Santa Maria.

Long Island has some 40 communities along its length (more than any other Bahamian island) with over 3,500 residents of very different ethnic backgrounds. Some of the most physically attractive people in The Bahamas come from Long Island. Here one can find descendants from many different peoples that have migrated to The Bahamas over the centuries from pirates and slaves to French missionaries and Greek sponge fishermen.

Long Island has always been known for its livestock, particularly Scottish "black face" sheep and thoroughbred horses, both introduced to the island over two hundred years ago. At one time there were numerous large estates on the island with extensive stone wall pastures, the ruins of which can still be seen today. The islanders have always been big on raising sheep, mutton being an excellent local dish, and have long been known as "sheep runners." Many Long Islanders are still involved with the fishing and sponging industry. A curious note for those interested in tilling the soil. Long Island farmers, as many farmers throughout The Bahamas, plant their crops by the phases of the moon. Certain phases cause higher tides resulting in a higher water table, this brings the water closer to the plants roots.

Tides in Long Island are quite varied. Tides at *Calabash Bay* and *Joe Sound* tend to run approximately 45 minutes to 1 hour behind Nassau tides while *Salt Pond* tides are 2½ hours later than Nassau tides and tides in the vicinity of Newfound Harbour are approximately 1¾ hours after Nassau.

Approaches

Cape Santa Maria - clears reefs off NW tip of:
23° 42.00' N, 75° 21.50' W

From the *Eastern Channel* entrance to *Elizabeth Harbour* in the Exumas a course of 68° for approximately 22 nautical miles will bring you to the waypoint west of *Calabash Bay* (those skippers wishing to detour around Cape Santa Maria may take up a heading of 60° to clear the Cape Santa Maria reef waypoint at 23° 42.00' N, 75° 21.50' W). From this position you may enter between the reefs (see *Cape Santa Maria* and *Calabash Bay*) to anchor just off the beach at *Calabash Bay*. Those wishing to anchor just below *Cape Santa Maria* may proceed another mile northeast to the waypoint marking the anchorage off the beach just below the light and beacon. From *Conch Cay Cut*, the western entrance to *Elizabeth Harbour*, a course of 78° will bring you to the waypoint to clear the reefs at Cape Santa Maria.

From Conception Island, a course of 242° for 15.4 nautical miles will also bring you to the waypoint to clear the reefs at Cape Santa Maria. *Dollar Harbour* lies 90° at 5.62 nautical miles from Nuevitas Rocks.

Clarence Town bears 199° at 31.1 miles from Port Nelson at Rum Cay while *Little Harbour* bears 186° at a distance of 39.2 miles. The southern point of Long Island lies at a distance of approximately 47.5 miles on a generally south/southwest heading but use caution if running this route as you need to parallel the southeastern shore of Long Island. Don't head directly for that waypoint from Port Nelson as you will run aground on Long Island; that's something you probably won't want to do.

From Bird Rock at Crooked Island, Clarence Town bears 303º at a distance of 36.3 miles, Little Harbour lies on a course of 293º, 26.9 miles distant, and the southern tip of Long Island bears 275º at 27.4 nautical miles distant. From French Wells, Clarence Town bears 314º at a distance of 44.1 miles, *Little Harbour* lies on a course of 309º, 33.7 miles distant, and the southern tip of Long Island bears 294º at 31.6 nautical miles distant.

Skippers transiting the areas between Cape Santa Maria, Conception Island, Rum Cay, San Salvador, and the entire eastern shore of Long Island must be aware that a branch of the *North Equatorial Current* called the *Antilles Current* generally sets in a northwesterly direction through here from .5 to .75 knots.

A special note for vessels transiting the waters between the Jumentos, Long Island, and the Crooked/Acklins District in the vicinity of the *Crooked Island Passage*. At an approximate position at 22º 50' N, 74º 48' W, lies the center of the *Diana Bank*. The approximately 100 square miles of *Diana Bank* lies west of the southern tip of Long Cay, south/southeast of the southern tip of Long Island, and east of *Nurse Channel*. There is a shallow bank, 35'-600' deep, lying in the midst of much deeper water, 1800'-6000' deep. With a strong swell in any direction the seas on top of the bank can get very rough as the water is pushed up the sides of this underwater obstruction. If you are experiencing rough seas in your transit of this area, by all means avoid the area of *Diana Bank*. If the seas are calm try fishing on the bank.

Calabash Bay, Joe Sound

Cape Santa Maria - clears reefs off NW tip of:
23º 42.00' N, 75º 21.50' W

Cape Santa Maria anchorage - ¾ nm W of:
23º 39.70' N, 75º 21.60' W

Calabash Bay - ½ nm W of 90º entrance:
23º 38.70' N, 75º 21.40' W

Joe Sound - ½ nm SW of entrance:
23º 36.85' N, 75º 21.55' W

At the northern tip of Long Island is Cape Santa Maria, named after Columbus' flagship which allegedly ran aground on the reefs hereabouts. The cape is a beautiful headland where stunning white cliffs with a series of caves and a beautiful white sand beach lie to leeward. Off the point an immense reef system marks the meeting place of *Exuma Sound* and the *Atlantic Ocean*. The reef structure to the northwest of the Cape is awash at low water and almost always breaking. There is a passage through the reefs just north of *Cape Santa Maria* but it is not recommended except for shallow draft vessels with experienced pilots, in excellent visibility and with very settled weather. *Calabash Bay* is the usual anchorage for boats bound south from George Town who wish to wait a day or so to round *Cape Santa Maria*. The bay, with its beautiful 2-mile long beach, is best as a lee anchorage with good protection for east to south although some swell works its way in around the Cape.

Navigational Information

Approaching from George Town, Exuma, your first sight of this area will likely be the high headlands of Newton Cay (see Chart LI-1). On the northern tip of Galliot Cay you will soon spot the neat rows of buildings that make up the *Cape Santa Maria Resort*. A waypoint at 23º 38.70' N, 75º 21.40' W, will place you approximately ½ nautical mile west of the entrance through the reefs off Galliot Cay and the anchorage at *Calabash Bay*. From this waypoint line up the conspicuous white house with the peaked-roof on a course of 90º and follow it in leaving the very conspicuous brown bar to port. The entrance is very wide and the only obstruction is the shallow brown bar just to the north. The white house lies approximately ½ mile south of the *Cape Santa Maria Resort* and sits by itself under some casuarinas. It has a flagpole on its north side and a windmill on its south side.

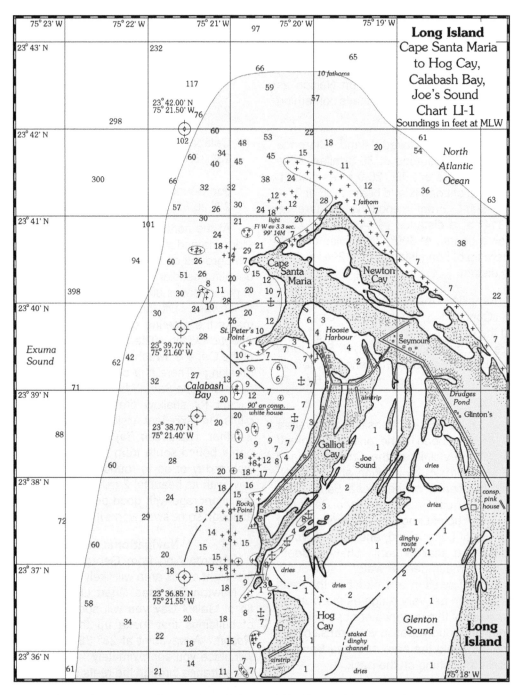

You can anchor about 100-150 yards off the beach in 6'-10' of water over one of the prettiest white sand bottoms you will ever see. You can anchor quite a ways south of the white house (actually anywhere along Galliot Cay south of the house) or you can anchor almost as far north as the resort before the water shoals. The anchorage just under *Cape Santa Maria Light* also offers good holding over a sandy bottom. To enter this anchorage proceed northeast another mile to a waypoint at 23° 39.70' N, 75° 21.60' W. From this waypoint eyeball your way in to the anchorage off the beach keeping the conspicuous brown reef well off your port side and staying north of St. Peter's Point. Both of these anchorages tend to be surgy and are no place to be in a norther. Even in strong east or southeast winds these two anchorages may get too uncomfortable for you. If that happens, of if bad weather threatens, you should round the southern tip of Galliot Cay and enter *Joe Sound*.

The entrance to *Joe Sound* is through a very narrow cut that is hard to see except from straight on. A waypoint at 23° 36.85' N, 75° 21.55' W will place you approximately ¾ mile southwest of the cut. Vessels anchored in *Calabash Bay* wishing to gain access to *Joe Sound* may coast south between Galliot Cay and the outlying shallow reefs being careful to avoid the shallow bar just off Rocky Point. The entrance lies about ¼ mile south of the very distinctive angular white houses. Never attempt this cut at night unless you are very familiar with it. As I mentioned earlier the cut is extremely narrow although a friend of mine, the owner of a 50' trimaran with a 30', beam claims he goes in and out at high tide. Enter the cut (7' at high tide) being careful to avoid the rocks on the southern side of cut. Once in the channel, slightly favoring the southern side, follow the slight curve until you pass into the deeper water (7'-9') on the other side. When you are through the cut you may turn to port and anchor wherever your draft will allow. Shallow draft vessels can go further up into *Joe Sound*, really nothing more than a creek. The sides dry at low water with about 6'-9' in the deep water passage.

A small anchorage also sits just to the south of the entrance channel. About ½ mile north of the entrance, after crossing a 5' bar and between the two groups of mangroves, vessels will find 9' at low water before the creek shoals. A dozen boats can sit comfortably in here and ride out even the fiercest frontal passage, safe from the fury of the seas but open to the wind. Just south of Galliot Cay is a fine anchorage in the lee of Hog Cay with room for four to six boats, a nice, calm anchorage even in very strong north/northeast to south/southeast winds. Here you can anchor in 7'-8' at low water but be prepared for some surge, not always, but sometimes. Hog Cay is privately owned and visits ashore must be by invitation only. Hog Cay is home to one of the largest, if not the largest, flock of West Indian Whistling Ducks in The Bahamas. The owners, I am told, leave out food for their feathered, quacking, friends.

When you are ready to depart *Joe Sound*, simply head west to avoid the reefs lying west off the cape and Galliot Cay. Those skippers leaving from Calabash Bay and wishing to round Cape Santa Maria may pass through the reefs just south of St. Peter's Point but only with good visibility. The shallow reefs are clearly defined and there is plenty of deep water between them. If in doubt use the traditional way out, put the white house with the flagpole on your stern and steer 270° until you are clear of the reefs. Then head for the waypoint to clear Cape Santa Maria reefs making sure you are keeping the reefs west of the Cape well to starboard.

What You Will Find Ashore

About ¼ mile north of the white cliffs below *Cape Santa Maria Light* are some caves and one very beautiful grotto into which you can take your dinghy if there is no surge. A hole in the roof allows sunlight in and creates a very dramatic effect. Watch out for submerged rocks upon entering this grotto and never attempt it with a surge running.

Ashore, the *Cape Santa Maria Beach Resort And Villas* (800-663-7090, resort@capesantamaria.com, http://capesantamarina.com) boasts 20 beachfront villas, internet access, trash receptacles, a public telephone, laundry service, and excellent dining in the *Cape Santa Maria Beach House*. Boaters can make lunch or dinner reservations on VHF ch. 16 by calling *Cape Santa Maria*. The resort also has small sailboat rentals, windsurfers, snorkeling gear, and deep-sea and bonefishing packages. Just north of the resort the a dirt road leads over to *Cape Santa Maria Light* and the *Columbus Monument* which looks like a day beacon from the water.

Medical Assistance

If you have a medical emergency contact *Cape Santa Maria Resort* for assistance.

Seymours

Just south of Cape Santa Maria and north of Galliot Cay is the very attractive settlement of Seymours where many of the inhabitants have their houses built on high ground. Some residents say that from this vantage point on a clear day you can see Conception Island and Rum Cay on the horizon.

Dinghy Dock

You can gain access to Seymours via the small dock that lies north of Galliot Cay facing *Hoosie Harbour*.

Provisioning

Provisions can be found at *Pratt's* in Seymours.

Dining

For a cold one visit the *Last Stop* in Seymours.

Glinton's

Just south of Seymours lies Glinton's where the remains of a Lucayan village was found which enabled archaeologists to once and for all establish Lucayan occupation on Long Island. The all-age school for the nearby communities is also located in Glinton's.

Medical Assistance

There is a clinic in Glinton's when the doctor visits on Tuesdays and Fridays.

Provisioning

For groceries try the *Rose Haven Meat Market*, and *Barbie's Ice Cream Shoppe* which also serves food and drink.

Burnt Ground

Just a little further south lies the settlement of Burnt Ground, home to the ruins of a 200-year old building, a two-story structure that is one of the oldest structures on Long Island. Most of the people in Burnt Ground work in Stella Maris, just south along the main highway.

Dinghy Dock

Skippers anchored at *Joe Sound* can easily access Burnt Ground by dinghy. From *Joe Sound*, follow the deep blue creek just off the small house with the wrecked dock, on a rising mid-tide or better, eastward until the blue water begins to shallow. Here, keep the offlying rocks to port and pass over the shallow bar until you are in the deeper water (3') of *Glenton Sound*. From this point steer straight for the large bright pink house on the northern end of *Glenton Sound*.

Dinghy skippers can also round the southern tip of Hog Cay and follow the blue dinghy channel as it snakes between shallow sandbanks that dry at low water. The channel is marked with stakes by local fishermen but is very easy to see in good visibility. Once at the pink house you will find a large concrete dock where you can safely leave your dink (sometimes you can purchase fish or lobster from the local fishermen here). This area almost dries at low water so be sure you don't get caught by the tide. From the dock, walk to the road and take a right. In town you will find a Post Office, a garage, a shell shop, and a straw works store.

Provisioning and Fuel

In Burnt Ground you will find *Adderly's Supply and Gas Station*, a small but well-stocked grocery store that even sells kerosene and some hardware supplies. Here too you will find the *B.G. Convenience Store, Burt's Dry Goods,* and the *MGS Food Store*.

Dining

If you want to grab a bite to eat in Burnt Ground you can visit the *Sabrina Bar and Grill, Fu Chan Restaurant,* or *Pratt's Restaurant and Bar,*

Dove Cay Passage

Dove Cay Passage - NW waypoint:
23° 34.61' N, 75° 21.15' W

Dove Cay Passage - W waypoint:
23° 33.53' N, 75° 20.83' W

From *Calabash Bay* you can sail south in the lee of Long Island past Simms all the way to *Thompson's Bay* and *Salt Pond* with few obstructions. The hardest part will be the short stretch from Hog Cay to Dove Cay, or if heading northward in the lee of Long Island, from Dove Cay to Hog Cay.

Navigational Information

Vessels heading south from Hog Cay or *Joe Sound* can choose from either of two routes depending upon their draft, visibility, and the skipper's ability to read water depths. Vessels with drafts of less than 6' can round Hog Cay very close and take up a heading of 165° for the westernmost tip of Dove Cay (see Chart LI-2). Watch your leeway and make sure that the current or the wind does not set you west of this route. Put Hog Cay on your stern and the western tip of Dove Cay on your bow and steer approximately 165°. This route is good for drafts of less than 6' with good visibility and a rising, almost high tide. The helmsperson must have good visibility and the ability to read water depths to run this route. Once you round Hog Cay heading south you will be in 12' of water that will begin to shallow to 5'-6' at low water in places along this stretch, particularly off Dove Cay. Just south of Hog Cay you must negotiate some scattered heads for a few hundred yards and then the bottom remains sandy. The tricky part awaits you as you round Dove Cay and you will need good light (as in NOT IN YOUR EYES) to negotiate this last section.

As you approach Dove Cay you will notice some shallower water to your west, ignore it, it does not affect you. Pass close to the western tip of Dove Cay in water that goes from 4' at low water to 12'. You will see the small offlying rocks just southwest of Dove Cay. There is a deep channel that passes very, very close to the western end of those rocks that you must find. It is a slightly deeper blue than the surrounding shallows. To the east is a shallow bar, to the west is a shallow bar, you must pass between the two close enough to the westernmost of the small rocks to toss this book onto it from your cockpit. You will pass over a bar here with 3'-5' over it at low water and then you will once again be in deeper water in the range of 7' at MLW. This bar is the shallowest spot on this route. On a good high tide 6' can pass over it easily, but I cannot recommend that a 6' draft attempt this route. Shoaling can occur which would make this route impassable for drafts of 6' or more. This route is very difficult to run in the early morning light as the sun is right in your eyes and you will not be able to pick out the deeper water, even an experienced pilot who can read the water may have trouble discerning where to go the first time.

Vessels heading northward around Dove Cay should run the above-mentioned route in reverse. Take the westernmost of the Dove Cay rocks close to starboard and then take up a heading of 345° for Hog Cay. Pass the southern tip of Hog Cay to starboard between Hog Cay and the distinctive brown shoal to its southwest.

Captains who have been scared off by my description of this route, or who have deeper drafts, or possibly just more sense, may take a more roundabout course as shown on Chart LI-2. From Hog Cay follow the curvature of the sandbank around towards Dove Cay. I have shown a couple of waypoints on the chart to help the navigator with their job if the banks become indistinct. Strong winds sometimes stir up silt in the water and make eyeball navigation all but impossible. Please do not simply steer waypoint to waypoint, you may run across an arm of the sandbank that I have misrepresented or one that has moved. Use your eyes. If you don't have good visibility, by all means, consider postponing your trip until you do.

You will notice by the chart that there is a large, shallow sandbank with some scattered heads well west of Dove Cay. This bank extends south and southeast for quite a few miles with only a few breaks of water over 6'. Take care if you find yourself west of this bank. It has not been accurately charted for its entire length.

Catamarans and shallow draft vessels, 3' and less, may find a comfortable secluded anchorage along the southeastern shore of *Glenton Sound* just northeast of Dove Cay in 4'-6' of water. From Dove Cay, steer northeastward, keeping Dove Cay

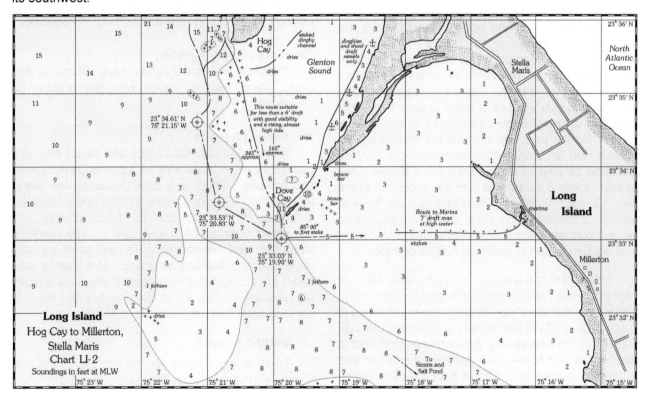

to starboard, paralleling the line of Dove Cay and the cays to its northeast. As you approach the mainland of Long Island you must negotiate a narrow passage between two shallow banks. This area has 1'-2' at low water. To your port you will notice that vast areas are dry at low water so don't stray too far that way. Eyeball your way between the shoals and you will be back in water that gets progressively deeper from 2' to 6' as you approach the marked anchorages on Chart LI-2. There is a lot of vegetation along this shore so be prepared for bugs. Also, don't forget to use an anchor light as some fishermen use this route to and from the dock west of Burnt Ground.

Stella Maris

W of entrance to marina channel:
23° 33.03' N, 75° 19.90' W

Stella Maris, *Star of the Sea*, is a huge resort complex lying about halfway between Dove Cay and Simms along Long Island's western shore. The resort is home to a full-service marina, the last before the Turks and Caicos, and the airstrip has regular flights to and from south Florida. Stella Maris is a *Port of Entry* and yachts can clear *Customs* and *Immigration* at the *Stella Maris Marina*.

Navigational Information

The marina cannot be seen from the normal routes of boats passing around Dove Cay as shown on Chart LI-2. If bound north or south along the western shore, a waypoint at 23° 33.03' N, 75° 19.90' W will place you approximately ½ mile southwest of Dove Cay and approximately 3½ miles west of the entrance to the marina. From this waypoint steer 85°-90° and you will see a large orange buoy; just past it is a row of stakes that lead into the marina. Except for the very first one, all the stakes will be topped with an orange Styrofoam float but they do not show up well on radar. Take these stakes close to port (within 2 yards) and with the exception of the one 3½' spot shown on Chart LI-2 you will have at least 4' at low water the entire way to the marina on an approximate course of 90°-95°. At the last stake you will turn to port to enter the marina complex.

A draft of 6' can easily make it into *Stella Maris* at high tide while vessels with drafts over 6' may wish to call the marina for advice although the marina tries to discourage drafts of over 6' from entering the channel. Either way, be sure you call the marina on VHF prior to your arrival and to secure accommodations. As you enter the marina proper the fuel dock (gas and diesel)

will be to starboard and the slips directly in front and to port of you. Well to port is a narrow "S" shaped canal that works its way around the marina and is an excellent hurricane hole where several local boats rode out *Hurricane Lilly* with no damage. The canal is 6'-7' deep at low water and there is 7'-8' at the docks.

What You Will Find Ashore

Marina

Stella Maris Marina is a full-service marina with full electric and RO water available. The marina offers public phones dockside and phone cards are available in the office. Marine guests are permitted to avail themselves of the amenities offered by the hotel including complimentary *Wi-Fi* and bicycle usage. The marina also has freshwater showers, water, and can handle all your garbage needs.

The repair staff offer fine workmanship or you can do your own. The marina railway can haul a vessel of 100' LOA and a 6' draft. The marina also has a more conventional 40-ton travel-lift and a lift for multihulls (to 23' wide). Boaters wishing to do their own bottom jobs are welcome to bring their paint and supplies and have at it although the marina requests that they do all serious underwater repairs for safety's sake. The marina has a full-service machine shop where they build and rebuild engines, transmissions, and manufacture specialty metal parts for the commercial fishing boats of Long Island (including *TIG* welding).

Customs and *Immigration*

Customs and *Immigration* have offices at the *Stella Maris Resort*, check with the marina for clearance.

Mechanical Repairs

The marina can repair gas and diesel engines, outboards motors, as well as do fiberglass repairs and painting. There is a local dealer on the island at *Harding's Supply Centre* in Thompson Bay for outboards and parts can be flown directly into the resort complex on a daily basis. The marina's alternator and starter shop is as good as any anywhere and better than most. The marina also offers dry storage of small boats. If you have a faulty refrigeration system it can also be brought back to working order here at *Stella Maris Marina*.

Getting Around

There is regular bus service into Seymours and Simms with buses leaving the marina at approximately

0700, 0900, 1200, and again at about 1600. This is an excellent way for boaters on a budget to get to town to shop and spend some time. Taxis are also available at all hours. Car rentals are available through the hotel desk, contact the marina for more information.

Propane

Propane tanks that need refilling can be handled though *Stella Maris Marina*.

Medical Assistance

If you have a medical emergency you can contact *Stella Maris Marina* for assistance.

Diving

The dive shop at the marina offers excellent snorkeling and reef dive trips as well as a fantastic shark dive where the dive masters hand feed what are described as "friendly" bull sharks. The dive shop has free snorkeling gear for hotel guests as well as two complimentary boat trips per week. The shop is able to fill and test your tank for you and they have a concrete SCUBA training pool (saltwater) 15' deep for those who need a refresher course or wish to take advantage of their *PADI* open water course. The dive operators can take you to dive sites like the wreck of the *M.S. Comberbach*, a 103' steel freighter that had been prepared for safe diving before being sunk, one mile offshore on *Cape Santa Maria Reef*.

Another popular spot is *Flamingo Tongue Reef* where thousands of flamingo tongue shells litter the bottom here hence the name. This reef lies some 6 miles from Stella Maris about ½ mile offshore in 25' of water. *The West Bar* is a very primitive coral garden in the shape of a bar 600' long and 300' wide lying within ½ mile of 2 beautiful beaches. Here you will spy a variety of brain, Staghorn, and towering pillar corals in 15' of water.

Poseidon's Point lies just a few minutes from Stella Maris and boasts massive brain corals, Elkhorn and Staghorn coral in water from 3'-30' deep. The dive shop can also arrange for trips to *Southampton Reef* at Conception Island where you can dive on the remains of a wrecked freighter which sank over 90 years ago. The 300' long hull lies in 25' of water with its prominent engines, boilers, anchors, and props.

There are some excellent snorkeling sights just off the eastern shore of Long Island at the resort. *Coral Gardens* lies in 3'-25' of water just at the northern end of the resort with signs to direct you. Almost at the southern end is the *Eagle Ray Reef* lying in 3' to 30' of water, also with signs to direct you.

Laundry

Across the street from the marina is the *Speed Queen Laundromat*. You can also send your laundry to the resort but this will be quite expensive.

Provisioning

If you walk to the road from the marina and take a right you will see a small grocery store across the street with some meats and limited groceries. On the resort property is a small general store. There is a small convenience store south of *Stella Maris*, in Millerton.

Dining

Just south of the marina is *Potcakes*, a bar and grill serving sandwiches and pizza. Dining is also available at the resort (at *The Tennis Club Restaurant*) with courtesy transportation provided.

The Stella Maris Resort

The *Stella Maris Resort* is often described in brochures and guides as a plantation style resort. This is actually quite a fitting description since the resort sits on what was once *Adderley's Plantation*, a Loyalist cotton plantation now residing in ruin. There are three buildings that are left intact to the roofline situated just to the north of the resort complex right off the main road. The resort offers several different packages from honeymoon specials to bonefishing and diving packages.

The resort spans Long Island from the western shore on the *Great Bahama Bank* to the eastern shore on the *Atlantic Ocean* with beaches on both shores. For information contact the front desk or call 800-426-0466 in the U.S. or 242-336-2106 locally. (reservations@stellamarisresort.com). Accommodations (60) range from rooms to apartments, cottages, and townhouses and from two bedroom villas to bungalows.

The resort has a large cave that is home to the weekly *Cave Party* with open fires, great food, live music and dancing. Spelunkers may wish to check it out at a less crowded moment. Signs at the resort will direct you to the cave.

Stella Maris to Thompson's Bay

Simms - ¾ nm SW of settlement:
23° 28.10' N, 75° 14.90' W

Navigational Information

From the waypoint at Dove Cay it is possible for a cruising boat to sail directly for Thompson Bay and the waypoint off Indian Hole Point in water that gets progressively deeper, 7' at Dove Cay to over 16' in places as you approach *Thompson Bay*. It is also possible for boats to sail close to shore in the lee of the land in 7' at low water. The major obstruction is the rocky bar that extends west of Ferguson Point as shown on Chart LI-3. Once past this rocky bar you can cruise right past Simms heading southward staying just few hundred yards offshore in places, even less around Bain's Bluff. From Simms simply follow the shoreline, basically running from one point of land to the next staying about 200 yards off each point. When leaving Simms and heading northward for Dove Cay remember to give Ferguson Point a wide berth. Vessels heading to Simms from the waypoint (23° 24.93' N, 75° 21.62' W) at Sandy Cay (also known as White Cay) at the southern tip of the Exumas, a course of 70° for 11.2 miles will bring you to a waypoint at 23° 28.10' N, 75° 14.90' W, approximately ¾ mile southwest of the Simms settlement. Head in towards the settlement and anchor wherever you prefer in 7' at low water.

If you are experiencing uncomfortable conditions while anchored off Simms, say perhaps that it is blowing east to southeast at 20 knots, the water has white caps, and you are just miserable, there is some relief. Head south about a mile or so and anchor in the lee of Bain's Bluff, the bold headland just south of Simms. Here you will find two or three nice places to anchor in calm water with good holding in 7'-9'. The shore around the bluff is full of small caves and cave holes awaiting your exploration as you wait for the winds to subside. From your cockpit you can see the ruins of some pasture walls, sometimes called "margins" that were built by slave labor and date to the Loyalist days of the late 1700s and early 1800s.

The first inhabited settlement south of Simms is Old Neils, one of the few settlements located on the eastern shore of Long Island. The original settlers preferred the western shore for its accessibility and for protection against hurricanes. Just south of Old Neils is Wemyss where only two families remain, living amidst the ruins of a 200-year old plantation. South of Weymss are Miller's and Mckann's, predominantly farming and fishing communities.

Simms and Bains

Simms is one of the oldest settlements on the island and was named after the first family that settled the area in the 1700s. The government center for northern Long Island is in Simms where you will find a *Police Station, Post Office*, a *Batelco* office, and the *Magistrate's* office.

Laundry

Laundry service is available through some local ladies but you can also send your laundry to the resort at Stella Maris but this will be quite expensive.

Dining

On the main road just outside the *Alligator Bay* property is *Anna's Away Restaurant*. Here you will also find the wonderful *Blue Chip Restaurant and Bar*, while north of town you'll find *Deal's Beach Bar*. In Bains you can grab a bite at *Jeraldine's Jerk Pit*

Medical Assistance

There is a community clinic located in Simms and they can be reached by phone at 242-338-8488.

The clinic is open from 0900-1700, Mondays and Wednesdays, and from 0900-1200 on Thursdays with one doctor and three nurses in attendance.

Provisioning

An agricultural packing-house is located in Simms and is a good spot to shop for fresh veggies where once a week the mail boat arrives to pick up the fresh produce. In town you can pick up some groceries at *CM's Total Mart*, the *MGS Food Store*, *O&S Soda and Beer*, *Anita's Takeaway*, and *Cartwright's Grocery*. Just north of Bain's Bluff is the settlement of Bains where you can get groceries at the *Rose Haven Food Fair*. There is also a fish processing plant on *Doctor's Creek*.

Thompson's Bay, Salt Pond

Salt Pond - ¼ nm SW of Indian Hole Point:
23º 20.70' N, 75º 10.30' W

Further south lies Salt Pond and Hardings, which are considered one town. Salt Pond, lying along *Thompson's Bay*, is a favorite destination of many cruisers who venture through the Exumas and central Bahamas and is named for the numerous old salt ponds found in the area. Many cruisers make this area their primary destination in their yearly cruise and use it as a base from which to explore surrounding waters. Usually, when a boater speaks of *Thompson's Bay* or Salt Pond they are considered to be one and the same. One would judge Salt Pond to be a fishing community by the number of fishing boats anchored in *Thompson's Bay* in the off-season. This is reflected in the economy of Salt Pond which is heavily dependent upon the richness of the catch.

The anchorage at Salt Pond is shallow with less than 6' at low water in spots. The harbour is open to the southwest but offers excellent protection from all other directions. I have anchored there in 25-30

Thompson's Bay, Salt Pond   Photo courtesy of Captain Paul Harding

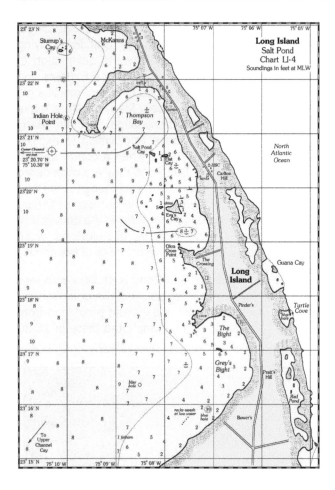

head east into *Thompson's Bay*. Most cruisers tend to anchor in the northeastern end of *Thompson's Bay* in 6'-8' at low water.

The public dock is about a mile south of this anchorage and some cruisers like to anchor off that area in 5'-6'. The commercial fishing boats tend to anchor in the vicinity of the town dock, for obvious reasons. South of town is a small bay known as The Bight with areas of water that are 6'-7' deep at low water. The best way to reach this anchorage is by going out and around the small cays in the middle of *Thompson's Bay* and head in on the beach staying just north of the point.

Vessels seeking shelter from southwest winds can find some protection in the lee of Salt Pond Cay and Eva's Cay. If you plan to anchor in the lee of Eva's Cay watch out for the submerged wreck of an old Haitian boat that lies approximately 200-300 yards northeast of the grounded wreck of the old mailboat *Seaker* lying close in behind Eva's Cay. The submerged Haitian boat sits in about 3½'-5' of water and has a metal pipe that juts out above water at low tide.

Near Salt Pond Cay lies the *boiling hole* at approximately 23° 20.20' N, 75° 07.69' W. This hole is very small but is very deep and water just *boils* out of it when the tide is running strong. South of the town dock and just north of The Crossing is a nice anchorage with depths of 7'-8' in places. The best way to gain access to this anchorage is by heading west around the offlying cays in the center of *Thompson's Bay*. A draft of 6' can be taken from just off the towndock at high water to the anchorage also. There are a few small, deep holes in this anchorage that are good for snapper fishing.

What You Will Find Ashore

A couple of final words about the *Thompson's Bay* area. First, the settlement known as *Thompson's Bay* actually is in the area of the *Thompson's Bay Inn*. Salt Pond is just about 1½ miles further south in the general vicinity of the school. If you ask a local for directions to Salt Pond they will direct you to the school. Second, most experienced cruisers to the *Thompson's Bay* area usually will not run their watermakers in the bay. The bottom of *Thompson's Bay* is great holding but the top layer is very fine silt. A little wind and the silt gets very stirred up. This can clog filters and damage pumps.

knots out of the southwest and although it was quite choppy, the anchorage provides good holding and some lee can be found (if it is not all taken by the Long Island fishing boats) behind the two small cays in the harbour. Relief from northwest winds can be found in the lee of Indian Hole Point at the northwestern end of *Thompson's Bay*.

Navigational Information

To enter *Thompson's Bay* as shown on Chart LI-4, a waypoint at 23° 20.70' N, 75° 10.30' W, will place you approximately ½ mile southwest of Indian Hole Point. Vessels heading to *Thompson Bay* from the northern end of Long Island, Dove Cay or Simms, can head directly for this waypoint in water that gets deeper the closer you get to Salt Pond. Vessels heading to Salt Pond from Exuma can head directly to this waypoint from the waypoint (23° 24.93' N, 75° 21.62' W) off Sandy Cay, also known as White Cay, at the southern tip of the Exumas. It is a straight run and the only obstruction may be a small arm of the Sandy Cay shoal that juts into your path and is easily seen and rounded. From the Indian Hole waypoint

Just north of town you can visit Salt Pond's extensive cave system. To find the caves go north along the main road about ¼-½ mile to the top of the next rise. By the house along the road you will find a path through the bush that leads west to *Thompson's Bay*. Follow the path for the two-minute walk to the water's edge, turn south (left), and walk about 10 yards, then walk back into the bush and there will be the entrance. A flashlight is necessary to enjoy the caves. If you take the road leading east you will come to a beautiful double bay with great scenery, shelling, and sheltered swimming.

Provisioning

Next to the *Esso* station is *Harding's Seafood* where you can purchase fresh fish, conch, or lobster when available. Also nearby is *Hillside Grocery*. Ice and frozen seafood are both available at *Atlantic Fisheries*.

Hillside Supply has a great selection of delicious edibles and the Saturday Farmer's Market offers some of the best of the island's produce and crafts.

Fuel

Just to the south is an *Esso* gas station but you'll have to jerry jug it as there is no fuel dock.

Dining

For exquisite dining (or lodging) visit the *Bahamian Village* or *Club Thompson Bay*. South of Salt Pond is The Bight where you will find the *Midway Inn Club and Restaurant*. Some of the best food around is prepared by Tryphena Bowe Knowles at the *Thompson's Bay Inn*.

VHF

There is a local VHF net from 0800-0815 on VHF ch. 18 daily.

The Long Island Regatta

In late May or early June, Salt Pond hosts the *Long Island Regatta* (http://www.grottobaybahamas.com/longislandregatta.html). The week-long party is a homecoming of sorts for native sons and daughters and is highlighted by four days of Bahamian sloop racing, partying, dancing, and marathon Gin and Coconut Water drinking. It has been said that after regatta there is not a single green coconut left on Long Island. Some of the greatest Bahamian sloops were built right here on Long Island by the late Rupert

Knowles. Rupert built the famous *Tida Wave* and the *Lady Muriel*,

The Comer Channel

Comer Channel #1:
23º 20.82' N, 75º 19.95' W

Comer Channel #2:
23º 19.53' N, 75º 24.00' W

Comer Channel #3 - W end of Comer Channel:
23º 20.30' N, 75º 32.00' W

Navigational Information

From Salt Pond, vessels of deep draft can take *Comer Channel*, almost 7' at MLW, westward until they reach a point directly south of *Hog Cay Cut* and thence take up a course for Nuevitas Rocks at the northern tip of the Jumentos. In this fashion you can keep the large, very obvious sandbank, on your port side. From *Thompson's Bay*, begin at the Indian Hole waypoint at 23º 20.70' N, 75º 10.30' W, which places you approximately ½ mile southwest of Indian Hole Point. Head generally westward, approximately 271° T and you will pick up the *Comer Channel*.

As you head westward you will notice that *Comer Channel* is sort of like a funnel with 7' down its center. To port will be the huge white sandbank known locally as *South Pointa Bank*. As you head westward you will see Sandy Cay (AKA White Cay, the southernmost of the Exumas) appear on the horizon. Keep it to starboard. If you drift too far south you will notice you are getting in the shallower water of the *South Pointa Bank*. If you are too far north of the channel you will also be getting into shallow water or even going up on the conspicuous brown bar known as *Red Bar*. A good clue that you are in the *Comer Channel* is the sea fans under your keel. They are harmless to your vessel and if they lean west you will know that the tide is going out and if they lean east you will know that the tide is rising. When you are south of Hog Cay in the Exumas you will notice that Hog Cay and Little Exuma Island appear as one cay. As *Hog Cay Cut* opens, look for the conspicuous palm tree on O'Brien's Cay, you will notice the blue water on the other side of the cut. Once *Hog Cay Cut* closes, you may begin to steer southwest for approximately one mile. Keep a sharp lookout to port to keep off the *South Pointa Bank*.

From this point you may steer south for approximately four miles to clear the bank. From this position you can take up an approximate course of southeast for Nuevitas Rocks taking the cays and light to starboard. From Nuevitas you can steer generally east to the waypoint off *Dollar Harbour* keeping off the bank (if you stay south of 23º 09.90' N you will be south of the extent of the one fathom line). If you wish to anchor for the night while on this route simply head east or south in the lee of the bank and anchor where your draft permits. If you get a chance you may wish to look for the wreck of the old Haitian power vessel that went aground on *South Pointa Bank*. For years its superstructure was above low water but storms and hurricanes have destroyed it and only its hull remains.

A final note on *Comer Channel*. Over the years the channel has seemed to silt in somewhat. Many yachts claim they have found less than 7' in its center, more like 5' at MLW. I have personally found less than 7' in several areas of the *Comer Channel*. This may be that I, like other skippers, was simply off course or it may be an indication of shoaling. If in doubt about whether to use it or not ask some of the fishing boats that anchor in Salt Pond, if anybody would know the current condition of *Comer Channel* it would be them.

For those of you who are in need of waypoints to stay in the *Comer Channel* here they are. From the Indian Hole waypoint you may head generally west to the *Comer Channel* #1 waypoint at 23º 20.82' N, 75º 19.95' W. From here steer a little south of west to the *Comer Channel* #2 waypoint at 23º 19.53' N, 75º 24.00' W, which lies south/southeast of Sandy Cay (White Cay). From this position steer a little north of west to reach *Comer Channel* #3 waypoint at 23º 20.30' N, 75º 32.00' W which lies a little over three miles south of *Hog Cay Cut* and is the western end of the *Comer Channel*. Vessels heading to Salt Pond via the *Comer Channel* from the Jumentos should use this as their starting waypoint. Vessels heading south to the Jumentos can use this as their starting waypoint.

Thompson's Bay

What You Will Find Ashore

Much of the land south of Salt Pond is generation land; title being owned by various families, the primary names being Darville, Dean, Cartwright, Burrows, and Knowles. They all seem to be related and there is much truth to their saying that "Everyone on Long Island is related." The best way to visit these communities is by renting a car or hitchhiking,

you won't have to wait long for a ride. Although the communities may be spread apart, they are all along the island's main road. The best way to see the island is to rent a car and take your time exploring each and every community. By the way, as you drive along keep a sharp eye out for the numerous goats and sheep that will wander in front of your vehicle causing you to slam on the brakes to avoid the little bleating critters.

South of Salt Pond lies a large bay known as The Bight as shown on Chart LI-4. Here you will find a very large blue hole lying just offshore and approximately 100 yards long and perhaps half that wide. I sounded it again and again and found depths of 39' at low water but local fishermen tell me there is a small hole in the center that is very, very deep. Ashore, right off the main highway, are the ruins of *St. Mary's Anglican Church*, said to be the oldest church building on Long Island. It is said that the church was built by the Spaniards.

Just south of Salt Pond, at Pinder's, there is a road leading eastward across the island to the Atlantic side where you will find Guana Cay. There is no safe anchorage along the eastern shore in the area so the only access you will have to Guana Cay is by land. Here you will find a beautiful protected shallow bay perfect for snorkeling and shelling along the long beach. A short swim over to Guana Cay will reveal a palm grove, a pretty little beach, and an abandoned hut. Here you can hand feed the small iguanas that populate the cay giving it its name. On the oceanside you can snorkel the old wreck of a steel freighter that came to rest on the rocks off Guana Cay in 15' of water.

Gray's

Six miles south of Salt Pond and well inland lies Gray's. Here you will find a branch of the *Royal Bank of Canada* as wells as the *Falcon's Rest Bar and Liquor Store*. The local inhabitants are primarily involved with the raising of sheep for market. Here you will find the ruins of three houses that once were part of *Gray's Plantation*. Between Gray's and Clarence Town, some 20 miles to the southeast are a number of small communities. Places like Andersons, Old Grays, Lower Deadman's Cay, Scrub Hill (yes there is also one north of Simms), and Stevens are home to only a few families each.

What You Will Find Ashore

In lower Deadman's Cay you will find the *J. B. Supermarket, Furniture, and Gas Station* with groceries, hardware, and fresh produce. Here you will also find *Carroll's Grocery*, the *Twilight Club,* and *Cartwright's Garage and Auto Parts*.

Deadman's Cay to South End

Deadman's Cays - NW end of channel:
23° 14.40' N, 75° 12.75' W

Deadman's Cays - SE end of channel:
23° 11.75' N, 75° 10.35' W

The larger communities such as Deadman's Cay, Buckleys, Mangrove Bush, and Cartwright are all located in a small area within a five-mile radius. All these settlements are located in an area of shallow water well south of *Salt Pond* only suitable for shoal draft vessels, dinghies, and small outboard powered boats. The *Junkers* and *Jerry Wells Landing*, located just north of Deadman's Cay are the only places where boats can unload supplies and fish.

On the highway south of *Salt Pond* sits Deadman's Cay, the top producer of sugar bananas for Nassau. Besides sugar bananas the area produces some very tasty mangoes. Long Island's main airport, other than the one at Stella Maris, is in Deadman's Cay with service from *Bahamasair* and some local charter companies with daily flights to Nassau.

Spelunkers may want to visit the nearby *Deadman's Cay Cave* where stalagmites and stalactites abound. The cave goes in two directions, one branch that appears to head directly for the ocean has never been completely explored. Just beyond Cartwrights is Hamiltons where a series of limestone caves were discovered with Lucayan carvings on the walls.

Why the area is called Deadman's Cay is up in the air. One version is that pirates marooned somebody or bodies on one of the local cays. Another story says that a cholera epidemic in the late 1700s to the early 1800s killed a number of the local inhabitants. They were apparently buried on the offlying Upper Channel Cay, which is why some old-timers won't set foot on Upper Channel Cay.

Navigational Information

Shallow draft vessels can head southeastward from Upper Channel Cay towards Lower Deadman's

Cay to anchor off Snapper Creek Cay as shown on Chart LI-5A. From a waypoint at 23° 14.40' N, 75° 12.75' W, head southeastward (approximately 138° T) passing south of Upper Channel Cay as shown on the chart as you make your way for a waypoint at 23° 11.75' N, 75° 10.35' W, which brings you to a position northwest of Snapper Creek Cay where you can pick up the channel of deeper water that leads around the cay's western tip and carries on along the southern shore of Snapper Creek Cay. Pilotage by eye is essential on this shallow water route as the controlling depth is only 3' at MLW, you'll have to play the tides very carefully here (the tend to average approximately 3.5 hours after Nassau tides). Don't try to anchor off the southwestern tip of Snapper Creek Cay in the area shown as *The Boilers* as the holding is poor and the bottom is scoured and hard packed.

What You Will Find Ashore

Buckleys lies just south of Deadman's Cay and is home to the only high school on the island. Buses travel the entire island bringing students here on a daily basis. The main *Batelco* station is located here. Buckley's is also home to a branch of the *Royal Bank of Canada, The Long Island Historical Museum and Library*, the *Queen's Highway Liquor Store*. Pettys is a very important community as it is the home to the only movie theater on Long Island. Quite often there are few clues as to which settlement you are actually

in, there are very few town signs in southern Long Island.

Medical Assistance

There is a clinic in Deadman's Cay and in Hamiltons you'll find the *Pharr-More Pharmacy.*

Mechanical Repairs

Hamiltons is home to the *Fisherman's Marine Center* (an *Evinrude* dealer). In Mangrove Bush you'll find *A & M Electrical Supplies, Knowle's Supply,* and *Under the Sea Marine Supplies,* a well-stocked marine supply store that also sells *Yamaha* outboards (337-0199).

Laundry

There's a laundromat located in Cartwright's, Buckley's, and in Hamilton's (*The Wash House*).

Provisioning

In Deadman's Cay you'll find the *J&M Food Store, Carroll's,* and *CT's Convenience Store*. In Hamiltons is *Long Island Wholesale Groceries*, and *Summer Seafood* where you can purchase conch, grouper, and lobster in season. In nearby Pettys you can shop at the well-stocked *Sea Winds Super Market, Treco's Supermarket*, and *Pineapple Square.*

Dining

At the airport is the *Sierra Club* with food, drinks, and dancing while in Deadman's Cay *Max's Conch Bar* has some of the best seafood (you have to try their conch salad) on Long Island. For good takeaway, visit *Forest 2* on *Queen's Highway*. Between Pettys and Mangrove Bush is the *Hillside Tavern Bar and Restaurant* where you can sample some of the best mutton you will find anywhere. IN Mangrove Bush you can grab something to eat at Kooter's serving breakfast, lunch, and dinner, as well as ice cream.

Propane

If you need propane while in Deadman's Cay contact Rudy Turnquest at 337-0026.

Dean's Blue Hole to Gordons

Further south you will come to a place that I consider a must see, especially before access is denied due to construction. As you drive south from Mangrove Bush you will pass a pink wall with white trim. Here you will see a nice road leading east over the ridge. The signs may tell you that this is the *Turtle Cove* development and plans include housing, a hotel, golf course, and a marina. If the chain is not blocking the drive follow it eastward over the ridge where you will come to a picturesque little cove. This is not *Turtle Cove* but the small cove north of it. Follow the road as it curves past the house and it will take you to a small gazebo with a picnic table on the southern end of this cove. Just before the gazebo another road leads off to the right. Follow this one about ¼ mile for a superb sight. When the road ends walk about another 100 yards and you will be standing on the beautiful beach at *Turtle Cove*, originally called *Eastern Harbour*. Look to your left and you will see a rocky cliff and a stunning deep blue pocket of calm water, *Dean's Blue Hole* (sometimes shown as *Bain's Blue Hole*). This is touted as the *World's Deepest Blue Hole* and the *8th Largest Underwater Cavern*. Divers have penetrated it to 220' and sounded it with lead lines at

Dean's Blue Hole   Photo by Author

Church at Clarence Town   Photo by Author

over 660'. Bring your snorkeling or SCUBA gear and check it out. You must visit this place, it is absolutely gorgeous (I'm running out of adjectives for some of these places). A couple of years ago a freestyle deep diving record was set here. At the entrance to *Dean's Blue Hole* is *Lloyd's*, a large restaurant and bar. The next community is Clarence Town, which is covered in the next section on the eastern shore of Long Island.

South is the town of Dunmore, named after Lord Dunmore. The shining white church on the hilltop is an excellent landmark in the rough surrounding terrain. Near Dunmore are the ruins of an old Loyalist plantation, some walls and two large hexagonal pillars that may have been part of a gate. Some of the ruins of the old Dunmore Plantation are still standing including parts of the main house with a fireplace, chimney, and sketches of sailboats on the walls. Just to the right of the pillars are some open holes that usually fill with water during rising tides. These seem to indicate that Long Island may have an extensive cave system connected to the sea and running all through the island. Locals say that when the tide is running you can hear "a rumbling noise." Long Islanders call these phenomena "Beaten Holes" and they are found in many places on Long Island. Speaking of caves, here you will find *Dunmore's Cave* which was used by Lucayan Indians and Pirates. In Dunmore you can stop at the *Sweet P Restaurant and Bar* for food and/or drink. Further south are some smaller settlements such as Taits, Molly Well, Berrys, Cabbage Point, and Ford.

A little further along the road you will come to Hard Bargain where there is a road leading to the abandoned *Diamond Crystal Salt Pans*, where salt was big business until recently. Now you will only find fish and shrimp farms with the harbour being off limits to cruisers except in an emergency, and even then the owners are not too thrilled about your being there.

Further south is the village of Mortimers. Most of the fishermen in southern Long Island live in Mortimers and Gordons. In Mortimers the fishermen bring their small boats two miles up the creek at day's end. There are approximately 120 people living here, three churches, a school, *Mortimer's Grocery*, *Berry's Food Store*, and the *Mid Way Bar*. The fishermen here have easy access to the large schools of grouper that inhabit the waters of southern Long Island. Mortimer's is home to *Cartwright's Cave*, once inhabited by Lucayan Indians. It is sometimes

referred to as *Duho Cave*, duhos being ceremonial stools use by the Lucayan Indians. You can inquire about guided tours in town.

Gordons should probably be called "Watsonville" as the only family living there is named Watson. The Watsons in Gordons make a living from fishing and hunting wild hogs. Yes, that's right, wild hog's. In Long Island, wild hogs are hunted with trained dogs that can sense a hog's presence and chase and corner the animal. If possible, the hunter will tie up the hog's feet and bring it home alive. If the animal is out of control the hunter must shoot the hog to protect his dogs. If the animal is brought back alive he will be fed until ripe for slaughter. The *Gordons Convenience Store* is next to the water's edge for any cruisers wishing to dinghy up the creek in search of some small groceries, you can also check out the *Ivis Food Store*.

The road ends rather abruptly after Gordons so pay attention if you're driving. At the end of the road is a small causeway that leads west over to the beach and it is worth a view. Here you will see the nice anchorage shown on Chart LI-8 (see the section *South End*) for those wishing a lee before heading to Crooked Island across the *Crooked Island Passage*.

Dollar Harbour

Dollar Harbour - ¾ nm S of:
23° 10.00' N, 75° 15.55' W

Navigational Information
Along the western shore of Long Island, a string of cays stretches from the Jumentos and Nuevitas Rocks eastward to Long Island itself. Just off the mainland of Long Island can be found an excellent anchorage at *Dollar Harbour* (see Chart LI-5). The only way to reach the area for vessels of 3' draft or more is to approach from the west at Nuevitas Rocks or from the south or southeast along the southeastern shore of Long Island.

Vessels with less than a 3' draft can, by playing the tide, gain access to the *Dollar Harbour* area directly from *Salt Pond*. From *Salt Pond* you may head directly for Upper Channel Cay. Pass west of Upper Channel Cay and work your way around its western tip in 8' of water keeping the conspicuous brown bar to starboard. The water will shallow to 1'-2' or so for a stretch of half a mile or more until you will pick up the conspicuous deep blue water, 7' and more) that winds its way to the small cut between Conch Cay and Wells Point. Most of the surrounding waters dry at low tide and every now and then you'll see a mangrove bush that has taken root. Pass between Conch Cay and Wells Point and head westward paralleling the shoreline of Conch Cay and Dollar Cay staying about 50-100 yards off in 2'-3' of water at low tide. Once you arrive at the deep blue water between Conch Cay and Dollar Cay turn to starboard and anchor wherever you prefer. The deep blue water meanders quite a ways northwestward with smaller branches leading off in various directions. This entire area is ripe for exploring by shallow draft vessels. There are many shallow passages (called *The Snakes*) that lead to deeper blue water between the various cays that offer good protection from fronts for shallow draft vessels that can venture up the twisting, turning, shallow creeks.

Deeper draft vessels, vessels with drafts of over 3', must approach *Dollar Harbour* from the south. A waypoint at 23° 10.00' N, 75° 15.55' W, will place you approximately ¾ mile south of the entrance to *Dollar Harbour*. From this position steer towards

the eastern tip of Sandy Cay. You will be able to see a channel of slightly deeper, slightly bluer water between the sandbanks to your port and starboard. This channel of blue water is what you will want to enter but first you must pass over a bar with almost 5' over it at low water. After that you must steer around a few large patch reefs that are easily seen. Never attempt this passage in poor visibility, at night, or in a strong onshore swell as a slight miscalculation may not be forgiving to your keel. Once past the bar work your way to the area between Sandy Cay and Dollar Cay. There is a very obvious sand bar in the middle of the two cays and you can pass it on either side in 5' at low water to gain the deeper water just beyond. Once inside you will have excellent holding in a sandy bottom but be prepared for current.

What You Will Find Ashore

This entire area, known as *Newfound Harbour* is a haven for birdwatchers. You may wonder why this area is called a "harbor" as it dries in so many places and mangroves are currently sprouting up in

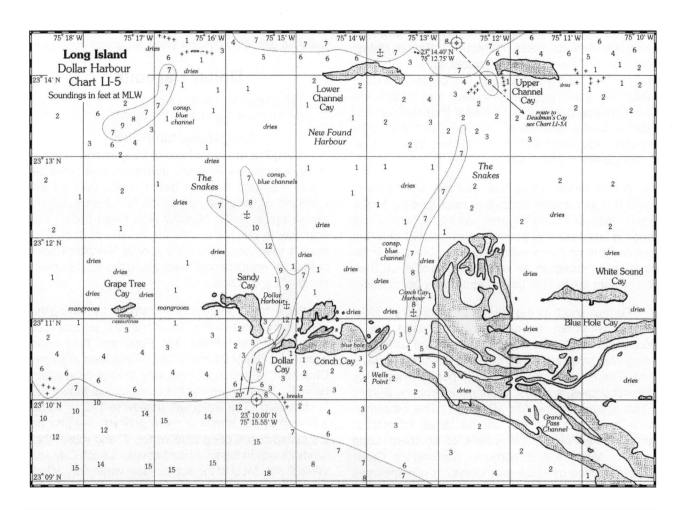

the shallows that are filling in west of Grape Tree Cay and between Grape Tree Cay and Sandy Cay. Up until a decade or so ago the harbour was deeper and vessels of 5' draft could pass through it but various storms left their mark and it is now a vast shallow bonefish marl. The Spanish were some of the first visitors to the *Newfound Harbour* area and on one of the cays (I am told it is near Wells Point though I have not found it) is said to be a well with stone around it and Spanish writing. Conch Cay was once farmed by the local population from the mainland.

The Eastern Shore

The eastern shore of Long Island is sometimes skipped by cruising yachts due to its lack of good harbours. Most simply pass it by on their way to and from the southern islands. The only two places for refuge on Long Island's rugged, inhospitable, windward shore is at Clarence Town and a little further south at *Little Harbour*. It is a long haul, approximately 41 miles, from *Cape Santa Maria*, along the eastern shore to Clarence Town, and even longer for cruisers bound for Crooked Island.

Some skippers heading for points south, such as Crooked Island, opt to take the mailboat route on the western side of the Exumas and Long Island thereby avoiding the area to windward of Long Island. The problem with the eastern shore of Long Island is the *Atlantic Ocean* ground swell. When it is running it can make coming into port nerve wracking to say the least. If a significant ground swell is running your safest port on the eastern shore is at Clarence Town (with *Little Harbour* a close second). I have been told that north of Clarence Town vessels can anchor behind Guana Cay passing either south or north of Guana Cay, but you should never attempt it with a ground swell running. I have never anchored behind Guana Cay and therefore cannot recommend it as an anchorage, I would rather suggest you anchor at Clarence Town, but I merely mention it for your knowledge in case of emergency.

Clarence Town

Clarence Town - ½ nm NW of Booby Rock:
23° 07.35' N, 74° 57.65' W

The spires of the two churches in Clarence Town can be seen from far out at sea making a good landmark to home in on. The two churches are definitely worth seeing and were built by the same man, Father Jerome, who built the Hermitage on Cat

Island. When he has known as Jerome Hawes, an Anglican missionary, he built *St. Paul's Church*. Later he converted to Catholicism and became Father Jerome. He returned to Long Island and in an effort to outdo his earlier construction he built the stunning, white *St. Peter's Church*. If you want to check out the huge cave system north of town, call *Cave Man* on VHF ch. 16 for a guide.

Navigational Information

The entrance to the harbour at Clarence Town is not too complicated. As shown on Chart LI-6, a waypoint at 23° 07.35' N, 74° 57.65' W, will place you approximately ¼ mile northwest of the entrance proper. As you can see by the chart, a good skipper can work his way into the anchorage in other ways than by the standard route that people have been using for years. This is fine, it may be easier for you to do that. But if you get confused and have to call someone ashore and ask for directions they will only be able to relate to the usual route for the entrance. From the waypoint, line up the southwestern tip of Cash's Cay, formerly Strachan's Cay but now named after its new owner, and head towards it on a course of 155°. When the white stand that used to be *Harbour Point Light* (east of the prominent stand of palm trees) bears 200° take up that heading to avoid *Conch Spit* which lies southwest of Cash's Cay. You will notice the seas breaking in the vicinity of Harbour Point so don't get too close to it, there's a lot of rocks and heads just off this point. When you can clear *Conch Spit*, take up a heading of 155° again on the southeastern point of the long beach. When you are abeam of the town dock and Sandy Point on Cash's Cay, you can turn to starboard to anchor off the town dock or turn to port to anchor past Sandy Point south of Cash's Cay in the lee of the reef. If you decide to anchor south of Cash's Cay use extreme caution, there is a submarine cable leading to Cash's Cay that lies across the anchorage as shown on the chart. Sometimes you can see it from your deck, most times not. Take care when setting your anchor here.

In settled weather you may wish to anchor just off the mailboat dock in grass and sand keeping an eye out for the submarine cable. If winds are strong out of the east you will probably be better off just south of Cash's Cay and east of Sandy Point. Here the reef breaks the seas and they don't have a chance to build very much before they reach this anchorage with its good holding sand/grass bottom. If you choose to anchor at the mailboat dock in strong easterly winds you will find the small fetch allows the seas to build

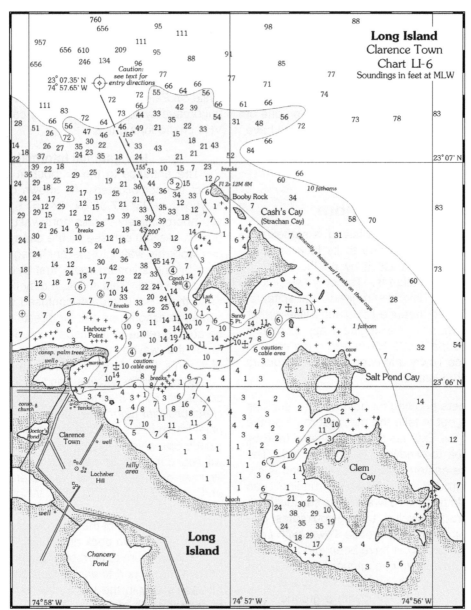

Long Island
Clarence Town
Chart LI-6
Soundings in feet at MLW

Clarence Town and Flying Fish Marina

slightly making for a lot of movement at anchor. You'll find that it's a little calmer if you anchor south of Cash's Cay.

If you wish to ride out a front at the mailboat dock you will have good protection except from strong north/northeast to east winds. The best anchorage for a frontal passage is south of Cash's Cay. My personal preference, if I have a window, is to head south about 10 miles to *Little Harbour* (see the next section *Little Harbour*), a well-protected refuge.

What You Will Find Ashore

Marina
The *Flying Fish Marina* (242-337-3430, or info@flyingfishmarina.com), is located on the waterfront in Clarence Town and is a great place to stop or stay. The marina can handle vessels with drafts to 9' with full electric and water at every slip (16). The marina offers diesel and gasoline at their fuel dock, *Outer Edge Grill* restaurant (242-337-3445), and a laundry.

Laundry
There is a laundry service at the marina.

Mechanical Repairs
If you need mechanical help you can contact the marina or If you need a good mechanic contact Henry Major at the *Shell* station (242-337-3936), Carlos Milander at *Milander's Auto* (242-337-3227), Red Major at the *Oasis Bakery* (242-338-3003), Andrew Cartwright (242-337-2424), or Rudolph Pratt (242-338-2378) who actually lives in Cabbage Point. *Milander's* also carries some basic marine supplies.

Fuel
Clarence Town is your last chance for fuel until you reach Crooked Island, Matthew Town on Inagua, *Abraham's Bay* on Mayaguana, or Provo in the Turks and Caicos Island group. If there is no fuel at the marina Rudolph Pratt can also deliver fuel to your vessel. Rudolph can be reached by phone at 242-338-2378.

Provisioning
Just up from the town dock is the *Agricultural Packing House* where you can purchase fresh produce and fish when available (usually Tuesdays and Wednesdays). You can also find a good selection of groceries at *Harbour Grocery (delivers to the marina)*, and the *True Value Food Store*.

Dining
If you are at the marina, stop in at the *Outer Edge Grill*. Next door to the packing house is the *Harbour View Restaurant and Satellite Lounge*, the place in town for dining. Others include the *Skieta OK Bar*, and the *Oasis Bakery and Restaurant* (also rents cars). Close to the marina is the *Rowdy Boys Bar and Grill*.

Medical Assistance
On the main road is the *Government Complex* and the *Community Clinic*.

Little Harbour

Little Harbour - ½ nm E of entrance:
22° 58.65' N, 74° 50.30' W

Not enough can be said about this small anchorage. Little Harbour offers excellent protection in all wind directions and you can ride out even the fiercest frontal passage here. The anchorage lies about 10 miles southeast of Clarence Town. You'll know you're getting close when you see the conspicuous long house sitting atop a ridge about seven miles south of Clarence Town. *Little Harbour* lies a little over two miles south of that house, the entrance being just south of the very visible rusty remains of an old freighter wrecked on Long Island's eastern shore. The entrance to this picturesque harbour as shown on Chart LI-7 is easy to enter even with 6' following seas. To enter take the southernmost of the two openings, between the unnamed cay and the mainland of Long Island favoring the northern side of the entrance between the two. There were once two rock cairns ashore that you would pass between, nowadays they've been torn down and a couple of white stakes take their place, one on the small cay to the north, and two stakes on the mainland to the south of the entrance. Do not attempt this entrance in strong easterly weather or with a heavy ground swell running, instead head north to Clarence Town or south around the southern tip of Long Island to anchor in its lee. If a ground swell is running and you are inside Little Harbour, stay put until it abates.

Navigational Information
A waypoint at 22° 58.65' N, 74° 50.30 W, will place you approximately ½ mile east of the narrow, inconspicuous entrance. The best water at the entrance lies about ¾ of the way north across the entrance from the mainland tip. Line up the opening on a heading of 270° and you will have 11' through

here at low water. If a sea is running you will notice it breaking south of you about halfway across the opening and also around the small cay that lies to the north of the entrance. Use caution when entering as some rocky ledges and heads line the sides of the entrance channel. Once inside look to port and you will see the hull of a small sailboat high on the rocks.

Another interesting wreck lies on the small cay about one mile south of the entrance to *Little Harbour*. Here you will find the hull of a boat, very much high and dry, sitting atop the cay. It will certainly make you wonder what forces of nature it took to place it there.

In east through south to west winds the best anchorage is in *Camel Bay* at the south end of *Little*

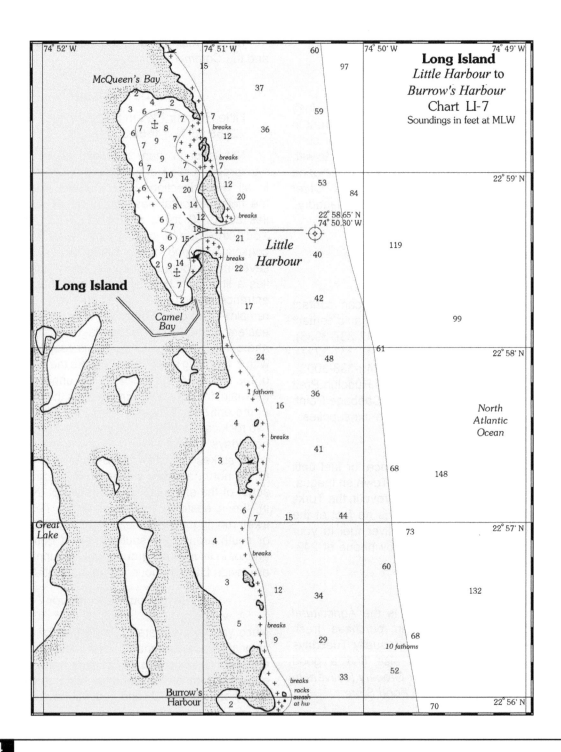

Harbour. Once inside the harbour, turn to port and tuck in wherever your draft will allow. In strong easterly winds the harbour can get a little rolly, just a little uncomfortable, but nothing a bridle won't cure. In the event of a frontal passage you can tuck in at the north end of the harbour at *McQueen's Bay* and enjoy the calm while anchored in a good holding sandy bottom. Once the wind comes into the east you must move south to *Camel Bay* to get out of the incoming swell. To access McQueen's Bay, once inside steer northward keeping an eye out for the shallow reef area northwest of the cay at the entrance and a few scattered heads that are easily seen and avoided.

What You Will Find Ashore

There are no communities in *Little Harbour* although some local fisherman often leave their boats there. There is a picturesque cactus and wildflower lined trail leading to the nearby community of Roses as well as a road from *Camel Bay.* At William Darville's *Carpenter Arms* you will find good conversation as well as fresh bread and *Dean's Food Store* can perhaps help you out with some limited groceries. You are likely to see some wild goats ashore, especially around *Camel Bay.* The waters of *Little Harbour* itself are home to a lot of large and small sea turtles. South of *Little Harbour* are two more small harbors that are only viable in settled weather and if your draft is 4' or less. In any type of seas their entrances break all the way across. Local knowledge, or the ability to read the water, coupled with good visibility, calm waters, and nerves of steel will get you inside. *Little Harbour* is a much better anchorage, easier to enter and leave, and it offers very good protection.

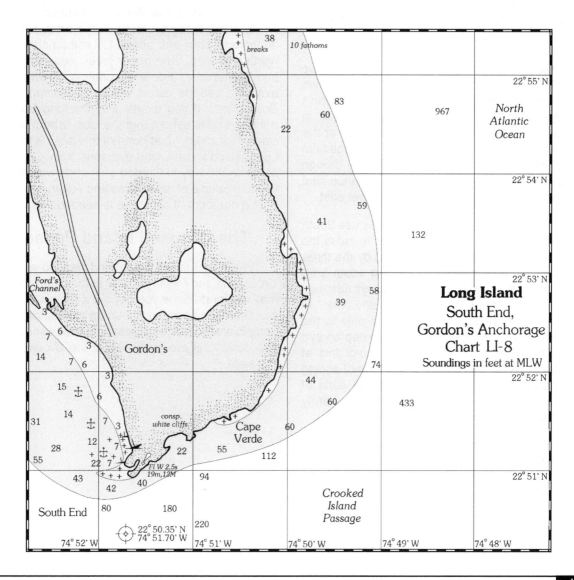

South End

Southern tip of Long Island - ½ nm S of:
22º 50.35' N, 74º 51.70' W

Many vessels, mine included, if headed for Crooked Island and points south, sometimes opt to take the route in the lee of Long Island instead of the usual Conception-Rum-Mayaguana route so favored by those in a hurry. I will usually leave George Town, pass through *Hog Cay Cut*, take Nuevitas Rocks to port, and anchor overnight in *Dollar Harbour*. I leave the next morning and work my way southeastward in the lee of Long Island to anchor just north of South End. Bear in mind that this is only to be done with a weather window of two days or more (although *Dollar Harbour* and French Wells are both good harbours in any wind, you will be completely exposed from south through west to just east of north at South End/Gordon's Anchorage). Allow one day to get to South End, one more day to get to French Wells at Crooked Island. I have gone from *Dollar Harbour*, around South End, and on to French Wells in 12 hours but it is a trip of about 60 or so miles. It may be easier for some skippers to break that down into two shorter legs. Sometimes I'll go straight to Gordon's Anchorage from Nuevitas Rocks and get there at about the same time as other boats who left at the same time I did arrived at Rum Cay. At this point I'm about 50 miles south of their position even though we've both traveled about the same distance that day, however they are about one mile further east.

Many fishing boats and Haitian vessels use South End as a waiting spot for good weather to cross the *Crooked Island Passage*, this is verified by the three wrecks along the shoreline. If heading south from *Dollar Harbour* to South End you can always turn east to anchor in the lee of Long Island at any time. In some places the shallows stretch out a mile to the west of the shore and you must always keep an eye out for the occasional head, never attempt this at night though. A favorite spot is at *Calloway Landing* where there used to be a light. Once, all sorts of sailing vessels from Nassau called here, now hardly anyone stops.

Navigational Information
From Crooked Island or points south, A waypoint at 22º 50.35' N, 74º 51.70' W, will place you approximately ½ mile south of the southwest point of Long Island as shown on Chart LI-8. From this position head northwest around the southwest tip of Long Island giving the shallow, very visible reef a good berth. Once past the reef turn to starboard and tuck in behind the reef wherever your draft will allow. This is called the *Gordon's Anchorage* and is a good spot in northeast through southeast winds although you may get some roll from strong southeast seas bending around the reef which breaks most of these seas. If that happens you'll probably want to rig a bridle.

If you are approaching from the north, say from *Dollar Harbour*, head for the above mentioned waypoint and about a mile before you reach it you will see the long beach and anchorage off the southwest tip of Long Island. If headed to this area from *Dollar Harbour,* keep a good watch out for Comer Rock, West Comer Rock, and Long Rocks lying about two miles west of Long Island and about half the distance from *Dollar Harbour* to South End.

What You Will Find Ashore
There are some creeks in the area, just off the anchorage area and about 1½ miles north that are worth exploring. The upper creek leads to Gordon's and Mortimer's. For a description of what little is available see the earlier section *Deadman's Cay to South End*. If you dinghy into the long beach you will see a table ashore that the local fishermen use to clean their catch. Just north of this table is the end of Long Island's main road that runs from *Cape Santa Maria* all the way to Gordon's. A short walk will bring you to a couple of residences and you may be able to bum a ride north if someone is headed that way.

The Crooked Island Passage

When you leave South End headed across the *Crooked Island Passage*, bear in mind that conditions may moderate once you get out a couple of miles or so. Often the seas "hump" up on the southern end of Long Island sometimes creating a false sense of what sea conditions are really like in the *Crooked Island Passage*.

The Jumentos

Ports of Entry: Duncan Town
Fuel: ask at Duncan Town
Haul-Out: None
Diesel Repairs: ask at Duncan Town
Outboard Repairs: Duncan Town
Propane: None
Provisions: Duncan Town (limited)
Important Lights:
Nuevitas Rocks: Fl W ev 4 sec
Flamingo Cay: Fl W ev 6 sec
Ragged Island: Fl W ev 3 sec
Cay Santo Domingo: Fl W ev 5 sec
Cay Lobos Lighthouse: Gp. Fl (2) W ev 10 sec

I have a nagging feeling deep down that I shouldn't tell anyone how to get to this lovely, unspoiled island chain. I really want to keep this one for myself. The Jumentos have all the flavor of the most pristine islands of the Exumas Cays but without all the hordes of cruisers, and yet, if needed, George Town is only a day or two away. Here is solitude. Here is natural beauty. Here you can relax, enjoy life at your own pace, and rarely see another human being except for the local fishermen who frequent these islands in great numbers. This is my favorite island chain in the entire Bahamas. Giving away the navigational information to allow cruisers to have a safe, enjoyable, memorable cruise through these cays is like giving away my daughter. Please take care of her.

When you are cruising The Bahamas you will often meet people who will give you the impression that they are old and knowledgeable Bahamas veterans, informing you early on in the conversation how long they've been cruising here and offering advice on every topic under the sun related to the islands. In fact, this is the very impression that they enjoy giving. Unfortunately, quite a few people dole out misleading information with an air of authenticity whose only purpose is not so much to assist you as it is to boost their status in your eyes. Be careful, these types can be outright dangerous if not simply ludicrous. One couple I know are snowbirds, spending their summers in the north and their winters in George Town, doing this regularly for years. I have known them to shake their heads and tell cruisers headed for the Jumentos "No, the water is too shallow for you there." You may also hear that there are no safe anchorages in which to weather a front in the winter cruising season. These people that have been encouraging these misplaced notions only show

their ignorance of this beautiful island chain. Many of the passages between the islands are over 30'-40' deep and there are two excellent spots for riding out fronts, more if you have a shallow draft vessel. True Bahamas veterans are out cruising and enjoying the islands, not growing a reef on their anchor chains as they confuse other skippers who seek the benefit of their experience. Read on and you will soon see the myths exploded and the truth laid bare. The next time you see these so-called experts holding court at *Chat and Chill* or *Two Turtles*, tell them where to go. Tell them to go to the Jumentos. On second thought, maybe you shouldn't tell them to come here. Maybe you should tell them that they are correct, it is too shallow, and yes, there are no places to weather a front. Then slip through *Hog Cay Cut* and head back to paradise.

The Jumentos, once called the *Yumettos*, are a croissant-shaped chain of islands approximately 110 miles long that lie at the southeastern edge of the Great Bahama Bank at the western edge of the *Crooked Island Passage*. The entire island chain is often called the Ragged Island Range although they are most often referred to as the Jumentos with the Ragged Island Range sometimes spoken of as a separate entity. With the exception of Jamaica Cay where a new resort is being planned, the only inhabitants of the cays reside in the Ragged Island area at its only settlement of Duncan Town. As a side note, *jumento* in my Spanish dictionary means *donkey*.

The Jumentos are an ideal place for cruisers wishing to get off the beaten path, to visit unspoiled islands free from commercial development, and to enjoy superb fishing, diving, and beachcombing. When cruising the Jumentos you will rarely see another cruising boat although this will surely change as more and more visitors to George Town, Exuma begin to venture in that direction. During lobster season, from August 1 through April 1, you will probably only see fishing boats from Long Island, Nassau, or Exuma, in the anchorages up and down the cays. There are a few large cays in the northern Jumentos with the majority of the larger cays lying in the southern Jumentos in the area of Ragged Island and northwards. Many of the passages in between are wide open to the deep water of the *Crooked Island Passage* with a few small cays spread over a very large area. These areas are prone to heavy seas in strong easterly winds, even well out onto the banks you may experience large seas. Strong currents and tides abound in all the cuts from the banks out to the *Crooked Island Passage*. Do not take this warning lightly. If you think a rage in Exuma can be rough, you have yet to see one in the Jumentos. Wind against tide in some of these cuts sometimes makes for some truly awesome waves, and a ground swell against the tide, even with little or no wind, can do the same.

From George Town it is possible to pass through *Hog Cay Cut* and head southward, cruise the Jumentos to Ragged Island and then go offshore across the *Crooked Island Passage* to Long Cay or Castle Cay in the Crooked/Acklins group. Another possibility is to head down island to Ragged Island, then return along the string of cays past Nuevitas Rocks and further east along the western shore of Long Island to anchor at Dollar Harbour or off Long Island's southern tip. From here it is only 30 some odd miles or so to Landrail Point or French Wells in the Crooked/Acklins group.

Tides in the central and southern Jumentos and the Ragged Island area are approximately 15 minutes later than Nassau. Tides in the area of Nuevitas Rocks are approximately ¾ hour later than Nassau.

A word about fishing in the Jumentos. You will find grouper, hogfish, and conch quite easily. Lobster on the other hand may be quite scarce. I don't know why, perhaps the area is fished so thoroughly by the commercial boats during the season that few are left for the cruisers. This is not to say that lobsters cannot be found, you just have to look harder, longer, and maybe even deeper, either that or look where the commercial guys don't.

Approaches

Exumas; Hog Cay Cut- ¼ nm S:
23° 23.50' N, 75° 30.92' W

From a waypoint just south of *Hog Cay Cut* in the Exumas, it is approximately 15.7 nautical miles on a course of 157° to Nuevitas Rocks, 14.8 nautical miles on a course of 188° for Pear Cay, and 24.6 nautical miles on a course of 216° to the waypoint west of Water Cay. Along these routes you will find water that progressively gets deeper, from 4'-6' just south and west of *Hog Cay Cut*, to 25'-35' and more as you approach the islands themselves. These routes are relatively free from navigational hazards for the first 10-15 miles from *Hog Cay Cut*, however, as you approach the northern Jumentos you will begin to see patch reefs and scattered heads. Initially

these heads and reefs are not a threat but as you approach the cays they begin to get closer and closer to the surface. For instance, if heading to Water Cay, straying east of your courseline may put you on the shallow bank that lies just north of the No Name Cays (see Chart JU-3). Although I have made every endeavor to chart the waters correctly in the vicinity of the cays themselves, I cannot chart every bit of water between the Jumentos and Exuma. If you're heading from *Hog Cay Cut* to Nuevitas Rocks, a popular route that I like, just south of the *Comer Channel* you'll find a shallow area with about 3'-4' over it at MLW. A short jog to the west will get you around this shoal and then you can return to your heading for Nuevitas Rocks. There may well be shallow areas along and either side of the course lines mentioned that I have missed. The prudent navigator will keep a sharp lookout for scattered shallow reefs, heads, and sandbanks, and steer around them.

One final note on *Hog Cay Cut*. Ideally, when headed to the Jumentos from George Town, Exuma, you should plan to anchor just north of *Hog Cay Cut* between West Rock and Little Exuma Island, and pass through the cut on a rising tide early the next morning (unless you draw less than 3'). This allows you to make landfall in the Jumentos about midday or later depending on the speed of your vessel. Unfortunately high tide is not always so gracious, often making its appearance later in the day (tides at *Hog Cay Cut* usually run 30 minutes to an hour later than George Town). If this is the case, you may wish to pass through *Hog Cay Cut* and anchor on the other side. **NEVER ATTEMPT TO TRAVEL THE BANKS FROM HOG CAY CUT TO THE NORTHERN JUMENTOS AT NIGHT.** In calm winds, vessels with a 5'-6' draft would have to proceed about two miles on their courseline to find water deep enough in which to anchor safely (9'-11' at high tide). If the wind is blowing, say 12 to 15 knots or more, anchoring on the banks can be a real experience, one I usually prefer to avoid. If you feel the same you may consider passing through *Hog Cay Cut* and heading northwestward along the shoreline of Little Exuma Island past the Ferry, approximately 10 miles or so from *Hog Cay Cut*. Here you can find shelter from the prevailing east to southeast winds behind the small cays north of The Ferry. If headed to Water Cay or Flamingo Cay the next morning, this delay will add about five miles to your trip but it is a fair exchange for a pleasant night's sleep. (For more information on *Hog Cay Cut* and the cays north of The Ferry, see *The Exuma Guide, 3rd ed.* Stephen J. Pavlidis, Seaworthy Publications, ISBN 978-1-892399-31-1

Vessels wishing to gain access to the Jumentos from the central Exumas can pass west of *Galliot Bank* and take the mailboat route past Hawksbill Rock to Water Cay, Flamingo Cay, or Nuevitas Rocks. If headed for Nuevitas Rocks it would be shorter to head inside *Jewfish Cut* off the western shore of Great Exuma. Nuevitas Rocks bears approximately 270° at a distance from 5.62 miles from Dollar Harbour at Long Island (for information concerning routes from Long Island via the *Comer Channel*, see the chapter *Long Island, The Comer Channel*). Vessels bound to the Jumentos or Ragged Island from the southern islands of The Bahamas will find them usually downwind. For instance, from French Wells at Crooked Island, Raccoon Cut bears 264° at a distance of 84 nautical miles.

A special note for vessels transiting the *Crooked Island Passage* between the Jumentos and the Crooked/Acklins District. At an approximate position at 22° 50' N, 74° 48' W, lies the center of the *Diana Bank*. The approximately 100 square miles of *Diana Bank* lies west of the southern tip of Long Cay, south/southeast of the southern tip of Long Island, and east of *Nurse Channel* in the Jumentos. *Diana Bank* is shallow, only about 35'-600' deep, lying in the midst of much deeper water, 1800'-6000' deep. With a strong swell in any direction the seas on top of the bank can

get very rough as the water is pushed up the sides of this underwater obstruction. If you are experiencing rough seas in your transit of this area, by all means avoid the area of *Diana Bank*. If the seas are calm, quite unusual hereabouts, try fishing on the bank.

Nuevitas Rocks to Water Cay

Nuevitas Rocks - banks side- ½ nm N of:
23° 10.00' N, 75°22.10' W

Nuevitas Rocks-offshore side - ½ nm SE of:
23° 09.30' N, 75° 21.60' W

Pear Cay Pass - ½ nm NNW of:
23° 08.65' N, 75° 31.20' W

Pear Cay Pass - ½ nm SE of:
23° 07.80' N, 75° 30.65' W

Water Cay Cut - ¼ nm SE of:
23° 02.20' N, 75° 40.35' W

Water Cay-banks side - ¾ nm NW of:
23° 02.00' N, 75° 44.00' W

Navigational Information
We will begin out tour of the Jumentos from north to south. From *Hog Cay Cut* it is approximately 15.7 nautical miles to Nuevitas Rocks (Chart JU-1) on a course of 156°. If you are en route past Nuevitas from the *Comer Channel*, *Hog Cay Cut*, or Hawksbill

The Jumentos
Nuevitas Rocks to
No Bush Cay
Chart JU-1
Soundings in feet at MLW

Rock, to the southern tip of Long Island or across the *Crooked Island Passage* to the Crooked/Acklins group, a waypoint at 23° 10.00' N, 75° 22.10' W will place you approximately ½ mile northeast of the light on Nuevitas Rocks. Keep Nuevitas Rocks to starboard until out in the deeper water and then take up the course to your destination. If approaching from the *Crooked Island Passage*, a waypoint at 23° 09.30' N, 75° 21.60' W will place you approximately ½ mile southeast of Nuevitas Rocks. In northbound towards *Hog Cay Cut* keep Nuevitas Rocks to port.

From Nuevitas Rocks westward lie a string of small cays and rocks leading to Water Cay (Chart JU-2 and Chart JU-3). There is little to attract cruisers except some lee anchorages at Pear Cay and Stony Cay, as well as excellent diving and fishing. You may see some Long Island fishermen working this area during lobster season. Their usual routine is for the big boat to head west down *Comer Channel* and then south to Water Cay while the divers head straight across in their small *Whalers* and dive the reefs along the way. This way they don't waste a day in transit.

Pear Cay lies west/southwest of Nuevitas Rocks some 9 miles. If approaching from *Hog Cay Cut*, a waypoint at 23° 08.65' N, 75° 31.20' W will place you approximately ½ mile north of *Pear Cay Pass* and north/northeast of Pear Cay. If headed for deeper water keep Pear Cay to starboard and head out Pear Cay Pass between Pear Cay and the unnamed cay to its east. If approaching from the *Crooked Island Passage* towards Hog Cay Cut or other points north, a waypoint at 23° 07.80' N, 75° 30.65' W, will place you approximately ½ mile southeast of Pear Cay Pass. Keep Pear Cay to port and pass between Pear Cay and the unnamed cay to its east.

The southernmost of the No Name Cays (Chart JU-3) lies just north of Little Water Cay and slightly to seaward of its neighbors. This cay is ringed by the ruins of an old pasture wall that dates to Loyalist days. Along its northern shore are the ruins of an old building, all that is left is the footings.

Just south of the No Name Cays is a deep-water cut that allows access to the Water Cay anchorages from offshore. A waypoint at 23° 02.20' N 75° 40.35' W, will place you approximately ¼ mile southeast of the cut. Pass between the southernmost of the No Name Cays as shown on Chart JU-3 and the northernmost of the small cays lying north of Little Water Cay. Head roughly northwest through the

center of this cut until you pass the last of the small cays to port. At that point you may turn to port to parallel the string of small rocks to Little Water Cay and Water Cay.

Just north of Water Cay sits Little Water Cay. On its western shore is a small cove known as Moxey Harbour. Here a small creek leads eastward into a small lake that was once used as a hurricane hole. About fifty years ago you could take a 6' draft into a 10' deep mangrove lined pond. The renowned Capt. Henry Moxey once spent 15 stormbound days in this harbour that Linton Rigg named after him. Moxey Harbour has now filled in to the east with mangroves and they have all but closed off the entrance to the lake save for a narrow, shallow creek. There is still enough room for one small, shallow draft vessel, say perhaps a small sloop or catamaran, to anchor in 3'-7' of water in the prevailing winds just before you reach the mangroves. Watch your swing room as there are rocky shallows on both sides of you.

As a first stop on your southbound cruise through the Jumentos you should definitely consider Water Cay. Although Pear Cay and Stony Cay offer adequate lee anchorages that are very nice in calm weather, the anchorage at Water Cay is the first truly comfortable anchorage in strong north to almost south winds that you will find in your cruise southward through these islands. Along the shore of Water Cay are some very prominent white cliffs that make up three distinct hills which are easily seen from offshore, sometimes from as far as 10 miles away.

A waypoint at 23° 02.00' N, 75° 44.00 W, will place you approximately 1 nautical mile northwest of the anchorage at Water Cay as shown on Chart JU-4. From here, head in towards the shore of Little Water Cay or the northern end of Water Cay, you will have deep water (15'-17') right up to the shoreline. Pass the point off Water Cay and anchor anywhere along the shore of Water Cay. The best spot is just inside the northern cove, inside the point. This offers the best protection and the least surge. The Water Cay anchorage is excellent for the prevailing east/southeast winds as well as north and northeast, but this is no place to be in a frontal passage. If a front threatens you need to get your vessel to Buena Vista Cay (37 nautical miles south of Water Cay) or Raccoon Cay (5 nautical miles south of Buena Vista Cay) for protection. If caught out in oncoming westerly weather your only option is to do what some of the local fishing boats do, tuck in along the eastern

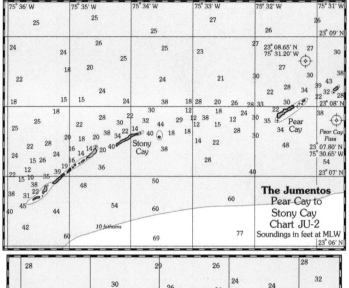

The Jumentos
Pear Cay to
Stony Cay
Chart JU-2
Soundings in feet at MLW

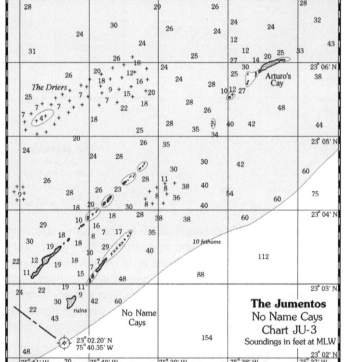

The Jumentos
No Name Cays
Chart JU-3
Soundings in feet at MLW

Cave at Flamingo Cay   Photo by Author

shore of some of these cays wherever your draft will allow and expect a somewhat rolly time until the westerly winds calm the seas in the *Crooked Island Passage* and give you a more comfortable lee. As soon as the winds begin to approach the north, shoot around to the southern or western side of your chosen refuge and tuck in wherever possible.

The holding along the entire length of Water Cay is fair to good. The sand is very hard and you must dive your anchor, especially if you expect any sort of a blow. One can also gain access from the southern end of Water Cay but the entrances there are narrow and only 7'-9' deep at MLW. It is safer to head northward up the western shore of Water Cay about ½ mile off, staying clear of the off lying shallow reefs and enter the anchorage from the west as shown on Chart JU-4.

You can also enter the anchorages at Water Cay from offshore via the cut lying south of Water Cay, between Water Cay and Melita Cay. Pass between the two and parallel the shoreline of Water Cay northeastward staying clear of the reefs that lie off its southwestern shore. If this entrance to the banks does not interest you, it is possible to enter the wide and deep cut lying south of Melita Cay to Lanzadera Cay. This cut is over 40' deep and a mile wide with only a small reef area lying just southwest of Melita Cay as a hazard.

What You Will Find Ashore

Water Cay is actually two cays separated by a narrow creek. This water in this creek flows strongly in and out with the tide and it is luxurious just to sit in and enjoy the flow. In extremely heavy weather seas break over the low-lying land just to the north of the creek and one should not anchor in its vicinity if a strong blow is forecast.

South of the last hill is a very small beach. Here you will find a path that leads over the island and also up along the ridge of the cliffs giving you a spectacular view in all directions. Look for mussels along the shoreline here.

Water Cay offers some excellent diving easily accessible by dinghy from the anchorage. Off the western shore of Water Cay are a few shallow reefs, excellent for snorkeling and

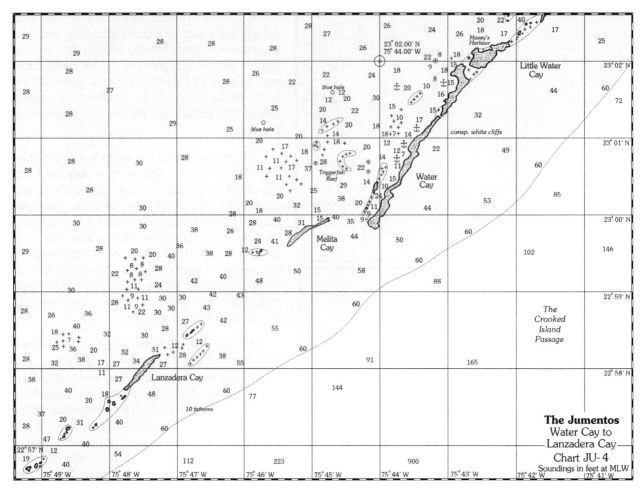

The Jumentos
Water Cay to
Lanzadera Cay
Chart JU- 4
Soundings in feet at MLW

fishing. One in particular, *Triggerfish Reef* abounds in large trigger fish, hence its name. There are a lot of reefs in the deeper waters (12'-20') surrounding Little Water Cay and Water Cay that make for excellent spearfishing and the banks are home to a plentiful supply of conch.

SCUBA enthusiasts will want to check out the two blue holes in the area, both within about three miles of the anchorage as shown on Chart JU-4. The first hole lies at 23º 01.59' N, 75º 44.68' W, about 1½ nautical miles west of the anchorage. This hole, the smaller of the two, is only about 48' deep with a sandy bottom. This hole is surrounded by reefs about 12' deep and the walls of the hole itself are vertical reef structure with many small holes and tunnels. There is no noticeable current in the hole itself and the hole is full of grouper, snapper, and sharks.

The second blue hole at 23º 01.20' N, 75º 45.73' W, lies just about one nautical mile west/southwest of the first blue hole. This hole is truly spectacular having almost vertical walls plunging to 122' with many holes,

tunnels, and crevices to hide the numerous large groupers, permits, and other marine life that inhabit it. Watch out for sharks here also. At the southeastern end of the hole there is a ledge where the hole heads even deeper downward. A handline and some conch for bait would probably bring up enough for a few meals at either of these two holes.

Water Cay to Flamingo Cay

Flamingo Cut- ¼ nm W of:
22º 54.30' N, 75º 51.00' W

Flamingo Cay-1 nm NW of:
22º 54.30' N, 75º 53.10' W

Just south of Water Cay lies Melita Cay. Anchored at Water Cay in moderate to strong easterly winds, you can watch waves crash into the eastern shore of Melita Cay and shoot skyward to fantastic heights. Southward of Water Cay to Flamingo Cay lie Melita Cay, Lanzadera Cay (Chart JU-4), and Torzon Cay (Chart JU-5). These cays offer little to visiting cruisers

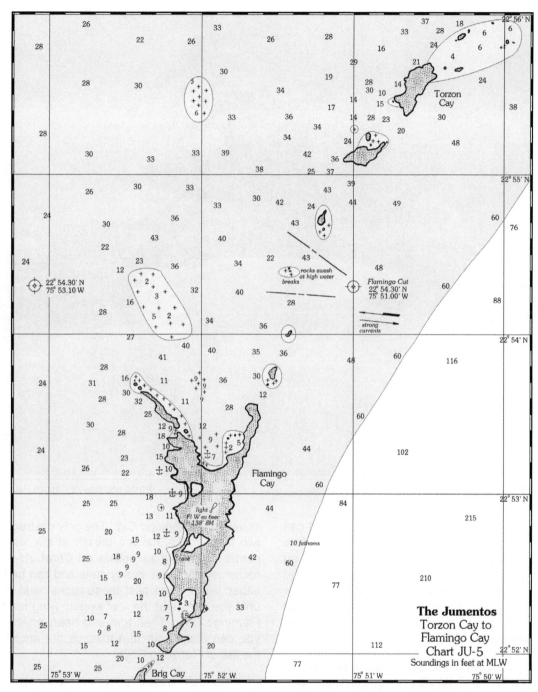

The Jumentos
Torzon Cay to
Flamingo Cay
Chart JU-5
Soundings in feet at MLW

except a lee if caught out in heavy east/southeast winds.

Navigational Information

South of Torzon Cay lies Flamingo Cay, largest of the northern cays of the Jumentos and a must stop on your Jumentos cruise. Flamingo Cay, sometimes called *Fillimingo* by the locals, is easily recognized by its high bluffs. From Water Cay there are several different routes from which to choose to gain Flamingo

Cay. Your choice will depend upon sea and wind conditions, and your own personal preference. From Water Cay you can pass outside into deeper water at any of the deep cuts south of Water Cay. There are no hazards on this route except the cuts themselves, which are deep and have a lot of current. Another choice is to parallel the inside of the small cays southwest of Water Cay to Flamingo Cay. Here again, all the cuts have a lot of current that can sweep you off your courseline before you know it.

Flamingo Cay from the north   Photo courtesy of Captain Paul Harding

If you choose to sail down on the banks you can head west of Water Cay about 1½-2 miles before taking up a course to parallel the cays southwestward to Flamingo Cay. This is a better route if the wind is kicking up. The only hazards when leaving Water Cay are the reefs just southwest and west of Water Cay and a small reef (6' at MLW) not shown on the charts in this guide, at 22° 57.00' N, 75° 50.56' W.

For skippers using the banks route, a waypoint at 22° 54.30' N, 75° 53.10' W, will place you just northwest of the anchorages that lie along the western shore of Flamingo Cay. If paralleling the western shore of the cays from Water Cay southwestward, watch out for the large reef that lies just north of the small cays that stretch northwest of Flamingo Cay as shown on Chart JU-5. From this waypoint pass south of those same offlying cays and enter the anchorage area.

From offshore, a waypoint at 22° 54.30' N, 75° 51.00' W, will place you approximately ½ mile to

seaward of *Flamingo Cut*. The only obstruction is the two large rocks that are awash at low water in the center of the cut as shown on Chart JU-5. These rocks usually break in any seas and can be taken on either side. Once past these rocks head northwest until you can clear the reef system lying northwest of Flamingo Cay. Then turn and head southward until you can make your turn towards the anchorages in the lee of Flamingo Cay.

You can anchor anywhere along the western shore of Flamingo Cay in winds of any strength out of the northeast to southeast. At the northern end there is a small cove, which would be suitable for a small, shallow draft vessel, say, perhaps a catamaran, to enjoy. In the cove south of it is the wreck of the *John Davis*. Just south of the *John Davis* is a pretty cove, my favorite, with a trio of palm trees ashore, and deep water very close in to the beach. This anchorage has good holding (it is still a good idea to dive on your anchor folks) and is the least prone to surge along this western shore. Ashore and to the north you will find the ruins of small house, a dry well, and a burial site. Just behind the well is a small cave that leads down about 10' to a small room that has enough room for four or five people to enjoy a sit down dinner. There are some other ruins in the area including some old graves, but one must cut a trail to them and the area is thick with poisonwood.

What You Will Find Ashore

South of this beach is another large cove, just north of the cave, that is just a little shallower than the one just mentioned. Here you will find a trail leading up the hill to the light (Fl W ev 6 sec, 138', 8M-the light is in such a state of disrepair that only a complete overhaul or replacement will get it back in working order again-don't plan on that happening any time in the near future). Just south of this anchorage sits a very special cave that can be entered by dinghy. Three natural holes in the roof of the cave allow streams of light to enter the cave making this a very peaceful little grotto. Along the back wall is another window leading out onto the back side of a hill overlooking a lake. This window can be reached from the beach just north of the cave and from here you can climb right down onto the conch shell floor of the cave.

At the northern end of Flamingo Cay is a beautiful beach and a good anchorage in winds from southeast to southwest. In strong winds from east to southeast there can be a bit of surge. You will obviously not want to be here in any northerly wind. To enter the anchorage you can turn to port as you come in Flamingo Cut and steer right up to the beach to anchor in 6'-9'. From the west you can pass north of the offlying reef northwest of Flamingo Cay or pass between it and the small rocks stretching northwest of Flamingo Cay. There is a dinghy channel between Flamingo Cay and the first rock leading off to the northwest. On the beach at this anchorage you will find the wreckage of a small, single engine amphibious plane.

At the southern end of Flamingo Cay lie two very conspicuous, large dome shaped rocks. Between them and Flamingo Cay is a pocket of water 15' deep at the end of the creek that separates Flamingo Cay from its southern tip. Between these rocks and Flamingo Cay a shallow draft vessel of 2'-3' draft could find protection from a frontal passage in about 3' of water. Care must be used if you attempt to tie up in here. The anchorage shoals quickly to the

north and is quite rocky. Check it out by dinghy first or head south to Buena Vista Cay if a front threatens. This area is a breeding ground and nursery for nurse sharks that frequent the area in May and June.

Divers will want to check out the numerous small heads lying along the western shore of Flamingo Cay well out into the anchorage area. Just northeast of the small cays lying northwest of Flamingo Cay is a beautiful Elkhorn and Staghorn coral reef whose top dries at low water.

To Buena Vista Cay

Man Of War Shoal - outer break-N of:
22° 48.75' N, 75° 54.66' W

Man Of War Shoal - inner break-N of:
22° 48.75' N, 75° 54.00' W

Man Of War Shoal - outer break-S of:
22° 48.05' N, 75° 54.66' W

Man Of War Shoal - inner break-S of:
22° 48.05' N, 75° 54.00' W

Jamaica Cay - ½ nm W of:
22° 44.55' N, 75° 55.10' W

Nurse Channel - ½ nm W of Channel Cay:
22° 31.30' N, 75° 50.40' W

Nurse Cay - ½ nm W of:
22° 28.60' N, 75° 51.70' W

Navigational Information

South of Flamingo Cay to Man of War Cay (as shown on Chart JU-6) are a small string of cays with narrow but deep cuts between most. I do not recommend these cuts for use if you wish to gain access to Flamingo Cay unless you have absolutely calm conditions and good visibility. It is far safer to use *Flamingo Cut*.

The first cay immediately south of Flamingo Cay is called Brigantine Cay, or more often Brig Cay, and the cleft in it is called *Brig Cay Cut*. Many, many years ago a brigantine was caught off Brig Cay in a gale and was unable to claw her way to windward. Flirting with disaster the Captain spied the narrow opening in the cay and estimated it to be just a few yards wider than his spars. He squared away and sailed right through the cut to a safe anchorage in the lee along the western shore.

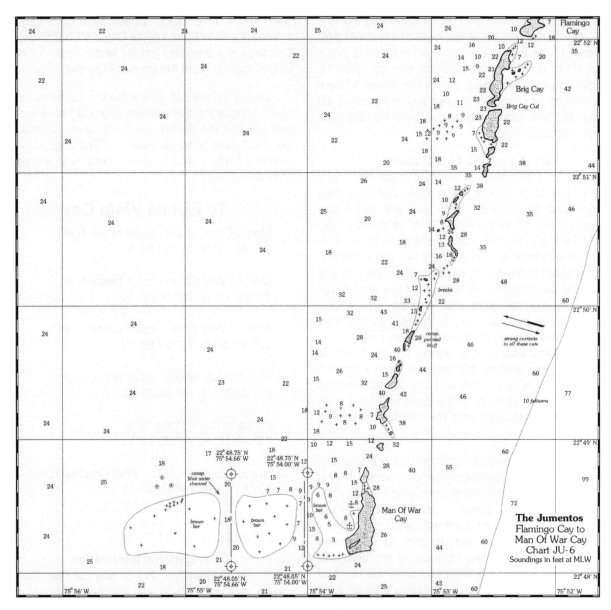

The Jumentos
Flamingo Cay to
Man Of War Cay
Chart JU-6
Soundings in feet at MLW

Man of War Cay offers some small lee in strong east to southeast winds just off the rocky beach on its western shore. There is a small cave in the cliff to the north of the beach and the wreckage of some small boats ashore.

Off the southwestern tip of Man of War Cay is a reef that stretches westward out onto the banks for approximately two miles. Vessels headed south to Jamaica Cay, your next recommended stop, can pass either out into deep water to avoid this shallow brown bar or head out onto the banks to bypass the shallows or go right through them the way the Mailboats do. If you wish to head out onto the banks to bypass the reef you must go to at least 75° 56'.00

W to clear the western tip of the reef before you head southwards to Jamaica Cay. If you wish to act like a mailboat, then read on.

There are two passages through this reef that you can take to avoid heading further west onto the bank. If you wish to parallel the string of cays as you head north or south you can take the inside route, just off

Man of War Cay. Approximately ¼ mile west of the southwest tip of Man of War Cay is a small break in the reef and a deep blue channel that leads through it. From the south the channel is much easier to discern. If you stay in the center of the channel you will have 9' at low water all the way through. The northern end is much harder to distinguish, especially if the light is in your eyes. The northern end of the channel lies between two brown bars just west of the northern tip of Man of War Cay. a waypoint at 22° 48.75' N, 75° 54.00' W will place you in the approximate area to search for the deep channel by eye, approximately ¼ mile north of it. As you look southward you will see the deep blue water of the channel and you must line up with that and steer between the two brown bars in 9' at MLW. I have run right down 75° 54.00' W keeping an eye on the two brown bars. From the south, a waypoint at 22° 48.05' N, 75° 54.00' W, will place you just south of the southern end of the channel where you should easily pick up the deeper blue water by eye in good visibility.

If you cannot read the water that well (and how did you get this far if you can't?) you may wish to try the other break in the reef that lies approximately 1 mile west of Man of War Cay. This break is a much more conspicuous deep blue channel with 17'-22' throughout. A waypoint at 22° 48.75' N, 75° 54.66' W, will place you approximately ¼ mile north of the cut. Head southward in the middle of the deep, wide, dark blue channel and you will soon be back in deep water. If you are approaching from the south,

a waypoint at 22° 48.05' N, 75° 54.66' W, will place you approximately ¼ mile south of the cut. From this position head north through the cut and you will soon be back in deep water. There, that wasn't so hard was it? You can now qualify to take the exam to drive a mailboat.

Man of War Cay has what appears to be a very pretty beach on its southwestern shore but as you approach you will notice that it is extremely rocky and may not be worth the trouble to land. There is a small cave hole on the small hill north of the beach and the wreckage of some small boats ashore. *Man of War Channel* (Chart JU-7), deep and wide, lies just south of Man of War Cay and stretches southward some three miles or so to Jamaica Cay with no hazards except rough conditions when strong wind or swell opposes the tide, but you can say that about all the cuts in The Bahamas.

A waypoint at 22° 44.55' N, 75° 55.10' W, will place you approximately ½ mile west of Jamaica Cay. To enter the anchorage at Jamaica Cay as shown on Chart JU-7A, you can pass either north or south of the small rock that lies just northwest of the house on Jamaica Cay. You can anchor off the northwestern shore of Jamaica Cay or just below the house in the small cove in 13' (see next paragraph about moorings). Both anchorages are subject to swell and have a grass/sand bottom. There is a small cove on the southern side of the island where you can tuck in during northerly/northeasterly weather. Although some protection from west/southwest winds can be found in the lee of the large rocks lying just to the west of the cay, this anchorage is not recommended for a frontal passage, better to head south to Buena Vista Cay or preferably, Raccoon Cay.

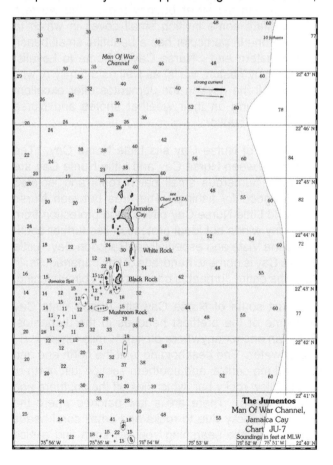

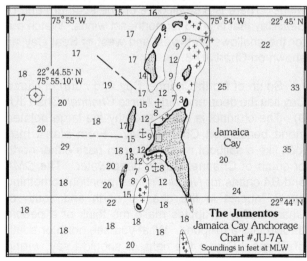

Jamaica Cay is the only cay north of Ragged Island that is inhabited. Here you may sometimes find Perseus ("Everybody calls me Percy!") Wilson. Percy is in the midst of transforming Jamaica Cay in to what will someday soon be quite a resort. He is building 15 one-bedroom cottages, 5 two-bedroom cottages, and a fuel dock. In the near future he will be placing moorings west of his house in that anchorage area between his house and the small cay to the west. This he says, will save whatever reef is left. If you do plan to anchor at Jamaica Cay, you may want to anchor out of the reef area. Percy currently has two large tanker trucks on shore for diesel and gasoline. If you need fuel he may be able to help you even though his fuel dock is not yet open. Percy also owns *Percy's Eagle's Nest*, the famous bar built into an airplane body just south of Duncan Town (you will read more on that in the section on Duncan Town and Ragged Island).

From Jamaica Cay southward it is a long haul, approximately 15 miles, over very exposed water until you reach the lee of Nurse Cay. Between Jamaica Cay and Nurse Cay are a lot of very small cays and rocks with the only decent lee available at Seal Cay (Chart JU-8). One can go south from Jamaica Cay either on the inside in water ranging from 7' to over 40' or outside in the deeper waters of the *Crooked Island Passage*. If you plan to parallel the cays be sure to keep an eye out for small rocks as shown on Charts JU-7 and JU-8, especially in the vicinity of *Jamaica Spit*, south of Jamaica Cay and southwest of Black Rock. Here depths range from 7' to 30' with scattered patch reefs. Farther south you will find some rocks that are barely out of the water at high tide and easily seen in good visibility. The anchorage in the lee of Seal Cay can be a little surgy in strong winds. There is a small cove on the southern end of Seal Cay that is good for northeast winds. Watch out for the shallows northwest and west of Seal Cay as shown on Chart JU-8.

South of North Channel Cay and north of Nurse Cay lies the deep and wide *Nurse Channel* (Chart JU-9). The channel is easily seen by the large pointed stone beacon on Channel Cay. From afar it may look like a sailboat mast. You can pass either north or south of Channel Cay in deep water. The *DMA* and *BA* charts for *Nurse Channel* mention something about "ripples in the channel north and south of Channel Cay. Ripples make me think of a pebble thrown into a millpond. What you see north or south of Channel Cay in the right, or should I say, wrong

conditions is certainly not ripples. As in most of the cuts in the Jumentos, a strong wind opposing an outgoing tide makes for some truly horrendous seas in the cuts. You can have the same conditions with little or no wind but a strong ground swell running. Seas in the cuts in these conditions can be anywhere from 6'-10' high and very close together. These are definitely not ripples. Use caution in these conditions. When such seas are in evidence you can still head north or south out on the banks. These "ripples" are confined to the areas of the cuts only. Don't forget that a strong easterly wind can create 6' seas well out onto the banks.

Once you reach the lee of Nurse Cay (Chart JU-10) you will again have smooth, calm seas in which to sail. A waypoint at 22° 28.60' N, 75° 51.70' W will place you approximately one mile west of Nurse Cay. Nurse Cay is named after the nurse sharks that once frequented the small creek on its southern shores in May and June to mate. That creek has since filled in and its mouth is now a beach. Nurse Cay is a beautiful cay that upon closer examination looks a bit out of place here. This is not your normal Bahamian scrub-covered cay, its shores are rather steep-to and covered with tall silver buttonwoods. The western shore offers some inviting small coves in which to anchor, one in particular has a beautiful small beach at its eastern end. Nurse Cay is home to Loyalist ruins (many pasture walls) as well as a family of wild goats. All the cays in the Jumentos offer excellent beachcombing on their weather shores and Nurse Cay is no exception.

South of Nurse Cay sits Little Nurse Cay. The waters between Nurse Cay and Little Nurse Cay are home to numerous small patch reefs and isolated heads, good for fishing. The area between Nurse Cay and Little Nurse Cay offers good protection from northerly winds but ideal protection lies further south at Buena Vista and especially at Raccoon Cay. Little Nurse Cay is home to hundreds of tiny bananaquits, in fact, the entire Jumentos offer excellent birdwatching.

Just south of Nurse Cay sits Buena Vista Cay with one of the prettiest beaches in the Jumentos. You can anchor anywhere off its 1½ mile length in 6'-12' of water. The best holding is at the north end and around the central and southern section just north of the shallow rocky bar, which lies off the southern end of the beach. There are a few patches where the holding is tricky due to rocks and small coral heads but with a little searching you will soon find a nice

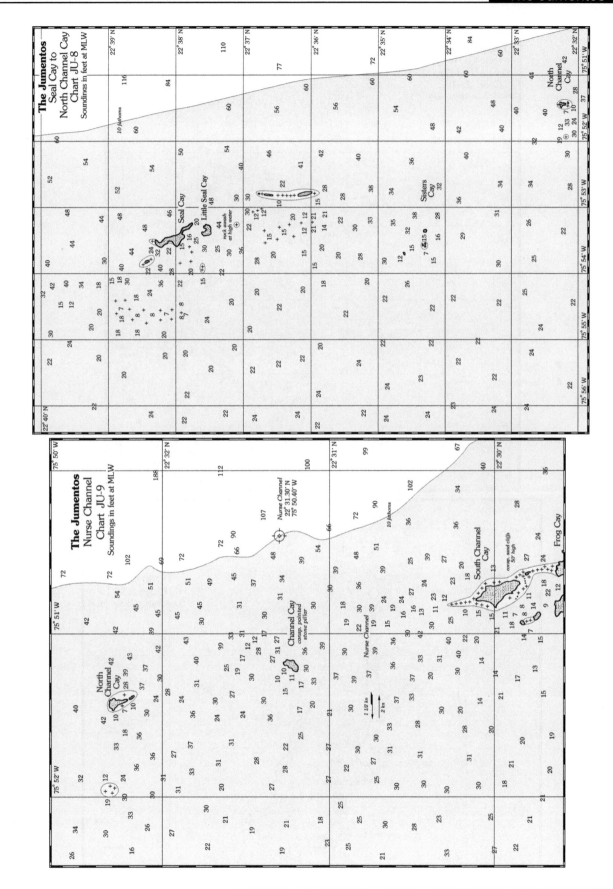

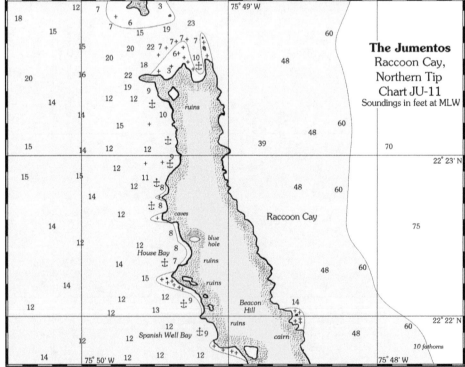

The Jumentos
Frog Cay to
Buena Vista Cay
Chart JU-10
Soundings in feet at MLW

22° 28.60' N
75° 51.70' W

Frog Cay
Knife Cay
Nurse Cay
Little Nurse Cay
Buena Vista Cay
Low Water Harbour Cay
Raccoon Cay

The Jumentos
Raccoon Cay,
Northern Tip
Chart JU-11
Soundings in feet at MLW

Raccoon Cay
ruins
caves
blue hole
House Bay
ruins
ruins
Beacon Hill
ruins
cairn
Spanish Well Bay
10 fathoms

plot of sand to set your anchor in. Holding is good though it's still a good idea to dive on your anchor. This anchorage is excellent even in strong east winds. Strong northeast or southeast winds, above 20 knots, causes a small surge to work its way around the points to roll you, not dangerously mind you, but sometimes very uncomfortably.

Buena Vista is home to goats, chickens, and I am told, a wild horse although I have not seen it or any sign of it, although I have seen a trio of pink flamingos off the point at the north end of the anchorage and many tropic birds performing their Springtime aerial mating rituals off the windward shore. Ashore you will find a trail marked by a white steel pipe about halfway down the beach that leads to a tiny cavern in the small hill.

Vessels seeking shelter from a frontal passage can pass south of Buena Vista and anchor in the deep channel between Low Water Harbour Cay and Buena Vista Cay (see Chart JU-10). Try to tuck up into the north as far as you can. The holding here is poor in places as the bottom is scoured so dive on your anchor. This area is open somewhat to the southwest but once the wind is into the west and northwest you are protected. When the wind shifts to the northeast you should immediately head back around to the western shore of Buena Vista and tuck into the calm pocket at the northern end of the beach.

Just south of Low Water Harbour Cay is a series of small, unnamed cays. There is a pass between low Water Harbour Cay and the first cay to its south with 6' at low water. Between this cay and the one to its east is a small pocket of slightly deeper water where one shallow draft vessel could find shelter from a front. Once again, as the wind clocks into the north, head back to the northern end of the beach on Buena Vista.

Raccoon Cay to Ragged Island

Raccoon Cut-¾ nm NNE of:
22° 21.45' N, 75° 47.00' W

Hog Cay-¼ nm W of southernmost beach:
22° 14.60' N, 75° 45.50' W

Little Ragged Island-¾ nm SW of:
22° 08.65' N, 75° 40.00' W

Raccoon Cay is a little over three miles long and is similar to Nurse Cay in that its western shore is home

to a growth of silver buttonwoods. The island is home to numerous ruins and pasture walls, a small house at the south end of house bay, and more buildings on the hills above *House Bay*. At the southern end of the cay are some ruins of a wall 6' high and 7' thick. The Ragged Islanders say there is a cemetery amidst the ruins and Bob and Anita on the *M/V Janice L* found a cemetery marker here. There are no raccoons on the cay but plenty of goats that the Ragged Islanders hunt. Raccoon Cay was once worked for salt and large boats would enter Raccoon Cut and anchor in the lee of Johnson Cay to take on their cargo of that commodity from Raccoon Cay and Ragged Island. The old Loyalist salt pond found just inland still has the walled slots for the sluice gate intact. There is a walled well at Spanish Well Bay, presumably named after Spanish seafarers who made use of its waters.

Navigational Information
From Buena Vista Cay the approach to Raccoon Cay is fairly simple (Chart JU-11), clear the southern point of Buena Vista Cay and head straight for Raccoon Cay, no waypoints needed, none given. At the northern end of Raccoon Cay is a small cove good in south to southwest winds. In east to southeast the anchorage is quite rolly. The entrance is narrow, between a shallow reef area lying off the northern shore of Raccoon Cay, as shown on Chart JU-11 and the reef and rocks extending northward from the northeastern tip of Raccoon Cay. Once inside you will find about 10' over hard sand. Dive on your anchor here! Proceeding southward along the western shore of Raccoon Cay you will find quite a few small coves in which to drop your hook. Most are a little surgy in strong (20+ knots) northeast to southeast winds The prettiest anchorage is in House Bay just north of Pimlico Cay. From here you can go ashore and explore the ruins on the hill and the old salt pond.

Vessels seeking shelter from a frontal passage have an excellent harbor between Raccoon Cay and Nairn Cay but one must play the winds correctly. Here, though open to the southeast and south, you will find protection from southwest through northeast. Once the wind is in the northeast it is time to consider moving back to the beach at Buena Vista or the western shore of Raccoon Cay. If a front threatens and the wind is still southeast to south, you should consider moving to the beautiful anchorage in the small cove on the northern shore of Johnson Cay. Although this is a surgy anchorage in easterly weather it is very calm in southeast to southwest. The entrance to Johnson

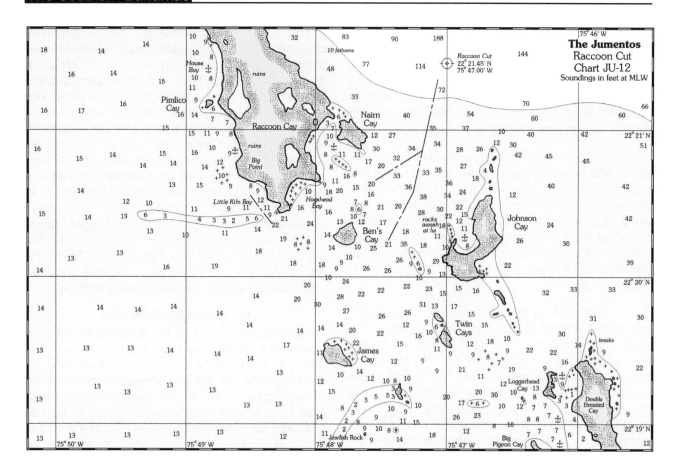

The Jumentos
Raccoon Cut
Chart JU-12
Soundings in feet at MLW

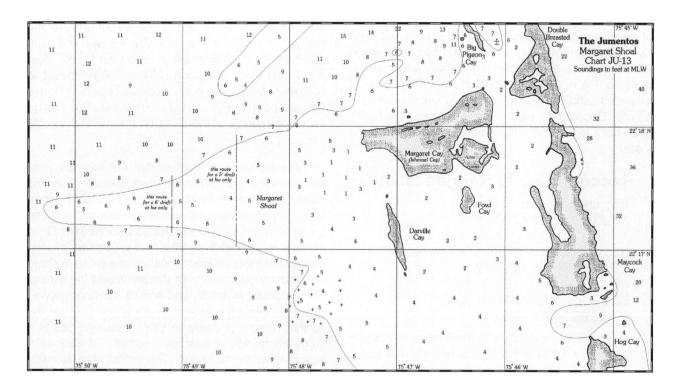

The Jumentos
Margaret Shoal
Chart JU-13
Soundings in feet at MLW

Cay is fairly straightforward between the rocks that are awash off its northwestern tip and the string of cays leading northeastward from Johnson Spit. Use caution when rounding the rocks that are awash at low water, I have heard of a boat that was holed here. There is 8'-10' however between Johnson Cay and the small rock that lies just off its northwestern tip.

Once inside Johnson Cay you should plan to ride out the pre-frontal winds from southeast to west. This is exactly when the anchorage at Nairn Cay is the roughest. Once the wind comes into the southwest to west, preferably west, grit your teeth and tough it out for the one mile run to the anchorage between Raccoon Cay and Nairn Cay, but not at night. Once safely inside (watch out for the rocky bar in the middle of the entrance as shown on Chart JU-12), you will once again be in calm water. The reason you should sit at Johnson Cay is because Nairn can be very rough in southeast through just southwest winds. If sitting at Nairn Cay during those conditions appeals to you more than crossing Raccoon Cut in westerly weather, (for the most part Ben's Cay will give you a slight lee), by all means make yourself at home. I only offer these suggestions, it is up to each skipper to make the correct decisions concerning the safety of his or her own vessel.

Boats wishing to gain entry to the banks through *Raccoon Cut* will find it fairly easy and deep. A waypoint at 22° 21.45' N, 75° 47.00' W, will place you approximately ½ nautical mile northeast of the cut and well north of Johnson Spit, the shallow breaking area that lies northward of Johnson Cay as shown on Chart JU-12. Steer southwestward between Nairn Cay and Johnson Cay. You can then take Ben's Cay on either side, to the north if you wish to head up to the anchorages off the western shore of Raccoon Cay, or to the south if you plan to head around Margaret Shoal and southward.

Keep an eye out for the shallow area just north and east of Ben's Cay, in an easterly sea rollers will heap up and break upon it.

Vessels transiting the western shore of Raccoon Cay must negotiate a shallow bar that stretches westward approximately 1½ miles from the southwestern tip of Raccoon Cay. Those vessels with drafts of less than 8' can pass between the shoal and Raccoon Cay at low water staying about 50-100 yards off Raccoon Cay. The ability to read the water would come in handy here as the shoal is very visible.

South of Johnson Cay sits Double Breasted Cay where you will find a small and surgy anchorage between its northern tip and Loggerhead Cay. This anchorage is protected from southeast to west but not the place to be in any northerly wind. Another nice anchorage in settled weather is south of Loggerhead Cay in the bight between Big Pigeon Cay, sometimes called Golding Cay, and Double Breasted Cay.

Shallow draft vessels can of course explore the waters much closer to Double Breasted Cay and find better shelter in its lee. This anchorage offers a little lee from west winds in the shelter of Big Pigeon Cay. Wild goats roam the shores of Double Breasted and good beachcombing abounds on the windward side of the island, in fact I have heard of people finding bales of marijuana on the eastern beach of Double Breasted Cay (no joke intended).

Margaret Cay, sometimes called Ishmael Cay, lies south of Raccoon Cut and west of Double Breasted Cay and stretches in an east/west direction. It is home to a family of goats, numerous mosquitoes, caves, large stands of lignumvitae, ruins on the southeastern tip, and is accessible only by dinghy.

Vessels heading south from *Raccoon Cut* to Hog Cay, Ragged Island, or Little Ragged Island must negotiate the large, westward stretching *Margaret Shoal*, a huge shallow sandbank stretching almost three miles out onto the banks. Shallow draft vessels, 3' or less, can shorten their trip by using the tide and cutting across the narrow bank at least ½ mile west of Margaret Cay. I draw 5' and I cross the bank at high tide anywhere west of 75° 48.50' W by steering south down that longitude. But only a rising, almost high tide. A 6' draft can cross *Margaret Shoal* at 75° 49.00' W. If you are a skipper of great wisdom and don't wish to gamble on a shortcut you must go to 75° 50.00' W where you can head south in relative comfort just west of the shoal.

Once past the western end of *Margaret Shoal* you can begin steering southeast towards Hog Cay paralleling *Margaret Shoal* on your port side. The shoal edges out near Darville Cay and the unnamed rocks lying between Darville Cay and Hog Cay. Once past the shoal it is best to steer to the southern end of Hog Cay. You will see some large whitish cliffs in the center of Hog Cay, don't steer for those, steer for the second beach south of the cliffs.

A waypoint at 22° 14.60' N, 75° 45.50' W, sits almost a half mile west of the beach at Hog Cay and is as good a spot as any to head for. Use caution when headed for this spot though. Make sure the currents don't sweep you north towards the southern edge of *Margaret Shoal* or south towards the shallow area that lies southwest of Hog Cay. You can anchor off either of the two beaches or under the white cliffs at Hog Cay. Do not head straight for the cliffs, head for the beach and then when just off Hog Cay, steer northward in the deeper water between *Margaret Shoal* and the Hog Cay towards the cliff. The beaches offer the least surge and good holding in soft grass/sand. The anchorage off Hog Cay offers better protection in prevailing conditions than Ragged Island Harbour and they are but a short dinghy ride from the entrance to Duncan Town.

Hog Cay is covered in a dense growth and was used for raising cattle, primarily Brahma bulls in the 1970s and 1980s. One Ragged Islander told me a story of a *Defence Force* vessel that landed on Hog Cay whose crew killed a Brahma Bull and only took the hindquarters. The owner was furious when he found out and he filed a claim with the government asking for $50,000 saying the unfortunate creature was his prime breeding bull. I was told he received some compensation but no amount was mentioned. There are still some wild goats on the cay. There are quite a few ruins on the southern shore of Hog Cay just east of Hog Point. At the north end of the second beach to the north are the ruins of a pasture wall. Follow this wall to an old salt pond, from there you can follow the trail to the eastern shore where you will find some offlying reefs that form some sheltered pools ideal for snorkeling.

Ragged Island

Little Ragged Island-¾ nm SW of:
22° 08.65' N, 75° 40.00' W

Ragged Islanders are not dependent on the tourist trade, some still work the salt ponds in the area and of course many fish. From the abolition of slavery up until the 1960s, Ragged Island relied heavily on the salt trade with Cuba and Haiti. Ragged Islanders received fruits, vegetables, and other goods that they could not produce in exchange for their salt and fish. After Castro came to power the salt industry went into decline to the point that there is virtually no production today at all except for personal consumption. Part of the reason is that there is no access to Duncan Town due to the shallowness of the waters. As a result the islands population has declined from about 500 in the 1950s to about 100 inhabitants today. The amount

of uninhabited houses give silent testimony to a more active past.

Today the economy of Ragged Island is based on the richness of the sealife in the surrounding waters. I talked to a marine biologist who was involved with grouper studies in Nassau and the Exumas who told me that the majority of groupers in the Nassau markets come from the Jumentos and the Ragged Island areas. As a side note, the last monk seal seen in The Bahamas was spotted off Ragged Island in 1957.

Ragged Islanders are quite a different breed altogether than can be found in the rest of The Bahamas. Here people talk to you as equals, neither up or down, and are extremely friendly and helpful. Duncan Towners have been by themselves so long, so very few cruising boats as well as Bahamians visit this area, that they have become fiercely independent. The Ragged Islanders have a strong feeling of being forgotten by their own government, they received no assistance after Hurricane Kate in 1985. Nevertheless, they are determined to restore the island to some semblance of its former glory. They are confident that with a new harbour trade that could be revived, new jobs created, and the youth of the island would be more interested in staying put and working towards a revitalization of the community.

Duncan Towners look forward to increased yacht traffic and the financial boom that it will bring. It will be up to you, the cruiser that visits this cay, to insure that you hold up your end of the bargain and don't become a burden as some thoughtless cruisers in other areas have done. Drop your trash off at the town dock, someone will pick it up and take it to the dump. Don't play the ugly, insensitive, tourist. Ragged Islanders are truly warm people, respect shown will be respect returned. These folks are truly different than any other Bahamians you will meet.

Navigational Information
South of Hog Cay lies *Ragged Island Harbour* and the entrance to Duncan Town as shown on Chart JU-14. I do not recommend the cut between Hog Cay and Ragged Island unless you are familiar with the waters of this area or are adept at reading the waters of this area. There are three reefs guarding the entrance to this cut, two at the eastern end that make up what is called the *Outer Bar Reef*, and one inside directly between Hog Cay and Ragged Island called the *Inner Bar Reef*.

If entering from offshore come in on a southwesterly course passing southeast of the rock beacon on *Black Rock Reef*. This course takes you inside the *Outer Bar Reefs*. Southwest of the beacon lies the dangerous and extensive *Inner Bar Reef*, which is easily seen as it breaks with almost any sea. Although the northern side is best, you can pass to either side of it. Watch out for the shallow spot, 5' at low water, lying southwest of the reef and north of Gun Point. There is a new light on Black Rock, sometime shown as Bulva Rock (see Chart JU-14).

An often surgy lee anchorage can be found just west of the northwestern tip of Ragged Island in *Ragged Island Harbour*, just below the conspicuous diesel tank that fuels the power generator and *Batelco* office in Duncan Town.

Ragged Island is approximately 4 miles long lying in a NW/SSE direction. Duncan Town, the only settlement, lies at the south end of a natural bay of shallow water. The settlement was named after Duncan Taylor, a Loyalist who discovered the island's charms in the early 18th century. Taylor, with his brother's help, built the salt ponds in the town's vicinity with slave labor and many of the inhabitants of Duncan Town are direct descendants of the slaves and bear their names. Here you will find names like Lockhart, Munroe, Curling, Wilson, Moxey, and Maycock.

Skippers wishing to enter the waters of Duncan Town from Hog Cay should head south from Hog Cay past Pigeon Rock, Pass Cay, (with its conspicuous large cross), and enter the shallow bank just west of Salt Cay, sometimes called Pigeon Cay. Pass Cay, sometimes called Bishop Cay, has a very conspicuous wooden cross on it. I have been told that a Catholic Bishop, some say a Church of England Bishop, drowned here. The telling has it that his body was not found, only his clothes. The cross was erected in his memory.

As you enter the shallow banks northwest of Salt Cay you will begin to see a white channel between two grassy shoals. This is the channel to follow, it has been swept clean by the constant outboard traffic hence the white sand bottom. The channel begins to bend to the southeast at Baachus Point and you will enter the dredged portion of the channel. You may see the remains of the old channel heading off to the east as you enter the dredged portion. Do not follow the old channel, it will just shallow out. In years

past, small sloops would sail down this channel into town. Old timers can tell you of days when there were upwards of 100 small sloops in the harbour awaiting salt to carry out to ships waiting at *Raccoon Cut* or *Ragged Island Harbour*. Follow the dredged channel into the basin and tie up to the town dock but be sure to leave room for fishing boats. There are spots in the channel that are well over 6' deep at high water while the inner harbour barely carries 5'-6', mostly 3'-4'.

What You Will Find Ashore

Straight up the steep hill from the dock sits the pink *Government Building*. This may well be your first stop. Lovely Charlene, the secretary, will be happy to tell you where to go for what you need. Here you may also see the Duncan Town jail, little more than one tiny cell that has been so little used that it is now a storage room, a pleasant testimony to Duncan Town.

High on a hill south of town is a simple masonry mound designed with thirteen steps all around. The inscription reads as follows:

In memory of ICELY, LLOYD
and one seaman of H.M.S. THUNDER,
who were drowned near the Brothers Rocks.
23/1/31

Medical Assistance

Up the hill to the right is the clinic; the nurse comes in the afternoon but if you need her ask anyone you see.

Mechanical Repairs

If you need a repairman for your outboard engine, contact Alpheas Nespitt, known as *Fish*, or Derek Carter, who uses the handle *Monkey Man* on the VHF.

Dining

On the main road you can dine at *Sheila's Fisherman's Lounge*. Nearby is the *Ponderosa Bar and Grill*. A short walk out of town, though easily accessible by dinghy if you land on the beach at *Southside Bay* (Chart JU-15), is the famous *Percy's Eagle's Nest*. Here Percy Wilson (Remember Percy from Jamaica Cay?), owns and operates the unique bar that is constructed using a DC-3 as its focal point. The bar is once again open so stop in and have a cold one, and say hello to Percy.

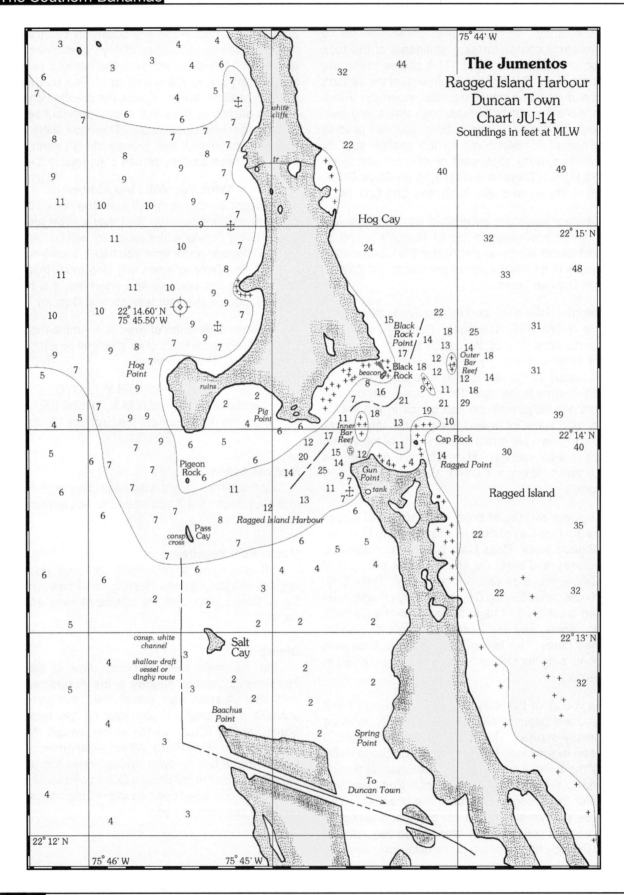

The Jumentos
Ragged Island Harbour
Duncan Town
Chart JU-14
Soundings in feet at MLW

Hog Cay

white cliffs

tr

22° 14.60' N
75° 45.50' W

Hog Point

ruins

Black Rock Point

Black Rock

beacon

Outer Bar Reef

Pig Point

Inner Bar Reef

Cap Rock

Ragged Point

Gun Point

tank

Pigeon Rock

Ragged Island Harbour

Pass Cay

consp cross

Ragged Island

consp. white channel

shallow draft vessel or dinghy route

Salt Cay

Baachus Point

Spring Point

To Duncan Town

22° 15' N

22° 14' N

22° 13' N

22° 12' N

75° 44' W

75° 46' W

75° 45' W

Provisioning

To the left of the *Batelco* tower is *Louie's Sweet Shop* with great bread and pies made to order (but you'll have to order in advance). On the main road is *Angie's Grocery*. Across from the clinic is *Maxine's*, a small but well-stocked grocery and dry goods store. Cephas Maycock, owner of the *Ponderosa Bar and Grill*, also sells fresh produce when he can get them from the mailboat. *Louisa's Sweet Place* is the spot to go for fresh bread and baked goods to order.

RO Water

Water is available at the *Government Building*, please ask first, the community has a new R/O plant strictly for community usage.

Fuel

If you need gasoline, ask Charlene at the *Government Building* or Maxine Wallace if they know of anybody who can let you have a few gallons. Bear in mind that everybody here gets their fuel in 55-gallon drums from the mailboat and it is a rare and valuable commodity, their fishing boats depend upon having an ample supply of gasoline. If you need diesel you may be able to persuade Leander Maycock, who runs the *Batelco* office, to allow you to purchase a few gallons from their supply.

Garbage

If you have sealed bags of garbage, leave them at the concrete dock and someone will take them away.

Navigational Information

Vessels headed south to Little Ragged Island must pass west of Ragged Island to clear the shallows lying just off the western shore. There is a pleasant anchorage off the northwest tip of Little Ragged Island and another in *Southside Bay* in settled weather as shown on Chart JU-15. Lockhart Cay, just north of Little Ragged Island, was once the home to a boat building facility many years ago. The small harbour to its west is called *Boat Harbour* and is often used as a hurricane hole. Ask any Ragged Islander how to find the twisting route into its semi-safe water.

If approaching Little Ragged Island from offshore a waypoint at 22° 08.65' N, 75° 40.00' W, will place you a little over a mile southeast of Little Ragged Island. From here head southwest and pass around the small rocks lying south of Little Ragged Island and head up the western shore at least a quarter mile off. Watch out for the reef off the southwest tip of Little Ragged Island as shown on Chart JU-16.

If passing south of Little Ragged Island keep a sharp lookout for Hobson Breaker. A dangerous rock that dries at low water, Hobson Breaker lies approximately two miles south of Little Ragged Island. By the way, you're only about 60 miles from Cuba here.

Little Ragged Island is privately owned as plans for a resort/cottages complex are in the works. For more information ask Percy. Off the eastern shore of Little Ragged Island is a white limestone cliff called *Lover's Leap*, a perfect spot for distraught lovers.

Cay Verde lies approximately 35 miles east/southeast of Little Ragged Island across the *Columbus Bank*, at the southeast tip of the *Great Bahama Bank* and *West Channel*, the channel that lies to the west of the Mira Por Vos Cays. Cay Verde is a surgy anchorage at best but is a fair lee for vessels headed to Great Inagua or the *Windward Passage*. Approximately 30 miles south of Little Ragged Island lies Santa Domingo Cay at the southern tip of the *Great Bahama Bank* at its junction with the western end of the *Old Bahama Channel*. The fishing around these cays is outstanding as evidenced by the amount of illegal Cuban and Hispaniolian fishermen who frequent this area. The *Royal Bahamas Defence Force* has regular patrols in the southern waters of The Bahamas to fight poaching by non-Bahamian fishing vessels. From Ragged Island southeastward to Inagua the VHF is often filled with Cuban, Dominican, and Haitian voices.

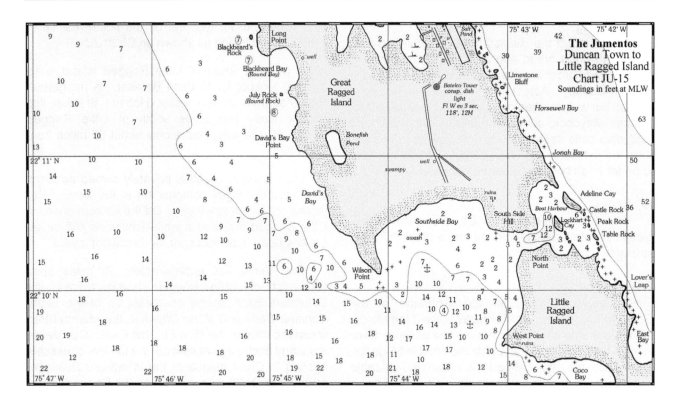

The Jumentos
Duncan Town to
Little Ragged Island
Chart JU-15
Soundings in feet at MLW

The Jumentos
Little Ragged Island
to Hobson Breaker
Chart JU-16
Soundings in feet at MLW

Crooked Island District

Ports of Entry: None
Fuel: Crooked Island
Haul-Out: None
Diesel Repairs: Crooked Island
Outboard Repairs: Crooked Island
Propane: Crooked Island
Provisions: Crooked Island
Important Lights:
Bird Rock Lighthouse: Fl W ev 15 sec
Attwood Harbour: Fl W ev 5 sec
Hell Gate: Fl W ev 6 sec
Windsor Point: Fl W ev 3 sec
Castle Island Lighthouse: Gp. Fl (2) W ev 20 sec

Though all the others we had seen were beautiful, green and fertile, this was even more so. It has large and very green trees, and great lagoons, around which these trees stand in marvelous groves. Here and there throughout the island the trees and plants are as green as Andalusia in April. The singing of small birds is so sweet that no one could ever wish to leave this place. Flocks of parrots darken the sun and there is a marvelous variety of large and small birds.
Christopher Columbus,
describing Crooked Island

The Crooked Island District is composed of three major islands, Crooked Island, Acklins Island, and Long Cay, which together encompass approximately 260 square miles of land lying inside twice that amount of shallow water. On some old charts the cays are called *The Fragrant Islands*. When Columbus visited the island group on October 21, 1492, the rich aroma of the cascarilla bark caused him to think that he had discovered the Spice Islands of the Indies. It is said that Columbus was directed to Crooked Island by Lucayan Indians who spoke of an island called *Samoete* and of gold being found there. Finding no such island or gold, Columbus continued on toward Cuba. Columbus christened Crooked Island *Isabella* after his Queen and named Portland Harbour *Cabo Hermoso* or *Beautiful Cape*.

The islands and cays that make up the Crooked/Acklins group are still untouched by large developments and retain much of their natural flavor. Acklins is a very peaceful, undisturbed, quiet island where the residents say you have to "...make your own sunshine," in other words you are on your own. The cays are home for flocks of pink flamingos,

osprey, egrets, and herons and the waters of some of the interior sections of the *Bight of Acklins* are excellent for bonefish and tarpon.

In the 1800s the Crooked Island District was more populated than any other Bahamian Islands. Albert Town on Long Cay was a *Port of Entry* and was heavily visited by commercial vessels. At this time Crooked Island had a population of 3,000-4,000, Acklins boasted 3,000-4,000, and Long Cay was home to almost 2,000 people. When steam replaced sail power as the principal means of ship propulsion and the shipping routes changed accordingly, the huge population of the district quickly dissipated, almost overnight, to other economically healthier areas. Today's population of over 1,200 Crooked/Acklins Islanders is far less than the original inhabitants, the Lucayan Indians. Over 30 Lucayan Indian sites have been found on Acklins Island and over 10 on Crooked Island.

Spelunkers will note that Crooked Island is noted for its extensive cave system. Today the primary export of the Crooked Island group is cascarilla and madeira bark, the base for the aperitif, *Campari*.

Approaches

The Crooked Island District lies approximately 300 nautical miles southeast of Nassau. When approaching from the northwest the first sight you will likely see is the 112' tall white lighthouse on Bird Rock lying off the northwest tip of Crooked Island or the high bluffs on the northern end of Crooked Island. Bird Rock, Chart CA-1, is home to the bright white lighthouse known as *Bird Rock Light*. Standing 112' tall and constructed of native limestone mined just behind Gun Bluff on the northern shore of Crooked Island, *Bird Rock Light* may appear to be a sailboat from far off. The light flashes white every 15 seconds and is visible for 23 nautical miles. The light is automated, but I don't think its batteries are checked very often. The last few times I've been by Bird Rock the light came on at sunset, winked a few times, and then was dark the rest of the night. Consider the light unreliable at best.

From Clarence Town, Long Island a course of 123° for 36.3 nautical miles will bring you to the waypoint north of Bird Rock. From Clarence Town, French Wells bears 134° at a distance of 44.1 miles. Bird Rock lies 26.9 miles from *Little Harbour*, Long Island, on a course of 113°, while French Wells bears 129° at a distance of 33.7 miles from Little Harbour. A course 114° for 31.6 nautical miles will bring you from the southern tip of Long Island to French Wells, while a course of 95° for 27.4 miles places you at the waypoint north of Bird Rock. The southern tip of Long Cay lies 32.6 nautical miles distant on a course of 132° from South End, Long Island. French Wells lies 84.0 nautical miles from *Raccoon Cut* in the Jumentos on a course of 84°. Bird Rock bears 158° at 53.2 miles from Port Nelson, Rum Cay.

The waypoint north of the northwestern tip of Bird Rock is 36.6 miles from the Propeller Cay anchorage at Samana Cay on a course of 260° and 27.4 miles from Attwood Harbour on a course of 293°.

Castle Island bears 338° at a distance of 75.2 miles from Matthew Town, Great Inagua, and 319° at a distance of 38.9 nautical miles from *Hogsty Reef*.

A special note for vessels transiting the waters between the Jumentos, Long Island, and the Crooked/ Acklins District: at an approximate position at 22° 50' N, 74° 48' W, lies the center of the *Diana Bank*. The approximately 100 square miles of the *Diana Bank* lies west of the southern tip of Long Cay, south/ southeast of the southern tip of Long Island, and west of *Nurse Channel* in the Jumentos. *Diana Bank* is a shallow sandbank, 35'-600' deep, lying in the midst of much deeper water, 1800'-6000' deep. With a strong swell in any direction the seas on top of the bank can get very rough as the water is pushed up the sides of this underwater obstruction. If you are experiencing rough seas in your transit of this area, by all means avoid the area of *Diana Bank*. If the seas are calm, quite unusual hereabouts, try fishing on the bank.

Concerning the Passages

The *Crooked Island Passage* is a deep and very busy thoroughfare that funnels vessels from the open Atlantic to the Jumentos, Ragged Island, Cuba, and Hispaniola. Vessels wishing to transit *Crooked Island Passage* southward are advised to steer 188° from a position 10 miles due east of San Salvador. On this route you will pass Bird Rock abeam at 6½ nautical miles. As you come abeam of *Windsor Light* at 7 nautical miles distance alter your course to 169° for 26 nautical miles to pass between Mira Por Vos and Castle Island through the *Mira Por Vos Passage*. When you are abeam of *Castle Rock Light* at 4 nautical miles distance you can alter your course once again to 165° to pass west of Cabo Maisi, Cuba.

There is an area north and northwest of Bird Rock where the *Antilles Current* meets the current

flowing through the *Crooked Island Passage*. Natural factors such as the wind, the tide, and the moon act on this area with unpredictable results. The normally northwest flowing *Antilles Current* may sometimes not flow northwest, and sea conditions can get downright nasty compared to other waters just a few miles away. If you are in this general area and note an odd current, cross-sea, or unusually suspect rough waters you might be in this very active zone. Don't panic, you'll soon pass through it.

Use caution when transiting the *Mira Por Vos Passage*. The currents generally set in a southwesterly direction directly onto the Mira Por Vos reefs. The prudent navigator should favor the steep-to Castle Island shore. If the currents should happen to be setting in a northeasterly direction (this is rare but it does happen) favor the Mira Por Vos side of the passage.

Crooked Island

Crooked Island takes its name from the lands twisted shape over hills and cliffs and through creeks and lakes. Although its 92 square miles make it larger than New Providence it only has a population of around 650. The shores of Crooked Island offers three different cruising grounds. To the north lies the reef protected windward side of the island. There are few natural harbours on this route for vessels of any draft and reef entrances are few and far between.

The leeward or western shore of Crooked Island is where most cruisers visit. The eastern shore of Crooked Island lies on the edge of the *Bight of Acklins* and generally only shoal draft vessels and dinghies transit this area except for some vessels seeking a safe lee in westerly winds off Long Cay, and of course those hardy cruisers transiting eastward towards the rarely visited western shore of Acklins Island. Let's begin our exploration of Crooked Island along its western shore, from Bird Rock to Long Cay.

Bird Rock to Landrail Point

Bird Rock - ¼ nm N of NW tip of reef:
22° 51.85' N, 74° 22.10' W

Portland Harbour - ½ nm W of entrance:
22° 50.40' N, 74° 21.90' W

Landrail Point - ½ nm W of anchorage off beach:
22° 49.10' N, 74° 21.40' W

Navigational Information

The first landfall most southbound vessels make is Bird Rock, which lies just northwest of *Portland Harbour* and Pittstown. The reef-encircled basin of *Portland Harbour* (Chart CA-1) is a fair anchorage but there is a very uncomfortable surge that works its way through here at times. This anchorage is well protected in winds from south/southeast through south to west/southwest. Is has been said that Columbus' three ships anchored here in 1492. If you wish to enter *Portland Harbour* a waypoint at 22° 50.40' N, 74° 21.90' W, will place you approximately ½ mile west of the entrance. The best water is approximately two-thirds of the distance from Pittstown to Bird Rock.

Favor the Bird Rock side of the channel heading eastward. Once inside turn to starboard and anchor wherever your draft will allow making sure to avoid the scattered reefs. Never attempt this entry at night or in poor visibility.

A better anchorage for today's skipper lies just south at Pittstown or 2½ miles further south at Landrail Point in sand and grass. The best anchorage, and with the easiest access, is about halfway down the long beach that lies just south of Pittstown. This is a lee side anchorage only and skippers should beware that they must move in the event of a frontal passage when the wind comes around to south of east. A

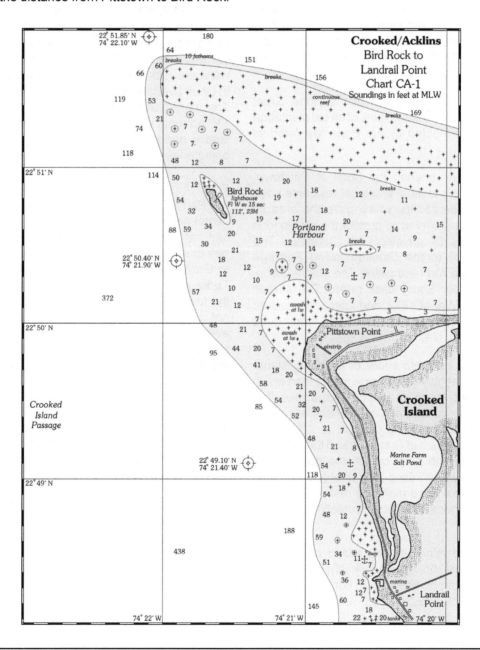

waypoint at 22° 49.10' N, 74° 21.40' W, will place you approximately ½ mile west of the beach just north of Landrail Point.

What You Will Find Ashore

Pittstown is home to a large group of primarily Canadian snowbirds and pilots as there is a large airstrip nearby. The first post office in the Bahamas was built here when William Pitt was Prime Minister of England and the remains of its walls are now part of *Pittstown Landings* which offers very nice accommodations with 12 rooms available. For more information contact *Pittstown* on VHF ch. 16. During the era of the *Napoleonic Wars* this post office served to deliver mail for the *West India Squadron* of the British fleet. This area was once surrounded by some 40 cotton plantations of 3,000 acres during the Loyalist years of 1783-1835 when some 1,200 slaves worked the local land.

History buffs will want to visit the *Hope Great House*, the centerpiece of the ruins of an old plantation which are now protected by the *Bahamas National Trust*.

Gun Bluff, just beyond the hotel at Pittstown, was once a pirate's lookout and local residents have found cannon thereabouts, which gave the area its name. These guns served to protect the plantations against the raids by privateers and pirates. The northern entrance to the *Crooked Island Passage* was guarded by a fort here called *The Marine Farm*. The U.S. Privateer *Saucy Jack* raided *The Marine Farm* during the War of 1812, and later she attacked again only to be driven off by newer and larger guns brought down from Nassau.

Between the northern shore of Crooked Island, from Gun Bluff westward to Pittstown, and then south to Landrail Point, there is a large inland lake that serves little or no current purpose. Plans are being hotly discussed to dredge a channel to it from the northern shore just west of Gun Bluff, and then another south of Pittstown to flush out all the debris, thus creating a deep water inland lake with good access. This would make a large marina a real possibility as well as offering good hurricane protection for boats and boaters.

The Crooked Island/Acklins Island area is fast becoming a prime bonefishing destination. For an excellent diving, tarpon fishing, and bonefishing guide contact Junior McKinney, *Ocean View,* or his brother Elton McKinney, *Blue Thunder* on VHF ch. 16. If

deep-sea fishing interests you more, you can contact Robbie Gibson, *Thunderbird* on the VHF to help you with your deep sea angling for dolphin, wahoo, tuna, and marlin.

Landrail Point sells no alcohol or tobacco as most of the residents are *Seventh Day Adventists*. The town is the commercial center of Crooked Island and has the usual government dock where the mailboat calls once a week, a church, a food store, a gas station, and a restaurant.

Marina

There is a small "marina" lying about ¼ mile north of the fuel tanks. It has a very narrow entrance that winds back into a small basin. A 30' long boat would be hard pressed to maneuver its way in here with 4' at low water inside and 3' at the bar at the entrance. The walls are rock and fenders are required. If you wish to tie up overnight call *Early Bird* for more information. The marina offers no amenities, no power, no cable TV, no running water, simply a place to tie up to the land if needed. As of this writing the marina was being enlarged to accommodate more small boats.

Fuel

Earl Scavella's gas station sells diesel, gas, and kerosene as well as a few basic food items. For fuel call *Early Bird* on the VHF. Unless someone befriends you in Mayaguana, or if you're headed to Great Inagua, this is the last fuel stop before the Turks and Caicos Islands. If you wish to tie up at the fuel dock that sits just south of the fuel tanks, it's not a good idea as it is very rusty and not what the average sail or motor yacht would care to tie to, you should consider med-mooring and backing in towards the dock so Kenneth Scavella can pass a long hose out to your boat by rope so you can fill your tanks.

It is possible for a small boat to enter and tie up in the marina for easy access to the fuel truck. For obvious reasons don't ask Kenneth to bring the fuel truck over to the marina for 10 or 15 gallons, instead walk the few yards to the gas station and jerry jug it back to your boat. It won't be long and someone will happen by and be glad to give you and your jerry jugs of water and gas a ride back to the marina or beach. The gas station has a faucet for well water, some may say it is a bit brackish, but I've used it for washing and find it excellent. The price is right also, it's free.

Provisioning

Next to the gas station is *Scavella's Supermarket* for your grocery needs. It may not be as well-stocked as *Exuma Markets* in George Town, but you can certainly get a few basics and frozen meats (best to wait until the day after the mailboat arrives).

Dining

You can dine out nearby at *Gibson's Lunch Room* which sits under the huge sapodilla tree just south of the fuel dock. Marina Gibson runs the place and serves excellent Bahamian dishes and delicious home-baked bread in an "at home" atmosphere. You haven't experienced Crooked Island if you haven't met Marina and had a meal with her at the *Lunch Room*. Be sure to call ahead if you intend to dine out, Marina answers to *Lunch Room* or *BASRA* as she and her son are the local *BASRA* representatives. You can have your mail sent to you care of Gibson's but expect a wait of 3-4 weeks. Have your mail sent C/O *Gibson's Lunch Room*, Landrail Point, Crooked Island, Bahamas. You can also place a telephone call from the *Lunch Room* and even take a fresh water shower.

Mechanical Repairs

If you need a diesel mechanic you can contact Timothy Thompson, *Cold Front* on the VHF, and if you are in need of an outboard mechanic contact Clinton Scavella whose VHF handle is *Snow White*.

Medical Assistance

There is a medical clinic at Landrail Point, the *Landrail Point Community Clinic*, at 242-344-2166.

French Wells

French Wells-1¼ nm NW of entrance:
22° 41.40' N, 74° 18.90' W

Just about a half-mile south of Landrail Point are some small bluffs that are deeply undercut. These are full of small cave-like openings that are perfect

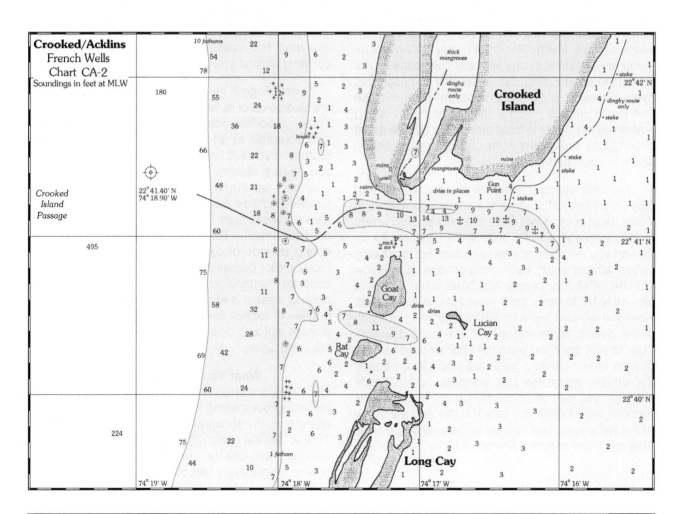

for diving and exploration. Never bring the big boat in here, there are far too many shallow reefs. When heading south along the shore of Crooked Island south of Landrail Point give the land a berth of at least a mile to avoid the shallow reefs and sandbars which lie well to the west in places.

Off the southern tip of Crooked Island, between Crooked Island and Long Cay, is French Wells, named by the French for its fresh water supply. Here you will find the ruins of an old fortification including an old cannon. A lovely sight, if you are fortunate, is to wake up and see a flock of pink flamingos wading in the shallows near the anchorage.

Navigational Information

A waypoint at 22° 41.40' N, 74° 18.90' W, will place you approximately 1 nautical mile west of the entrance to the anchorage at French Wells as shown on Chart CA-2 (if you're approaching from the north, from Landrail Point, beware the reef that lies approximately ¾ mile north of the entrance to French Wells, it usually breaks in seas from south through north). The entrance into the anchorage of French Wells should only be attempted in good visibility, never at night, and never with a heavy following sea. If you are caught in strong westerly conditions do not attempt to enter French Wells, not that you might not make it in safely, but rather to avoid any small mistake that would put you up on a shallow bank. In strong westerlies it is better to head around the southern end of Long Cay and anchor in the calm lee off its eastern shore to await better conditions.

From the waypoint, steer towards the N tip of Goat Cay which lies just south of the anchorage at French Wells (bear in mind that there is a very strong current that flows in and out of this cut so be prepared for it). To port you will see a shallow sandbar that looks very yellow, almost white. East of this sandbar is a narrow channel of slightly deeper and bluer water that arcs around N-NE towards the S-shore of Crooked Island. Here you will also see a brown bar that lies just south of the deeper water and arcs in the same direction. Turn to port after you pass the shallow sandbar and use the brown bar as a guide keeping it to starboard, the deeper water lies just along its northern side although you can steer directly on top of the brown (grassy) bar. Follow the darker water and the curve of the bar around until you are in the anchorage area. This route can handle a 5' draft at MLW.

Once inside you'll notice a deeper blue channel on the northern side of the anchorage area, while south of that the bottom is darker with grass. Both offer good holding, but between the two is a shallow bar with 4'-5' over it at MLW (see Chart CA-2). Sometimes the tide at French Wells lags Nassau by as little as thirty minutes and by as much as two hours.

The western end of the anchorage area is a bit rocky, you will find much better holding at the eastern end of the anchorage, near or east of the bend as shown on Chart CA-2. As I have mentioned, there is a very strong current through here so you'll sleep better if you use two anchors in a Bahamian moor (though I often anchor here with one and get away with it). The current is so strong (2½-3½ knots or more) that even in winds of 25-30 knots you may be turned beam to or even stern to the wind. Even in strong winds from the east the banks offer little protection and you can get some small wind-blown seas in here, nothing dangerous as long as your anchors are set well, though they can be uncomfortable. During any period of strong winds you will spend approximately 12 hours out of every 24 on an outgoing tide. This means that when the winds opposed the tidal flow you may find yourself sailing around and around, spinning around your anchor and tangling your lines.

Linton Rigg in his *Cruising The Bahamas*, the first cruising guide of its kind to the Bahamas, calls French Wells "a perfect ocean-locked harbour." As nasty and miserable as all this may sound, this is the best protection you will find in all around conditions unless you have a shallow draft vessel and can gunkhole your way up the small creeks that abound in the Crooked/Acklins area. Keep an eye on your anchor lines and keep them from fouling each other and don't cuss too much. This is a very beautiful anchorage during periods of calm to moderate winds. Some locals prefer Portland Harbour for frontal passages. I consider *Portland Harbour* unacceptable in anything north of west, it is wide open to the northwest through northeast except for the protection that the reefs provide which is downright little though it does break the large seas.

What You Will Find Ashore

There is a small creek that winds its way through the mangroves along the eastern shore of Crooked Island from the anchorage at French Wells northward. This is an excellent dinghy trip and shallow draft vessels could use the creek as a possible hurricane hole, provided there was no accompanying surge. At the eastern end of the anchorage area are some small trees used as marker stakes to lead you northward along the eastern shore of this southern leg of Crooked Island. The water taxi uses this route on Tuesdays and Saturdays to ferry passengers between Albert Town and *Church Grove Landing* on the days that a plane is scheduled to land at the airstrip. If you are so inclined, you can follow the taxi and acquaint yourself with the route if you are having trouble finding it. This route leads past Church Grove Landing where you can get ashore and hoof it for about 2 miles to a road that leads from Landrail Point eastward through Church Grove where you'll find the *Tiger Bar*. The terrain is pretty rough on your shoes, it's much easier to dinghy up to Landrail Point on a good day and try to hitch a ride. Further north on the water taxi route you will find Turtle Sound, a gunkholer's delight. Divers will want to investigate the blue holes and fishermen will want to tangle with the large tarpon that inhabit these shallow waters. Even in French Wells you may see tarpon frolicking about the anchorage along with large rays leaping out of the waters around your boat.

On the southwest tip of Crooked Island as shown on Chart CA-2, is a small cairn. If you follow the sandy trail that leads inland for about 100 yards you will come to two more cairns with a stone arrow in the ground pointing in the direction of a fresh water well about 50 yards away. The well has plenty of fresh water that, while it may not be drinkable, it certainly is suitable for washing. There is even a clothesline that someone has strung up in the trees around it. If you wash your laundry or dishes here take care not to let soapy water re-enter the well. If you walk, or dinghy, northward along the beach past the cairn you will discover what is one of my absolute favorite beaches in all the Bahamas. Once the large, flat, slabs of limestone run out, you will find a beautiful, curving, white sand beach stretching northward for a couple of miles. The few patches of casuarinas dotting the shore offer shade while the fine sandy bottom makes for excellent swimming. This is as pretty a beach as you could expect to find in the islands, possibly all it needs to be perfect would be a few palm trees, but not being a perfect world, it's certainly close enough for this beach bum.

Just inside the entrance to French Wells on northern side is a narrow, mangrove lined creek that you can follow northwards into the interior of Crooked Island for a couple of miles. The creek is over 6' deep in places and can get quite narrow. A wonderful place to explore, you will find plenty of sea life, and bugs so bring some repellent on warm, windless days.

Here Fishy Fishy...

The islands of the Bahamas are inhabited by a warm, proud people, the descendants of slaves, Seminole Indians, French missionaries, English and Scottish settlers, pirates, and a few expatriated Americans, Canadians, and Europeans. Bahamians are by nature very religious, although some of the younger folks may dress like rappers, rastas, or gangbangers, there is one primary difference between them and their role models, the Bahamians will most likely be in Church on Sunday.

Here you'll meet Princes and Kings. You'll meet folks like Prince Johnson, Prince Albert, and the King, Elvis. In fact, on Long Island it is said that everybody has a cousin named Elvis. You'll meet folks like Flash, Ice, Burn, Zippy, Dee, Doo Dah, Boog-a-Lou, Iron Head, and Tubby.

At Crooked Island you might cross paths with Junior, his radio handle is *Ocean View,* and he or his daughter always monitor VHF ch. 16. I first met Junior while anchored at French Wells just south of Crooked Island. Junior is one of the Rev. McKinney's sons. One day the good Reverend asked me if I had met his son and I replied "Junior? Sure, I met him just the other day!" The Reverend's face slowly took on a painful expression and he sadly shook his said and he slowly said "No. Elton." It seems that Junior may be a bit of a black sheep in his very religious family. Junior is definitely his own man and you will quickly come across that realization within minutes of meeting him.

Junior and his brother Elton are fishing and diving guides for visitors to the Crooked Island District but Junior would rather be fishing by himself than doing just about anything else. Junior, like most Crooked Islanders tells the state of the tide not by the height of the water along the rocks, but rather by the position of the moon. Most Crooked Islanders have a very good relationship with the moon. Some can tell what kind of a day they will have by whether the moon is "...on the right or on the left." But Junior is not so different from most Bahamian fisherman. His skill with a handline certainly pays for his day's expenses. He rarely comes home without a cooler full of grouper, grunts, or snapper. What is so special about Junior as a fisherman must be seen to be appreciated.

When Junior baits his hook and tosses his line overboard he is transformed. He is no longer a mere fisherman. Junior becomes a warrior engaged in mortal combat where there can be only one winner. His fishing style borders upon a martial art. Standing in his boat, Junior deftly tosses his bait into a likely looking spot and immediately takes an "on guard" stance. Junior leans ever so slightly into the direction of his cast, his fingers deftly feeling for the slightest tug on his line, his eyes glued to the spot where his bait landed. All his senses are on full alert. His body perfectly still. From a hundred yards away, you cannot help feel the tension. You can almost hear his thoughts calling out to the fish. "Here fishy-fishy..." Silently he watches. Patiently he waits. Suddenly Junior feels something that to a person of less experience may just seem like the current nudging the bait. But Junior knows what it is. It is his adversary come calling. This is what Junior is here for. His worthy opponent has again tried to outsmart him and failed. In the blink of an eye Junior's upper torso straightens up and his arms flail about in a blur as he pulls his line in hand over hand and boats his catch. After placing his prize in the cooler Junior silently baits his hook and takes to the battle again. Watching. Waiting. Here fishy-fishy...

Long Cay

Albert Town - ½ nm WNW of:
22° 36.35' N, 74° 21.50' W

Long Cay - turning point to head E across Bight:
22° 34.65' N, 74° 16.90' W

Long Cay - 1¼ nm S of stake leading to dock:
22° 34.10' N, 74° 19.90' W

Long Cay - S tip- ¾ nm S of Windsor Point:
22° 31.65' N, 74° 22.80' W

Long Cay was once known as Fortune Island and the name fit it very well indeed as in the early years of its history is was a rendezvous for the windward wreckers. Albert Town was a *Port of Entry* and the island's most prosperous settlement in the heyday of the early 1800s before the coming of steam power. Long Cay served as a clearing-house for sailing ships in those days. The water is deep and the ships could just anchor right off shore in the lee of the island. The commercial shipping activity created a very healthy economy and the town even had streetlights for the carriages of its residents. There was a railway

system to assist in moving shipments when the great steamers of the *Hamburg-American Line* stopped at Albert Town.

The island became a ghost town of sorts almost overnight when steam power became the prevalent means of propulsion and the population of almost 2,000 in the mid-1800s has dwindled to less than 30 today. The eastern part of Long Cay is a sanctuary for pink flamingos which can also be seen at French Wells on the southern tip of Crooked Island. Long Cay is also host to a fresh water pond, one of the few in the Bahamas.

Navigational Information

Heading south from French Wells keep at least 1½ miles off Long Cay to avoid the shallows and reefs lying just to the west of the land as shown on Chart CA-3. These shallows stretch out almost a mile in places and reach as far south as two miles south of Albert Town. A waypoint at 22° 36.35' N, 74° 21.50' W, will place you approximately ½ mile northwest of Albert Town, which sits amid a long grove of palm trees that are easily seen from offshore. Another landmark is the prominent Fortune Hill, which is visible from over 10 miles away. I wish I could brag about the anchorage off Albert Town and tell you how safe it is but it would be a lie. The waters off Albert Town are strewn with shallow reefs and heads that stretch westward for over ¼ mile. If you wish to anchor off Albert Town do it well offshore and dinghy in. Better yet, anchor off the eastern shore and walk across or dinghy down from French Wells. There is almost always a surge off Albert Town.

What You Will Find Ashore

As you approach Albert Town you can tie up to the small concrete wharf (use extreme caution here) and walk up the path to the settlement. The first thing you will notice is the old cemetery on the hill overlooking the *Crooked Island Passage*. There is a good freshwater well just up the road that you are welcome to use. The only store is Stephen Rose's *Ready Money Store* just up from the dock a ways. Stephen is a former mailboat owner and captain and is an excellent source of information about these waters. At his store you will find a limited selection of supplies but you can purchase beer, which is unavailable at Landrail Point. The *Batelco* office is open every day from 0900 to 1700. There is a small fish processing plant here that ships directly to Nassau on the mailboat. Call *Windsor* on VHF ch. 16 to order fresh bread.

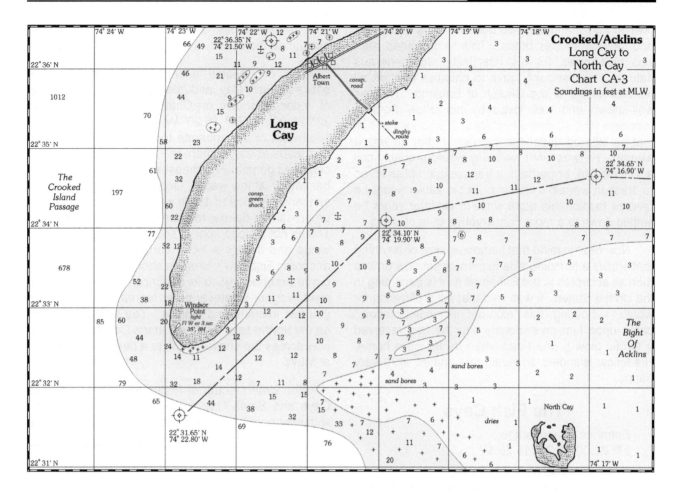

If you are headed southward from Albert Town the reefs stop about two miles south. From there southward the coast is steep sided, about 30-40' high, with many undercuts and small cave holes ideal for dinghy exploration. On the southern point of Long Cay at Windsor Point is *Long Cay Light*, which flashes white every 3 seconds, is 35' high, and is visible for 8 miles. If you are intending to round the southern tip of Long Cay to anchor off its eastern shore give Windsor Point a wide berth, at least ½ mile as there is a shallow, reef strewn area just off its southern tip.

A very good anchorage in westerly conditions, or even in light prevailing winds, is off the eastern shore of Long Cay. There is a lot of current here so be sure to set your anchors well. Large conch abound and you may even see some pink flamingos. A waypoint at 22° 31.65' N, 74° 22.80' W, places you approximately ¾ mile south of Windsor Point and in a position to head northeast along the eastern shore of Long Cay. Parallel the eastern shore of Long Cay and anchor wherever your draft and the sea conditions allow. In the vicinity of a small green shack

on shore you will see three small islands. These are man-made in the sense that they are nothing more than large piles of conch shells with mangroves now growing out of them. North of the conch shell islands you will see a very conspicuous road that cuts over the ridge and leads down to a tiny dock with a very shallow small boat channel marked by a stake. You can tie your dinghy up here and hike the road across to Albert Town. On the way you will pass the ruins of Douglas Town, the old railroad, and the ruins of the old Catholic church atop a hill to the south.

Miss

Not all of the most interesting characters in the Bahamas are still with us. A century ago, there lived in Albert Town, Long Cay, a large man who was one of the pillars of his community, an upright citizen, an entrepreneur, and a bit of a curiosity to his fellow islanders as well as to visitors. He was very involved in his community serving on the *School Committee*, the *Board of Health*, and the *Board of Works*. He was also one of the richest men on Fortune Island owning and managing two businesses, a schooner, and several smaller boats. This kind-hearted man was well-known for his hospitality and generous nature. He unselfishly gave to charities and left all his real estate to the Church of England. He was well-known and well loved by his fellow Fortune Islanders who all called him *Miss*. It was said of him that he labored under the impression that he was a woman. He was what we today would probably call a transvestite, or perhaps a transsexual. Miss loved to dress in women's clothing. In his earlier years he favored fashionable attire while in his later years he settled down to a more conservative style of dress.

Now bear in mind that homosexuality, or anything that shows a feminine side to men, is not now or was then as accepted in the Bahamas as it is becoming in the United States. It was said that his preference for women's clothing, this "extraordinary hallucination," came upon him mysteriously after he had received a terrific blow to the head when he fell off a horse. His fellow islanders accepted this and all were very happy.

The Fish Cays

Entrance to anchorage:
22° 28.00' N, 74° 16.20' W

Navigational Information

Southeast of Long Cay lies a string of small islands called the Fish Cays as shown on Chart CA-4. The waters to their east are shallow with many sand bores and are virtually impassable except for small boats. Some of the areas between the cays, east of the cays, and to seaward of the cays to the one fathom line dry at low water. These shallow waters are teeming with sea fans and you may even find some conch. Along the western shores of these cays the drop-off offers excellent trolling and diving opportunities for the adventure loving SCUBA diver. There are numerous shallow water reefs with abundant marine life waiting to become your dinner. Just southeast of Long Cay lies North Cay with its large reef/sandbar off its northwest tip. Give it a wide berth.

South of North Cay, the larger Fish Cay is home to a large population of small iguanas. One would think that the Guana Cays (which actually does have a small colony of iguanas), which lie just to the south of Fish Cay, would be their home instead. Rather, the better fishing is around the Guana Cays. Doesn't

quite make sense does it? Perhaps someone misnamed the cays?

The only viable anchorage in the area lies between Fish Cay and the Guana Cays in 8'-12' of water as shown on Chart CA-4. A waypoint at 22° 28.00' N, 74° 16.20' W, will place you ¼ mile southwest of the entrance to the dark blue channel that leads to the anchorage. From this position you can head generally northeast-east/northeast across a bar with 7' at low water. Once past the bar, and the sea fans that inhabit it, you will find the depths getting progressively deeper to about 12' between the cays. This is not a good spot in southerly to northwesterly winds and there's a lot of current here so use two anchors. Fish Cay's western shore has an absolutely gorgeous beach, good for beachcombing, sunbathing, swimming, or whatever other recreational diversions you can imagine and employ. You can also anchor on the northwestern side of Guana Cay, working your way across the shallow bank to a deeper area with 7' at MLW.

The waters south of Fish Cay, between Guana Cays and South Cay are very shallow and strewn with sandbores as are the waters to the east of these

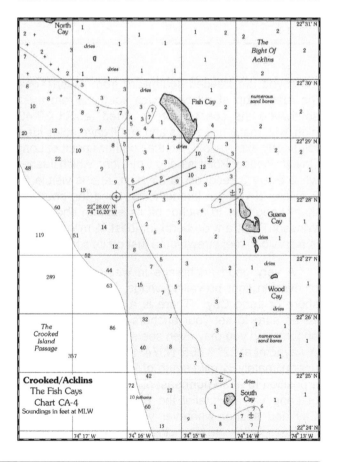

cays. There's little here for cruising vessels but plenty for dinghy exploration, lots of sea fans, conch, and marine life. However there are two anchorages, one south of and one north of, the lovely beach surrounded South Cay, but these anchorages are best only in light prevailing winds.

The Bight of Acklins

One of the most rarely visited areas of the Bahamas is the *Bight of Acklins* (a National Park) and the western shore of Acklins Island. Most cruisers are discouraged by the two words that describe the Bight of Acklins so well: remote and shallow, Most of the communities on Acklins Island dot the western shore of Acklins Island adjoining the *Bight of Acklins* and by playing the tides, vessels with drafts of less than 5' can pass southward along the western shore of Acklins Island to exit back into deeper water just north of Salina Point and Jamaica Bay. The western shore of Acklin's Island has places where the water is 8' deep, but the further south you travel, the shallower the water gets. You were once able to travel southward along the western shore of Acklin's with a 6' draft all the way to Castle Island and points south. I believe those days may be over. If you can prove me wrong, please contact me with details of your passage. You can email me at stevepavlidis@hotmail.com.

A word of warning about the waters in the *Bight of Acklins*. In the northern areas of the *Bight of Acklins*, strong northerly winds tends to push all the water out of the area to the extent that you may have a low tide for a day or two in the upper reaches of the bight, especially in *Turtle Sound*. The tides along the northwestern shore of Acklins Island around Spring Point lag the tides at Nassau by about 3 hours while at Jamaica Cay they are 1 hour and 15 minutes behind Nassau. The area along the western shore of Acklins Island is very safe in strong easterly winds; you can find good shelter from northeast through southeast, however you will be open to any westerly winds (although in the more southerly areas you will get some protection from a shallow bank that lies west of Acklins). If strong westerly winds threaten you can find some shelter in the lee of Long Cay as shown on Chart CA-3.

Crossing the Bight

Long Cay - turning point to head E across Bight: 22° 34.65' N, 74° 16.90' W

Long Cay - 1¼ nm S of stake leading to dock: 22° 34.10' N, 74° 19.90' W

Camel Point - 3 nm NNE of: 22° 30.00' N, 73° 59.50' W

Skippers wishing to cross the *Bight of Acklins* eastward towards the western shore of Acklins Island must do so from the eastern shore of Long Cay (unless you draw less than 4', then you can pass northwards along the western shore of Acklins from Castle Island). North of the conch shell islands mentioned in the previous section on Long Cay and shown on Chart CA-3, you will see a very conspicuous road that cuts over the ridge and leads down to a tiny dock with a very shallow small boat channel marked by a stake leading to it. The mailboat puts this road astern and steers 90° to head to Acklins Island. Skippers wishing to head across the bight of Acklins may use the following waypoints as shown on Chart CA-3. From the waypoint south of Windsor Point head to a waypoint at 22° 34.10' N, 74° 19.90' W. From this position head to a waypoint at 22° 34.65' N, 74° 16.90' W from which you can take up a course to a waypoint at 22° 30.00' N, 73° 59.50' W (see Chart CA-5) which will bring you to a position approximately 6 miles southwest of Snug Corner and 2½ miles northwest of Spring Point.

Snug Corner to Spring Point

Snug Corner - 1 nm SW of 22° 32.00' N, 73° 54.25' W

Camel Point - 3 nm NNE of: 22° 30.00' N, 73° 59.50' W

Navigational Information

Most of the communities on Acklins Island dot the western shore of Acklins Island adjoining the Bight of Acklins. Just south of where the mangroves begin sits Snug Corner, parts of which were once called Mason Bay, but which are now mostly abandoned. As shown on Chart CA-5, a waypoint at 22° 30.00' N, 73° 59.50' W, will place you approximately 6 miles southwest of Snug Corner and 2½ miles northwest of Spring Point settlement.

From this waypoint, if your draft is 3' or less, you work your way to Snug Corner where you can anchor

Crooked/Acklins
Snug Corner to
Camel Point
Chart CA-5
Soundings in feet at MLW

The Bight Of Acklins

22°33.00' N
22°32.00' N
22°31.00' N
22°30.00' N
22°29.00' N
22°28.00' N

22°30.00' N 73°59.50' W
22°32.00' N 73°54.25' W

Snug Corner
Masons Bay
Goodwill
Mason's Bay
Harry Creek Point
dries
blue hole
Jumba Hole
Golden Grove
blue hole
Cold Rock
North Atlantic Ocean
Camel Point
Cord of Wood Point
Ground Nut Point
Spring Point Settlement
Batelco tower Fl R
Pleasant Point

74°00.00' W 73°59.00' W 73°58.00' W 73°57.00' W 73°56.00' W 73°55.00' W 73°54.00' W 73°53.00' W

off the town dock. Vessels of greater drafts can work their way south to anchor as close to Spring Point settlement as their draft allows. You can land your dinghy at the concrete jetty at Snug Corner near the hand-dredged channel or on the beach by the Central Guest House in Mason's Bay. At Spring Point you can tie up at the concrete jetty near the Batelco office or at the government dock at Camel Point (see Chart CA-6).

What You Will Find Ashore

In Snug Corner the residents say they have the best of both worlds. . . they have the same number of dance halls as they do churches. There is a blue hole in the Bight just north of Snug Corner. If you would like a bonefishing guide contact James Bain at the *Top Choice Bonefish Lodge* in *Mason's Bay*.

Approximately six miles south/southwest of Snug Corner lies Spring Point, the principal settlement on Acklins Island. This area is rich in fertile soil and was the first area settled on Acklins Island with the plantations that were located here primarily interested in growing tobacco and cotton.

Spring Point hosts a sailing regatta for Bahamian B and C class sloops every *August Monday, Bahamian Independence Day*.

Fuel

If you need gas see Mr. Bain in Snug Corner. Spring Point has a fuel dock where the mailboat docks once a week. The *Shell* gas station is only open on Tuesdays and Saturdays, when the flights from *Bahamasair* land (or you can visit *Nai's Restaurant* to jerry jug some gasoline or you can contact Felix at *Batelco* on VHF ch. 16).

Provisioning

If you need some groceries you can sample the limited selection at *Forbes Variety* in Snug Corner. In Spring Point visit *McKinney's* for bottled spirits, groceries, car rentals (call *Big Mac* on VFH ch. 16), and hardware items.

Medical Assistance

There's a government clinic with a nurse on duty at Mason's Bay. If you have a medical emergency telephone 242-344-3615. There is also a government clinic with a nurse and doctor on duty in Spring Point (once again, if it's an emergency telephone 242-344-3615).

Dining

Curtis Hanna's (*Red Devil* on VHF) *Airport Inn* is the most popular eating and socializing spot in Acklins. Here you will also find *Nai's Guest House* with 6 rooms available and a wonderful restaurant where you can also pick up some ice and grocery items. Or you can try *Rollex*, the local restaurant/bar that also rents cars.

Camel Point to Jamaica Cay

Camel Point - ¾ nm W of:
22° 27.00' N, 74° 01.00' W

Jamaica Cay - 1 nm N of:
22° 24.50' N, 74° 06.40' W

Turning Point - Camel Point to Jamaica Cay:
22° 24.40' N, 74° 02.55' W

Jamaica Cay - ½ nm W of:
22° 20.30' N, 74° 09.00' W

Navigational Information

Heading south from Spring Point you'll round Camel Point (sometimes shown as Spring Point) as shown on Chart CA-5 and in more detail on Chart CA-6. You can anchor in the lee of Camel Point in prevailing winds, or head southward a bit more to work your way as far to the east as your draft allows in Delectable Bay. Tie up your dinghy to the concrete jetty and take a short walk inland down a rock path where you'll find the town of Delectable Bay separated from the *Bight of Acklins* by a large salt pan. The residents here are involved with sponging

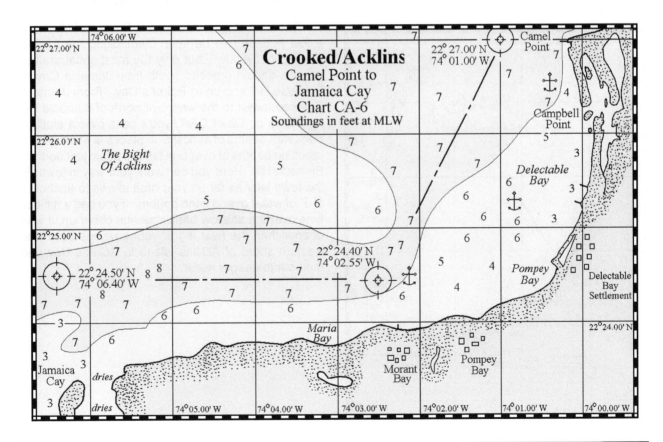

and growing aloe, called *halawis*, for shipment to Nassau. If you're hungry you have little choice but to dine at *Cooper's Restaurant* in town.

A little further south of Delectable Bay is the settlement of Pompey Bay. One hundred years ago Pompey Bay was the most active town in the district and the rock walls marking the old plantation boundaries are still in place. The tall triple-turreted church on the shore is the only semi-complete structure from the past and stands in contrast to the high school, the only one on Acklins Island. Just a little further south sits the large concrete dock marking Morant Bay, now deserted. Four feet can access the dock at high tide.

Heading south to Jamaica Cay involves a bit of piloting as you play the tide to work your way through a small bottle neck of 7' deep water between two shallow sandbanks as shown on Chart CA-6. I've given a waypoint for this route but I suggest that you pilot your way through by eye instead of navigating exclusively by GPS.

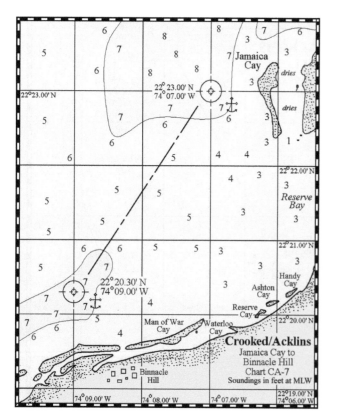

Jamaica Cay to Binnacle Hill

Binnacle Hill - ¾ nm NW of:
22° 23.00' N, 74° 07.00' W

Jamaica Cay - ½ nm W of:
22° 20.30' N, 74° 09.00' W

Cotton Bay Cay - 1 nm W of:
22° 18.40' N, 74° 12.25' W

Rokers Cay - start of route to Rokers Cay:
22° 17.85' N, 74° 16.25' W

Rokers Cay - 2 nm NW of:
22° 16.50' N, 74° 13.50' W

Navigational Information

Just around the point is Jamaica Cay where you can anchor in 5'-7' at MLW over a sand bottom as shown on Chart CA-7. In this area, from Jamaica Cay southward to Roker's Cay, one can find protection from the westerly winds of a frontal passage by the large, shallow sandbank that lies to the west of Acklins Island. Jamaica Cay in uninhabited and is a perfect spot to get away from it all, solitude, gin-clear water for swimming, and no other boats in sight save the passing of the occasional fishing boat.

The next stop southbound is Binnacle Hill where a few houses can be seen overlooking the flats in the *Bight of Acklins*, but only the most shoal draft of vessels should proceed south from Jamaica Cay to Binnacle Hill and on to Roker's Cay. From Jamaica Cay southwest to the waypoint north of Binnacle Hill as shown on Chart CA-7, you'll pass over a shallow bank with depths of almost 5' in places at MLW before reaching depths of over one fathom again just north of Binnacle Hill. Here you can work your way in towards the town jetty as far as your draft allows to anchor in 5'-7' of water over a sand bottom. If you had a difficult time over the shallow bank passage cheer up, it was deeper than the next leg of your passage down the western shore of Acklins Island to Roker's Cay and then out to deeper water.

Chart CA-8 (map):

74°17.00' W | 74°16.00' W | 74°15.00' W | 74°14.00' W | 74°13.00' W | 74°12.00' W | 74°11.00' W

Crooked/Acklins
Cotton Bay Cay to
Rokers Cay
Chart CA-8
Soundings in feet at MLW

22°20.00' N
22°19.00' N
22°18.00' N
22°17.00' N
22°16.00' N

Cotton Bay Cay
dries
Rokers Cay

22° 18.40' N
74° 12.25' W

22° 17.85' N
74° 16.25' W

10 fathom (PA)

22° 16.50' N
74° 13.50' W

Caution:
Scattered rocks
and coral heads

74° 10.00' W

Cotton Bay Cay to Roker's Cay

Cotton Bay Cay - 1 nm W of:
22° 18.40' N, 74° 12.25' W

Rokers Cay - start of route to Rokers Cay:
22° 17.85' N, 74° 16.25' W

Rokers Cay - 2 nm NW of:
22° 16.50' N, 74° 13.50' W

Navigational Information

Heading south from Binnacle Hill you'll pass west of Cotton Bay Cay as shown on Chart CA-8 to work your way to a waypoint at 22° 16.50' N, 74° 13.50' W, which places you almost 2 miles west/northwest of Roker's Cay. There are no safe anchorages along this leg unless you have very little draft and can tuck your way in along the western shore of Acklins Island. From Cotton Bay Cay you'll pass over a shallow sand bank to the waypoint mentioned where you'll find depths of 4'-5' at MLW. Use extreme caution when traversing these waters, keep a sharp eye out, and proceed slowly and cautiously. From the waypoint you can head northwest to a waypoint at 22° 17.85'

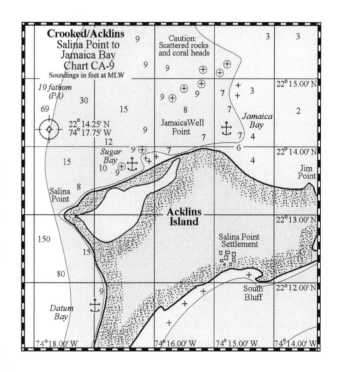

Crooked/Acklins
Salina Point to
Jamaica Bay
Chart CA-9
Soundings in feet at MLW

10 fathom (PA)

22° 14.25' N
74° 17.75' W

Sugar Bay
Salina Point

Acklins Island

Datum Bay

Caution:
Scattered rocks
and coral heads

22°15.00' N
22°14.00' N
22°13.00' N
22°12.00' N

Jamaica Bay
JamaicaWell Point
Jim Point

Salina Point Settlement
South Bluff

74°18.00' W | 74°16.00' W | 74°15.00' W | 74°14.00' W

N, 74° 16.25' W, which places you in over 10 fathoms west of the shallow banks of Acklins Island. Congratulations, you've just had a remarkable voyage from Long Cay to the western shore of Acklins Island and back to deep water, a unique passage similar in scope to running inside the reef at Andros, and one to which few other Bahamas cruisers can lay claim.

Jamaica Bay

Jamaica Bay - 3 nm W of anchorage:
22° 14.25' N, 74° 17.75' W

Navigational Information

Off the southeastern tip of Acklins lies *Jamaica Bay*, a delightful lee anchorage providing adequate shelter in the prevailing northeast to southeast winds. For vessels with drafts of over 3', the only entrance to this anchorage is from the west, from a position just north of Salina Point as shown on Chart CA-9. A waypoint at 22° 14.25' N, 74° 17.75' W, places you a mile north of Salina Point and approximately 3 miles west of the anchorage in Jamaica Bay.

From the waypoint as shown on the chart, head eastward passing north of Sugar Bay (where you can find some protection from east-southeast winds in the lee of a shoal) past Jamaica Well Point to anchor in *Jamaica Bay* wherever your draft allows.

What You Will Find Ashore

Southeast of the anchorage you'll see a concrete jetty where you can land your dinghy for the two mile walk to the Salina Point settlement that lies on the eastern shore of Acklins Island. Salina Point, the settlement, not the point of land, is the largest and most prosperous community on Acklins Island despite being so remote. In town you'll find a small store with a very limited selection of groceries and fresh bread as well as a government clinic with a nurse on call. If you're hungry you can get a bite to eat at the *Blue Bird Restaurant* in town.

Vessels can find a bit of a lee to anchor in *Datum Bay* as shown on Chart CA-9, however it is prone to surge and can be very uncomfortable even when anchored close in to shore.

Castle Island

Castle Island - ½ nm NW of anchorage:
22° 08.50' N, 74° 20.40' W

Castle Island - ¼ nm S of Mudian Harbour:
22° 07.00' N, 74° 19.00' W

Castle Island lies along the western edge of the *Mira Por Vos Passage* and just off the southern tip of Acklins Island. The N end of the island is rather high and hilly becoming low and sandy as it stretches southward. The cut between Castle Island and Acklins Island is guarded by a large reef system and this passage is suitable for shoal draft vessels or dinghies only.

The huge (135') red and white barber-pole that is *Castle Island Lighthouse* (GP. FL W-2 ev 20 sec, 130', 22m) is one of the most important lights in the Caribbean due to the tremendous amount of boat traffic plying the waters of the *Crooked Island Passage*, the *Windward Passage*, and the *Old Bahama Channel* along the Cuban coast. The light was manually operated until Bahamian independence in 1973, today it is all battery and solar powered. If you wish to visit the cay you will notice the recent ruins of the light keeper's homes, cooking rooms, and the boathouse with its railway leading to the water. You can climb to the top of the lighthouse for some spectacular views and sunsets.

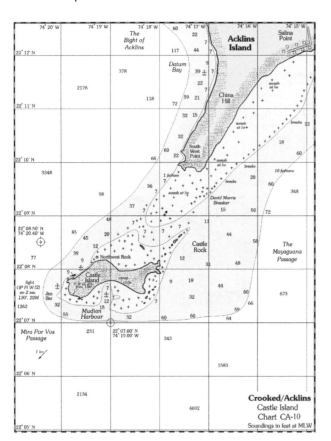

On the beach is the wreck of an old Belizean freighter. The ship, and sometimes the beach itself, are strewn with shoes. Closer examination of the hold will reveal clothes and shoes. One cruiser I know entered the hold to find a pair of boot soles, the right and left in the correct placement, floating in the dark water. Frightened that she had found a dead body she called to her companion and they soon discovered that the boots were simply floating upside down.

Navigational Information

Anchorages can be found on the banks west of Castle Island or east if the need arises. A waypoint at 22° 08.50' N, 74° 20.40' W will place you approximately ½ mile northwest of the anchorage on the western shore of Castle Island as shown on Chart CA-10. There is a small reef encircled anchorage called *Mudian Harbour* (a corruption of *Bermudian Harbour*) on the southern side of Castle Island that is good in winds from the northwest to the north/northeast. The entrance is through a break in the reef approximately ½ mile east of the lighthouse. Two white beacons on the northwest side of the harbour form a range (003°) for the entrance channel, which can carry 9' at low water. A waypoint at 22° 07.00' N, 74° 19.00' W, will place you approximately ¼ mile south of the entrance

to *Mudian Harbour*. Vessels can also anchor north of Castle Island at *Datum Bay* in easterly conditions, but it can get quite rolly in southeasterlies.

Mira Por Vos

Mira Por Vos - 1 nm W of:
22° 07.00' N, 74° 32.50' W

The Spanish named this tiny group of islets and reefs well, *Mira Por Vos* means "watch out for yourself" and should be taken to heart when visiting this group. This 40-square mile area, unlit and unmarked, is best skipped unless you require shelter or seek to test the excellent fishing that abounds in the area. The islands only inhabitants are flocks of nesting sea birds. The area was once much more dangerous until the *Imperial Lighthouse Service* constructed the lighthouse on Castle Island.

Navigational Information

Mira Por Vos, Chart CA-11, lies about 7 miles west of Castle Island at its closest point and is essentially a large shallow bank less than 60' deep and thick with scattered heads and reefs. Land masses consist of a number of small barren reefs and rocks scarcely visible above water, the largest being only ½ mile long. The fishing is superb on the *Mira Por Vos Bank* but this is not a place to ride out any type of threatening weather.

South Cay is the largest island and a temporary anchorage can be found in its lee if absolutely necessary. There is a shallow rocky bar extending from South Cay to Northeast Rocks that must be avoided. You can anchor in the lee of Northeast Rocks which in strong prevailing winds is actually quite calm. Two miles to the northwest of Northeast Rocks lies North Rock, a brown booby rookery but not much of an anchorage.

A waypoint at 22° 07.00' N, 74° 32.50' W, will place you approximately 1 mile west of the *Mira Por Vos Bank*. From this position you may head east to Northeast Rock, southeast to South Cay, or northeast to North Rock.

The Northern Shore - Crooked

Bird Rock - ¼ nm N of NW tip of reef:
22° 51.85' N, 74° 22.10' W

North of Acklins Island - clear of NE Reef:
22° 48.00' N, 73° 47.00' W

Travel close in along the northern shore of Crooked Island should only be attempted in good light and settled weather due to the absence of good protection and the abundance of shallow offshore reefs stretching eastward for over 25 miles with only an occasional break. There are only three anchorages along this route that I can in all honesty recommend and all should only be considered when seeking relief from the prevailing northeast to southeast winds. The north shore of Crooked Island and Acklins is no place to be caught in a fierce frontal passage if it can be avoided. The breaks in the reef are hard to find in poor visibility and heavy seas. Use extreme caution if you plan to enter any of the harbours along the northern shore.

Navigational Information

Vessels heading east along the northern shore of Crooked Island must first round Bird Rock and the reef just to its north. A waypoint at 22° 51.85' N, 74° 22.10' W, will place you approximately ¼ mile north of the northwest tip of this reef as shown on Chart CA-1. From this position, or preferably from north of this position, you can begin to head east avoiding the reef that bears away east/southeast along the shore of Crooked Island.

What You Will Find Ashore

Heading eastward along the northern shore some seven miles from Gun Bluff is Moss Town. Moss Town is accessible only by small boat from *Attwood Creek*, a shallow mangrove lined tidal creek. The town is a cluster of small houses decorated with yellow elder, the *National Flower* of the Bahamas. From the top of the hill in Moss Town you can gaze upon the brilliant blue-green waters of *Turtle Sound*, accessible from the southern part of Crooked Island at French Wells. Years ago fisherman could navigate the maze of twisting shallow mangrove creeks from *Turtle Sound* to gain access to Moss Town from various landing stations. The only station that is still in use is *#1*, which connects with Cabbage Hill via a long road.

Turtle Sound is a very attractive small boat anchorage with tall cliffs, mangrove lined waterways, and blooming cactus ashore. Cabbage Hill is the most populous of Crooked Island's settlements. There you will find *The Crooked Island Lodge* (http://crookedislandlodge.com/) with 6 rooms available, the *T & S Guest House, T & S Grocery and Hardware Store* (with some limited marine supplies), two churches, *The One-Stop Shopping Center*, an auto repair shop, a barber shop, a beauty salon, and three

bars including the *Bloom of the Valley Bar and Night Club,* which is actually located in Johnny Hill. You can get gasoline in Cabbage Hill at Ezekiel Thompson's when it's available, he'll also deliver to Church Grove Landing for you and he can arrange to have your propane tanks shipped to Nassau for refilling.

Farther east is Colonel Hill, the capital of the Crooked Island District and at the top of the hill you will see the Commissioner's home and just below it the small government complex consisting of a post office, the *Commissioner's Office*, the *Police Station*, a government clinic, the *National Insurance Office*, the central high school, and several teacher's residences. Here you will find *Sunny Lea*, a restaurant, guest house, bakery, and store all in one and run by Mrs. Eunice Deleveaux.

The entrance to the unnamed harbour at Colonel Hill is through a small reef passage northeast of McKay's Bluff. I cannot recommend this passage. The reef passage itself is not difficult bearing 205° on the conspicuous palm trees standing on McKay's Hill. The problem begins when you turn back to the east

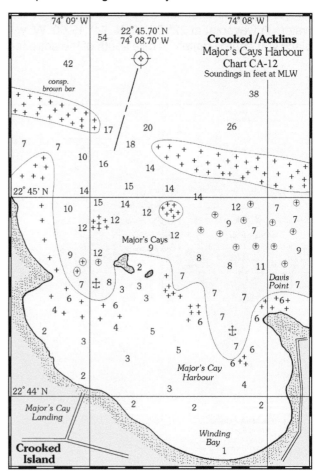

to pass McKay's Bluff to anchor in its lee. You must negotiate a series of reefs will small, narrow breaks between them. It is possible to pass over them with 6' at low water but you must certainly know how to read the water as you will be passing over reef while trying to dodge many shallow heads. Shallow draft vessels should have no problems. If you do plan to anchor west of McKay's Bluff, once you round the point you will find an uninhabited anchorage with shelter from east through south to west. On the southwest section of the bluff is a cave, only accessible by small boat, with a wide mouth and a series of natural skylights inside. Just outside the cave is a large lignum vitae tree covered with bromeliads. West of Colonel Hill is the airstrip with flights on Tuesdays and Saturdays.

Major's Cay

Major's Cays - ½ nm north of entrance :
22º 45.70' N, 74º 08.70' W

Navigational Information

Just past Colonel Hill along the northern shore you will come to Major's Cay with its impressive white church sitting high on a hill. Entrance into *Major's Cay Harbour* as shown on Chart CA-12 is relatively easy. The anchorage has 7'-12' over a sandy bottom and the town lies approximately one mile inland down a sandy path. The primary landmark in this area is the prominent wedge-shaped cliff at McKay's Bluff, which lies approximately 12 miles southeast of Bird Rock. From this landmark head east for approximately 2 miles until the next break in the reef lines up with the two small cays bearing south. A waypoint at 22º 45.70' N, 74º 08.70' W, will place you approximately ¼ mile north of the entrance. Use caution when entering this and any harbour entrance along the north side of Crooked Island. This particular cut is wide, deep, and easily seen. Steer roughly south/ southwest and keep an eye out for the reefs on either side. The best anchorage is in about 7'-12' over a sandy bottom between the point and the small cays.

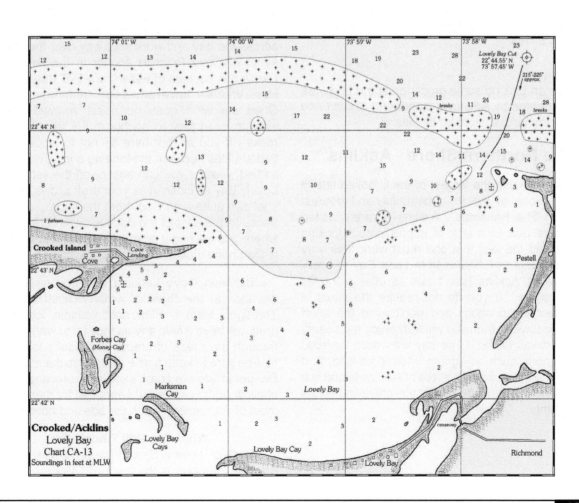

Another option is to anchor east of Major's Cays in the lee of Davis Point in 7' at mean low water.

The small towns west of Major's Cay, Bullets Hill, Thompson Hill and True Blue were at one time the largest communities on Crooked Island. At one time there were more people in these three communities than the entire population (1200+) of today's Crooked Island.

There is an anchorage shown in *The Yachtsman's Guide to the Bahamas* just off True Blue and Brown's but I cannot recommend it. The anchorage, although it has good holding, offers no protection in the prevailing east to southeast winds and there is nothing ashore of interest. Brown's is deserted, only ruins on the shore today, and the waters off the beach are strewn with small, shallow patch reefs to avoid. Much better anchorages are at Major's Cay and *Attwood Harbour*.

What You Will Find Ashore

Dining
Here you will find the *Peace and Plenty Bar*, the bright orange *Peace and Plenty Bar* is actually someone's home and you must go around back for a drink and a chat.

Provisioning
You can pick up some groceries at the huge (as big as a garage by American standards) *South Land Grocery*, the largest store on the island.

The Northern Shore - Acklins

Acklins Island, the largest of the Crooked Island District, is one of the most beautiful, and poorest islands in The Bahamas. Acklins is rarely visited by cruisers due to a lack of sophisticated docking facilities and the fact that one must work their way across the *Bight of Acklins* from Long Cay to really access what Acklins Island has to offer along its western shore. If you do not require the latest in marina accommodations and don't mind the short jaunt to windward, then you will truly enjoy the beauty that is Acklins Island. The cay was once covered in hardwoods such as lignum vitae, braziletto, and ebony. The entire eastern shore of Acklins Island is a beachcomber's paradise due to the prevailing winds and currents.

Lovely Bay

Lovely Bay - ½ nm NNE of entrance:
22° 44.55' N, 73° 57.45' W

Along the northern shore of Acklins Island you will find anchorages at *Lovely Bay* and at Attwood Harbour. *Lovely Bay* offers a good anchorage in prevailing winds as well as a good lee in winds from west to north.

Navigational Information
Lovely Bay is just that...lovely. There is a wide, deep break in the reef just north of the three rocks lying northeast of the Lovely Bay settlement. A waypoint at 22° 44.55' N, 73° 57.45' W, will place you approximately ½ mile northeast of this break as shown on Chart CA-13. Eyeball the opening and once you have located it, steer approximately 225° through the break in the reef and avoid the small patch reefs that lie on the inside of the fringing reef.

If you seek shelter from northeast to east winds you can anchor just south of the three rocks just to starboard. If you proceed to *Lovely Bay* steer clear of the patch reefs that dot the area. If you have a draft of 5' or less and seek shelter from a front head west across the bay and work your way over the shallows south of Cove Point to anchor in the lee of *Cove Landing* in pockets of water from 5'-6' deep at MLW. Here you will have protection from west to north. Once the wind goes northeast you will probably want to head east to anchor in the lee of the three rocks. If you anchor here try not to block the ferry that shuttles between the landing and *Lovely Bay*. In settled weather you can anchor off the settlement of Lovely Bay as close in as your draft allows, the water shallows quite a way out from the shore. Just a few paces to the east of the dock lies the center of town where you will find a small store and a bar which also is the phone station.

Between Cove Landing and *Lovely Bay* is an entrance to the *Bight of Acklins* called *The Going Through*. Here shallow draft vessels, less than 3' draft, will have a field day as they try to work their way through the maze of creeks and tidal passages. A hint-be sure to keep a mile away from the mangroves. Deeper inside are some excellent hurricane holes for shallow draft vessels but searching for them will take most of your time. Watch the tide and have fun.

What You Will Find Ashore
East of *Lovely Bay*, between *Lovely Bay* and Attwood Harbour, is the town of Chesters. Shallow

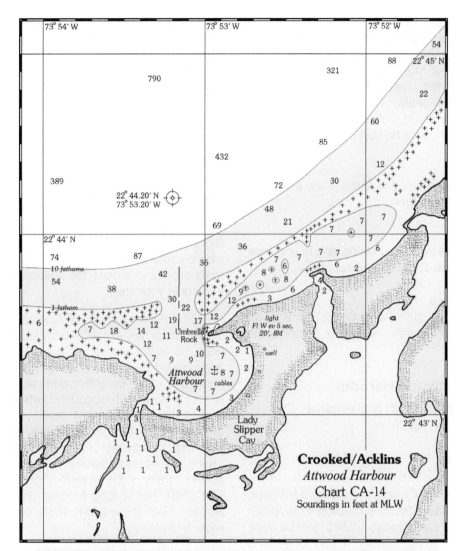

73° 54' W   73° 53' W   73° 52' W

Crooked/Acklins
Attwood Harbour
Chart CA-14
Soundings in feet at MLW

Attwood Harbour

Photo Courtesy of Paul Harding

draft vessels can gain access to Chester's by heading east inside the reef from *Lovely Bay*. Chester's is probably most famous for its boatbuilding. Here the legendary Frank Moss, now retired and living in Nassau, built wooden boats with his bare hands for most of his 80 plus years. He has a 70-footer and a 100-footer to his credit, building them right on the beach. In his latter years he built only dinghies.

Provisioning

You can purchase food at *Moss' Store* and there is a phone available in town.

Fuel

If you need gasoline you may be able to convince someone to sell you some of their supply.

Medical Assistance

If you have a medical emergency there is an unstaffed clinic in Chesters where a doctor visits twice a month.

Attwood Harbour

Attwood Harbour - ½ nm N of entrance:
22° 44.20' N, 73° 53.20' W

North of Acklins Island - clear of NE Reef:
22° 50.00' N, 73° 47.00' W

Four miles east of Chester's is *Attwood Harbour*, a lovely curving bay offering protection from winds from the east-northeast through south to almost west. Attwood Harbour is not exactly a part of Acklins Island, it actually is situated on Lady Slipper Cay. There is a light at the entrance but like most lights in the outer islands, it should be considered unreliable. The best anchoring is in the northeast corner of the harbour. Although the outlying reefs and shallow entrance channel break most of the seas entering the harbour, *Attwood Harbour* is not the best spot to ride out a frontal passage. I have ridden out a weak front there and would not wish to be inside during a fierce 30+ knot, norther. Van Sant calls *Attwood Harbour* a deathtrap in a norther; he is not exaggerating.

Navigational Information

A waypoint at 22° 44.20' N, 73° 53.20' W, will place you approximately ½ mile north of the entrance to *Attwood Harbour* as shown on Chart CA-14. The break through the reef is wide and deep and very straightforward and easy to see. Never attempt this entrance at night! From the waypoint head south.

Your landmark will be Umbrella Rock and the light on the point on your port side. The deep water begins approximately 150 yards west of Umbrella Rock. Pilot your way in by eye and drop your hook in the eastern end of the harbour in 7'-10' in good holding sand.

Ashore you will see two small buildings that house cable equipment sitting just inland of the beautiful beach. About 50 yards south of the northern tip of the eastern beach is a path leading inland about 30-50 yards to a concrete lined well. This well has excellent water for washing and showers. In a pinch you could boil it and drink it. There is a small creek with a 1' bar at the entrance that winds back into the Bight of Acklins. There are some small pools inside where you will find 3'-4' at MLW. There are plenty of reefs around to arouse the interest of the divers and anglers in your crew.

Off the northeast tip of Acklins Island lies a reef strewn area known as Northeast Point and Hells Gate. Give this area a WIDE berth. These reefs are a graveyard for boats. Here you will find acres and acres of Elkhorn coral that dries at low water. There is simply no way through the reefs and you must go around them, way around them! A waypoint at 22° 50.00' N, 73° 47.00' W, will place you in deep water well north of Northeast Point and its surrounding reef. There are no settlements, no anchorages, and no access to any of the eastern shore of Acklins Island. The shore has a long fringing reef along its entire length. Give the eastern shore of Acklins Island a wide, wide berth.

What You Will Find Ashore

On the mainland of Acklins Island is the small settlement of Pinefield, sitting south of Hell Gate on the northeastern tip of Acklins Island. Most residents are fishermen who use their small boats in the mangrove creeks north of the settlement. In town you will find the Williamsons with a wingless plane in their yard. The plane crashed close to their property and Holston Williamson keeps it in good shape, applying a new coat of a paint every time he paints his house. The Williamsons have two guest houses which they rent to visitors year round. A few miles south of Pinefield is Hard Hill, the highest point on Acklins Island. Residents say that on a clear day they can see the Plana Cays to the east. Here in Hard Hill the main road running north to south on Acklins really begins.

Samana Cay

Ports of Entry: None
Fuel: None
Haul-Out: None
Diesel Repairs: None
Outboard Repairs: None
Propane: None
Provisions: None
Important Lights: None

Samana is an uninhabited and very isolated little cay lying about 20 nautical miles north-northeast of *Attwood Harbour* on Acklins Island. There is a large body of evidence pointing to this 9-mile long cay as being Columbus' first landing site in the New World, not San Salvador as is the popular belief (See the section *San Salvador*). The cay was once populated by Lucayan Indians before the raiding Spanish decimated the population. Ashore you will find the ruins of an old settlement, a few fishermen's huts, and a well that is now brackish, and a cave on the eastern end. In later years the island was called *Attwood Cay* and eventually became *Samana*. The waters surrounding the cay are thick with coral reefs that have claimed many a vessel. You can still see the remains of an old freighter on the northeast side of Samana Cay's eastern reef.

In the past Samana was actively farmed by Acklins Islanders. The farmers would stay for extended periods of time and large boats would sail to Samana to pick up the Cascarilla bark, conch, fish, crabs, and crops that the farmers harvested. This practice eventually ceased in the 1950s and Samana was rarely visited except by passing yachts for the next quarter of a century. The practice was revived in 1983 and carries on today so you might not be alone when you visit here. On the shores of Fisherman's Bay you will see the wooden shacks used by today's fishermen standing next to the stone ruins of past buildings.

There is once again an active interest by fishermen in search of fish, lobster, conch, and land crabs, sometimes staying weeks at a time in the renovated shacks in *Fisherman's Bay*. While anchored in the Propeller Cay anchorage one year, I met two fisherman from Lovely Bay that came over in a 16' boat with a 30 horsepower outboard in search of black land crabs. The white crabs have more meat than the smaller black crabs but the meat is sweeter in the black crabs. The two gentlemen had four huge bags of crabs that they told me would net them $110

a bag in Nassau. They asked me if I had any gas to spare and I told them I was down to my last 10 gallons but I could let them have 3 gallons. I did not ask for any recompense but they soon returned with a gallon size bag full of cleaned conch that took three days to finish. In the outer islands courtesy shown is often rewarded many times over.

Approaches

Samana is generally low and sandy along its western shore with a conspicuous white bluff along its southern shore. From *Attwood Harbour* it is 20.4 nm on a course of 33° to the waypoint south of Propeller Cay. From Betsy Bay, Mayaguana, the Propeller Cay anchorage lies 50 miles away on a course of 326°. From Bird Rock, northwest of Crooked Island, Propeller Cay bears 80° at a distance of 36.6 nautical miles. West Plana bears 357° at 28.2 miles, but you must exercise extreme caution on this route to avoid the reefs off the northeastern tip (*Northeast Reef*) of Acklins Island.

A note on the passage between Acklins Island and Samana. The *Antilles Current* runs strong along the northeastern shores of The Bahamas, roughly at a speed of ½ knot but often higher. Through the 20 mile stretch between Acklins and Samana the *Antilles Current* is funneled somewhat with a resulting increase in speed to about ¾ knot at times. At times this current acts like the *Gulf Stream* in the sense that at its center, along its *axis*, the seas are generally higher than at its northern or southern edges.

Another interesting note, an Acklins Islander told me that there is a spot in the center of this passage with only 90' of water over it. He told me the bank lies on a bearing of 210° from Propeller Cay, "…just as you make out the land, about 12 miles out from Acklins." I have searched for this area, a possible pinnacle, but have found no evidence of it. That does not mean that it doesn't exist. If you are in the area and notice anything strange in the sea conditions, this bank may have something to do with it. If you find it please contact me with its coordinates. An acknowledgment in and a free copy of the next edition of this guide will be your reward.

Propeller Cay Anchorage

Propeller Cay anchorage - ½ nm S of entrance:
23° 03.10' N, 73° 44.35' W

Samana Cay, pronounced *Sa-MAN-a*, not *Sah-ma-NAH*, as the city in the Dominican Republic is called, offers good protection to vessels headed north or south if a frontal passage threatens. The best anchorage by far is in the lee of Propeller Cay off Samana Cay's southern shore. Please note that you may find charts with Propeller Cay listed as Pimlico Cay or even Prickly Cay so don't be confused. This anchorage is open to the southwest and it can get pretty choppy inside with a stiff southwest wind blowing. Although a reef breaks the truly big seas on the outside, inside the anchorage you may find a 3' chop in winds of 25 knots and more.

Some skippers praise the *Columbus Anchorage* west of *Fisherman's Bay*, but I find it not well protected, it's open from the southeast through south to the west-northwest. As you can see, in prevailing conditions there is little protection here, use it only as a settled weather anchorage and watch out for reefs

upon your approach. The *Columbus Anchorage* lies just west of the end of the fringing reef that lies south of *Fisherman's Bay*. If you are not happy here the anchorage at Propeller Cay offers excellent protection and is not that difficult to enter if you have good visibility.

Navigational Information

For entrance into the Propeller Cay anchorage as shown on Chart CA-15, a waypoint at 23° 03.10' N, 73° 44.35' W, will place you approximately ½ mile south of the entrance to the anchorage behind Propeller Cay. A good landmark as you approach are the very conspicuous white cliffs that lie just northeast of Propeller Cay. From the waypoint head northward until you can pick up the channel which you should approach on a heading of approximately 350°-360°. The northern end of the slightly winding channel lies about 50-75 yards east of the northeastern tip of Propeller Cay. The moderate current flows east and

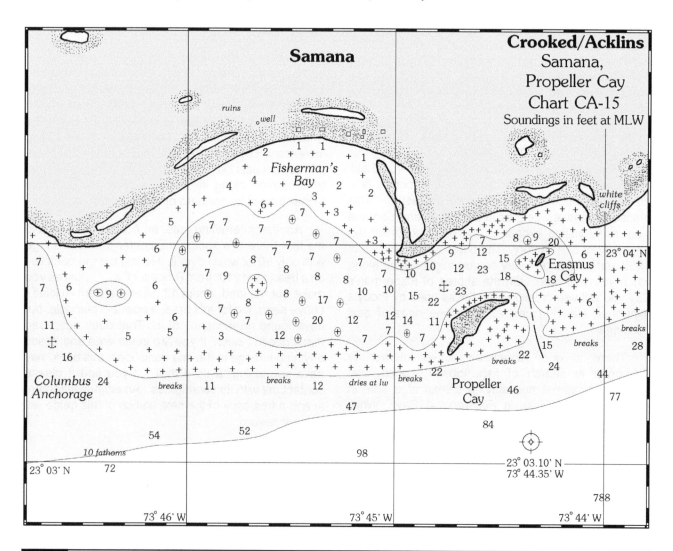

west across the channel and through the anchorage as well.

The ability to read the water is essential here but if you have made it this far you are probably pretty fair at picking out reefs and heads from sand. Never attempt this channel at night or with a heavy following sea, one small mistake and you will be up on the reef before you know it. This is a narrow channel, only about 40'-75' wide with a least depth of 9', but the bottom is easily seen as its green color (indicating sand) stands out from the surrounding brown reefs. A good idea is to approach the reefs and steer parallel to them about 100 yards off, if weather permits, to eyeball the channel before you attempt to enter. Take your time and give the channel a good once over to familiarize yourself with it. If time and weather conditions permit you may wish to dinghy the channel first. Some skippers mark the channel with floats, often leaving them behind when they leave. Never, I repeat **NEVER**, trust any range or buoys you see in this vicinity. Trust only what your eyes tell you! As you make out the channel approach it on a heading of approximately 350º-360º. This heading is not that important, what is important is what you see and what your depth sounder indicates, trust your eyes. The channel makes two small doglegs before rounding the reef at the northwestern tip of Propeller Cay. Watch our for the shallow yellow coral amidst darker coral that lies to port just as you begin your entrance to the

channel, this head is just awash at low water. Once you clear Propeller Cay round to port, not too soon mind you, you'll find excellent holding in soft sand in 10'-25' of water.

What You Will Find Ashore
The shore of Propeller Cay is surrounded by beautiful reefs as are the beaches of Samana just north of Propeller Cay. Good snorkeling and fishing abound in this area and there are beautiful reefs everywhere. If you wish to land your dinghy the best spot is at the northeastern end of *Fisherman's Bay* just west of the entrance to the shallow creek area west of the palm trees. This area is very shallow and strewn with small rocks, conch shells, conch pens, and small patch reefs so use caution. A better spot, particularly if you wish to use the beach for swimming, is about ¼ mile east of the conspicuous white cliffs. Here the close in reefs break and you can beach your dinghy on a very nice, deep, sandy beach. The northern shore of Samana is excellent for beachcombing.

As I mentioned earlier, there is a moderate current that runs east-west through this anchorage. It is not as strong as the current at French Wells, but it can make your stay a little rolly. In east or west winds you will lie to the wind and not get much roll unless the wind pipes up. In any other winds you will be turned slightly to the current, not much, you'll barely notice, only enough to make the accompanying roll

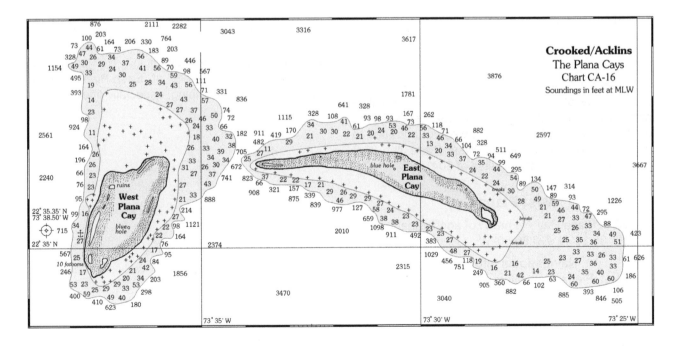

uncomfortable. To make the best use of the shelter offered, and to cut down on roll, you can either lie to a bridle and adjust your position to the incoming surge, or you can play musical chairs and move around the anchorage. In winds from ENE through SSW the best anchorage with the least roll is close in the lee of Propeller Cay (watch out for the reefs along the shore). In winds from NE through N to W your best spot is on the northern side of the anchorage as close as you can get to shore (again, watch out for the inshore reefs). In strong SW to W winds, well, just pray they don't last long as there is no real lee and you will have to endure some chop depending on the wind strength.

The Plana Cays

Fuel: None
Haul-Out: None
Diesel Repairs: None
Outboard Repairs: None
Propane: None
Provisions: None
Ports of Entry: None
Important Lights: None

Between Acklins and Mayaguana on the western side of the *Mayaguana Passage* lie the Plana Cays, sometimes called the French Cays. These two small reef fringed islands, West Plana Cay and East Plana Cay, actually the tops of two distinct seamount-like risings of the sea floor, stretch east to west for approximately 9 miles. They offer a lee side anchorage along with good fishing, diving and exploring possibilities ashore.

Approaches

From Samana, the anchorage at West Plana lies on a course of 177° at a distance of 28.2 nautical miles. Betsy Bay, Mayaguana, lies 29.7 miles distant on a course of 296°. From the western entrance to Abraham's Bay, Mayaguana, West Plana lies 36.3 nautical miles away on a course of 304°.

West Plana Cay

West Plana Cay - ½ nm W of anchorage:
22° 35.35' N, 73° 38.50' W

Navigational Information
West Plana Cay offers some lee protection in northeasterly or easterly blows. I wish I could tell you this is an excellent lee anchorage but it is not. I prefer to avoid it unless I have to stop, but you might appreciate West Plana Cay more than I do. This a rolly anchorage at times, but a good lee from the prevailing winds if needed, and there are several heads in the neighborhood to dive. The anchorage is just off the beach on the western shore of West Plana Cay. A waypoint at 22° 35.35' N, 73° 38.50' W, will place you approximately 1 mile west of the beach on the western shore of West Plana as shown on Chart CA-16. Simply head in for a point in the middle of the beach and drop the hook in sand with good holding. Watch out for the occasional scattered coral head through here.

What You Will Find Ashore
West Plana Cay is a very lush island, especially when compared to East Plana Cay. Along the northern shore of West Plana Cay you will find large piles of rocks washed up from past hurricanes. There are some old buildings on the cay that were built and are occasionally used by farmers and fishermen from Crooked Island.

Crooked and Acklins Islanders have set up a permanent camp of sorts on West Plana where they come for stretches of two months at a time to harvest Cascarilla bark which is used in the Italian aperitif *Campari*. During this period the harvesters cut, soak, dry, and bag the bark for shipment to Nassau and eventually to Italy. While on the cay they also catch conch, fish, and crabs.

East Plana Cay

East Plana Cay can be used as a lee in northerly winds. Find a place close in to shore and drop your hook avoiding the reefs closer in. The long beach along the northern shore of East Plana Cay is excellent for beachcombing, especially after a blow.

Mayaguana

Ports of Entry:

Abraham's Bay
Fuel: *Abraham's Bay*
Haul-Out: None
Diesel Repairs: *Abraham's Bay*
Outboard Repairs: Pirate's Well
Propane: *Abraham's Bay*
Provisions: Abraham's Bay
Important Lights:
Guano Pt., *Abraham's Bay*: Fl W ev 3 sec
Northwest Point: Fl W ev 5 sec

Mayaguana is almost as primitive as its ancient Lucayan name, which was shown on some early charts as *Mariguana*. Some local residents tell me that the name is not Lucayan in origin, rather that the island is named after the many green iguanas found on Booby Cay lying off the eastern shore of Mayaguana. Of course the term *iguana* itself is Lucayan in origin. The island was uninhabited until around 1812 when a group of Turks Islanders settled here and many of today's residents can trace their heritage to those early inhabitants.

The United States Government leased bases in Mayaguana for 99 years from the British government in exchange for 40 old destroyers as part of World War II's *Lend Lease* program. Although no base was ever really developed, an *Air-Sea Rescue Station* of the *Caribbean Division* of the *U.S. Air Force* was set up and maintained at Abraham's Bay on the south side of the island. This area was the site of a *U.S. Missile Tracking Station*, now long abandoned, which boosted the population of Mayaguana to over 3,000 for a few years. *Abraham's Bay* was sounded and a chart drawn up in 1941 (which is still in wide use today although the latitude and longitude lines are off considerably). A wireless station was also established at the same time on the western side of the island at *Betsy Bay*.

Mayaguana boasts one of the world's best shelling spots along its weather shore and *Abraham's Bay* is a favorite stopover for those skippers bound to or from the Caribbean. Magnificent wall dives surround this tiny island (Did I say tiny? It's 24 miles long and 6 miles wide) with the drop off just a few hundred feet offshore in some places while the offshore reefs are alive with food fish and lobsters (I have heard some local fishermen boast that the best fishing is along the northern and eastern reefs).

The island itself is thickly wooded and rather low-lying for the most part although it hills rise here and there throughout the land mass with the eastern end being generally more hilly and steep-to.

Approaches

Betsy Bay, Mayaguana bears 146° at a distance of 50.0 nautical miles from the Propeller Cay anchorage at Samana Cay, and 29.7 miles on a course of 116° from the southern tip of West Plana Cay. The western entrance to *Abraham's Bay* lies approximately 36.3 miles distant on a course of 124° from the southern tip of West Plana Cay.

From the waypoint at the western end of *Sandbore Channel* off Provo in the Turks and Caicos, the eastern entrance to *Abraham's Bay* bears 330° at a distance of 46.4 miles. Southeast Point, Mayaguana lies 37.7 miles distant on a course of 337° from the waypoint off *Sandbore Channel*.

Northwest Point to Start Bay

Northwest Point-1½ nm W of light:
22° 27.10' N, 73° 09.90' W

Start Bay-½ nm SW of best holding:
22° 20.30' N, 73° 05.30' W

For vessels heading southward across the *Mayaguana Passage* from Acklins, Samana Cay, or the Plana Cays, Northwest Point and *Betsy Bay* make good stopovers at the end of a long day. *Abraham's Bay* lies almost twenty miles away around Devil's Point and in prevailing winds (with no chance of a westerly shift) many cruisers opt to anchor off Northwest Point, at *Betsy Bay*, or at Pirates Well for the night and then proceed to *Abraham's Bay* the next morning.

Navigational Information

A waypoint at 22° 27.10' N, 73° 09.90' W, will place you approximately 1½ miles west of Northwest Point as shown on Chart MG-1. From here you have a choice of destinations; you can head through the cut to Pirates Well, anchor just below the light (Fl W ev 5 sec, 70', 12M) at Northwest Point, or head another two miles southeast and anchor off the settlement of *Betsy Bay*. My personal favorite in light easterly weather, simply because it's easiest, is to anchor off the small rocky beach just south of the light at Northwest Point in 15' of water. Here, with the help of a bridle arrangement, you will get less roll than you will at *Betsy Bay*. The bottom is sand with scattered rocks and coral so pick a good sandy spot to drop your hook and hope that your rode doesn't wrap around a coral head or rock if the wind shifts. Years ago there was a whale skeleton that washed ashore off the point, you may still find a piece of it strewn about.

About ½ mile south of the light you will see what appears to be a marina with a range leading into its entrance channel. This is a private dock used only by the mailboat and there is usually no one around so there is no use in trying to hail somebody on the VHF. Although there is 8' of water at the entrance and 10' inside, the sides are sharp rock and coral and not a place you would want to tie to except perhaps in an emergency. I should add that this place is open to the west and would be a deathtrap in a strong westerly.

If you wish to anchor at *Betsy Bay* head southeast about two miles to anchor off the settlement in water from 15'-40' deep. The very conspicuous *Batelco*

tower and huge satellite dish, which is sometimes your first landfall when approaching from the northwest, mark the settlement. Here too the water is strewn with coral and rocks so take care in setting your anchor, the holding is good when you find a sandy spot. The anchorage at *Betsy Bay* is better in southeast winds than the anchorage south of *Northwest Point Light* though I like the anchorage by the light better in light easterly winds. There is a long beach just south of *Betsy Bay* that offers good protection in southeast winds but don't stray in too close as there is a rocky bar lying parallel to the beach about 50 yards or so out from the beach.

Another option is to pass through the cut in the reef lying north of Northwest Point and anchor off Lower Pirates Well. The cut lies about 100 yards north of Northwest Point and has a minimum depth of 8' at MLW. Never try this cut in poor visibility or with a heavy onshore (westerly) swell as it breaks all the way across the cut and you won't be able to see

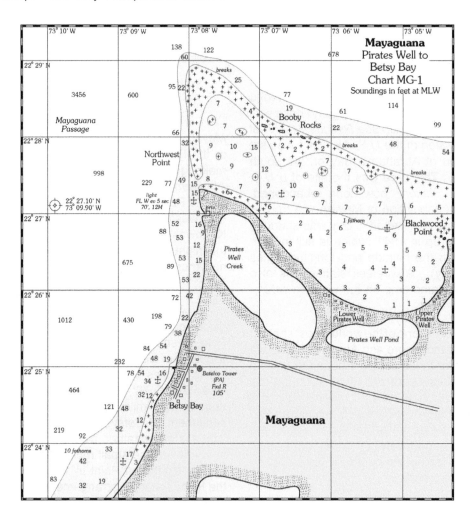

the channel. Once through the cut head eastward along the northern shore, not too close in) and anchor wherever you draft allows off Lower Pirates Well, the first community to starboard just east of the very conspicuous hotel. The two communities of Upper Pirates Well and Lower Pirates Well are usually just called Pirates Well. At one time you could take a 5' draft well into the bay to anchor off the shore of Upper Pirates Well, which sits under the very pretty grove of coconut palms at the southeastern end of the bay. Today, unless you have a shoal draft multihull, you can't get very close at all.

The entire northern shore of Mayaguana offers good beachcombing with a few very nice beaches. The coast has a few small, snug anchorages for small boats, but the cuts through the reefs are narrow, intricate, and very difficult to see. The Booby Rocks are aptly named as they are home to a colony of brown boobies.

When you have had your fill of this area and decide to move on to *Start Bay* or *Abraham's Bay* you can pass close in to the western shore of Mayaguana and round Devil's Point just a few hundred yards off. As you round Devil's Point you will immediately find yourself in the grip of a very strong current, sometimes as strong as two knots or more depending on wind speed and direction. This current runs very close in to Devil's Point, but as you head more towards *Start*

Bay or *Broken Bay* you will find yourself free of its effects. The only anchorage in this area is at *Start Bay* where you can anchor in good holding sand. Although it is possible to anchor anywhere between *Broken Bay* and Start Point, *Start Bay*, as shown on Chart MG-2 has the best holding and least rock and coral clutter.

Once again, find a nice sandy spot in which to drop your hook. A waypoint at 22° 20.30' N, 73° 05.30' W, will place you approximately ¼ mile southwest of the best holding. *Start Bay* has the advantage of being easy to leave at night for a passage to Provo or northward. There is an almost continuous brown bar that often breaks lying about 50 yards offshore almost the entire length of the bay from *Broken Bay* to *Russell's Bay* so don't try to tuck in too close. This anchorage is good in north through east winds, but it's time to move when the wind goes southeast and builds. At the southeast end of the bay at Start Point is the small dock and pilings where the fuel ship ties up to unload diesel and gasoline for Mayaguana

What You Will Find Ashore
If you need a guide, call *Bain Boys* on the VHF.

Provisioning
Upper and Lower Pirates Well are lovely communities with a small but friendly population. In

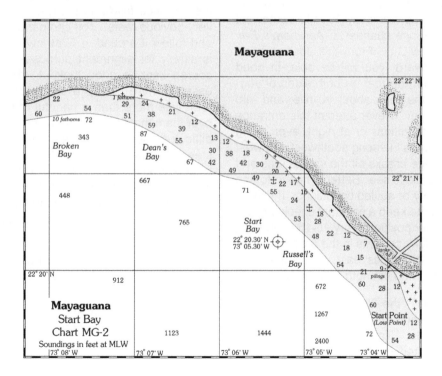

Lower Pirates Well you will find *Gibson's Food Fair* and *Brown's Convenience Store*.

Mechanical Repairs

If you need an outboard mechanic call *Bain Boys* on the VHF and ask to speak to Stafford Bain Jr.

Abraham's Bay

Abraham's Bay - inner waypoint E entrance:
22º 21.07' N, 72º 58.45' W

Abraham's Bay-¼ nm SSE of E entrance:
22º 20.80' N, 72º 58.30' W

Abraham's Bay-¼ nm NE of W entrance:
22º 19.80' N, 73º 02.50' W

Abraham's Bay-¼ nm SW of W entrance:
22º 19.25' N, 73º 03.40' W

Southeast Point-1 nm WSW of anchorage:
22º 16.70' N, 72º 48.40' W

Navigational Information

As you head eastward around Start Point for *Abraham's Bay* the reef begins just past the fuel dock and continues, with only two breaks, to Guano Point just south of the settlement of Abraham's Bay. If approaching from the west the western entrance to *Abraham's Bay* is the widest, deepest, and easiest to enter. A waypoint at 22º 19.25' N, 73º 03.40' W, will place you approximately ¼ mile southwest of the western entrance channel to *Abraham's Bay* as shown on Chart MG-3. From this position head generally northeastward (you will be able, in good visibility, to make out the reef on both sides of you) until you are past the reef, about ¾ mile, and into *Abraham's Bay* proper. Never attempt this entrance in strong onshore conditions or at night, even using waypoints. Sometimes in strong southwest and west weather this entrance breaks all the way across and the break is impossible to see. Better to heave-to and wait for good visibility or settled conditions. If you do heave-to remember to keep a constant check on your position, plotting your position every 10-15 minutes at least as there are fluky currents in the area that push sometimes west, sometimes east, and sometimes north depending on wind strength and direction.

In March of 1997, the 36' sloop *Hey Jude* was hove to eight miles south of *Abraham's Bay* in strong west/northwest winds. Taking positions every 30-40 minutes she drifted east and then north. She

finally wound up on the southwestern tip of the reef, a total loss; don't let this happen to you. If you are leaving the western entrance to *Abraham's Bay*, a waypoint at 22º 19.80' N, 73º 02.50' W, will place you approximately ¼ mile northeast of the entrance, a good spot to work your way southwest from as you leave *Abraham's Bay*.

The eastern entrance to *Abraham's Bay,* just southwest of Guano Point, is narrower than the western entrance and there is a shallow rock lying almost in mid-channel. A waypoint at 22º 20.80' N, 72º 58.30' W, will place you approximately ¼ mile south/southeast of the entrance channel. Never attempt this channel at night, in poor visibility, or with a heavy onshore swell running, you'll never see the channel. Government charts of this area show what appear to be two small cays on either side of the channel entrance. CAUTION: There are no such cays. The areas they show as cays are actually stands of Elkhorn Coral that dry at low water and have a height of approximately ½'-1' above MLW. With good visibility you will have no problem entering this channel.

From the waypoint given above, head to an inner waypoint that lies halfway between the two stands of coral at the mouth of the eastern entrance at 22º 21.07' N, 72º 58.45' W. If things don't look right to you, ignore the waypoint and trust your eyes and your depthsounder. From this position head into the entrance following the green water between the very obvious reefs. You can parallel the western reef and follow it around in 7' at low water. This course is simply for alignment purposes, as you steer this course keep a good lookout. Pilotage by eye is essential here. Keep a sharp lookout for the small reef, little more than a handful of rocks, with only 4' over them that lies almost mid-channel, it can be very difficult to see. Once past the small reef you can steer to starboard keeping the small sandbar shown to port to anchor in 7' at low water or pass west of the sandbar to anchor in 7' at low water a little further out. The light on Guano Point flashes white every 3 seconds, is 13' tall, and is supposed to be visible for 8 nautical miles.

The best anchorage is all the way in to the eastern end of *Abraham's Bay* where you can anchor in 6'-9' of water in places. Keep a sharp eye out as you navigate eastward in *Abraham's Bay*. The bay has quite a few shallow spots and rocky heads here and there, all easily seen in good light. Never attempt this

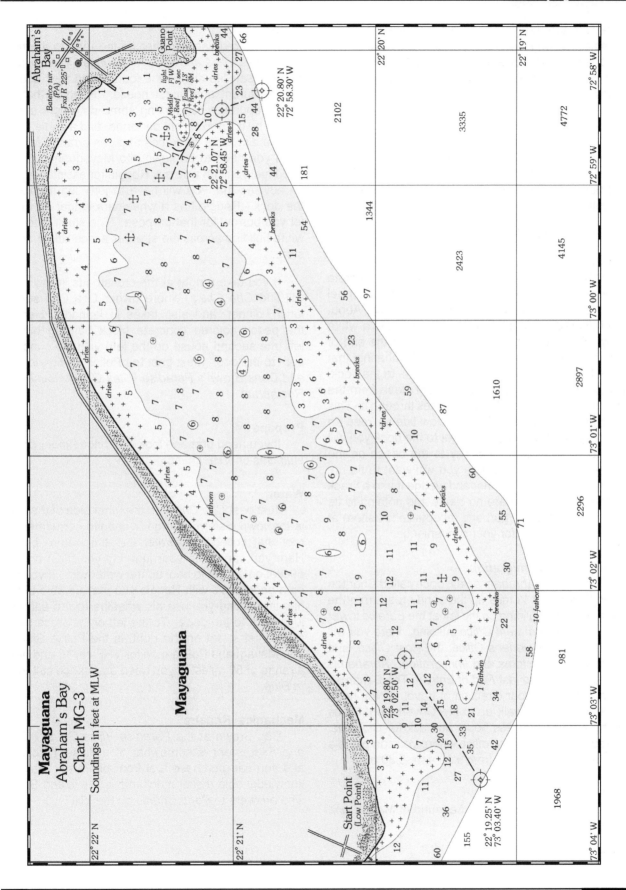

Mayaguana
Abraham's Bay
Chart MG-3
Soundings in feet at MLW

Mayaguana

Abraham's Bay

Batelco tur. light
(PA)
Fxd R 225'

Guano Point

light
Fl W
3 sec
13'
8M

East Reef
Middle Reef

22° 20.80' N
72° 58.30' W

22° 21.07' N
72° 58.45' W

22° 19.80' N
73° 02.50' W

Start Point
(Low Point)

22° 19.25' N
73° 03.40' W

1 fathom

1 fathom

10 fathoms

dries
breaks

22° 22' N
22° 21' N

22° 20' N
22° 19' N

73° 04' W
73° 03' W
73° 02' W
73° 01' W
73° 00' W
72° 59' W
72° 58' W

route with the morning sun right in your eyes, you'll be aground long before you see the shallows. At the eastern end of the harbour the bottom is strewn with rocks and small heads so be sure to pick a good sandy spot to drop your hook. The holding is good here when you are set in the sand though a constant roll is evident, more so in stronger winds. A bridle arrangement is helpful although during periods of strong winds, say 20+ knots, if you adjust your bridle to the wind waves you will roll from the swell and if you adjust for the swell coming in from the reef you will roll to the wind waves.

What You Will Find Ashore

Dinghy Dock

Visitors to town can dinghy in to the large concrete dock to tie up and visit ashore. The dinghy channel is narrow and extremely shallow at low water. About two hundred yards southwest of the dock is a white buoy. From the white buoy steer toward the end of the dock until you can pick up the white channel that leads between two shallow grassy areas to the dock. The channel is sandy white and kept clean from the amount of outboard traffic that passes through it. This channel has about 1' of water at low tide so keep an eye on your prop. When you get to the dock you will find some steps about halfway to the beach on the western side. This is where you will want to tie up. Pull out your dinghy anchor and wedge it into a crack on the dock as there are no cleats and nothing to tie to. A large concrete garbage receptacle is ashore at the end of the dock for your convenience.

Customs and *Immigration*

The town of *Abraham's Bay*, once called Charlton Town, lies about ¼ mile up the sandy road from the dock. The first building on the left at the *Batelco* tower is the pink *Government Office* building. Here you will find the *Commissioner's Office*, the *Post Office*, and the offices of *Customs* and *Immigration*. *Abraham's Bay* is the first and last *Port of Entry* in The Bahamas depending upon your direction of travel. If you need to clear in or out, walk up to the *Government Office* during normal business hours and ask for *Customs*. Next door is the *Batelco* office where you can place a call seven days a week from 9:30 a.m.-5:30 p.m.

Fuel

Diesel and gasoline can be found at *Mayaguana Petrol*.

Dining

A hundred yards further up the road to the right is *Reggie's Villas and Satellite Lounge*. The building with the satellite dish is the lounge and next door is the restaurant and guest house. Reggie Charlton has a reputation for serving some downright strong drinks, he is an excellent bartender and a genial host. Reggie also sells cigarettes and can arrange for any parts you need to be flown into Mayaguana. If you need fuel you can also ask Reggie for assistance, but be advised that you will have to jerry jug it back to the dock. Reggie has a wheelbarrow that he might let you borrow for that purpose. The small blue and white building across the street is a nice little grocery store.

If you take a right at the crossroads in town you will find *Cha Cha's*, where owner Cha Cha serves lunch, dinner, and also takes in laundry. Hers is the peach colored concrete block building on the left (the second house on the left) with the concrete path to the door. Just past the Police Station *is Cap and Doris Brown's Paradise Villas Guest House and Restaurant*.

Propane

If you need propane look up Prince Pinder or hail *Gulf Gas* on VHF ch. 16

Water

Just past *Cha Cha's* on the other side of the road is the town cistern, a large V-shaped corrugated tin roof that collects rainwater into the cistern below. Here you can fill up your jugs but you must bring a bucket on a rope to haul up the water with. If you are on a good basis with Reggie you may be able to talk him into letting you use his wheelbarrow to cart you jugs back to the dock. To the left of the crossroads, at the first street on the right, is the Police Station. The Mayaguana Police monitor VHF ch. 16 and have a range of 50 miles. If you need assistance call *Boys In Blue*.

Mechanical Repairs

Cap Brown at the *Paradise Villas Guest House and Restaurant* is somewhat of a diesel mechanic and you can purchase fuel from him also. Another knowledgeable diesel mechanic is Cleveland Brown who answers to *Papa Charlie* on the VHF.

Provisioning

Options for provisions are *Brook's Dry Goods* and *Loraine's Variety Store*, both in *Abraham's Bay*, *Bain's Convenience Store* in Pirate's Well, and *L&L Groceries* in *Betsy Bay*.

Medical Clinic

The phone number for the medical clinic is 242-339-3109.

Southeast Point

Navigational Information

Many cruisers on their way to Provo usually leave *Abraham's Bay* and anchor in the lee of Southeast Point for a few hours to make a nighttime departure for Provo that much easier and shorter. A waypoint at 22° 16.70' N, 72° 48.40' W, as shown on Chart MG-4, will place you approximately 1 mile west/southwest of the anchorage area. Anchor off the beach in the shelter of the reef and you will be fairly comfortable in light to moderate northeast to east winds. Strong east

winds make this an uneasy anchorage. Winds and/or seas out of the southeast may make this anchorage anywhere from uncomfortable to downright untenable. If you anchor here awaiting your departure for Provo you might wish to explore the wreck of the sailboat *Amie* which lies on a beach about 2 miles northwest of Southeast Point. I have seen pink flamingos wading in the shallows that dry about a mile northwest of the wreck.

To the east of the main island of Mayaguana lies Booby Cay. Booby Cay, a National Park, besides being a home to brown boobies, is also home to a colony of small rock iguanas. These are the same iguanas that are found 50 miles to the southeast at Little Water Cay northeast of Provo. There is a small anchorage just inside the reef between Mayaguana and Booby Cay offering little save some shelter from westerly winds. The entrance through the reef is narrow and hard to find.

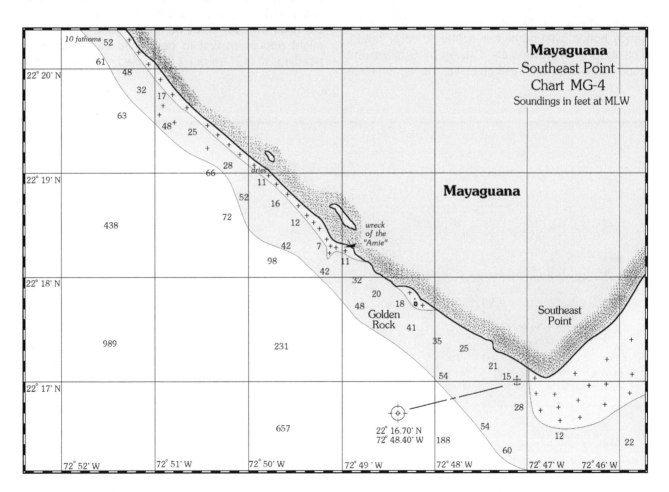

Hogsty Reef

Ports of Entry: None
Fuel: None
Haul-Out: None
Diesel Repairs: None
Outboard Repairs: None
Propane: None
Provisions: None
Important Lights:
Northwest Cay: Fl W ev 4 sec

Hogsty Reef was once shown on old charts as *Les Etoiles* and its present name was given to the area by early buccaneers. *Hogsty Reef*, along with *Glover Reef* and *Lighthouse Reef* off Belize and the *Cay Sal Bank*, is the closest thing that you will find to a true coral atoll in the *North Atlantic Ocean*. To understand how rare this is one must bear in mind that there are over 400 atolls scattered around the *Pacific* and *Indian Oceans*.

Hogsty Reef, a Protected Area, is basically a horseshoe-shaped outer reef enclosing an inner lagoon where the depths range from 6'-35' over a sandy bottom with numerous scattered coral heads. The area is approximately 3 miles by 5 miles and good sized seas can build up inside the lagoon even

though the outer reefs breaks the ocean swells. The fringing reef rises almost straight up from mile deep water so rapidly that skippers rarely see the breakers from over a mile away and don't even come up on soundings until 100 yards from the reef itself.

Visitors to *Hogsty Reef* today are primarily fishermen taking advantage of the abundance of sea life in the vicinity, and cruisers seeking shelter. Do not attempt to use this anchorage in a strong blow from any direction unless absolutely necessary.

The outer reef offers excellent diving opportunities, but only for the experienced diver due to the tidal conditions, sea swells, and strong current. The inner lagoon makes for excellent snorkeling and fishing over the scattered coral heads.

Approaches

The most visible landmark during the daytime is the rusting remains of an old Liberty ship stranded on the northern reef by a hurricane in 1963. Little remains today and every years brings further deterioration to the hulk, one day it will be all but gone. The wreck might appear at first to be a ship underway on a heading of 142° so don't be misled. The wreck lies

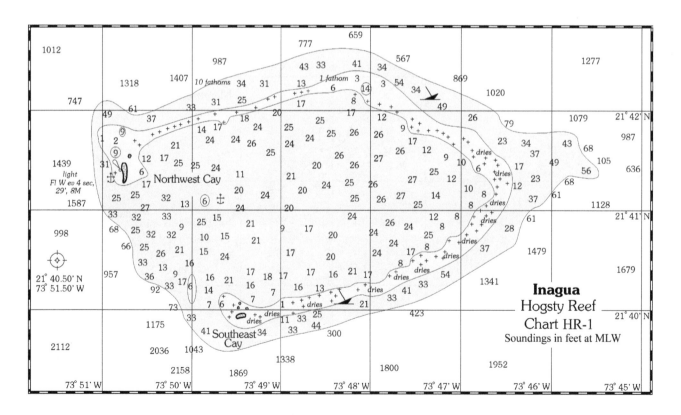

Inagua
Hogsty Reef
Chart HR-1
Soundings in feet at MLW

approximately 4 miles east of the entrance to the lagoon, which lies just south of Northwest Cay.

Almost visible is the 29' tall red and white banded light tower standing on Northwest Cay flashing white every 4 seconds and which is visible for approximately 8 nautical miles.

Hogsty Reef lies approximately halfway between Castle Island in the Crooked/Acklins District and Northwest Point at Great Inagua. From Castle Island a course of 139° for 38.8 miles will bring you to the waypoint off the western edge of *Hogsty Reef* (see Chart HR-1). From Matthew Town, Great Inagua, the same waypoint bears 356° at a distance of 44.2 nautical miles.

Hogsty Reef

Hogsty Reef-1 nm W of entrance to lagoon:
21° 40.50' N, 73° 51.50' W

Navigational Information

The entrance to the reef enclosed basin is fairly simple, it lies between Northwest Cay and Southeast Cay, which actually lies at the southwestern tip of *Hogsty Reef* as shown on Chart HR-1. A fair lee anchorage can be found along the western shore of Northwest Cay in 8'-30' of water as shown on the chart. The two cays are little more than a couple of hundred yards long each and offer little protection when the wind and seas are up. In more settled weather you can anchor in the center of the lagoon in 6'-35' of water, but take care to avoid the scattered coral heads.

A waypoint at 21° 40.50' N, 73° 51.50' W, will place you approximately one mile west of the entrance to the lagoon lying between Northwest Cay and Southeast Cay. From the waypoint head generally east/northeast to enter the lagoon or simply steer for Northwest Cay to anchor in its lee. Remember, *Hogsty Reef* is no place to be when severe weather threatens, it is best avoided if conditions are forecast to deteriorate.

Great Inagua

Ports of Entry:

Matthew Town
Fuel: Matthew Town
Haul-Out: None
Diesel Repairs: ask at Matthew Town
Outboard Repairs: ask at Matthew Town
Propane: Matthew Town
Provisions: Matthew Town
Important Lights:
Matthew Town: Gp. Fl (2) W ev 10 sec

Lying almost within sight of the mountains of Cuba and only 60 miles from Hispaniola, Great Inagua, the third largest and southernmost of the Bahama islands, is approximately 40 miles long and 20 miles wide at its widest part. Great Inagua is generally low lying, flat and wooded except for a few scrub covered hills along the eastern shore. Both Little Inagua and Great Inagua are fringed by reefs along their eastern shores, a graveyard for all manner of vessels. Great Inagua is fairly dry, most people use cisterns for catching rainwater while incoming salt ships sometimes bring fresh water to the island.

Great Inagua was discovered by the captain and crew of the *Pinta* on Columbus' first voyage to the New World in 1492. The captain, Martin Alonzo Pinzón, had deserted Columbus in Cuba to search for gold in Hispaniola when he came across Great Inagua and named the island *Bebeque*. Some say Great Inagua's name is a corruption of *heneagua*, which is derived from the early Spanish explorer's word for a salty site, the way the Spaniards viewed Great Inagua and which has changed little in 500 years, Great Inagua is known far and wide for its salt production. Others say that the island's moniker is a corruption of the name of one of the island's many residents, the iguana.

Approaches

From Castle Island off the southern tip of Acklins Island, Matthew Town bears 158° at a distance of 75.2 nautical miles, while from the waypoint at Hogsty Reef Matthew Town bears 176° at a distance of 44.2 nautical miles.

If you are approaching from Little Inagua you must round Northwest Point (see Chart IN-1) well off before turning southward towards Matthew Town. The waypoint off Northwest Point lies 38.8 nautical miles on a course of 248° from the anchorage at Little Inagua. If you are approaching the waypoint off Northwest Point from Little Inagua, be sure to keep a sharp lookout as you approach within 10 miles of Northwest Point, there are several reefs lying northeast of the point that you must take care to avoid.

Great Inagua

Great Inagua is sort of the Wild West of The Bahamas and it is definitely not set up for heavy tourism. This isolated island is rarely visited by cruisers except those heading to and from the Caribbean who often stop to clear in or out of The Bahamas or top off their fuel tanks here. With the exception of three 100' high hills the terrain is flat and harsh and has more cacti than any other Bahamian island. Wild donkey's, cows, and hogs roam the land, the donkeys in particular being plagued to no end by the mosquitoes such that it is not unusual to see a donkey wade out until only his head is above the water. As the mosquitoes swarm over the donkey's exposed head he will dunk his head and shake it to get some short-lived relief from the troublesome pests.

Great Inagua's principal claim to fame is shared by some 60,000 pink flamingos and the *Morton Salt Company*. Great Inagua was once called the *El Dorado* of The Bahamas due to its highly productive salt industry, the second largest in the world. Little is known of the early history of Great Inagua, there is evidence of a prosperous salt industry as early as 1803, and some say salt was a commodity here as early as the 1600s. Wrecking seemed to be prosperous in Great Inagua as elsewhere throughout The Bahamas for a period of time. Henri Christophe, the Emperor of Haiti, built a summer palace at Northeast Point in the early 1800s to take advantage of Great Inagua's close proximity to Haiti and he is rumored to have rowed back and forth the entire 110 miles from Haiti. There is a spot near Northeast Point called Christoph where there are still some ruins to be found, and it is said that the Emperor hid a cache of gold in the area.

In 1849, a company upgraded salt production on Great Inagua by using mule-powered rail cars. The salt itself, now seen in huge piles that are easily see from far out to sea, was kept in a specially built storage building called the *Salt House*. Above the door to the *Salt House*, which still stands today, is a unique brick design crafted of bricks imported from the sunken remains of the old pirate haven of Port

Royal, Jamaica. Just before the end of World War I, the population of Great Inagua numbered around 5,000 and Matthew Town was a principal *Port of Entry* for ships plying the waters of the Windward Passage and the Caribbean. Ships from both the *Hamburg-American Line* and the *Netherlands Steamship Company* regularly made stops at Great Inagua to take on salt, supplies, and laborers. The unionization of stevedores and migrant workers stopped a lot of the shipping activity around Great Inagua and the economy suffered somewhat until the arrival of the Erikson brothers.

The modern history of Great Inagua can be traced back to 1936 and the arrival of the Erikson brothers who arrived on the island, much to the hostile discontent of the local inhabitants, with tractors, trucks, bulldozers, and modern salt production machinery. The Erikson brothers built up the salt works in the space of only 12 years to where they were, and still are, one of the most successful salt producers in the world. The salt industry on Great Inagua had flourished during the American Civil War and until sometime thereafter and the price of salt during this period rose from $.60 to $1.00 a bushel, or somewhere in the neighborhood of $18 to $30 a ton. Matthew Town was at its peak during these years with a population of over 7,000 who lived in lavish luxury for such an out of the way place as Great Inagua. The happy islanders flourished with horse drawn carriages and moonlight balls, French fashions, and even a polo team.

When the price of salt plummeted to a low of $3 per ton the salt economy collapsed and Matthew Town virtually became a ghost town. Many islanders shipped out to work on the Panama Canal, the Mexican railroads, the *Hamburg-American Line*, the *Royal Netherlands Line*, or the mahogany industry in central America. So few people were left on the island to work that the Erikson brothers had to import laborers from the nearby Turks and Caicos islands to build a workforce sufficient to man all their machinery. The Eriksons were successful in revitalizing the salt industry to such a degree that it caught the interest of the giant *Morton Salt Company* who bought out the Eriksons in 1955. For a firsthand account of the Erikson years and the lifestyle of the residents of Great Inagua during that period, read *Great Inagua* by Margery O. Erikson (*Capriole Press*, Garrison, N.Y., 1987), it is an excellent account of those years.

Today, *Morton Bahamas, Ltd.* (*MBL*), employs over 300 people and operates some 80 salt ponds covering 12,000 acres. It is the second largest solar salt operation in the world and produces over a million pounds of salt every year. On Great Inagua, dikes hold back shallow, but extensive, reservoirs that hold water pumped from the sea for evaporation and the seawater is channeled from one reservoir to another by a series of pumps and aqueducts. The tropical sun evaporates the moisture as the seawater transforms first into a concentrated brine and finally into layers of almost pure salt which are raked up into huge white pyramids so easily seen from offshore. Besides regular salt for consumer use, Great Inagua produces a larger, coarser grain the size of peanuts for scientific and industrial applications. Today, Matthew Town's population is nowhere near the numbers of a century ago, but stands proud at over 1,200 people.

Great Inagua is also home to a mercury driven, kerosene fueled, 25,000 candlepower lighthouse that was built in 1870, much to the dismay of wreckers who were put out of business by the presence of the light. The light is one of two of the last manually operated light in The Bahamas, but it was no help to a scientist named Gilbert Klingel whose *Spray* replica was wrecked on Great Inagua in a gale in the 1920s. On his way to a scientific expedition in the West Indies when shipwrecked, Klingel decided to use his salvaged equipment to study Great Inagua. Klingel stayed on for 6 months taking botanical specimens and wrote an excellent natural history book entitled *Inagua: The Ocean Isle*.

Northwest Point, Man of War Bay

Northwest Point - ½ nm NNW of:
21° 07.10' N, 73° 40.10' W

Navigational Information

At the northwestern tip of Great Inagua lies Northwest Point as shown on Chart IN-1. Vessels headed for Matthew Town or the *Windward Passage* via the western shore of Great Inagua can make for a waypoint at 21° 07.10' N, 73° 40.10' W, which places you approximately ½ mile north/northwest of Northwest Point. Vessels headed to this waypoint from Little Inagua or Mayaguana should keep an eye out for the reefs north of Great Inagua and northeast of *Alfred Sound* and Northwest Point as shown on the chart.

There is a fair anchorage inside *Alfred Sound* that is good in winds from east through south to west, which is great in the early stages of a frontal passage, but not a good spot in strong winds from the northwest

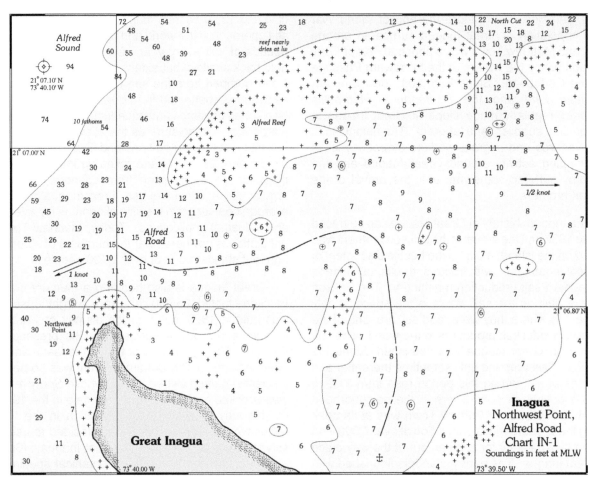

Inagua
Northwest Point,
Alfred Road
Chart IN-1
Soundings in feet at MLW

through north to the northeast. Great Inagua suffers from a lack of an all-weather anchorage, your only choices during a frontal passage are in *Alfred Sound*, north of *Molasses Reef* (more on that in a moment), or leaving Great Inagua altogether.

The entrance to the anchorage at the southern end of *Alfred Sound* weaves through a break in the reef and around some smaller heads and patch reefs and should never be attempted at night or in periods of poor visibility. Use caution if anchored here, if the wind shifts into the north while you're anchored here at night you'll have to tough it out anchored off a lee shore until daylight because you won't be able to find your way out in the dark. To enter the anchorage from the waypoint just given north/northwest of Northwest Point, head to a point lying just east of Northwest Point at *Alfred Road*, the gap between Northwest Point and the southwestern tip of *Alfred Reef*.

Beware of a 1-knot tidal current that sets northeast and southwest across *Alfred Road*. Once through the gap work your way eastward rounding the tip of the

unnamed reef shown on the chart. Once clear of this reef turn to starboard and work your way in as close as your draft allows to the northern shore of Great Inagua.

Another entrance lies west of *Alfred Road* and the waypoint. *North Cut* (see Chart IN-1) is plenty deep for the average cruising boat, it's about 15' at low water, but it is narrow, *Alfred Road* is a much safer entrance.

Northeast of *North Cut* is Sheep Cay (not shown on the chart), which I have heard touted as a leeward anchorage. I cannot do the same, the narrow entrance through the reef just east of Sheep Cay is hard to find, even in good visibility and it is restricted to drafts of less than 4' at low water.

Just south of Northwest Point, along the northwestern shore of " between Northwest Point and Devil's Point just north of Matthew Town is large, curving *Man of War Bay*. In winds from northeast to southeast this is a good lee anchorage though there are quite a few reefs off the shoreline, especially along the northern shore of the bay. The northern shore is high and offers a fair lee in winds from the north to northeast, and you can expect a surge anywhere in the bay. The southern shore of *Man of War Bay* should not be considered as an anchorage in southerly winds as the water is relatively deep close in to shore. In southerly conditions it's better to use the anchorage at *Alfred Sound* instead.

Matthew Town

Matthew Town-¾ nm W of:
20° 57.10' N, 73° 41.50' W

Navigational Information

Matthew Town is the principal settlement on Great Inagua and the waters are fairly deep close in to shore. A waypoint at 20° 57.10' N, 73° 41.50' W, will place you approximately ¾ mile west of the town dock as shown on Chart IN-2. From the waypoint head east and anchor wherever your draft allows.

The anchorage here is a good lee in light to moderate prevailing winds though there is often a surge. If a front approaches you must go elsewhere, either to *Alfred Sound* or in the lee of *Molasses Reef*. The Erikson brothers made several attempts to build jetties here, but met with disaster as gale after gale destroyed their finest efforts. For those wanting to

land a dinghy here the best thing to do is to head north of town into the small dredged harbor where you can tie up (for a fee-get a receipt) and walk or hitch a ride into town, only a few minutes away. The entrance to the harbor is on a course of 126° on the small pole at the southeastern end of the harbor. Use caution upon entry as rock ledges line both sides of the narrow entrance channel that barely takes 5' at low water. Never attempt to use the small, 200' by 200' harbor as a refuge in a frontal passage, it is a deathtrap as the wrecks inside will testify.

What You Will Find Ashore

Customs and *Immigration*

Matthew Town is a *Port of Entry* and clearance can be obtained at the pink *Customs* office near the town dock.

Fuel

The local *Shell* station will arrange for fuel (gas or diesel) to be delivered to the southern wall of the small harbor if needed. *Shell Trading Ltd.* is the largest gas station and auto parts outlet but you can also find fuel at the *Crystal Service Station* near the harbor, and *Winston Burrows Gas Station*.

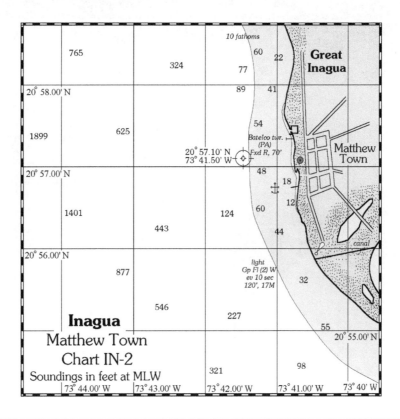

Dining

In town you'll find several restaurants. The *Topp's Restaurant and Bar*, owned by Cleveland Palacious, serves up good Bahamian food and is quite the night spot. Cleveland monitors VHF ch. 16 for those in need of local information. On the other side of town is Sheddie Fox's *Hide Out Café*, one of the more popular spots for nighttime entertainment in Matthew Town. Other good stops are the *Cosy Corner*, *Crystal Ruins*, *Pour More*, the *Last Stop Takeaway*, *Grace's Takeaway, and the Snake Pit*. The *Main House* is a 4-room hotel owned by *MBL*, and accommodations can also be found at the *Crystal Beach Hotel* and *Walker's Guest House*.

Provisions and Propane

If you need propane stop in at the *Inagua General Store* where you can also pick up some groceries before making the next leg of your voyage. *MBL* also owns a store here, *Ingraham's Variety Store*. There are branch offices of the *Royal Bank of Canada* and *The Bank of the Bahamas*. If you'd like a night out

you might want to visit the *Old Salt Theater*, which sometimes presents films and slideshows.

Medical Assistance

There's also a clinic with a doctor and a nurse in Matthew Town and a library/museum in town as well.

Inagua National Park

In 1963, the *Bahamas National Trust* convinced the Government of The Bahamas to set aside 287 square miles of the interior of Great Inagua as a preserve for the long necked, and equally long legged, pink flamingo. Thus was born *Inagua National Park* complete with a Warden and encompassing 12-mile long Lake Windsor and numerous mangrove salinas, the breeding and feeding grounds for the pink flamingo. Resident Warden Henry Nixon has his hands full protecting the lives of some 60,000 pink flamingos. Henry's father, Jimmy Nixon, has been protecting "fillymingos" here since 1952, first as an Audubon Warden and more recently as the Park Warden. Jimmy retired leaving Henry to battle

Salt mounds on Great Inagua

Photo Courtesy of Nicolas Popov

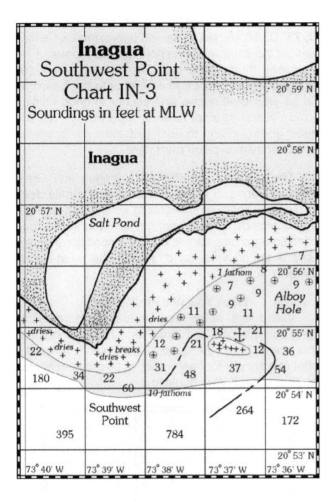

Inagua
Southwest Point
Chart IN-3
Soundings in feet at MLW

Nearby *Union Creek* is a 7-square mile hawksbill and green turtle preserve that was organized by the *Caribbean Conservation Society* and the late Sam Nixon. The purpose of the project is to develop a breeding and research grounds for the pelagic sea turtles. The *Caribbean Conservation Society* and The *Bahamas Ministry of Agriculture and Fisheries* release thousands of newly hatched baby turtles into the waters of Great Inagua in hopes that they will grow to maturity and return to nest on Great Inagua. *Union Creek* also protects the habitat of the Bahamian parrot which only lives on Great Inagua and Great Abaco. The Great Inagua parrot nests in trees unlike their Abaco cousins who nest on the ground. Ask around Matthew Town as there are several people who can arrange tours for you, though it is best to contact Henry Nixon himself.

Southwest Point

With the exception of the anchorage at Alfred Sound inside Northwest Point (see Chart IN-1), the only other place on Great Inagua to offer any sort of protection from southwest winds is approximately 2 miles east of Southwest Point in the lee of *Molasses Reef* as shown on Chart IN-3. I cannot recommend this spot in strong southwesterlies as I have never experienced those winds at this location and the local opinions differ. Some folks say it's a good place to anchor while most say no, stay away in those conditions. I am inclined to believe the nay-sayers in this instance. I would not relish the thought of riding out a prefrontal wind shift to the west behind *Molasses Reef*, but since this is the only protection available I have sounded the area and offer the results here.

Navigational Information

From Matthew Town parallel the coastline of Great Inagua southeastward towards Southwest Point staying at least ½ mile off the reef-strewn shore. Many places along this reef dry and once past Southwest Point the waters closer in to the shore are literally strewn with small heads and patch reefs. Pilotage by eye is essential here.

Round Southwest Point giving it a wide berth, at least ½ mile, and head east approximately 2½ miles until you are past the very visible *Molasses Reef* where you can round up into its lee. You can also pass between *Molasses Reef* and the reef-strewn shore, but it's not advisable, it's easier to pass south of *Molasses Reef* and enter its lee from the east. You won't be able to get close to the southern shore of

poachers on a daily basis as "fillymingo steak" seems to be quite tasty. In ancient Roman times flamingo tongue was a delicacy while here on Great Inagua Nixon can tell you tales of "fillymingo" roundups when entire families ran around chasing the tasty pink birds. Besides worrying about poachers, the Warden has to keep an eye on the wild boars as they have a taste for "fillymingo" as well. The pink flamingos do not breed in great numbers, usually laying just one egg per year. For this reason The *Bahamas National Trust* has begun a hatchling program with 10,000 flamingos being born in one year. The flamingos feed mostly on brine shrimp which helps to maintain their unique pink color. The flamingo may be the only vertebrate that eats standing straight up with its head upside down. Henry Nixon can arrange jeep tours of the Park and you may stay in rather Spartan surroundings in *Basil's Bunkhouse* at *Flamingo Camp* (the *Arthur Vernay Camp*) while you're visiting there.

Great Inagua as the waters are shallow and full of dangerous heads and small patch reefs, but you can still gain some lee by tucking in as close as your draft and nerves allow.

Little Inagua

Ports of Entry: None
Fuel: None
Haul-Out: None
Diesel Repairs: None
Outboard Repairs: None
Propane: None
Provisions: None
Important Lights: None

Little Inagua lies a little over 5 miles north of Northeast Point on Great Inagua and is seldom visited by the typical cruising yacht. The island is relatively flat with a small ridge just inshore that encircles most of the island. The inhospitable eastern shore is guarded by a very shallow and dangerous fringing reef extending from the northwestern tip of Little Inagua southward along the eastern shore to the southern tip of the island.

Approaches

If approaching Little Inagua form the southern end of West Caicos at the western edge of the Caicos Bank, steer to a point north of Little Inagua. From there you can pass to the west of Little Inagua to head southward along the island's western shore to the anchorage off the southwestern coast. An added benefit to cruisers approaching from the east are the *Pinnacles* lying northeast and east of Little Inagua. The Pinnacles are actually the tops of undersea mountains that rise to within 90' of the surface. They are not a hazard to navigation, but they are good fishing grounds so troll a line across here. A lot of the sportfishermen from the Turks and Caicos venture here for the piscatorial action.

Little Inagua

Little Inagua-½ nm W of anchorage:
21° 26.50' N, 73° 03.50' W

Navigational Information
The only anchorage at Little Inagua is in the lee of the island, anywhere along the southwestern shore, but there is no shelter here from westerly winds. The anchorage is only good in winds from the northeast through the southeast, and some swell may work its way in during periods of stronger winds.

As shown on Chart IN-4, a waypoint at 21° 26.50' N, 73° 03.50' W, will place you approximately ½ mile west of the southwestern shore of Little Inagua. Find your way through the break in the reef, you'll see scattered heads about, and head in to the beach as far as your draft allows and anchor in good holding sand. Never attempt to enter here at night as you need good visibility to spot and miss the scattered heads and small patch reefs here.

The passage between Little Inagua and Great Inagua is about 5 miles wide and over a mile deep in places. There is a westward setting current here and this piece of water can get very rough in strong conditions so take care to avoid it if conditions dictate (say a strong west wind against the west-setting current).

What You Will Find Ashore
Inland are some very interesting formations. Here you will find 100' Royal Palms rising out of holes that are at times 30' deep. These same holes are often a reservoir for fresh water if you are in need, but boil the water before drinking it.

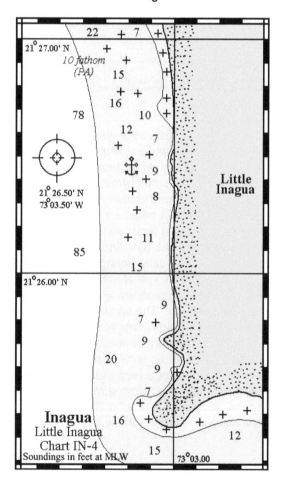

The Caicos Islands

Don Reynolds © 1997   HAITIEN SMAKIE

The Thornless Escape

A Prescription

By Captain David Matthews

S/V TAO

When you've done Stocking Island, up the hill
And told your lies at Chat and Chill,
Checked Peace and Plenty, Two T's in turn,
Now put Chicken Harbour to the stern.

Dreaded cold front's on the way,
Wind's gone south, it's time to say,
Conception Island here we come,
Your eastern side will be some fun."

Feeling smug's a wee bit catching
Wind a' howling, but seas not matching
Raise a glass, boat's set to go
All waiting for Herb's weather window.

Frontal passage does its thing,
Back of the front has a certain ring.
Reefed main and spitfire is our dream,
Just love that breeze abaft the beam.

Now we're out where the big boys play,
Making easting it's safe to say,
It sure beats slogging it under power,
Rum-time soon passing Bird Rock tower.

Shore-leave over, diesel to the top,
Ready now for the next wee hop

ttwood thirty seems slow to close,
Motorsailing madness, wind on the nose.

Northeast Breakers to starboard side,
West Plana's fine after this wild ride,
Barrel sponges, big guys, stories told,
Best SCUBA in the western world.

Behold a miracle, the sea got smooth,
Get this wagon in the groove.
On to Mayaguana's northwest side,
West wind coming, nowhere to hide.

Wind and current, the choppy situation,
Acknowledge Caicos Passage's reputation.
But we're smokin' now and doing fine,
Ticking miles off the ole rhumb line.

Following sea and sails are light,
Surf Sellar's Cut and hang a right.
Customs' coming out and hooks are down,
Passage complete with nary a frown.

Marine sunrise, hot water we've got,
Tiki Hut breakfast hits the spot.
IGA shopping and e-mail that works,
Welcome to Provo, Toast of the Turks!

A Brief History

The *Bahamas Platform*, of which the Turks and Caicos are a part, was created by the shifting of the Earth's plates, a process known as *plate tectonics*, approximately 11-25 million years ago during the era known as the *Miocene*. During the *Pleistocene Era*, about two million years ago, the rise and fall of the sea level segregated the islands of this archipelago. The cays themselves are basically limestone that was laid down as windblown deposits during the *Tertiary*, approximately 1 to 2 million years ago. Most of the current aspect of The Turks and Caicos Islands has been produced in geologically recent times by coral formation. The cays themselves are generally flat with few hills over a hundred feet high and their external limestone is worn razor sharp by the action of wind and wave. Several of the cays are honeycombed with caves and cave holes.

The first inhabitants of the Turks and Caicos Islands of which there is any record of were the Tainos. The Tainos were Arawakan in origin and sprang from South America where their descendants are still to be found in parts of Venezuela and the Guianas. The Arawaks colonized the Caribbean in dugout canoes, a specimen of which in Jamaica was 96' long with an 8' beam and may have carried as many as 150 rowers. The relatively peaceful Tainos, although they were brave warriors, were forced to keep on the move by the presence of the far fiercer Caribs. The Caribs were a cannibalistic group whose chief purpose seemed to be murdering the Arawakan men, enslaving their women, and castrating the young Tainos and fattening them with rich diets and preventing them from engaging in any form of labor to ensure their tender flesh. The Carib religion promised a paradise for the courageous warrior wherein the Arawaks he killed would serve him as slaves while assuring the coward that he would be doomed to a hell wherein he would eternally serve a Taino master. A handful of Caribs survive to this day in Dominica though even less is known of their early culture than the Arawakans.

In their search for peace, the Tainos pushed their canoes northward into the Caribbean, reaching Hispaniola around 200 A.D. and then settling in Cuba and Jamaica over the next two hundred years. They reached the Turks and Caicos and The Bahamas sometime around 700-900 A.D. in the last wave of their migration. Here they became known as *luddu-cairi* or *luko-kayo,* meaning *island people*. We know them today as the Lucayans.

The Caribs were never far behind the Lucayans. By the time Columbus reached the New World, the Caribs had conquered the Lesser Antilles and were raiding Puerto Rico and Hispaniola. Columbus noted scars on the bodies of some of the Lucayans and through sign language was told that people on neighboring islands wanted to capture them and that they had defended themselves.

The Lucayans built circular, conical houses of wood and thatch, and survived on conch, fish, native game and plants. They were basket makers and were adept at manufacturing polished stone implements. Lucayan pottery is called *palmettoware* and it was tempered with bits of conch shell to improve the quality (Lucayan pottery has turned up at several archeological sites throughout the Turks and Caicos Islands since 1912, unfortunately, most of these early finds were removed from the country or simply turned up missing). With the exception of some small gold decorations, the Lucayans had no knowledge of the use of metal. They slept in hammocks, a habit that Spanish seamen soon picked up. And there seems to have been some commerce between the Lucayans on Middle Caicos and their Taino cousins in Cuba and Hispaniola.

The Lucayans were a handsome people, almost oriental in appearance, with broad faces and foreheads flattened in infancy by tying them to boards. This practice was designed to add distinction to their appearance as well as hardening the bone as protection against blows. Mayans and Egyptians shared this unique custom at one time, as did an Indian tribe in Montana called the Flatheads. Lucayans wore their coarse hair in bangs in the front and long in the back. For the most part they wore no clothing, although they painted their faces and sometimes their entire bodies with red, black, and white pigments. They decorated themselves with tattoos, necklaces, bracelets, bones, and feathers. Their chiefs, or *caciques*, were allowed to practice polygamy and served as chief, judge, and priest in their culture. The Lucayans had a class structure and the *caciques* enjoyed all the benefits afforded to their position. The *cacique*'s canoe was the only one that was painted; when traveling by land, they were borne on litters while their children were carried on the shoulders of their servants. After death, the *cacique* was buried along with sufficient supplies for the journey to *Coyaba* along with one or two of his favorite wives.

The Lucayans were lovers of peace and simple pleasures with a gentle and generous nature, sharing anything they had with Columbus and his men. Next to singing and dancing, the Lucayans loved *batos*, an organized ball game similar to volleyball and soccer. The remains of a Lucayan ball court were found on the island of Middle Caicos. Ball courts have been found in Puerto Rico and points farther south but never this far north.

Though they had no written language, their spoken language was described as "soft and not less liquid than Latin." Some 20 Lucayan words and their derivatives survive to this day. Avocado, barbecue, canoe, Carib, cannibal, cassava, cay, guava, hammock, hurricane, iguana, maize, manatee, pirogue, potato, and tobacco all are Lucayan in origin. The Lucayans had their own names for the islands of the Turks and Caicos as well. The Caicos Islands were referred to as *Yucayo* while Providenciales was *Yucacanuco*, West Caicos was *Macubiza*, Middle Caicos was *Aniana*, East Caicos was *Quana*, and South Caicos was known as *Caciba*. The Turks Islands were called *Babueca* by the Lucayans while Grand Turk was known as *Amuana* (and if you accept the *Grand Turk Landfall Theory*, it was known as *Guanahani*), Salt Cay was called *Canamani*, Cotton Cay was *Macarei*, and Great Sand Cay was known as *Cacina*.

It was the Lucayans who taught Columbus' crew their custom of smoking the *cohiba* plant in their strange y-shaped pipes called *tobacco*. The tubes of the Y were inserted in their nostrils and the smoke inhaled until the smoker fell into a stupor. The Spaniards quickly picked up this habit although they did not inhale to the point of intoxication. Although Columbus never reported seeing the Lucayans smoke, in his log he described a leaf that he found a native carrying in his canoe as being highly valued by the Lucayans.

Columbus originally thought the Lucayans had no religion and believed that they would readily become Christians. But the Lucayans actually had a highly developed religion with two supreme beings, a male and a female, and a belief in an afterlife. They also believed in numerous spirit beings called *zemis* who lived in sacred trees, carved images, and in the relics of the dead. These *zemis* had to be appeased with great festivals in their honor. To induce visions of the future, the Lucayans ground into a powder a potent narcotic called *yopo* that they then snorted up the nostrils. A similar drug is still in use by Amerindians in Venezuela to this day (I'll give you three guesses as to what drug this may be). A Lucayan chief under the influence of *yopo*, foresaw the destruction of his civilization by "…strange blonde men in winged canoes."

The discovery of the New World by Columbus (who had blonde, almost white hair) in 1492, sounded the death knell for the Lucayan civilization. Columbus brought back seven Lucayan captives in chains, but two escaped en-route, some say on Providenciales. One returned to Europe with Columbus and was baptized at the Cathedral of Barcelona with the King and Queen of Spain standing as godparents. He took the name Diego Colón and returned with Columbus to the New World in the fall of 1493, where he served as Columbus' interpreter.

It was not long before King Ferdinand of Spain authorized raiding parties to the "useless islands." The Spaniards made some 500 journeys to the islands of The Bahamas and the Turks and Caicos to enslave the Lucayans for their mines and plantations in Cuba and Hispaniola. By 1513, within one generation, no Lucayans were estimated to be left in the Turks and Caicos Islands. The Spanish historian Herrera tells us that when Ponce de León arrived in Grand Turk in late 1512 he could only find one Lucayan to assist him in his search for the fountain of youth on Bimini. Maps of that period show Grand Turk called *Del Viejo* or *Old Man*. By contrast, in 1517 there were an estimated 20,000-40,000 Lucayans in The Bahamas and their price fluctuated at about 4 gold pesos each. The asking price skyrocketed to 150 gold pesos each for these excellent divers when rich pearl beds were discovered off Venezuela and Trinidad. The Spaniards played upon an Arawak superstition and enticed many Lucayans to board ships with promises of returning them to South America, their ancient homeland and the place where their souls would go when they died; *Coyaba*. Many Lucayans did not go willingly, choosing instead to fight the heavily armed Spaniards. Others, even mothers with small children, committed suicide by drinking the juice of the cassava plant to avoid a life of wretchedness at the hands of the cruel Spaniards. The rest died of starvation and ill treatment while in bondage and only a very few lived to old age. By the early 1520s, this peaceful, innocent civilization, that had lived only to satisfy nature without all the trappings of laws and governments, was obliterated from the face of the earth and sadly reduced to a footnote in history.

After the time of the Lucayans, the Turks and Caicos had few visitors save a few Spanish ships stopping in the Turks Islands for salt. The first Englishman to make mention of the island group was Captain John Hawkins of Plymouth, a well-known privateer who passed by the Caicos group in 1564 in search of salt. The islands re-entered history in the middle of the 17th Century when salt rakers from Bermuda decided to use three of the Turks Islands for an entrepreneurial venture. In the 1640s they created salt ponds on Salt Cay, Grand Turk, and South Caicos, and their endeavor was successful enough to create the basis for the local economy for the next two centuries. Even today, some consider the fine, white Turk's Island salt the preferred preservative and seasoning. From about 1678 onwards, Bermudian salt rakers of British descent were populating the islands, at first only in the dry season, and later on, living on the islands full-time. They immediately set out to destroy all the trees, seeking to increase salt production.

At first the salt rakers collected salt for their own use, but as their commodity increased in value it became the backbone of the Bermudian economy for over 100 years. Settlers on these islands during this time lived primarily off their salt production, fishing, and wrecking. While The Bahamas severed its ties with Bermuda in 1663, the salt rakers in the Turks and Caicos continued to maintain a link with the island. Several petitions were submitted to Parliament to annex these islands to Bermuda but all were turned down.

As Spanish shipping activity increased in the New World, the era of privateering began. Spanish ships laden with the riches of the New World would pass through the waters of the Turks and Caicos and The Bahamas on their way back to Spain making wrecking very profitable in these waters. It was said that if a crewman were lucky enough to survive the wreck, it was uncertain as to whether he would survive the wreckers. If the Spanish knew of the location of their wrecks they would send crews to salvage the valuables. Bahamian and Turks Island wreckers would drive off the intruders and loot what they had salvaged.

As Captains became wise to the ways of the wreckers, wrecks became fewer and fewer, the privateers had to find other uses for their talents. This was not difficult, the era of the buccaneers was in full swing.

The original buccaneers (*boucaniers*), the forerunners of the pirates, were based just south of the Turks and Caicos Islands at Tortuga. They were a wild group of men from France, Holland, and England, indentured servants, seafarers, and adventurers. They wore colorful, picturesque garb and hunted the semi-wild cattle and pigs on the island, descendents of escapees from Spanish farms. They roasted the meat over fires called *boucans* and would sell this smoked meat product, along with hides and tallow, to passing ships. Hispaniola soon became the location of a huge illicit meat and hides trade. The *boucaniers* quickly learned to live less off hunting and rely more on their commerce with Spanish ships, first in canoes, then "acquiring" ships, and finally in small flotillas.

From 1629 to 1641, English buccaneers were organized as a company, using the island of Providence off the Nicaraguan coast as a base. The 1630s were a prosperous era for the Providence based buccaneers. Their prosperity ended abruptly in 1641, when the Spanish invaded the island and massacred every settler they could find. The few who escaped shifted their base of operations to Tortuga, an island off the northern coast of Hispaniola just south of the Turks and Caicos Islands. Recruits from every European trading nation began to pour in. By the middle 1600s the buccaneers formed armed bands who were accustomed to hardship, had strong codes of honor that they chose to live by, and were extremely well led. For over 75 years these buccaneers were the scourge of the Spanish fleet. In the 1640s, a buccaneer from Normandy who called himself Pierre Le Grand, often called the "Father of Piracy in the West Indies," boldly captured a Spanish galleon in the passage between Tortuga and the *Caicos Bank* while her crew slept. Le Grand and his 28 men approached the galleon in an old dilapidated raft, not far from sinking when the captain of the galleon spied their craft. Laughing at the condition of their vessel and the ragtag crew, the captain said he would not fear them even if they were the size of his own galleon. Le Grand had bored holes in the bottom of his boat to insure that his men were properly motivated, that either they would take the galleon or the sea would take them. Le Grand and his men pulled alongside the galleon and wedged the big ship's rudder and climbed aboard just as their own little boat sank beneath the waves. Le Grand and his men took the ship without a shot and Le Grand himself burst into the officer's cabin in the midst of a quiet card game. Le Grand took the ship to France after allowing those of the galleon's crew who would not join his ranks to depart on the island of Hispaniola. Pierre Le Grand is believed to be the only pirate to have ever taken a galleon. After Le Grand and his men divvied up their spoils, they retired from the sea and Le Grand was said to have lived happily to a ripe old age.

Most prominent of the buccaneers were Edward Mansfield and the legendary Sir Henry Morgan. In 1664, Mansfield and Morgan set up a base in Nassau and were received quite favorably. Nassau came to be quite the haven for the wandering buccaneers. Mansfield's early and untimely death created confusion in the leadership of the buccaneers and Morgan set them off on a course of plunder and profit. The years between 1671 and 1686 were a time of buccaneer ascendancy as the buccaneers gained major European finance against the Spanish Empire. After the capture of Jamaica in 1655, Port Royal, just outside of Kingston, became the headquarters for English buccaneers and remained so for 20 years. Under Sir Thomas Modyford and Sir Henry Morgan their achievements reached a climax. The *Treaty of Madrid* with Spain in 1670, the death of Sir Henry Morgan in 1688, and finally the destruction by earthquake of Port Royal in 1692 dispersed these Jamaican-based buccaneers.

There is no fine line as to when the buccaneers became pirates. *Webster's* offers little difference between the two. History suggests that the code of honor of the early buccaneers was forgotten and the bands degenerated into piracy. The buccaneers had articles called *chasseparties* that allocated duties, rewards, and compensations. In all things, their brotherhood was expected to observe a rigid code of honor called *la coutume de la côte*, which roughly translated means, *the custom of the coast*. Despite their code and the *chasseparties*, the English and French buccaneers were always quarreling. The number of English buccaneers at Tortuga having to rely on French protection increased year by year. The Jamaica and Carolina legislatures passed severe acts against them and the buccaneers became less and less particular about their prey. By 1685 their own people were even calling them pirates. Whatever unity there was between the British and French buccaneers dissolved when their two countries went to war after William of Orange ascended the English Throne in 1689. This struggle was to last 126 years with only one long break. Loyal English were no longer welcome in Hispaniola and when the Anglo-French fighting reached the Caribbean in 1691, the

last of the English pirates left the safety of Tortuga and settled in areas of The Bahamas and the Turks and Caicos. Most of their activity was centered in the Nassau area but roaming pirates are said to have consistently used areas such as Parrot Cay, French Cay, and Grand Turk as bases from which to stage raids. By 1713, there were an estimated 1,000 active pirates operating in the waters of The Bahamas and the Turks and Caicos. One interesting theory about how the Turks Islands received their name suggests that in the 16th and 17th centuries, under the leadership of the two Barbarosa brothers, a band of Barbary pirates operated out of these waters. Originating in Constantinople, the brothers eventually settled on an uninhabited salt island that the Spanish later referred to as Grand Turk.

Some of the most notorious pirates to be found in the pages of history have been reported as lurking in Turks and Caicos waters over the years. Mary Read and Anne Bonney, the "lady" pirates who sailed with Calico Jack Rackham, Stede Bonnet the Gentleman Pirate, Benjamin Hornigold, Charles Vane, Captain Kidd, L'Olonnois, and Edward Teach who was much better known as Blackbeard. If any one pirate could embody the spirit of the era and of piracy itself, none would be better suited for it than Blackbeard. From 1713 until 1716 he teamed up with Benjamin Hornigold and was based in Nassau along with Captains Jennings, Burgess, and White. Blackbeard's independent pirate career lasted only two short years, from 1716 when he acquired his first ship, the *Queen Anne's Revenge*, until his death in the Carolinas in 1718.

Jean-David Rau, who named himself L'Olonnois after his birthplace in les Sables D'Olonne in Brittany, was one of the old guard, one of the last of the original *boucaniers* of Tortuga, and one of the most ruthless psychopathic pirates in history. He is said to have used French Cay, just south of Providenciales, as a hideout to wait on Spanish vessels heading northward through the *Windward Passage*. Recently the gentleman who started that rumor has since withdrawn his original statement though it is possible that L'Olonnois actually might have stayed there. Such a reputation did he create for himself that Spanish sailors would rather die fighting or drowning than to fall into his hands. If a captive would not tell L'Olonnois what he wished to know, L'Olonnois would often cut him to pieces and pull out his tongue. He had been known to hack a man to pieces one slice at a time, first a finger, then a hand, then an arm, until there was nothing left to remove, or the poor fellow died. He also practiced *woolding*, that is, tying a piece of rope around a man's head and twisting it tighter and tighter with a stick until his eyes popped out. L'Olonnois was the scourge of Central and South America from the Yucatan to Venezuela. His most famous torment involved a Spanish crew that remained silent concerning a route into a town in Central America, the main road being blocked and heavily protected. L'Olonnois ripped open one man's chest and began to gnaw on his still beating heart telling the rest of his hostages "I will serve you alike if you do not show me another way."

L'Olonnois met a fitting end. After an engagement with a Spanish flotilla that nearly decimated his band of buccaneers, he and some of his crew took to land working their way into the jungles of the Central and Southern America. Here cannibals made a meal of him and all but five of his surviving crew.

A stranger piratical trio than Calico Jack Rackham, Anne Bonney, and Mary Read would be hard to find. Anne Bonney and her penniless sailor husband moved to Nassau seeking employment. There she meet Calico Jack Rackham who soon swept her off her feet. She eloped with Rackham, heading off to sea in men's clothes. Calico Jack put her ashore with friends in Jamaica when she became pregnant until such time as she gave birth and could rejoin him. She later accompanied Rackham on all his later exploits. Mary Read, raised as a boy by her grandmother, joined an army unit as a cadet and fought bravely. She fell in love and eventually married another soldier, who at first did not realize that she was a woman. After her husband died she again dressed up as a man and went on board a vessel bound for the West Indies.

Read soon joined up with a band of privateers under Woodes Rogers on the island of Providence. Mary Read claimed she detested the life of the pirate; however, when some of the crew mutinied and returned to their former lifestyle, with them went Mary Read. She wound up on board Calico Jack's ship and no one had guessed she was a woman. And then along came Anne Bonney. Bonney thought Read was a rather handsome fellow and became enamored of her, forcing her to reveal her secret. Jealous Calico Jack, noticed the partiality Bonney was showing to Read and threatened to shoot him/her. Once again her secret was revealed. Mary Read later fell in love with another crew member and

revealed herself to him. When her lover fell into a disagreement with another crew member and the two were to duel ashore in two hours, Read found out and engaged the crew member in an argument and promptly killed him.

In 1719, Calico Jack was finally captured and removed from his ship. During the battle Anne Bonney, Mary Read, and one other crew member were the last fighters on deck, the rest of the crew fleeing below. Mary Read tried in vain to rouse the crew, finally killing one and wounding another before the lady buccaneers were captured. Rackham, who at this point was estranged from his mate, had taken to enjoying a bush hallucinogen and was removed from his below decks hiding place in a stupor. In court, when asked how they pled, Mary Read and Anne Bonney promptly announced, "My Lord, we plead our bellies!" Both women were pregnant and English law at the time forbade hanging a mother to be, no matter how serious her crime. Mary Read later became ill and died in prison, thereby cheating the hangman. Anne Bonney, through the intercession of some notable Jamaican planters, escaped the noose and was never executed. Calico Jack, while awaiting execution, was allowed a brief visit from Anne Bonney. Instead of consoling Rackham, she only told him that she was sorry to see him here and that if he had fought like a man he would not have to die like a dog. Anne Bonney wound up in Virginia, married with children. Parrot Cay, a corruption of Pirate Cay, is said to be one of Rackham, Bonney's, and Read's favorite hideouts. Legend also had it that in 1850, the English Captain Delaney recovered over $130,000 in pirate loot from Sand Cay.

When Woodes Rogers began to break up the pirate presence in The Bahamas, fewer and fewer brethren of the coast visited the nearby Turks and Caicos Islands. Some privateering and wrecking continued through the remainder of the 18th and into the 19th centuries. Details of this era are sketchy at best, but it is known that in 1725 Grand Turk was seasonally occupied by upwards of 1,000 laborers raking salt, fishing for turtles, and wrecking.

Spain occupied the Turks Islands in 1710, even as the salt rakers prospered. France claimed the Turks and Caicos Islands in 1753 and erected wooden columns on them bearing her coat of arms. The crew of a British vessel from Charleston, Carolina, destroyed these columns the following year. France later occupied Grand Turk and Salt Cay from 1778 to 1783 as the salt rakers continued their flourishing enterprise. During the American Revolution, Bermudian Salt Rakers ignored the British blockade and shipped salt to Washington's armies.

In 1766, in spite of the Bermudian's objections, The Bahamas government extended its jurisdiction to the Turks and Caicos Islands, while on the North American continent a rebellion was brewing. The *Stamp Act* of 1765 was the beginning of the end of British rule in the colonies. The American Revolution was getting underway and it was as much a revolt as it was a civil war. An estimated 20% of the population of the colonies was fiercely loyal to the Crown and hostile to the American cause.

Known as Tories, the Loyalists favored reconciliation with the Crown. Many stood to lose jobs, commerce, or prestige if the upstart rebels were victorious. Many Loyalists suffered greatly at the hands of the Patriots. Some were socially ostracized and their businesses boycotted; others who refused to sign loyalty oaths to the rebellion were accused of treason and often had all their land and possessions confiscated. Still more were tarred and feathered in the name of Patriotism.

Many Loyalists were sent to the notorious *Simsburg Copper Mines* in Connecticut. They worked in holes 150' below the surface and so many died there that the mine was known as the "Catacombs of Loyalty." The Patriots became even more hostile and vengeful after the defeat of Cornwallis at Yorktown in 1781. Many Loyalists sought refuge in eastern Florida, as Florida was not involved in the American Revolution.

In 1783, just before the end of the American Revolution, a French contingent seized the Turks Islands. They successfully repelled a counter attack by the Captain of the *HMS Albemarle,* the young Horatio Nelson. The French had little influence on the islands and *Treaty of Versailles* on January 20, 1783 restored The Bahamas and the Turks and Caicos to England and gave Florida to Spain. The Loyalists in Florida felt cheated that Florida was being traded for The Bahamas and were irate at having to move again. No longer feeling safe in the colonies, the Loyalists looked elsewhere for safe haven.

Most of the Loyalists that arrived in the Turks and Caicos had holdings in the South Carolina and Georgia area. Probably the best known of these Loyalists was Wade Stubbs who emigrated from Gasworth in England's County Cheshire to East Florida, near St. Augustine between 1775 and 1778. When the Loyalists fled the mainland, the Crown granted 72 of them approximately 18,000 acres on North and Middle Caicos. Stubbs received 860 acres, the second largest of the 332 grants given, fashioned from the 10,090 acres on North Caicos. He initially called his plantation "Bellefield." In 1790 Wade Stubbs convinced his brother Thomas to leave Cheshire and join him. Thomas built a plantation called Cheshire Hall on Blue Caicos, what is today known as Providenciales

Thomas Stubbs started out growing Anguilla or long staple Sea Island cotton. Anguilla cotton grew to the size of small, bushy trees and produced a high quality cotton. Many of these plants still survive today in the bush on North and Middle Caicos. For several years the plantations flourished and were producing large yields; land values soared from £9,450 for a tract to over £70,000 per tract. Soon yields began getting smaller and smaller. The problems in production came from removing the sticky seeds from the cotton bolls, the chenille bugs that devoured the sweet leaves, and the fact that cotton quickly strips the soil of nutrients mandating long fallow periods of manuring to maintain yields. Eli Whitney's cotton gin solved the first problem in 1793, but the other two problems caused the downfall of the cotton business in the Turks and Caicos Islands. Also, a devastating hurricane in 1813 added to the abandonment of the plantations. Thomas Stubbs' *Cheshire Hall* cotton plantation was hit harder than most by the chenille bug and fertilization problems, and in 1810 he sold Cheshire Hall.

In 1791, Wade Stubbs was named a *Justice of the Peace* and as the years went by, added to his holdings of land and slaves, he was quite the Loyalist success story. He had purchased other plantations from other Loyalists who were deserting them and had so much land that he could leave vast tracts of land to fallow as yields fell. He purchased the Haulover Plantation on Middle Caicos after the original owners left. Cotton on that estate was still being raised within the memory of people still living today. Stubbs success was in part due to the fact that he raised enough stock to supply his fields with manure. So successful and important was this cotton trade that after the independence of Haiti in 1799, the British government built Fort George on a small cay just southwest of North Caicos to protect the cotton industry.

In 1800, 14 of Wades Stubbs' slaves stole one of his sloops and escaped. After 1806, Stubbs referred to *Bellefield* as *Wade's Green*, a name indicating his affection for the land and his prosperity. Wade Stubbs died in 1822 and was buried in a stone crypt behind *St. Thomas' Church* on Grand Turk. At the time of his death Wade Stubbs owned over 3,000 acres on North Caicos, 5,000 acres on Providenciales, and even more land on Middle Caicos, including Haulover. He had 384 slaves, all but 8 of whom were in the Caicos Islands. Some of his estate went to his nephew Henshell Stubbs, a Grand Turk salt producer, but most went to his namesake cousin, another Wade Stubbs, who continued living at *Wade's Green* until about 1850. After emancipation in 1833, the Stubbs slaves, some farming and some working in salt in the Turks, were freed and the plantations came to disrepair and disuse. In 1882 the government of the Turks and Caicos Islands purchased 1,800 acres of *Wade's Green* for division into 25-acre parcels to encourage farming. In 1885 the Stubbs house was refurbished as a combination courthouse, jail, and quarters for a magistrate who was posted there to stimulate the faltering settlement.

Between the years of 1827 and 1847 a salt tax was producing a quarter of the revenue of The Bahamas and Turks islanders were indignant. None of the money they paid in taxes was going to help their islands and the price of salt dropped considerably though the Salt Tax stayed the same. Though they were represented in Nassau, the distance and travel time involved limited the time a representative actually sat in Assembly. Although a mailboat reached Long Cay once a month and Grand Turk only four times a year, the only Bahamians they ever saw were tax collectors. Several boats bound for Jamaica passed through on a regular basis however and the Turks islanders grew to feel more kinship with Kingston than with Nassau.

After continuing complaints to the Crown an investigation was in order. The Governor of The Bahamas, George B. Matthew, made a perilous 18-day voyage from Nassau to Grand Turk which convinced him of the difficulties in transportation, communication, and life in general in these harsh islands. Separation was recommended. In 1848, the Turks and Caicos Islands were granted a separate charter providing for internal self-government subject to the Governor of Jamaica, a more pleasing proposition for the Turks islanders than continuing Bahamian rule.

The next few years were marked by prosperity in the salt business and the new government seemed to be working well. Then, in the evening of September 30, 1866, a devastating hurricane hit Grand Turk. By morning 63 were dead, over 750 homes destroyed, and more than a million bushels of salt were washed away. The country and its economy were literally left in ruins and the salt market became depressed in the ensuing years. In 1872 the islanders petitioned Queen Victoria to annex the Turks and Caicos Islands to Jamaica, which she did in 1873.

Over the following years the Turks and Caicos islanders continued to run their own affairs to a large extent. Unfortunately, Jamaican rule became no more popular than the preceding Bahamian rule. In reality, little was gained in the islands by their bond to Jamaica. When Jamaica became independent in 1962, the people of the Turks and Caicos Islands overwhelmingly wished to become a British Crown Colony. They got their wish. Also in 1962, John Glenn, after his famous space flight, first set foot back on planet Earth at Grand Turk.

Today the islands enjoy autonomous internal rule although the Governor is appointed by the Queen. Since undergoing massive economic development from 1967, the Turks and Caicos Islands have emerged as a world-class tourism destination and a major offshore financial center.

In 1976, the first constitution was granted to the islands creating a ministerial form of government. The present constitution did not come into being until March 4th, 1988. The Turks and Caicos Islands are a parliamentary democracy implementing the traditional Westminster model. The government consists of a governor, appointed by the Crown, who acts as the Queen's representative and is responsible for internal security, external affairs, defense, and certain judicial matters. The Legislative Council (LegCo) consists of 13 elected members serving four-year terms, three appointed members, a Speaker who is selected from outside or from the elected or appointed members who are not Executive Council (ExCo) members. The Executive Council, which is responsible for the day-to-day business of government, consists of the Governor, Attorney General, Chief Secretary, Financial Secretary, and the Chief Minister and his cabinet of four appointed ministers selected from the elected members of the Legislative Council.

In recent decades many Turks and Caicos islanders left their homes to find work in The Bahamas leaving huge gaps in the work force at home which are quite often filled by workers from Haiti and the Dominican Republic. With the huge tourism boom on Providenciales, this is slowly changing, as more and more native sons and daughters are finding adequate employment in their homeland. The tourism boom is increasing steadily with each passing year; one can only foresee prosperous times ahead for the Turks and Caicos islanders.

The constitution of 1976 was amended in recent years, but in any case has now been suspended since August 2009 and the Islands are now under the direct rule of Great Britain pending a further revision.

The Caicos Islands

Ports of Entry:
Providenciales, South Caicos, North Caicos
Fuel: Providenciales, South Caicos
Haul-Out: Providenciales
Diesel Repairs: Grand Turk, Providenciales, Salt Cay, South Caicos
Outboard Repairs: Grand Turk, Providenciales, South Caicos
Propane: Grand Turk, North Caicos, Providenciales, South Caicos
Provisions: Grand Turk, North Caicos, Middle Caicos, Providenciales, South Caicos
Important Lights:
North West Pt., Providenciales: Gp Fl (3) W 15s
Providenciales, Bird Cay: Fl W ev 10 sec
Cape Comete, E. Caicos: Gp Fl (2) W ev 20 sec
West Caicos, Southwest Point: Q R
French Cay: Fl R
South Caicos: Fxd W
Long Cay, east end: Fl R ev 2.5 sec
Dove Cay, west end: Fl G ev 2.5 sec
Bush Cay: Gp Fl (2) W ev 10 sec

The Caicos Islands, for the most part, lie on the northern edge of the huge *Caicos Bank* west of the Turks Islands and separated from their sister cays by the ocean deep *Turks Island Passage*. The Turks and Caicos archipelago lies approximately 575 miles southeast of Miami and about 450 miles northeast of Jamaica. The majority of the land area, population, tourist industry, and yachting scene in the Turks and Caicos Islands are located in the Caicos Islands themselves, specifically on Providenciales.

Some say the Caicos Islands derived their name from *Caya Hica*, the Lucayan words for *String of Islands*, while others say the term is said to be derived from the Spanish *cayos* meaning rocky islands, while still others say the name *Caicos* is Lucayan in origin.

Limestone caves abound in the Turks & Caicos Islands where spelunking is becoming a popular activity. Some of the best caverns are on East and Middle Caicos, the latter of which is also home to some dazzling surface formations of limestone. Several valuable archaeological sites containing pre-Columbian artifacts have recently been found in some of the caves on Middle Caicos.

A very unusual and interesting phenomena occurs on a monthly basis after a full moon throughout the Caicos Islands. Look for an ebb tide about 3-6 nights after a full moon. About 1 hour after sunset, for around 15 minutes, the marine worm *Odontosyllis enopia* performs a sparkling mating ritual. Simply called *Glowworms*, the female of the species releases an egg mass that spirals to the surface emitting a pulsating pale green luminescence. The male, also glowing, does a zigzag sort of maneuver until he encounters these egg masses, causing an even brighter green flow. The number of mating displays may change from month to month but the spawning cycle is dictated by the lunar and solar patterns happening only a few nights of the month. This is a fascinating ritual to watch and most charter boat operators offer sunset glowworm cruises complete with dinner and drinks.

Approaches

Abraham's Bay - ¼ nm SSE of E entrance:
22° 20.80' N, 72° 58.30' W

Southeast Point - 1 nm WSW of anchorage:
22° 16.70' N, 72° 48.40' W

Vessels approaching the Caicos Islands from The Bahamas usually make Mayaguana their last stop in this island chain as they work their way south to Provo. From the waypoint at the eastern entrance to *Abraham's Bay*, 22° 21.70'N, 72° 58.45'W, the entrance to *Sandbore Channel* lies 46.6 miles away on a course of 150° while *Leeward Cut* bears 134° at 54.1 nautical miles distant. Bruce Van Sant, in his *Gentleman's Guide to Passages South*, suggests using Southeast Point as a staging area and leaving from there instead of the slightly longer run from *Abraham's Bay*. This is not a bad idea, but perhaps

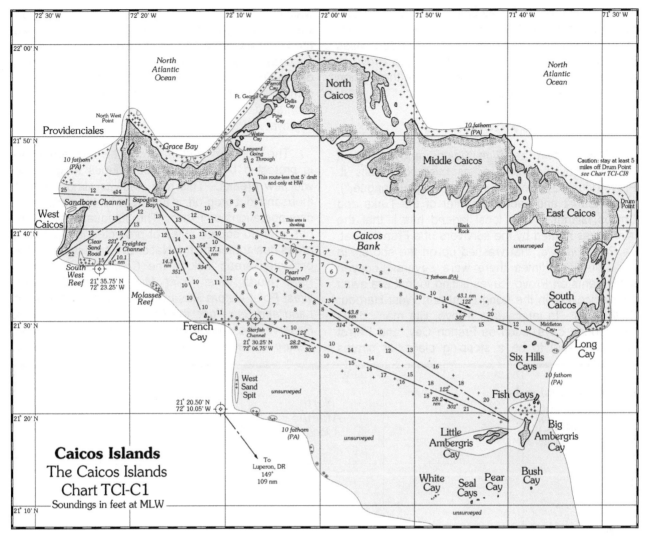

Caicos Islands
The Caicos Islands
Chart TCI-C1
Soundings in feet at MLW

a bit outdated for today's crop of cruisers. Although staging at Southeast Point gives you a better angle on the wind and shortens the overall distance (if you don't count the over 11 miles traveled from *Abraham's Bay* to Southeast Point), most cruisers today don't bother with wind angles and simply turn on the engine and motorsail from *Abraham's Bay* or *Start Bay* to Provo. In southeast winds the reef at Southeast Point gives you no protection whatsoever, and the only protection you have at Southeast Point is from winds from the northeast to east (unless you want tuck into the northerly part of the bay in northerly winds). From the waypoint at Southeast Point, Mayaguana, 22° 16.70'N, 72° 48.40'W, *Sandbore Channel* bears 157° at a distance of 37.6 nautical miles while *Leeward Cut* bears 135° at 44 miles. The primary hazards on the route from Mayaguana to *Sellar's Pond*, *Stubbs Cut*, or *Leeward Cut* are the reefs off North West Point on Providenciales. A waypoint at 21° 53.10'N, 72°

19.90'W, will place you approximately ½ mile north of the reefs in deep water. If your route takes you to *Sellar's Pond*, *Stubbs Cut*, or *Leeward Cut*, especially at night, do not venture south of this waypoint until east of 72° 17' W. Also, bear in mind that when you head towards *Sandbore Channel*, once at the entrance you still have more than nine miles of easting to make before you reach the safety of the anchorage at *Sapodilla Bay*.

Vessels heading for the *Caicos Banks* from the Turks Islands must first cross the deep *Turks Island Passage*, sometimes called the *Columbus Passage*. From the *Front Street* anchorage at Grand Turk, the waypoint at the entrance to Cockburn Harbour on South Caicos bears 281° at a distance of 21.1 nautical miles. From Salt Cay, Cockburn Harbour bears 306° at 19.3 miles, while from Great Sand Cay it bears 328° at 22.7 miles distant. *Long Cay Cut* at the south end of Long Cay bears 275º at 23.4 miles from the Front Street anchorage at Grand Turk, 298º at 20.6 miles from Salt Cay, and 320º at 22.9 miles from Great Sand Cay. Vessels heading to Provo or from across the *Caicos Bank* should see the section entitled *Routes Across the Caicos Bank.*

Providenciales

Once known as *Blue Caicos* and *Provident Caicos*, Providenciales, or as everybody calls it, Provo ("Just say Provo mon, don' hurt your tongue."), is the tourist and yachting center of the Turks and Caicos Islands. One local legend has it that the island was named by the survivors of a French boat, *La Providentielle*, that washed up on the shore. In pre-Columbian times there were several Lucayan settlements on Provo; caves dating to that era await your discovery in the Long Point and West Harbour Bluff areas. In later years, Provo, like many of its neighboring cays, such as French Cay, and Parrot Cay, was said to be a stopping place for pirates

waiting to ambush treasure laden vessels plying the waters of the *Caicos Passage*. As in The Bahamas, the Loyalists came and went next. They found less success in the Turks and Caicos Islands than they did in The Bahamas, primarily due to its more arid climate. The ruins of the Loyalist era *Cheshire Hall Plantation* lie near the *Market Place* on *Leeward Highway.*

The northern and most of the western shore is protected by an almost continuous fringing reef with few breaks. This reef, with its almost vertical thousand foot drop-off, is the focus for the multitude of dive operations on Provo. The 38 square mile island has over 30 square miles of protected land and sea areas designated by the National Parks system. The protected areas include the *Chalk Sound National Park*, *North West Point Marine Park*, the *North West Point Nature Reserve*, the *Princess Alexandra Land and Sea Park,* the *Princess Alexandra Nature Reserve*, the *Pigeon Pond and Frenchman's Creek Nature Reserve*, the *Cheshire Hall Loyalist Ruins,*

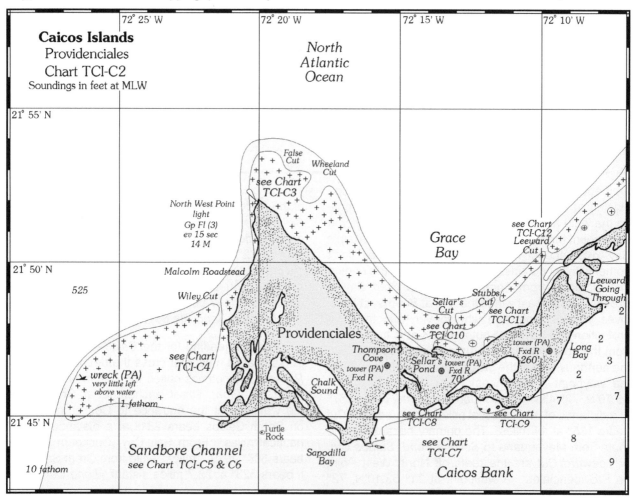

and *Sapodilla Hill*, with its stones engraved by shipwrecked sailors.

The three oldest settlements on the island are The Bight and Blue Hills on the northern shore and Five Cays on the southern shore. The Bight and Blue Hills were built around fresh water supplies and these locations give one a real feeling of a Caribbean settlement. Blue Hills had a notorious reputation as the wrecking capital of the island until just after the American Civil War. Nearby *North West Reef* contributed much to this profession and to the reputation of the community. Five Cays is primarily a fishing settlement with a large Haitian population. As recently as 1960, these three villages were all there was to Providenciales. It was on Provo that the economy of the Turks and Caicos first experienced its rebirth in the late 1960s, as tourism began to take over from the steadily declining salt industry.

In 1966, a Swedish surveyor named Bengt Soderqvist met with Fritz Luddington, who had been flying over the island for many years. Fritz was once the owner of the Two Turtles Inn in George Town, Exuma, Bahamas. These two shared their interests with other developers of vision. The government allowed the group to lease/purchase some 4,000 acres on Providenciales. In October of 1966, the seven investors, affectionately called the *Seven Dwarfs*, arrived on Providenciales on a boat of the same name. Tommy Coleman was the advance man for Fritz Luddington and his *Provident Ltd.* group. The other five investors were Julia Barber, Rogers Morton, Peter Thompson, Theodore Roosevelt III, and Richard DuPont. *Provident Ltd.* had certain obligations to meet to satisfy the government in order to receive the acreage, and these were met by 1971, scarcely five years from the inception of the project. This included the dredging of *Sellar's Pond* (now home to *Turtle Cove Marina*) and the creation of a channel to the sea, the building of roads to connect the three settlements of Blue Hills, The Bight, and Five Cays, the construction of a hotel and jetty at Five Cays, and the employment of a certain number of the local population. The jetty was actually constructed at *South Dock* as Five Cays was too shallow.

Provident Ltd. laid the early groundwork for the boom that was to come, and Provo is still right in the midst of that tourism boom. Resorts, marinas, restaurants, condos, residential projects, dive operations, a casino, and several shopping centers have all sprung up in recent years, and the end is

nowhere in sight. Provo serves more than 100,000 visitors annually and it is a truly cosmopolitan island where you will find native Turks and Caicos islanders (*Belongers*), American, European, and Canadian expatriates, Haitians, Dominicans, and a variety of other nationalities and cultures. There are several major resorts, a casino, and one posh golf course.

Many cruisers have a love/hate relationship with Provo. Just as you cannot judge The Bahamas by Nassau, if you don't like Provo don't judge all the islands of the Turks and Caicos group by her standards. You'll find that many residents on the other islands in the Turks and Caicos archipelago often say that Provo is too cosmopolitan, that it tries to be too American. Indeed, Provo has a livelier nightlife, and more hustle and bustle than Grand Turk and South Caicos, and may give one the impression of being more of a suburb of Florida than a Caribbean hideaway. You will find that the rest of the islands of the Turks and Caicos have a much more laid-back out-island feel to them. A final note; if you are having any packages or mail sent to you in the Turks and Caicos and especially Provo, have them sent by *UPS* or *FedEx*, never by regular mail delivery, don't even think of sending it first class or airmail. It might take weeks. Even going by *UPS* or *FedEx* may pose a danger, although not common. I once ordered a part from a major marine supplier and told them to *FedEx* it to me in the Turks and Caicos Islands. Somehow, I still don't know how, it got to me even though it was addressed to the Cocos Keeling Islands. I've had other friends who found their mail had been forwarded to St. Kitts instead of the Turks and Caicos Islands, while others have had packages shipped to Turkey. You'd think that in this modern age…

North West Point, Sandbore Channel

North West Point, Provo - ½ nm N of reef:
21° 53.10' N, 72° 19.90' W

Malcolm Roadstead - ½ nm W of anchorage:
21° 49.85' N, 72° 20.80' W

Wiley Cut - ¼ nm NNW of cut:
21° 48.85' N, 72° 21.35' W

Navigational Information

Vessels approaching *Sapodilla Bay* and the western shore of Providenciales from Mayaguana or the Plana Cays will have no obstructions. If headed to Leeward Going Through or *Turtle Cove Marina* at *Sellar's Pond* on the northern shore of Provo on

Grace Bay, you must take care to avoid the reefs off North West Point as shown on Chart TCI-C2. A good rule of thumb is not to head south of 21° 53'N until east of 72° 17'W.

South of North West Point on the western shore of Providenciales is a great anchorage in prevailing winds with quite an amusing history. *Malcolm Roadstead* offers a deep, reef-clear entrance right up to the beach as shown on Chart TCI-C3. Columbus is said to have anchored here in October of 1492. You too can anchor right off the beach in 8'-15' of water just off the new resort (don't try to anchor here with winds or seas with any northerly component to them.). A waypoint at 21° 49.85'N, 72° 20.80'W will place you approximately ½ mile west of the anchorage. From this position simply head in towards shore and anchor wherever your draft allows just off the beach. A good landmark to look for is the first large hill south of North West Point: it has a very distinctive white sandy road running vertically down its western face and the anchorage lies about ¼-½ mile south of the hill.

There are several mooring balls here that are suitable for boats of 60' in length and larger. These are primarily for the local dive boats but cruisers are permitted to use one if no commercial vessel requires it. There is good diving at, around, and near each mooring so be sure to avail yourself of the opportunity to view steep walls alive with corals.

Until recent years, this area was home to the *Tiki Huts,* shown on some charts as *Atlantic Village,* which were originally the set of a French game show called *Pago Pago.* The theme was a South Pacific island where contestants could win various prizes by completing several tasks. Just offshore is a dive site that consists of a large metal cage left over by the show. Contestants were required to dive down into the cage to catch small plastic pearls that were released into the water by a huge artificial "sponge" inside this cage. Nearby were several mermaids with SCUBA tanks to offer air to the divers when they needed a breath, bracelet-like rings that the divers earned were traded underwater for breaths of air. However there was one bad mermaid who would signal a diver over for a breath and then swim away. This was done to add a bit of excitement to the show. You can imagine the problems they might have had with this format. The show filmed less than a dozen episodes that are sometimes still shown today on the local cable TV station. Today, this area is the home to the *Amanyara Resort,* a private, world class resort

featuring individual villas, each with a private chef and swimming pool!

Just south of *Malcolm Roadstead* is narrow *Wiley Cut* just north of Wiley Point. Vessels with drafts of less than 6' can, with the tide, work their way along the western shore of Provo from *Wiley Cut* to West Harbour Bluff on the inside of the reef, but I do not recommend this route for the average cruiser. This route is dangerous and should only be attempted by the skilled reef-navigator with excellent visibility and calm conditions. By using this route you'll save only a little time by not going around the reef to the mouth of the *Sandbore Channel* and the risk involved is not worth the few minutes saved. I only show this passage because it can be done and several local charter and dive boats use this reef-strewn route.

A waypoint at 21° 48.85'N, 72°, 21.35'W, will place you approximately ¼ mile north/northwest of *Wiley Cut* as shown on Chart TCI-C4. Never, I repeat NEVER, attempt this route with the sun directly in your eyes, with heavy following seas, or during periods of poor visibility and cloudy, murky water. Head in through the cut on a heading of SSE-SE keeping between the two very visible reefs. Work your way around Wiley Point as shown on Chart TCI-C4 steering between the numerous shallow heads and patch reefs that are strewn across the northern section of this route and, believe me, they are thick through here. Keep working your way southward, zigzagging between the heads, reefs, and shallow bars that begin to thin out along with the water around *North Creek.* Do not attempt to follow the courseline exactly as drawn on Chart TCI-C4: it is only for reference. Your actual route will be a little more winding with little resemblance to the courseline on the chart. Use your eyes through here, nothing else will get you through. Just north of *North Creek,* boats drawing less than 4' have the option of continuing southward paralleling the shore closer in to work your way through the shallows west of the area between *Well Creek* and Bone Fish Point. Vessels drawing over 5' are advised to head further west (as shown on the chart) around the shallows and through *Turtle Channel.* Vessels can anchor on the western side of West Harbour Bluff in prevailing winds but you cannot tuck in close to the beach unless you draw less than 3'. Once past West Harbour Bluff you can turn eastward to proceed to *Sapodilla Bay* as shown on Chart TCI-C6.

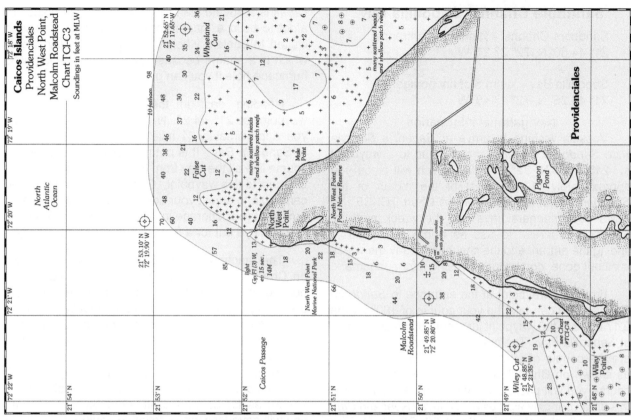

Caicos Islands
Providenciales
North West Point,
Malcolm Roadstead
Chart TCI-C3
Soundings in feet at MLW

North
Atlantic
Ocean

Caicos Passage

Wheeland
Cut

False
Cut

Mule
Point

North
West
Point

North West Point
Pond Nature Reserve

Pigeon
Pond

comp. condos
with pointed roofs

many scattered heads
and shallow patch reefs

North West Point
Marine National Park

Malcolm
Roadstead

Wiley Cut

Wiley
Point

Providenciales

see Chart
#TCI-C4

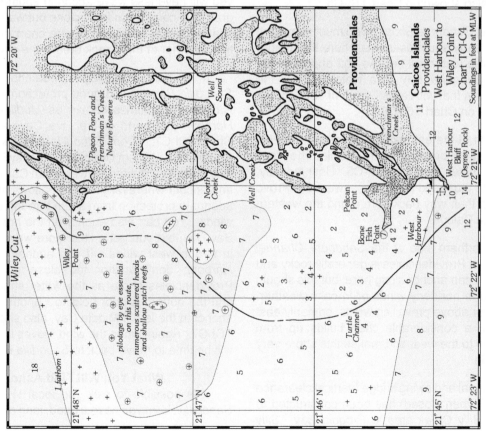

Caicos Islands
Providenciales
West Harbour to
Wiley Point
Chart TCI-C4
Soundings in feet at MLW

Providenciales

Pigeon Pond and
Frenchman's Creek
Nature Reserve

Well
Sound

North
Creek

Well Creek

Frenchman's
Creek

West Harbour
Bluff
(Osprey Rock)

Pelican
Point

Bone
Fish
Point

West
Harbour

Turtle
Channel

Wiley Cut

Wiley
Point

pilotage by eye essential
on this route,
numerous scattered heads
and shallow patch reefs

1 fathom

Sandbore Channel, Sapodilla Bay

Sandbore Channel - ¾ nm W of entrance:
21° 44.50' N, 72° 27.25' W

Sapodilla Bay - ¼ nm S of anchorage:
21° 44.25' N, 72° 17.40' W

Navigational Information

Vessels wishing to arrive at *Sapodilla Bay* via wide *Sandbore Channel* should head to a waypoint at 21° 44.50'N, 72° 27.25'W, which will place you approximately ¾ mile west of the mouth of the *Sandbore Channel* as shown on Chart TCI-C5. In years past mariners have had the wreck north of *Sandbore Channel* to use as a navigation aid in finding the entrance to the channel. Today the wreck is all but gone, don't count on using it for a landmark.

From this waypoint at the entrance to *Sandbore Channel* you can take up your course of 100° for the 9.17 miles to the waypoint just south of the anchorage at *Sapodilla Bay*. The only obstructions on this route are the couple of shallow rocks at *Sandbore Shoal* as shown on Chart TCI-C5, but if you stay on your course you will pass well north of these. Once past this area your only worries are *Halfway Reef* and *Bluff Shoal*, both also shown on Chart TCI-C5.

Once past *Sandbore Shoal*, if you must stray from your course, stray south as that is where the deeper obstruction-free water will be. As you approach the Turtle Rock/*Sapodilla Bay* area watch out for the scattered heads that will lie well north of your course line as shown on Chart TCI-C6.

Just south of the entrance to *Sandbore Channel* is another smaller break in the reef called the *Pony Channel*, as shown on Chart TCI-C5. Until recently, the only boats that used this channel were the Provo dive boats on their way back from diving the western shore of West Caicos.

On the northern side of the *Sandbore Channel* the shoreline of Providenciales is generally rocky and steep-to. One can anchor along here, but this should only be done in northerly winds or in calm weather. In moderate or above prevailing winds, primarily east to southeast, a considerable chop builds up from *Sapodilla Bay* to the west and makes this shore very uncomfortable.

A small canal and swing bridge (vertical clearance only about 5' when closed) has been constructed to connect the *Silly Creek* area to *Proggin Bay*. *Silly Creek* is a private planned community and plans are afoot to build a marina inside. Currently access is limited to boaters who own property at *Silly Creek*, which is a shame because *Silly Creek* is a fantastic hurricane hole if you can get in there.

Heading east in the *Sandbore Channel*, a waypoint at 21° 44.25' N, 72° 17.40' W, will place you approximately ¼ mile south of the anchorage at *Sapodilla Bay*. It is not necessary to keep on the course line all the way from the entrance to *Sandbore Channel* to this waypoint. Once past Turtle Rock you can begin to adjust your course more north of east to arrive at the anchorage in *Sapodilla Bay* but you must keep an eye out for a few scattered, shallow heads.

The anchorage at *Sapodilla Bay*, as shown on Chart TCI-C6, although shallow, has very good holding in soft sand, but I see so many skippers anchoring too far south and west, virtually out of the small protection that the point offers, most likely this is due to their deeper drafts. *Sapodilla Bay* is good in north through east winds, but when the wind goes into the southeast, the waves work their way right around the point and can make it a bit uncomfortable. If you anchor as far as your draft will allow to the north; you will have less wave action in southeast winds. A draft of 5' can tuck in fairly close but watch out for the shallow wreck on shown on the chart; on a very low tide a corner of this wreck breaks the surface.

If a frontal passage threatens, cruisers in *Sapodilla Bay* will find good protection in *Bermudian Harbour*, sometimes shown as *Mudjian* or *Mudjon Harbour*, just north of the Five Cays as shown on Chart TCI-C7. From *Sapodilla Bay* head east past *South Dock*, William Dean Cay, Pussey Cay, and Sim Cay. Head northward between Sim Cay and Bay Cay and anchor wherever your draft allows and you'll find adequate protection from south through west to north winds. You can also anchor on the northern side of Bay Cay, but you get a little more wave action there in strong west winds. If you anchor in *Bermudian Harbour*, don't anchor too close in towards the Providenciales shore as the water shallows quickly and the bottom is poor holding. Another option is to anchor in the lee of Middle Cay, also shown on Chart TCI-C7. Again, when the wind moves into the north it will be time to move back to *Sapodilla Bay*.

What You Will Find Ashore

It is possible to pick up local *Wi-Fi* service in *Sapodilla Bay* if you have a good, long range antenna.

Chart TCI-C5 (upper)

72° 27' W 72° 26' W 72° 25' W 72° 24' W 72° 23' W 72° 22' W 72° 21' W

21° 46' N

10 fathoms

wreck (P.A.)
very little
breaks above water

numerous scattered heads
and shallow patch reefs

scattered heads and
shallow patch reefs

see Chart
TCI-C4

Pigeon Pond &
Frenchman's Creek
Nature Reserve

continuous
reef
dries at LW

1 fathom

Providenciales

West
Harbour

21° 45' N

**Sandbore
Channel**

21° 44.50' N
72° 27.25' W

Halfway
Reef

West
Harbour
Bluff

Bluff
Shoal

100° mag.
To
Sapodilla Bay

Sandbore Shoal

21° 44' N

Pony
Channel
21° 43.40' N
72° 27.30' W

21° 43.40' N
72° 26.75' W

21° 43' N

10 fathoms

1 fathom

dries
at lw

Stinger
Bay

Cove
Point

Logwood
Point

Caicos Islands
Providenciales
Sandbore Channel
Western Entrance
Chart TCI-C5
Soundings in feet at MLW

dries
at lw

Bernard
Bay

**West
Caicos**

Chart TCI-C6 (lower)

To
Leeward
Highway

Providenciales

Isaac Cay
Long Cay

Five
Cays

Pappa
Cay

Pigeon Pond &
Frenchman's Creek
Nature Reserve

Frenchman's
Creek

Chalk Sound
National Park

Five
Cays
Bay

dries

21° 46' N

swing bridge

Silly
Creek

see Chart
TCI-C7

West
Harbour
Bluff
(Osprey
Rock)

Proggin
Bay

Taylor
Bay

Stubbs
Creek

Simon
Point

21° 45' N

Sapodilla
Bay

Customs

conspic.
white
tanks

Middle
Cay

Bermudian
Harbour

Turtle
Rock

280° mag.

Boggy
Cove

South
Dock

William
Dean
Cay

Pussey
Cay

Sim
Cay

Bay Cay

To
Sandbore
Channel

21° 44.25' N
72° 17.40' W

21° 44' N

21° 43' N

Caicos Islands
Providenciales
Sandbore Channel,
Sapodilla Bay
Chart TCI-C6
Soundings in feet at MLW

72° 21' W 72° 20' W 72° 19' W 72° 18' W 72° 17' W 72° 16' W

On the hill overlooking *Sapodilla Bay* is the old *Provo Aquatic Center* at the southeastern end of the bay. The center has not been open in a few years and many cruisers are under the mistaken idea that they can clear in there or use the dock. The building is private now and the dock is reserved for the occasional dive boat to load and unload passengers, but several cruisers have been using the dock to tie up while in town. Please note that the property, including the dock, are private and off limits to cruisers.

On the top of *Sapodilla Hill* are several stones that were engraved by shipwrecked sailors and can be accessed from the hotel side of the hill or from the gravel road by the old *Aquatic Center* using a steep, rocky trail.

Vessels arriving at *Sapodilla Bay* and wishing to clear *Customs* are now advised to dinghy in to shore just north of the private dock and walk to the *Customs* office, a walk of about a mile. You can head east, towards the main road and take a right, you'll see the *South Dock* complex. From the area north of the private dock you can walk to the path to a cross path, turn right, then left, and over the hill you'll find *South Dock*. The guard at the gate where the *Customs* office is located, will ask to see your passport and then direct you to the *Customs* office, you can't miss it, it's a large two-story green building to your left as you enter (see photo).

As an alternative to a long walk, you can take your dinghy around Gussie Point, less than ½ mile to the east and land where you can or tie up to the dock if it's empty and no freighters are due. A short walk of about one hundred or so yards brings you to the *Customs* office. *Immigration* is now located upstairs in the *Customs* building.

It would be a good idea to secure the contents of your dinghy here as I have had cruisers tell me that they had their dinghies searched for valuables when left here; so leave nothing aboard that can wander off easily. I always leave my dink here and have never been troubled by theft or any appearance of attempted theft. Of course, I'm usually carrying all sorts of weapons to leave at *Customs* and that could be why my dink isn't bothered by whoever is messing around in our boats (you must leave your weapons with *Customs* for safe-keeping until you clear out of the Turks and Caicos). Clearance itself is usually painless and quick; for more information on clearing in see the section *Customs and Immigration* in the chapter *The Basics*.

The *Customs* office is manned Monday through Friday and on weekends if commercial traffic is expected. You can try to contact *Customs* by calling *Harbourmaster* on VHF ch. 16, but you may or may not receive a reply. More than likely you'll receive a response from *South Side Marina* (east of *Sapodilla Bay* at *Cooper Jack Bight*) who monitor VHF ch. 16, 24/7, and are more than happy to help cruisers. *South Side Marina* also hosts a daily VHF net every morning at 0730 on VHF ch. 18.

Some of the buses and jitneys will try to get as much as they can for their service from the unwary tourist. By all means, agree on a price before boarding the bus or taxi or you will find that you may have made a grievous and expensive error.

The closest restaurant to *Sapodilla Bay* is at the *Las Brisas Resort*, just a short walk to the west on *Silly Creek Road* (the road just behind the beach at *Sapodilla Bay*). There is a small convenience store located on the town side of the intersection of *Silly Creek Road* and *South Dock Road,* the road that runs from town to the *South Dock* complex. There is also a new *Quality* store here.

If you need a diesel mechanic try *Caribbean Marine Diesel* based at the *Caicos Marina and Shipyard*; you can phone owner Mike Speers at 941-5903.

The facilities that abound on Provo itself could fill an entire book, and you will find pamphlets and small magazines and papers all over town advertising this and that. I will endeavor to give you a brief description of what is to be found on Provo, but only if you promise not to swear at me in the event that I missed some special or favorite place of yours. I haven't been to each and every store and building on the island, most certainly, and I have not dined at every restaurant; that would take a long time and a lot of money and my publisher would not go for that! So with that in mind, let's head up the *South Dock Road* from *Sapodilla Bay* towards the main road on the island, *Leeward Highway*, and I'll try to give you a mini-tour of what's available on Provo.

From *Sapodilla Bay* and the docking facilities at *South Dock,* the *South Dock Road* winds up and over the gentle hills northward toward *Leeward Highway*. Heading north from the intersection of the *South Dock Road* and the road leading up to the *Aquatic Center* and *Silly Creek,* you'll find a small road that leads off to the right. The road does not look inviting

The anchorage at *Sapodilla Bay*

and it appears to only lead into the parking lot of a small plant, but if you see a small sign that says "The Learning Center," that's your road, follow the signs. Take a right and walk up the hill as the small, rough road curves a bit to the right. At the top of the hill you'll see the greenhouses of *Island Fresh Produce*, the Provo hydroponics center. Fantastic hydroponic vegetables are grown here and sold to restaurants and grocery stores all over the island. *Island Fresh* (941-3903) does not sell retail, only wholesale, but they are happy to sell to the cruiser (what a great attitude!); you'll have to purchase a small minimum quantity, at least a pound of whatever you choose (restaurants must purchase a minimum of two pounds). The hydroponics center can be hard to find but fret not, their produce can usually be found at the *IGA* on *Leeward Highway*.

As you pass over the hills you'll get an absolutely gorgeous view of beautiful *Chalk Sound* and its vivid green waters. About a mile or so north of the *Shell* complex is a *Texaco* station on your left. Just before

the *South Dock Road* joins the *Leeward Highway* you'll see *Kishco* on the right. This is a small dry-goods store with all sorts of home-related goodies for sale. The main *Kishco* store is now located on *Leeward Highway* and although it does not supply foodstuffs, it is the cheapest place on the island to buy wine. A couple of years ago *Kishco* purchased the entire contents of a hurricane damaged wine warehouse and today they are able to sell good wine with damaged labels at two bottles for the price of one!

Before long you'll come to the intersection at the *Leeward Highway*. The *Leeward Highway* is the main road that stretches from the airport on the western end of the cay all the way to the *Conch Farm* at the eastern end of Provo and you'll find located along this 4-lane highway the bulk of the business on Provo. To your right at the intersection of *South Dock Road* and *Leeward Highway* is *Lamont's Barbecue and Grill* for takeout food, or if you choose, eat outside at one of their tables.

If you take a left at *Leeward Highway* you will be on the *Old Airport Road* where immediately on your right you will see *The Wine Cellar* (http://winecellar.tc/) a barber shop, and a beauty parlor as well. For good island cuisine try the *Hole in the Wall Restaurant and Bar* at *William's Plaza* on the *Old Airport Road*. *Hole in the Wall* specializes in local cuisine and offers free pickup and drop off, just phone 941-4136

If you take a right on *Leeward Highway* from *South Dock Road* you will have several miles of stores and restaurants before you. On the left, just past *The Wine Cellar* is *Airport Road* which leads (where else?) to the *Fritz Luddington International Airport*. At the airport you can rent a car, visit any of several small shops, or, if you're hungry, you might want to stop at *Fast Eddies* for seafood and native dishes. At the *Airport Inn Plaza* you'll also find the *Indian Plaza Restaurant* with exotic Indian dishes and vegetarian delights.

Proceeding eastward on *Leeward Highway* from the *Airport Road*, you will now enter the downtown area and *Leeward Highway* widens from two lanes to four and is very well lit at night. "Downtown" is little more than a few stores and small mall-like centers along the *Leeward Highway* at what is known as *Butterfield Square*. On the north side of *Leeward Highway* you will see the yellow *TCI First Bank Building* which also houses some government offices, and several other shops. Next door is the *American Airlines* office and *Immigration*. A must stop is *Tasty Temptations*, open at 6:30 every morning until mid-afternoon serving fresh buns, rolls, bread, croissants, and sandwiches.

Across the street, on the southern side of *Leeward Highway*, is the *Town Center Mall* where you'll find *Rosie's Place* (the old *KFC* building), a computer service shop, and the *Island Pride Supermarket*, a great provisioning stop with a good deli and everything from frozen foods to fresh meats and veggies as well as fresh milk, orange juice, and ice cream. Next door to *Island Pride* is the new *Immigration* office in a large orange building that simply says "*Sam's*" on the front.

Just past *Butterfield Square* on the northern side of the road a *Shell* station just before the intersection with *Blue Hills Road*. *Blue Hills Road* takes you northward along the gorgeous *Grace Bay* shoreline through Blue Hills and northwards to North West Point via the new *Millenium Highway*.

Blue Hills is a lovely little community, the oldest one on the island, located on the edge of *Grace Bay* and bordering Blue Hills Road from *Leeward Highway* all the way to where the road turns into a sandy track past *Reef Harbour*. As you turn onto *Blue Hills Road* at the roundabout you'll see a black building on your left. Just behind this building is a gentleman who rebuilds electrical equipment, particularly alternators.

Here you'll find the *Government Clinic*, the *Provo Food Fair*, *Rigby's Variety Store*, and *Where It's At* where you can find fine Jamaican and native dishes. Along here you'll find *Computer Line*, a good spot for computer parts and Internet access.

As a cruiser, your primary stop might well be *Walkin Marine*, the only boating supply store on the island (but it is a good one). *Walkin Marine* is an *OMC* dealer and carries a good supply of outboard parts as well as most anything you need such as wire, *5200*, stainless steel nuts and bolts, line, anchors, fishing supplies, and frozen bait. They also perform service work on all outboard motors. For more info ask at the store or call *Walkin Marine* on VHF ch. 16 and ask for Sherlock.

Just past where *Blue Hills Road* does a 90° at *Grace Bay* you'll find *Da Conch Shack*, the only true island style beach front restaurant on Provo. Here you can have the freshest conch and conch salad found almost anywhere, right out of the bay to your plate. *South Side Marina* offers a weekly trip to *Da Conch Shack* from their marina at *Cooper Jack Bight*.

A bit west sits *Pub on the Bay* offering excellent native cooking and "just catched" seafood served to you right on the beach under palm thatched tiki huts. You've gotta try *Pub on the Bay*. Another fine eatery is *Henry's Road Runner Restaurant and Bar* specializing in local dishes. There is a strong Haitian influence in Blue Hills; one gentleman I talked to estimated it to be about 50% Haitian. Further west on *Blue Hills Road*, just past the *Three Queens Bar*, look to seaward and you will see several sailboats in various stages of construction. The Dean family, primarily James Pringle Dean and James Dean, has been building sloops here on the beach for over 30 years and racing them regularly in the local regattas.

Back on the *Leeward Highway*, as you continue east you'll come to a *First Caribbean Bank Branch*. Across the street is the *Market Place* where you will find several nice gift shops, a jeweler, and a DVD rental store.

Continuing down *Leeward Highway* the shops begin to spread out more and more. You'll pass places like *Provo Building Supply* and the *Rigby Medical Center*. Look for the medical center to be replaced soon by a new hospital just behind the current center.

South of *Leeward Highway*, where, on the hills above Five Cays, you'll find *TC Gas* where you can get your propane filled while you wait, and *Tibor's Machine Shop*, who used to be on the *Old Airport Road*.

Heading east from *Market Square* you'll come to a huge *DO-IT Center* (http://www.doitcenterprovo.com/), much like a *Home-Depot* in the United States. Moving eastward once again on *Leeward Highway*, those provisioning might want to visit *Price Club Supermarket* with its huge stock of groceries and dry goods sold in bulk. *Price Club Supermarket* moved here from *South Dock Road* and their new large building houses even more goodies than their old place. If provisioning in Provo, you'll find the prices generally equivalent to Nassau prices, with some items priced close to stateside prices.

A little farther eastward and you will come to *Quality Food Centre* (scheduled to move to *South Dock Road* and become the closest grocery store to the *Sapodilla Bay* anchorage; http://www.qualityfc.com/), *Menzies Medical Center*, and the former site of *Chez Woo Chinese Restaurant*, formerly *Hey Jose's Mexican Restaurant*. There are several small gift shops next to *Chez Woo* and at the end of the small strip mall and a photography studio. Heading westward, from *Hey Jose's* to *Sapodilla Bay*, take your first left, just past *Quality Supermarket* and *Menzies Medical Center* (a top quality medical center), and then take your first right.

A little east of *Chez Woo* you will come to *Suzie Turn* at *Suzie Turn Plaza*. The area around the turn-off from *Leeward Highway* to *Turtle Cove Marina* and the *Miramar Resort* is called *Suzie Turn*, because Suzie, a secretary who used to work in *Turtle Cove*, could never remember where the turn was. Her friends felt for her and put up a sign that read "Suzie, turn!" Both the sign and Suzie are long gone but the area still bears her name, as does *Suzie Turn Plaza*, home of *CompTCI*, a good spot for Internet access. More on *Turtle Cove Marina* a little later.

On the southern side of *Leeward Highway*, next door to *Bayview Motors*, you'll find a *NAPA* auto parts store if you need any items that may be useful on a boat (I can think of plenty). One word of warning however: no refunds, all sales are final, even if they gave you the wrong part. Next door to NAPA is *Angela's Top O' The Cove Deli* serving breakfast and lunch, and dinner (all to go), along with baked goods, meats, beverages, gourmet coffees, homemade desserts, pizza, soups and sandwiches, and quiche. Just past *Suzie Turn Plaza*, on the left side of *Leeward Highway* is the office of *Lime*, the local cable and wireless company. Further east on *Leeward Highway* is *PizzaPizza* at the new *Multiplex Cinema Plaza*. The cinema shows the latest movies on four screens.

On the right hand side of *Leeward Highway* is the huge *Graceway IGA* supermarket, a great place for provisioning in Provo. The store is large, even by US standards, and has just about anything you could want including a deli with fresh baked goods. Cruisers buying $50 or more in groceries get free delivery. Located in the same complex is a bank and the new location of *The Unicorn Bookstore*, THE place to go for reading materials (lots of kid's stuff too!), recent periodicals, used and new books, and lots of guides for the Caribbean. They also carry Bob Gascoine's charts and *The Turks and Caicos Guide*.

About ¾ mile past *IGA*, on the left, is *Pablo's Laundromat* where you can drop off your laundry for same day service (currently $6 per load, it's cheaper at *South Side Marina*). If you're staying at *Turtle Cove Marina*, there is a man that will pick up your laundry for you and drop it off at *Pablo's* for about $4 per load. Just past *Pablo's* as you head east is *A&J's Groceries*.

FedEx will likely have moved to their new location near *IGA*. You can have your items shipped here and pick them up, just remember to mark all incoming supplies as ship's stores for a *Vessel in Transit*.

Just past *Pratt Road* on the northern side of *Leeward Highway* is the large *Business Solutions* store, sort of an "Office Depot" type of establishment. *Business Solutions* not only sells office and computer supplies, they also repair computers and can even print boat cards for you.

Still eastward on *Leeward Highway* is *Kathleen's Seven Eleven Convenience Store*, though it is much more than its name implies. *Kathleen's* is more like a regular grocery store than a convenience store as you might be used to in the U.S. or Canada. Here you can find lots of veggies, packaged foods, drinks, ice cream, and frozen meats, but the prices are slightly higher than *IGA* and *Island Pride*. Nearby, on the northern side of *Leeward Highway*, by the electrical power station, is *Neely's Restaurant and Bar*. *Neely's*, formerly *Dora's*, serves up delicious native seafood and chicken dishes for breakfast, lunch, and dinner and the seafood buffet on Mondays and Thursdays is not to be missed.

The turnoff to *Grace Bay* is well-marked, as are all the side roads leading off *Leeward Highway*. The *Grace Bay* turnoff is at the roundabout where *Leeward Highway* goes from 4-lanes down to 2-lanes. Continuing eastward, *Leeward Highway* is a 2-lane road but it is now paved all the way to the *Conch Farm* at Leeward Going Through. Taking a right on *Long Bay Hills Road* will take you to the *Caicos Marina and Shipyard*. As you drive down the rough road you'll crest a hill and on the right is *Sea Sage Hill Drive* where you'll want to visit *The Hole*, a naturally formed limestone hole 40' across and over 80' deep. There's a swimming hole at the bottom for those who dare to climb down the ropes to reach it.

Leaving *Leeward Highway* (before the Long Bay Hills turnoff at the roundabout where the highway goes from 4-lanes to 2) and going north towards the resorts on *Grace Bay* you'll find the *Grace Bay Pharmacy* (http://www.gracebaypharmacy.com/) where you can access the Internet, or visit an art gallery. Here too is the new *IGA Gourmet Store* where the upper end market items are beautifully presented. Just before where this road meets the highway you'll find *Almara's Craft Centre*, a colorful collection of small shops selling all manner of T-shirts, hats, and non-island made crafts.

This road ends rather quickly at the intersection of the *Bight Road*, where, if you turn left, you'll find *Bella Luna*, a multi-storied, Italian restaurant with a huge area for outside dining and glass walls permitting a wonderful view of *Grace Bay* even in inclement weather. *Bella Luna* is the place to go for true Italian food and good service in an elegant atmosphere.

Heading westward you will find the *Saltmills Mall*, and *Danny Buoy's Irish Pub and Sports Bar* (http://www.dannybuoys.com/db/). The mall boasts the *Big Al's Burgers* (http://bigalsislandgrill.com/) and several boutiques and gift shops such as *Peaches*, *Step in Style*, *Blue*, *Treasures*, and *Caribbean Creations*. On the upper floor is the National *Health Insurance Board*

and the *Athletic Club Gym*. Nearby, *La Petite Place* is undergoing a makeover and remains mostly vacant.

Further west on the *Bight Road* you will pass the area known as Kingston (where *Annie's* is the place to go for local cooking although they maintain irregular business hours) and the *Beaches Resort* and *Le Deck* resorts. *Beaches* has a good deal for divers. For a set fee you get to go on a two-tank dive as well as have the complete use of the *Beaches* complex for one day. Swimming pool, beach, tennis court, and the opportunity to sample some outstanding dining are all yours for this one low price. Keep heading west and the *Bight Road* will bring you through the settlement of The Bight and onward to the *Turtle Cove Marina* complex, which we will discuss in a moment.

If you were to turn to the right, eastward, at the intersection of the *Bight Road*, immediately on your right is the *Ports of Call* shopping and dining area. This is one of the most popular stops on Provo and the highlight for most is *Barefoot Café* with their *Sunday BBQ Bash*. Wednesday nights they serve up an all-you-can-eat buffet, and not to be outdone, *Calico Jacks'* offers an *All-You-Can-Eat Pasta Night* on Mondays. Shoppers will delight at the offerings of the *Night and Day Boutique*, and *Provo Fun Cycles*. If you wish to work off the fancy meals you've been dining on, there is a gym upstairs at *Ports of Call*. Right next door to *Ports of Call*, just a bit to the east, is another shopping/dining mall, *La Petite Place*, where you can visit Juice, serving all sorts of freshly squeezed fruit and vegetable juices, fruit and herbal teas, and smoothies. Nearly all of the restaurants here at Ports of Call have free *Wi-Fi* for their customers, just ask for the password.

Heading east from Ports of Call you will pass many of the Grace Bay resorts such as the elegant Grace Bay Club (https://gracebayresorts.com/gracebayclub/) with its extremely formal Anacaona Restaurant (formal attire only, no children under 12). Opposite the Grace Bay Club, behind the beautiful grounds of the Sunshine Nursery, is the Coco Bistro (http://www.cocobistro.tc/) where you can dine under the palms. All the brochures about this place never mention the mosquitoes and no-see-ums. If you plan to dine here, and you should, choose a very windy night. Even better, maybe the bistro should put a can of insect repellant on every table.

Along the same road are the Wymara, West Bay Club (http://www.thewestbayclub.com/), the Turks and Caicos Club, and Coral Gardens where the Somewhere Cafe serves Tex-Mex food and breakfast all day.

A little further east is the huge Club Med complex. Club Med is very private, it is not open to the general public, but for a fee you can become a member for a day and have access to their complex. If you just want to visit for a meal, I can recommend the Sunday All-You-Can-Eat Lunch Buffet. For $35 per person, 18 and older, you get to help yourself to a huge buffet, enjoy a Mimosa, and drink unlimited beer, wine, juices, and sodas. That's unlimited beer and wine folks! People should be beating a path for this one.

Just east of Club Med is the Provo Golf Club, an 18-hole championship course with an attractive clubhouse that is open to members and non-members alike (http://www.provogolfclub.com/). The golf course uses over 300,000 gallons of RO water a day to maintain its lush fairways and greens. The Arab backers that financed the golf course had to do something for the island to be allowed to construct the golf course so he built the Provo Water Company which benefits the course as well as the islanders. In 1996 the course was rated one of the top ten golf courses in the Caribbean. If you don't want to play golf, but want to dine at the club, stop in at the Fairways Bar and Grill and watch the duffers hard at play.

Across the street is the Ocean Club, a luxury condominium project. Now you will enter the Leeward area where a huge planned community development project is ongoing. The Leeward Highway ends at Leeward Marina and Leeward Going Through which we will discuss in greater detail in the section The Caicos Cays-Leeward Going Through to North Caicos.

The Southern Shore

Cooper Jack Bight - ½ nm SW of entrance:
21° 45.05' N, 72° 14.00' W

Caicos Marina/Shipyard - 1 nm SSE of entrance:
21° 44.80' N, 72° 10.30' W

Bay Cay - 1 nm ESE of:
21° 43.75' N, 72° 14.00' W

There are two good marine facilities on the southern shore of Providenciales including the only haul-out yard in the Turks and Caicos at this time.

These services are easily accessible from *Sapodilla Bay* with only a few small reefs and shoals, easily seen in good light, to avoid. Don't try to head eastward to the marinas at *Discovery Bay* or Juba Point with the sun right in your eyes first thing in the morning. Bear in mind that strong northeast winds for a day or two can keep the tides low on the southern shore of Providenciales while strong southerly winds will give the area higher tides than normal.

Navigational Information

As of this writing the closest marina facilities to Sapodilla Bay are at the *South Side Marina* and *Harbour Club Marina* (649-941-5748), both located in Cooper Jack Bight, sometimes called Discovery Bay (a draft of 7' can enter the marina at high tide). While *South Side Marina* is a full-service marina, *Harbour Club Marina* is private and is usually filled up with local dive boats.

To reach *South Side Marina* and *Harbour Club Marina* head east from *Sapodilla Bay* past the Five Cays, William Dean Cay, Pussey Cay, Sim Cay, Middle Cay, and Bay Cay, passing south of them as shown on Chart TCI-C6 and Chart TCI-C7. Once past Bay Cay you can take up an approximate northeast heading to a waypoint at 21° 45.05' N, 72° 14.00' W, placing you approximately ¼ nautical mile southwest of the entrance channel into the canals of *Cooper Jack Bight* and the marina as shown on Chart TCI-C8. Before heading out from *Sapodilla Bay* for either *South Side Marina* or *Caicos Marina and Shipyard* it might be a good idea to hail them on the VHF to let them know you are headed their way.

This area is often called *Discovery Bay*, primarily by the realtors and developers responsible for such things. From the waypoint in *Cooper Jack Bight* you will be able to look northeastward and see the marina complex hiding just inland. At this point, you can head generally NE past Cooper Jack Rock until you pick up the markers leading in to the marina. Watch out for scattered heads and shallow bars on this route, the whole southern shore of Providenciales has numerous scattered heads and bars strewn about that are easily seen in good light and avoided. Be sure to take the point and its shallow sandbar well to starboard. Round into the deeper water of the entrance channel (there is a small range set up on shore for this purpose, if you're confused contact *South Side Marina* on VHF for instructions) and proceed to the marinas that lie straight ahead.

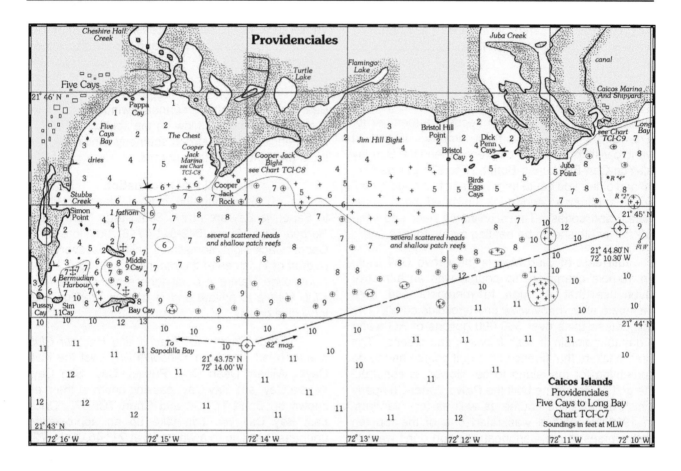

South Side Marina suggests using the following route and waypoints (unverified by me). First, hail the marina on VHF ch. 16 (working channel 18) to advise the marina staff of your approach. Starting at a waypoint at 21° 43.50' N, 72° 14.65' W, set a course of 30° magnetic for 1.8 nm to a second waypoint at 21° 45.26 N, 72° 13.98' W. At this point the marina's marker buoys (lit at night) should be visible over your starboard bow. Keep close to the buoys (red, right, returning), and then pass through between the red and green markers and immediately turn 90° to port to enter the marina.

What You Will Find Ashore

To your left, as the canals of Discovery Bay bear away, you will see the new Provo Marine Biology Education Center. Turtle Lake at the end of the canals is a good bonefishing spot. South Side Marina and Harbour Club Marina lie just ahead and to starboard. As I mentioned earlier, Harbour Club is private, but South Side Marina (http://www.southsidemarina-tci.com/) is a full-service cruiser-friendly marina (run by cruisers for cruisers).

Owner Bob Pratt and Manager Simon Anderson have worked overtime to upgrade the services at the marina and make it a true cruiser's destination, clean, quiet, and with a "family" atmosphere. One of their services is the voluntary monitoring of VHF ch. 16 on a 24/7 basis in case of emergencies. We all can feel safer knowing that the marina is listening and able to arrange assistance. The marina also hosts a daily VHF net on ch. 18 at 0730.

South Side Marina offers diesel, gas, and 2 stroke oil, as well as dockside electric and RO water. They have floating docks with 20 slips capable of handling vessels up to 65' LOA with a 6' draft (and in fact have docked two vessels of over 90' LOA). Ashore you will find bathrooms and showers, a laundry room with a self-service washer and dryer, Wi-Fi, a book exchange, ice, TV hook up, temporary cell phone rental, daily happy hours in the gazebo, and weekly cruisers' barbeques on Wednesday. South Side offers free rides to the grocery store for guests of the marina. Cruisers are welcome to use the dinghy dock at the marina for a fee of $5 per day. The use of holding tanks while in the marina is mandatory but the marina does not have a pump out facility so you will have to go elsewhere for that. *South Side Marina* can be reached at (649-231-4747, or southsidemarina@ gmail.com).

The marina is home to *Bob's Bar* (open nightly from 1700-2100), a popular eating and drinking establishment where you will meet lots of locals and ex-pats and hear their tales. Their marina store sells *Wavey Line Charts*, courtesy flags, and T-shirts, and the marina staff can help with onward voyage planning. Next day propane fills are available.

Well east of *Cooper Jack Bight* is Juba Point and the well-marked entrance to the *Caicos Marina and Shipyard* (http://www.caicosmarina.com/) where a draft of 6' can enter just past low tide. In 1986, Canadian investor Ted Trump built this marina with the goal of making it the largest marina complex in the Caribbean, and today new owners are in the process of upgrading and expanding the services with plans for more slips and even a playground for the kiddies. *Caicos Marina and Shipyard*, the only place to haul a boat (a 75-ton travel-lift and a 20-ton forklift) between Stella Maris and George Town in The Bahamas, and Puerto Rico. They also sell diesel, gas, ice, sodas, and RO water. The marina has a small laundry, public telephone, Internet access, and they can handle your mail and fax needs. The yard can handle all sorts of hull related work such as fiberglass repairs, strut work, welding, painting, interior repairs, and even motor work in their newly refurbished eco-friendly yard.

Dockage is side-to along their 500' dock and with the installation of their new floating docks, *Caicos Marina and Shipyard* is able to accommodate approximately 24 vessels with full electric, Wi-Fi, pump out, and RO water. Their large shed has now been converted into stacked dry-storage for smaller boats and the marina now offers long-term wet and dry storage of cruising boats including a care-taking service to run your engine, pump the bilge, and charge the batteries. The *Caicos Marina and Shipyard* can be reached by VHF on Ch. 16, or by phone at 649-946-5600, by fax at 649-946-5390, and by email at caicosmarinashp@tciway.tc. The Providenciales *Police Marine Division* is based at the *Caicos Marina and Shipyard*. The marina is also an agent for *Grace Bay Car Rentals* (http://www.gracebaycarrentals. com/). Look for the marina to open a bar and restaurant in the near future.

Housed on the marina property is Mike Speer's *Caribbean Marine Diesel* where you can have your engine serviced or replaced, welding done, and have your prop straightened. You can telephone *Caribbean Marine Diesel* for service if your boat can't make it to the marina at 941-5903. If you need welding and/ or fabrication in steel, aluminum, or stainless steel, call Mike Robertson at *Osprey Marine Services* at 946-5122. Mike is one of the best welders and fabricators on the island and can also help you with any woodworking repairs as well as minor rigging and hull repairs.

Navigational Information
To find Juba Point and the *Shipyard* from the Sapodilla waypoint steer 108° for 3.2 miles, past the Five Cays, William Dean Cay, Pussey Cay, Sim Cay, Middle Cay, and Bay Cay, to a waypoint at 21° 43.75'N, 72° 14.00'W, as shown on Chart TCI-C7. The best way to describe the route to the *Shipyard* is to use the natural land formations themselves instead of waypoints. From the waypoint southeast of Bay Cay, look to the north and east. That last point of land that you see to the east is Juba Point. Heading just north of east on a course of approximately 82°, a line of dark spots, shallow patch reefs and rocky bars, will lie parallel to this route. Keep south of all the dark spots that you see (the line of shallow reefs) keeping them well off your port side as the deeper, obstruction free water lies to their south. The actual course line has you passing north of one of the dark reefs, but it is fine to pass it to the south as well. The course here is not as important as staying in the clear blue/green water and avoiding any dark patches that you see.

As you approach Juba Point you will notice what looks like a huge white "I" seemingly carved into the hillside. Actually it is a sandy road with a vertical trail leading down to a sandy beach. As you take the huge white "I" on your port beam, the *Shipyard* entrance channel lies approximately ¾ mile to the east. At this point you should be able to make out the cranes and perhaps even the entrance channel markers of *Caicos Marina and Shipyard*. From here you can work your way to a waypoint at 21° 44.80' N, 72° 10.30' W, which will place you a little over 1 nautical mile south of the entrance channel leading into the *Caicos Marina and Shipyard* as shown in the blow-up on Chart TCI-C7 and Chart TCI-C9. From this waypoint you should see the outer sea buoy (white light atop) and the two red markers between it and the shore. From this position, the entrance channel is approximately 1 nautical mile distant on

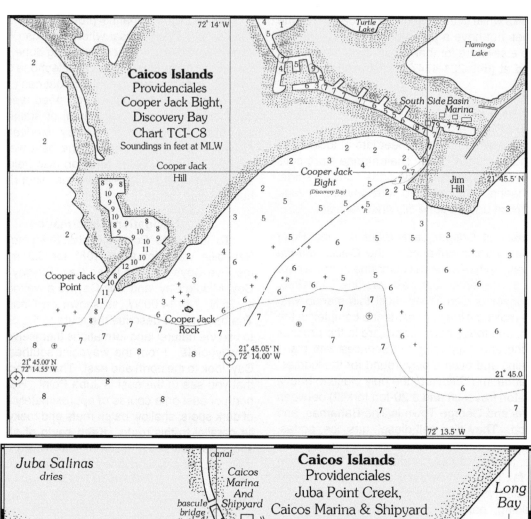

Caicos Islands
Providenciales
Cooper Jack Bight,
Discovery Bay
Chart TCI-C8
Soundings in feet at MLW

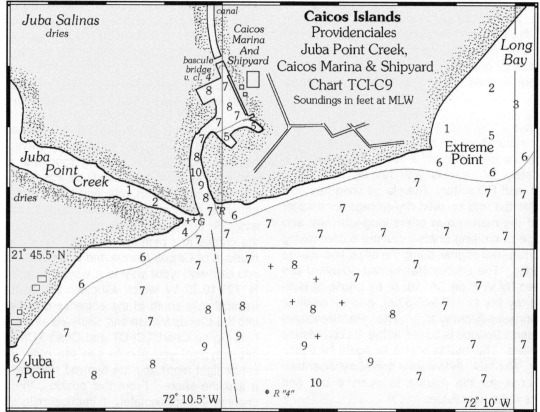

Caicos Islands
Providenciales
Juba Point Creek,
Caicos Marina & Shipyard
Chart TCI-C9
Soundings in feet at MLW

an approximate course of 345º magnetic (but as you will notice, the course actually bends more northward after R "4").

The channel mouth is marked by tall red and green striped pilings (red-right-returning), and as you approach the entrance keep a lookout for any stray heads in the surrounding waters. There is a shallow spot between the channel markers that carries 6' at low water. The channel curves to the east as you approach the marina complex with its huge building and tall cranes that are usually the first sight of the marina from seaward. The two small coves southeast of the marina dock and lift are private and are not part of the marina complex; they would make a fair hurricane hole if needed. A canal heads northward from the marina past a small bridge towards a number of private homes in the Long Bay Hills area, but draft is limited to about 3'-4' at MLW. This too would be a nice spot to ride out a hurricane.

Now if you insist on waypoints for this route then here you are: from the *Sapodilla Bay* waypoint head 108º for 3.2 nautical miles to a waypoint southeast of *Bay Cay* at 21º 43.75'N, 72º 14.00'W, as shown on Chart TCI-C7. From this waypoint steer 82º for 3.6 nautical miles to a waypoint at 21º 44.80' N, 72º 10.30' W. This is the outer waypoint for your route to the *Shipyard*. From this waypoint keep the red markers to starboard as you approach the entrance channel as shown on Chart TCI-C9. Keep a sharp lookout for the reefs that abound on the N side of this courseline.

Northern Shore, Grace Bay

North West Point - ½ nm N of reef:
21º 53.10' N, 72º 19.90' W

Wheeland Cut - ½ nm NNE of cut:
21º 52.65' N, 72º 17.65' W

Stubb's Cut - ¼ nm NW of cut:
21º 48.93' N, 72º 11.30' W

Grace Bay, the large body of water on the northern shore of Providenciales, is the location for most of the tourism infrastructure as well as being a fantastic sailing ground in its own right. Here you can get the full effect of the prevailing east/southeast winds, but with very little sea. *Grace Bay* is named after Gracie Jane Hinson, usually just called Grace, who was born in Grand Turk in 1873. In 1892 Grace married Hugh Houston Hutchings, also a native of Grand Turk. The

couple spent their honeymoon at a small cottage on the beach on the north shore of Providenciales near the settlement called The Bight, then called Blue Hills. Grace was a very beautiful woman and the couple's visit was quite an occasion for the few inhabitants of the area. After the couple returned to Grand Turk, the people of Blue Hills referred to the beach as *Grace Beach* and the waters as *Grace Bay*, as they are known today.

Navigational Information

As mentioned earlier, vessels approaching *Sapodilla Bay* and the western shore of Providenciales from Mayaguana or The Plana Cays will have no obstructions. If headed to Leeward Going Through or *Turtle Cove Marina* at *Sellar's Pond* on the northern shore of Provo on *Grace Bay*, you must take care to avoid the reefs off North West Point as shown on Chart TCI-C2. A good rule of thumb is not to head south of 21º 53'N until east of 72º 17'W. A waypoint at 21º 53.10'N, 72º 19.90'W, will place you approximately ½ mile north of the reefs in deep water. If your route takes you to *Sellar's Pond*, *Stubbs Cut*, or *Leeward Cut*, especially at night, do not venture south of this waypoint until east of 72º 17' W.

Just east of North West Point as shown on Chart TCI-C3, is *Wheeland Cut*. Vessels drawing less than 4' can enter this cut and pass eastward between the outer reef and the northern shore of Providenciales, that is if they can pick their way through the shallow reef that winds itself from Provo out to the barrier reef just southeast of *Wheeland Cut*. I do not recommend this route as there is nothing to gain by taking it, but everything to lose. There are numerous shallow patch reefs, coral heads, and rocky bars between the reef and the shore that you must avoid along this route. The best water is just inside the reef, staying north of the shoreline until in the vicinity of the high hills just west of Sellar's Pond. The only boats that actually use this route are the local fishermen and a few of the dive boat operators. And by all means stay out of *False Cut*- it is exactly that. It can lead even small outboard powered boats (yes, I mean dinghies) to destruction. From *False Cut* to North West Point the area is literally STREWN with dangerous *shallow* reefs, many of which dry out at low water or lie just inches below the surface.

This area is a great snorkel spot in settled weather, but use extreme caution; these waters are thick with heads just waiting for the unwary dinghy. The heads are especially thick close to the point. The

North West Point Light (Gp Fl-3 W, ev 15 sec, 15M) is once again out of operation and when it will be repaired is anybody's guess.

The center of the yachting scene in *Grace Bay* is located at *Turtle Cove Marina* in *Sellar's Pond*. There are two routes to *Turtle Cove Marina* from outside the reef, but the best one is the primary route through *Sellar's Cut* as shown on Chart TCI-C10. A secondary route - and this one is usually only used by those skippers with good weather, even better visibility, and a fearless desire to sail around and through reefs paralleling the beach - is to pass through the reef via *Stubbs Cut* and head westward towards *Sellar's Cut* on the inside of the reef. We will discuss entering *Stubbs Cut* in a moment, but for now, let me just say that once inside *Stubbs Cut*, the skipper can parallel the beach close in, keeping all the white dive site buoys to starboard as you approach *Sellar's Cut*.

Off the *Beaches Resort* you will have to keep further offshore and steer between several small patch reefs and heads to gain *English Cut* as shown on Chart TCI-C10.

For those skippers wishing to enter through *Sellar's Cut*, a waypoint at 21° 48.40'N, 72° 12.40'W, will place you approximately ¼ mile north of the green daymark that defines the entrance channel through *Sellar's Cut* as shown on Chart TCI-C10. There are supposed to be a matching set of red and green markers here, but wind and wave seems to remove one or the other every year. Remember that as you approach the cut and find yourself wondering where the other marker is. Always remember that any floating aid to navigation mentioned in this book is subject to disappearing or moving between the time we go to print and the time you arrive at your destination. Storms, high winds and seas, all combine to play

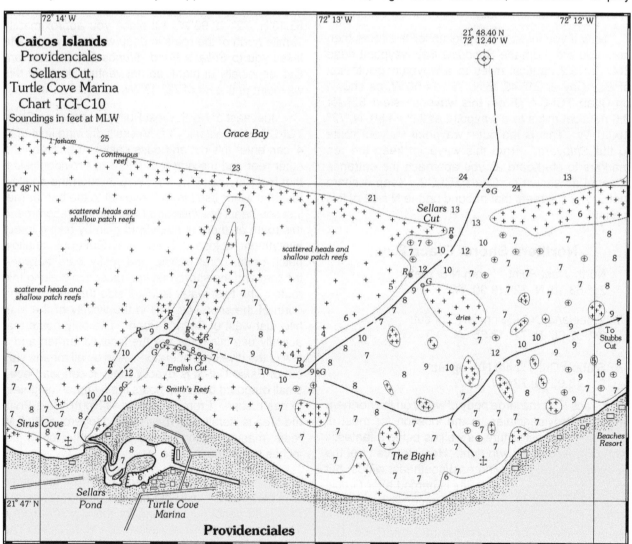

havoc on floating aids along the northern shore of Provo from *Sellar's Cut* to *Leeward Cut*.

From the waypoint at *Sellars Cut* head generally southward until you can pass between the outer green daymark (red right returning), in 13'-22' of water and follow the rest of the markers in as shown on the chart. At one time you had a choice of two routes to take when inside the reef, the more northerly route has been discontinued and the markers removed in favor of the far easier *English Cut*. I have run both routes and much prefer *English Cut*, which, though narrow (a 52' long by 30' wide trimaran can make it through with no problem) has a minimum depth of 7' and is far shorter. Once through *English Cut* keep the green markers to port as you head towards the marina entrance. Watch out for the shallow heads lying just north of the shoreline about 100 yards northeast of the entrance to the pond. The winding entrance channel itself is narrow and has a shallow sandbar at its eastern entrance, on your port side when entering, and a rocky bar across the channel on your starboard side. Once inside, give the final inner turn on your port side a wide berth before rounding to port into the pond itself.

Never attempt *Sellar's Cut* with a strong northerly swell; in these conditions the cut will break all the way across and any mishap at this point could be disastrous. If unsure about how to enter *Sellar's Cut* and the entrance to *Turtle Cove Marina*, call the marina on VHF ch. 16 and the dockmaster will be happy to have someone come out to lead you in. At this time there is no charge for this service but a tip is expected, and very well deserved as you will see.

There used to be a nice anchorage in *Sirus Cove* just west of the entrance to *Sellar's Pond* and *Turtle Cove Marina*. It's a calm spot in moderate prevailing conditions, though the bottom is a bit grassy, and it offered an excellent opportunity for cruisers to avail themselves of all that *Turtle Cove* has to offer by dinghy. There is some question as to whether the National Park Wardens will allow you to anchor there even though the dive boats use the anchorage for their guests.

Another good anchorage is in *The Bight* just south of the *Beaches Resort*. This spot has good holding and adequate protection from the prevailing wind and swell. Snorkelers will love to investigate *Smith's Reef*, the large area lying between *English Cut* and the shoreline. *Smith's Reef* is a favorite local

dive spot where you can explore several shallow water patch reefs and numerous scattered heads that are frequented by snorkelers from both the resorts and the local dive operations. In fact, between the barrier reef and the shoreline are many shallow reefs marked by white buoys. These are all active dive sites and the buoys are for the dive boats to tie to. You can take your dinghy out to these reefs and see for free what the charterers and other tourists pay a lot of money to view.

What You Will Find Ashore

Turtle Cove Marina has 106 slips, sells diesel and gas, and can handle a 188' vessel with a 7.5' draft. The marina is a port of entry so if you need to clear in the dockmaster can arrange for a Customs officer to visit your boat. The marina offers *Wi-Fi*, propane fills, and hosts the annual *Provo International Billfish Tournament* in mid-summer and sells fishing licenses year-round. In years past cruisers could anchor in Sellar's Pond, but the sandbar that once filled the center is now part of the marina, and docks have been constructed around its circumference effectively ending the anchoring in the pond. *Turtle Cove Marina* can be reached at (649-941-3781, or tcmarina@ tciway.tc).

The complex surrounding the marina has just about anything a cruiser could want; what isn't there is only a short taxi ride away, or perhaps you would rather rent a scooter or car from *Scooter Bob's* (649-946-4648) on the marina grounds. *Scooter Bob's* has some of the most competitive rental prices on the island and also has a good line of fishing tackle and baits. Scooter Bob's is one of four auto rental companies on the island who will deliver to any marina. The others are *Tropical Auto Rental* (649-946-5300), *Grace Bay Autos*, and *Rent a Buggy* (649-946-4158).

Also on site is *The Tiki Hut* (649-941-5341), a very nice outdoor bar and grill combo, and *mango Reef Restaurant* (946-946-8200) serving economical lunches and eloquent dinners with great homemade ice cream. The *Tiki Hut* is very popular and offers a *West Indian Curry Night* on Mondays, and a *Chicken and Rib Night* on Wednesdays, while the *Anchorage* offers *Peking Duck Night* on Mondays, *Mussels Night* on Tuesdays, and a *Sushi and Sashimi Night* on Saturdays, and a *Sunday Brunch* until 1400.

The *Coco Bistro* (649-946-5369) although a bit pricey is first class dining experience. For casual elegant dining on Grace Bay Beach visit *Bay Bistro* (649-946-5396) at Sibonné Beach Hotel.

Provo Turtle Divers (649-946-4232) formerly *Art Pickering's Turtle Divers*) operates out of *Turtle Cove* for those wanting to explore the fine reef diving in Grace Bay or West Caicos. There are numerous other small gift shops, boutiques and salons in the surrounding complex including *Tipsy's Liquors.*

Across the street from the marina you'll find the steep natural stone stairs that lead up to the *Miramar Resort*, formerly the *Erebus Inn* (when it was named after a giant butterfly which when touched brings you good luck), is truly elegant and its *Magnolia Wine Bar and Restaurant* (649-941-5108) is nothing short of first class with an absolutely stunning view of *Grace Bay.* I suggest going there just for the view, but I personally avoid the staircase from *Turtle Cove Marina.* Perhaps if I made better use of *Bodywise*, the complete gym that is located at the *Miramar Resort*, the steep staircase known as *Cardiac Hill* might not be so exhausting.

Of course, the time I spend at *Turtle Cove* in *Sharkbites* probably doesn't help. Situated on the eastern end of the marina property, the Friday evening happy hour with two for one drinks and complimentary munchies is a regular stop for me when I' m on Provo. *Sharkbites* also offers a Wednesday night *Fish & Chips Night.* I sincerely believe, and I may have tried them all, that *Sharkbites* has THE BEST chicken wings on the island of Providenciales. I've heard it said that they also have the island's best hamburgers but I can't seem to get past the wings to try the burgers. Check out the money shark and the card shark hanging from the ceiling in *Sharkbites.* Nearby is a DVD rental store, Tropical Upholstery (for canvas and upholstery repairs) and *Baci*, an Italian style eatery with excellent espresso.

About a mile to the west of *Sellar's Pond*, around the next point (Cove Point), lies the almost hidden entrance to the dredged creeks of *Thompson Cove* as shown on Chart TCI-C2, a very, very private residential community. The sign that welcomes you at the entrance says it all: "Private. Unauthorized boats will be removed." *Thompson Cove* would make a great hurricane hole with excellent protection in its narrow creeks (5'-7' at MLW) that are protected on all sides by high hills. If you had permission you could probably tie up to someone's unused dock or simply head up one of the channels to secure yourself.

Drafts of less than 5' can wiggle their way into *Thompson Cove* on a high tide by heading west from Sellar's Pond in 7' of water dodging the occasional head or small reef that you will come across. As you approach the next point there will be a rocky bar that works its way west/northwest from the point. A small white buoy marks a narrow cut through the reef to port. Enter the cut at high tide and work your way in towards the narrow entrance to *Thompson Cove.* Five feet can make it in with a good visibility and a high tide of at least 2 ½'; needless to say the ability to read the water is essential here.

Navigational Information

To the east of *Sellar's Cut* is the wide and deep *Stubbs Cut*, sometimes called *Club Med Cut.* When *Leeward Cut* and *Sellar's Cut* are breaking, *Stubb's Cut* may still be passable. A waypoint at 21º 48.93'N, 72º 11.30'W, will place you approximately ¼ mile northwest of the cut as shown on Chart TCI-C11. From this waypoint look ashore and you will see a large red and white tower, the *Cable and Wireless* tower that sits in the Long Bay Hills area (260' with a fixed red light at night). Put the tower on your bow and steer 140º magnetic to enter the cut. An alternative method of entry is to line up the tower and the red roofed building that lies just below it on the beach. The eastern end of this building is elevated and pointed. Line up the tower directly behind this raised portion of this roof or slightly to the east of it, between the roof and the trees, and come in on that heading.

Once inside, watch out for the shallow bars to starboard. Once inside *Stubb's Cut* you can head northeastward to Leeward Going Through as shown on Chart TCI-C12 or southwest towards *English Cut* as shown on Chart TCI-10. If heading to *English Cut* you can cruise close in to shore keeping the line of white dive buoys to starboard. Once in the vicinity of the *Sandal's Beaches Resort* you will have to keep offshore a little more as shown on the chart. If headed to Leeward Going Through there are fewer obstructions as shown on the charts.

Every Thursday night there is a huge new party for locals, ex-pats, and tourists, *The Turks and Caicos Fish Fry.* The party begins about 1730 and lasts till 2130 or later at *Bight Park* on *Lower Bight Road.* A US$10-per-person taxi ride from any *Grace Bay* resort will help you get to this family friendly event. The food, served up by several small vendors and residents is unbeatable as is the steel band music!

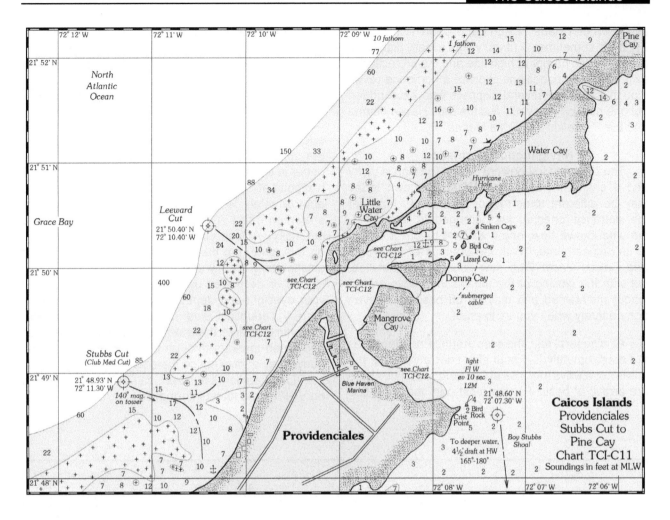

The Caicos Cays

Leeward Going Through to North Caicos

Ft. George Cut - ½ nm NW of cut:
21° 53.70' N, 72° 07.90' W

Leeward Cut - ½ nm NW of cut:
21° 50.40' N, 72° 10.40' W

Deep water on Banks for shortcut to Leeward:
21° 45.50' N, 72° 07.00' W

Stretching from the northeast tip of Provo to the tip of North Caicos lie a small group of barrier islands. These unassuming little gems surrounded by settings of finely powdered beaches and warm, blue waters, are some of the prettiest sites in the entire archipelago. From the air, they take on the appearance of a delicate necklace suspended between the two points of land. Little Water Cay, Water Cay, Pine Cay, Fort George

Cay, Dellis Cay, and Parrot Cay: these names include both uninhabited wild life preserves (the domain of the *Turks and Caicos National Parks*) as well as award-winning and internationally recognized luxury resorts.

Each island is blessed with gorgeous beaches, swirling sand flats, and plenty of shallow coral reefs. The most beautiful and protected anchorages in the Caicos Islands can be found in between these cays and all are within a short dinghy ride of each other. A word of warning: the ability to read water is essential here as you will travel over some shallow sandbars before you will be able to enjoy the deeper protected water of the anchorages. Never try these entrances with the light in your eyes; you'll have little chance of discerning the shallow water from the deeper water.

The area that is sometimes called the Caicos Cays, stretches from the northeast end of Providenciales to North Caicos. The best anchorage for those wishing to spend time on Provo is at Leeward Going Through as shown on Charts TCI-C11 and Chart TCI-C12. A 7½' draft, sometimes 8' (if you've got a really high tide), can enter this harbor at high tide and the protection is excellent in all conditions short of a hurricane (even though I know of several skippers who have ridden out one here). Here you'll find the *Blue Haven Marina* and the *S. Walkin and Sons Marina.*

Navigational Information

The entrance to Leeward Going Through is tricky and it changes frequently. What is shown today may be different tomorrow or next week, however the entrance channel was dredged in late 2004, but who knows how long it will last before it silts in to its original state. With the opening of the *Turks and Caicos Yacht Club* new buoys were installed, but with the closing of the marina the buoys are no longer maintained and may be off position or even gone entirely when you try to enter.

As a general rule, the tides around Providenciales are approximately ½-1 hour after tides at Nassau, but this is not always the case at Leeward. The tides here are erratic at best. For the most part, the flood tide does not flow as long as the ebb tide. I have seen the flood last only three hours in strong southeast winds. Use caution if attempting to figure the tides.

If bound for the anchorage at Leeward Going Through there are several entrances through the reef. *Leeward Cut* is the closest but in a strong northerly swell it breaks all the way across, effectively closing the cut. *Stubbs Cut* or *Fort George Cut* would be better in those conditions, though not much better. A waypoint at 21° 50.40'N, 72° 10.40'W, will place you approximately ½ mile northwest of Leeward Cut as shown on Chart TCI-C11. This is where it begins to get tricky. At last report, new markers were installed on this route, but the markers have a reputation for disappearing shortly after they are set in place, often moved or destroyed by huge northerly swells. Use your eyesight and depthsounder to get you through here. If in doubt call *Blue Haven Marina* for assistance. From time to time there will be a combination of red and green markers through here. Bear in mind that buoys may or may not be there as you approach. As I mentioned earlier, if in doubt, call *Blue Haven Marina* on VHF for the latest information.

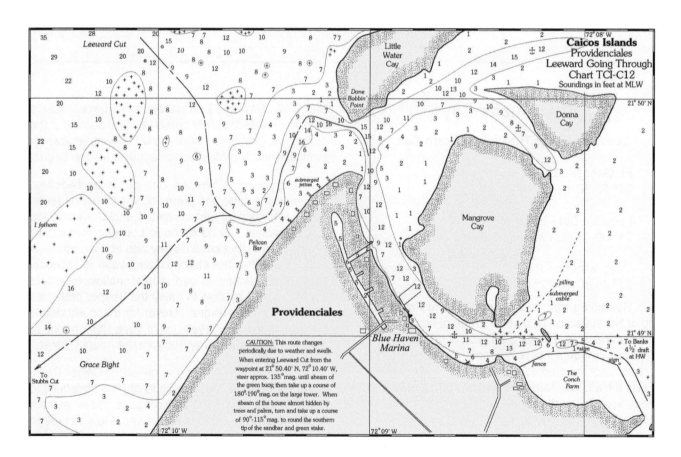

From the waypoint, enter *Leeward Cut* on an approximate heading of 135º-140º magnetic. The heading here is not as important as staying south of the very shallow reef on the north side of the cut. This reef is easily seen in good visibility and is usually breaking. Once inside the reef you will see a small patch reef as shown on Chart TCI-C12. Keep this reef to port and turn to starboard to steer towards the huge red and white striped *Cable and Wireless* tower (260', Fxd R) to the south on a heading of approximately 180º-190º. As you are heading south look ashore and you will see a string of houses leading south from the northeast tip of Providenciales. There is one residence that is almost hidden by trees with several palms lining the shoreward side of the home. Just in front of this house is a shallow sandbar that works southward from Little Water Cay. Round this shoal well to the south and head northeastward between the sandbar and the shore. If you can't discern the shoal, head in on the house that I just mentioned on an approximate heading of 90º-115º keeping an eye out for the shallow bar to port. Pass between the shallow bar to port and then, swinging wide back towards *Leeward Cut,* avoid the shallows off the beach as shown on the chart and work your way towards the cut between Little Water Cay and Providenciales. Pass between the two and then you can turn to starboard to head into Leeward Going Through and the anchorage.

The best anchorage used to be just to the north of the newly expanded marina docks. If you wish to anchor south of the docks, be advised that about 150 yards south of the docks the bottom gets rocky with scattered coral heads littering the bottom. There are small, scattered heads throughout the anchorage at Leeward Going Through, even north of the marina, but they are a little thicker south of the docks. Diving to check on your anchor here is advised.

There is a fair bit of current in Leeward Going Through and two anchors set in a Bahamian moor are absolutely necessary, unless you like to untangle your lines when they get wrapped around the stray head.

When anchored at Leeward Going Through and bad weather threatens, you will need to keep an eye out for incoming vessels, as the skippers of many of the local dive boats bring their craft in here to anchor when inclement weather threatens. While many of these skippers have a captain's license and are in fact veteran seamen, a captain's license is not required

in the Turks and Caicos Islands and a few of these "captains" have little concern about where and how they anchor their unattended boats. Some of these skippers simply drop an anchor and head to shore.

What You Will Find Ashore

The large *Blue Haven Marina and Resort* complex (the former *Niki Beach Resort and Marina*) dominates the area and offers slips for vessels to 220' LOA with full electric, a fuel dock, water, pump outs, cable TV, restaurant and bar, a volleyball court, horseshoe pit, large scale chess set, and a pool with a swim-up bar. The marina monitors VHF ch. 16 and 14 and can be reached by phone at 649-946-9910, or you can visit their website at http://www.bluehaventci.com/ or email them at contact@bluehaventci.com.

Just south of the docks at Leeward Going Through is *Walkin Marina*. The marina is only suitable for shallow draft vessels, and small powerboats and has no fuel dock. You can reach the marina by phone at 649-946-8898. Here you can take a ferry to North Caicos where you can rent a car to visit both North Caicos and Middle Caicos (connected by a causeway), and have lunch at any of several restaurants on the island before returning on the last ferry to Provo at 1630. You can also visit the growing tourist and marina complex on the north side of North Caicos.

South of Heaving Down Rock, the ramp where the small barges load and unload about ½ mile south of the marina, you will notice a large area with pilings in the water and nets stretched between them. This is the *Conch Farm*, established in 1984 to commercially grow the queen conch, *strombus gigas*. The life cycle from egg to adult takes about four years. The *Conch Farm* has successfully developed hatchery and juvenile rearing techniques, and the *Farm* has a current inventory of approximately 1.5 million conch in all stages of their growth cycle. Theirs is the only such facility in the world. The *Conch Farm* has guided tours and a *Conch Boutique* and restaurant. South of Mangrove Cay and east of the Conch Farm is a submerged cable in 1'-3' of water at low tide. This cable is easily seen and definitely something to avoid.

From the dock at *Leeward* you can get on any one of several charter boats for a wonderful day trip to North Caicos or if you desire, any other island in the chain from Middle Caicos, to South Caicos and even Grand Turk. Here you can find *Silver Deep* (649-946-5612) who will take you just about anywhere you want

to go in these islands: North Caicos, Middle Caicos, East Caicos, South Caicos, Grand Turk, and even to Salt Cay. Owner Arthur Dean and his brothers will be happy to take you to any of these spots from Leeward. For more information call 941-5595 or check in at the *Silver Deep* office at *Leeward*. Not to be outdone, *J & B Tours*, also at *Leeward*, has several Island exploration charters that will take you in and around Provo and all the way to South Caicos if you like. For more info, check their office or call 946-5047. *J & B Tours* also sells fishing licenses. Both *Silver Deep* and *Big Blue* (649-946-5034) offer charter dive trips.

Navigational Information

Vessels drawing 5' or less and wishing to head out onto the *Caicos Banks* from Leeward Going Through can do so at high tide, and only at high tide. The last year or so has seen a supply boat with a 5' draft enter Leeward Going Through from the *Caicos Bank*, this has helped this route a lot since the supply boat has basically "dredged" a 5' deep channel for us. Since it is easy to get Nassau tides by SSB and ham radio (see the section on *Weather* in the chapter *The Basics*). A vessel drawing 4½' will need a tide of over 2'-2½', that is a 2.6'-3.1' above datum Nassau tide or

equivalent. Remember that tides here are generally .6' less than tides in Nassau and approximately one hour later. A 5' draft needs a tide of the equivalent of a Nassau above datum tide of 3.6' and more, not rare, but definitely not common. I have traveled this route with a Nassau tide of 3.8' above datum and saw nothing less than 5' the entire route. Bear in mind that wind direction sometimes affects the tides on the banks south of Provo. A few days of northwest through northeast wind may cause an unusually low tide on the southern shore of Provo while a strong southeast to southwest wind will have the reverse effect. The prudent mariner will likely check the route at high tide by dinghy the day prior to his planned departure.

From Leeward Going Through, head south toward the *Conch Farm* as shown on Chart TCI-C12, passing between the small unnamed cay and the *Conch Farm* (don't try this route in the early morning with the sun in your eyes; you won't be able to see a thing). Keep the first sign and the conspicuous brown shoal that parallels the *Conch Farm* fence to starboard. Once past the first sign, head for the second sign staying about 75'-100' off the fence. There are a couple of shallow heads on this part of the route, but they should lie well to port if you keep your course close to a line between the two signs that parallel the fence. Once past the second sign, keep parallel to the fence as you head towards Bird Rock keeping about 50-100 yards east of the rock. As you come abeam of Bird Rock steer approximately southeast until about two hundred yards or so south of the rock, to avoid a shallow sand patch lying just south and southeast of Bird Rock. From this position you can take up a course of anywhere between 165º-200º to cross shallow *Boy Stubbs Shoal*; the deeper water seems to be on a course of about 180º-200º. The shallowest part of this route lies between ½ mile and 2 miles south of Bird Rock across shallow *Boy Stubbs Shoal*. The bottom is not quite flat through here, there are several "humps" in the bottom and if you are too early or if the tide is too low, you will likely keep bumping over them as you power your way through, but don't worry as they're all soft sand.

Keep on your course for several miles, dodging any black or brown patches you see, until you reach deeper water, anywhere from 7' and above, generally in the area of 21º 45.50' N-21º 46.00' N. This route is a terrific shortcut if you're headed to *Sapodilla Bay*. I believe that if enough sailboats come through here we'll eventually have a pretty nice channel dredged (but don't try it with a winged keel, they tend to act as an anchor).

If you are in *Sapodilla Bay*, *South Side Marina*, or *Caicos Marina and Shipyard* and wish to avail yourself of this shortcut to Leeward, head ENE past the shipyard to a waypoint at 21º 45.50'N, 72º 07.00'W. Watch out for scattered heads and shallow patch reefs along this route. Once in the general vicinity of the waypoint, head for a waypoint at 21º 48.60'N, 72º 07.30'W, approximately ¼ mile east/southeast of Bird Rock. From this position simply follow the above mentioned directions in reverse.

What You Will Find Ashore

Just North of Leeward Going Through lies Little Water Cay, a very popular picnic spot for locals and cruisers; logs show that the island is visited annually by over 17,000 tourists. The island lies within the boundaries of the *Princess Alexandra National Park* and has been set aside as a nature preserve for about 1,500-2,000 of the rare and endangered Turks Island rock iguanas (*Cyclura carinata*) as well as a variety of bird life. When Loyalists and Salt Rakers first inhabited the Turks and Caicos Islands, their pet dogs decimated the indigenous iguana population on these cays, until the only place you can find them today is on the uninhabited cays such as Little Water Cay. As the *Meridian Club* (http://www.meridianclub.com/) was being built on Pine Cay in 1973, an iguana survey showed a population of 15,000 on the cay.

By 1976 nearly all the iguanas were gone due to predation by cats and dogs introduced during construction. A 1995 survey showed only one iguana, a few burrows, and several tracks along the northeast coast. A new problem has occurred by the creation of the sand bridges between Little Water Cay, Water Cay, and Pine Cay over the last several decades. Speculation concerning the feral cats on Pine Cay suggests that it is only a matter of time before they work their way down to Little Water Cay.

From the small beach on the southern shore of the cay there is a nice boardwalk that takes you through the interior of the cay to view the local vegetation and the island's population of iguanas. The nature trail on the northern shore of the island, best reached from the *Grace Bay* side of the cay and within easy dinghy distance from Leeward, is the most scenic in terms of animal life. If you visit the cay, please stay on the boardwalk; do not feed, touch, or harass the iguana in anyway, and please do not bring a cat or dog ashore. A bit of Turks and Caicos Island folklore that has to be seen to be believed has it that the iguanas in these islands will dance to music. Try it and see, grab a few cans or bottles and tap out a rhythm, or perhaps bring along a boom box with your favorite CD and play DJ for these creatures. The waters between Little Water Cay, Donna Cay, and Mangrove Cay as shown on Chart TCI-C12 are deep and make for a very good though current-ridden anchorage. Two anchors are a must here. The only problem with this anchorage area occurs on the weekends when the locals tend to water ski through here. Donna Cay was once part of Mangrove Cay until Hurricane Donna changed the landscape along these islands, hence the name of the cay.

North of Little Water Cay, and connected to Little Water Cay since Hurricane Donna, is the uninhabited Water Cay. Just off its western shore, as shown on Chart TCI-C11, is the wreck of an old barge in 4' of water. The barge was being towed along the shore when it broke loose and came to rest in its current location. On the northern shore of Water Cay are some very nice beaches and sheer rock ledges that are wonderful for snorkeling or just swimming. In prevailing winds these beaches are very calm, though sometimes a swell can work its way over the reef to push your anchored dinghy ashore. These very beaches were the background for the 1987 *Sports Illustrated Swimsuit Edition*.

Pine Cay lies just to the north of Water Cay and is named after the Cuban Pine which thrives on the edges of the island's freshwater ponds. Once a separate cay, Pine Cay was joined to Water Cay by Hurricane Donna, as was Little Water Cay. Pine Cay is best known for being the home of the *Meridian Club*, an extremely exclusive total-getaway resort constructed in 1973. No phone, no TV, just peace and quiet and pristine beach. No loud vehicles are allowed, only golf carts and bicycles. The island itself has several distinctive zones of vegetation, shared mainly by palmettos and pines. On the islands northern end there are a few brackish lakes inhabited by several species of (once) saltwater fish, also a legacy of Hurricane Donna.

Pine Cay was also the site of an ancient Lucayan settlement, and in the 18th and 19th centuries is said to have been used as a hideout for pirates. Pine Cay is private and visits ashore must be by invitation only, although access to the beach up to the dune line is allowed. You can anchor off the beach, a somewhat surgy anchorage at times, on the western shore of Pine Cay wherever your draft allows, but only in prevailing winds. You can also pick up a dive boat mooring if they are available and not needed by a commercial vessel. If you're interested in name-dropping, it is said that Bill Cosby and Denzel Washington frequent Pine Cay, and that Jimmy Buffet has a passion for bonefishing in the nearby waters.

Navigational Information

Further north, the Pine Cay, Fort George Cay, Dellis Cay, and Parrot Cay anchorages can be easily accessed by sea via *Fort George Cut* as shown on Chart TCI-C13. Vessels wishing to visit the area from Leeward Going Through can do so by venturing northeast inside the reef. As shown on Chart #'s TCI-C11, Chart C12, and chart C13, the route lies between the reef and Water Cay and Pine Cay. There are only a few shallow reefs and a couple of sandbars to watch out for. Stay away from any dark spots you see; these will likely be heads or small patch reefs.

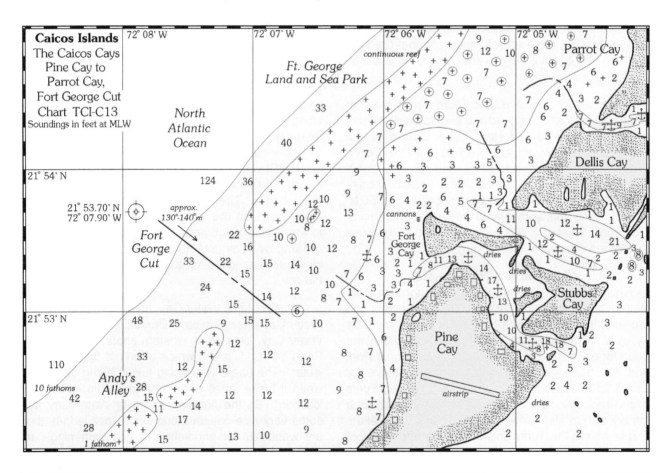

For skippers entering through *Fort George Cut*, a waypoint at 21° 53.70'N, 72° 07.90'W, will place you approximately ½ mile northwest of *Fort George Cut*. Enter the cut on an approximate heading of 130°-140° magnetic. The heading here is not so important as simply staying between the reefs, but not to worry, *Fort George Cut* is wide and deep. Once inside you can head southward to Leeward or Water Cay, or northward to Dellis Cay and Parrot Cay. About a mile southwest of Fort George Cay is another smaller break in the reef known as Andy's Alley. This very visible bright blue cut is about 100 yards wide and has a minimum depth of 11'. To find Andy's Alley look for the southern end of the beach on Pine Cay, and when approaching the usually breaking reef, look for the bright blue cut.

What You Will Find Ashore

Fort George Cay is a *National Historic Site* that dates back to 1798-1812. To protect the cotton production on North and Middle Caicos, settlers built Fort George and set up cannons to defend their main port of export in anticipation of attack by pirates and Americans. Today, thanks to *Hurricane Donna*, the same cannons that were poised to protect the islands now lie in about 3'-4' of water, making for an excellent snorkel. Look for them about 50 yards south of the small beach on the northwestern tip of Fort George Cay about 50' offshore. There are three of these two hundred-year-old cannons, all pointing to seaward; you can't miss them. You can anchor west of Fort George Cay wherever your draft allows, but only in settled weather, and watch out for a surge coming in over the reef. There is a wonderful, deep, uncrowded anchorage between Fort George Cay and Pine Cay that only sees some small boat traffic from the resort on Pine Cay. This is an extremely difficult anchorage to enter: it has shallowed to the point that only drafts of less than 5' can enter, and that's on a high tide.

As little as three or four years ago, drafts of 5'-6' could enter here, but as with all the cuts along this section of the Caicos Cays, what is deep today may be quite shallow tomorrow. After entering Fort George Cut head northeastward until you can take up an approximate southeast heading towards the point on Pine Cay as shown on Chart TCI-13. There is really no way to describe the entrance here other than to say that it curves around generally back towards the northeast until you reach the darker, deeper water between the cays. A high tide, excellent visibility and the ability to read water are what will get you through here. There are several sandbars that you must

zigzag between and some shallow grassy patches that give a false impression of being deeper than they look. Once inside you will find a deep anchorage that goes well eastward between Pine Cay and Stubbs Cay and even out onto the Caicos Bank a bit. As usual, put down two anchors for the current.

Dellis Cay, named after a Greek sponger from Hydra named John Dellis, was the center of a small but thriving sponging industry on the cay in the late 1800s. The cay is subject to a unique pattern of tide and current, giving this island the nod when it comes to some of the best beachcombing in the Turks and Caicos Islands. Beautiful white sandy beaches surround Dellis Cay; ashore you may find the ruins of an old fish processing plant. There is a good, deep anchorage between Dellis Cay and Fort George Cay that can be accessed by vessels with drafts of less than 5'. Excellent, and I do mean excellent, visibility as well as a healthy dollop of patience is required to find the channel, as the sandbars change often and you will have to do quite a bit of zigzagging. Only try this just before high tide and remember that there may be no one around to help you should you run aground.

Navigational Information

As shown on Chart TCI-C13, head northeastward from *Fort George Cut* between the reef and Fort George Cay, avoiding the large shallow bar that sits northwest of Fort George Cay and the small shallow reefs between the bar and the outer barrier reef. Line up the southwestern tip of Dellis Cay and head in on it on a heading of 140° magnetic. You will probably have to dodge some shallow spots as all these sandbars change frequently in this stretch of cays. As you approach the southwestern tip of Dellis Cay you will find that you also have to pass between two shallow yellow colored sandy bars, 1'-2' at MLW. One works out westward from Dellis Cay, the other also lies east/west just a little northwest of the first bar. You will have to turn to starboard to pass between the two to make it into the deeper water at the entrance to the anchorage. The anchorage itself has two arms, one on the Dellis Cay side, one on the Stubbs Cay side. Both offer good protection, though I prefer the anchorage on the Dellis Cay side.

In recent years, Dellis Cay was acquired by a Turkish developer and became part of an elaborate Ponzi scheme. Wealthy clients were offered exclusive homes yet no infrastructure was ever completed. The developer has had his assets frozen pending investigation.

North of Dellis Cay and southwest of North Caicos lies Parrot Cay. Some say that Parrot Cay is a corruption of "Pirates Cay," where legendary pirates such as Calico Jack Rackham, Annie Bonney, Mary Read, and Blackbeard are said to have visited. An 18th century house still stands on this 300-acre private island. There was an attempt at growing cotton on Parrot Cay in 1918, but it lasted only a few years. Along Parrot Cay's northern shore you will see the red roofs of a prestigious modern resort that was deserted but is now being reopened.

There is an nice anchorage lying between Parrot Cay and Dellis Cay that is much easier to access than the anchorage between Fort George Cay and Pine Cay. A vessel with a draft of 5'-6' can enter here with the tide; the only dangers are the numerous (though easily seen in good light) shallow heads and small patch reefs that dot the waters between the reef and Dellis Cay and Parrot Cay. Good visibility is essential but a cool head and nerves of steel are just as important. As shown on Chart TCI-C13, work your way north inside the reef from Fort George Cut, taking care to avoid the many shallow heads and patch reefs. When you are north of the cut between Parrot Cay and Dellis Cay you will notice the darker water inside the cut and a small arm of it heading out north/northwest towards the reef. You will want to line up the northern point of Dellis Cay and take up an approximate heading of south/southeast on it. The heading here is not as important as trying to picture how the deeper water flows out over the sandbar. This channel, 4' in places at MLW, is your only way in if you draw 5'-6'. Once inside, the deeper water goes well eastward to the eastern end of Dellis Cay, with only a slight zigzag.

West Caicos

Pony Channel - ¼ nm W of:
21° 43.40' N, 72° 27.30' W

Pony Channel - ¼ nm E of:
21° 43.40' N, 72° 26.75' W

West Caicos Marina - ¼ nm NW of entrance:
21° 42.00' N, 72° 28.00' W

West Caicos - ¾ nm S of Southwest Point:
21° 36.75' N, 72° 29.00' W

Freighter Channel - SW waypoint:
21° 35.75' N, 72° 23.25' W

West Caicos, lying approximately 10 miles southwest of Providenciales and *Sapodilla Bay*, was originally called *Macubiza* by the Lucayans and *Petite Caique* by the French. The waters off the western shore of the island offer miles of superb wall-diving and imposing limestone cliffs, a favorite spot for the numerous dive boats operating out of nearby Provo. In years past, West Caicos was allegedly a haven for pirates that would attack homeward bound French boats returning from Haiti. A French Captain in 1753 wrote that West Caicos was "abounding in the white beaked Bahamian parrot." It is said that Nelson captured a French sailing vessel off West Caicos in 1777 when he commanded the sloop *Little Lucy*. The tourist brochures say that Delvin's Cove at the northern end of West Caicos was a hideout for the infamous pirate Delvin or Dulien but I was unable to find any reference to a pirate by that name.

On the western shore you will find the ruins of Yankee Town where in the mid-1800s a flourishing community of sisal workers lived. In 1849, 18 acres were planted at Spencerville on the northern coast of West Caicos and proved so successful that over 1,000 acres of sisal were eventually being grown on the island. If you look around you will find the ruins of a sisal press, railway, steam engines, and several limestone buildings dating to the late 1800s and early 1900s when 70 salt and sisal workers lived and worked here. At a cost of over $30,000, the government constructed the railway and a saltwater canal to the salinas but the sisal project was halted at the beginning of the American Civil War. The old railway stretches across West Caicos in an east/west direction and if you hike the causeway you may see some of the pink flamingos, osprey, and herons that live along the shores of Lake Catherine, a nature reserve. The Dominican dictator Trujillo tried to buy West Caicos a few years prior to his assassination. It is believed that he wanted the island for a hideaway, but the deal fell through when clear title could not be found. In 1973 *Esso* planned to build a huge oil refinery on the cay, but plans were abandoned when the owner suddenly died. You can anchor off Yankee Town in settled weather or in light to moderate prevailing east/southeast winds. Stronger winds create a bit more surge in the anchorage.

Navigational Information
Vessels approaching *West Caicos Marina* from *Sapodilla Bay* should head west, out *Sandbore Channel* to the waypoint shown and then turn southward to the waypoint off the marina. There is

another option, *Pony Channel*, just north of the reef that borders the northwestern shore of West Caicos, but this route is not recommended except for the experienced reef navigator with good visibility, and calm conditions. Approaching from *Sapodilla Bay* you'll have deep water all the way to a waypoint at 21° 43.40' N, 72° 26.75' W, which places you approximately ¼ mile east of *Pony Channel* as shown on Chart TCI-C5. From the waypoint head west passing north of the reef and south of a smaller shoal as shown on the chart. Vessels heading for *Sapodilla Bay* from *West Caicos Marina* can follow this route in reverse. From *West Caicos Marina* parallel the reef north/northwest to a waypoint at 21° 43.40' N, 72° 27.30' W, which places you approximately ¼ mile west of *Pony Channel*. Head east through the channel for about ½ mile and then set your course for *Sapodilla Bay*.

The entrance to the *West Caicos Marina* itself lies through a natural break in the reef just west of Company Point. A waypoint at 21° 42.00' N, 72° 28.00' W, will place you approximately ¼ nautical mile northwest of the entrance channel leading into the marina as shown on Chart TCI-C14A. From the waypoint pass between the entrance jetties and enter the marina basin. Use extreme caution, there are shallow reefs on both sides of the channel, and if that were not enough to worry about, Provo dive boats use the channel to pass to and from the western shore of West Caicos. The dive boats usually don't slow down for cruising vessels and a dangerous situation could come about if one was headed outward from *Bernard Bay* as you were headed into the marina. Keep your eyes open here and let's avoid any problems. The marina is just part of a much larger project involving condos and all the amenities, most located near the southern end of West Caicos.

There is a nice lee anchorage off the northwestern tip of West Caicos that is often used by locals as well as the dive boat operators working out of Provo. The anchorage in *Bernard Bay* that is shown on Charts TCI-C5 and Chart TCI-C14 lies just off a beautiful beach and is a great spot in settled weather and in east to southeast winds. The anchorage can be gained through a small winding break in the reef off Company Point as shown on Chart TCI-C14 and in greater detail on Chart TCI-C14A. You can also reach *Bernard Bay* from the *Sandbore Channel* area directly from *Sapodilla Bay* as shown on Chart TCI-C5. Both routes require good light and you'll have to dodge several coral heads and small patch reefs in water

that is less than 6' deep (at MLW) in places, but you may find that the end result is worth your effort. If you don't wish to try the cut at Company Point, you might consider anchoring south of Company Point along the western shore of West Caicos as shown on the chart and taking a short dinghy ride in to the beach.

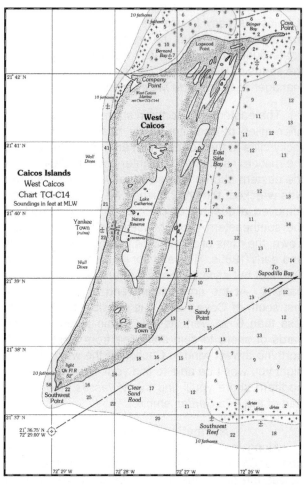

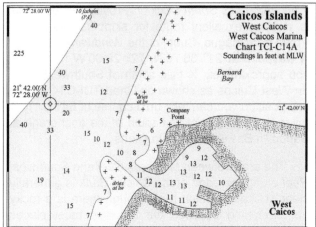

What You Will Find Ashore

The *West Caicos Marina* started out well but along the way something went awry. It seems that funding was lost with the demise of the financing company and the entire project was on hold for almost the last two years. The current situation is that the marina is closed and nobody is permitted ashore on the marina grounds, however the owners have no problem with transient vessels anchoring inside the marina's basin. It is just as easy to use the dive buoys just off the marina but they must be made available for dive boats during daylight hours. For the latest info on the status of *West Caicos Marina* contact Simon, the manager at *South Side Marina* on Provo.

The eastern and northern shores of West Caicos offer miles of beautiful sandy beaches with a few rocky cliffs at the northeastern and southern tips and the rusty ruins of an old freighter about midway down the eastern shore. It is said that when this freighter was wrecked, the crew opened the safe aboard and removed a quantity of silver bars. Atop a bluff on the southeastern shore of West Caicos stands Star Town, the ruins of an old *DEA* base during the 1970s and early 1980s. The site got its name from the two Quonset hut style buildings that are laid out in a star pattern. At the northeastern end of West Caicos, just south of Cove Point, it is possible for a draft of less than 6' to work its way within a few hundred yards of shore to gain some lee from west through north/northwest winds. Caution: if the wind shifts at night you won't be able to find your way out. On the northern shore you'll find the *Molasses Reef Hotel*, part of the *Ritz-Carlton* empire.

Navigational Information

Along the eastern shore of West Caicos is the popular *Clear Sand Road,* the channel from the ocean across the banks that is often used by the freighter traffic that uses *South Dock* on Providenciales. This is also an excellent route for skippers heading to Provo from Inagua, Cuba, or the *Windward Passage*. A waypoint at 21° 36.75'N, 72° 29.00'W, will place you approximately ¾ mile south of Southwest Point on West Caicos as shown on Chart TCI-C14. From this position you can take up a course of 64° for 13.1 miles to the waypoint just south of the anchorage at *Sapodilla Bay* with no obstructions.

The area between *Molasses Reef* and *Southwest Reef* along the edge of the *Caicos Bank* is generally clear of shallow patch reefs though there is a rocky bar stretching between the two. In most places

this bar has 15'-20' over it and does not pose a navigational hazard to the average cruising boat. There is a channel through here as shown on Chart TCI-C1 that is simply called the *Freighter Channel*. It is often used by commercial vessels headed to *South Dock* on Provo and leads in from the sea between *Southwest Reef* and *Molasses Reef* with a least depth of 12' near *South Dock*.

Capt. Dave Matthews of the trimaran *Tao* has been sailing these waters for over 25 years and suggests that if you are off the southern end of West Caicos and cannot find refuge from strong northeast winds you can tuck up under the lee of *Southwest Reef* for some protection from the seas (parts of the reef and bars to its north dry at low water). For shelter from W-NW winds and seas you can anchor in the lee of Sandy Point as shown on the chart.

French Cay

French Cay - ½ nm W of anchorage:
21° 30.60' N, 72° 12.70' W

French Cay - ¾ nm SW of anchorage:
21° 29.75' N, 72° 12.65' W

French Cay was originally called Cay Blondell at the beginning of the 1600s. Blondell was a French surveyor in Haiti who was commissioned to study the feasibility of building a navigational landmark on the cay to assist those vessels en route to and from the *Windward Passage*. The French lost several ships in the vicinity over the years, including one three-decked merchantman laden with treasure from Hispaniola. Blondell stressed the importance of building some sort of structure on French Cay to keep mariners from confusing it with West Caicos and West Sandspit, but nothing ever came of his efforts. Over the intervening years, French Cay's greatest claim to fame is that the pirate Francoise L'Olonnois is said to have occasionally used the island as a base from which to raid ships en route to and from the nearby *Windward Passage*.

Today French Cay is a protected bird sanctuary and you will understand why when you visit. Hundreds of gulls, boobies, and terns call this tiny sliver of rock and sand on the edge of the *Caicos Bank* home, swarming over and around it throughout the day. Until recently, a permit from the *DECR* was required to set foot upon the island, today however landing on French Cay is prohibited.

In the waters surrounding French Cay nurse sharks mate each summer so give them a wide berth if you happen to be there at the same time; they are usually not aggressive unless molested. The island itself is rather low-lying and sandy, with excellent snorkeling along its southwest side. French Cay has gotten quite popular with dive boats operating on a daily basis out of Providenciales.

Navigational Information

As you approach French Cay, you will probably not sight this low-lying island until about five miles away. Your first sight of it will probably be the top of the light standing on the southwestern part of the cay (Fl R, 10'). From the waypoint just south of the anchorage at *Sapodilla Bay*, steer 171° for 14.3 miles to a waypoint at 21° 30.60'N, 72° 12.70'W, which places you approximately ½ mile west of the anchorage on the western shore of French Cay as

shown on Chart TCI-C15. On this route the water depths range from about 16' just south of *Sapodilla Bay* to about 10' just north of French Cay, and there are no obstructions. As you approach French Cay from these 10' depths, the water gets progressively deeper as you head for the edge of the *Caicos Bank*.

If arriving from offshore head to a waypoint at 21° 29.75'N, 72° 12.65'W, which places you approximately ¾ mile southwest of the anchorage area and on the edge of the *Caicos Bank*. From the entrance waypoint to *Caicos Marina and Shipyard* at Juba Point, French Cay bears 197° at a distance of 14.8 nautical miles.

If headed to *Sapodilla Bay* from French Cay you will begin to make out the hills of Providenciales from more than 10 miles away. The conspicuous twin white fuel tanks at the *Texaco* yard east of the green

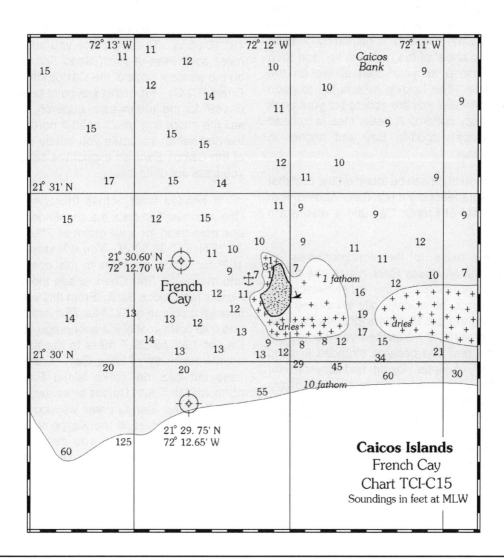

Caicos Islands
French Cay
Chart TCI-C15
Soundings in feet at MLW

customs building at *South Dock* are your landmarks if you are making for *Sapodilla Bay*, but don't confuse them with the several white houses that lie to the east of *Sapodilla Bay*. Another good landmark as you get closer is the huge crane at South Dock just west of the white tanks. As I said, there are no obstructions on this route; I have run this route at night from French Cay to *Sapodilla Bay*, but I cannot recommend that others do so.

What You Will Find Ashore

The northern section of the anchorage area tends to be rocky and grassy, but if you set your anchor well in the surrounding sand you will stay put. The best holding is in the sandy holes in the grassy areas in the center of the anchorage area. In moderate east/southeast winds you might get a bit of a surge around the southwestern tip of French Cay, if so, it's very easy to rig a bridle for a comfortable night.

A bit of a lee anchorage is available from southwest through west winds off the northeastern shore of French Cay. Entrance is gained by heading north around the shoal of the northern tip, and then heading in as close as your draft allows on the northeastern side. The holding here is fair to good depending on how well you are able to set your hook in the rocky/grassy bottom. A better idea is to head northward towards *Sapodilla Bay* and anchor in *Bermudian Harbour*.

Excellent snorkeling can be found on the reef that lies south and southeast of French Cay. Another reef lies well southeast of French Cay and is also worth exploration.

Just a few miles to the north/northwest of French Cay is the *Molasses Reef Wreck,* the oldest shipwreck in the Americas and the first shipwreck site in the Caribbean to be scientifically excavated and exhibited. Measuring just 19 meters long, the caravel, having safely crossed the treacherous Atlantic, ran aground on the reef and became stranded in sand in about 15'-20' of water, laying undiscovered for some 400 years until it was found by treasure divers in 1976. Some unscrupulous salvager tried to gain financially from the excavation by claiming the ship was the *Pinta*, Columbus' flagship on his 1492 voyage of discovery. The claim was soon proven to be false and the government of the Turks and Caicos Islands took over the salvage and identification process. A government permit was issued to the *Institute of Nautical Archaeology* at *Texas A&M's*

National Museum under the direction of Dr. Donald H. Keith. Irate treasure hunters then tried to dynamite the site with, fortunately, minimal damage. Dating of Lucayan pottery pieces found on the site placed the ship on the reef prior to 1513 (remember, all the Lucayans were forcibly removed from the Turks and Caicos Islands by 1513) and researchers speculated that the ship was a slaver en route to Hispaniola. The ship was armed with state-of-the-art weapons of the period and the national museum on Grand Turk now displays the largest selection of 16th century wrought iron breech loading cannons in the world.

Navigational Information

From French Cay, with the right wind, you can sail right off the bank for Inagua, Little Inagua, Haiti, Manzanillo or Luperón in the DR, or to the *Windward Passage* and Cuba. If you are bound for Manzanillo, a course of 179° for 101.5 nautical miles will bring you to the entrance to Manzanillo. If bound for Luperón from French Cay, head out into the deeper water off the Caicos Banks and head for a waypoint at 21° 20.50'N, 72° 10.05'W. This will place you approximately two miles southwest of *West Sand Spit*, a shallow area on the western edge of the *Caicos Bank* as shown on Chart TCI-C1. From this waypoint take up a heading of 149° for the 109 miles to Luperón. If you intend to sail the entire way you'll need a northeast wind. For the first half of this route you will be sailing in the lee of the *Caicos Bank* so expect the seas to build once you pass out of its lee.

If headed west across the banks from French Cay you must first clear the shoal north of French Cay and then head for a waypoint at *Star Channel* at 21° 30.25'N, 72° 06.60'W. You will steer approximately 102° for almost six miles to this position. For more information on *Star Channel* see the section *Routes Across the Caicos Bank*. From this waypoint you can take up a course of 123° for 28 miles to the waypoint one mile northwest of the anchorage at Big Ambergris Cay or 104° for 29.7 miles to the anchorage at the southwestern tip of Long Cay. From here you can pass out into the *Turks Island Passage* to head northward to South Caicos or eastward to the Turks. Also from the *Star Channel* waypoint you can steer 113° for 28.1 miles to the waypoint just north of the Fish Cays. From here you can head out across the *Turks Island Passage* to Great Sand Cay if you choose.

North Caicos

North Caicos, located only 12 miles from Provo, is about 44 square miles in area. Its 1,500 inhabitants primarily live in the four settlements that are connected by the King's Highway, which runs the length of the island. The southern shore of the island is primarily mangroves and tidal flats, home to flocks of flamingos, bonefish, and tarpon. Thanks to its abundant rainfall, North Caicos is known as the garden center of the Turks and Caicos Islands. At one time, extensive farms fed all of the islanders with crops transported by inter-island trading sloops.

Navigational Information

There are no deep draft anchorages at North Caicos; the closest for a 5'-6' draft is between Parrot Cay and Dellis Cay as shown on Chart TCI-C13. There are several day charters that run out of *Leeward Marina* that can provide lunch and transportation, either scooters or jeeps, for those interested in taking a tour of this beautiful cay. The entire northern shore of North Caicos is protected by an offshore barrier reef, but a vessel with a draft of less than 6' can work its way through the reef at *Ropier Cut* (see Chart TCI-C16) in an emergency. That route, as are almost all the inshore routes between Parrot Cay eastward to East Caicos, is literally strewn with shallow coral heads and shoals. If you choose to dinghy to the island you can rent a car from Pat Hamilton at 946-7141 or from *Old Nick Rental Cars* at 946-7358.

What You Will Find Ashore

Along the northwestern shore of North Caicos, Three Mary's Cays is a great snorkeling spot near Sandy Point where you'll also find ospreys and their nesting sites. The cays are a protected sanctuary and visits ashore are by *DECR* permit only. Sandy Point is a small fishing/farming community of only about 40-50 residents, where, in the early 1900s, guano miners discovered a cave containing ancient Lucayan artifacts, including a stone idol. The community is tucked in behind the lush vegetation of the cay and the casual visitor might not even see the buildings. At the dock by the small harbor sits an old rusting crane, while to the right sits a huge old wooden hull. There used to be a blue hole tucked into the mangroves right off this harbor, but it was filled in during a hurricane. Located here is the *North Caicos Yacht Club and Marina*, a small but very nice marina built to support the condos and home owners here. Basically it is just a dredged canal with concrete sides, there are no amenities (except for a small local

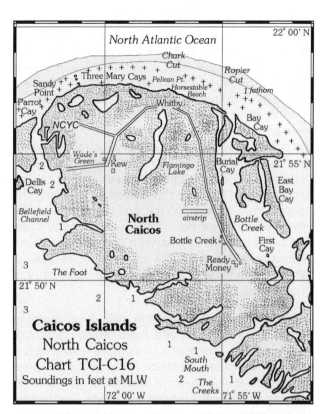

store selling basic food and drinks) and the marina is not open for cruisers at the time of this writing.

Most visitors make their first stop at Whitby where you'll find *Whitby Plaza*, a resort area located along the northern shore. Three hotels here offer fine lodging and meals to those who wish to get away from the hustle and bustle of Provo. Here you'll find a tourist information center; a great spot to begin your exploration of North Caicos. You'll probably want to check out the *North Caicos Art Center*, where you can find great buys on very nice native arts and crafts as well as silk paintings and pareos by local islanders. You might want to call ahead to make sure they'll be open as they really don't stick to a schedule. Call Alveira at 946-7120 or Regina at 946-7360.

Don't miss dining at *Papa Grunt's Seafood Restaurant* for great food. You might also want to sample the choices at *Marina View* and the *Ocean Club*. Directly across from *Whitby Plaza* is *Flamingo Pond* where you can view and photograph hundreds of West Indian flamingos. To find the pond, take the *Whitby Highway* heading east to the beach roads and you will come to *Flamingo Lookout* with its sign and small covered viewing platforms. Aircraft flying out of the nearby airstrip have been restricted from flying across the pond to the delight of the flamingos and flamingo enthusiasts. The *Prospect of Whitby Hotel* serves Italian cuisine with dinner reservations requested at what is really *Club Vacanza*, a mini *Club Med* for Italians just west of Whitby. The *Prospect of Whitby Hotel* is named after the famous *Prospect of Whitby Pub* that overlooks the Thames River in London. The nearby *Pelican Beach Resort* (http://www.pelicanbeach.tc/) has a great view overlooking the pine-fringed shore. The family-run resort has 12 rooms and serves excellent native meals in a modern restaurant. The bar attracts locals as well as tourists and guests on the cay. If you need fresh bread look up Wealthy Forbes in Whitby; just ask anyone in the village where to find her. For those who prefer a bed and breakfast inn, try *Joanne's Bed and Breakfast*. *Horsestable Beach* on the northern shore east of Whitby offers miles of beautiful private beaches. For groceries try *KJ Variety Store*.

The settlement at Kew, the agricultural center of North Caicos, is named after the botanical gardens at Kew, England. There is a clinic (https://www.visittci.com/kew-clinic), a *Post Office*, and a public phone on *Forbes Street* in the heart of Kew. Between Bellefield Landing and Kew you will find the *Cosmic Farm* where North Caicos farmers grow fresh fruits, vegetables, and herbs and welcome all visitors. Another mile up the *Cosmic Farm Road* are the ruins of Wade's Green. As the road ends you will find a sign with a map and instructions on how to proceed by foot. Bring a good pair of shoes as the walk from the road to the ruins can be rough. A team of archaeologists from *UCLA* excavated the ruins in 1989, and now visitors can see some of the finest Loyalist ruins in the Turks and Caicos Islands including a courtyard and jail. A small general store is on the left as you approach the Wade's Green ruins. Stop in for a cold drink and meet Cecelia, who sells her own wonderful basketwork. If you feel adventurous, spend the night in Kew as their only tourist and don't miss eating at *Ma Sue's* where Susan Butterfield will serve you up some truly authentic North Caicos fare, as well as sell you groceries, fruit, veggies, and frozen goods. At the other end of Kew, on the road from Whitby, you'll find *Forbes' Variety Store* where owner Elizabeth Forbes sells a wide range of household and auto supplies. If you wish to purchase fish and veggies in season, try Farmer John at 946-7381.

Further east along the main road, Bottle Creek offers up its own Loyalist ruins at the *Belvedere Plantation*. Bottle Creek is a small fishing community that borders *Bottle Creek* on the *King's Highway*.

The creek is protected from the *North Atlantic Ocean* swells by the Bay Islands and their fringing Elkhorn reefs. In case of emergency there is a small medical facility by the high school in the heart of Bottle Creek at High Rock, just up from the government dock, or you can call *Government Nurse* on VHF ch. 16. At the airport north of Bottle Creek you will find some pretty good food at the *Super D Café*. Along *Creek Road*, the lower road in Bottle Creek, are several old, historic houses, many of them still inhabited. If you need fresh fish and veggies in season contact Peter the Haitian at 946-7303. If you want a loaf of fresh bread try Iona Gardiner (who also offers some very nice basketry) at the *Aquatic Restaurant,* on *Kings Road,* at 946-7272.

You can also get some fine native cuisine at *Titter's Restaurant* ran by "Titters" whose pea soup and steamed conch is to die for. *Titter's* is right next to the airport. If you're into dominos you'll want to visit the *Two Son's Restaurant*. Another good eating establishment is *Wendy's Restaurant*, no relation to the chain though. If you plan to stay overnight try *Gordon Black's Guest House*. For groceries try *Speed's Grocery* or *My Dee's Variety Store*. For those in search of cool libation, try *Ellie Smith's*, *Albert Grey's*, *Dar Williams'*, and *Nash's Bar and Pool Hall*. South of Bottle Creek, near Ready Money, stand the tallest pine forests in the Turks and Caicos Islands. Off the eastern shore of North Caicos, the Bay Islands are a national park boasting miles of pristine beaches. Iguanas on the nearby East Bays Cays are an outstanding example of the natural diversity of this green island. Towards the mouth of Bottle Creek sits the small village of Major's Hill, where everyone is named Gardiner. Look for big changes in the Bottle Creek area over the next few years. I've seen the plans for a dredged channel, 12' deep, into Bottle Creek that will lead to a large upscale marina and resort/condo complex called *Mare Bella*. As of this writing financing has been arranged, but construction has not begun.

Divers will want to note that diving along the north shore of North Caicos, as in the other islands, takes the form of spur and groove formations that drop in a mini-wall from 30-70 feet. This is the same barrier reef that stretches across the entire northern boundary of the Caicos Islands, and the diving is similar to that found on the north shore of Providenciales. This area sees far fewer divers than the sites at Provo or West Caicos, with a subsequent increase in marine life. Expect an excellent fish population with the occasional larger visitor.

Middle Caicos

Middle Caicos, often called Grande Caicos, is the largest cay in the Turks and Caicos Island group and the least exposed to tourists of all the inhabited cays. Middle Caicos can boast the most dramatic shoreline of any of the Caicos group with towering limestone cliffs along its windward shore, only broken by a few small beaches with gentle rolling hills in the background. You can now drive or bike from Middle Caicos to North Caicos on the only causeway in the Turks and Caicos southwest of Mudjin Harbour as shown on Chart TCI-C17.

Navigational Information

A vessel with a draft of 6' or less can work its way through the offshore barrier reef at *Ferguson Cut* (see Chart TCI-C17) to anchor off the northern shore in an emergency. The area is littered with shallow coral heads and shoals, so good light is necessary. The anchorage would be a lee at best and only in south to southwest winds. There are also cuts northwest of Gambol Point (*Gamble Cut*) and just off the northeastern tip of the island (*Big Cut*). For the most part these cuts are usable and should only be attempted in an emergency and preferably if you can get some local assistance by VHF. Vessels heading east or west in the vicinity of Middle Caicos must give the northeastern tip of Middle Caicos just east of Gambol Point a wide berth of three miles or more. The water is shallow, about 20'-35', northeastward from Middle Caicos in this vicinity (see Chart TCI-C17).

What You Will Find Ashore

There are only three villages on the island, home to about 270 people and recently linked with a new paved road. In a recent nationwide cooperative effort,

pastel colored paints have been provided to the island's homeowners to paint all the inhabited homes on Middle Caicos. Daily air service and weekend ferry service to North Caicos are the only links to the other populated islands in the Turks and Caicos Islands. Between North Caicos and Middle Caicos is an area that is known as the *"Crossing Over Place."* Here you'll find a trail where, at low tide, one can walk from North Caicos to Middle Caicos just as the residents have been doing for centuries. The trail begins just west of the *Blue Horizon Resort* (http://bhresort.com/) and meanders along the bluffs along the northwestern shore of Middle Caicos. If you don't feel like walking across, a ferry at Pine Barrel Landing provides service between Middle and North Caicos on Fridays, Saturdays, and Sundays.

Middle Caicos is a spelunker's delight where the 12,000 year old *Village Cave* or *Conch Bar Caves* a national park, offer over 15 miles of above sea level caves. For a local guide, try Herbert Niat; his intimate knowledge of these caves is worth the trouble of seeking him out. Ask him to take you to *Indian Cave* at King Hill where you will see an impressive 60' high cathedral ceiling. Here you'll find roots spiraling down from the ceiling to the rich soil of the floor between massive limestone arches. Artifacts found in these caves by a team from the University of Indiana headed by Sean Sullivan prove that Middle Caicos had an estimated 4,000 Lucayan Indians that thrived in pre-Columbian times. There is also evidence of a Lucayan ceremonial and trading center. Researchers have discovered over 38 Lucayan sites on Middle Caicos alone. And in 1977-1978, archaeologists unearthed a rare Lucayan ball court near Armstrong Pond. Ball courts have been found in Puerto Rico and points farther south, but never this far north. For great description of the ball game and how it was played by the ancient Lucayans, read the first chapter of James Michener's *Caribbean*.

The island's Northwest Point is a combination of beautiful inlets, marshes, mangroves and inland ponds that serves as a haven for birdlife. Conch Bar is the largest of the three settlements on Middle Caicos and is home to the island's only airstrip. Both *Taylor's Guest House* and *Arthur's Guest House* offer fine accommodations for the weary visitor. Nearby Mudjian Harbour, a corruption of the name Bermudian Harbour, offers a beautiful half-moon beach set against a backdrop of breathtaking limestone cliffs and is one of the most photographed sites in the

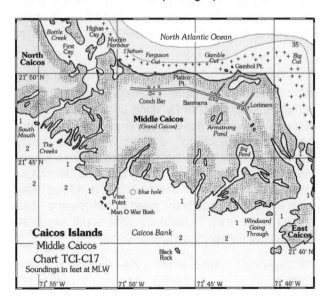

Turks and Caicos Islands. The nearby *Blue Horizon Resort* offers five fully equipped villas overlooking this scenic panorama. Future plans call for condo building sites and an enlarged resort. For good local food try *Carey's Restaurant* or *T&J Boutique*, which doubles as a gift shop.

East of Conch Bar, just a scant distance from the northern reef-fringed shore, sits Bambarra, a small community with a very unique history. In 1841, the Spanish slaver *Esperanza* wrecked on the reef at Breezy Point. The surviving freed slaves settled in the Caicos Islands, while some of the survivors traveled to Grand Turk for employment.

The following year another Spanish slaver, the *Gambia,* with a hold full of slaves from Bambarra in Africa, wrecked in The Bahamas. The survivors were sent to Middle Caicos, where they founded the settlement of Bambarra situated about five miles east of Conch Bar. The name refers to the Bambarra people who lived on the shores of the *Niger River* in West Africa. From offshore, Bambarra is barely visible, some of its buildings dotting the high ridge behind some casuarinas. The only store is Emmanuel Hall's well-stocked little grocery store.

Bambarra is home to the *Middle Caicos Expo*, an annual event held in mid to late August that some say is the best party in the Turks and Caicos. The *M.C. Expo* is a homecoming of sorts for Bambarrans who have moved away for employment. The activity centers along the thatched huts in the shade of the casuarina trees on the beach where vendors set up shacks to serve food and drink. Events include a sailing regatta, dominos, a beauty pageant and a tug of war. Pelican Cay, about ½ mile offshore, can be reached at LW by a sand "road" that disappears at HW.

Further east is the third and most remote of the Middle Caicos settlements, Lorimers, a very traditional settlement named after Dr. John Lorimers, a Loyalist plantation owner whose grave is nearby. Lorimers has a school, a church, a clinic with twice-weekly visits by a doctor from South Caicos, a government built water tank and two wells, *Big Well* and *Dark Night Well*. There are no stores here but residents may have an item that you are in need of, ask around. The creeks to the east of Lorimers offer some excellent bonefishing and exploring possibilities.

Divers will want to explore the blue hole near the south shore of middle Caicos just northeast of Man O

War Bush as shown on Chart TCI-C16. This dive site is best visited from Leeward Going Through by small boat or from one of the anchorages in the area of Fort George Cay. The hole is about 400 yards in diameter and over 200' deep and is surrounded by shallow banks rich in sea life, including sharks and rays.

East Caicos

Jacksonville Cut - ¼ nm N of:
21° 47.00' N, 71° 35.90' W

East Caicos holds the distinction of being the largest uninhabited island in the Turks and Caicos Islands. Like West Caicos, East Caicos is now an uninhabited paradise, though there was once a considerable bit of industry here. The ancient Lucayans once settled here and there are several caves on the island adorned with Lucayan artwork. Near Jacksonville there are several caves where skeletons have been found. In a cave known as "New No. 1," there are prehistoric petroglyphs on the walls. Loyalists settled here in 1791, but as elsewhere, didn't last more than a few decades.

The sisal industry flourished following the Loyalists, finally collapsing in the late 1820s. In the 1960s, a newspaper Tycoon rebuilt the ruins of the

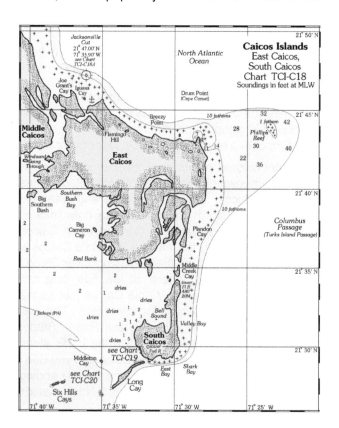

old Jacksonville Plantation on the northern tip of the island where railroad tracks stand in silent testament to a former life. Jacksonville was once the home of the *East Caicos Sisal Company* and the *J. N. Reynolds Cattle Farm*. Today the most noteworthy inhabitants are the feral cows and donkeys that still roam this island's 18-square miles, descendants of the animals used by the early farmers. Nearby Iguana Cay boasts, as you have probably guessed by now, a large colony of iguanas. Due to the shallow waters and even shallower reefs, East Caicos is rarely visited, except by small boat or dinghy.

Navigational Information

A vessel with a draft of less than 6' can work its way through *Jacksonville Cut* to anchor between Iguana Cay and East Caicos in *Jackson Cut Bay* as shown on Chart TCI-C18A. A waypoint at 21°

47.00'N, 71° 35.90'W places you approximately ¼ mile north of the cut as shown on Chart TCI-C18. After you work your way through the break in the reef you will then have to pick your way through a minefield of shallow coral heads until you can anchor in the deeper water between Iguana Cay and the mainland of East Caicos. This anchorage is great in winds from east through south to west though a bit of swell works through from the open Atlantic in moderate and stronger winds. Shallow draft boats can work their way over a shoal (1' at MLW) to anchor in 6' between East Caicos and Joe Grant's Cay as shown on the chart.

Iguana Cay was the site of Lucayan settlement over 600 years ago. Researchers recently found the 1841 wreck of an old slave ship, a 100' brigantine called the *Trouvadore*, in the waters of *Jacksonville*

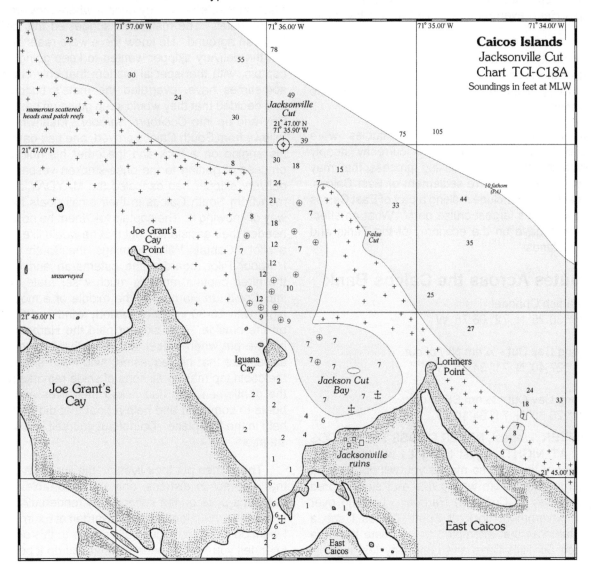

Caicos Islands
Jacksonville Cut
Chart TCI-C18A
Soundings in feet at MLW

Cut. This shipwreck holds particular significance to the Turks and Caicos Islanders, many of whom can trace their roots to the surviving slaves (there was

only one casualty, a woman who was shot on the beach after the shipwreck).

What You Will Find Ashore

Though swamps and mangroves inundate much of the island, you can find the highest point of the entire Turks and Caicos Islands here on East Caicos: *Flamingo Hill*, which rises to a height of 230' and overlooks the deadly *Phillip's Reef*. *Phillip's Reef* and nearby Haulover Point have been the home of numerous wrecks over the years. When transiting the area north and east of East Caicos, mariners are advised to pass to the east of *Phillip's Reef*. It is possible to pass inshore of *Phillips Reef* in water from 22'-30' deep, but it is so much safer to pass east of *Phillip's Reef*, even though you'll travel a few more miles.

There is a splendid 17 mile beach on the north coast of the island that is usually only used by sea turtles to lay their eggs because of the large mosquito population.

In the late 1990s, feasibility studies were completed, and developers are currently deeply involved in the decision-making process that may eventually lead to the re-settlement of East Caicos. Plans are said to include making a part of East Caicos into "the world's largest cruise port." What an effect that would have on the economy of the Turks and Caicos Islands!

Routes Across the Caicos Bank

Starfish Channel:
21° 30.25' N, 72° 06.75' W

Long Cay Cut - ½ nm NW of cut:
21° 27.40' N, 71° 34.75' W

Long Cay Cut - ½ nm SE of cut:
21° 26.60' N, 71° 34.10' W

NEVER, I repeat, **NEVER CROSS THE** *CAICOS BANK* **AT NIGHT!** I just thought I would mention that right at the start so maybe you will not forget it and tempt fate. I am writing this as I sit anchored off Long Cay in *Cockburn Harbour*. Looking over at the government dock at South Caicos I see a 42' catamaran that attempted to negotiate the area between Six Hills Cays and Long Cay last night in

a nice east wind of 25 knots on the nose, no moon, and only a spotlight to locate the scattered heads and reefs that you often find on the *Caicos Bank*. Please note that on a moonless night you cannot pick out the reefs with a spotlight unless they are breaking and they probably won't be doing that. The cat, with a delivery crew aboard, promptly ran aground on one of the several reefs in the area and the Captain put out a MAYDAY distress call on VHF. ch.16; they immediately received word from South Caicos that help was on the way.

The folks at South Caicos are seamen; they make their living from the sea and they know what it is like to be in trouble at sea. Soon two small boats set out to render assistance in the rapidly deteriorating weather. Before they could arrive at the stricken vessel the captain was able to get his boat off the reef and the mate suggested that they anchor where they were in 15' of water. The mate also suggested this before they ran aground. He knew there were reefs around but the delivery skipper wanted to keep going. The captain, with that special wisdom that only captains sometimes have, overruled the mate's suggestion and decided that they would keep going on past Long Cay and up into *Cockburn Harbour*. Meanwhile the fellows from South Caicos arrived, one had damaged his engine on a rock and the other his hull in the process of getting to the once-stricken vessel. The delivery skipper had canceled the MAYDAY but the men from South Caicos in their small boats had no way of knowing it. The captain told them he no longer needed their assistance, but that he would like to hire a pilot. Captain Willis Jennings, the South Caicos Harbour Pilot, boarded the catamaran and guided the hired captain, and his much wiser mate, safely into *Cockburn Harbour* in the middle of a moonless night with 25-30 knots of easterly wind and 8' seas on the outside. The skipper paid the Harbour Pilot his fee but when presented with a bill for the other assistance that he requested, said hired skipper hit the cabin top making all sorts of snide remarks about the gentlemen who had risked their lives and their boats to come out and help a boat that did not need help in the first place. Do not put yourself in a similar situation.

Those men put their lives on the line for a vessel that was not in distress, only uncomfortable. Who can put a price on the service they rendered? In my tenure as a volunteer assistant warden at Exuma Park I went on a dozen rescue calls similar to this one and I can tell you from experience that you do it because you have to, because somebody has to help and you are the only one there to do it. Were the warden and I to put a price on the services we rendered, I am sure it would seem staggering to the average boater, but then again they weren't out there in the wind and the seas. I know a certain salvager in The Bahamas who would not have stirred from his bed without being guaranteed twice what the good men of South Caicos asked for. Do not let this happen to you. **DO NOT CROSS THE CAICOS BANK AT NIGHT!** There, now that I'm finished getting up on my soapbox, let us continue.

I've always considered local knowledge the best knowledge when it comes to navigating any waters anywhere, and the *Caicos Bank* is no exception. The local knowledge here is that when crossing the *Caicos Bank*, if you can see land to the north, you are too far north towards the shallower water - good advice when crossing from Provo to South Caicos, Long Cay, Six Hills Cays, or the Ambergris Cays. There are several routes to choose from depending on your draft as shown back on Chart TCI-C1. As I just mentioned, and probably cannot repeat often enough, none of these routes should be attempted at night as you may come across the stray coral head or small patch reef anywhere on the *Caicos Bank*. If you see any dark patches of water, by all means steer around them. Even in areas on the *Caicos Bank* where the heads and patch reefs are particularly thick you can always find deeper water between them and plenty of room to steer around them. One pleasant sight that you'll find on the *Caicos Bank* is the phenomenon of the *Emerald Cloud*. On certain days when the sun and the clouds are right the bottoms of the clouds take on a lovely green hue. What happens is that the green

NEVER cross the Caicos Bank at night

water of the bank is reflected off the underside of the cloud giving its emerald appearance.

Navigational Information
From the waypoint at *Sapodilla Bay*, a heading of 122° for 43.1 nautical miles will bring you to a waypoint at 21° 27.40'N, 71° 34.75'W, approximately ½ mile inside *Long Cay Cut* and just west of the southern end of Long Cay as shown on Chart TCI-C20. In the first edition of this guide I mentioned that this route across the *Caicos Bank* could accommodate drafts of less than 7' at MLW and drafts of up to 8½' with the tide and was the easiest and preferred route across the bank. Although still easy, areas of the route have shallowed to the point that the controlling depth as shown on Chart TCI-C1 is a bit over 5' at MLW and 6½' with the tide, which limits the use of this route to fewer vessels. The shallower areas are on the northern side of this route between 72° 07' W and 72° 00' W, so if you find the water getting progressively thinner, try heading a bit south of the courseline. You will still have to steer through some scattered heads in the vicinity of 72° 05'W through 71° 55'W, but once east of this area you will find the heads more scattered. Depending on the wind direction, you can anchor north or south of the Six Hills Cays. This pair of cays with a small rock between them is easily identified, the six hills, three hills on each cay. Here you'll find good snorkeling on the reefs on the southern side of the cays but getting the hook to set here can sometimes be a pain. There are several areas of rock and grass but if you look around a bit you'll find a good sandy spot in which to drop your hook.

You can anchor in the lee of the southern tip of Long Cay in easterly winds, but keep a good eye out for the scattered heads and patch reefs in the area, as shown on the chart. If you have enough time you can head out *Long Cay Cut* into the deeper water of the *Turks Island Passage* and head northeast to enter into protected *Cockburn Harbour* at South Caicos (see next section *South Caicos*). When heading out through *Long Cay Cut*, watch out for the rocks south of Long Cay and the large breaking reef lying southwest of the cay as shown on Chart TCI-C20. Skippers with shallow drafts or those who love a challenge can pass north of *Middleton Bar* and then parallel it on its north shore to work in along the northwestern tip of Long Cay into *Cockburn Harbour*. I do not recommend this route unless: A) you absolutely have to be in South Caicos and conditions do not allow an outside transit of Long Cay; B) you have a draft of less than 5' and you are attempting to round or cross the bar at high tide; and C) you are simply adventurous and like a challenge. If you are attempting to round *Middleton Bar*, a waypoint at 21° 30.90'N, 71° 36.10'W will place you approximately ¼ mile northwest of the shallow northwestern end of the bar. From this position head generally southeast keeping in the deeper water on the northern side of the bar until you begin to find the deeper water closer in towards Long Cay. If you headed south from *Leeward Going Through* across *Boy Stubbs Shoal* and enjoyed that passage, you'll love this one. You would not be able to guess by looking at the island, but Middleton Cay was once home to Lucayan Indians. Recent digs have unearthed a Lucayan site on this tiny cay.

Vessels heading to the Ambergris Cays from *Sapodilla Bay* (as shown on Chart TCI-C1) can steer 134° for 43.8 miles from the *Sapodilla Bay* waypoint to a waypoint at 21° 19.75'N, 71° 39.75'W. This waypoint places you approximately 1 mile northwest of the anchorage between Little Ambergris and Big Ambergris as shown on Chart TCI-C21. Of course, if you are heading from Big Ambergris to *Sapodilla Bay* you will steer 314° for 43.8 miles to reach the waypoint south of the *Sapodilla Bay* anchorage. This route takes you through the *Pearl Channel*, which lies between two relatively shallow banks with about 6' at MLW.

The more traditional routes across the *Caicos Bank* make use of the *Starfish Channel*, which lies south of the major area of shallows on the bank. From *Sapodilla Bay* take up a course of 154° for 17.1 nautical miles to a waypoint in *Starfish Channel* at 21° 30.25'N, 72° 06.75'W. If bound for Long Cay from *Starfish Channel*, take up a course of 104° for 30 nautical miles, which will bring you to the anchorage off the southwestern tip of Long Cay. A note of caution on this route; take care not to run up on the Six Hills Cays, you can pass them on either their north side or their south side, but you cannot go straight through them. Your course north or south of the Six Hills Cays will depend on whether you are heading for the waypoint at the anchorage off the southwestern tip of Long Cay, or if you are heading for the deep-water waypoint at *Long Cay Cut.*

From the waypoint at *Starfish Channel* a course of 122° for 28. 2 miles will bring you to the anchorage between Big Ambergris Cay and Little Ambergris Cay. If you're at French Cay and wish to head to Ambergris Cay, this is also a good route to take. One can also head east of French Cay, past the shallow reefs to work your way up onto the banks about 4-5

miles east/southeast of French Cay where you can take up a course to the Ambergris anchorage. There will be several areas of heads lying just to the east of French Cay that you will have to dodge.

Vessels heading toward Long Cay and the route across the *Caicos Bank* towards *Sapodilla Bay* and Providenciales can head to a waypoint at 21° 26.60'N, 71° 34.10'W placing you ½ mile southeast of *Long Cay Cut.* Pass between the southern tip of Long Cay (watch out for the rocks off its southern tip) and the reef lying just southwest of Long Cay as shown on Chart TCI-C20. Work your way up inside of Long Cay, as shown on the chart, to take up your course of 302° to *Sapodilla Bay.*

South Caicos

Cockburn Harbour - ¼ nm SE of:
21° 28.70' N, 71° 31.70' W

South Caicos, or Big South as some of its residents describe their island, is relatively small, only 8½ square miles, but it is quite densely populated by Turks and Caicos Islands standards. Most of the island's 1,200 inhabitants live in Cockburn Harbour, which should not be confused with Cockburn Town on Grand Turk. Cockburn Harbour, or East Harbour as it is sometimes called, dates to Bermudian Salt Raker days. The salt pans north and east of the town now lie abandoned since the failure of the salt industry in the 1960s. South Caicos is home to what is known as the *Boiling Hole*, a natural ocean hole where the water that boils out contains a high degree of salinity, making it perfect for salt production. The Boiling Hole fed the salt pans that once made South Caicos the Turks and Caicos' largest producer of salt. Today most of her people rely on the sea for their livelihood and South Caicos exports large numbers of conch and lobster to the United States and France through her two fish processing plants. Some sport-fishermen call South Caicos the big fish capital of the Turks and Caicos, with the larger pelagics often seen here in great numbers. A vertical wall wraps around the southern edge of South Caicos, then extends the length of Long Cay and is often reputed to have the finest diving in the Turks and Caicos. On the northern tip of the island is the 480' tall red and white antenna of the old *U.S. Coast Guard Loran Station, NMA-5,* that is now a private station that transmits in Spanish at 50,000 watts, a great landmark that flashes red at night. Don't confuse it with the much shorter (260') red and white *Cable and Wireless* tower at the southern end of the island at Cockburn Harbour that has a fixed red light at its top.

Navigational Information

Cockburn Harbour, one of the best natural harbors in the Turks and Caicos Islands, is a working harbor with a regular fleet of fishing boats and trading vessels bound to and from Haiti and the Dominican Republic. It's not unusual to walk down the streets of town and hear Creole on one corner and Spanish on the next. The entrance to the harbor is lighted and easy to enter, even at night. If approaching Cockburn Harbour from the north, stand off South Caicos at least a mile or more to avoid the fringing reefs. The entrance to *Cockburn Harbour* will lie about a mile or so south of the long unfinished hotel on the southeastern shore of South Caicos. A waypoint at 21° 28.70'N, 71° 31.70'W, will place you approximately ¼ mile southeast of the entrance channel between Long Cay

and Dove Cay as shown on Chart TCI-C19. A good landmark is the huge green house with the pointed roof on the hill and the conspicuous white concrete light tower. The light tower shows a fixed white light at 90' above sea level from 90°-180°.

Cockburn Harbour has received a bad rap as having poor holding but those that reported bad holding have simply been anchoring in the wrong spots. I have ridden out fronts with prolonged winds of over 30 knots here without a problem. The holding, if your anchor is set well, is good throughout with the exception of a few places. At the eastern end of the harbor near Dove Cay, and close in along the southern shore of South Caicos, there are several areas of what the locals call "slate," hard, crusty, scoured sand that is difficult to get an anchor to set in. The best holding is at the western end of the harbor, between the remains of an old buoy and the shore.

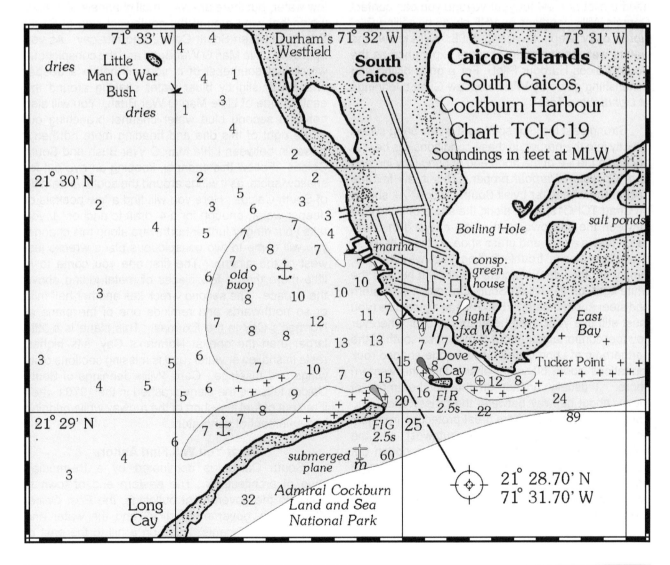

You will notice that this is where the locals anchor their boats, even during hurricanes. I am told that the old buoy drifted into *Cockburn Harbour* from Puerto Rico during *Hurricane David* back in the 1970s and has been in its present position ever since.

Close in to the South Caicos shoreline you must avoid several submerged railways west of *Sea View Marina* between the marina and the wooden dock with the small wooden building on the end. *Cockburn Harbour* offers excellent protection, even in strong winds, as the banks to the west and northwest dry in places at low water. However, if I knew a strong front was heading my way with westerly winds of 40 knots or more, and if I had the time, I would try to get over to Grand Turk to tuck into *North Creek* for the best protection and the most comfort. In periods of light or no wind, you might need to set a bridle to keep from rolling as there is a little current in the harbor. If you need a pilot or crew for your voyage you can contact Captain Willis Jennings on VHF ch. 16 by calling *Pilot House* or by telephone at 946-3308. Willis knows the waters well, having over 20 years experience as the South Caicos Harbour Pilot. For a good diving and bonefishing guide try Willis' nephew Gilbert Jennings at *Lightbourne Taxi.*

Strong east through southeast winds bring swells directly into the harbor; in these conditions it is best to anchor in the lee of the north end of Long Cay instead of in *Cockburn Harbour* proper. This is my favorite anchorage whenever I visit South Caicos. As shown on Chart TCI-C19, head along the shore of Long Cay between the shallows west of the cay and the dark patch that is a rock and grass shoal a little to its west. If you are having trouble finding your way in here, simply put the white concrete tower (that houses the white light) on the hill on South Caicos on your stern and steer approximately 250°-255° as a guideline (you must still use your eyes here) and anchor wherever you feel comfortable. About ½ mile or so south of the northern tip of Long Cay are two wedge-shaped rock formations about 50 yards apart along the western shore. I usually anchor off the southernmost of these, about halfway between the grassy shoal and Long Cay. This spot offers great protection from just north of east through south to southwest, and the holding is excellent in soft sand. I have ridden out several fronts here with sustained southwest through northwest winds of 30-40 knots and my one CQR did not budge; yes, the holding here is excellent. *Long Bar* and *Middleton Bar* break the larger seas and all you wind up with off Long Cay is a 2'-3' chop. When

the wind goes into the northwest the best spot is at the far western end of *Cockburn Harbour*, where you can find good protection in the lee of Man O War Bush and the large bank area surrounding it that dries at low water. You'll get some chop in a strong westerly here, but nothing dangerous. The *School for Field Studies* at South Caicos wishes to remind boaters to please not anchor in the large turtle grass beds in the area west of Long Cay; these are study sites for their students. There is plenty of good clean sand to drop the hook in, so please avoid the large turtle grass beds.

Vessels drawing less than 4' can find a nice alternative anchorage west of *Cockburn Harbour*, but for safety's sake you should check out the approach by dinghy beforehand. Just before high tide head towards Little Man O War Bush, keeping it just off your port bow. Most of the water around this cay dries at low water, but there are two small channels of deeper water that wind around the southwest side of South Caicos between South Caicos and this cay. As you approach Little Man O War Bush and the conspicuous wreck just southeast of it, you will notice a deeper channel of slightly bluer water snaking around the eastern side of Little Man O War Bush. You will also notice a second blue water channel branching out to the right of this one and heading more northerly, closer in between Little Man O War Bush and South Caicos. Follow this channel, keeping an eye out for shallow spots, as it winds around the southwestern tip of South Caicos. Here you will find a few pockets of deeper water, enough for a 4' draft to anchor. If you take your dinghy further northward along this channel you will come to two conspicuous plane wrecks just west of the airstrip. The first one you come to is little more than a few pieces of metal jutting above the surface. The second wreck lies another half mile or so northwards and reminds one of the plane at Norman's Cay in the Exumas. This plane is a little larger than the one at Norman's Cay, sits higher, rests in shallower water, and is missing sections of its wings and fuselage. Capt. Willis Jennings of South Caicos tells me the plane crashed in the 1970s when it ran out of fuel just short of the runway while bringing in a shipment of generators.

What You Will Find Ashore
South Caicos is dominated by a Bermudian style of architecture. The eastern end of town is home to the government buildings, the *Post Office*, *Courthouse*, government clinic, and the water and fisheries departments. High on a hill to the east of

these buildings is the *Residency*, an 18th century structure that was the district commissioner's home and is now *Mae's Bed and Breakfast*. You can't miss *Mae's*. It's the huge green house with the pointed roof that was your landfall as you approached *Cockburn Harbour*. Call first if you wish to dine here. Just to the east is a cemetery with several old gravestones. Throughout town you'll see many wooden jetties, warehouses, and churches that date back over 2+++00 years. Along the eastern shore of South Caicos northeast of *Mae's* are the unfinished remains of a huge hotel complex sitting on the ridge above the beautiful beach at *East Bay* where you'll find good beachcombing after a northeast through southeast blow. The Norwegian investors backed out of this hotel project around 1988; today it stands unfinished, but it remains a great landmark. There is a trail from *Mae's* leading to the beach.

On the northern shore of *Cockburn Harbour* you will see a large concrete dock with several conspicuous storage tanks. This is the *Sea View Marina* where owner Captain Lewis Cox and his son Norman are your hosts. You can get fuel right at the dock, or, if you draw too much to come alongside (7' at low water), either Lewis or Norman will be glad to meet you at the government dock with their 2,500-gallon fuel truck. The marina offers free overnight dockage, yes, that's right, free overnight dockage with or without fuel purchase, but the dock can only handle up to three boats - weather permitting. When was the last time you heard of a marina offering free dockage? Thirty-amp 110v power is available and fresh water can be trucked in with a 55-gallon minimum. If you need just a few gallons, Norman says he can help you right from his tank.

You can also arrange for fuel from *Pinnacle Fuel Suppliers* (649-946-3283), and *Charlie Alpha (VHF ch. 16)*, Captain Bruce Lightbourne and his *ESSO* fuel truck for delivery to the government dock. *Charlie Alpha* will also deliver groceries and fuel to your boat if you are at anchor.

Sea View Marina can also hold your mail for you, arrange a *FedEx* or *UPS* package delivery through Provo, supply a diesel or outboard mechanic, arrange a propane tank fill, and even rent you a car. There's little that Lewis and Norman can't do for visiting boaters. Their very well-stocked *Sea View Market* is the best on the island with fresh fruits and veggies, frozen meats, ice cream, all sorts of dry goods, some small boating supplies, and a phone just outside

the front door. Next door, their *Café Columbus* is currently closed and they don't know when they will re-open it. For more info call *Sea View Marina* on VHF ch. 16.

For a taxi you can use ch. 16 to raise *Glinton's Taxi*; owner Bertram Glinton will be happy to take you all over the island at a very reasonable price. For an interesting history lesson, ask Bertram about his years in salt production. You can also try *Lightbourne Taxi*, *Hillside Taxi*, or *Wee 10 Base*. Garbage can be placed in the dumpsters on the street in front of the *Sea View Marina* or by the fish factory docks. Across the street from the *Sea View Marina* is *Anita's Bakery* at *Anita's on the Bay* where owner Anita Clarke bakes wonderful fresh bread; she can even whip up something for you to eat in a pinch.

If you need Internet access there is a small computer shop near the end of the town dock.

You will notice that almost everyone in South Caicos has a smile and a hello for you. This community is as far from Provo in distance as it is in atmosphere. I cannot say enough about the wonderful people that are South Caicos' true treasure. This is my favorite island in the entire Turks and Caicos archipelago. I once found myself in dire straits in my data acquisition vessel when my automatic bilge pump burned out and my sixteen-footer was swamped at dawn after all-night 40-knot squalls. I received more than enough help from the good people of South Caicos and none wanted anything in return. All they wanted was the chance to help somebody. They informed me that, after all, that's what we are all here for, to help each other. South Caicos and her people will always hold a dear spot in my heart, especially my good friends Capt. Willis Jennings and Marvin. By the way Marvin, if you're reading this, I still have those plugs and they're still working fine. Oh, and hello to you too, Willis!

As you walk around town it's not unusual to see donkeys, cows, or dogs competing for the road with you and the occasional car or motorcycle. As for bars, *Miss Trudy's Jetaway Bar* is the place for nightlife in South Caicos. For good native food *Muriel's* is the best and she is just east of the *Immigration* office and government dock. Another stop is *Carver's Restaurant* behind *Bayside Auto Parts* across from the *Wee 10 Market* also just east of the *Sea View Marina*. You can also try the *Eastern Inn* for good takeaway food. *First Caribbean Bank* has an office in town, though they are only open on Wednesdays from 0900 till 1300. Next to the bank is *Myrna Lee's Restaurant*. For hardware or lumber try the new *G & H Hardware and Lumber Co*. On the airport road at the salt pans is the *Pond View Restaurant*, a good choice for lunch or dinner. Other options are *Ocean Haven*, *Love's* on the *Airport Road*, and *Miss May's Bed and Breakfast*.

High on a hill above the harbor is the *Admiral's Arm Inn*, a charming and historical location that was the first hotel built in the Turks and Caicos Islands. Until about 35 years ago, the *Inn* was being used to process cotton. With the disappearance of the owner, Diane, her brother could not keep the inn going, and despite his best efforts, the inn and its garden became a pasture for goats and donkeys. Today the inn serves as housing for students in the *School for Field Studies Program* and it's still worth a visit. The large pink two-story building next door is the *Club Caribe Harbour and Beach Resort*, the only hotel on the island. The *Club Caribe Sunset Bar and Restaurant* has large glass windows with a stunning view of the rocky cliffs and turquoise waters of the harbor below.

Club Caribe has the only dive operation on the island and it is here that you can get all your diving questions about South Caicos answered. The diving off South Caicos includes wall dives as well as some beautiful shallow water reefs and coral gardens teeming with marine life.

Just off Long Cay, as shown on Chart TCI-C19, is a dive site known as the *Plane Wreck*, a *Convair* 340 lying in about 60' of water. The wreck is situated approximately 300 yards off the cay, actually just opposite the first rock formation on the shoreline south of the entrance to *Cockburn Harbour,* and is marked by a buoy. Please don't tie your big boat to this buoy, it only strong enough for small boats and dinghies.

Another interesting site is the *Eagle's Nest*, named for the community of stingrays that lives amidst its unusual seascape of sand channels and ledges. Ask about the shallow water dive sites such as *Lion's Head Rock*, *Boulder Ground*, and the *Admiral's Aquarium*. As I mentioned earlier, ask for Gilbert Jennings at *Lightbourne Taxi* for a knowledgeable diving guide.

Just west of the *Sea View Marina* are several concrete and rip-rap jetties for small boats to tie to; this is where you'll want to tie up your dinghy, but be sure to use a stern anchor to keep your bow off the concrete wall in the surge. At the head of the docks is one of the two fish factories in town. The second, just to the west, lies at the head of the wooden dock with the small wooden building on the end. Just up the hill from the fish factories is the *Cham B Grocery Store* and around the corner is *Hillside Grocery*.

In late May, South Caicos is host to one heck of a big party, the annual *South Caicos Regatta*. People from all over the Turks and Caicos Islands flock to Cockburn Harbour for this colorful, energetic festival. The excitement builds during the Saturday morning sloop races and climaxes Saturday afternoon and night with music, dancing, donkey races, and maypole dancing. If you are in the area do not miss this event.

The Southern Cays

Fish Cays - ¾ nm N of:
21° 23.50' N, 71° 37.25' W

West Sand Spit - 2 nm SW of:
21° 20.50' N, 72° 10.05' W

Big Ambergris Cay - 1 nm NW of anchorage:
21° 19.75' N, 71° 39.75' W

The Southern Cays is the name given to the numerous small islands that lie on the Caicos Bank to the south of Six Hills Cays and Long Cay, stretching about 20 miles south and southwest of Cockburn Harbour on South Caicos. There are three groups, the Fish Cays, the Ambergris Cays, and the Seal Cays. With the exception of the Ambergris Cays these cays are rarely visited except by local fishermen and divers.

Navigational Information
The Fish Cays are small, rocky, and offer little to passing yachtsmen. The largest of the three is worthy of a dinghy trip if you are interested in cactus and lizards, and there is a beautiful Elkhorn coral reef off this cay's northwest shore. You can actually anchor on the western side of this cay in settled weather or prevailing winds, but you'll have to thread your way through some coral heads and small reefs. The cay is covered in prickly pear cactus and is a nesting site for Sooty Terns in the summer months. There are three small beaches on the western shore and several shallow reefs that are excellent for snorkelers and fishermen. If passing through from *Sapodilla Bay* to the *Turks Island Passage*, a waypoint at 21° 23.50'N, 71° 37.25'W, will place you approximately ¾ mile north of the Fish Cays in good water as shown

on Chart TCI-C21. From here you can head straight to the Turks Islands or the Dominican Republic.

Between the Fish Cays and the Ambergris Cays are numerous coral reefs and heads, some lying just inches below the water's surface; the water in between them, though 25'-35' deep in places, is affected by strong and sometimes confused tidal currents. If you are headed west onto the *Caicos Bank* and wish to anchor south of the Fish Cays between the Ambergris Cays, the best idea is to do what the locals do. Head west on the bank until Little Ambergris is abeam and then head south. This will get you past the majority of the shallow reefs that lie between the Fish Cays and Big Ambergris Cay. This area is a cartographer's nightmare. There is absolutely no way that I could show each and every reef in this area on Chart TCI-C21 at that scale. A word to the wise usually being sufficient, I would suggest you avoid this area unless you can read the water well and don't mind a little white knuckle maneuvering. It is possible to leave the anchorage between Little and Big Ambergris and work your way through these reefs to gain the deeper water of the *Turks Island Passage*, but it might be prudent to avoid them altogether. The choice is yours; I can only advise.

A waypoint at 21° 19.75'N, 71° 39.75'W, will place you approximately one mile northwest of the anchorage that lies between Big Ambergris and Little Ambergris Cay. Watch for scattered heads and shallow patch reefs in this area. The anchorage has great holding, but the shallows stretch out a good bit off the shore of both cays. A 5' draft can usually get within ½ mile of Big Ambergris Cay for good protection from east and southeast winds just off the house and small dock. If you anchor just north of the buildings on Big Ambergris, you can tuck in a little closer but there are a few more shallow reefs to avoid. If you head north from here to round the Fish Cays, once again it is best to do it just like the locals do. Put the eastern end of Little Ambergris on your stern as you head north to avoid the majority of the shallow reefs between the Fish Cays and Big Ambergris Cay.

What You Will Find Ashore
The Ambergris Cays, Big Ambergris (East Ambergris) and Little Ambergris (West Ambergris) are named after the wax-like substance that is excreted by the humpback whales that pass through the Turks Island Passage and often found on the windward shore of Big Ambergris. Big Ambergris and Little Ambergris are as distinctly different as night and

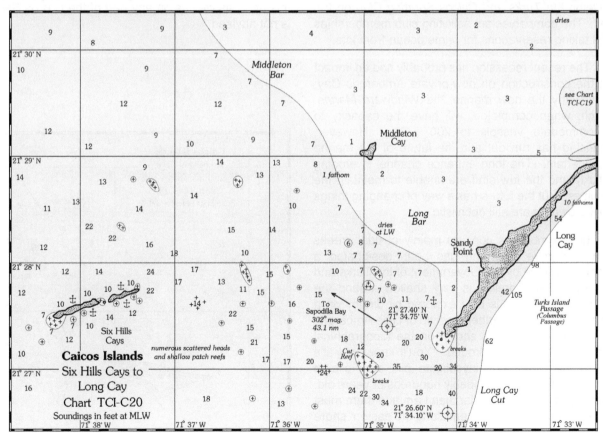

day. The easternmost cay, Big Ambergris, is slightly hilly (max. elevation 96') while its neighbor one mile to the west, Little Ambergris, is larger in area but quite lower in elevation. There are some ruins of pasture walls and a couple of buildings on the southern end of the Big Ambergris, remnants of earlier inhabitants of the cay. John Lightbourne purchased Big Ambergris Cay from The Bahamas in 1811 and sold it in 1837 for 6,000 bushels of salt. The island was used for the growing of sisal until the late 1800s. Following the taking of the first whale in the Turks and Caicos Islands on Feb. 4, 1846, a whaling lookout post was established on Big Ambergris Cay. Later on the island was used as a sisal plantation. Today you'll find a colony of rock iguanas inhabiting the cay along with a lot of Turk's Head Cactus. On the eastern shore is a beautiful beach in Long Cay that is excellent for beachcombing. Grab a comb and have at it!

Big plans are in the works for Big Ambergris Cay. In 1995, the cay was purchased by a group of investors who had a goal or establishing a marina and resort on the island. This did not work out for one reason or another, but in 2002 the *Dolan, Pollak, and Schram Development Company* visited the island and signed an agreement with *Ambergris Cay Ltd.* to develop the *Turks and Caicos Sporting Club* on the cay. The companies are soliciting club memberships and taking reservations for prime ocean-front lots.

The recent recession has probably had an impact on the construction on now-private Ambergris Cay, particularly the new marina, the *Windward Marina*, which, when completed, will have the capacity to accommodate vessels to 200' LOA. However, financing has run out and the future of the marina is uncertain. The long entrance channel is eroding quickly and the few staff are unable to maintain the facilities. But the future has a way of changing things so the owners are still optimistic.

Little Ambergris consists mainly of tidal creeks and mangrove flats and has been designated a *Nature Reserve* by the Government of the Turks and Caicos. The shoreline is very shallow around the entire island and it is best explored by dinghy on a rising tide. Off the northeastern tip of Little Ambergris Cay is an area that is shown on the topographical maps as the Conch Ground. You'll know why it's called that when you investigate pile after pile of conch shells that are probably hundreds of years old. These piles are much taller than I am and there must be at least two dozen of them along the eastern shore

of Little Ambergris; it is quite a sight. The surrounding dune and rock structure support a large colony of rock iguanas. Hawksbill and green turtles use the western shore of Little Ambergris Cay for nesting sites during the spring and early summer months; please do not disturb any turtles you may see there and don't dig in the sand for their nests. These cays are often used as a stopover before heading to Luperón, which isn't a bad idea, the reef snorkeling, at its worst, is fantastic.

South of the Ambergris Cays the banks are studded with numerous coral heads that reach up from 20' depths to break the surface. Just south of Big Ambergris Cay lies Bush Cay (as shown on Chart TCI-C1), a protected sanctuary (visits ashore require a permit from the *DECR*) and this tiny tree covered island has a navigational light tower. The Seal Cays, another protected sanctuary, are named after the now extinct West Indian monk seal and primarily used as fishing ground by Caicos fishermen along the area surrounding White Cay. These cays lie south and southwest of the Ambergris Cays and stretch for 10 miles between Bush Cay and White Cay. The waters surrounding these cays are strewn with shallow reefs that rise from 40'-60' to dry at low water in numerous places. Travel at night on the *Caicos Bank* south of this area, as well as on any part of the *Caicos Bank,* is not advised.

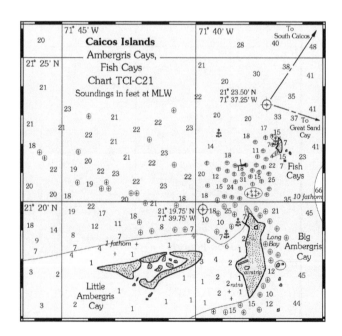

The Turks Islands

Ports of Entry:
Grand Turk (*South Base*)
Fuel: Grand Turk
Haul-Out: None
Diesel Repairs: Grand Turk, Salt Cay
Outboard Repairs: Grand Turk
Propane: Grand Turk
Provisions: Grand Turk

Important Lights:
Grand Turk Lighthouse: Fl W ev 7.5 sec
Salt Cay, Northwest Point: Gp Fl (4) W ev 20 sec
Great Sand Cay: Fl W ev 2 sec

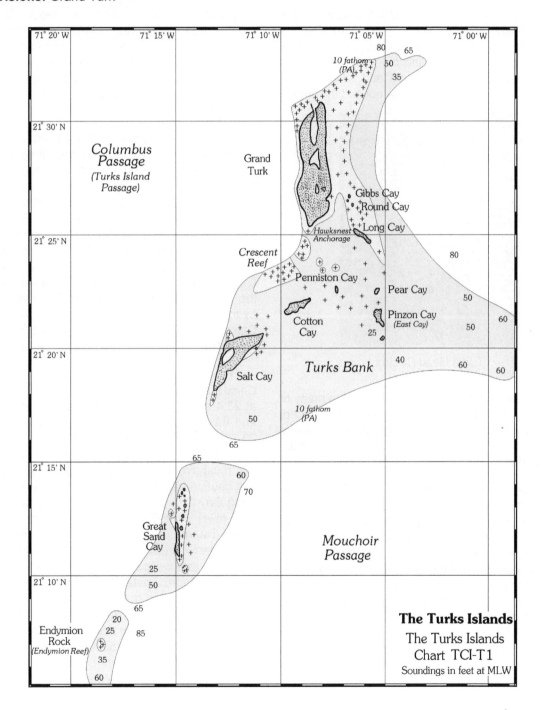

The Turks Islands
Chart TCI-T1
Soundings in feet at MLW

To the east of the deep *Turks Island Passage*, sometimes called the *Columbus Passage*, lies the *Turks Bank* and the Turks Islands themselves, once called the "Salt Islands." Here you will find the capital of the Turks and Caicos on Grand Turk, the largest of the Turks Islands and one of only two inhabited islands in the group. The *Turks Bank* is some 36 miles long and varies in width from three to fifteen miles. The sandy bottom is littered with coral heads and patch reefs making for some excellent diving opportunities. The name of the group is said to come from Sir William Phipps, who named them after the native Turk's Cap or Turk's Head Cactus (*Melocactus intortus*) in 1687. Phipps and his men were in the area recovering 26 tons of gold and silver from a wrecked Spanish galleon when he noticed the cactus

Turks Head Cactus

that reminded him of a Turkish fez. Sadly so many of these turk's cap cacti have been dug up that except for the few in private gardens and establishments, they are only found growing in the more remote sections of the island group.

Another opinion as to the origin of the name suggests that it comes from a time when the islands were used as hideouts for various pirates, some of whom were said to be of Turkish descent. It has been suggested that in the 16th and 17th centuries, under the leadership of the two Barbarosa brothers, a band of Barbary pirates operated out of these waters. Originating in Constantinople, the brothers eventually settled on an uninhabited salt island that the Spanish later referred to as Grand Turk. There is no concrete proof of that occupation but either way, an occasional letter or parcel sometimes is mistakenly sent to Istanbul or Ankara for processing.

Approaches

The *Turks Island Passage* is a 25 mile wide, 7,000' deep trench connecting the Caribbean and the southwest north Atlantic and separating the Turks Islands from the Caicos Islands. The tidal current in the Turks Island passage is often fickle; usually it flows northward through the passage at ½-1 knot, but at other times, depending on the wind strength and direction, its speed increases and its direction may vary from north/northwest to northeast. During the months of January through March, an estimated 3,000 humpback whales traverse the *Turks Island Passage* to their winter breeding grounds that stretch from the *Silver Banks* to Samaná in the DR. Use caution when around these magnificent creatures and please don't harass them.

From the waypoint at the mouth of Cockburn Harbour on South Caicos, the *Front Street* anchorage at Grand Turk bears 101° at 21.1 miles, *South Dock* bears 107° at 21.2 miles, and the western entrance to *Big Cut* bears 110° at 21.3 nautical miles distant. From South Caicos the waypoint for entry into the protected anchorage at *North Creek* on Grand Turk bears 93° at a distance of 21.8 miles, but don't simply plug in that waypoint and go. As you approach Grand Turk you must take care to avoid the reef off the northwestern point of Grand Turk that is marked by the steel remains of an old ship. Also from South Caicos, Salt Cay bears 126° at 19.3 miles, while Great Sand Cay bears 148° at 22.7 miles distant.

From *Long Cay Cut* on the western edge of the *Caicos Bank* the *Front Street* anchorage bears 95° at 23.4 miles, *South Dock* bears 101° at 23.3 miles, and the western entrance to *Big Cut* bears 104° at 23.3 miles. The entrance waypoint for *North Creek* bears 88° at a distance of 24.3 miles. Once again, you must avoid the northwest reef off Grand Turk so use caution as you approach Grand Turk. Also from Long Cay Cut, Salt Cay bears 118° at a distance of 20.6 miles while Great Sand Cay bears 140° at 22.9 miles distant. If approaching from Luperón in the Dominican Republic, a course of 176° for 77 miles will bring you to a waypoint at 21° 10.80'N, 71° 15.50'W, which lies approximately ¾ mile southwest of the reef at the southern end of Great Sand Cay. From Puerto Plata, a course of 167° for 86 miles will bring you to the same position. Near this waypoint be sure to keep west of the small trio of rocks shown on Chart TCI-T6 as the Three Marys. From Luperón, the waypoint at 21° 17.60'N, 71° 14.10'W that lies approximately ¾

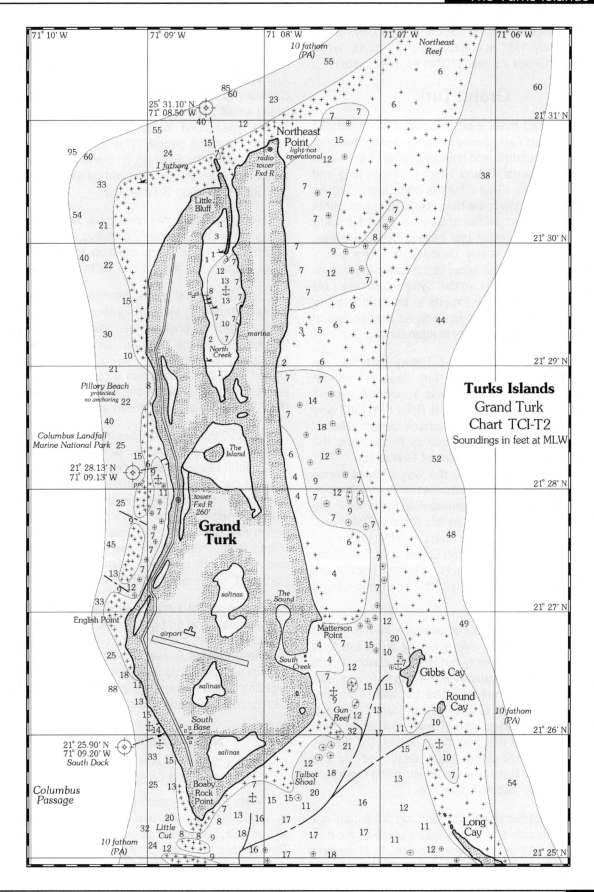

71° 10' W   71° 09' W   71 08' W   71° 07' W   71° 06' W

10 fathom (PA)   55

Northeast Reef   6

85 60   60

23   25° 31.10' N 71° 08.50' W   40   55   12   Northeast Point   light not operational   15   6   21° 31' N

95   60   24   1 fathom   15   7   radio tower Fxd R   12   38

33   54   21   Little Bluff   1   3   7   7   21° 30' N

40   22   1   12   7   9   12

15   13   7   7   7

30   8   13   10   7   marina   7   3   5   6   44

10   2   7   North Creek

21   1   2   6   21° 29' N

Pillory Beach protected, no anchoring 22   8   14   7

40   18   **Turks Islands**
Grand Turk
Chart TCI-T2
Soundings in feet at MLW

Columbus Landfall Marine National Park 25   The Island   6   12   52

15   21° 28.13' N 71° 09.13' W   6   pvc   4   9   7   21° 28' N

25   tower Fxd R 260'   11   12   9   48

9   7   **Grand Turk**   8   6

45   7   7

13   7   4   7

12   salinas   7   21° 27' N

33   The Sound   12   49

English Point   Matterson Point   15   20

airport   10   Gibbs Cay

25   4   12   15   15   Round Cay   10 fathom (PA)

18   South Creek   8   15   21° 26' N

88   11   salinas   9   13   10   54

13   South Base   Gun Reef   12   13   11   10

15   32   17   7

14   21   15   10

21° 25.90' N 71° 09.20' W South Dock   33   15   salinas   12   18   13

25   13   Boaby Rock Point   Talbot Shoal   20   16   12   11   Long Cay

Columbus Passage   20   13   16   17   17   11   12

32   Little Cut   8   18   17   54

10 fathom (PA)   24   12   9   16   17   18   12   21° 25' N

mile southwest of the reef south of Salt Cay, bears approximately 178° at a distance of 83 miles while from Puerto Plata it bears 170° at 92 miles distant.

Grand Turk

Twenty-two miles east of South Caicos, across the 7,000' deep *Turks Island Passage*, lies the historic, commercial, cultural, and political capital of the Turks and Caicos islands, Grand Turk. Six miles long and three miles wide, Grand Turk is often argued to be Columbus' first stop in the New World. Most accounts put Columbus' first landfall at San Salvador, but there is a growing movement that believe that Columbus' Guanahani was in reality Grand Turk. The theory has been getting some acceptance and in December of 1989 a *Grand Turk Landfall Symposium* was held in Grand Turk. Several experts in the field, leading Spanish historians, and even a direct descendant of Christopher Columbus were in attendance.

The *Grand Turk Landfall Theory* was first put forward by the nineteenth century Spanish historian Fernández de Navarrete and is supported, among others, by the works of Robert Power in 1982 and local Turks and Caicos historians Josiah Marvel of Providenciales, an associate of Power, and the late Herbert E. "Bertie" Sadler of Grand Turk. This theory has gained much in the way of acceptance in the last two decades but, as with all theories concerning Columbus' *Guanahani,* its basis lies in the descriptions of the islands as laid down in Columbus' log, the *Diario* (for more information on this theory you can visit the *Public Library* on Grand Turk and check out Herbert E. Sadler's seven volume *Turks Island Landfall* series on the history of the Turks and Caicos Islands).

The descriptions of *Guanahani* in the *Diario* can be interpreted to give a strong argument to a Grant Turk landfall theory but there is absolutely no physical evidence whatsoever pointing to Grand Turk as a possible *Guanahani*. The Lucayan sites that have been found on Grand Turk predate Columbus by almost 500 years though many valuable sites, including the one that may have proven the theory, could have unknowingly been destroyed by the Bermudian Salt Rakers when constructing Cockburn Town in the 17th and 18th centuries.

The descriptions in Columbus' log are simply not enough to classify any one particular place as the true *Guanahani* as they can be interpreted to fit several

locations. Most experts point to San Salvador in the Bahamas as being Columbus' *Guanahani* and they are supported by some strong physical evidence. Archaeologists have dated Lucayan sites on San Salvador to the end of the 15th century and have also found small beads and brass bells that were similar to the types used by the Spanish for trading that date to the same period. This firmly establishes the Lucayans and the Spanish on the island at the same time and presents the most compelling argument for San Salvador being *Guanahani.*

However until some researcher somewhere digs up some artifact saying "Columbus arrived here on October 12, 1492," or something to that effect, all these theories will remain exactly that - just theories.

Grand Turk first gained prominence in the 1600s for its salt-making stations. There was a time when Grand Turk's harbor was the main shelter for British vessels out on the business of the empire in this particular part of the world. In more recent times, the United States Air Force had a base on the southern end of the island, while the U.S. Navy had a base (Pan Am Base) at the northern end.

In 1950 the United States built a missile tracking station on Grand Turk which remained until 1981. In 1962, John Glenn, after his famous space flight, first set foot back on planet Earth at Grand Turk. LBJ, the Vice President at the time, came to Grand Turk to welcome home the first American to orbit our planet. Glenn was picked up approximately 160 miles east of Grand Turk. Over the next few years five Gemini and one Apollo craft splashed down in the waters north, northeast, and east of Grand Turk.

Sailors might be interested in this bit of Turks Island trivia. The first great American Merchantman to trade with the Orient was the *Grand Turk*. The 300-ton three-masted vessel boasted 22 guns and was originally designed as a privateer. The *Grand Turk* is probably better known as the ship seen on bottles of *Old Spice* after-shave and cologne.

North Creek Anchorage

North Creek - ¼ nm N of entrance:
21° 31.10' N, 71° 08.50' W

North Creek is sometimes called *Columbus Lake* by supporters of the *Grand Turk Landfall Theory* .If at all possible, I suggest that everyone who visits Grand Turk, if your draft allows, should anchor in this well-

Entrance Channel to the anchorage in *North Creek*

Photo by Author

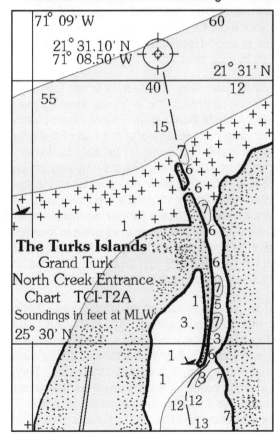

71° 09' W
21° 31.10' N
71° 08.50' W
60
21° 31' N
40
12
55
15
7
6
6
7
1
6
1
6
The Turks Islands
Grand Turk
North Creek Entrance
Chart TCI-T2A
7
5
Soundings in feet at MLW
3.
7
25° 30' N
3
1
6
1
3
7
12
12
13
7

Lighthouse Park at *North Creek*

protected harbor to explore this marvelous island. Here boats with drafts of 5½' will find excellent holding in 10'-15' of water with protection from every direction and only a relatively few bugs on calm nights. Have I convinced you yet? Sounds too good to be true, right? It almost is.

Due to storms over the last several years, the depths in the channel have changed. When this guide was first published you could take a draft of 6½' into this anchorage, today, the entrance channel limits entry to vessels of 5½' at high water.

The hardest part about gaining access to this anchorage is finding a weather window to permit entry at certain times of the year, primarily the winter months. The entrance channel is easily blocked by northerly swells that tend to break all the way across the narrow mouth, making the channel impassable. Now just because you have light east or southeast winds as you approach Grand Turk, do not assume you can easily enter the channel. Swells from frontal passages that did not make it as far south as the Turks and Caicos Islands or from large storms to the north can easily build and spend themselves along the northern shore of Grand Turk. One day I approached the entrance with a long, lazy 8' northerly swell running in calm wind conditions and could not even get close to the cut. That lazy swell had been transformed into huge crashing breakers along the entire northern shore of Grand Turk. On another occasion I had a light east/southeast breeze of less than 10 knots and a 4'-6' northeasterly swell and had no problem entering. Sometimes you just have to get close enough to take a good long look at the cut before deciding to proceed. Or you can call *Flamingo Cove* or *MPL* on VHF ch. 16 and perhaps if they have seen the cut that day they can tell you whether the cut is passable; they can also arrange a pilot for a fee. Some yachtsmen enter *North Creek* under the mistaken impression that they can clear *Customs* and *Immigration* once inside. If you need to clear in at Grand Turk you must do so at the new freighter dock on the southwestern side of the island at *South Base*.

Navigational Information

When approaching the northern shore of Grand Turk from the west or the north your landmarks will be the large red and white checkerboard water tower, the old and unused lighthouse on Northeast Point, and the radio antenna that shows a fixed red light at night.

As you approach the northern shore from the west, the actual entrance will be hard to discern against the background of the shoreline, but it will appear to lie below the white-roofed building that sits about ¼ mile south of the water tower. A waypoint at 21° 31.10'N, 71° 08.50'W, will place you approximately ½ mile north of the narrow entrance channel and the jetty as shown on Chart TCI-T2 and on the blow-up, Chart TCI-T2A. At the time of this writing there were two white PVC stakes near the end of the jetty that lies on the western side of the entrance channel. Captain Bob Gascoine set these PVC stakes up as a range to help you line up your entry. This may change at any time, so use caution.

In normal conditions the swells will break across the reefs to the east and the west of the channel with lighter action actually in the channel itself. The prudent mariner will likely pass by the entrance once or twice at a close but safe distance to get a good feel for the way the channel lies. The channel is the only entrance to the lake inside and all the water goes in and out of this one channel with the tide, so expect a lot of current. You'll have better steerage if you go against the tidal flow but I have done both and had no difficulties. However, if it is your first time, I recommend going against the flow, or if possible to time your entry for high water, slack, or just as the tide begins to ebb. Never attempt this entry with the sun directly in your eyes.

When you have decided to enter the channel, line up and approach the entrance keeping the jetty close to your starboard side. The entrance channel is narrow, about 75' wide along the end of the jetty but it widens inside. You should be able to discern the deeper, bluer water alongside the jetty and the yellow and brown of the shallow rocky water to the east of the channel. The reefs to the east and west of the entrance channel stretch farther northward than the end of the jetty so keep your eyes open to avoid them. Enter the channel keeping close to the jetty, but not too close; you'll have 6' just inside the entrance and 8' in places through this first section at MLW.

The jetty is made up of large rocks, blocks of concrete, dredged materials, and numerous rusty car and truck frames, engine blocks, axles, and one small front-end loader. Any of these can easily damage the inattentive skipper's vessel if too close. The jetty has a small break in it as it reaches the shore, so don't confuse this with the channel you are in. The break is shallow and has the top of a large rock in the center of it at high water. Both sides of the channel shallow slightly at this break so keep to the center of the visible channel if at all possible and you'll have 5' at MLW. Proceed along the entrance channel paralleling the jetty and as you pass between the jetty and the shoreline to the east the channel will widen a bit. Favor the jetty side as the eastern shore is very shallow and the channel still follows close to the jetty.

As the anchorage comes into view you will notice that the jetty has a large rusty crane on it as well as a barge at its southern end that also has a crane on it. Between these two cranes you will find the shallowest spots in the entrance channel. The bottom through here is sand and the current has built up over a dozen or so shallow sand mounds (easily seen in good light) that lie perpendicular to your course and stretching from the jetty to the shallows of the eastern shore. These sand mounds, one or two of which only have about 3'-3½' of water over them at MLW, are not very wide and if you bump you will likely be able to power over them. Sometimes there are shallower spots on one side or the other of these mounds so you might be able to zigzag your way through. Depths between these mounds are generally 6'-7' at MLW. As I mentioned earlier, 5½' can enter here but if you don't choose a good tide to enter on you might have to power your way over these humps. I believe that in an emergency, a 6' draft could enter here on an extremely high tide if the skipper didn't mind powering over these humps. The only problem would be that this same skipper would then need another extremely high tide to get back out.

As you approach the end of the jetty by the remains of the huge barge and crane, don't get careless, you have one or two more obstacles to avoid. At the eastern end of the entrance channel, across from the end of the jetty, lies a huge piece of steel bar that once marked the eastern end of the entrance channel. Instead of being exactly vertical, this bar leans over and is awash at high water and only about 6" of it juts above the surface at low tide. This steel bar could do a lot of damage to your boat, so keep an eye out for it and don't stray too close to it. Just as you reach the end of the entrance channel at the barge you will come upon a grassy shoal that is not shown on other charts of the area. The reason for this is that it has just appeared over the last few years. The shoal, easily seen in good light, only has 3' of water over it in most places. If you have a high tide you can pass it on either side, but if the tide is low

you can only pass between the shoal and the end of the jetty in 5'-6' at MLW close in to the jetty.

Once around the grassy shoal area you will be in 8'-15' of water and you can anchor wherever your draft allows and you feel comfortable. The anchorage shallows west and northwest of the end of the jetty and south of the *Flamingo Cove Marina* dock on the eastern shore of the lake. You'll see several boats moored around the periphery of the anchorage and if you wish to explore the edges of *North Creek*, keep on the lookout for bits of floating line; these are mooring lines that no longer have floats on them. The *Flamingo Cove Marina* has been severely damaged by storms but is still functional and willing to do whatever is necessary to welcome visitors. The marina can accept vessels to 40' LOA with 5' at MLW. Transportation to town can be arranged.

About midway down the western shore is a government dock at North Wells where the police boat is kept. You are not allowed to tie to this dock, but you can dinghy in to the beach just north of the dock to leave your dinghy while you walk or hitchhike the mile or so into town. About 150 yards south/southeast of the police dock is a submerged wreck in 7' of water, so keep an eye out for it if you are in that vicinity. There is also a floating line next to the wreck with no float attached; you'll want to avoid it and keep that poly line out of your prop.

What You Will Find Ashore
If you take the road along the eastern shore of *North Creek* you will come to the ruins of the old U.S. Navy base and the *Grand Turk Lighthouse*. In the mid-19th century, at the height of the industrial revolution, this entire lighthouse was cast in iron in England and then shipped to Grand Turk. The light was reassembled on a bluff overlooking *Northeast Reef* in 1852-1854 and is credited with helping to sustain the lucrative salt industry in the Turks salt islands as well as saving countless ships. Today this one hundred and fifty-year-old lighthouse, the Silent Sentinel, awaits restoration. To get there by car, follow *Lighthouse Road* past the *Coral Reef Club* with its palm-tree shaded, hillside units, restaurant, swimming pool, and tennis court. Drive up The Ridge, Grand Turk's better residential area, past the entrance to *Flamingo Cove Marina* and you will come to the entrance of the abandoned U.S. base. Here you can take the dirt road to the left of the fence to reach the lighthouse. Watch out for the feral donkeys as you approach the old base.

Divers on the nearby *Northeast Reef* might find the huge sections of railway that a sinking ship jettisoned on the reef in 1912.

High on the ridge at the southeastern end of *North Creek* is the red roofed *Island House*, a Mediterranean style villa featuring air-conditioned units with a swimming pool and a great view of the anchorage. Just south of the *Island House* is a *Texaco* gas station where you can jerry jug fuel to your dinghy on the shore below it. The nearby *Arches of Grand Turk* is newly constructed and features four 2-story townhouses that are perfect for those looking for quiet accommodations.

Just west of the northwestern shore of *North Creek*, Brian Riggs and other researchers found a Lucayan Indian site that was carbon-dated to 700 A.D., predating a site in Inagua that was estimated to be from around 900 A.D. A local dive instructor, Captain Bob Gascoine, who lived aboard his *Aquanaut* in the upper reaches of *North Creek*, found an ancient Lucayan paddle preserved under layers of mangrove leaves in the northwestern corner of *North Creek*. The paddle was dated to around 1100 A.D.; although off the island now for scientific evaluation and restoration, the paddle will soon be on exhibit at the *National Museum* in Grand Turk. This leaves Captain Bob once again up *North Creek* without a paddle (with apologies to Piers Xanthony).

A note for birdwatchers, there is a large flock of pink flamingos that are often seen in the area of the shallows around the entrance to *North Creek*.

Front Street Anchorage

Cockburn Town, and South Base

Front Street anchorage - ¼ nm W of reef:
21° 28.13' N, 71° 09.13' W

South Dock - ¼ nm WSW of end of dock:
21° 25.90' N, 71° 09.20' W

The western shore of Grand Turk offers a fair lee anchorage just below the large *Cable and Wireless* tower. There are several breaks in the reef here and vessels with drafts to 8' can enter and anchor just off the heart of *Front Street*. The western shore of Grand Turk is a national park and vessels over 60' LOA are not allowed to anchor here except in two designated areas near the freighter dock by *South Base* as shown on Chart TCI-T2. The western shore of Grand Turk is

only tenable in winds from northeast to southeast. If a front threatens it is time to move around to the north side to enter *North Creek* or head south to anchor off the southeastern shore of Grand Turk at *Hawksnest Anchorage*, or in the lee of the island at *South Creek*.

The anchorages along the western shore of Grand Turk near *Front Street* can be quite surgy at times and that is one reason I recommend the *North Creek* anchorage so strongly. Another reason is the number of shallow bars and rocky shoals that lie between the reef and the shore. I much prefer to anchor in *North Creek* if at all possible.

Navigational Information

A waypoint at 21° 28.13' N, 71° 09.13' W, will place you approximately ¼ mile west of the break in the reef at the *Front Street* anchorage (sometimes shown as the *Turk's Head Anchorage*). There are actually three breaks through the reef here. The waypoint will place you just off the northernmost one, the widest of the three. None of these reef entrances should be attempted early in the morning with the sun right in your eyes; good visibility is necessary anytime you attempt to pass through any break in any reef anywhere. The northernmost cut, the one most boaters use, is marked on its southern side by a white PVC marker at the time of this writing. If the marker is still there when you are, keep it to starboard when passing through this wide cut.

If in doubt as to which side to take it on, check it out first by dinghy or call *MPL* on VHF ch. 16 or any of the dive shops on VHF ch. 68 for the latest in local knowledge. The cut itself has a minimum depth of 6' at MLW and is easily seen in good light. Any of these three cuts can be used to gain entry to the anchorage area inside the reef, but be warned that there are several shoals and rocky bars between the reef and the shoreline that you must avoid if you attempt to maneuver north or south along the shoreline.

About ½ mile north of the waypoint for the *Front Street* anchorage there used to be a nice anchorage just off *Pillory Beach*. The entrance is through a wide gap in the reef that is easily seen in good light and the holding good just off the resort. The Grant Turk landfall theory recognizes this as the place where Columbus first set foot in the New World and the area is now protected and no anchoring is permitted.

What You Will Find Ashore

If you have anchored near the dock, you can land your dinghy on the beach by the dock. If you need a

SCUBA tank filled, any dive shop can handle that for you (several dive shops are located near the beach south of the anchorage). There is Wi-Fi available if you have a good antenna.

Since 1766, the seat of Government for the Turks and Caicos Islands has been located in Cockburn Town on the western shore of Grand Turk. Although its legal name is Cockburn Town, everyone usually just says Grand Turk when referring to the island or the town. Cockburn Town, pronounced Co'burn Town, was first established by Bermudian Salt Rakers and the architecture hints of that heritage as well as others that influenced this British colony over the last 330-odd years. The houses on Grand Turk all reflect a lovely Old World charm; Duke and Front Streets are lined with historic 18th and 19th century landmarks that reflect the Bermudian architecture style of the salt era. The sidewalks of Cockburn Town are paved with cobblestones and the streetlamps are restored antiques, suitable for display in other places, but hard at work here.

The town itself is well suited for a walking or bicycling tour (it's not unusual to find people bicycling around town going about their everyday business), and almost every building has a walled courtyard meant to keep wandering donkeys from munching on the foliage. Today the occasional donkey is a rarity. Most of the 100 plus donkeys were moved to the northeast end of the island in 1995 and some were spayed and neutered to control their rate of growth. These donkeys are the descendants of those that the Bermudian Salt Rakers brought with them to haul the salt carts around the island. At one time there were over 800 donkeys roaming the streets of Grand Turk. Some folks will gladly tell you tales about the infamous Buster. It seems that Buster had a reputation for having an aggressive sexual drive and was known to bite women on the rear. To be perfectly honest, Buster would bite just about anybody. Buster got to be such a pain (no pun intended), that he had to be put to sleep.

If you need medical assistance the Grand Turk Hospital, north of the Front Street anchorage, is open 24/7 and can be reached by phone at 649-946-2040, 649-943-1212, and 649-946-2333 (in an emergency). Also in Cockburn Town is the Downtown Clinic (649-946-2328) open from 0800-1230 and 1400-1630.

There are several couriers located on Grand Turk. FedEx has an office here (at Harbour House on Front Street) and can be reached at 649-946-2542. DHL can be reached at 649-946-4352 and has daily service from Provo. UPS only has an incoming package service (Cee's Warehouse Groceries).

There are two banks on Grand Turk; First Caribbean International Bank and Scotia Bank. Both are on Front Street and both have ATM's.

For provisions your choices are Cee's Warehouse Groceries and Sundries, Dot's Food Fair and D&G Wholesale, all on Pont St. with the 7/11 Grocery just around the corner. On Frith St. you will find Sarah's Shopping Centre and Sunset Pharmacy while on West Road you'll find Robinson's Foods.

Front Street is the heart and soul of Cockburn Town, with several government offices and many businesses located along this seaside promenade. You may see a lot of folks riding bicycles, but not on narrow, one way, Front Street. The southern end of Front Street effectively starts at the southern end of Pond Street (and is called Duke Street at this point). Just southeast of the end is the Building Materials store, a large hardware store that also rents cars. Here you'll also find K's Drugs for over the counter medications. A block south of Building Materials is the Diplomat Café, home to fine native cuisine and a popular spot. As you proceed up Duke Street the first place you will come Cecil Ingram's Sea Eye Diving (ci@tciway.tc) is one of only three dive operations on the island and is wholly Turks and Caicos owned and operated.

As you proceed north you will notice a few private residences mixed in with the businesses along the Grand Turk waterfront. Next you'll come to Captain Kirk's Guesthouse (No relation to Captain James T. Kirk of the Starship Enterprise) and MPL, the local Yamaha distributor, Carolina Skiff dealer, and the only outlet for marine supplies on Grand Turk. If you need a diesel or outboard mechanic call MPL on VHF ch. 16 and ask for Kirk. Kirk and his wife Leah also run Flamingo Cove Marina on North Creek. Next door is the Osprey Beach Hotel (http://www.ospreybeachhotel.com/) offering the Courtyard Café where you can dine on excellent home cooking in the cool shade of their courtyard. On Wednesdays and Sundays, owner Jenny Smith offers a barbecue with live entertainment. Next door is Oasis Divers where owners Everett Freites and Dale Barker love to pamper their guests on dives around Grand Turk and Salt Cay. Nearby is the famous Salt Raker's Inn, the 150 year old home of a Bermudian shipwright that is now a 12-room hotel with restaurant (http://www.saltrakerinn.com/).

Your next stop is the recently restored *Turk's Head Inne* (http://www.turksheadinne.com/), originally built in 1840. All seven of the hotel's rooms are individually furnished with genuine antiques in keeping with the hotel's unique history as the original home of the island's salt overseer, then serving as the British governor's guesthouse and also as the American Consulate. Many of the rooms have a private balcony with a sea view or a private garden patio as well as air-conditioning and cable TV. Guests of the hotel also have access to the governor's private golf course. The restaurant is highly rated by islanders and visitors alike, and serves up some of the best in international and local cuisine served in elegant surroundings. You'll want to try the *Turks Head Inne Bar & Restaurant* for a meal in the beautiful shaded garden that surrounds the hotel, an excellent spot to beat the heat with an ice cold drink, or dine indoors on their upstairs deck. Just north of the inn is *X's Place*, a unique art gallery with antiques and crafts available. Next door is *Sadler's Seaview Apartments* offering beautiful ocean views in a private garden setting.

At this point *Duke Street* curves to the sea and actually becomes *Front Street*; the seawall is all that separates you from the *Turks Island Passage*. On your right is the huge *Lime* (formerly *Cable and Wireless*) complex and to your left is the anchorage just off the town. The 260' tower is topped with a fixed red light at night. Here you can purchase phone cards, place a call, and even send or receive a fax.

Northward you'll come to the *Arawak House* and the *Public Treasury* where you can purchase Turks and Caicos commemorative coin sets. Next door is the *Shell Shack* where owner Doug Gordon makes some of the most unique shell jewelry you'll find anywhere, you must check out the *Shell Shack*. Next door, the *Beachcomber Guest House* (http://www.saltcay.org/beachcomber/), is a charming bed and breakfast inn right on *Front Street*.

Next you will come to the government complex on *Front Street*. Here, in the center of the historic district, is the hub of some of the Turks and Caicos government though most offices have moved to the *South Base* complex. The bright blue West Indian flavored *Post Office*, the Bermudian accented *Legislative Council*, and several other government offices still open for business here every day. In

1989, these buildings were renovated, a new brick forecourt was laid, and numerous trees and shrubs were planted along *Front Street*. Just behind the post office on *Pond Street*, the road that parallels *Front Street* and the town salinas, is the new Courthouse where you are welcome to sit in on court hearings as long as you are properly dressed (ladies no slacks, men no shorts, and no T-shirts on either of you).

Outside the government compound you will see some ceremonial cannons and the Turks and Caicos national flag. The flag consists of the Union Jack on a blue background along with the Turks and Caicos coat of arms depicting a flamingo, pelican, queen conch, turk's cap cactus, and a spiny lobster. A predecessor to the current flag showed the emblem of salt and sailing ships that was the official flag of the Turks and Caicos Islands during the salt days. One of the salt stacks on the emblem had an entrance resembling the entrance to an Eskimo igloo. The flag maker commissioned for this job mistakenly thought the Turks and Caicos Islands were near the North Pole.

Further down *Front Street* you'll pass *St. Mary's Anglican Church* and its memorial to the Turks and Caicos islanders who died in World Wars I and II. The other Anglican Church on the island is *St. Thomas* situated next to the Anglican cemetery. If you head east on *Moxey Street* by the Courthouse you will cross the pond and the pink building on your right will be *City Market*, a pretty nice little grocery store. A note about shopping in Grand Turk. The plane comes in on Wednesdays and the fresh fruits, veggies, and meats that arrive then will show up on the shelves that afternoon and there are usually some left the next day also. In other words, Tuesday is not the day to shop for fresh goodies on Grand Turk. Passing *City Market*, take your second right at the two story yellow building on *Frith Street* and *Sarah's Shopping Center* will be on your right. *Sarah's* has fresh veggies, fruits, milk, ice cream, and frozen meats as well as some bulk goods. Grocery shopping on Grand Turk involves going to each of these stores as no one particular store is likely to have it all. If you head north on *Pond Street* from the courthouse and take the next right at Church Folly you will come to *Missick's Bakery*, *Neville's Auto Parts*, and the *Philatelic Bureau*. The Turks and Caicos Islands are known far and wide to stamp enthusiasts for their colorful postage stamps and a visit to the *Philatelic Bureau* is a must for anyone with an interest in the Turks and Caicos series of postage stamps.

Back on *Front Street*, your next stop on your northward journey is the *Victoria Public Library*. Here you can check out a book for a small deposit and they have quite a selection of reading material as well as reference books. If you have any books that you would care to donate, by all means please do. The nearby *Library Tennis Court* hosts several concerts and variety shows each year. You will now come to the intersection of *Front Street* and *Prison Folly*, the wide road that takes you one block east to the old prison and a new modern office development.

Next is the *Harbour House* where you will find the local *FedEx* office. Garbage is a problem on Grand Turk. There used to be several dumpsters scattered about the island but they have all rusted. Today all garbage pickup is done on a door to door basis, though you might see the odd can bolted to a power pole but they won't hold much. For boaters, it has been suggested that you take your bagged garbage to a wooden walled outdoor receptacle next to *Scotia Bank*. This is where everybody in the *Harbour House* leaves their garbage and it must make do for the occasional cruiser too. Behind the Harbour House on *Pond Street* is *Caribe West Discount Liquors*, a *FedEx* office, and *Cee's Warehouse Groceries*. *Cee's* is a great place to stop to pick up bulk goods with excellent prices on cases of sodas. *Cee's* is also the island's *UPS* agent (incoming packages only).

After *Harbour House* the one-way section of *Front Street* ends at the *Odd Fellow's Lodge*, a two-story building with a large eye painted on one side. The *Lodge* is one of Grand Turks several *Masonic Lodges* and it is said that the proclamation of the emancipation of slavery was read from the veranda of this building on August 1, 1838. Northward from here is the old *Customs Shed* which houses the *Turks and Caicos Islands Tourist Board* so if you need tourist related information, this will be a handy place to stop.

A great place to eat is next, the *Poop Deck*, a great local hangout serving some of the best native cuisine at affordable prices with an ever-changing daily special. Across the street is *TIMCO, Turks Islands Importers*, where you can get some fresh and frozen foods, as well as cases of sodas, and alcoholic beverages. Next door is *A-1 Business Machines*, a *Canon* dealer where you can pick up computer and office supplies and have minor repairs made.

I'm sorry to report that Peanut's Butterfields has passed away and her well known *Pepper Pot Snack Shop* has closed, so you'll have to go elsewhere for *Dragon Stout* and *rhythm pills*. East of Peanut's old place on *Pond Street* is *Dot's Food Fair, Dot's Liquor Store,* and *Dot's Gift Shop*. *Dot's Food Fair* is a very well stocked grocery and dry goods store with fresh produce, canned goods, ice cream, fresh meats, non-prescription drugs, and a selection of beers. *Dot's Boutique and General Merchandise* on *Pond Street* carries clothes, household furnishings, office supplies and books.

Heading north from *Pond Street* you'll come to Mitch Rolling's *Blue Water Divers* (mrolling@tciway. tc). Mitch also owns the *Eagle Ray Recording Studio* that he built in the basement of his home. Mitch, who is known as the singing divemaster, and his friend Dave, another singing divemaster, have released an album entitled *Grand Turk Blues*. Mitch performs at the nearby *Osprey Beach Hotel* during their Wednesday and Sunday night barbecues.

Next to *Blue Water Divers* is the *Guinep House*, one of the oldest stone buildings on the island and named after the large tree in the front yard. *The Guinep House*, situated on *Front Street* directly facing the sea and the *Columbus National Marine Park*, is the home of the *Turks and Caicos National Museum* (http://tcmuseum.org/) and was constructed of ship's timbers in Bermudian seafarer's tradition. The building itself is fully air-conditioned and on those hot afternoons it's a perfect place to escape to and cool down. But relief from the climate is not the only reason one should pay a visit to the museum. The *Turks and Caicos National Museum*, opened in 1991, has recorded in its archives and displays, the cultural history of the Turks and Caicos Islands, their discovery, the impact of the early European settlers, and the role that the islands played in the great 20th century space race. Tools and pottery that date back to Lucayan times will give you an idea of how these peaceful people lived. The museum proudly displays an extremely well presented marine reef replica with many interesting facts on reefs and reef fish. But the museum's centerpiece is its fascinating collection of artifacts from the *Molasses Reef Wreck*, the oldest shipwreck in the Americas and the first shipwreck site in the Caribbean to be scientifically excavated.

Measuring just 19 meters long, the caravel, having safely crossed the treacherous Atlantic, ran aground on the reef and sank in about 15'-20' of water, laying undiscovered for some 400 years until it was found by treasure divers in 1976. An unscrupulous salvager tried to gain financially from the excavation by claiming the ship was the *Pinta*, one of Columbus' original three ships. The claim was soon proven to be false and the government of the Turks and Caicos Islands took over the salvage and identification process. A government permit was issued to the *Institute of Nautical Archaeology* at *Texas A&M's National Museum* under the direction of Dr. Donald H. Keith. Irate treasure hunters then tried to dynamite the site but their efforts resulted in minimal damage.

Dating of Lucayan pottery pieces found on the site placed the ship on the reef prior to 1513 (remember, all the Lucayans were forcibly removed from the Turks and Caicos islands by 1513) and researchers speculated that the ship was a slaver en route to Hispaniola. The ship was armed with state-of-the-art weapons of the period, and the *National Museum* can boast to having the largest selection of 16th century wrought iron, breech-loading cannons in the world. Following the salvage, cataloguing and preservation of the 2,000-plus artifacts comprising selections of arms, tools, personal effects and pottery, the artifacts were returned to Grand Turk, where they are now exhibited at the museum with the ship's huge anchor hanging from the wall as the centerpiece of the exhibit.

The Turks and Caicos National Museum has a new newsletter, the *Astrolabe*, and plans are afoot to build a complementary museum in Provo, not a duplicate, but one with different offerings oriented to the Caicos group of islands. Definitely stop in and visit the museum's Director Barry Dressel and Manager Brian Riggs and visit the gift shop, with its locally made crafts and selection of Caribbean books located on the second floor.

North of the museum, shoppers might want to visit one of the last fish processing plants in the Turks and Caicos Islands, the *Sea View Fish Market*. Owner Jonathon Missick has been fishing these waters since he was nine years old. Jonathon is an excellent source of fishing tales if you can find the time to listen. He can tell you how the fishing was big on Grand Turk before the "old people died away." Next door is Captain Sam Seymour's tiny but well stocked *Pilot House Store*.

If you head east from here you will come to *Pond Road*. Take a left on *Pond Road*, which now becomes *Hospital Road*, and you'll find *The Regal Begal* a few blocks north. This is probably the best place on the island for local dishes johnnycake, boiled fish, peas and rice, and anything made with conch.

Just north of the *Front Street* area on the western shore of Grand Turk is the *Bohio Dive Resort* (the old *Guanahani Beach Resort*) on *Pillory Beach; www.BohioResort.com*), thought by some to be the first place Columbus set foot in the New World. The resort has *Guanahani Restaurant* and the *Ike & Donkey Beach Bar*.

If you were to drive south from *Front Street* towards the southern end of the island you will pass the airport and soon come to *Government House*, the governor's residence that is called simply *Waterloo*. *Waterloo* was built in 1815 (the same year as the *Battle of Waterloo*) and is not open to the public except by special invitation. The cabinet, the *Executive Council*, meets every week at the governor's office, a small modern single-story building with its own entrance marked *Governor's Office*. Just past the white wall that surrounds *Waterloo* and the governor's private golf course is the entrance to *Governor's Beach*, a beautiful sandy beach with a backdrop of shady casuarinas. As of winter 2002, a 72-room hotel/resort complex is still planned for construction on *Governor's Beach*. The plantation styled edifice is to have elements of Bermudian and Grand Turk architecture to retain the quaint character of Grand Turk while it caters to the upscale tourist clientele.

Navigational Information

A little further south is the entrance to *South Dock* and the huge *South Base* government complex which houses *Immigration*, *Customs*, and several other prime governmental agencies. Your first sight of Grand Turk when approaching from South Caicos or points south will probably be the huge white bulbous *FAA* antenna that at first glance resembles a water tank high on the hill above *South Base*. The large *FAA* antenna there has a fixed red light at its top. The new concrete *South Dock,* just south of the older steel dock, is the place you'll need to tie up to clear in at Grand Turk. If you need fuel call *Texaco I* on VHF ch. 16 and they will deliver fuel to the dock for you.

A waypoint at 21° 25.90'N, 71° 09.20'W will place you approximately ¼ mile west/southwest of the new *South Dock*. If your intent is to clear in call *Grand Turk Harbourmaster* on VHF ch. 16 for instructions. If you only need fuel and have already cleared in elsewhere call *Texaco 1* for instructions. Vessels over 60' are allowed to anchor in the vicinity of the dock between latitude 21° 26.12' N and 25°25.85' N. The dock itself is designed for vessels to 275' with drafts of 12' at the bow and 15' at the stern.

What You Will Find Ashore

South Base today is the *Carnival Cruise Ship Port* and center for a burgeoning tourist industry. Just to the east of *South Base*, along the road that leads southward around the complex, is a remarkable sight, especially for sailors who use wind generators aboard. Here is a 75' tall, red and white striped wind powered generator that was built with a grant from the Canadian government. The 5 kilowatt AC generator is a vertical tower with two blades that resemble an eggbeater. The top is buoyed by wires and the whole contraption revolves with an incredible amount of noise (and I thought my old *Windbugger* was noisy!). It takes 17 knots of wind for the unit to create enough power to be efficient; less than 17 knots and the unit is not even turned on.

Just south of *South Base* is the *Arawak Inn and Beach Club* located at one of Grand Turk's best beach diving locations on a secluded stretch of white sandy beach on the southwest side of Grand Turk. The *Inn* features 14 air-conditioned units right on the beach, cable TV, a fresh water pool, a beach bar and restaurant, horseback riding, and a daily shuttle service into Cockburn Town. Wade into the water and out a few hundred yards and you can dive on the pristine Grand Turk Wall that hosts a magnificent array of marine life.

Divers will also want to check out the old South Dock and the area called *The Pits*. The old steel *South Dock* was constructed in the mid-1950s to service the island's shipping and the U.S. missile tracking station on Grand Turk. Over the years, *South Base* garbage, cargo, and all manner of flotsam and jetsam associated with the exchange of freight have settled in the surrounding waters. A variety of marine creatures have taken to calling this garbage dump home and can be viewed and photographed in their natural environment. Please exercise caution as some of the debris, such as monofilament fishing line left by careless fishermen, may entangle and trap the unwary diver.

Grand Turk celebrates a couple of unique holidays such as the *McCartney Day* celebrations on June 5th. James Alexander George Smith (JAGS) McCartney inspired Turks and Caicos Islanders to be proud of their heritage. McCartney witnessed a certain pride

that Jamaicans had in their roots and endeavored to bring the same pride to his people in the Turks and Caicos Islands. The *Grand Turks Cactus Festival* has replaced the yearly carnival as one of the most popular events of the year. The *Cactus Festival* features sports, dancing, art, and costume contests as well as an island beauty pageant.

Hawksnest Anchorage

Big Cut - ¼ nm NW of:
21° 24.60' N, 71° 09.25' W

Along the southeastern shoreline of Grand Turk is the historic *Hawksnest Anchorage* as shown on Chart TCI-T2, a good shelter from westerly winds. Hawksnest Anchorage offers good protection in winds from west/southwest through northwest to north, while safe anchorage can also be found in the lee of Gibbs Cay in northeast through southeast winds. Vessels can also seek shelter from westerly winds further north along the eastern shore of Grand Turk past the entrance to *South Creek*, as shown on Chart TCI-T2. Although these anchorages can get very surgy at times, the holding is good. Entrance to these anchorages is through one of several cuts through the reef south of Grand Turk.

Navigational Information

Hawksnest Anchorage, once called *Reef Harbour*, for all practical purposes lies off the southeastern shore of Grand Turk, but, is sometimes shown on some older charts as lying between Grand Turk and Cotton Cay, protected by a reef to the west, and Long Cay and a reef to the east. *Turks Island Landfall* theorists claim that this is the anchorage that Columbus claimed would hold "all the ships in Christendom." Entrance for larger vessels of 10' draft is south of the reef between Salt Cay and Cotton Cay from the west and south of Pinzon Cay (once called Breeches Island and sometimes still referred to as East Cay) in the east. The U.S. Navy surveyed *Hawksnest Anchorage* during World War II with an eye to establishing an anti-submarine tracking base for *Catalina Flying Boats*, but nothing came of it.

Today, entrance to the *Hawksnest Anchorage* for the average cruising boat is through one of several breaks in the reef south of Grand Turk. Just south of Boaby Rock Point on Grand Turk is *Little Cut*, sometimes called *Small Cut* on some charts. As well as being shallower and narrower than *Big Cut*, *Little Cut* is often hard to pick out, which is why I recommend *Big Cut* for someone not familiar with these waters.

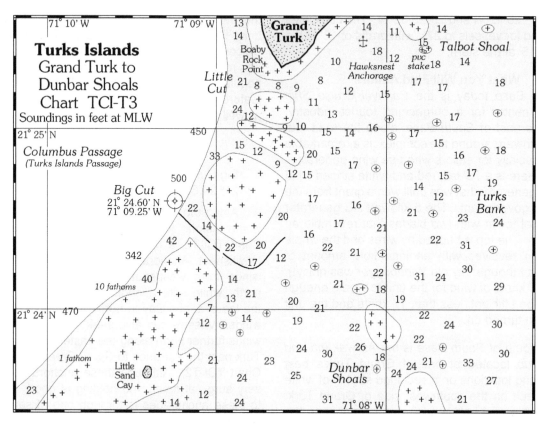

Turks Islands
Grand Turk to
Dunbar Shoals
Chart TCI-T3
Soundings in feet at MLW

Columbus Passage
(Turks Islands Passage)

Big Cut
21° 24.60' N
71° 09.25' W

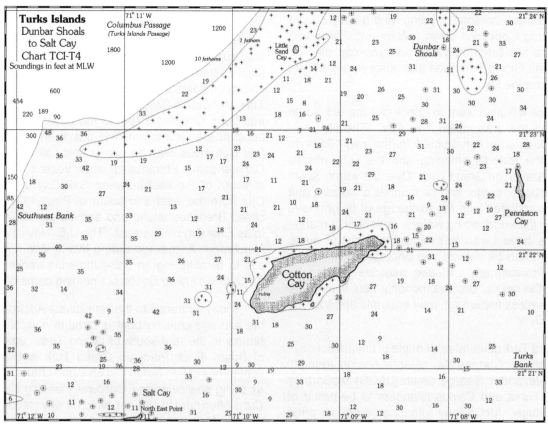

Turks Islands
Dunbar Shoals
to Salt Cay
Chart TCI-T4
Soundings in feet at MLW

Columbus Passage
(Turks Islands Passage)

A waypoint at 21° 24.60'N, 71° 09.25'W, will place you approximately ¼ mile northwest of *Big Cut* (sometimes shown as *Great Cut*) as shown on Chart TCI-T3.

From this waypoint look southeast and you will see three cays about a mile or two distant. Line up with the center of the southernmost cay and head in on it on an approximate heading of 135°. Once again, I must advise that this heading is just for orientation; you must use your eyes to pilot through the reef here. The reef to the south, on your starboard side as you head southeast, is the shallowest and the easiest to see.

Once inside, begin to steer north/northeast to anchor in Hawksnest Anchorage proper in northwest and northerly winds, taking care to avoid the eastern side of the reefs you just passed through. If the winds are southwest to west, continue northeast around *Talbot Shoal* and *Gun Reef* to anchor in the lee of Grand Turk just south of the entrance to *South Creek* (where Lucayan Indians once kept their canoes) as shown on Chart TCI-T2. As you pass *Talbot Shoal* keep an eye out for the buoy that marks the very shallow reef of its southern tip. You can actually pass between this reef and *Talbot Shoal* but it is so much easier and safer just to round the buoy in deeper water and be done with it. Bear in mind that the buoy may be long gone by the time you cruise these waters; use extreme caution through here.

The only problem with the anchorage south of *South Creek*, other than the surge, is that you are right in the flight path to the airstrip and you will be buzzed all day long by plane after plane, including a few large jets. The well-lit building with the huge fence west of the mouth of *South Creek* is the new prison. If you seek a lee in moderate northeast to southeast winds you can anchor in the lee of Gibbs Cay with good protection but watch out for a few scattered heads in the vicinity. A word of warning: these anchorages along the southeastern shore of Grand Turk can get quite rolly when there is no wind to keep you perpendicular to the ever-present surge.

What You Will Find Ashore

The small islands of Gibbs Cay and Round Cay were once called *The Twins* and later *The Sisters* on a French chart that dates to the mid-18th century and are today protected under the national park ordinance as a bird sanctuary. During the early summer months, sooty and Noddy Terns nest here and raise their young. These islands once played a small part in the defense of Grand Turk. At the summit of Gibbs Cay you will find the ruins of a lookout post which, with the canon placement on Gun Hill on the mainland of Grand Turk, served as a line of defense for Grand Turk. Gibbs Cay was the location of a French gun emplacement in 1780 called Ft. Castries and was later used as a fort by Turks islanders in fear of a French invasion of Hispaniola in 1791. The offshore Elkhorn coral reefs offer some excellent shallow water snorkeling and even some small tunnels as well as some very friendly sting rays.

Long Cay, once called Pelican Island, lies about 1½ miles southeast of Grand Turk, as shown on Chart TCI-T2. This uninhabited island is a sanctuary for the Turks and Caicos rock iguana, the same creature that is also found on Little Water Cay northeast of Provo at Leeward Going Through. Visitors to this 1½ mile long narrow cay must apply for a permit from the *DECR*, in Grand Turk. A little further south is Pear Cay, once called Bird Island, whose rocky shoreline has little to offer save for some excellent snorkeling and diving on the reefs off its western shore. In settled weather you can anchor in the small reef-encircled harbor between Long Cay and Round Cay, but you may need to set a bridle to keep from rolling with the surge.

At 65' in elevation, Martin Alonzo Pinzon Cay, usually just called Pinzon Cay and formerly known as East Cay, is the highest of the Turks Island group. The island is named after the pilot of the *Pinta* on Columbus' first voyage to the New World. The only inhabitants of this cay were those who manned a lookout post here and treasure hunters that based here in 1970 while searching for treasure on the *Silver Banks*. The ruins of their base camp are still visible on the southwestern shore of the island. There is somewhat of a surgy lee anchorage along the northwestern shore. There is a small blow hole on the eastern side surrounded by several small rocky pools that are perfect for bathing. Pinzon Cay is home to a magnificent growth of the native Turk's Head Cactus, one of the only remaining places in the islands where they are still found in the wild.

Cotton Cay, as shown on Chart TCI-T4, is the largest and lushest of the uninhabited Turks Islands. The island is privately owned, but access is allowed as of this writing. The cay was once owned by the Harriot Family of Salt Cay fame and as such was used as a retreat and for cattle grazing. Ashore you will find the ruins of their support buildings and many pasture walls. A beautiful subterranean grotto leads to a rock enclosed cove near the ruins of the old house on the western shore of the island. Recently two Lucayan sites were found on Cotton Cay as well as two sites on nearby Long Cay. Just to the east of Cotton Cay lies Penniston Cay, whose rocky shores offer little to the cruising skipper. Tropic Birds frequent the southern shore in spring and early summer.

Salt Cay

Salt Cay - ¼ nm W of Deane's Dock:
21° 19.90' N, 71° 13.25' W

Salt Cay - ¾ SW of S end:
21° 17.60' N, 71° 14.10' W

Seven miles southeast of Grand Turk lies what some tourist brochures refer to as "the land that time forgot." Salt Cay was originally called *Caiceman* or *Canamani* by the ancient Lucayans and later known as *Petite Saline* by the French. Little on the cay has changed since 1900 when the salt industry flourished. The large inland salt pond that still dominates Salt Cay's land area was the attraction and the focus for commerce on Salt Cay for hundreds of years from the time of the Lucayan traders, to the Bermudian Salt Rakers who first arrived in 1645, to even more modern times when Salt Cay was still a busy port well into the 1960s. The skeletons of old windmills that pumped brine into the flats still stand in the salt ponds while nearby giant salt piles sit unused and untouched for years. In 1845, Salt Cay was the home of the *Turks Island Whaling Company*. The remains of the *Taylor House*, the old whale watching outpost, still sits on the highest spot on Salt Cay on Taylor Hill along the eastern shore, and is easily seen from anywhere on the cay.

Captured whales were taken ashore at *Whale House Bay* on the eastern shore for processing of their meat, oil, and ambergris of which a 150-lb. chunk sold for $20,000 in New York in 1955. But that was then and this is now; and nowadays an estimated 3,000 humpback whales pass by unmolested between January and March on their way to their winter breeding grounds on the *Mouchoir* and *Silver Banks* that lie east and southeast of the Turks Islands, and the humpbacks are still bringing money into Salt Cay every season. The *Windmills Hotel* has become a favorite of whale watchers due to Salt Cay's prime location at the eastern edge of the *Columbus Passage*. If you don't wish to bring your boat to Salt Cay, you can leave your boat in the *North Creek* anchorage at Grand Turk and take the weekly ferry to Salt Cay (please check the schedule days on their web site at: https://www.visittci.com/salt-cay-community-ferry).

Recently some local residents and a couple of American investors began an attempt to resume salt production on Salt Cay. A company called *Sun Crystals Trading Company* has leased 250 acres of Salt Cay and plans to employ modern technology in the salt production process, while employing 40 local residents. Four salinas and most of the windmills will remain as mementos of the past. Donkeys, vital to salt production in the early years on Salt Cay, will not be used - to avoid contamination. The finer grades of salt produced is intended for use in water treatment and cattle feed, while the lower grades of salt will be used for snow and ice removal in northern climes.

Today a few dozen cars wander the roads, and the streets are used as much by cows and donkeys as people (it wasn't until 1989 that a fence was built around the airport to keep donkeys off the runway).

Unfortunately, the recent government allowed an Eastern European developer to secure large parcels of Salt Cay. The project is now on hold thanks to the intersession of the current Governor, Gordon Wetherell. Governor Wetherell has ordered that no further work is permitted on Salt Cay until a current set of criminal investigations has been completed against the owner. It is said that the owner has already made a deal with a resort company based in the Far East. Beautiful beaches border much of the Salt Cay shoreline, while herons and other birds feed in the salinas and in the marshlands to the south. The distinctively Bermudian style homes, all with dusty but neatly swept dirt yards, set a unique tone and style. Salt Cay is a vestige of the old Turks and Caicos, a window to a simpler and slower time. It has been said that Salt Cay is "...what the Caribbean used to be." Salt Cay, often regarded as a living museum of industrial archaeology of the Salt Raker era, has been designated a *UNESCO World Heritage Site* to preserve the history and culture of this tiny island. This ensures that all future development on Salt Cay must be in absolute harmony with its historic past.

You will probably notice that the island is primarily inhabited by the very old and the very young; those in the middle, for the most part, are off on the other islands seeking their fortunes. The 200 or so residents that remain are all very friendly and quick with a bit of conversation for the passing stranger. The sign at the airport says it all: *Bon Voyage! Return by any means!* Salt Cay is one of those islands that, no matter how long you stay, you find that you really did not stay long enough. I am certainly guilty of that.

Navigational Information

A waypoint at 21° 19.90'N, 71° 13.25'W, will place you approximately ¼ mile west of *Deane's Dock* as shown on Chart TCI-T5. If approaching from the south or east your first sight will probably be of the huge *White House* that absolutely dominates the Salt Cay shoreline. The holding along the eastern shore of Salt Cay can only be rated as poor to fair with a light layer of sand mixed with rocks and other rubble over a rock bottom. You can anchor anywhere along Salt Cay's western shore between *Deane's Dock* and the *White House*; the holding is about the same. The entire western shore of Salt Cay is quite rocky as you get closer in to shore. The southern third of the western shore has a few more sandy patches to set your anchor in but I never feel comfortable anchoring off Salt Cay's western shore.

My favorite anchorage, and one that is rarely taken advantage of by visiting cruisers, is in *North Bay* just off beautiful North Beach on the northern shore of Salt Cay. The entrance is gained by going north of the reef at North West Point and working your way in towards the beach, dodging the few coral heads and small patch reefs that are easily seen in good light. Don't try this route early in the morning with the sun in your eyes. The holding is good in sand, but the anchorage is only good in southeast to southwest winds and a little surge might work its way in during periods of stronger winds. This anchorage is not recommended with winds from west through north to east or with the threat of a wind shift to those directions during the night, as you won't find your way out in the dark.

Deane's Dock is well protected but open to the southwest. The entrance is over a rocky bottom with only 4' at low water at the entrance, with anywhere between 2'-4' at MLW along the walls where you could tie up once you get around the shallow spot in the center. If you should tie up inside during a frontal passage, expect a strong surge to move you about quite a bit. For information on how to enter the dock call *Salt Cay Divers* on VHF ch. 16. If you need gas, diesel, or groceries, you can get all three at Nathan Smith's place just southeast of *Deane's Dock* by the

large fuel tanks. If you need a diesel mechanic ask for Perry Tolbert. If you require medical assistance not of a severe nature, you can visit the Salt Cay clinic located by the school. They are open every weekday morning and are staffed by a resident nurse.

What You Will Find Ashore

The anchorage on Salt Cay's western shore is just off the only settlement on Salt Cay, Balfour Town. Balfour Town is divided into two sections, the north side and the south side. On the north side you can find Leon Wilson's *One Down One to Go Restaurant*, also known as the *Big W*. Leon, former chairman of the *Turks and Caicos Tourist Board* and the unofficial "Ambassador of Good Will" for Salt Cay, serves great chicken, conch, and hamburgers. In town you'll also find the government clinic, well-staffed by Muriel and her assistant Coralene, with a government doctor visiting about every three weeks. Right in the middle of Balfour Town is Irene Been-Legget's *Halfway House*. The tourist brochures boast that Irene's hospitality and excellent cooking has convinced more than one of her guests to retire to Salt Cay. The *Mt. Pleasant Guest House* is also a good stop for cold refreshments in their bar or patio restaurant.

One of the hottest eateries on the island is the *Green Flash Cafe* (greenflashwhales@gmail.com) near the dock. Check out their weekly *Wednesday Wing Night* and sign up for a Glow Worm night or a whale watching trip. The *Island Thyme Bistro and Internet Cafe* (http://www.islandthyme.tc/) offers good food as well as internet access. The *Coral Reef Cafe* located at the *Salt Cay Divers Shop* has free *Wi-Fi*. The *Smuggler's Tavern* at *Pirate's Hideaway by the Sea* (http://www.saltcay.tc/) offers some unique twists on native dishes, while *Pat's* serves up more traditional fare for breakfast, lunch, and dinner in a garden setting. If you need some groceries you can try *H&P Mercantile*, *Ship to Shore Groceries*, *Smith's*, *Pat's*, or *Nettie's Groceries*.

On the western shore of Salt Cay you will find the impressive *White House*, the ancestral home of the Harriots, Bermudian salt merchants. When the hurricane of September 1813 destroyed the old Harriot home with a 15' tidal surge, the Harriot clan decided to build a structure that would withstand whatever nature threw its way. The two-story house, the oldest standing building on the cay, was constructed between 1834 and 1840. The house was built of stone with the seaward edge in the shape of a ship's prow to protect it from heavy waves on

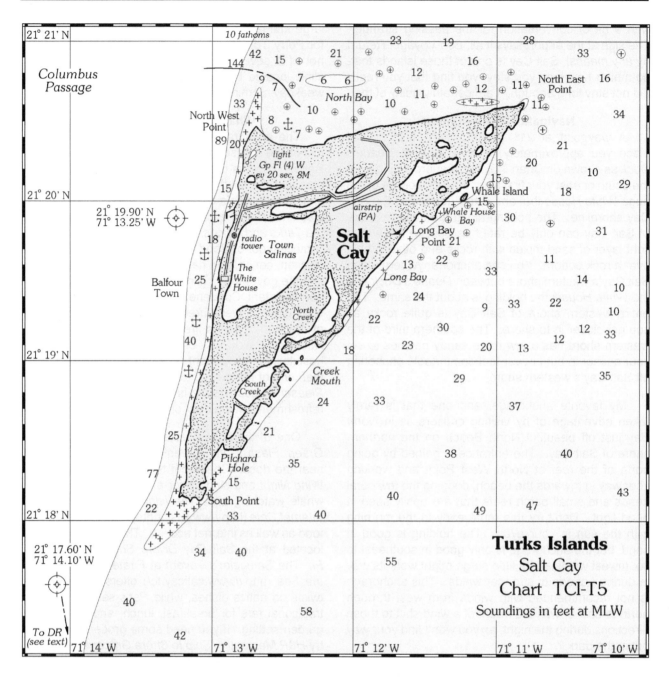

Turks Islands
Salt Cay
Chart TCI-T5
Soundings in feet at MLW

the side-walls and possible flooding. The entire first floor was used for salt storage and even today, salt can still be seen in the interior of the first floor. The pointed roof was fashioned by shipwrights with massive wooden beams reinforced with stout knees. She appears able to withstand quite a lot of torture and has over the last 150 years. In 1940 and 1941, *Paramount Pictures* filmed *Bahama Passage* starring Madeleine Carroll and Sterling Hayden on Salt Cay with the *White House* starring in several scenes. Also in town you can find the *Brown House*, an old wooden

hotel. *The Brown House* has a beautiful veranda and currently has caretakers who rent out smaller, private homes nearby.

Salt Cay's *North Beach* is one of the most beautiful beaches in the entire Turks and Caicos archipelago. The *Windmills Plantation*, a small but luxurious resort and now a growing condo concern, sits on the beach, just a short walk from the airport. Good food and accommodations can also be found at Bryan Sheedy's *Mt. Pleasant Guest House* (more about Bryan in a moment), and at the *Castaway's Beach House* with a half-dozen getaway cottages right on the beach.

Salt Cay is an almost virgin diving area. The island is blessed with a wall drop-off running the length of its western shore. Local residents Ollie Been and Debbie Manos run the very relaxed *Salt Cay Divers* (*http://ww.saltcaydivers.tc/*) and they will be happy to be your guides to Salt Cay's wealth of dive sites, including the much acclaimed wreck of the *H.M.S. Endymion*. Lying about 15 miles southwest of Salt Cay near Endymion Rock as shown on Chart TCI-T1 and Chart TCI-T7, the *H.M.S. Endymion*, a 140', wooden-hulled British Man-of-War lies in only 25' of water near Endymion Rock, sometimes called *Endymion Reef*. She was carrying reinforcements to the islands during a war with France when she went down in 1790 after hitting the reef and was only recently discovered. Divers can explore her 18 nine-foot long cannons, her four 15' anchors, her huge bronze keel bolts that can testify as to the size of the warship, and all sorts of other debris lying scattered about the nearby and for seabed. Needless to say, settled weather is necessary to visit this site.

Military personnel from the bases on Grand Turk used to dive on the wreck site in the 1950s, but over the next few decades it was all but forgotten. Bryan Sheedy, an American who owns and operates the *Mount Pleasant Guest House* (http://www. mountpleasantguesthouse.com/) on Salt Cay, rediscovered the wreck in 1991. The *Mount Pleasant Guest House* was built in 1830 and is simply chock full of fine furniture, pewter artifacts, original paintings, and bicycles that you can rent to tour the island. The *Mt. Pleasant Guest House* also offers horseback riding. Bryan, a rodeo rider in his youth, used to run *Porpoise Divers* before turning over the operation to Ollie and Debbie, who renamed it *Salt Cay Divers*.

The eastern shore of Salt Cay is very rocky and is best explored by dinghy on a calm day. In the salinas along the eastern shore are two blue holes lying almost side by side. The blue holes are only about 20'-30' in diameter and who knows how deep. One diver has reportedly entered the holes to a depth of 250' without seeing bottom.

On *Southwest Beach* the *Sunset Reef* has two air-conditioned units with TV, CD, complimentary bicycles, whale watching deck, and golf cart rentals available.

Those skippers bound for the Dominican Republic can head south of Salt Cay to a waypoint at 21° 17.60 N, 71° 14.10'W, approximately ¾ mile southwest of the reef south of Salt Cay. From this position you can take up a course of 178° for the 83-mile run to Luperón or a course of 170° for approximately 92 miles to Puerto Plata. This route will carry you over part of the *Turks Bank* that lies east of Great Sand Cay; you should have water at or near 10 fathoms in its vicinity. If you begin to get into water much less than this you have perhaps drifted to far to the west, nearer the eastern shore of Great Sand Cay. If this happens simply head a little more east until in deeper water.

Great Sand Cay

West Bay - ½ nm W of anchorage:
21° 11.65' N, 71° 15.50' W

Great Sand Cay - ¾ nm SW of S end:
21° 10.80' N, 71° 15.50' W

Great Sand Cay, commonly called Big Sand Cay (it seems as if nobody calls it Great Sand Cay anymore even though that is its name) and shown on some older charts as Seal Cay, was once a habitat for the West Indian monk seal and the manatee, the former hunted to extinction and the latter well on its way. Legend has it that Spanish treasure is buried on the cay and it is claimed that a British captain named Delaney recovered $130,000 in pirate treasure from a cave on Great Sand Cay in 1850.

Great Sand Cay is a desert paradise. Iguanas and curly-tailed lizards roam the prickly pear cactus decorated landscape. Twice a year green and hawksbill turtles nest on the beautiful western beach south of the light and nurse sharks gather in the shallow lagoon during their mating season. On the eastern shore of the island a great stone arch called *The Looking Glass*, carved from the limestone by the flow of the ocean's waters, stands in mute testimony to the sea's power. The dangerous reefs southwest of Sand Cay took their toll on so many passing ships that a light was finally established on the cay in 1848. Nonetheless ships still continued to pile up on nearby *Endymion Reef*. The eastern shore offers excellent beachcombing; there is all manner of flotsam and jetsam that has washed ashore on the cay from the open Atlantic. As with so many of the land parks in the island chain, visitors are supposed to have a permit from the *DECR* in Grand Turk to walk ashore.

Navigational Information

If heading south from Salt Cay, be sure to keep west a bit to avoid the reefs north of Great Sand Cay as shown on Chart TCI-T6. The large light tower (*Fl W ev 2 sec, 85' 10M*, usually not working) on Beacon Hill just north of the beach is easily seen from seaward and makes a great landmark from any direction. A waypoint 21° 11.65'N, 71° 15.50'W, will place you approximately ½ mile west of the anchorage off the beach in *West Bay*, as shown on Chart TCI-T6. From this waypoint, head in towards the beach and anchor wherever your draft allows. This is a great anchorage in winds from northeast to southeast, though some surge can make it quite rolly at times. The holding is good in sand and there are plenty of reefs, heads, and ledges to snorkel north and east of Big Sand Cay.

Those skippers bound for the Dominican Republic can head south of Great Sand Cay to a waypoint at 21° 10.80'N, 71° 15.50'W, approximately ¾ mile southwest of the reef at the southern end of Great Sand Cay. From this position you can take up a course of 176° for the 77-mile run to Luperón or a course of 167° for approximately 86 miles to Puerto Plata. Be sure to keep the small trio of rocks shown on Chart TCI-T6 as the Three Marys well to port when heading southeastward towards the DR. Also, don't stray near the vicinity of the *Endymion Reef* (or Endymion Rock as it is sometimes shown) as shown on Chart TCI-T1. The water over the reef is between 4' and 8' in places. It's best to give it a wide berth to the west or pass between it and Great Sand Cay.

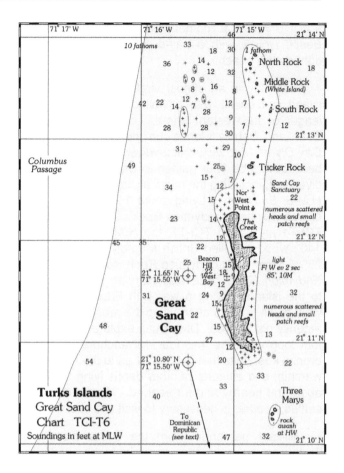

The Dominican Republic

The Dominican Republic

Ports of Entry: Barahona, Manzanillo, Luperón, Cofresi (*Ocean World Marina*), Puerto Plata, Samaná, *Puerto Bahia Marina*, Salinas, Santo Domingo, Boca Chica, Casa de Campo
Fuel: Luperón, Cofresi, Puerto Plata, Samaná, La Romana, Boca Chica, Casa de Campo, Cap Cana
Haul-Out: Luperón, Boca Chica, Haina
Diesel Repairs: Luperón, Cofresi, Puerto Plata, Boca Chica, Cap Cana, Casa de Campo
Outboard Repairs: Luperón, Cofresi, Puerto Plata,
Boca Chica, Cap Cana, Casa de Campo
Propane: Luperón, Cofresi, Puerto Plata, Samaná,
Boca Chica, Cap Cana, Casa de Campo
Provisions: Luperón, Cofresi, Puerto Plata, Samaná, Boca Chica, Cap Cana, Casa de Campo, Santiago, Santo Domingo
Important Lights:
Luperón-head of dock: Gp. Fl R ev 10s
Ocean World Marina Sea Buoy: Fl W
Puerto Plata Sea Buoy: Fl R
Punta Fortaleza: Fl W ev 6 sec
Puerto Plata Range: Fl R
Cayo Vigia: Fl R

This section is not intended to be a cruising guide to the Dominican Republic - far from it. Rather, I offer the three most popular destinations that cruisers visit before or after their Turks and Caicos cruise. First we will discuss Luperón, by far the most popular stopover in the Dominican Republic, and arguably the best hurricane hole in the Caribbean. Next we'll visit the relatively new *Ocean World Marina* complex at Cofresi. And finally we will cover Puerto Plata, the commercial center of the northern coast of the Dominican Republic (usually just called the DR). I urge all mariners plying these waters to carry adequate charts of the Dominican Republic aboard. As for routing information along the northern coast of the DR between Luperón and Samaná, I will not even attempt to offer any suggestions for this route save to say that I suggest you get a copy of Bruce Van Sant's *The Gentleman's Guide To Passages South* and follow the advice contained therein.

Located on the northern edge of the Caribbean Sea, the Dominican Republic (*Republica Dominicana*) occupies the eastern two-thirds of the island of Hispaniola, the second largest island of the Antilles.

Although it shares a border with Haiti, the two vastly different countries and cultures have little in common. While the inhabitants of Haiti have French and African cultural roots, the population of the Dominican Republic has a mixture of African, Amerindian, and Caucasian roots, and the culture and language is Hispanic. Economically the DR is far more developed than Haiti, with a much higher standard of living and quite free of the unrest that plagues Haiti. The principal religion is Roman Catholic and the Church is very influential on several issues such as education, divorce, and birth control; but its overall influence has diminished over the years.

The Dominican Republic has three major metropolitan areas. Santo Domingo, with a population of over two million, is the capital and lies on the southern coast. On the northern coast lies Puerto Plata, one of the DR's main tourist draws, with some 60,000 year-round residents. Santiago, located in the central highlands, is the country's leading industrial center, with a population of over 250,000. Sosúa, near Puerto Plata, and La Romana and Punta Cana, at the eastern end of the island, all have growing resort populations. The rest of the DR's seven-million-plus population lives in or around a dozen or so smaller towns and villages.

The economy of the DR is dominated by agriculture, with 56% of the country used for crops or pasture. Small farmers produce staple foods such as plantains, beans, and sweet potatoes. Agricultural products account for two thirds of export earnings. The rest comes largely from minerals, like bauxite, nickel, and gold. The DR is among the top ten gold producing countries of the world and has the largest single gold mine in the Western Hemisphere. The income from the export of these metals is about equal to the amount spent on imported petroleum. Most of the remaining imports are manufactured goods such as machinery, chemicals, and foodstuffs.

In recent years the government has made great efforts to improve the economy by stimulating the tourist industry and today more than 500,000 tourists visit the country each year to enjoy the climate and the beautiful beaches. The DR has a little bit of everything for everyone. Its main cities offer all kinds of attractions, from its breathtaking landscapes and pristine beaches, to its modern shopping malls and exciting nightlife. But by far, the most attractive feature of the DR is the friendliness of its people.

Visitors will probably want to visit some of the better known historical sites in the DR. In Santo Domingo you can check out *Columbus' Castle* (*Alcazar*), the *St. Francis Monastery*, the *Cathedral of Santo Domingo*, the *Museum of Royal Houses*, *Columbus Square*, the *Ozama Fortress*, *El Faro a Colón* (the *Columbus Lighthouse*), and the first street ever built in the new world, Calle Las Damas. The *Autonomous University of Santo Domingo* (*UASD*), is the oldest university in the Americas dating back to 1538. In Puerto Plata, *Fort San Felipe* bears witness to Nicolás de Ovando's founding of that city in 1502.

There are 16 national parks, 9 natural monuments, and 7 reserves in the Dominican Republic, all under the control of the *Dirección Nacional de Parques*. Among the most popular is *Bermudez National Park* at *Duarte Peak*. A word of warning here; the strenuous hike up and down *Duarte*, the highest mountain in the Caribbean at 10,417 feet, takes at least two days. *Los Haitises National Park*, located on the southern shore of Samaná Bay (Bahía de San Lorenzo), is a protected coastal region known for its mangrove swamps, its caves with Taino rock paintings, and strange rock formations called *mogotes* that emerge from the sea and are unmatched for their eerie beauty.

The *National Park of the East*, southeast of La Romana, is of great interest to those who want to explore prehistoric caves, some of which boast pre-Columbian petroglyphs. Not far off its beautiful beaches lies Isla Saona, which has several excellent hiking trails. The *Reserva Antropológica de las Cuevas de Borbén* was extended in 1996 to protect the *El Pomier* caves, in San Cristóbal, under threat from limestone quarrying. The caves are of enormous archaeological value, with over 4,000 wall paintings and 5,000 rock drawings. Cave #1 contains 590 pictograms, making it superior to any other cave painting site in the Caribbean. Other places of interest are the *Los Tres Ojos National Park*, the *Marine Mammals Sanctuary*, the *National Botanical Garden*, and the *Parque Zoológico Nacional*. The *Reservas Científicas*, the *Scientific Reserves*, include lakes, patches of forest and the *Banco de la Plata*, the enormous *Silver Banks* where hump-backed whales migrate from the Arctic every year to mate and give birth. About 50 boats conduct trips to the *Silver Banks* out of Samaná.

Since the Dominican Republic is located just south of the *Tropic of Cancer*, the temperature varies little from season to season. Average temperatures range from 80º-95º F during the day to the low 70's at night. Although the DR is in the tropics, the trade winds, the surrounding ocean, and high elevations combine in some areas to produce a climate that is far from typical of the tropics. In fact, frost is common on the highest peaks of the *Cordillera Central*. In most areas, however, temperatures are moderately high and vary little from season to season. Rainfall is normally greatest on the mountain slopes over which the easterly trade winds blow and decreases on the opposite slopes and in the major valleys. Annual precipitation averages about 60 inches, but the mountainous areas receive considerably more moisture. The rainy season is from June to November.

Citizens of the United States and Canada may enter the DR with a passport, no Visa is required. Minors may enter with only an original birth certificate. Cuban residents of the United States may enter with their U.S. residency card and additional official photo-bearing document. American and Canadian visitors are required to purchase a tourist card for US$10 upon entry. If you're heading to the DR from the Turks and Caicos or the Bahamas, remember to get a departure clearance when leaving those waters. Visitors leaving by air are required to pay a US$27 departure tax. Personal electronics are admitted into the Dominican Republic, although professional video equipment, television cameras, and other related items may need special clearance. Guns will need to be checked in when entering. For more detailed info on clearing in or out of the DR, see the section on *Customs and Immigration* in the chapter *The Basics*.

After clearing into the DR you will probably want to exchange your dollars for pesos. Don't change more money than you plan to spend. Only 30% of Dominican currency exchanged by visitors can be changed back into dollars upon departure (a tip - save your currency exchange receipts). Although it's extremely tempting, one should avoid changing money on the black market. Absolutely no more than US$5,000 may be taken out of the country when you leave. Arrests have been made for even small currency-law violations. Foreign currency can be changed into Dominican pesos at *Banco de Reservas* booths at the airports, major hotels, or at commercial banks. Banking hours are 0830 to 1500, Monday through Friday. Airport booths remain open to service all incoming flights, up to 24 hours if necessary. Traveler's checks and major credit cards are widely accepted. Cash advances are available at some commercial banks. When tipping, a 10%

gratuity (as well as an 8% sales tax) is often included in the bill. Please note that the practice of tipping taxi drivers is not the custom in the DR but it is widely practiced, and just as widely appreciated. As for provisioning, you'll want to check out the excellent deals on wine, rum, cigars, and *El Presidente* beer. Bear in mind that the DR practices the Latin tradition of the siesta. Many shops close for long lunches from 12:30 P.M. to 2:30 P.M. However, major shopping centers, supermarkets, and stores frequented by visitors usually remain open from 9 A.M. to 7 P.M. In the DR you'll find *Atlantic Standard Time* in effect year round, so the time here is one hour ahead of *Eastern Standard Time* in the Fall and Winter and the same as *Eastern Daylight Time* in the Spring and Summer. Electricity is 110 volt, 60 cycle.

Baseball is a passion in the DR; there are more baseball players from the Dominican Republic playing in the North American major leagues than from any other Caribbean nation. Most major league clubs maintain small baseball camps in the Dominican Republic, and the DR's professional winter league draws many U.S. players.

The famous *Merengue Festival* is a lively celebration of the country's national music, with *Merengue* bands performing at most major hotels and along the Santo Domingo Malecón. This huge party takes place from the last week in July through the first week of August. The term *Merengue* refers both to the music and the dance, which evolved in the Dominican countryside among the happy people of a divided island. The history of the *Merengue* is woven into the fabric of Dominican history itself. This Afro-Caribbean dance became part of country life and is still danced today around the squares of small villages, next to bonfires on secluded beaches, in ballrooms, and in nightclubs throughout the world. In the traditional countryside settings, the music is provided by a *Perico Ripiao*, a small band made up of an accordion, a drum, a guiro and a box bass. Puerto Plata's *Merengue Festival* is held during the second week of October. Christmas celebrations begin in early December and end on *Epiphany Day*, Jan. 6..

Americans needing the assistance of the *U.S. Embassy* in Santo Domingo can telephone 809-541-2171, or fax the embassy at 809-686-7437 (http://santodomingo.usembassy.gov/). In Santo Domingo the embassy sits at the corner of *Calle Cesar Nicolas Penson* and *Calle Leopoldo Navarro* The Dominican Republic postal service boasts over 190 branches and is the least expensive (although slowest) way of sending and receiving international mail. The postal service also has a higher priced express mail service similar to the *U.S.P.S. Priority Mail*. Private couriers include *DHL*, *FedEx*, *UPS*, and several local P.O. Box courier services such as *Express Parcel Service*. There are 120 AM radio stations on the island, 6 HF stations, and 18 television stations scattered about. Amateur radio operators can get a 30-day reciprocal (HI) for no charge upon clearing in.

Divers will be happy to know that the waters surrounding the island of Hispaniola hold some 400 shipwrecks that have produced many valuable artifacts over the years. The DR is great place for beginner divers as well as for serious underwater explorers. Although the North coast near Puerto Plata and Sosua might prove disappointing for the experienced diver due to the extensive damage the reefs there have suffered, the southern shore and the eastern side of the island offers dive sites to satisfy the most demanding diver. *La Caleta Underwater Park* is located just a short boat ride from Boca Chica and there divers will enjoy good viz and a fertile underwater life. Divers may also visit the wreck of the *Hickory*, an old treasure hunting ship. Isla Catalina is a good spot for wall diving and large fish. Isla Saona is also a great spot for the larger marine creatures. As tourism develops on the island, diving in the Dominican Republic might soon become very popular and the dive sites more crowded.

The Future

Big changes are in the works for the Dominican Republic. First, design and development has begun on the *Amber Cove Cruise Center* which will accommodate up to two cruise vessels, or 10,000 people daily in the *Bay of Maimón* just west of Cofresi and Puerto Plata, and east of Luperón. There is also a new highway under construction that will service Puerto Plata, Cambioso (and its pristine beach), and what may become the Punta Alma project near Luperón. The highway will make the trip to the airport at Puerto Plata much faster. New high tension power lines are being installed to bring 24-hour per day electricity to Luperón.

A Brief History

The island that we know as Hispaniola was first inhabited by Ciboney Indians and later by Taino Indians who still occupied the island when Christopher Columbus discovered it on December 5, 1492. The native Indians had named the island *Quisqueya* but Columbus changed its name to Hispaniola (from *Isla Espanola,* the "Spanish Island"). Columbus lived here for many years prior to his death, and his remains are said to be buried in the *Cathedral of Santo Domingo* in Santo Domingo. Christopher Columbus' brother Bartholomew founded Santo Domingo in 1496, making the city the oldest permanently occupied settlement in the Americas.

At that time there were more than a million native Taino Indians on the island but within 50 years most had died of starvation, overwork in the gold mines, and epidemics of European diseases. The gold that could be obtained using the 16th century mining techniques was exhausted by 1530. Spain lost interest in Santo Domingo soon after the discoveries of Mexico and Peru. The Spaniards who remained on the island turned to cultivating sugar cane, using black slaves imported from Africa.

In 1697, Spain ceded the western third of Hispaniola to France. By the end of the 1700's, the new French possession known as St. Domingue was one of the world's richest colonies, producing vast quantities of sugar and cotton. By 1795 France had gained control of the entire island but slave uprisings in the western section in 1804 led to the creation of Haiti, the world's first black republic. In 1814 Spain regained control of the eastern part of the island, but the Dominicans declared their independence in 1821. In 1822 the Haitians invaded the Dominican Republic and ruled it by force for almost 22 years, but the Dominicans did not lie down and accept this intervention. They launched the *Trinitaria*, a secret society founded by Juan Pablo Duarte, and under the leadership of Ramon Matias Mella and Francisco del Rosario Sanchez, the Spanish-speaking inhabitants of the east rebelled against the Haitians and proclaimed their independence on February 27, 1844, calling their nation the Dominican Republic. This period of occupation is often considered the cause of an antagonism that still separates Dominicans from Haitians. One favorable consequence of Haitian rule, however, was the freeing of slaves in the DR.

Unhappily, liberation from the Haitians did little to bring peace and economic progress to the DR. During the rest of the 19th century, the Dominican Republic suffered severe economic difficulties, scores of revolutions, armed invasions from Haiti, and another period of Spanish domination from 1861 to 1865. Money was borrowed and spent recklessly by corrupt governments, and by 1916 the country was in political and economic chaos.

In 1905, the United States established partial control of the Dominican economy to protect American investors. Increasing debts and internal disorders resulted in the occupation of the DR by U.S. Marines in 1916 in order to restore order and protect the approaches to the Panama Canal. This occupation lasted for eight years, and, though there was opposition to it, the enforced political stability permitted major social and economic advances.

In 1924, the U.S. occupation ended; in 1930 there was another revolution and the DR fell into the hands of a dictator, Gen. Rafael Leonidas Trujillo Molina. For nearly 31 years, until his assassination in 1961, Trujillo headed a ruthless police state. At the cost of political freedom, the DR had another period of imposed stability that, combined with favorable sugar prices, stimulated impressive economic growth. In December 1962 the first free elections in nearly 40 years brought the leftist Juan Bosch to the presidency. His reform program led to his overthrow by the military in September 1963.

Five years of political turmoil after Trujillo's death led to another intervention by the United States. When Bosch's supporters attempted to restore him to power in 1965, civil war broke out, and U.S. troops were sent in to restore order and the status quo and ease U.S. concerns about the possibility of a Cuban-style Communist takeover. Since then the political scene has been relatively orderly, with freely elected presidents. In 1966, Joaquin Balaguer was elected president. His right wing authoritarian rule continued until the election of 1978, when Antonio Guzman defeated Balaguer in a very controversial election. Guzman was in turn defeated by Salvador Jorge Blanco in 1982. Balaguer, elderly and blind, was narrowly reelected in 1986 and 1990. In 1988 Blanco was convicted of corruption in absentia and in 1992 was sentenced to 20 years in prison.

Much wealth has been generated, but it has always been unequally distributed. The bulk of the population remains poor and undernourished. In the 1980s the low price of sugar in the world market brought on a series of economic crises. Under Salvador Jorge Blanco, who was president from 1982 to 1986, the government instituted an austerity program. Wage controls and the removal of food subsidies led to rioting in 1984. Economic difficulties persisted in the debt-ridden nation through the 1990 election, in which Balaguer defeated his long-time opponent, Juan Bosch. Austerity measures dictated by the International Monetary Fund were still in force in 1992. The 1991 deportation of illegal Haitian immigrants worsened relations with Haiti.

Medical Help

In the DR, the phone number for a medical emergency is 911, but don't count on it working all the time. Most medical centers are bi-lingual, many accept international insurance, and the costs can be 1/3 of the prices in the U.S. All the clinics are free to residents of the Dominican Republic and cruisers, but the more serious medical problems, such as those that require a visit or a stay at one of the hospitals in Puerto Plata or Santiago can cost quite a bit. Most medical insurance is accepted throughout the DR and drugs that can only be acquired by prescription in the US, are available without a prescription in the DR, and most are very inexpensive. It helps to know the Spanish translation of the drug when you head for the *pharmacia*.

There is a medical clinic in Luperón where two of the three doctors in residence speak passable English. The clinic is located at the end of *Calle Luperón*, two blocks south of *Verizon* and then three blocks southwest. While the clinic can deal with most basic health problems, for testing you will be referred to the *Laboratory Luperón*, just across from the *guagua park*. If you have your samples in before 1200 you can usually get the results by 1700. If you need a dentist try the *Medicon Dental Implant Center, Independencia No. 9*, (phone 888-848-7639, ext: 24368).

If you need medical attention in Puerto Plata visit *Centro Médico Bournigal* (809-586-2342, Fax: 809-586-6104 or email them at info@bournigal-hospital.com).

In Santiago you can find medical attention at *HOMS*, the *Hospital Metropolitano de Santiago, Duarte Highway* Km 2.8 (829-947-2222 Ext. 5000, Fax: 829-947-2223, or you can reach them by email at info@homshospital.com, http://www.homshospital.com/).

In Sosúa or Cabarete you can visit the *Medical Center Carretera Sosua-Cabarete* Km 1, Sosúa, 809-571-4696, or you can reach them by email at cmc.sosua@gmail.com. In Cabarete visit *Servi-Med* Dr.

Gidion or Dr. Naurio Carretera, *Cabarete 25* (809-571-2903). If you need a vet in Sosúa or Cabarete, visit *Dr. Bob's*, on the main road from Sosúa to Cabarete. (24-hour phone number 809-430-5503). After *El Choco Road* you will come to a *Coastal* gas station, just past the station is the *Dr. Bob's* sign.

In Samaná, Dominican Republic, quality medical care can be found at the *Centro Medico de Especialidades Samaná* (with ambulance service), located at *Calle Coronel Andrés Díaz No.06,* phone: 809-538-3999, 809-538-3888, or fax them at 809 538-2424 (http://cmes.com.do/). The *International Medical Center* (info@internationalmedicalcenter.com) is located in the *Plaza Pueblo Principe,* Local 4, in the heart of downtown Samaná and is open 24/7 (809-552-1117, Fax: 809-538 2675). If you need a dentist in Samaná, visit Dr. Elizabeth Frias de Martinez, her clinic (*Miami Family Dental*) is located at *Calle Peter Vander Horst No.2* (809-538-3180, Cell: 809-988-1705.

In Santo Domingo, *Clinica Abreau*, (http://clinicaabreu.com.do/) at *Calle Arzobispo Portes No. 853,* has 24-hour emergency service and free treatment for foreigners (809-688-4411). the *El Hospital Docente Padre Billinil* is located on *Calle Padre Billini y Santomé, Zona Colonial*, and offers free consultations (809-333-5656, . If you need an ambulance call *Movi-Med Ambulance Evacuation Service* at 809-532-0000.

The Northern Coast

The northern coast of the Dominican Republic is popular with cruisers headed to the Caribbean, although many tend to skip it when returning. Since the officials in the Dominican Republic are a bit more open to cruising boats along this shore, the anchorages here are much more inviting as more than just an overnight stopover. We will explore the northern coast from west to east.

Luperón

Luperón - 1 nm N of entrance:
19° 55.50' N, 70° 56.51' W

By far, the nearest, most popular destination when heading to the Caribbean from the Turks and Caicos, is Luperón. In years past we would have to give that honor to Puerto Plata; but since Luperón became an official port of entry, Puerto Plata's yacht traffic has dropped off considerably. Luperón was named after General Luperón, who was one of the Dominican Republic's greatest heroes. In 1879, under his leadership, the country was reorganized and set on the road to economic recovery. Luperón, which is sometimes shown as Puerto Blanco on some charts, is usually the name given to this entire area, but most insist that Puerto Blanco is the bay and Luperón is the town. Either way, it is a favorite stop for cruisers bound north or south.

This tiny harbor is one of the best hurricane holes in the Caribbean and many cruisers tend to call it home for the season staying months at a time. I know a couple who might just spend the rest of their lives there. They love the cheap rum, wine, and dining as well as the secure protection that Luperón has to offer. The people love boaters in Luperón; boaters really help the economy here and the locals appreciate it and go out of their way to be accommodating. There is a boater's net every Sunday and Wednesday on VHF. Ch.72, at 0800. Here you can pick up the latest info about what's going locally including business announcements, upcoming festivities, boat gear sales, and info on who's just arrived in the harbor. VHF ch. 68 is used for all local communications, usually only the Navy uses ch. 16.

Navigational Information
From Great Sand Cay in the Turks and Caicos Islands, the waypoint off Luperón bears approximately 176° at a distance of 77 nautical miles. If approaching from the waypoint just south of Great Sand Cay you can head directly for this waypoint with no dangers. Your first sign of impending landfall may well be while you are still 20 miles north of the Dominican Republic. Cabo Isabella is clearly seen as the highest spot around. As you approach the entrance to the bay at Luperón, keep Cabo Isabella to starboard. There are some hills to both the right and left of the entrance channel, but the very conspicuous light-colored roof of a hotel/resort complex makes another good landmark. Keep the hotel well to starboard; the entrance to Luperón lies approximately ½ - ¾ mile to the east of the hotel.

If the wind is right, usually out of the southeast, your dog may alert you to your impending landfall from many miles out to sea. Suddenly the air will be filled with the aroma of dirt, trees, animals, and smoke and you might find your dog sniffing the air trying to figure out where these new scents are coming from. If your sniffer is up to snuff you too might be sniffing the air along with your pooch. Quite a refreshing change

if you've gotten used to the dry, almost desert-like islands of the Turks and Caicos.

As shown on Chart DR-1, the entrance to Luperón lies between a large shoal area on the western side of the entrance and another area to the eastern side of the entrance. Caution is called for when entering the channel to Luperón, in poor light the shoals are difficult to make out.

Approaching the entrance slowly in the morning light, you may be able to make out the shoal fairly easily, as the water may still be clear then. Later during the day, as the winds pick up (about 0900 the breeze fills in and blows all day until around sunset); it gets a little harder to discern the shoal from offshore.

From the waypoint at 19° 55.50' N, 70° 56.51' W (approximately one mile north of the entrance channel), a good course is to keep the eastern cliff close on your port bow until you can make out the buoy that now marks the shoal on your starboard side. As of this writing there are two buoys (and bear in mind that this may change at any time) and the westernmost buoy is in shallow water and should be kept WELL to starboard upon entering. Keep an eye out for the breaking shoal off the eastern shore and take the westernmost buoy to starboard upon entering. The entrance channel leading into the anchorage is often hard to make out until you get fairly close and it opens up before you.

As you approach the entrance, keep close to the eastern shoreline where the deeper water lies and keep the buoys well to starboard. Once inside you'll see *Caño Quitano* to the east, but do not enter that harbor at this time (though many cruisers leaving Luperón anchor just inside the entrance to ease a night departure).

As the entrance to the inner harbor opens up to starboard, pass roughly midway between the northern and southern shore watching out for the shoals off each one. As you enter the harbor the deeper water lies along the mangroves on the southeastern shore. If you pass along those mangroves you'll avoid the large, shallow mud shoals that plague the center of the harbor and change and grow with each passing season. The shoals rise up from 20' depths to lie about 1'-2' under the surface; use caution as lots of folks run aground here. Boats can anchor anywhere in the harbor, near the marina or by the town dock. Usually where there is a large gap with no boats you'll find a shoal so keep your eyes open. The water in the

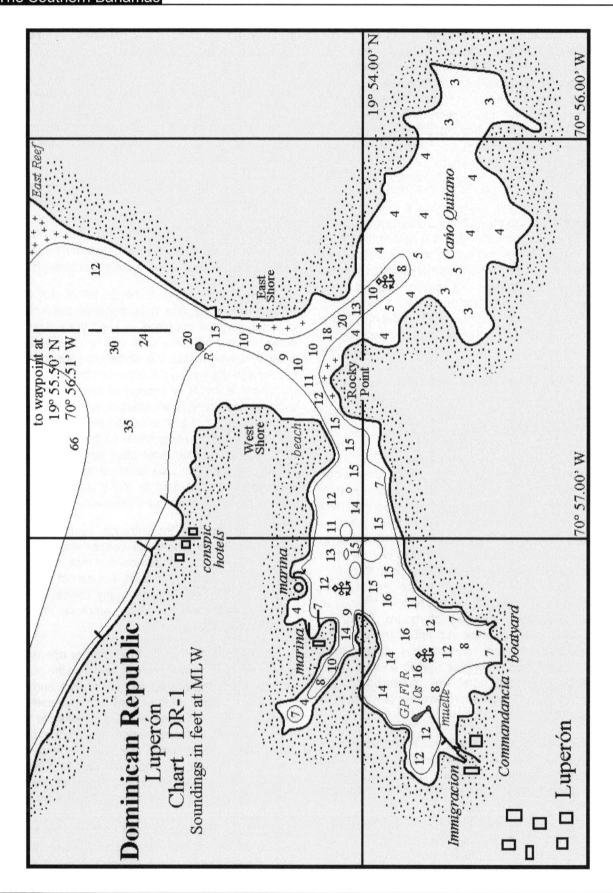

Dominican Republic
Luperón
Chart DR-1
Soundings in feet at MLW

to waypoint at
19° 55.50' N
70° 56.51' W

66   35

24
30
15

East Reef

12

East Shore

R 20   15   10

20   9

9   18   20   13

10   11   10   4   4   5

12   5   4   8

15   10   5   4   4

15   West Shore   beach   Rocky Point   3   5

15   4   4   3   3   4

15   4   Caño Quitano   4

14   15   7   4   3

15   7

14   12   11   3   3   3

12   13   15

marina   15

12   marina   15   15

marina   4   7   16   15   11

14   9   16

8   10   16   12   7

8   14   16   8   7

4   GP Fl R   8   12   7

7   14   10s   muelle   7

12   16   Commandancia   boatyard

12   12   Immigracion

conspic.
hotels

Luperón

19° 54.00' N

70° 56.00' W

70° 57.00' W

harbor is muddy brown and the visibility is nil. The bottom here is basically mud and the holding is great, but it takes a few days for your anchor to set here. Boats drag frequently as people often forget that they are anchoring in 20' of water and fail to put out enough scope. But if you do drag, unless you run into another boat or the dock, it's all mud and mangroves around you to act as a cushion. The town dock is marked with a red light (GP Fl R, ev 10 sec.) that works well although it is not visible outside the harbor.

What You Will Find Ashore

If you need to clear in, it would be convenient for the officials if you anchored near the town dock (*muelle*) at the southwestern end of the anchorage. After anchoring, hoist your "Q" flag and sometime during the day the *Commandancia's* official will come out to your boat to clear you in. This person will likely say he is with the "Navy" and may or may not have a translator with him. A lot of boats simply take their papers into town to clear in and save the *Commandante's* men a trip out (you know how impatient we cruisers can be), and I've done that myself. Sometimes it's okay, while at other times the *Commandante* may tell you to go back to your boat and wait (which has also happened to me). At the time of this writing standard procedure is to wait for the *Commandante*.

After the *Commandante* and his entourage have cleared you (*Agriculture* will be along as well: at the time of this writing there is no fee for the Navy clearance, but you will have to pay for *Agriculture*), you must now go to the *Immigration* office and all aboard must come into town to clear.

The dinghy dock is in the SW corner of the harbor at Luperón, it lies on the NW side of the *muelle*. You can also get water here and drop off garbage for a fee. Just up from the dinghy dock on the road into town is a small blue trailer, this is the *Immigracíon* office. You will have to pay a fee per person aboard, and a fee for the boat (please note that all fees are subject to change depending on time and the exchange rate of the peso versus the American dollar). The *Immigracíon* office is also where you'll find the *Ports* representative and have to pay for harbor clearance. Across the street, over the small bridge and up the hill is the *Commandancia's* office, this is where' you'll need to go to get a *despacho* when you clear out.

When clearing out you must obtain a *despacho*. On the day of your departure, one hour before you plan to leave, you must go to the *Port Authority* office to pay your bill. Take that receipt to the *Commandancia*

to obtain your *despacho*. The *Commandante*, or his representative, will then come to your boat for an inspection and give you your *despacho* which is supposed to be good for 24 hours, but you may be told that you should leave within an hour. However, if you have an engine problem what can be done? Stay overnight and leave in the morning if you desire, but don't tell anybody that I suggested this. I have also left the main anchorage in Luperón and anchored overnight in *Caño Quintano*, leaving at first light the next morning.

In a small cove that lies just to starboard off the entrance channel is the *Marina Puerto Blanco*, the oldest, marina in the harbor. The marina has a small boat dock with room for about 10-15 boats and it usually stays full. The bar at the marina is a popular hangout for cruisers with Wednesday night pot lucks, daily happy hours from 1700-1900 PM, and other events during the week such as the Sunday nautical swap meet where cruisers buy and sell their no-longer-needed charts, courtesy flags, and all manner of used boat gear that's been sitting in various lockers doing nothing but taking up room. There is electricity and water dockside, but be prepared for frequent power outages. There is also a dinghy dock where you can get water for washing. Some folks will drink this water but I don't recommend it; bottled water is sold here as well as throughout town in 5 gallon bottles. You can drop off your laundry here for what is usually same-day service. The marina also has showers and car and truck rentals. You can phone the marina at 809-571-8644.

High atop a ridge across and to the east of the *Puerto Blanco Marina* is the newer *Luperón Marina and Yacht Club* with their dock and 69 steps that lead up the hill to the restaurant and bar. The restaurant has a great view and good access to any breeze that might be blowing. There is limited dockage and free internet access. The marina offers a clearance service, call ahead on VHF ch. 68 for entry instructions and to let the marina know that you need clearance. The docks have water, electricity, showers, and the marina also offers ice, a laundry service, and *Wi-Fi*.

A short walk north of the marinas is the *Caribbean Village Luperón*, the beachfront resort that you used as a landmark when approaching Luperón. The resort is spread over 16 lush, landscaped acres, with gorgeous views of the *Atlantic Ocean*. The large resort boasts 441 beautifully appointed air-conditioned rooms. The resort offers SCUBA lessons in their pool, bicycles, windsurfing, snorkeling, sailing, tennis, a gym with sauna and *Jacuzzi*, aerobics, table tennis, billiards, and horseback riding on the beach. Also on-site are several boutiques, a buffet-type restaurant, a beach restaurant, and a disco. There is some nice snorkeling along the jetties by the hotel, but be forewarned: if you walk the beaches in the DR

you will sometimes find vendors hawking their wares. They're usually very friendly and understand a firm no. This is not much of a problem in Luperón, as the vendors are not allowed on the beach. It tends to be more of a problem from Puerto Plata eastward.

Shopping in Luperón

Just watching the world go by in Luperón

Luperón Marina and Yacht Club

At the southern end of the anchorage area, southeast of the government dock, is *Marina Tropical* and its haulout yard. The marina has a 30-ton lift, a *Cono-Lift*, which is basically a hydraulic trailer, limited water, showers, toilets, power (intermittent), workshops, and a bar. The yard can haul boats to 47' LOA. You can reach the marina by phone at 829-440-9926, or email them at marinatropical.dr@gmail.com.

Just inland from the *muelle* and the dinghy dock is the town of Luperón. Not much bigger than South Caicos, Luperón is quite a bit busier, and much more alive. Everywhere you go you'll find people talking, music playing, and cars and motorcycles roaring by. Many people live in homes that also house their business where they might sell fruits and veggies, rum, water, roasted chickens, or sodas. Prices are great in the DR and Luperón is no exception. You can easily find rum at $3-$4 a bottle, wine for $2-$3 a bottle, and a carton of DR produced cigarettes for half of what an equivalent brand would cost in the States (and I'm told they taste as good as US brands). You can eat out for next to nothing; a lunch in one of the more inexpensive places will run you in the neighborhood of $2-$4. I love *Laisa's* just in from *Verizon* on the same side of the street. Almost directly across from *Verizon* is a great little restaurant on the corner that serves excellent food (lunch for four costs under US$25 there).

To start our tour of Luperón, let's begin with the first stop you will have to make; you must change your American dollars into pesos. The first rule is do not change very much more money than you plan to spend. Only 30% of Dominican currency exchanged by visitors can be changed back into dollars upon departure (a tip - save your currency exchange receipts). Although it's extremely tempting, one should avoid changing money on the black market; not to worry though, there is little if any black market activity in Luperón.

The *Claró* office in Luperón, *Altagrácia* (even though many people still call it *Codatel),* is the most convenient place to exchange your dollars although there are others (*Alejandro Pharmacia* and *Alexandria's Gift Shoppe* to name just a couple). To find *Claró*, walk into town on the main road from the government dock. As you enter town it splits and *Duarte Street* forks off straight in front of you on your right hand side. Follow *Duarte Street* for two blocks and *Altagrácia* will be on your left. *Altagrácia* is also

a great place to go for Internet access although most of the gringo restaurants have *Wi-Fi.*

Next, you'll want to know how to get around Luperón; the easiest way of course is by foot. The town lies just up from the town dock and is only about a mile long. But if you want to get anywhere else, or if you have to pick up something, you have your choice of several different modes of transportation. For those on a budget, and the adventurous, there are the *motorconchos.* These are small motorcycles that roar around town all day and most of the night. If you need a *motorconcho*, they hang out all day long at *Codatel.*

Next up in the conveyance chain are the taxis and *guaguas* (basically cars are taxis and minivans are *guaguas).* The taxis are the priciest means of transportation but they will take you wherever you wish to go. A motorconcho from town to the hotel costs 15 pesos; a taxi costs 100 pesos. As anywhere in the DR, you should negotiate for a better deal, but the taxi drivers seem to stand pretty steadfast. It would pay to rent a van with others for the most economical method. *Guagua*s can be found in town at the *guagua park, parquecito,* the small park at the end of town away from the town dock. If you want to get to Puerto Plata this is the way to go, but you must leave Luperón with enough time to shop at the other end.

With the exception of the *pharmacia* and the larger grocery stores, most places close from noon till two for siesta. The *guaguas* run all day but only when they're full; they are truly an experience. You're likely to find yourself stuffed into a minivan with 16 other people, a dog, a chicken, and a couple of goats. If headed to Puerto Plata, take a *guagua* to Imbert (home of the closest bank and *ATM* machine though you can draw pesos at *Codatel* on your *Visa* card) and pick up a bus there that's headed to Puerto Plata. If you need a trusted taxi driver, try *Nino's Taxi* to go to Puerto Plata or Santiago; his phone is 809-493-6950.

If headed to Santo Domingo, there is a daily bus available from Luperón, it leaves about 1330 and the trip takes about 7 hours. One final note: if you are planning on doing major provisioning, you should consider renting a van for the day; you won't be able to carry a lot on a *guagua.*

If headed to Puerto Plata, take a *guagua* to Imbert (home of the closest bank and *ATM* machine though you can draw pesos at *Codatel* on your *Visa* card) and pick up a bus there that's headed to Puerto Plata. If headed to Santo Domingo, there is a daily bus available from Luperón, it leaves about 1330 and the trip takes about 7 hours. One final note: if you are planning on doing major provisioning, you should consider renting a van for the day; you won't be able to carry a lot on a *guagua*. Call José for van rentals (see the next paragraph).

In Luperón you can rent a car or motorcycle from José Virgilio Rodriquez, known around town as José Villo (bee-yo), of *José's Adventure Tours*. José is a very enterprising young man who can get you whatever you need, diesel, water, propane, and even act as your translator. I am told that I must mention that he is very handsome (okay all you ladies, don't knock on his door all at once). You can reach José on VHF ch. 68, or you can phone him on his cell phone at 458-9506, or at his home at 571-8624, or you can fax José at 571-8082. José is a government licensed tour guide (one must attend school for this) and *José's Adventure Tours* operates all over the Dominican Republic and features trips to Santo Domingo, the waterfalls, horseback riding, and shopping expeditions to Santiago. I cannot recommend a more valuable and trusted contact for you than José in Luperón. José is also in the process of opening up a *Casa de Cambio, House of Exchange* where you can change your dollars to pesos. As you approach town from the dinghy dock, the first house on the left is José's.

For car rentals you can also try *Odalis* (Pedro Odalis Cueto) on VHF ch. 68 or phone them at 223-3580, or you can speak to José, on VHF ch. 68. Now that you have your pesos, if you're like most cruisers you're ready to search out a place to eat. The typical Dominican meal consists of a meat, rice and beans, and plantains and can be had for about 75-90 pesos at the many *comedors* around town. As you walk around town you'll find many small shops selling notions, fruits, veggies, bottled water, roasted chicken, and all manner of goods. Every street has a place to eat and half the fun is discovering the best places. *Laisa's Pico de Pollo* is one of my favorites and may become one of yours as well.

A very popular spot is *Capt. Steve's Bar*, six blocks up from the dock. The ambiance is Mexican with food to go, *Wi-Fi*, motorcycles for rent, horse riding excursions, and many other activities. *Wendy's Bar* and *JR's Tropical Bistro* are both on the right as you enter town from the government dock. *Wendy's* has movie nights on Mondays and Tuesdays, *Karaoke* on Fridays, and all kinds of drink specials every day of the week. Wendy's is a gathering spot for the folks involved with the weekly gringos versus locals softball game. *JR's* has movie nights on Thursdays and Fridays, with trivia night on Wednesdays, and Tuesday is taco day. *JR's* is closed on Sundays and Mondays.

La Yola has a great atmosphere, cool breezes, and a two for one happy hour. The menu has reasonable prices for lunch and dinner and offers pizza with a good variety of toppings.

Now that you've filled your cruising tummy, you'll probably want to check out the shopping. But we'll discuss shopping in Luperón in a moment. First, let's start with some basic needs. There is a medical clinic in Luperón where two of the three doctors in residence speak passable English. The clinic is located at the end of *Calle Luperón*, two blocks south of *Verizon* and then three blocks southwest. While the clinic can deal with most basic health problems, for testing you will be referred to the *Laboratory Luperón*, just across from the *guagua park*. If you have your samples in before 1200 you can usually get the results by 1700. The prices are right here. A blood and fecal test is US$10 and the office visit is free. All the clinics are free to residents of the Dominican Republic and cruisers, but the more serious medical problems, such as those that require a visit or a stay at one of the hospitals in Puerto Plata or Santiago can cost quite a bit. Most medical insurance is accepted throughout the DR and drugs that can only be acquired by prescription in the US, are available without a prescription in the DR, and most are very inexpensive. It helps to know the Spanish translation of the drug when you head for the *pharmacia*. The folks at *Farmicia Danessa* on *Parque Central* are very knowledgeable and even have photo developing available.

If you need marine supplies visit *Banegra's*, located at *27 de Febrero*. Their supplies are limited but they do carry basics such as charts, filters, flags, and can even arrange canvas repairs. *Flaco* can also be counted on for sail and canvas repairs, they are located on *Calle Duarte*. *Calamity Canvas* is a cruiser owned business and owner Ron can handle your canvas repairs. Ron can be reached on VHF ch. 68 or by phone at 809-523-6987.

Persio Núñez at *Núñez & Núñez* in Santiago has a nice machine shop and rebuilds gasoline as well as diesel engines. His number is 809-522-8202, or 522-2200. There is a small welding shop on the right as you approach Luperón from the town dock. If you need a good refrigeration man, look up Mariano in town. For major diesel problems Mike is your best bet, and Santiago has almost anything you need to repair your engine.

Gasoline and diesel are usually both easily available at the gas station in town, though if Luperón is out, you may have to get a taxi to El Estrecho to visit the station there. You can haul your own jerry cans, but the gas station is on the road to Imbert, all the way on the other side of town, about a mile from the dinghy dock. You'll find several Dominicans hanging around the dock that will take your cans and fill them for you, usually for about a $.25 a gallon more. These very innovative young men will bring 55-gallon drums of fuel out to your boat and siphon the diesel into your tank. ALWAYS use a *Baja Filter* to clean any fuel going into your tanks when in the Dominican Republic.

It's usually easiest to call *Papo* on VHF ch. 68 and Papo will deliver fuel, water, propane, or anything else you need to your boat, Papo will make your life at anchor much easier. Another option is to hire a *motorconcho* for a few pesos. The only problem with that is that you must hang on to the bike and the gas cans while en route. Rafael or Handy Andy (VHF ch. 68) an also deliver fuel or water to your boat, as well as clean the bottom of your vessel.

If you need propane, the propane fill station is past the cockfight arena (a busy place on a Friday afternoon), just past the gas station. You'll notice it by the conspicuous white propane tank. The normal way to get propane is hire a *motorconcho* for a few pesos. Once again, if you need propane, you can call *Papo* on VHF ch. 68 for same day service.

There are several Internet cafes in town: *Claro, Codatel* (*Calle Duarte*), *Orange, Punto Internet, Independencia, Capt. Steve's Bar, JDMax*, and *Puerto Blanco Marina*. There is Wi-Fi in the anchorage for US$12 per week, US$30 per month, and plans for longer periods. Test the reception where you are anchored before signing up for a plan.

Independencia has mail service, and you can have your mail sent to you care of Anna Lopez's store, *Casa Lopez*, on the corner just up from *Verizon*. Make sure it is addressed to Ana Lopez, Casa Lopez, your boat name, #36 Calle Duarte, Luperón, Dominican

Republic. Ana is the *UPS* representative here and her phone number is 809-836-1042.

If you need your laundry done, there are laundry services at *Puerto Blanco Marina* and also at *Captain Steve's Bar*. Lydia also does laundry and she is located just up the street from the *Immigration* office.

Now let's talk about the shopping in Luperón. To begin with, the produce trucks that regularly run to the marina have some of the best deals. Listen for their call on VHF ch. 68. If they don't have what you want tell them and they'll bring it next time. As you walk around town you'll notice fruit and vegetable stands (and small gift shops) everywhere and everyone is willing to deal. You'll have no problem finding mangoes, avocados, cucumbers, tomatoes, yucca, plantains, potatoes, carrots, onions and large, fresh pineapples that go for about 10 pesos. Broccoli and lettuce are hard to find in Luperón. In town, the *Supermercado* will take special orders and deliver to the marina or town dock for free, and.. they speak English! *La Economica*, the local veggie market, has fresh produce delivered on Tuesdays and Fridays; selections depend on the season. Near the government dock in town is the *Able Mini Market* where you can pick up food, beer, rum, and soft drinks.

Cigar smokers will want to sample the DR's great cigars. Cigarette smokers will appreciate the fact that Dominican *Marlboros* are very inexpensive; I am told that they taste the same as U.S.-manufactured *Marlboros*. *Nacionals* are another great deal. Rum is cheap in the DR, and *Brugal* is one of the better rums to be found. For cheaper wines and spirits not available in Luperón, a trip to Puerto Plata is called for, especially a visit to the rum factory. Certain items such as bacon, cheese, broccoli, lettuce, powdered drinks (not milk), butter (not canned margarine), packaged meats, deli meats, cake mixes, canned cream, and yeast are difficult to find in Luperón. A once a month trip to Puerto Plata or Santiago will be all you need to stock up on these items if you are planning to stay a while.

We've all heard about the provisioning in Puerto Plata. You can also get anything you need in Santiago, though it is a bit farther away. The *ferreterías* and *supermercados* are literally brimming with all kinds of goodies for the cruiser with big eyes and pockets full of pesos. *La Sirena* (formerly *Pola*) and *Nacionale* are the two largest stores and are stocked like *Super*

Walmarts back in the states. You can have lunch there while you do your shopping; both have nice cafeterias. *Nacionale* even has a *Baskin Robbins* for those who crave their 53 flavors. One final note: it's cheaper to buy local brands whenever possible, especially locally manufactured toilet paper that goes for about a third of the cost of U.S. toilet paper. *Ochoa* is a huge hardware store in Santiago that carries almost anything you need.

If you like horseback riding you must visit *Mario's Ranch*. Mario will pick you up and take you on half day and full day horseback riding trips or you can contact José to set up a trip to Mario's.

West of Luperón, reachable by a new road, is the town of La Isabela. Here, on his second voyage to the New World in 1493, Columbus founded the first European town in the Americas with the first court and where the first Mass was said in the New World. Today, only the layout of the town is visible, but there is a small hotel by the ruins.

The *Dirección Nacional de Parques* is undertaking the restoration and excavation of La Isabela. To get to La Isabela from Puerto Plata you can either take a tour from Puerto Plata, or take a *carro público* from *Villanueva y Kundhard* in Puerto Plata to the village of La Isabela. To get to La Isabela from Luperón, either make local arrangements with a taxi, get a rental car, or travel to Puerto Plata to hook up with a tour group. Between La Isabela and Monte Cristi are the lovely beaches of Punta Rucia and Estero Honda.

Ocean World Marina

Marina - ½ nm NE of entrance:
19° 50.05' N, 70° 43.65' W

Approximately seven miles east of Luperón, and two miles west of Puerto Plata, is the entrance for a top notch, world class marina, *Ocean World Marina*, located at Cofresi.

Navigational Information

A waypoint at 19° 50.05' N, 70° 43.65' W, will place you approximately ½ mile northeast of the entrance channel into *Ocean World Marina* as shown on Chart DR-2 (you will see the yellow sea buoy located at 19° 50.095' N, 70° 43.535' W). The entrance channel offers no problems in normal to moderate weather however, in heavy northerly swells the entrance may break all the way across making entrance dangerous if not impossible. Once inside you will be as snug as

a bug in a rug, as long as you don't mind some surge when those northerly swells are running.

From the waypoint it's a straight shot down the channel keeping between the red and green buoys. Bear in mind that the marina frequently loses buoys during winter storms so the actual configuration you see may differ from what is on the chart in this guide. You can stray south of the green buoys and still be in nearly 20' of water all the way to the breakwater, but by no means stray outside the red buoy line which mark a shallow, breaking reef (*Palometa Reef* - you'll see it to starboard upon entry). Favor the green markers upon entry.

If you need assistance in entering the marina, give *Ocean World Marina* a hail on the VHF and the Dockmaster, Randall, will talk you in.

What You Will Find Ashore

The 35-acre *Ocean World Marina* complex is truly a class establishment with a very friendly and helpful staff. The marina has 104 slips and can accommodate vessels to 250' in length with drafts of just under 12'. If you need to clear in or clear out, *Customs* is located on-site and will come out to your boat to assist you in the process. The yard has a 35-ton lift.

In 2008, the government of the Dominican Republic passed a new law concerning the boarding of foreign vessels seeking clearance. At this time that law pertains only to vessels clearing in at marinas such as *Ocean World* or *Cap Cana*. The law states that only two officials may board your boat and they are not permitted to ask for "donations." It will be wonderful when the officials in Luperón will be required to abide by such regulations.

Also on-site you'll find a fuel dock, a pump-out station, quality electrical service (30-400 amp, single and three-phase), RO water at the dock, 24-hour security, personal concierge service, car rentals, mail and package delivery, weather and fax services in the marina office, the *Poseidon Restaurant*, the *Octopus Bar and Grill*, a pool with a swim-up bar, a laundry (dry-cleaning is available), Wi-Fi at your boat or internet access at the office, *Lighthouse Cocktail Lounge*, dockside telephone and cable TV, a casino, and by the time this guide is published there will also be a marine store (with fishing supplies) and a small grocery for you. There is a haul-out for small vessels and repair services as well. *Ocean World Marina* can be reached by phone at 809-970-3373, or

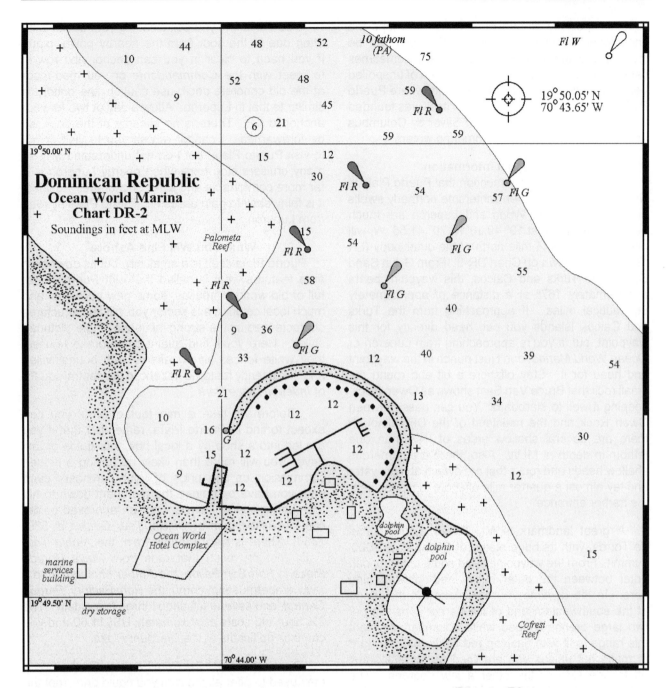

Dominican Republic
Ocean World Marina
Chart DR-2
Soundings in feet at MLW

you can contact them through their website at www. oceanworldmarina.com.

While staying at the marina you will receive complimentary admission to the *Ocean World Adventure Park* (http://www.oceanworld.net/) located next door. The park offers intimate dolphin, sea lion, and shark interaction programs; the dolphin habitat is the largest in the world with 12 million gallons of seawater in the main pool. There are several nearby restaurants to pique your culinary interests.

Puerto Plata

Puerto Plata - ¾ nm N of sea buoy:
19° 49.10' N, 70° 41.55' W

Puerto Plata, once the primary destination of cruisers southbound from the Turks and Caicos, is visited far less frequently today since Luperón has become a port of entry. Puerto Plata, with a population of about 60,000, is now primarily a commercial harbor and it shows. On land, Puerto Plata and almost the entire Atlantic coast of the DR is a very popular tourist haven, especially among Europeans. Perhaps the finest beaches in the Dominican Republic can be found along the superb Atlantic Coast, sometimes called the *Amber Coast*, a 75-mile strand of unspoiled beaches on the north side of the island, where Puerto Plata is the principal city. The town itself was founded in 1502 and was named *Port of Silver* by Columbus after being inspired by its shimmering waters.

Navigational Information

To begin with, let me mention that Puerto Plata is NOT a good harbor when wintertime northerly swells are running; *Ocean World* and Luperón are much better. A waypoint at 19° 49.10' N, 70° 41.55' W, will place you almost ½ mile north of the outer buoy (LR "2," Fl R) as shown on Chart DR-3. From Great Sand Cay in the Turks and Caicos, this waypoint bears approximately 167° at a distance of approximately 86 nautical miles. If approaching from the Turks and Caicos Islands you can head directly for this waypoint, but, if you're approaching from Luperón or *Ocean World Marina*, don't just punch in the waypoint and head for it. Stay offshore a bit and round the small rock that Bruce Van Sant shows as Owen Rock, keeping it well to starboard. You can pass between Owen Rock and the mainland of the DR, although there are several shallow areas of less than one fathom in depth at MLW. Also, there are numerous shallow heads and rocks that are awash at high water and lay almost a quarter mile offshore in places near the harbor entrance.

A great landmark is Mt. Torres, Loma Isabel de Torres, with its huge statue of Christ at its 2600' summit. From the waypoint, head south until you can enter between the outer buoys, red-right-returning here. In the daytime you can make out the range at the southwestern end of the harbor consisting of two large orange-capped white columns. At night this range is lit with flashing red lights that are hard to make out unless you are lined up correctly, just off to one side or the other a few degrees. The entry range is approximately 225° magnetic but the channel is deep, wide, and well-marked; but like all aids to navigation, they might not be there when you are. Don't stray east of the green markers, the water shallows rapidly in their area. The yacht anchorage area is shown on Chart DR-2 and lies just west of the large commercial dock. Expect a surge through here and a lot of roll from local traffic. The water can also be very sludge-like at times; once you leave Puerto Plata you might want to clean your waterline.

You'll also find yourself cleaning your decks quite often due to the soot from the nearby power plant. If you need to clear in you can anchor and row in to meet with the *Commandante* or you med-moor at the old concrete dock; use caution, the bottom is similar to that in Luperón. Allow a day or two for your anchor to set. There is no security at the dock, so be forewarned. I cannot advise you to visit or not to visit Puerto Plata, but I do not understand why so many cruisers stop here when nearby Luperón is a far more comfortable and safer anchorage. Besides, it is fairly easy to gain access to Puerto Plata by road from Luperón.

What You Will Find Ashore

Puerto Plata itself is a small city, but its downtown area features what is called the "old" Puerto Plata, full of old wooden houses, some new buildings, and much local color. In this sector you will find structures characterized by the strong influence of late Victorian styles. Here you'll find quaint gingerbread houses, their white fences simply aflame with bougainvillea and the recently restored gazebo in the central square of *Independence Park*.

Before we take a mini-tour of what you can expect to find in Puerto Plata, remember that if you are led into a shop by a local boy, tour guide or taxi driver, you will more than likely be paying a hidden commission on the price of your purchase, even after you have bargained the merchant down to his rock bottom price. If you want an approved guide, call the *Association of Official Tour Guides* at 586-2866. There is also a tourist train, the *Amber Tour Train* (not on rails!) that runs from *Playa Dorada Plaza* to *Fort San Felipe*, the *Amber Museum* (http://www.ambermuseum.com/), the *Rum Factory*, *Parque Central*, and several gift shops three times daily. The 2½ hour trip costs approximately US$11.50 and you can pick up tickets at the *Discount Plaza*.

By all means visit the *Rum Factory*. On their tours they used to offer all the rum you could drink (not the same today), and they used to have only three rules for those who partook of these tours. One, you had to wear a shirt. Two, you had to wear shoes. And three, you could not fall asleep while on the tour! If it's a hot day and ice cream sounds like a good idea, make your way to *Parque Central* and visit *Mariscos* for real Italian ice cream! In the center of town you can find the *Amber Museum* (*Duarte St.*) with some of the most remarkable specimens of this gemstone, the designated national gem. On an adjacent street you'll find the *House of Larimar* where you can have *Larimar*

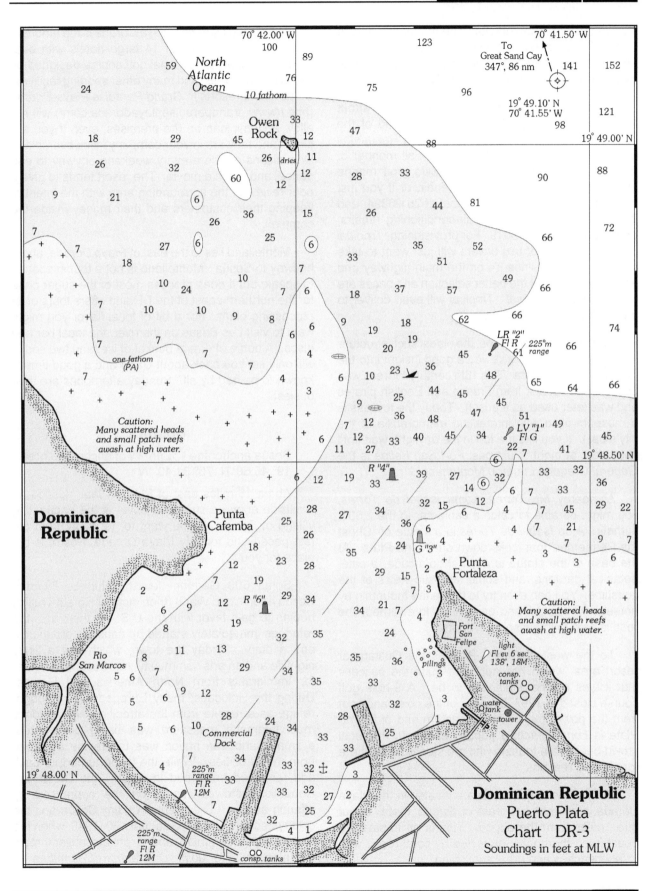

North Atlantic Ocean

Owen Rock

dries

10 fathom

one fathom (PA)

Caution:
Many scattered heads
and small patch reefs
awash at high water.

To Great Sand Cay
347°, 86 nm

141

19° 49.10' N
70° 41.55' W

19° 49.00' N

LR "2"
Fl R   225°m range

LV "1"
Fl G

R "4"

Dominican Republic

Punta Cafemba

19° 48.50' N

G "3"

Punta Fortaleza

Caution:
Many scattered heads
and small patch reefs
awash at high water.

Fort San Felipe

pilings

light
Fl ev 6 sec.
138', 18M

consp. tanks

water tank
tower

R "6"

Rio San Marcos

Commercial Dock

19° 48.00' N

225°m range
Fl R 12M

225°m range
Fl R 12M

consp. tanks

Dominican Republic
Puerto Plata
Chart   DR-3
Soundings in feet at MLW

jewelry custom made on-site. The mountains behind Puerto Plata contain the world's richest deposits of amber, a fossilized tree resin. Parts of these same mountains appeared in the movie *Jurassic Park*.

If you need marine supplies, just across the street from the haul out yard at the southern end of the harbor, west of the town dock, you'll find *Repuestos Maritimos*, 586-4728, a good stop for all manner of marine related goodies, fishing tackle, and marine electronics. If you need diesel repair, or if you just need parts, call *Laboratorio Diesel* at 261-6394, and if you need refrigeration or air-conditioning repairs, phone *Zelltec* at 533-5019. For provisioning, *Tropical* is the best. A lot of taxi drivers will just want to take you to *José Luis* since it's on the main highway and easier to get to, but the better selection and prices are to be found at *Tropical*. *Tropical* will even deliver to the dock or a house for you.

A visit to *Fort San Felipe*, the oldest such structure in the New World will give you a good insight into the history of Puerto Plata. This 16th century fortress was built to resist attack from French and English pirates and was later used as a prison. Today the fortress is a museum filled with interesting memorabilia of the city's past. If you like the fort in the daylight, wait until you see it at night. Just past *Fort San Felipe* is the *General Gregorio Luperón Monument*.

At nearby *Mt. Torres, Loma Isabel de Torres*, you might be able to catch a cable car to the 2,600' summit. Atop *Isabel de Torres* is a statue of "Christ the Redeemer" that looks down on Puerto Plata. At the base of the statue is a gift shop/arcade, a café, botanical gardens, and some fantastic views of the coastline. You can even try to tackle the mountain by horseback, bicycle, and car but be forewarned: the road is next to impassable in spots.

To the west of Puerto Plata is the Costambar resort area, which has not been quite the success that it was originally planned to be. A 9-hole golf course closed in 1997, because of the noise and soot from the power plant. At the eastern end of Puerto Plata is *Long Beach*, a popular spot with the local crowd but not the tourists who are steered elsewhere for obvious reasons.

Most of the major hotels are located in the Playa Dorada area that lies east of Puerto Plata, about three miles from the airport. This is an impressive beachfront, thoroughly protected by coral reefs, with lovely beaches and great snorkeling.

The *Grand Paradise Playa Dorada* is the umbrella name for the complex of 14 large hotels with over 3,300 rooms, an exceptional golf course designed by Robert Trent Jones, and many other sporting facilities. Some of the resorts in *Grand Paradise Playa Dorada* (http://www.grandparadiseplayadorada.com/) will not allow a Dominican on the premises, even if you are single and they are in your company. However, many Dominicans go there every weekend anyway to eat, dance, and catch a movie. The resort tends to give a poor review of the surrounding area with the intent of keeping their customers and their money inside the complex.

Montellano lies to the east of *Playa Dorada*, about halfway to Sosúa. Montellano is not a tourist spot so to speak, but it does process most of the sugar cane for the northern coast of the DR and offers tours of its processing plant. For a bit of local flavor you might want to visit Las Brisas on the river, the local bar and disco. A bottle of rum, a bucket of ice, and two sodas will only set you back about US$4 and a good time is known to be had by all. Sunday afternoons are their busiest.

Sosúa

Sosúa anchorage - ¼ nm W of anchorage area
19° 45.60' N, 70° 31.40' W

About 16 miles east of Puerto Plata, nestled on a hillside above a sheltered cove, is the enchanting village of Sosúa. If you want to get away from the fast paced and touristy Playa Dorada, Sosúa is the place for you.

Some 600 German Jewish refugees founded Sosúa after World War II (then dictator Rafael Trujillo, hoping to gain favor with the U.S., let them in). the refugees immediately started up sausage production and a dairy. Today the town, which has a lively nightlife and an arts community, has become a center for immigrants from North America and Europe. During the Holocaust many European Jews sought refuge as a respite from the atrocities. As history's most infamous massacre was being perpetrated, a small Caribbean nation was to provide a respite from the atrocities. While the world turned its back and remained immersed in apathy, the Dominican Republic bestowed mercy on the oppressed by offering asylum. They settled on tiny Sosúa and the colony became official on January 30, 1940, when the Dominican government and a private philanthropic organization, the *Joint Distribution Committee of*

New York, signed the DORSA (Dominican Republic Settlement Association) agreement and some 600 settlers moved in.

The atmosphere of warm hospitality found in this beautiful yet unfamiliar land was conducive to the flourishing of Jewish-owned businesses. So cordial were the locals that, over the years, the Jews assimilated their culture and co-mingled with them to create genuinely Dominican families where the Jewish traditions were still preserved and respected. What is most remarkable is the fact that after five decades, and despite the changes of government, the passing of generations and the advent of tourism, the spirit of the decree whereby the Jewish were given political asylum has remained untouched. Today, the few remaining Jews enjoy the same consideration, respect and freedom of religion as in the first days of the colony.

Navigational Information

As shown on Chart DR-4, a waypoint at 19° 45.60' N, 70° 31.40' W, will place you approximately ¼ nm W of the anchorage area outside the reef. Do not venture too close to shore as reef and rocks abound and the water shallows quickly.

The area is a national park and anchoring is not permitted. Local officials will approach your boat upon arrival and direct you to pick up a mooring.

What You Will Find Ashore

Sosúa is actually three villages straddling the bay: Los Charamicos to the south and El Batey to the north. They are not far apart and a walk through and between the two doesn't take long. Los Charamicos, where years ago the plantation workers lived, has a typical Dominican village atmosphere complete with lively restaurants and bars, street vendors, loud music, and screeching chickens.

El Batey, the part of town where the plantation owners lived, is the hub of tourist activity in Sosúa. Here you'll find upscale restaurants, bars, boutiques, and luxurious resort hotels (over 2,000 hotel rooms) and villas along with a large ex-pat community. Sosúa is popular with tourists from both North America and Europe because of its lovely beaches and dive sites. You can even take a taxi from Puerto Plata, it's only 4 miles for the airport in Puerto Plata.

If you need to exchange some money in Sosúa, your best bet is an ATM or you can visit Western Union (in El Batey), Playero, or Caribe Express, and Banco Santo Cruz.

If you need internet access, several hotels and restaurants (Britannia, Alberto`s, Bailey`s, Cubanos (http://sosuacigars.com/index.html), Bar Central, Cafe Tropical and many others) can accommodate you.

For good dining try Bailey's, the Brittannia Pub and Grill (a favorite of ex-pats, http://www.britanniapubsosua.com/), Germania Sosúa (for German fare, http://www.germania-sosua.com/), or the Waterfront Restaurant for great ocean views. Le Papillon (http://www.lepapillon-puertoplata.com/) offers tons of rustic and nautical ambiance as well as several aquariums. There are numerous fine restaurants in El Batey and finding the one that interests you the most is part of the fun of exploring the area.

A unique spot to visit is Castillo Mundo King, atop a hill with a view that is worth all the effort to get there. The castillo itself is filled with Dominican and Haitian art as well as UFO themes, an eclectic collection gathered by artist in residence Rolf Schulz (http://castillodelmundo.webs.com/).

Just east of Sosúa is Cabarete, one of the world's top windsurfing/kitesurfing spots. In the mid-1980's Cabarete was only an empty beach and a handful of old wooden houses. Then it was discovered to be the best windsurfing location in the Caribbean, and one of the best in the world. Today Cabarete hosts the annual Windsurfing World Cup.

For music lovers, Cabarete also hosts the Jazz-Blues Merengue Festival. On its mile-long main street, you will find a wide selection of windsurfing centers, hotels, restaurants, discos, and gift shops. Further east you'll find even more exotic, secluded beaches such as La Preciosa and Diamante.

Rio San Juan

Rio San Juan - ¼ nm W of anchorage area
19° 38.60' N, 70° 05.50' W

Rio San Juan is a good spot to overnight as you move east or west along the northern shore of the Dominican Republic. Never attempt to anchor here with winds or seas with any northerly component to them.

Navigational Information

As shown on Chart DR-5, a waypoint at 19° 38.60' N, 70° 50.50' W, will place you approximately ¼ nm W of anchorage area off the town amidst all

Castillo Mundo King, Sosúa

Sosúa

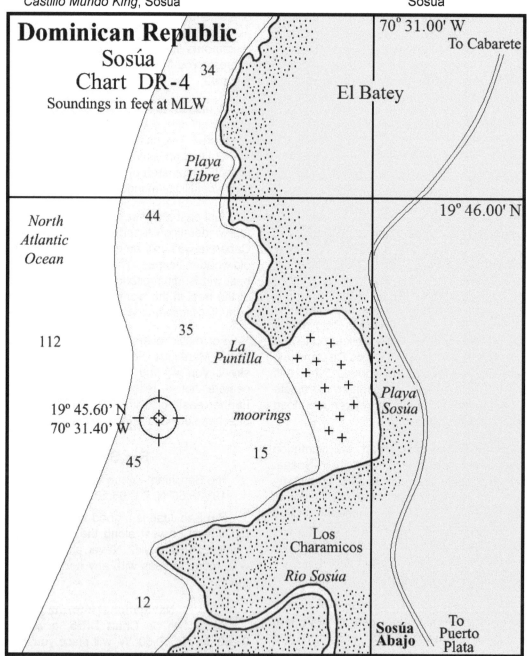

Dominican Republic
Sosúa
Chart DR-4
Soundings in feet at MLW

70° 31.00' W
To Cabarete

El Batey

34

Playa Libre

North Atlantic Ocean

44

19° 46.00' N

35

112

La Puntilla

Playa Sosúa

19° 45.60' N
70° 31.40' W

moorings

45

15

Los Charamicos

Rio Sosúa

12

Sosúa Abajo

To Puerto Plata

the local fishing boats. From the way point, work your way through the shoals (never try this at night) until you can turn south to anchor. Look for a sandy spot to drop your hook. South of here are numerous sandbars that are to be avoided.

Another anchorage is to the north and does not involve threading the needle through shoals; this spot is much better if you plan to leave at night. The bottom here is hard sand and rock.

What You Will Find Ashore
Rio San Juan has numerous hotels, restaurants, and small grocery stores. *Wi-Fi* is available at most hotels; many hotels have computers you can use.

There is no shortage of quality eateries, my favorite is *Arena Y Sol*, right on the beach, featuring fresh seafood from the nearby market. *Cheo's Café* features a local flavor to their cuisine and a good bet is their huge platter of grilled seafood for two. The *Café de Paris* features international cuisine, primarily French, and fresh seafood. For Spanish flavored dining visit *Corral del Pollo* and after dinner sidle up

to their coffee and cigar bar. The *Villa Belia Hotel* has an excellent restaurant and nearby *La Casona* features deep-fried pizza empanadas (http://www.villabelia.com/).

Located atop beautiful cliffs along the edge of the sea near Rio San Juan, the par 72 *Playa Grande Golf Course* (http://www.playagrande.com) is the last course designed by the legendary Robert Trent Jones Sr.

Puerto El Valle

(Escondido)
Puerto El Valle - 1¾ nm NNW of anchorage
19° 19.00' N, 69° 20.50' W

Moving east along the northern coast of the Dominican Republic, a good stop before rounding Cabo Samaná to head to Puerto Rico or to visit Santa Bárbara de Samaná, is the anchorage at Puerto El Valle. This anchorage is best in settled weather as some swell works its way into the bay making an

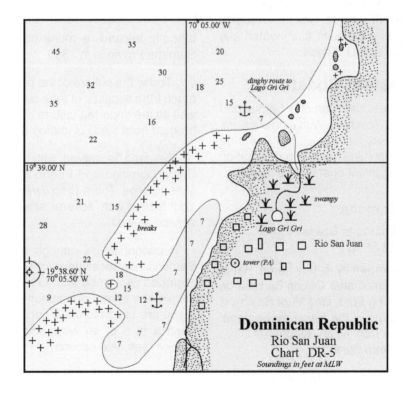

overnight stay uncomfortable. Never try to anchor here if seas from any northerly direction are forecast.

As Bruce Van Sant reports in his excellent work, *Passages South*, Puerto El Valle was reported as Escondido, or Puerto Escondido, on surveys by the *USS Eagle* in 1905-1906. Today, on most charts, it is shown as El Valle or Puerto El Valle, and we shall use that name here, but if you hear it called Escondido you will know that they are one and the same.

Navigational Information

As shown on Chart DR-6, a waypoint at 19° 19.00' N, 69° 20.50' W, will place you approximately 1¾ nm NNW of the anchorage area off *Playa El Valle*. From the waypoint head in a general SSE direction to anchor in the lee of the mountains just off the beach (*Playa el Valle*).

What You Will Find Ashore

Most folks don't come ashore at Puerto El Valle, cruisers tend to use the anchorage more for just an overnight layover, but those that do come ashore can enjoy *Claritzas Bar and Grill*.

Climbers and hikers will love the many mountains that are waiting on them, all with great views of the anchorage and the *North Atlantic Ocean*. Roughly two miles NE of town is a pleasant fresh-water lake that is worth a visit, *La Laguna Salada*.

The Eastern Coast

By far, most cruisers visit Samaná before and after crossing the *Mona Passage*. With a new marina to enjoy, and *Los Haitises* just across the *Bahía de Samaná*, the area is becoming more of a destination than a place for clearing in/out or staging a crossing.

Samaná

Samaná - ¼ nm S of Punta Gorda
19° 11.40' N, 69° 18.85' W

Samaná, or as it is known by its true name, Santa Bárbara de Samaná (named after Queen Bárbara de Braganza, the wife of King Ferdinand VI of Spain), is located on the north shore of the *Bahía de Samaná*, south of the NE tip of the Dominican Republic at Cabo Samaná and west of Punta Balandra.

Samaná was founded in 1756 and Canary Islanders were brought across the *Atlantic Ocean* to live here. Originally created as a Maritime District (similar to a Province), Santa Bárbara de Samaná

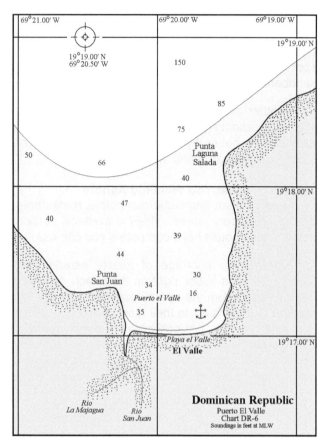

officially became a municipality and the capital of Samaná Province in 1865.

Today the culture of the people of Samaná draws much from aspects of their own ancestor's slavery as well as the imported culture of freed slaves that were brought from the U.S. during the Haitian occupation.

Samaná is served with daily bus service from Santo Domingo and Puerto Plata by two major bus lines, *Caribe Tours* (http://www.caribetours.com.do/) and *Metro*, with several smaller bus lines offering service as well.

I cannot stress enough the bad reputation that Samaná has received over the last few years. It is regarded as a good spot to have your dinghy stolen, so take the proper precautions when anchored there. If you are uncomfortable anchoring in Samaná, then head a mile or so west and stay at *Puerto Bahía Marina* (see next section).

Navigational Information

As shown on Chart DR-7, a waypoint at 19° 11.40' N, 69° 18.85' W, will place you approximately ¼ nm S of Punta Gorda in the *Bahía de Samaná*.

From the waypoint, head generally NW, working your way between the mainland to the north (to starboard side as you approach) and the string of islands (Cayo Paloma and Cayo Vigia) to port (avoiding the shoals and rocks close in). You can anchor off the town or off the northern shore of Cayo Vigia. The holding is good in the main anchorage, there is little current, and moorings abound (but there is still room to anchor). It is possible to anchor in *Bahía Escondida* but it is not recommended in prevailing winds as it affords little protection

When you clear in you will likely be asked to pay US$.70 per foot anchoring fee by the Department of Ports. This is a valid charge and is actually a dock usage fee that some folks decline to pay.

What You Will Find Ashore
There are two main government docks in town where you can tie up your dinghy (out of the way of the commercial operators please) but don't tile up to the smaller cruise ship tender dock to the east.

If you need Internet access, most of the hotels and many restaurants offer free *Wi-Fi*, and there are a few small Internet cafes in town. If you have a good *Wi-Fi* antenna you should be able to pick up *Wi-Fi* in the anchorage. Also in town is a hardware store, an

ice house, and the only watch repair service in this part of the Dominican Republic.

If you need groceries, the large and modern *Mimasa* supermarket is the place to go. It is located across the street from the *Scotia Bank* and is air-conditioned! Samaná also has a great farmer's market, *mercado*, in the center of town by the traffic light on the main road. This is the place for fresh produce, while at the rear of the market's central building you can pick up fresh seafood. You'll also find small butcher shops and all sorts of stalls selling everything from gifts to saddles.

If you find yourself in need of a pharmacy, visit *Pharmacy Giselle*, or the new pharmacy, *Carol Pharmacia* (809-562-6767), they deliver to *Puerto Bahía Marina*.

There are four main banks in town, *Scotia Bank*, *Banco Popular*, *Banco BHD*, and *Banco de Reserva*, and all are open Monday through Friday from 0900-1700, and on Saturdays from 0900-1200. All of the banks have ATMs that are open 24 hours (one is located just across the street from the government dock.

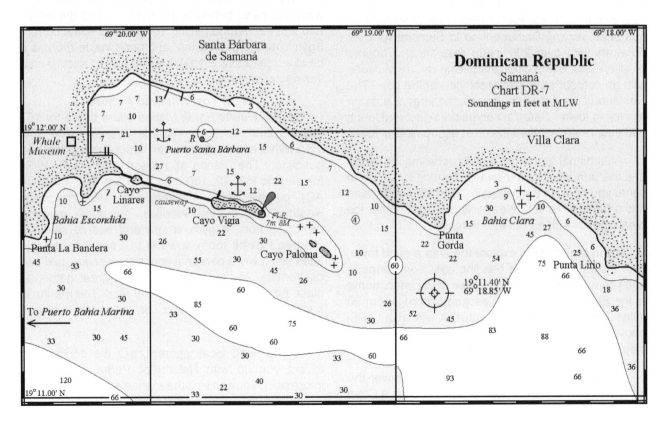

The most iconic sites in Samaná are *Los Puentes*, the famous *Bridges to Nowhere* that lead from the mainland to Cayo Vigía. The bridges, constructed in the 1960s, were intended to bring visitors to a casino complex that never materialized. In the 1980s, a restaurant opened for a few years but today little remains of that structure. Today however, the area is a boon for hikers and bikers with park benches and rest areas spread along its length.

Samaná is a popular spot for tourist excursions to observe humpback whales during their annual winter migration to the nearby waters. *Whale Samaná's* Kim Beddall runs whale watching tours from mid-January until late March aboard the *Pura Mia* from the dock in Samaná. For more information call Judy at 809-538-2494 or visit their website at http://www.whalesamana.com/.

On the western shore of the bay you will find the *Centro de la Naturaleza*, the *Whale Museum and Nature Center* (open Monday through Saturday from 0900-1400). Also nearby are zip line concessions and a group that will take you to swim with sea lions in the bay (http://samanazipline.com/).

If you are interested in dining in town, the following restaurants offer free *Wi-Fi* to their patrons. *Le Royal Snack* has a great view of the water as well as good food and a complete bar! *Chino Hotel & Restaurant* has been serving Chinese food in Samaná for over 30 years with over 200 menu selections. *Taberna Mediterranea* offers Spanish cuisine on the Malecón with an outdoor patio and great view of the bay. The *Restaurant La Antorcha* boasts the largest outdoor terrace in town. *Cafesito* serves breakfast and lunch and their breakfasts are the most economical in town.

After dinner you might wish to get some ice cream and the *Bon Ice Cream Parlor & Terrace* is hoping to serve you right on the *Malecón*. *Bon Ice Cream* also has a full service bar. Nearby is *Splash*, another ice cream parlor with an outdoor terrace.

If you are ready to explore the area around town, take the *El Portillo* road heading east from Samaná and you will soon come to the town of El Limon, home to the *El Limon Waterfall (Cascada Limon)*, about 20 miles from Samaná. The waterfall sits about 900' above sea level and drops over 120' into the crystal clear waters of a swimmable pool.

For those of you who are itching to discover the waters around Samaná, a good place to start is Cayo Levantado, approximately four miles SE of Samaná, where you can anchor for the day (no overnight anchoring is permitted here), dine ashore, enjoy the beach, and shop for local crafts. The island is popular with cruise ships so don't be surprised to see one in the nearby waters. At the eastern end of the island is the *Gran Bahía Hotel* and their restaurant is not open to cruisers, guests only.

Puerto Bahía Marina

Puerto Bahía Marina - ¼ nm SW of entrance
19° 11.40' N, 69° 21.40' W

Lying just to the west of Samaná is the well-protected *Puerto Bahía Marina*, a full service facility that is an excellent place for a layover before or after crossing the *Mona Passage* between Puerto Rico and the Dominican Republic. The marina is a *Port of Entry*, be sure to notify the marina by VHF (the marina monitors ch. 16) before entering and alert them that you will require clearance. If I were arriving and needed to clear, I would rather do it at the marina than anchoring in Samaná and clearing in town.

Navigational Information
As shown on Chart DR-8, a waypoint at 19° 11.40' N, 69° 21.40' W, will place you approximately ¼ nm SW of the marked entrance channel. From this waypoint head between the markers and the jetties and into the marina basin. You'll notice some current upon entering the marina, and once inside there is a bit of surge (and a 3' tidal rise and fall) so secure your vessel accordingly.

What You Will Find Ashore
Marina Puerto Bahía Marina offers space for 107 vessels and can accommodate vessels up to 150' LOA with drafts to 10', and can supply both diesel and gasoline. The marina and resort also offers *Wi-Fi*, full electric (30, 50, 100 amp, and 3-phase, 60 cycle AC), potable water, showers and restrooms, daily weather info, marine supplies, groceries, garbage pickup, a pool, a gym, a spa and beauty salon, a children's game room, a water taxi service, free taxi rides into town, a personal concierge service, taxi and car rentals, 24-hour security, and a great gathering place for fine dining, the *Cafe del Mar*. The marina is happy to assist guests with *Customs* and *Immigration* clearance.

If you need local laborers, ask the dockmaster to set you up with Nelson or Pedro. For more information you can visit the marina's website at *www.*

PuertoBahiaSamaná.com or telephone the marina at 809-503-6363.

Between the mountains and the marina sits the *Bannister Hotel* (http://www.thebannisterhotel.com/) featuring fine suites and equally impressive service for their patrons. The hotel is named after a British captain, Jack Bannister, who fought on nearby Cayo Levantado. The hotel offers free Wi-Fi and iPod docking stations in each room.

Bahía de San Lorenzo

Bahía de San Lorenzo - ¼ nm W of Punta Arena
19º 05.50' N, 69º 29.00' W

The most exciting locale awaiting your exploration is along the southern shore of *Bahía de Samaná*, approximately 12 miles SW of Samaná and *Puerto Bahía Marina*, the *Bahía de San Lorenzo*, the highlight of *Parque Nacional de los Haitises*, or simply, *Los Haitises*. You can take your own boat to the park or join a tour leaving from the dock in Samaná.

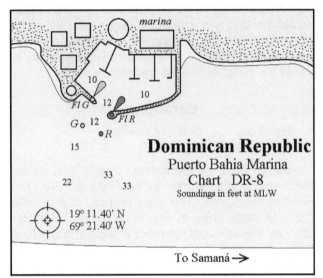

Mangrove creek, *Los Haitises*

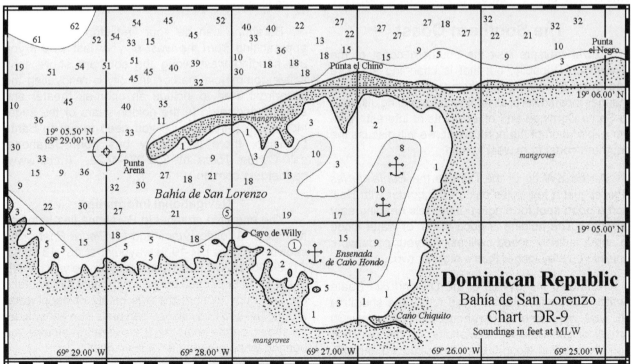

Navigational Information

As shown on Chart DR-9, a waypoint at 19º 05.50' N, 69º 29.00' W, will place you approximately ¼ nm W of Punta Arena. From the waypoint, head south and then east, passing south of the Punta Arena peninsula, working your way eastward to anchor where your draft allows in the lee of the mangroves. The bottom is mud but the holding is good.

What You Will Find Ashore

This national park covers 1600 square kilometers (only part of which is open to the public) in the SW corner of the *Bahía de Samaná* but the most popular area is the *Bahía de San Lorenzo,* consisting of 58 islands and numerous breathtaking, winding, mangrove-lined waterways.

Los Haitises is home to one of the most precious rainforests and mangrove reserves in the Caribbean. The term *Haitis* means highland in the Taino language but even though Tainos were known to have inhabited this region, the petroglyphs in some of the caves are thought to predate the Tainos.

Park officials may or may not come to your boat to collect a US$3.00 per person fee. If you avail yourself of the park dock, the officials there will collect the fee from you. The mangrove creeks and rivers will soon reveal their treasures to you as you take the time to explore; up these creeks you will find everything from small restaurants and bars to pre-Columbian cave art.

The Southern Coast

Fewer cruisers visit the southern coast of the Dominican Republic, but that is changing as more and more skippers are learning of the comfortable marinas located here, all within easy traveling distance to Santo Domingo and other points of interest. Like our exploration of the north coast, we will discuss the southern coast from west to east.

At the SW tip of the DR lies the *Bahía de las Aguilas* just a few miles east of the border with Haiti and a good spot for staging of vessels heading east or west. The holding is good in 15' of water close in and it is likely nobody will ask for your paperwork unless you stay longer than a night or two.

Rounding the SW tip of the DR and Isla Beata (watch out for fish traps), if you follow the shoreline NE you will come to Barahona, approximately 30 nm W of Las Salinas. Depending on the direction you are heading along the southern coast of the DR,

Barahona will be the first port of entry where cruisers can clear in, or the last port of entry for you to clear out.

A word of warning about the rivers of the Dominican Republic that meet the sea along this coast. While they may offer shelter for a hurricane, the trade-off here is that with the torrential rains that come with a hurricane or tropical storm, the rivers can become a place you won't want to be when the river rises by several feet and the current multiplies.

Vessels transiting the eastern coast of the DR from the *Bahía de Samaná* to the southern coast must remember they are cruising a dangerous lee shore with many reefs and shoals. Give the eastern shore a wide berth. Watch your weather windows and try to transit the coast before the tradewinds build.

Barahona

Barahona - ¼ nm NE of sea buoy
18º 13.30' N, 71º 04.00' W

Santa Cruz de Barahona, usually just called Barahona, is also known as *La Perla del Sur, The Pearl of the South*. This busy port city is a favorite place to stage trips to nearby eco-tourists haunts such as the *Jaragua-Bahoruco-Enriquillo Biosphere Reserve*, a UNESCO site, or *Lake Enriquillo*, one of the few saltwater lakes in the world inhabited by crocodiles.

Barahona can be your first stop in the DR if approaching from the west or your last stop if you are heading west along the southern shore. An active commercial harbor, the city is renovating the waterfront area to include an open-air theater and exhibits dedicated to the golden years of the sugar industry in Barahona. If you need to get to Santo Domingo, there is a daily bus from Barahona, call *Caribe Tours* at 809-221-4422 (http://www.caribetours.com.do/).

Navigational Information

The entrance channel to Barahona lies between two reefs, *Arrecife Yunca* and *La Piedra Prieta*. As shown on Chart DR-10, a waypoint at 18º 13.30' N, 71º 04.00' W, will place you approximately ¼ nm NE of the lit (Fl G 3s) sea buoy. From the waypoint take the sea buoy to port; there is plenty of deep water around the sea buoy so you can pass it on either side. As shown on the chart there is a lit range ashore, the bearing when entering is 243º magnetic.

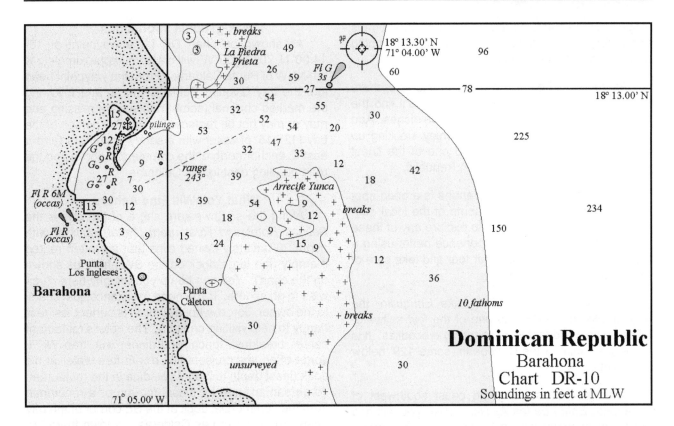

There is a protected anchorage in the small cove just past the *Club Nautico* docks as shown on the chart. Just follow the buoys into the anchorage area north of the town dock; use caution in poor visibility, the markers are red and green pillar buoys and unlit. Anchor in the NE corner of the cove, the holding is fair to good in a mud bottom. On the northern shore of the cove is a power plant and it is well-lit at night. The dock on the western shore is for coal vessels so do not anchor as to block access to it.

I don't recommend it, but you can tie up to the commercial dock (*muelle*) to the south but there is a charge for this, you will have to pay for 24 hours even if you only stay a fraction of that time. One good thing about the *muelle* is that the road at the end of the dock leads directly into town.

What You Will Find Ashore

Although the harbor at Barahona is commercial, there are still some amenities here for cruisers. If you need to clear in or out of the Dominican Republic it is easy enough to do here, but be forewarned that several cruisers have complained about officials overcharging for their services. The *Marina de Guerra* has an office located at the town dock, this is where you go to get your *despacho* to continue east or to leave the country if you are heading west. *Immigration* is located a few yards away from the *Marina de Guerra* office. The officials will usually come to your boat shortly after your arrival so you shouldn't have to go into town to look them up.

You can tie your dinghy to the town dock (high dock) or you can ask to use the dock at *Club Nautico* (US$10 per day, it's easier to deal with and much safer than the town dock). If you need fuel you will have to jerry-jug it in a taxi. A good idea is to ask for Fernando at *Club Nautico*; Fernando can act as your guide, or representative in finding fuel, and can arrange any transportation you may require.

If you need Internet access there is no Wi-Fi available but there is an Internet cafe in town. There are two banks in Barahona, the largest, *Banco Popular,* has an ATM. There are also two hardware stores in town as well as two churches located near the city park (*parque central*).

Barahona is a pretty good place for provisioning. The town offers two large supermarkets, *Jacobo* on the corner of *Calle Anaconda* and *Padre Ballini* and the other one just off the park. Barahona has a large fresh produce market where you can find all manner of locally made crafts, furniture, and produce (especially the plantains and coffee that Barahona is known for). If you want a quick snack while shopping there are plenty of hot food vendors.

As you would expect in a city of this size, there are many, many places to dine, and you'll find the local favorites are often seafood and rice dishes. And if you are a coffee lover, you will enjoy stocking up with Barahona coffee, considered one of the finest gourmet coffees of the Dominican Republic.

As I mentioned earlier, Barahona is a good spot to begin your explorations of some of the local eco-tourism hotspots. If you wish to explore any of these spots you might enjoy the experience better using a local travel agent to set up your tour and take care of the transportation and security.

The most popular site is *Lake Enriquillo*, the largest lake in the DR and one of the few saltwater lakes in the world that is inhabited by crocodiles. It is the lowest point in the Caribbean, some 129' below sea level.

Another spot is along the coast southwest of Barahona, *Bahía de las Aguilas*. Here you will find crystal clear water with a backdrop of lush, green mountains. Here you will not find a hotel. Here you will not find a restaurant. You will however, probably find turtles here, in the *Jaragua-Bahoruco-Enriquillo Biosphere Reserve* one of *UNESCO's World Network of Biosphere Reserves*.

Las Salinas

Las Salinas - ½ nm NNW of Punta Calderas
18° 14.00' N,   70° 33.00' W

On the southern shore of *Bahía de Calderas*, Las Salinas de Bani is set amid sandy beaches and mountain views with a working salt pond on the western peninsula.

Although there are officials here to clear you in and out, the authorities generally clear you for national transport, ie: for those traveling along the coast of the Dominican Republic. Once in a while you will find an official who doesn't mind clearing you in or out for international travel, but international clearance is much easier at Barahona (warning, see previous section), approximately 28 nm to the west, or at Boca Chica to the east. There is not an *Immigration* office in Las Salinas.

Navigational Information

As shown on chart DR-11, a waypoint at 18° 14.00' N, 70° 33.00' W, will place you approximately ½ nm NNW of Punta Calderas. From the waypoint head into the bay favoring Punta Calderas and following the marked channel (some markers are missing and may or may not be replaced) to the SW portion of the bay (12' -15' of water with a sandy bottom) or further east to anchor north of the commercial docks and the road heading east to Las Calderas.

What You Will Find Ashore

Along the southwestern shore of the bay is the *Salinas Hotel and Restaurant (Hotel Salinas)* with about 20 privately owned slips that are often rented if empty (the large dock on the SW shore as shown on the chart). You can tie up your dinghy here if you wish to go ashore. If you need assistance, just speak to the owner, Jorge, whose English is perfect, as he is happy to help visiting cruisers. The hotel's restaurant serves breakfast, lunch, and dinner with free Wi-Fi. Jorge often lets cruisers fill up with free water at his dock (least depth is 7.5') if you dine in the restaurant. Jorge can arrange for diesel for you or a repairman from the commercial dock at the SE corner of the bay nearer the town of Las Calderas. In town there are a few small bodegas and eateries as well as fresh produce.

Approximately 23 nm east of Las Salinas, is a small anchorage in the lee of a reef at Punta Palenque. The anchorage is best when winds are from the NE through the E. Anchor as far north as possible to avail yourself of the protection the reef affords. I cannot recommend Punta Palenque as an overnight anchorage, as cruisers are not quite welcome here and officials may visit you and deny permission for an overnight stay, even if you insist you are merely taking a rest stop. However, the local fishermen appreciate cruisers and will love to sell you part of their catch.

Puerto de Haina

Puerto de Haina - ¼ nm S of entrance channel
18° 24.60' N, 70° 01.05' W

Only about 7 nm SW of Santo Domingo is the entrance to Puerto de Haina, a large and busy commercial port situated on the *Rio Haina*. The area is known for crime and the only reason I mention it here is due to the marina and boatyard located just upriver. Do not consider this area a recommended

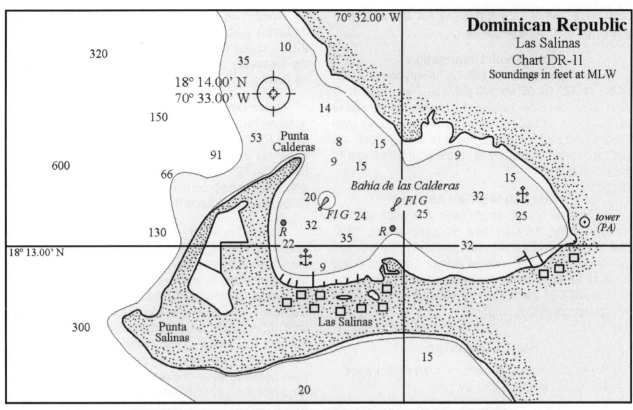

Dominican Republic
Las Salinas
Chart DR-11
Soundings in feet at MLW

70° 32.00' W

320

10

35

18° 14.00' N
70° 33.00' W

14

150

53   Punta
      Calderas

91

8   15

600

9   15

66

15

Bahía de las Calderas

20   *Fl G*   *Fl G*   32

Fl G 24   25   25

R

130   32   R

18° 13.00' N

22   35   32

9

tower
(PA)

300   Punta
       Salinas

Las Salinas

15

20

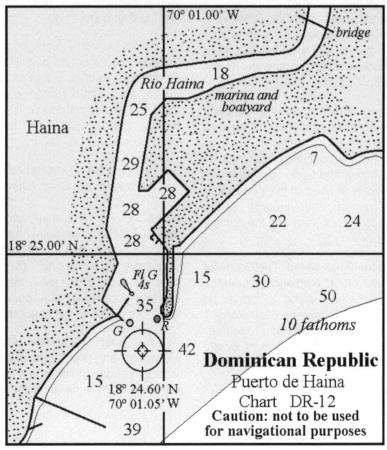

70° 01.00' W

bridge

18

Rio Haina

25   *marina and
      boatyard*

Haina

29   7

28

28   22   24

18° 25.00' N   28

*Fl G
4s*   15   30

35   50

G   R   *10 fathoms*

42   **Dominican Republic**
     Puerto de Haina
15   18° 24.60' N   Chart   DR-12
     70° 01.05' W   **Caution: not to be used
39   for navigational purposes**

anchorage, rather view it (the marina and boatyard) as an option in an emergency.

Navigational Information

As shown on Chart DR-12, a waypoint at 18° 24.60' N, 70° 01.05' W, will place you approximately ¼ nm S of entrance channel. From the waypoint pass between the jetties and head up river, staying mid-channel, and after the river turns to the east you will see the marina to starboard on the southern shore of the *Rio Haina*.

What You Will Find Ashore

As shown on the chart, here you will find *Club Nautico Haina*, on *Carretera Sánchez* at Km. 13½. The marina is popular with the local sportfishing crowd but the attraction for cruisers is their *TravelLift* in the event of an emergency haulout. You can phone the yard at 809-537-7969/3961, or you can email them at info@nauticohaina.cjb.net.

Santo Domingo

Santo Domingo - ¼ nm S of marked entrance
18° 27.50' N, 69° 53.50' W

Santo Domingo (actually Santo Domingo de Guzmán) the capital and largest city of the Dominican Republic, is best visited by rental car, with a tour group from any other marina, or by cruise ship from the state-of-the-art cruise terminal at Sansouci on the eastern shore of the *Rio Ozama*.

The facilities for cruisers are Spartan at best. There is one small marina along the river's eastern shore and another one to the west of Santo Domingo up the river at Haina (with a boatyard). But neither river is particularly attractive and I only mention them for those that find they are in need of the services in the area (mechanical, medical, or veterinary). By the way, there is no place to anchor here and the current can be strong at times.

Santo Domingo, sometimes called "The Gateway to the Caribbean," is the oldest continually inhabited European settlement in the New World. Founded on the eastern shore of the *Rio Ozama* by Bartholomew Columbus in 1496, the settlement was originally named La Nueva Isabela after the Queen of Spain, but the name was changed on August 5, 1498, in honor of St. Dominic.

Santo Domingo was important as a base for European expansion in the Caribbean, a starting point for expeditions to colonize Puerto Rico (led by Ponce de Leon), Cuba (led by Diego Velázquez de Cuéllar), the conquest of Mexico (led by Hernán Cortés), and the discovery of the *Pacific Ocean* by Vasco Núñez de Balboa.

Santo Domingo was destroyed by a hurricane in June of 1502, and was rebuilt on the opposite shore of the *Rio Ozama*. As the Spanish hold on Hispaniola began to dissolve, the city was captured by Francis Drake. In 1697, the Treaty of Ryswick acknowledged that France had dominion over the western third of Hispaniola, now known as Haiti.

Santo Domingo changed hands many times over the coming years, captured by the French, then Haitian rebels, then the Spanish retook the city until they were overthrown in 1821 when it became the capital of an independent nation, the Dominican Republic. However the city fell to Haitian invaders until after Spanish intercession, the city again became the capital in 1865 (although for the next 60 years it would be like a ping pong ball going back and forth between several dictators including Trujillo who renamed the city after himself. Finally, when Trujillo was assassinated in 1961, the city was once again named Santo Domingo.

Today, Santo Domingo is the cultural, financial, political, commercial and industrial center of the Dominican Republic, and is the major seaport for the nation. Santo Domingo approved legislation in 2005 to develop a huge cruise ship terminal and new marina and a decade later there is still much to be accomplished in this regard.

Navigational Information

As shown on Chart DR-13, a waypoint at 18° 27.50' N, 69° 53.50' W, will place you approximately ¼ nm S of the marked entrance channel between the jetties. From the waypoint head NE up the Rio Ozama past the cruise ship terminal staying midstream until you arrive at the marina. There is a lighted range to lead you in but it isn't really necessary for the average cruising boat as there is good water unless you get too close to the shore or jetties.

Just past the marina is a floating bridge (not shown on the chart) that blocks further inland river access to boats. There is a fair amount of current in the river, even more after strong rains.

What You Will Find Ashore

On the eastern shore of the river, north of the cruise ship terminal, lies *Rio Ozama Marina*, where all dockage is med moor with buoys for your bow (or stern) line. There are few amenities here but the owners have grand plans for the property, so who knows, maybe the future will bring about some very positive changes.

To explore Santo Domingo I suggest getting any of the better travel guides to the area, there is SO MUCH to see here starting with the *Malecón* and the *Christopher Columbus Lighthouse* (*Faro a Colón*).

If you need mechanical assistance for your boat you can call Tony Rodamentes (*Av. St. Martin*), at 809-688-2151. If you need marine supplies you can visit *Auto Marina* (*Av. Los Proceres*), 809-565-6576 (marinecenter@codetel.dom). If you require a hardware store, a good one can be found on *Av. John F. Kennedy*, the *Ferretería Americana*, and you can telephone them at 809-549-7777.

Heading east from Santo Domingo towards Boca Chica, you will find *La Caleta*, a national park lying just a few miles west of Boca Chica (see the Index Chart for the southern coast of the Dominican Republic). Once a popular stopover for cruisers, since 2013, no anchoring is permitted here to protect the reef. Although there are moorings for daytime diving use, no vessels are permitted to stay overnight.

Boca Chica

(San Andrés)

Boca Chica - 1¼ nm SE of entrance channel
18° 25.50' N, 69° 36.70' W

Approximately 18 nm east of Santo Domingo is the resort town of Boca Chica located in the small bay, *Bahía de Andrés*, lying NE of Cabo Caucedo. A good landmark is the conspicuous tall cranes ashore.

Boca Chica is the perfect spot on the south coast to explore Santo Domingo while enjoying a nice, comfortable marina. You can rent a car here and there is also excellent bus service connecting Boca Chica with Santo Domingo.

Navigational Information

The anchorage area, the moorings, and access to the marinas are protected by a long reef and the only access is by the marked channel at the western end of the shoal. If you require assistance hail *Marina*

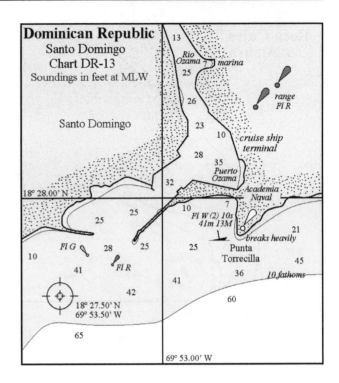

Zar-Par on VHF ch. 6 and they will send a boat to guide you (this service is not available at night).

As shown on Chart DR-14, a waypoint at 18° 25.50' N, 69° 36.70' W, will place you approximately 1¼ nm SE of the well-marked entrance channel. From the waypoint steer roughly NW (approximately 300° M) and enter the marked channel. You can avail yourself of the sectored light (*RWG*) but NEVER attempt to enter this channel at night unless you know these waters!

As you head into the well-marked channel you will pass the port area (Caucedo) well to port and avoid the end of the reef to starboard, once past the reef you can turn to starboard in the lee of La Piedra to head to the marinas. Favor the marina docks very closely as the water shoals to starboard and the channel is tight through here. The bottom here is mostly mud and sand and the controlling depth is 10' except when the wind is NE, then you can count on there be 1' less depth. If you draw more than 7' you should hail *Marina Zar-Par* on VHF ch. 6 for more information.

You can anchor in the lee of La Piedra but it is very small and space is limited. There are moorings available just off *Marina Zar-Par* but you cannot anchor further east off the public beach. If you take a mooring keep an eye on the depthsounder so that

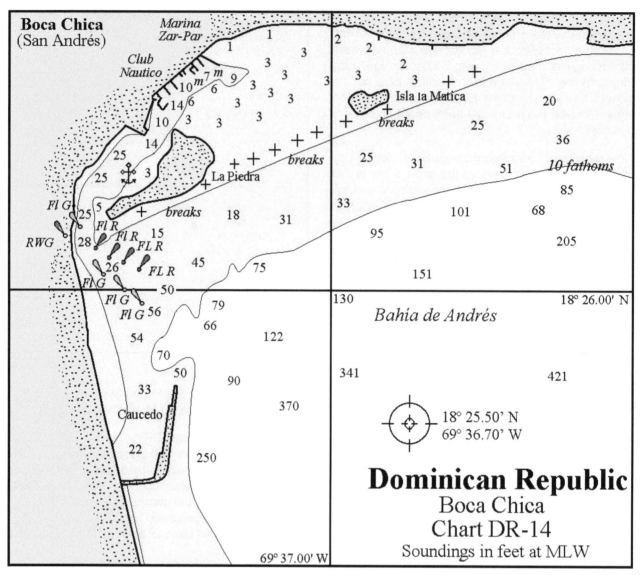

Boca Chica
(San Andrés)

Marina Zar-Par

Club Nautico

La Piedra

breaks

breaks

breaks

Fl G

Fl R

Fl R

Fl R

FL R

Fl G

Fl G

Fl G

RWG

Caucedo

Isla la Matica

breaks

Bahía de Andrés

18° 26.00' N

18° 25.50' N
69° 36.70' W

Dominican Republic
Boca Chica
Chart DR-14
Soundings in feet at MLW

10 fathoms

69° 37.00' W

you do not run aground when the tide changes. Bear in mind that on the weekends many Dominicans come out and play in the surrounding waters and the area from the front of the marina to La Piedra can be VERY busy, and some even say downright unsafe. If you take a mooring all the amenities of Marina Zar-Par are yours for the use. Moorings are for use by vessels less than 50' LOA due to the shallow waters. If a mooring line is missing please contact the marina and let them know.

What You Will Find Ashore

There are two marinas here, the private *Club Nautico de Santo Domingo* and *Marina Zar-Par*, both lying on the mainland shore just next to each other.

Club Nautico de Santo Domingo, although private, has a fuel dock, transient slips, water, showers, Wi-Fi, a restaurant, a pool, and a 70 ton *Travelift* for those needing a haulout. You can phone the marina at 809-683-2582, or visit their website at http://www.clubnautico.com.do/. *Club Nautico* tells me they can handle an 8'draft with the tide.

Marina Zar-Par is a relatively new full-service marina with an *Immigration* office located above the laundromat. Although the office is officially open 24-hours a day, cruisers are only handled from 0800-1800. If you intend to clear out from here, bear in mind that you are not permitted to leave after 1800 daily, you must leave as soon as your despacho has been issued (it's best to plan an early morning departure). The fuel dock is where you will handle your clearance paperwork and if you do not take a slip you will be charged for usage of the dock. The marina also offers a clearance service if you do not wish to deal with the paperwork for a fee of US$50. This fee covers clearance handling (but not the clearance fees), usage of the dock on the day you depart, and water. If you do not wish to use the fuel dock you can anchor in the lee of La Piedra and dinghy in to handle the formalities.

The marina offers full electric (30, 50, and 100 amp service), *Wi-Fi* (with a computer in the office that you can use if you don't have one), laundry, showers, free cable TV in the *Captain's Club* (located above the laundromat), fax service, a fuel dock, and 150 slips with some that can accommodate a vessel to 100', and all with 24-hour security.

The marina also offers courtesy rides to the airport as well as the grocery store in Boca Chica just east of the marina (the grocery store will bring you back to the marina). Free cell phone usage is also supplied for guests of the marina.

The boatyard has a 70-ton *TravelLift* that can accommodate drafts to 8' and beams of 28'. The yard/marina can also help you dispose of oil and batteries. You can phone the marina at 809-523-5858, or you can visit their website at www.marinazarpar.com

If you require marine supplies visit *Centro Marino, Av. Andres #3*, or call them at 809-523-6033, or email them at centro.marino@hotmail.com. For mechanical repairs try Juan Carlos Baez at *Technical Marine*, 809-805-8125.

If you need help with electrical or electronic problems, you can contact Ian Wilson at *Wilson Marina and Villa Services* at 809-743-9503. You can also contacted *Manuel Electric*, just across from the entrance to *Club Nautico* to the west, or call them at 809-523-9769.

In town there are several banks, grocery stores, and fine eateries (with a lot of Italian restaurants) and the marinas will be happy to tell you which ones are the best at the moment. The best place for groceries is *Olé*.

East of Boca Chica

Moving east from Boca Chica there are a couple of anchorages that deserve at least a mention here although they are not high on my list of quality destinations.

Approximately 18 nm east of Boca Chica is the *Rio Macoris* and the industrial town of San Pedro de Macoris. The river should never be entered at night due to large, unlit mooring buoys that are for ships awaiting entrance to the port in town. The river entrance channel is well-marked and easy to follow, but don't venture outside the channel to the east due to shoals and foul ground. If you wish to visit Sand Pedro de Macoris it is best done by rental car from Boca Chica or Casa de Campo.

Approximately 17 nm further east lies Isla Catalina (see the Dominican Republic, Southern Coast Index Chart) that offers a lee from winds from north through east to southeast (although the anchorage tends to be rolly in all but the best conditions). The island is popular with cruise ships and day trippers and can be quite busy when the fleet is in. Isla Catalina` is a good spot for wall diving and large fish.

Casa de Campo Marina

Casa de Campo Marina - ¼ nm SW of entrance
18° 23.60' N, 68° 54.40' W

Just east of Isla Catalina is the town of La Romana. While one can anchor in the river, it is not advisable due to strong currents and poor holding. Instead, head a few miles further east and get a slip at *Casa de Campo Marina* and visit La Romana by rental car or taxi (there is good shopping/provisioning in La Romana). The marina is only a few minutes away from the international airport in La Romana.

Navigational Information

As shown on Chart DR-15, a waypoint at 18° 23.60' N, 68° 54.40' W, will place you approximately ¼ nm SW of the well-marked entrance channel. From the waypoint head in a NNE direction and you will pick up the lit markers to guide you into the marina. You will notice the conspicuous red and white striped light at the end of the jetty to starboard upon entering. If you need help, hail the marina on VHF ch. 16 or 68 and they will send out a boat to guide you.

What You Will Find Ashore

Designed to become an international destination, the 370 slip *Casa de Campo Marina* is part of a much larger resort that also houses a haul-out yard, a yacht club, a sailing club, several yacht brokers, a plaza with many stores and theaters, and several fine restaurants on-site.

Some slips have finger piers while some are Med-moor, and the marina can accommodate vessels up to 250' LOA with depths ranging from 9'-15'. The tidal range is a mere 6" inside the protected harbor. The marina boasts two fueling stations (and 6 in-slip fueling points for vessels over 120"), full electric (110, 220, and 380 volt AC at 60 Hz), a laundry, cable TV, telephone, *Wi-Fi*, and golf carts for travel within the marine complex. On-site you will also find a pharmacy and bank, and of course the marina has 24-hour security. The dockmaster's office supplies mariners with daily weather reports and monitors a system of surveillance cameras to make your stay as comfortable and safe as possible.

The *IBC* boatyard has a 120-ton *TravelLift*, 25 different repair services, and a chandlery. All service personnel have been fully trained and certified and undergo regular training updates. The marina can be reached by phone at 809-523-2111/2112, or by email at marinacdc@verizon.net.do.

The sailing school, located on the *Rio Chavon*, has trained some 4,000 students in the DR and Italy since 1978 and is directed by Franco Pistone.

Located on the northeastern part of the marina complex, the marina is home to the *Casa de Campo Yacht Club*. Housed in a large and impressive Colonial-designed structure, the yacht club oversees many of the marina's activities including dinners and even international regattas. Inside you will feel like you have entered an old-style yacht club that reeks of old money and a century of sailing.

The marina also boasts several prime shopping areas on-site including the unique *Coconut Mall* housing a bank, a gourmet deli, rental cars, several restaurants and three cinemas. There are numerous fine international restaurants on the marina's grounds such as *The Azimut Café, Café Juanita, The Enoteca, Il Limoncello, Peperoni, Chinois, La Casita,* and *Mistral*.

To the west is the town of La Romana and it is a long walk or a short taxi ride away from the marina. For provisioning you can't go wrong at the huge, well-stocked, *Supermercado Jumbo* (http://jumbo.com.do/ofertas.aspx). Besides the normal range of groceries the store carries a large selection of fresh produce.

Approximately 4.5 nm east of *Casa de Campo Marina* is the small anchorage at Bayahibe. Primarily a fishing village, Bayahibe has become a homeport for commercial vessels taking tourists to nearby Isla Saona to the east (generally between 0900-1100 and 1500-1800).

The town is set up to cater to the tourists and you will find several gift shops here besides the usual plethora of bars and restaurants, most on the waterfront for the view. Bayahibe is not a port of entry and if you need to clear the local officials will direct you to *Casa de Campo Marina* and La Romana for clearance. The *Dominican Republic Coast Guard*, the *Marina de Guerra*, has an office in the tan building at the end of the public beach. The anchorage is pleasant enough save for a bit of a roll. There is a small fuel dock with 4' at MLW.

Isla Saona

Isla Saona - ½ nm NW of anchorage
18° 12.50' N, 68° 47.00' W

Isla Saona, a nature reserve, lies off the southeastern tip of the Dominican Republic and offers nothing in the way of services and amenities for the cruiser save for a good spot to drop the hook before or after crossing the *Mona Passage*.

Although Isla Saona is inhabited, many of her people cater to the tourists that arrive on daily shuttles from Bayahibe to enjoy the island's many beautiful white sand beaches. Quite a few still fish daily and don't be surprised if some come by your anchored boat to sell you some of their catch.

Navigational Information

NEVER attempt to bring your vessel between Isla Saona and the mainland of the Dominican Republic from the east, there is a huge reef system that can be treacherous. Although there is a deep water passage between the southern end of the reef and the tip of Isla Saona I do not recommend that anybody venture into these waters, the area between Isla Saona and the mainland, *Bahía Catalinita*, is best explored by dinghy from the anchorage on the NW shore of Isla Saona.

If approaching from the east, give the southern shore a wide berth, at least 2 miles, to avoid the huge reef shown on the chart as *Bujos del Caballo*. Also do not attempt to pass between *Bujos del Caballo* and Isla Saona.

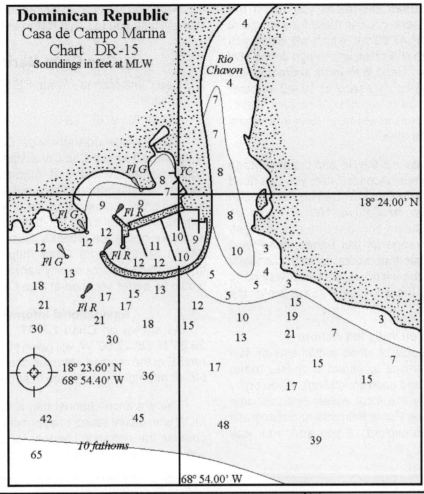

Dominican Republic
Casa de Campo Marina
Chart DR-15
Soundings in feet at MLW

Rio Chavon

18° 24.00' N

18° 23.60' N
68° 54.40' W

10 fathoms

68° 54.00' W

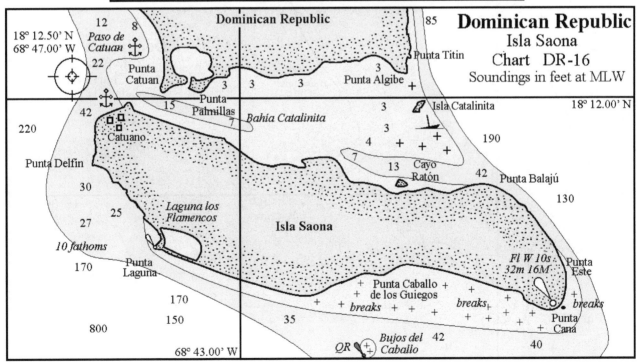

Dominican Republic

Dominican Republic
Isla Saona
Chart DR-16
Soundings in feet at MLW

18° 12.50' N
68° 47.00' W

Paso de Catuan

Punta Titin

Punta Algibe

Punta Catuan

Punta Palmillas

Bahía Catalinita

Isla Catalinita

18° 12.00' N

Catuano

190

Punta Delfin

Cayo Ratón

Punta Balajú

130

Laguna los Flamencos

Isla Saona

10 fathoms

Punta Laguna

Fl W 10s
32m 16M

Punta Este

Punta Caballo
de los Guiegos

breaks

breaks

breaks

Punta Cana

QR

Bujos del Caballo

68° 43.00' W

As shown on Chart DR-16, as you round the western tip of Isla Saona you can make for a waypoint at 18° 12.50' N, 68° 47.00' W, which will place you approximately ½ nm NW of the anchorage on the NW shore of Isla Saona. Head in towards shore and you can anchor in good holding sand in 10'-40' of clear water just off the small settlement of Catuano. Never attempt to anchor here in winds or seas from south through west to northeast.

If the wind moves into the NE and the anchorage at Isla Saona becomes uncomfortable, you can head west to Boca Chica or Casa de Campo, or you can anchor in the *Paso de Catuan*, NW of Punta de Catuan, but use caution and don't try this at night. If leaving the anchorage off Isla Saona, head west to avoid the sandbar that works its way northwest from the NW tip of the island, to work your way north and then east into the anchorage in the lee of the mainland.

What You Will Find Ashore

There are a couple of small settlements on Isla Saona but no amenities to attract a cruiser (other than fresh seafood and good snorkeling). If you enjoy exploring by dinghy the local waters will captivate you. To the ENE lies Punta Palmillas and numerous mangrove creeks to explore. If you work your way

eastward you will pick up a channel with 5'-6' of water that will take you to Cayo Raton and Isla Catalinita.

Cap Cana Marina

Cap Cana Marina - ½ nm SE of entrance channel

18° 29.85' N, 68° 22.00' W

On the windward shore of the Dominican Republic is the large 130-slip *Cap Cana Marina*, part of a huge condominium project that attracts upscale condo owners, sportfishermen, and cruisers prepping for, or arriving after, a crossing of the *Mona Passage*. The marina is a Port of Entry and the marina will assist you with your clearance process. Just to the north is the 34-slip *Marina Punta Cana* (http://www.puntacana.com/) which attracts mostly sportfishermen; cruisers would be better serviced at *Cap Cana Marina*.

Navigational Information

As shown on Chart DR-17, a waypoint at 18° 29.85' N, 68° 22.00' W, will place you approximately ½ nm SE of the marked entrance channel to the marina. Never attempt this entrance in strong easterly seas.

The entrance channel has a least depth of 7' at MLW with a tidal range of approximately 1.5'. Do not confuse the entrance channel for *Cap Cana Marina* with the entrance channel to *Punta Cana Marina*

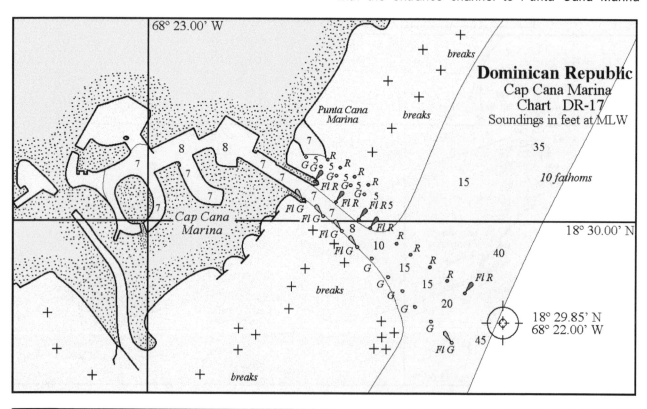

which lies just to the north. *Cap Cana Marina* offers a pilot service (0800-1800 daily) if needed; the marina can be reached on VHF ch. 16 or 72.

There are supposed to be 21 markers leading you into the marina but they may not all be there when you are trying to find your way into the marina.

What You Will Find Ashore

Cap Cana Marina (809-695-5539, info@ marinacapcana.com) was designed for larger sportfishing vessels, not the average cruising boat, and for that reason fendering can be difficult as many slips are alongside a wall with an overhang at the top. The dockmaster, Domingo, understands cruisers and he can be a big help when you tie up.

Cap Cana Marina has 130 slips (81 slips can handle vessels over 130' LOA), most with 40' long finger piers and full electric (110/220 volt 30 and 50 amp service along with three-phase electric to 480 volts and 100 amps). The marina can accommodate vessels to 150' LOA with a draft of 8'. Each slip has water, free Wi-Fi, and cable TV (not free). Vessels needing clearance should notify the marina by VHF (ch. 16 or 72.) prior to entry and follow their instructions. Usually the marina will direct you to the fuel dock where the officials will come aboard.

On the marina grounds you will find a dozen fine restaurants, a delicatessen, a laundry (a short golf cart ride away as are the showers), the *Sanctuary Spa* (http://sanctuarycapcana.com/), four beauty parlors, a fitness center, tennis courts, and a paddle ball and volleyball court. Nearby *Scape Park* (http://www.scapepark.com/en/) offers 74 acres of forest and 12 miles of hiking trails.

The marina maintains high quality service personnel on-site, or they can help you find an outside contractor if needed for everything from marine electronics to refrigeration, and hull painting. You can reach *Cap Cana Marina* by phone at 809-688-5587, or reach them by email at marina@capcana.com.

Situated just north of *Cap Cana Marina*, the poorly protected *Marina Punta Cana* is really not worth a stop unless by some chance *Cap Cana Marina* is full and you have no place else to go (little chance of that I believe). The entrance channel is difficult to make out but breaking seas will give you an idea where the break in the reef lies. An outer green buoy marks the channel entrance and several buoys line the entrance. The controlling depth in the entrance channel is 5' at MLW with 7' inside the marina basin (bear in mind that there is a 1.5' tidal range here). There always seems to be a swell in the marina basin and it can often be uncomfortable.

The marina offers 34 Med-moor slips, water, electricity, a fuel dock, a laundry, a swimming pool, and a nice international restaurant. You can contact the marina by phone at 809-959-2262 or by email at info@puntacana.com.

A Little Basic Spanish

(Just Enough to get you into Trouble)

While command of the Spanish language is not a prerequisite for happy cruising in the Dominican Republic, knowing a little will certainly help you get by better and everybody will love you for at least trying.

Buenos Dias. Good morning.
Buenas tardes. Good afternoon.
Buenas noches. Good night.
¿Cómo está usted? How are you?
¿Muy bien gracias, y usted? I am fine thank you, and you?
¿Como se llama? What is your name?
Me llamo es . . . My name is. . .
¿Habla usted inglés? Do you speak English?
¿Habla usted Español? Do you speak Spanish?
No muy bien. Not very well.
Muy poco. Very little.
¿Cómo se dice. . .? How do you say. . .?
No entiendo. I don't understand.
Escríbamela, por favor. Please write it down for me.
¿Donde está el. . .? Where is . . .?
anclaje-anchorage
arrecife-reef
bahia-bay
bajo-shoal
banco-bank
Capitán de Puerto-Harbormaster
caleta-cove
canal-channel
desembarcadero-landing
ducha-shower
embarcadero-wharf, quay
ferretería-hardware store
Immigración-Immigration
lavandería-laundry
mecánico-mechanic
médico-doctor
pasaje-passage
punta-point
rada-roadstead
supermercado-supermarket
telefono-telephone

¿Donde puedo comprar . . . ? Where can I buy...?
¿Tiene usted . . . ? Do you have. . . ?
Necesito. . . I need. . .
agua-water
azúcar-sugar
café-coffee

camarones-shrimp
carne-meat
cerveza-beer
cigarillos-cigarettes
fosforos-matches
fuego-a light
gasoil-diesel
gasolina-gasoline
huevos-eggs
jamón-ham
jugo-juice
leche-milk
limones-limes
mantequilla-butter
pan-bread
patatas-potatoes
plátanos-bananas (plantains)
pollo-chicken
propano-propane
queso-cheese
tomate-tomato
vino-wine

Colors
blanco-white
negro-black
azul-blue
rojo-red
verde-green
amarillo-yellow

Directions
aquí-here
allí-there
la derecha-right
la izquierda-left

Numbers
uno-1
dos-2
tres-3
quatro-4
cinco-5
seis-6
seite-7
ocho-8
nueve-9
diez-10
once-11
doce-12
trece-13
catorce-14

quince-15
diéz y seis-16
diéz y seite-17
diéz y ocho-18
diéz y nuevo-19
veinte-20
veinte y uno-21
treinta-30
uarenta-40
cincuenta-50
sesenta-60
setenta-70
ochenta-80
noventa-90
cien-100
ciento y uno-101
mil-1,000
mil uno-1,001

Days of the Week
Lunes-Monday
Martes-Tuesday
Miércoles-Wednesday
Juevos-Thursday
viernos-Friday
Sábado-Saturday
Domingo-Sunday
Ahora-Now

¿Quién? Who?
¿Qué? What?
¿Cuando? When?
¿Donde? Where?
¿Por qué? Why?
¿Cómo? How?
¿Qué lejos? How far is it?
    Está lejos. It's far.
    Está cerca. It's near.
¿Qué hora es? What time is it?
¿A qué hora? At what time?
Tengo hambre. I'm hungry.
Perdón. Excuse me.
¿Puede ayudarme? Can you help me?
¿Qué es eso? What is this (that)?
¿Cuánto cuesta? What does it cost?
Dame éste. Give me this one.
Dame eso. Give me that one.
No tengo dinero. I have no money.
¡No se mueva! Don't move!
¡Manos arriba! Put your hands up!

References

A Cruising Guide to the Caribbean and the Bahamas; Jerrems C. Hart and William T. Stone, Dodd, Mead and Company, New York, 1982

A Cruising Guide to the Exumas Cays Land And Sea Park; Stephen J. Pavlidis with Ray Darville, Night Flyer Enterprises, U.S.A. 1994

A General History of the Robberies and Murders of the Most Notorious Pirates: Daniel Defoe, (Capt. Charles Johnson). Routledge and Kegan Paul, Ltd., London, 1955

A History of the Bahamas; Michael Craton, Collins Press, London, 1969

A History of the Bahamas; Michael Craton, San Salvador Press, Ontario, Canada, 1986

A History of the Turks and Caicos: Prof. Josiah A. Marvel, unpublished monograph

American Practical Navigator; Nathaniel Bowditch, LL.D., DMA Hydrographic Center, 1977

An Essay on the Constitutional History of the Turks & Caicos Islands: Prof. Josiah A. Marvel and Leonora Harvey Missick, unpublished monograph

A Shipwreck Guide to the Bahamas and the Turks and Caicos, Vol. I: Tony A. Jaggers, American Southern Printing, Sarasota, FL, 1994

Bahamas Handbook and Businessmen's Manual; Sir Etienne Dupuch, Jr., Etienne Dupuch Jr., Publications Ltd., Nassau, Bahamas

Blackbeard the Pirate: Robert E. Lee and John Blair, Winston-Salem, NC, 1974

Coastal And Offshore Weather, The Essential Handbook; Chris Parker, Christopher Parker Jr., Green Cove Springs, FL. 2003.

Dictionary of Bahamian English; John A. Holm, Lexik House Pub., Cold Springs, NY, 1982

Diving, Snorkeling, & Visitors Guide to the Turks and Caicos Islands: Capt. Bob Gascoine, Graphic Reproductions, Miami, FL, 1991

Great Inagua; Margery O. Erikson, Capriole Press, Garrison, NY, 1987

HF Radio E-Mail For Idi-Yachts, Captain Marti Brown, Cruising Companion Publications, Marathon, FL 2003.

Island Expedition, The Central And Southern Bahamas; Nicolas and Dragan Popov, 1988, Graphic Media, Miami FL

Mystical Cat Island; Eris Moncur, Northstar Press, Miami, FL, 1996

Out Island Doctor; Dr. Evans W. Cottman, Hodder and Stoughton, London, 1963

Pirate Rascals of the Spanish Main: Addison B.C. Whipple, Doubleday and Co., New York, 1957

Pirates and Privateers of the Caribbean: Jennifer Marx, Krieger Publishing Company, Malabar, FL, 1992

Reptiles and Amphibians of The Bahamas; Bahamas National Trust, 1993

Sailing Directions For The Caribbean Sea; Pub. #147, Defense Mapping Agency, #SDPUB147

Secrets of the Bahamas Family Islands 1989; Nicolas Popov, Dragan Popov, & Jane Sydenham; Southern Boating Magazine, May 1989

The American Coast Pilot; Blunt, 1812

The Aranha Report on the Berry Islands; Land and Surveys Dept., Nassau, New Providence, Bahamas 1925

The Bahamas Handbook: Mary Moseley, The Nassau Guardian, Nassau, Bahamas, 1926

The Bahamas Rediscovered; Nicolas and Dragon Popov, Macmillan Press, Ltd. London 1992

The Book of Pirates: Brian Innes, Bancroft and Co., Ltd., 1966

The Buccaneers of the Americas: A. O. Esquemelin, George Rutledge & Sons, London, 1893

The Diario of Christopher Columbus' First Voyage to the Americas, 1492-1493: Fray Bartolomé de Las Casas,

Translated by Oliver Dunn and James E. Kelley Jr., Norman: University of Oklahoma Press, 1989

The Ephemeral Islands, A Natural History of the Bahamas; David G. Campbell, MacMillan Education, 1990

The Gentleman's Guide To Passages South; Bruise Van Sant, Cruising Guide Publications, 1989 and 1996

The Great Days of Piracy in the West Indies: George Woodbury, W.W. Norton and Co.

The Log of Christopher Columbus: Robert H. Fuson, Tab Books, Blue Ridge Summit, PA, 1987

The Ocean Almanac; Robert Hendrickson, Doubleday, New York, 1984

The Pirates: Douglas Botting, Time-Life Books, Alexandria, VA, 1978

The Pirates Own Book; published by A. & C. B . Edwards, New York, and Thomas, Cowperthwait, & Co., Philadelphia, 1842

The Pirates Who's Who: Phillip Gosse, Rio Grande Press, 1988

The Statute Law of The Bahamas; Revised Edition 1987, Chapter 355

The Story of the Turks and Caicos Islands: C.D. Hutchings 1977

The Turks and Caicos Islands, Lands of Discovery: Amelia Smithers, Macmillan Education, London, Second Edition, 1995

Turks and Caicos Islands: Paul G. Boultbee, World Bibliographical Series, Vol. 137, Clio Press, Oxford U.K./ ABC Clio, Santa Barbara, CA, U.S.A.

Turks and Caicos Pocket Guide: Julia Blake, Domy Graphix Ltd., 1997

Turks Islands Landfall, Vol. 1-7: Herbert E. Sadler, Grand Turk

Where the Trade Winds Blow; Bill Robinson, Charles Scribner's Sons, New York, 1963

Appendices

Appendix A: Navigational Lights

Navigational lights in the Bahamas should be considered unreliable at best. The actual characteristics of each light may differ from those published here and are subject to change without notice. It is not unusual for a light to be out of commission for long periods of time. Listing of lights reads from north to south. Please note that due to the efforts of Beryl Nelson of Providenciales, North West Point Light on Providenciales (Turks and Caicos Islands) is now working after years of disrepair.

LOCATION	LIGHT	COLOR	HT.	RANGE
The Southern Bahamas				
Cat Island				
Bennett's Harbour	Fl ev 4 sec	W	53'	12 nm
Smith's Bay	Fl ev 4 sec	W	38'	7 nm
Devil Point	Fl ev 5 sec	W	143'	12 nm
Half Moon Cay				
South shore	Fl ev 2½ sec	W	69'	13 nm
Conception Island				
Southwest Point	Fl ev 2 sec	W	84'	6 nm
Rum Cay				
Cottonfield Point	Fl ev 8 sec	WYR	75'	10 nm
Port Nelson Dock	Fxd	G	16'	5 nm
San Salvador				
Dixon Hill Lighthouse	Gp. Fl (2) 10 sec	W	163'	19 nm
Long Island				
Cape Santa Maria	Fl ev 3.3 sec	W	99'	14 nm
Clarence Tn. Booby R.	Fl ev 2 sec	W	41'	8 nm
South End	Fl ev 2½ sec	W	61'	12 nm
The Jumentos				
Nuevitas Rocks	Fl ev 4 sec	W	38'	10 nm
Flamingo Cay	Fl ev 6 sec	W	138'	8 nm
Bulva Rock (Black Rock)	Fl ev 3 sec	R	13'	4 nm
Ragged Island	Fl ev 3 sec	W	118'	12 nm
Cay Santo Domingo	Fl ev 5 sec	W	30'	7 nm
Cay Lobos Lighthouse	Gp. Fl (2) 10 sec	W	145'	22 nm
Crooked Island District				
Bird Rock Lighthouse	Fl ev 15 sec	W	112'	23 nm
Attwood Harbour	Fl ev 5 sec	W	20'	8 nm
Hell Gate	Fl ev 6 sec	W	56'	10 nm
Windsor Point	Fl ev 3 sec	W	35'	8 nm
Castle Island Lighthouse	Gp. Fl (2) 20 sec	W	130'	22 nm
Hogsty Reef				
Northwest Cay	Fl ev 4 sec	W	29'	8 nm
Mayaguana				
Guano Pt., Abrhm's Bay	Fl ev 3 sec	W	13'	8 nm
Northwest Point	Fl ev 5 sec	W	70'	12 nm
Great Inagua				
Matthew Town	Gp. Fl (2) 10 sec	W	120'	17 nm
The Turks and Caicos Islands				
The Caicos Islands				
North West Point, Providenciales	Gp Fl (3) 15 sec	W		14M

LOCATION	LIGHT	COLOR	HT.	RANGE
Providenciales, Bird Cay	Fl ev 10 sec	W		12M
Cape Comete, East Caicos	Gp Fl (2) 20 sec	W		12M
West Caicos, SW Point	Q	R	52'	
French Cay	Fl	R	10'	
South Caicos	Fxd	W	50'	9M
Long Cay, east end	Fl ev 2.5 sec	R		5M
Dove Cay, west end	Fl ev 2.5 sec	G		5M
Bush Cay	Gp Fl (2) 10 sec	W		14M
The Turks Islands				
Grand Turk Lighthouse	Fl ev 7.5 sec	W	108'	6M
Head of South Dock-front	Fl ev 3 sec	W & R	20'	3M
Head of South Dock-rear	Fl ev 3 sec		30'	3M
Salt Cay, NW Point	Gp Fl (4) 20 sec	W		8M
Great Sand Cay	Fl ev 2 sec	W	85'	10M
Dominican Republic				
Luperón - head of dock	GP Fl ev 10s	R	30'	3M
Ocean World Marina Sea Buoy	Fl	W		
Puerto Plata - sea buoy	Fl	R		
Punta Fortaleza	Fl ev 6 s	W	138'	8M
Puerto Plata Range	Fl	R		12M
Cayo Vigia	Fl	R	22'	8M

Appendix B: Marinas

Some of the marinas listed below may be untenable in certain winds and dockside depths listed may not reflect entrance channel depths at low water, check with the dockmaster prior to arrival. For cruisers seeking services "Nearby" may mean a walk or short taxi ride away.

MARINA	FUEL	GROCERY	DINING	E-MAIL or WEBSITE
		The Southern Bahamas		
Cat Island				
Hawk's Nest Resort	D & G	Yes	Yes	http://www.hawks-nest.com/
Flamingo Hills Resort	Still under construction			http://flamingohills.com/marina
Crooked/Acklins District				
Landrail Point Marina*	None	Nearby	Nearby	
Long Island				
Flying Fish Marina	D & G	Yes	Nearby	info@flyingfishmarina.com
Stella Maris Resort	D & G	Nearby	Nearby	jill@stellamarisresort.com
San Salvador				
Riding Rock Marina	D & G	Nearby	Nearby	info@ridingrock.com

* *Landrail Point Marina* is a small man-made harbour for the usage of small, outboard powered vessels.

MARINA	FUEL	GROCERY	DINING	E-MAIL or WEBSITE
		The Turks and Caicos Islands		
Ambergris Cay				
Windward Marina	Still under construction - lack of financing			
Blue Haven Marina	D & G	Nearby	Yes	contact@bluehaventci.com
Caicos Marina/Shipyard	D & G	No	No	info@caicosmarina.com
Harbour Club Marina	Private			harbourclub@tciway.tc
South Side Marina	D & G	Nearby	Nearby	southsidemarina@gmail.com
Turtle Cove Marina	D & G	Nearby	Yes	tcmarina@tciway.tc

MARINA	FUEL	GROCERY	DINING	E-MAIL or WEBSITE
Walkin Marine	Only suitable for smaller, shallow draft vessels			
South Caicos				
Seaview Marina	D & G	Yes	Nearby	
West Caicos				
West Caicos Marina	Closed awaiting financing, anchoring permissible inside marina			
Grand Turk				
Flamingo Cove	D	No	Nearby	
Deane's Dock	Nearby	Nearby	Nearby	

The Dominican Republic

MARINA	FUEL	GROCERY	DINING	E-MAIL or WEBSITE
Boca Chica				
Cl.Nautico Santo Dom.	D & G	Nearby	Nearby	info@clubnautico.com.do
Marina Zarpar	D & G	Nearby	Yes	info@marinazarpar.com
Cofresi				
Ocean World Marina	D & G	Yes	Yes	concierge@oceanworldmarina.com
Haina				
Club Nautico Haina	D & G	Nearby	Nearby	info@nauticohaina.cjb.net
La Romana				
Casa de Campo Marina	D & G	Yes	Yes	www.casadecampo.com.do/
Las Salinas				
Salinas Hotel & Marina	D & G	Nearby	Nearby	info@marinadesalinas.com
Luperón				
Luperón Marina & YC	None	Nearby	Yes	info@Luperonmarina.net
Puerto Blanco Marina	None	Nearby	Yes	puertoblancomarina@gmail.com
Marina Tropical	None	Nearby	Nearby	marinatropical.dr@gmail.com
Punta Cana				
Cap Cana Marina	D & G	Yes	Yes	info@marinacapcana.com
Marina de Punta Cana	D & G	Nearby	Yes	
Samaná				
Puerto Bahía Marina	D & G	Yes	Yes	www.puertobahiasamana.com
Santo Domingo				
La Marina del Rio Ozama	D & G	Nearby	Yes	

Appendix C: Service Facilities

As with any place, businesses come and go, sometimes seemingly overnight. Certain entries on this list may no longer exist by the time this is published. Listings in the Dominican Republic are listed by city and then "DR."

Appendix C-1: Southern Bahamas

The area code for all the islands of The Bahamas is 242.

FACILITY	LOCATION	PHONE	VHF CALL OR E-MAIL
Car Rentals			
AB Rent a Car	Matthew Town, Great Inagua	339-2224	ab_rentalcar@hotmail.com
C & S Car Rentals	Cockburn Town, San Salvador	331-2631	
Donny Newbold	Port Howe, Cat Island	342-5041	
Gilbert's Car Rentals	New Bight, Cat Island	342-3011	
Hawks Nest Marina	Hawks Nest Creek, Cat Island	342-7050	http://www.hawks-nest.com/

FACILITY	LOCATION	PHONE	VHF CALL OR E-MAIL
Ingraham's Car Rentals	Matthew Town, Great Inagua	339-1677	
Mr. T's Car Rentals	Deadman's Cay, Long Island	337-1054	
New Bight Car Rentals	New Bight, Cat Island	342-3514	
New Bight Shell	New Bight, Cat Island	342-3014	New Bight Service
Oasis Bakery	Clarence Town, Long Island	337-0003	Oasis Bakery
Ophelia's Car Rental	Deadman's Cay, Long Island	337-1042	Opheliasrentacar@yahoo.com
Riding Rock Marina	Cockburn Town, San Salvador	331-2631	info@ridingrock.com
Stella Maris Resort	Stella Maris, Long Island	338-2050	jill@stellamarisresort.com
Taylor's Garage	Burnt Ground, Long Island		
Taylor's Garage			
Thompson's Bay Inn	Salt Pond, Long Island		
William's Car Rentals	Glinton, Long Island	338-5002	
William's Garage			
Windsor Car Rentals	Stella Maris, Long Island		Windsor
Diesel Repair/Parts			
Andrew Cartwright	Cabbage Point, Long Island	337-2424	
Captain Black's Welding	Arthur's Town, Cat Island		
Cleveland Brown	Abraham's Bay, Mayaguana		Papa Charlie
Henry Major	Clarence Town, Long Island	337-3936	Harbour Master
Milander's Auto/Marine	Clarence Town, Long Island	337-3227	Milanders Auto
Red Major	Clarence Town, Long Island	338-3003	
Riding Rock Marina	Cockburn Town, San Salvador	331-2631	info@ridingrock.com
Stella Maris Resort	Stella Maris, Long Island	338-2050	jill@stellamarisresort.com
Timothy Thompson	Landrail Pt., Crooked Island		Cold Front
Electronics/Electrical			
JVC Electronics	Salt Pond, Long Island		
Fabrication/Welding			
Captain Black's Welding	Arthur's Town, Cat Island		
Stella Maris Resort	Stella Maris, Long Island	338-2050	jill@stellamarisresort.com
Haul Out			
Stella Maris Marina	Stella Maris, Long Island	338-2055	stellamarisresort.com/
Hull Repair/Painting			
Stella Maris Resort	Stella Maris, Long Island	338-2050	jill@stellamarisresort.com
Marine Supplies			
Milander's Auto/Marine	Clarence Town, Long Island		Milanders Auto
Stella Maris Resort	Stella Maris, Long Island	338-2050	jill@stellamarisresort.com
T & S Marine	Cabbage Hill, Crooked Island		
Under The Sea	Mangrove Bush, Long Island	337-0199	
Outboard Repair			
Alpheas Nespitt	Duncan Town, Ragged Island		Fish
Captain Black's	Arthur's Town, Cat Island		Snow White
Derek Carter	Duncan Town, Ragged Island		Monkey Man
Fisherman's Marine	Hamiltons, Long Island	337-6226	
Riding Rock Marina	Cockburn Town, San Salvador	331-2631	info@ridingrock.com
Stafford Bain Jr.	Pirates Well, Mayaguana		Bain Boys
Stella Maris Resort	Stella Maris, Long Island	338-2050	jill@stellamarisresort.com/
Under The Sea	Mangrove Bush, Long Island	337-0199	
Propane			
Inagua General Store	Matthew Town, Great Inagua	339-1460	
Nai's Service Station	Spring Point, Acklin's Island		
Prince Pinder	Abraham's Bay, Mayaguana		

FACILITY	LOCATION	PHONE	VHF CALL OR E-Mail
Propane Truck	Port Howe, Cat Island		
Rudy Turnquest	Deadman's Cay, Long Island	337-0026	
Shell Station	Cockburn Town, San Salvador		
Shell Station	New Bight, Cat Island		
Thompson's*	Cabbage Hill, Crooked Island		

* Propane tanks must be shipped to Nassau by mailboat, turnaround time approximately 2 weeks.

Appendix C-2: Turks and Caicos

All listings in the Turks and Caicos are area code 649.

FACILITY	LOCATION	PHONE	VHF CALL OR E-Mail
Car Rentals			
Al's Rent-A-Car	North Caicos	331-1947	
Avis	Provo (Airport)	946-4705	reservations@avis.tc
Bayside Cars & Buggies	Grace Bay	941-9010	info@baysidecarstci.com
Budget	Provo (Airport)	946-4079	budget@tciway.tc
Caicos Wheels	Prov0 (Airport)	946-8302	customerservice@caicoswheels.com
Dickenson's Car Rental	Grand Turk	241-1549	
Dutchie's Car Rental	Grand Turk	946-2244	
Fox Rent A Car	Provo (Airport)	941-8262	reservations@foxrentacar.com
Grace Bay Car Rentals	Providenciales	941-8500	info@gracebaycarrentals.com
Pat Hamilton	North Caicos	946-7141	
Hertz	Providenciales	941-5503	
Island Rent a Car	Providenciales	946-4993	
Karib Auto Rental	Grand Turk	346-8652	karibarental@gmail.com
KK & T's Auto Rentals	Providenciales	941-8377	info@kkntsautorentals.com
Majestic Taxi & Tours	Providenciales	231-7901	
Middle Caicos Rentals	Middle Caicos	946-6185	
Mitchell Car Rental	Grand Turk	946-1879	
Mystique	Providenciales	941-3910	p_mystique@tciway.tc
Old Nick Rental Cars	North Caicos	946-7358	
Paradise Scooters	Grace Bay	333-3333	info@paradisescooters.tc
Payless Car Rental	Provo (Airport)	946-8592	
Presidential Taxi Tours & Auto	Providenciales	246-8190	info@tcitaxi.com
Provo Rent a Car	Providenciales	946-4475	RentACar@provo.net
Rent a Buggy	Providenciales	946-4158	reservations@tciway.tc
Scooter Bob's	Providenciales	946-4684	info@scooterbobstci.com
Seabreeze Taxi & Tours	Grace Bay	245-9651	darnley@seabreezetaxiandtours.com
Seaview Marina	South Caicos	946-3245	
Sixt Rent a Car	Provo (Airport)	941-3966	
Sunrise Auto Rental	Providenciales	946-4705	
Superior Auto Rentals	North Caicos	232-2137	info@superiorautorentals.com
TC National Car Rental	Providenciales	946-4701	
Tony's Car Rental	Grand Turk	231-1806	thriller@tciway.tc
Tropical Auto Rental	Grand Turk	946-2095	tropical@tciway.tc
Tropical Auto Rental	Providenciales	946-5300	tropical@tciway.tc
Wet Money Tours	Grand Turk	331-3449	wetmoneyenterprise@gmail.com
Canvas & Upholstery			
Caribbean Marine & Diesel	South Side Marina	941-5903	caribmarinediesel@tciway.tc
Diesel Repair/Parts			

FACILITY	LOCATION	PHONE	VHF CALL OR E-Mail
Caicos Marina & Shipyard	Providenciales	946-5600	info@caicosmarina.com
Caribbean Marine Diesel	Marina, Provo	941-5903	caribmarinediesel@tciway.tc
MPL Enterprises	Grand Turk	431-0376	yamaha@yamaha.tc
Sea View Marina	South Caicos	946-3245	seaviewm@tciway.tc
Percy Tolbert	Salt Cay		

Diving

Aqua TCI	Grace Bay	946-1226	aquatci@live.com
Art Pickering Turtle Divers	Turtle Cove	946-4232	info@ProvoTurtleDivers.com
Big Blue Divers	Providenciales	946-5034	info@bigblueunlimited.com
Blue Water Divers	Grand Turk	946-2432	info@bigblueunlimited.com
Caicos Adventures	Providenciales	941-3346	divucrzy@tciway.tc
Club Caribe	South Caicos	946-3446	
Dive Provo	Providenciales	946-5040	diving@diveprovo.com
Flamingo Divers	Providenciales	946-4193	greatdiving@flamingodivers.com
Grand Turk Diving Co. Ltd	Grand Turk	946-1559	info@gtdiving.com
Oasis Divers	Grand Turk	946-1128	info@oasisdivers.com
Provo Turtle Divers	Providenciales	946-4232	info@ProvoTurtleDivers.com
Provo Wall Divers	Providenciales	941-5441	
Salt Cay Divers	Salt Cay	241-1009	scdivers@tciway.tc
Sea Eye Diving	Grand Turk	946-1407	ci@tciway.tc

Electronics/Electrical

Walkin Marine	Providenciales	946-4411	walkinmarine@tciway.tc

Fabrication/Welding

Caicos Marina & Shipyard	Providenciales	946-5600	info@caicosmarina.comc
Osprey Marine Services	Providenciales	946-5122	
Provo Steel	Providenciales	941-3112	provosteel@tciway.tc
Tibor's	Providenciales	941-5802	tibor@express.tc

Generators

Caicos Marina & Shipyard	Providenciales	946-5600	info@caicosmarina.com
Caribbean Marine & Diesel	South Side Mar.	941-5903	caribmarinediesel@tciway.tc
MPL Enterprises	Grand Turk	431-0376	yamaha@yamaha.tcHaul Out
Seaview Marina	South Caicos	946-3245	seaviewm@tciway.tc

Haul Out

Caicos Marina & Shipyard	Providenciales	946-5600	info@caicosmarina.com
Seaview Marina	South Caicos	946-3245	seaviewm@tciway.tc

Hull Repair/Painting

Caicos Marina & Shipyard	Providenciales	946-5600	caicosmarinashp@tciway.tc

Internet

Aqua Bar (Turtle Cove)	Providenciales	946-4763	
CompTCI	Providenciales	941-4266	Ken@comptci.tc
Computer Guys	Providenciales	946-4152	
Computer Line	Providenciales	941-5834	info@computerline.ci
Deluxe Business Center	Providenciales	941-8876	
Grace Bay Pharmacy	Providenciales	946-8242	
Turtle Cove Marina	Providenciales	941-3781	tcmarina@provo.net

Marine Supplies

Caicos Marina & Shipyard	Providenciales	946-5600	info@caicosmarina.com
MPL Enterprises	Grand Turk	431-0376	yamaha@yamaha.tc
Walkin Marine	Providenciales	946-4411	walkinmarine@tciway.tc

Outboard Repair

Caicos Marina & Shipyard	Providenciales	946-5600	info@caicosmarina.com

FACILITY	LOCATION	PHONE	VHF CALL OR E-Mail
CMPL Enterprises	Grand Turk	946-2227	
MPL Enterprises	Grand Turk	431-0376	yamaha@yamaha.tc
Seaview Marina	South Caicos	946-3245	seaviewm@tciway.tc
Walkin Marine	Providenciales	946-4411	walkinmarine@tciway.tc
Propane			
Caicos Oil Ltd	S. Dock Rd., Pro.	941-7872	info@caicosoil.com
Grand Turk Gas Depot	South Dock, G. T.	946-2532	
Seaview Marina	South Caicos	946-3245	South Caicos Marina
South Side Marina	Providenciales	241-2439	southsidemarina@gmail.com
TC Gas	Grand Turk	946-2532	
TC Gas	Providenciales	941-3585	
Turtle Cove Marina	Providenciales	941-3781	tcmarina@tciway.tc
Propellers			
Caribbean Marine & Diesel	S. Side Mar. Provo.	941-5903	caribmarinediesel@tciway.tc
Refrigeration			
Caribbean Marine & Diesel	S. Side Mar. Provo.	941-5903	caribmarinediesel@tciway.tc
Rigging			
Osprey Marine Serv.	Providenciales	946-5122	

Appendix C-3: Dominican Republic

All listings in the DR are area code 809, 829, or 849. As with any place, businesses come and go, sometimes seemingly overnight. Certain entries on this list may no longer exist by the time this is published or may have changed their names or phone numbers. All telephone numbers in the Dominican Republic are area code 809, 829, or 849.

FACILITY	LOCATION	PHONE	VHF CALL OR E-MAIL
Auto Rentals			
Ace	Puerto Plata (Airport)	809-586-0505	rent@acerentacar.com
Ace	Punta Cana (Airport)	809-959-1241	rent@acerentacar.com
Ace	Santiago	809-822-3872	rent@acerentacar.com
Ace	Santo Domingo (Airport)	809-549-0509	rent@acerentacar.com
Adventure Rent A Car	Santiago	809-612-5494	info@adventurerentcar.com
Adventure Rent A Car	Santo Domingo	809-549-1493	info@adventurerentcar.com
Adventure Rent A Car	Sosúa	809-586-0106	info@adventurerentcar.com
Avis	Santiago	809-582-7007	
Avis	Santiago (Airport)	809-233-8154	
Avis	Puerto Plata (Airport)	809-586-0214	
Estelvina Felipe (Dentist)	Luperón, DR		
Hertz	Puerto Plata (Airport)	809-586-0200	
Hertz	Punta Cana (Airport)	809-959-0365	
Hertz	Santo Domingo (Airport)	809-549-0454	
José	Luperón, DR	809-458-9506	José, VHF ch. 68
Lucke Car/Jeep Rental	Puerto Plata	809-568-0217	
National	Puerto Plata (Airport)	809-222-9058	
National	Punta Cana (Airport)	809-222-9058	
National	Santo Domingo (Airport)	809-222-9058	
Odalis	Luperón, DR	809-223-3580	Odalis, VHF ch. 68
OK Motors	Cabarete	809-571-1666	ok-motors@hotmail.com
Payless Car Rental	Puerto Plata (Airport)	800-586-0108	
Payless Car Rental	Punta Cana	800-959-0287	

FACILITY	LOCATION	PHONE	VHF CALL OR E-MAIL
Payless Car Rental	Santo Domingo (Airport)	800-549-8911	
Thrifty Car Rental	Puerto Plata (Airport)	809-333-4000	
Thrifty Car Rental	Punta Cana	809-466-2046	
Thrifty Car Rental	Santo Domingo (Airport)	809-549-0930	
Tropicar	Puerto Plata (Airport)	809-586-0242	reserve@tropi-car.com

Diesel Repair/Parts

Laboratorio Diesel	Puerto Plata	809-261-6394	
Marina Cap Cana	Cap Cana	809-695-5539	info@marinacapcana.com
Marina Casa de Campo	La Romana	809-523-2111	
Marina Zar-Par	Boca Chica	809-523-5858	info@marinazarpar.com
Núñez & Núñez	Santiago	809-582-2200	
Ocean World Marina	Puerto Plata	809-970-3373	
Repuestos Maritimos	Puerto Plata	809-586-4728	
Technical Marine	Boca Chica	809-805-8125	
Tony Rodamentes	Santo Domingo	809-688-2151	

Diving

Caribbean Divers	Boca Chica	809-854-3483	markushaemmerle2@yahoo.de
Coral Point Diving	Bayahibe	809-584-9655	info@coralpointdiving.com
Diwa Dive Center	Puerto Plata	809-261-3150	diwa.dominicana@yahoo.com
Dressel Divers	Puerto Plata	321-392-2338	info@dresseldivers.com
Northern Coast Diving	Sosúa	809-571-1028	info@northerncoastdiving.com
Scuba Fun Center	La Romana	809-833-0003	info@scubafun.info
Sea Pro Divers	Puerto Plata	809-710-3747	info@seaprowatersports.com
Sea Pro Divers	Punta Canta	809-754-3632	info@seaprowatersports.com
Treasure Divers	Boca Chica	809-523-5320	dive@treasure-divers.net

Electrical Repairs

Centro Marino	Boca Chica	809-523-6720	info@centromarinoforrest.com
Electro Nautica	Santo Domingo	809-328-1916	service@electronauticadr.com
Marina Cap Cana	Cap Cana	809-695-5539	info@marinacapcana.com
Marina Casa de Campo	La Romana	809-523-2111	harbourmaster@marinacasadecampo.com.do
Manuel Electric	Boca Chica	809-523-9769	
Marina Zar-Par	Boca Chica	809-523-5858	info@marinazarpar.com
Ocean World Marina	Puerto Plata	809-970-3373	
Repuestos Maritimos	Puerto Plata	809-586-4728	
Tony Rodamentes	Santo Domingo	809-688-2151	
Wilson Marine	Boca Chica	809-743-9503	

Fabrication/Welding

Kiko	Luperón		
Marina Cap Cana	Cap Cana	809-695-5539	info@marinacapcana.com
Marina Casa de Campo	La Romana	809-523-2111	harbourmaster@marinacasadecampo.com.do
Marina Zar-Par	Boca Chica	809-523-5858	info@marinazarpar.com
Núñez & Núñez	Santiago	809-582-2200	
Tony Rodamentes	Santo Domingo	809-688-2151	

Haul Out

Club Nautico de S. D.	Boca Chica	809-685-4940	
Marina Casa de Campo	La Romana	809-523-2111	harbourmaster@marinacasadecampo.com.do
Marina Zar-Par	Boca Chica	809-523-5858	info@marinazarpar.com
Ocean World Marina	Puerto Plata	809-970-3373	
Tropical Marina	Luperón	809-440-9926	marinatropical.dr@gmail.com
Tropical Marine	Luperón	809-440-9926	

FACILITY	LOCATION	PHONE	VHF CALL OR E-MAIL
Hull Repair/Painting			
Club Nautico de S. D.	Boca Chica	809-685-4940	
Marina Cap Cana	Cap Cana	809-695-5539	info@marinacapcana.com
Marina Casa de Campo	La Romana	809-523-2111	harbourmaster@marinacasadecampo.com.do
Marina Zar-Par	Boca Chica	809-523-5858	info@marinazarpar.com
Internet			
Hotel Salinas	Salinas		
Luperón Marina & YC	Luperón	809-771-2002	info@luperonmarina.net
Marina Cap Cana	Cap Cana	809-695-5539	info@marinacapcana.com
Marina Casa de Campo	La Romana	809-523-2111	harbourmaster@marinacasadecampo.com.do
Marina Zar-Par	Boca Chica	809-523-5858	info@marinazarpar.com
Pharmacia Vanessa	Luperón		
R&V Comunicaciones	Santo Domingo	809-687-8565	saladinfelix@yahoo.es
Verizon	Luperón		
Verizon	Luperón		
Marine Supplies			
Auto Marina	Santo Domingo	809-565-6576	info@automarina.com.do
Centro Marino	Boca Chica	809-523-6720	info@centromarinoforrest.com
Luperón Marine Supplies	Luperón		VHF ch. 68
Marina Casa de Campo	La Romana	809-523-2111	harbourmaster@marinacasadecampo.com.do
Outboard Repair			
Centro Marino	Boca Chica	809-523-6720	info@centromarinoforrest.com
Marina Cap Cana	Cap Cana	809-695-5539	info@marinacapcana.com
Marina Casa de Campo	La Romana	809-523-2111	harbourmaster@marinacasadecampo.com.do
Marina Zar-Par	Boca Chica	809-523-5858	info@marinazarpar.com
Ocean World Marina	Puerto Plata	809-970-3373	
Propane			
Any Motorconcho	Luperón		
José	Luperón	809-458-9506	José, VHF ch. 68
Marina Cap Cana	Cap Cana	809-695-5539	info@marinacapcana.com
Marina Casa de Campo	La Romana	809-523-2111	harbourmaster@marinacasadecampo.com.do
Papo	Luperón		Papo, VHF ch. 68
Propeller			
Marina Casa de Campo	La Romana	809-523-2111	harbourmaster@marinacasadecampo.com.do
Marina Zar-Par	Boca Chica	809-523-5858	info@marinazarpar.com
Refrigeration			
Electro Nautica	Santo Domingo	809-328-1916	service@electronauticadr.com
Marina Cap Cana	Cap Cana	809-695-5539	info@marinacapcana.com
Marina Casa de Campo	La Romana	809-523-2111	harbourmaster@marinacasadecampo.com.do
Marina Zar-Par	Boca Chica	809-523-5858	info@marinazarpar.com
Mercado del Sol	Luperón		
Zelltec	Puerto Plata	809-533-5019	
Rigging			
Marina Casa de Campo	La Romana	809-523-2111	harbourmaster@marinacasadecampo.com.do
Marina Zar-Par	Boca Chica	809-523-5858	info@marinazarpar.com
Sail and Canvas Repair			
Calamity Canvas	Luperón	809-523-6987	
Flaco	Luperón		El Flaco, VHF ch. 68
Mare Sailmaker	Punta Cana	809-307-3426	jenny@maresailmaker.com
Marina Casa de Campo	La Romana	809-523-2111	harbourmaster@marinacasadecampo.com.do
Marina Zar-Par	Boca Chica	809-523-5858	info@marinazarpar.com

Appendix D: Waypoints

__Caution__: Waypoints are not to be used for navigational purposes. The following waypoints are intended to place you in the general area of the described position. All routes, cuts, and anchorages must be negotiated by eyeball navigation. The author and publisher take no responsibility for the misuse of the following waypoints. Waypoints are listed from north to south. Latitude is "**North**" and longitude is "**West**." Datum used is WGS84.

WAYPOINT DESCRIPTION	LATITUDE	LONGITUDE
The Southern Bahamas		
Cat Island		
Arthur's Town - ½ nm SW of	24° 36.80'	75° 41.20'
Bennett's Harbour - ½ nm W of entrance	24° 33.75'	75° 39.00'
Alligator Point - ½ nm SW of southwestern tip	24° 31.00'	75° 41.50'
Smith's Bay - ¾ nm W of	24° 19.75'	75° 29.55'
Fernandez Bay - ¾ nm W of	24° 19.10'	75° 29.55'
Bonefish Point - ¾ nm SW of western tip of shoal	24° 16.50'	75° 28.90'
New Bight - ¾ nm SW of Batelco Tower	24° 16.75'	75° 25.75'
Old Bight - ¾ nm NW of anchorage	24° 13.40'	75° 25.20'
Hawks Nest Point - 1 nm W of point	24° 08.55'	75° 32.45'
Springfield Bay - 1.5 nm S of Dolphin Head	24° 07.00'	75° 24.50'
Half Moon Cay (Little San Salvador)		
West Bay - 1 nm W of anchorage	24° 34.48'	75° 58.60'
Little San Salvador - 1 nm S of light	24° 32.70'	75° 56.30'
Conception Island		
North of reef off northwestern tip of Conception Island	23° 55.18'	75° 05.40'
West Bay - ¾ nm W of anchorage	23° 51.00'	75° 08.00'
Southeast point - clears reef SE of Conception	23° 47.25'	75° 04.66'
Rum Cay		
Flamingo Bay - ¼ nm N of wreck at entrance to Bay	23° 42.45'	74° 56.80'
Sandy Point - clears Sandy Point for eastward jog to Port Nelson	23° 38.50'	74° 57.30'
Port Nelson - ¼ nm SW of western end of Sumner Point Reef	23° 37.75'	74° 51.20'
Rum Cay - 1½ nm SE of southeastern tip clear of reef	23° 37.00'	74° 47.00'
San Salvador		
Graham's Harbour - 1 nm W of entrance channel at Green Cay	24° 08.15'	74° 31.60'
Cockburn Town - 1 nm W of anchorage off town	24° 02.75'	74° 32.75'
French Bay- ¾ nm SW of Sandy Point	23° 56.10'	74° 34.80'
Long Island		
Cape Santa Maria - clears reefs off NW tip of the Cape	23° 42.00'	75° 21.50'
Cape Santa Maria anchorage - ¾ nm W of beach below light	23° 39.70'	75° 21.60'
Calabash Bay - ½ nm W of 90° entrance between the reefs	23° 38.70'	75° 21.40'
Joe Sound - ½ nm SW of entrance channel	23° 36.85'	75° 21.55'
Dove Cay Passage - NW waypoint	23° 34.61'	75° 21.15'
Dove Cay Passage - W waypoint	23° 33.53'	75° 20.83'
Dove Cay - W of entrance to Stella Maris Marina channel	23° 33.03'	75° 19.90'
Simms - ¾ nm SW of settlement	23° 28.10'	75° 14.90'
Comer Channel #1	23° 20.82'	75° 19.95'
Salt Pond, Long Island - ¼ nm SW of Indian Hole Point	23° 20.70'	75° 10.30'
Comer Channel #2	23° 19.53'	75° 24.00'
Comer Channel #3 - western end of Comer Channel	23° 20.30'	75° 32.00'
Deadman's Cays - NW end of channel	23° 14.40'	75° 12.75'

WAYPOINT DESCRIPTION	LATITUDE	LONGITUDE
Deadman's Cays - SE end of channel	23° 11.75'	75° 10.35'
Dollar Harbour - ¾ nm S of	23° 10.00'	75° 15.55'
Clarence Town - ½ nm NW of Booby Rock at entrance	23° 07.35'	74° 57.65'
Little Harbour - ½ nm E of entrance	22° 58.65'	74° 50.30'
Southern tip of Long Island - ½ nm S of	22° 50.35'	74° 51.70'

The Jumentos

WAYPOINT DESCRIPTION	LATITUDE	LONGITUDE
Nuevitas Rocks - banks side-½ nm N of	23° 10.00'	75° 22.10'
Nuevitas Rocks - offshore side-½ nm SE of	23° 09.30'	75° 21.60'
Pear Cay Pass - ½ nm NNW of	23° 08.65'	75° 31.20'
Pear Cay Pass - ½ nm SE of	23° 07.80'	75° 30.65'
Water Cay Cut - ¼ nm SE of	23° 02.20'	75° 40.35'
Water Cay; banks side - ¾ nm NW of	23° 02.00'	75° 44.00'
Flamingo Cut - ¼ nm W of	22° 54.30'	75° 51.00'
Flamingo Cay - 1 nm NW of	22° 54.30'	75° 53.10'
Man Of War Shoal - outer break-N of	22° 48.75'	75° 54.66'
Man of War Shoal - inner break-N of	22° 48.75'	75° 54.00'
Man of War Shoal - outer break-S of	22° 48.05'	75° 54.66'
Man of War Shoal - inner break-S of	22° 48.05'	75° 54.00'
Jamaica Cay - ½ nm W of	22° 44.55'	75° 55.10'
Nurse Channel - ½ nm W of Channel Cay	22° 31.30'	75° 50.40'
Nurse Cay - ½ nm W of	22° 28.60'	75° 51.70'
Raccoon Cut - ¾ nm NNE of	22° 21.45'	75° 47.00'
Hog Cay - ¼ nm W of southernmost beach	22° 14.60'	75° 45.50'
Little Ragged Island - ¾ nm SW of	22° 08.65'	75° 40.00'

Crooked Island District

WAYPOINT DESCRIPTION	LATITUDE	LONGITUDE
Bird Rock - ¼ nm N of northwestern tip of reef	22° 51.85'	74° 22.10'
ortland Harbour - ½ nm W of entrance SW of Bird Rock	22° 50.40'	74° 21.90'
Landrail Point - ½ nm W of anchorage off beach	22° 49.10'	74° 21.40'
North of Acklins Island - clear of Northeast Reef	22° 50.00'	73° 47.00'
Majors Cays - ½ nm north of entrance through reef	22° 45.70'	74° 08.70'
Lovely Bay - ½ nm NNE of entrance through reef	22° 44.55'	73° 57.45'
Attwood Harbour - ½ nm N of entrance through reef	22° 44.20'	73° 53.20'
French Wells - 1¼ nm NW of entrance	22° 41.40'	74° 18.90'
Albert Town - ½ nm WNW of	22° 36.35'	74° 21.50'
Long Cay - turning point to head east across Bight of Acklins	22° 34.65'	74° 16.90'
Long Cay - 1¼ nm south of stake leading to small dock	22° 34.10'	74° 19.90'
Bight of Acklins: Snug Corner - 1 nm SW of	22° 32.00'	73° 54.25'
Long Cay - southern tip - ¾ nm S of Windsor Point	22° 31.65'	74° 22.80'
Bight of Acklins: Camel Point - 3 nm NNE of	22° 30.00'	73° 59.50'
Anchorage between Fish Cay and Guana Cay - entrance	22° 28.00'	74° 16.20'
Bight of Acklins: Camel Point - ¾ nm W of	22° 27.00'	74° 01.00'
Bight of Acklins: Jamaica Cay - 1 nm N of	22° 24.50'	74° 06.40'
Bight of Acklins: Turning point - Camel Point to Jamaica Cay	22° 24.40'	74° 02.55'
Bight of Acklins: Binnacle Hill - ¾ nm NW of	22° 23.00'	74° 07.00'
Bight of Acklins: Jamaica Cay - ½ nm W of	22° 20.30'	74° 09.00'
Bight of Acklins: Cotton Bay Cay - 1 nm W of	22° 18.40'	74° 12.25'
Rokers Cay - deep water start of route to Rokers Cay	22° 17.85'	74° 16.25'
Bight of Acklins: Rokers Cay- 2 nm NW of, turn to Cotton Bay Cay	22° 16.50'	74° 13.50'
Jamaica Bay - 3 nm W of anchorage	22° 14.25'	74° 17.75'
Castle Island - ½ nm NW of anchorage on W shore	22° 08.50'	74° 20.40'
Castle Island - ¼ nm S of Mudian Harbour entrance	22° 07.00'	74° 19.00'

WAYPOINT DESCRIPTION	LATITUDE	LONGITUDE
Mira Por Vos - 1 nm W of Mira Por Vos Bank	22° 07.00'	74° 32.50'
Samana		
Propeller Cay anchorage - ½ nm S of entrance channel	23° 03.10'	73° 44.35'
Plana Cays		
West Plana Cay - ½ nm W of anchorage	22° 35.35'	73° 38.50'
Mayaguana		
Northwest Point - 1½ nm W of light	22° 27.10'	73° 09.90'
Abraham's Bay - inner waypoint at eastern entrance	22° 21.07'	72° 58.45'
Start Bay - ½ nm SW of best holding	22° 20.30'	73° 05.30'
Abraham's Bay - ¼ nm SSE of eastern entrance	22° 20.80'	72° 58.30'
Abraham's Bay - ¼ nm NE of western entrance	22° 19.80'	73° 02.50'
Abraham's Bay - ¼ nm SW of western entrance	22° 19.25'	73° 03.40'
Southeast Point - 1 nm WSW of anchorage	22° 16.70'	72° 48.40'
Hogsty Reef		
Hogsty Reef - 1 nm W of entrance to lagoon	21° 40.50'	73° 51.50'
Inagua		
Little Inagua - ½ nm W of anchorage	21° 26.50'	73° 03.50'
Northwest Point - ½ nm NNW of point	21° 07.10'	73° 40.10'
Matthew Town - ¾ nm W of	20° 57.10'	73° 41.50'

Turks and Caicos Islands

The Caicos Islands

	LATITUDE	LONGITUDE
Ft. George Cut - ½ nm NW of cut	21° 53.70'	72° 07.90'
North West Point, Providenciales - ½ nm N of reef in deep water	21° 53.10'	72° 19.90'
Wheeland Cut - ½ nm NNE of cut	21° 52.65'	72° 17.65'
Malcolm Roadstead - ½ nm W of anchorage	21° 49.85'	72° 20.80'
Leeward Cut - ½ nm NW of cut	21° 50.40'	72° 10.40'
Stubb's Cut - ¼ nm NW of cut	21° 48.93'	72° 11.30'
Wiley Cut - ¼ nm NNW of cut	21° 48.85'	72° 21.35'
Leeward Going Through - S entrance, ¼ nm ESE of Bird Rock	21° 48.60'	72° 07.30'
Sellar's Cut - ½ nm N of cut	21° 48.40'	72° 12.40'
Jacksonville Cut, East Caicos - ¼ nm N of cut	21° 47.00'	71° 35.90'
Deep water on Banks for shortcut to Leeward	21° 45.50'	72° 07.00'
Cooper Jack Bight - ½ nm SW of entrance to Discovery Bay	21° 45.05'	72° 14.00'
Turning point to Boatyard -1 nm SSE of entrance channel	21° 44.80'	72° 10.30'
Sandbore Channel - ¾ nm W of entrance	21° 44.50'	72° 27.25'
Sapodilla Bay - ¼ nm S of anchorage	21° 44.25'	72° 17.40'
Bay Cay - 1 nm ESE of, beginning of route to Boatyard	21° 43.75'	72° 14.00'
Pony Channel – ¼ nm W of	21° 43.40'	72° 27.30'
Pony Channel – ¼ nm E of	21° 43.40'	72° 26.75'
West Caicos Marina – ¼ nm NW of entrance channel	21° 42.00'	72° 28.00'
West Caicos, Clear Sand Road - ¾ nm S of Southwest Point	21° 36.75'	72° 29.00'
Freighter Channel - SW waypoint	21° 35.75'	72° 23.25'
French Cay - ½ nm W of anchorage	21° 30.60'	72° 12.70'
Starfish Channel	21° 30.25'	72° 06.75'
French Cay - ¾ SW of anchorage on edge of Caicos Bank	21° 29.75'	72° 12.65'
South Caicos, Cockburn Harbour - ¼ nm SE of entrance	21° 28.70'	71° 31.70'
Long Cay Cut - ½ nm NW of cut and anchorage area	21° 27.40'	71° 34.75'
Long Cay Cut - ½ nm SE of cut in Columbus Passage	21° 26.60'	71° 34.10'
Fish Cays - ¾ nm N of	21° 23.50'	71° 37.25'
West Sand Spit - 2 nm SW of	21° 20.50'	72° 10.05'
Big Ambergris Cay - 1 nm NW of anchorage	21° 19.75'	71° 39.75'

WAYPOINT DESCRIPTION	LATITUDE	LONGITUDE
The Turks Islands		
Grand Turk, North Creek - ¼ nm N of entrance channel at jetty	21° 31.10'	71° 08.50'
Grand Turk, Front Street anchorage - ¼ nm W of break in reef	21° 28.13'	71° 09.13'
Grand Turk, South Dock - ¼ nm WSW of end of dock	21° 25.90'	71° 09.20'
Big Cut - ¼ nm NW of	21° 24.60'	71° 09.25'
Salt Cay - ¼ nm W of Deane's Dock	21° 19.90'	71° 13.25'
Salt Cay - ¾ SW of S end, waypoint to take up course to DR	21° 17.60'	71° 14.10'
Great Sand Cay - ½ nm W of anchorage in West Bay	21° 11.65'	71° 15.50'
Great Sand Cay - ¾ SW of S end, waypoint to take up course to DR	21° 10.80'	71° 15.50'
The Dominican Republic		
Northern Coast		
Luperón - 1 nm N of entrance channel	19° 55.50'	70° 56.51'
Cofresi, *Ocean World Marina* - ½ nm NE of entrance	19° 50.05'	70° 43.65'
Puerto Plata - ¾ nm N of sea buoy	19° 49.10'	70° 41.55'
Sosúa anchorage - ¼ nm W of anchorage area	19° 45.60'	70° 31.40'
Rio San Juan - ¼ nm W of anchorage area	19° 38.60'	70° 05.50'
Puerto El Valle (Escondido) - 1¾ nm NNW of anchorage area	19° 19.00'	69° 20.50'
Eastern Coast		
Samaná - ¼ nm S of Punta Gorda	19° 11.40'	69° 18.85'
Puerto Bahía Marina - ¼ nm SW of entrance channel	19° 11.40'	69° 21.40'
Bahía de San Lorenzo - ¼ nm W of Punta Arena	19° 05.50'	69° 29.00'
Southern Coast		
Barahona - ¼ nm NE of sea buoy	18° 13.30'	71° 04.00'
Las Salinas - ½ nm NNW of Punta Calderas	18° 14.00'	70° 33.00'
Puerto de Haina - ¼ nm S of entrance between the jetties	18° 24.60'	70° 01.05'
Santo Domingo - ¼ nm S of entrance between the jetties	18° 27.50'	69° 53.50'
Boca Chica - 1¼ nm SE of marked entrance channel	18° 25.50'	69° 36.70'
Casa de Campo Marina - ¼ nm SW of marked entrance channel	18° 23.60'	68° 54.40'
Isla Saona - ½ nm NW of anchorage	18° 12.50'	68° 47.00'
Cap Cana Marina - ½ nm SE of entrance channel	18° 29.85'	68° 22.00'

Appendix E: Tidal Differences

All tides mentioned are based on Nassau tides. Times of tides in other locations vary from a few minutes to a few hours before or after Nassau tides. Time is "B" for before Nassau, and "L" for later than Nassau.

LOCATION	TIME HW	TIME LW
Abraham's Bay, Mayaguana	10 min. L	13 min. L
Allan's-Pensacola, Abacos	35 min L	45 min L
The Bight, Cat Island	35 min. B	35 min. B
Cat Cay, Biminis	23 min L	23 min L
Clarence Town, Long Island	49 min. L	54 min. L
Datum Bay, Acklins Island	15 min B	15 min B
Elbow Cay, Cay Sal Bank	1h 26 min. L	1h 31 min. L
Eleuthera, eastern shore	19 min. L	26 min. L
Eleuthera, western shore	2h 17 min. L	2h 36 min. L
Freeport, Grand Bahama	same	same
Fresh Creek, Andros	13 min. L	5 min. L
George Town, Exuma	20 min B	20 min B
Great Stirrup Cay, Berry Islands	25 min L	25 min L

LOCATION	TIME HW	TIME LW
Green Turtle Cay, Abacos	5 min L	5 min L
Guinchos Cay	14 min. L	19 min. L
Little Inagua	10 min L	10 min L
Mastic Point, Andros	5 min L	5 min L
Matthew Town, Great Inagua	15 min. L	15 min. L
Memory Rock, Abacos	24 min. L	29 min. L
North Bimini	13 min. L	25 min. L
North Cat Cay	30 min. L	35 min. L
Nurse Channel, Jumentos	15 min. L	10 min. L
Pelican Harbour, Abacos	26 min. L	31 min. L
Royal Island, Eleuthera	5 min L	5 min L
Salt Pond, Long Island	1.5 hour L	1.5 hour L
San Salvador	35 min. B	35 min. B
Ship Channel, Exuma	15 min B	15 min B
South Riding Rock, Biminis	40 min L	40 min L
Start Point, Mayaguana	25 min L	25 min L
Walker's Cay, Abaco	1h 25 min L	1h 25 min L

Appendix F: Metric Conversion

Visitors to The Bahamas and the Turks and Caicos Islands will find the metric system in use and many grocery items and fuel measured in liters and kilograms. As a rule of thumb, a meter is just a little longer than a yard and a liter is very close to a quart. If in doubt use the following table.

1 centimeter (cm) = 0.4 inch	1 inch = 2.54 centimeters
1 meter (m) = 3.28 feet	1 foot = 30.48 centimeters
1 meter = 0.55 fathoms	1 fathom = 1.83 meters
1 kilometer (km) = 0.62 miles	1 yard = .92 meters
1 kilometer = 0.54 nautical miles	1 nautical mile = 1.852 kilometers
1 liter (l) = 0.26 gallons	1 gallon = 3.79 liters
1 gram (g) = 0.035 ounces	1 ounce = 28.4 grams
1 metric ton = 1.1 tons	1 pound = 454 grams

Index

Industrious Hill 59
International Ramsar Bureau 31
Isabel de Torres 272, 274
Ishmael Cay. *See* Margaret Cay
Island House 244
Island Pride 200, 202
Isla Saona 259

J

Jackson Cut Bay 227
Jacksonville Cut 226–228, 309
Jamaica Bay 149, 152, 153, 308
Jamaica Cay 117, 125–128, 135, 149, 151, 152, 307, 308
Jamaica Spit 128
Jamaica Well Point 153
James Cay 132
Jewfish Wall 77
Joe Grant's Cay 227
Joe Sound 94–98, 307
Joe's Sound 96
Johnny Hill 156
Johnson Cay 131–133
JoJo 26
Juba Point 203, 205, 221
Jumentos 117, 118
Junkanoo 28

K

Kelly Bay 58
Kew 29, 224
King Hill 225
King's Highway 223, 224
Kingston 186, 189, 202
Knowles Village 59

L

La Caleta Underwater Park 260
Lady Slipper Cay 158
La Isabella 270
Lanzadera Cay 121, 122
La Providentielle 192
La Romana 258, 259
Leeward Cut 190, 191, 207, 209–213
Leeward Going Through 24, 26, 33, 193, 202, 207, 210–216, 226, 230, 251, 309
Leeward Highway 29, 192, 198–202
Leeward Marina 18, 212–214, 223, 299
Little Ambergris Cay 230, 235, 236
Little Cut 249

Little Harbour 113
Little Inagua 174, 175, 180
Little Nurse Cay 128
Little Ragged Island 131, 133, 134, 137, 307
Little San Salvador 65
Little Water Cay 120, 171, 122, 211, 213, 215, 251
Lockhart Cay 137
Loggerhead Cay 132
Long Bar 232
Long Bay 24, 79, 202, 207, 210
Long Bay Hills 24, 202, 207, 210
Long Cay 95, 119, 139, 140, 144, 146–149, 152, 157, 189–192, 222, 228–232, 234, 236, 249, 251, 255, 299, 308, 309
Long Island 95, 96
Long Point 192
Long Rocks 116
Lorimers 226
Los Haitises 281
Lovely Bay 158, 161, 308
Low Cay 81
Lower Deadman's Cay 106, 107
Lower Pirates Well 166–168
Low Water Harbour Cay 131
Loyalists 72, 188, 192, 215, 226, 227
Luperón 9, 14, 20, 24, 25, 30, 34, 222, 236, 238, 255, 256, 258, 262–272, 274, 275, 277, 309

M

Mailboa 29
mailboats 28, 29
Major's Cay 157
Major's Hill 224
Malcolm Roadstead 193, 194, 309
Mangrove Bush 31, 94, 106, 108, 301
Mangrove Cay 213, 215
Manhead Cay 83
Man of War Bay 176, 177
Man of War Cay 125–127
Man of War Point 64, 65
Man O War Bush 226, 232
Margaret Cay 132, 133
Margaret Shoal 132–134
Market Place 192, 200
Martini's Reef 77
Mason Bay. *See* Snug Corner
Mason's Bay 149, 150
Mastic Point 310
Matthew Town 113, 173–179, 298, 301, 308, 310
Mayaguana Passage 163, 165
Maycock Cay 132
McKay's Bluff 156

About the Author

Photo Courtesy of Danielle Courteau

Stephen J. Pavlidis has been cruising and living aboard since the winter of 1989.

Starting in the Exuma Cays over 20 years ago, Steve began his writing career with guides to the many fascinating destinations he visited. Many of his books stand alone to this day as the quintessential guides to the areas he covers.

His books are different than most other cruising guides in some very significant ways. All of the charts in Steve's books were created using data personally collected while visiting each area using a computerized system that interfaces GPS and depth soundings.

You can find out more about this exceptional author by visiting his Web site, www.Seaworthy.com where there is current news and information about Steve's latest projects, as well as contact information.

Other books by Stephen J. Pavlidis:

Life at Sea Level, ISBN 978-1-892399-33-5
The Exuma Guide, 3rd Edition, ISBN 978-1-892399-31-1
A Cruising Guide to the Leeward Islands, 2nd Edition, ISBN 978-1-892399-36-6
The Northern Bahamas Guide, ISBN 978-1-892399-28-1
The Northwest Caribbean Guide, 2nd Edition ISBN 978-1-892399-38-0
The Puerto Rico Guide, 3rd Edition, ISBN 978-1-892399-39-7
The Turks and Caicos Islands Guide, 3rd Edition, ISBN 978-1-892399-40-3
A Cruising Guide to the Virgin Islands, 2nd Edition, ISBN 978-1-892399-35-9
The Windward Islands Guide, 2nd Edition, ISBN 978-1-892399-37-3

About Don Reynolds

Photo Courtesy of Don Reynolds

Don Reynolds whose sketches grace this publication, was born in 1944. Don's love of the sea began at the age of 18 months while crossing the *North Atlantic Ocean* from England to America aboard the *HMS Queen Mary*.

Subsequent voyages continued from Puerto Rico to New York via transport aboard the *Pvt William H. Thomas* and across the *Pacific Ocean* aboard the *USS Yorktown* and continuing on with his home-built 36' Roberts cutter, *Ppalu*.

Don met Steve during a shakedown cruise to the Exumas in 1996, sharing sketches and knowledge of the area. *Ppalu* eventually took Don & Lynn (wife) up to the coast of Maine and back before sailing for the Med the next year. Having always worked as an artist, a dream was fully realized in Italy by sculpting marble in Pietrasanta while living aboard *Ppalu* for three years.

The return voyage out of the Med and down to Cape Verde and across again to the Windward Islands began the island hop back through the turquoise and blue waters of the Bahama outer islands.

Private and public art commissions consume the present day activities, but the next dream voyage is still alive and with luck, should come true... while *Ppalu* patiently waits on her mooring.

Lightning Source UK Ltd.
Milton Keynes UK
UKHW050944021122
411501UK00005B/31